THE DILEMMAS OF DISSIDENCE
IN EAST-CENTRAL EUROPE

Citizen Intellectuals and
Philosopher Kings

D1552920

THE DILEMMAS OF DISSIDENCE IN EAST-CENTRAL EUROPE

Citizen Intellectuals and Philosopher Kings

by
Barbara J. Falk

Central European University Press
Budapest New York

Published in 2003 by

Central European University Press

An imprint of the
Central European University Share Company
Nádor utca 11, H-1051 Budapest, Hungary
Tel: +36-1-327-3138 or 327-3000
Fax: +36-1-327-3183
E-mail: ceupress@ceu.hu
Website: www.ceupress.com

400 West 59th Street, New York NY 10019, USA
Tel: +1-212-547-6932
Fax: +1-212-548-4607
E-mail: mgreenwald@sorosny.org

ISBN 963 9241 38 5 cloth
ISBN 963 9241 39 3 paperback

Library of Congress Cataloging-in-Publication Data

Falk, Barbara J.
    The dilemmas of dissidence in East-Central Europe : citizen
intellectuals and philosopher kings / by Barbara J. Falk.
    p. cm.
Includes bibliographical references and index.
    ISBN—ISBN
    1. Europe, Eastern—Politics and government—1945–1989. 2. Europe,
Central—Politics and government—20th century. 3. Dissenters—Europe,
Eastern—History. 4. Europe, Eastern—Intellectual life—20th century.
I. Title.
    DJK50 .F35 2002
    943'.0009'045—dc21
                        2002011885

Printed in Hungary by
Akaprint

This book is dedicated to the memory of my grandmother Ada Troyer Vetter, and my dear friend and mentor H. Gordon Skilling, as well as the two people most central in my life today, my husband Jules Barry Bloch and my daughter Alannah Ada Bloch.

TABLE OF CONTENTS

List of Abbreviations   xi
Preface   xv
   A Note on Nomenclature   xxix
Acknowledgments   xxxiii

Chapter 1
INTRODUCTION   1

SECTION 1

Chapter 2
POLAND: THE HARBINGER
   OF CRISIS AND COLLAPSE   13
Intellectual Opposition in Poland: 1956–1965   13
The Catholic Church in Poland   18
The Students' Protest: March, 1968   22
The Workers' Protest: Gdańsk, 1970   27
The Events of June, 1976: Radom, Ursus, and Beyond   34
Komitet Obrony Robotników (KOR):
   The Workers' Defense Committee   35
The Alternative Civil Society?   40
Towarzystwo Kursów Naukowych (TKN):
   The Flying University   42
The Pope's Visit, 1979   43
Solidarity (*Solidarność*)   45
Intellectuals within Solidarity   49
Martial Law and its Aftermath   51
Solidarity Underground   53
Re-Legalization, the Roundtable Talks (RT),
   and Free Elections   56

Chapter 3

CZECHOSLOVAKIA: FROM INTERRUPTED
   TO VELVET REVOLUTION   59
Czechoslovak Stalinism and the Role of Intellectuals   59
The Economic Crisis of the 1960s   62
Proposals for Economic Reform   63
The Writers' Union and the Cultural Renaissance
   of the 1960s   65
The Student/Youth Movements and Strahov   68
The Prague Spring   70
The Action Program and Soviet Response   71
Independent Currents: The Untimely Rebirth
   of Civil Society   76
Čierna nad Tisou   77
Crisis: Soviet Mobilization and the Moscow Protocols   79
Normalization   80
The Underground Music Scene and the Trial of the PPU   84
The Helsinki Accords and Charter 77   88
Výbor na Obranu Nespravedlivě Stíhaných (VONS)   92
The "Underground University"   92
Samizdat Publishing and Distribution   94
Repression and Resistance in the Czech Lands
   and Slovakia in the 1980s   95
The Underground Church in Slovakia   100
The Tide Turns: "Just a Few Sentences"   102
The GDR Exodus and the Fall of the Wall   103
November 17 and the Birth of Civic Forum
   and Public against Violence   103
Havel na Hrad   106
The New Year's Address and the Consolidation
   of Democracy   107

Chapter 4

POST-1956 HUNGARY: REPRESSION, REFORM,
   AND ROUNDTABLE REVOLUTION   109
The Hungarian Revolution of 1956: Lessons and Legacies   109
Kádárite Communism   112
The Politics of Economic Reform: The NEM   113
Socialist Redistribution and the Second Economy   116

Intellectuals: On the Road to Class Power? 118
The Budapest School 122
"Populist" vs. "Democratic" Dissent 125
Beszélő and Hungarian Samizdat 130
Toward an Alliance: The Bibó *Festschrift* and Monor 135
Lakitelek 138
Intra-party and Election Reform 139
The Rebirth of Civil Society 142
Ellenzéki Kerekasztal (EKA) and the "Pacted Transition" 146
The "Four Yeses" Referendum 151
June 16, 1989: The Reburial of Imre Nagy 152

SECTION 2

Chapter 5
INTELLECTUALS IN POLAND:
THE TRADITION CONTINUES

THE TRADITION CONTINUES 157
Leszek Kołakowski: A Source of Hope amidst Hopelessness 157
Adam Michnik's Alliance Strategy: The Church and the Left 165
"A New Evolutionism" 177
Non-violence as Theory and Practice 180
Kuroń: A Bridge between Generations 184
Theorizing Civil Society: The Polish Case 192

Chapter 6
OPPOSITION INTELLECTUALS
IN CZECHOSLOVAKIA

IN CZECHOSLOVAKIA 199
Václav Havel's Theatre of the Absurd 199
The Evolution of "Living in Truth": Its Meaning
and Consequences 204
From Playwright to Dissident in Husák's Czechoslovakia 208
Theorizing Resistance: "The Power of the Powerless" 215
"Politics and Conscience" and the Destructive Capacities
of Technology 225
Largo Desolato, Temptation, and the Vaněk Plays 229
Letters to Olga: "Being" and the "Absolute" 236
The Decisive Influence of Jan Patočka 242
Václav Benda's "Parallel *Polis*" 247
The Collective *Oeuvre* of the Chartists 251
Theorizing Civil Society: The Czechoslovak Example 254

Chapter 7
THE DEMOCRATIC OPPOSITION IN HUNGARY   257
The Philosophical Legacy of György Lukács   257
The Influence of István Bibó   261
Kis and Bence: *Toward an East European Marxism?*   266
The Social Contract of *Beszélő* and "Radical Reformism"   277
Kis' Democratic Alternative   281
Miklós Haraszti: The Nature of Repression for Workers
    and Artists   290
Theorizing Civil Society: Konrád's *Antipolitics*   298

SECTION 3

Chapter 8
THE DISSIDENT CONTRIBUTION
    TO POLITICAL THEORY   313
Defining the Problem: Civil Society
    and the Shifting Boundaries of Public and Private   313
Toward a Reconstituted Public Sphere: Central European
    and Western Intersections in Theorizing Civil Society   316
Reappraising Civil Society: Feminist Critiques   325
Political Economy as Critique:
    The Dissidents Meet the Market   327
Dissident Thought as Reconstructed Liberalism   334
Political Theory Engages with Dissident Theory   348
Marginalization or Public Engagement: The Role of
    Central European Intellectuals in the Post-Communist Era   354

BIBLIOGRAPHY   365

Personal Interviews   397
Skilling Seminar, Toronto   398
Filmography/Videography   398

NOTES   399

INDEX   463

LIST OF ABBREVIATIONS

ANC	Anti Nuclear Campaign Hungary
COMECON	Council for Mutual Economic Cooperation
CPSU	Communist Party of the Soviet Union
CPCz	Communist Party of Czechoslovakia *(Komunistická Strana Československa)*
ČSM	Czechoslovak Student Union *(Československý svaz mládeže)*
EKA	Opposition Roundtable *(Ellenzéki Kerekasztal)*
END	European Nuclear Disarmament
Fidesz	Federation of Young Democrats *(Fiatal Demokraták Szövetsége)*
FJF	Independent Lawyers' Forum *(Független Jogász Fórum)*
HNF	Patriotic People's Front *(Hazafias Népfront)*
HOS	Movement for Civil Liberties *(Hnuti za Občanskou Svobodu)*
ISO	Initiative for Social Defense *(Iniciativa Socialní Obrany)*
KAN	Club of Non-Party Engagés *(Klub angažovaných nestraníků)*
KDNP	Christian Democratic People's Party *(Keresztény Demokrata Neppárt)*
KIK	Warsaw Club of Catholic Intelligentsia *(Klub Inteligencji Katolickiej)*
KISZ	Communist Youth Alliance *(Kommunista Ifjúsági Szövetség)*
KKK	Club of the Crooked Circle *(Klub Kryzwego Koła)*
KMT	Central Workers' Council of Greater Budapest *(Nagybudapesti Központi Munkástanács)*

KOR   Workers' Defense Committee
              (*Komitet Obrony Robotników*)
KSS-KOR   Social Self-Defense Committee
              (*Komitet Samoobrony Społecznej*)
KWZZ   Founding Committee for Free Trade Unions of the
              Coast (*Komitet Założycielski Wolnych Związków
              Zawodowych Wybrzeża*)
MDF   Hungarian Democratic Forum
              (*Magyar Demokrata Fórum*)
MKJL   John Lennon Peace Club (*Mírový Klub John Lennon*)
MKS   Interfactory Strike Committee
              (*Międzakładowy Komitet Strajkowy*)
MSZMP   Hungarian Socialist Workers' Party (*Magyar
              Szocialista Munkáspárt*)
NEM   New Economic Mechanism
NEP   New Economic Policy
NMS   Independent Peace Initiative
              (*Nezávislé Mírové Sdružení*)
NOW-a   Independent Publishing House
              (*Niezależna Oficyna Wydawnicza*)
OPZZ   Official Trade Union
              (*Ogólnopolskie Porozumienie Związków Zawodowych*)
PPS   Polish Socialist Party (*Polska Partia Socjalistyczna*)
PPU   Plastic People of the Universe ("The Plastics")
PZPR   Polish United Workers' Party (*Polska Zjednoczona
              Partia Robotnicza*)
RMP   Young Poland Movement (*Ruch Młodej Polski*)
ROPCiO   Movement for the Defense of Civil Rights
              (*Ruch Obrony Praw Człowieka i Obywatela*)
RT   Roundtable Talks
SČSS   Union of Czechoslovak Writers
              (*Svaz Československých Spisovatelů*)
SD   Democratic Party (*Stronnictwo Demokratyczne*)
SKS   Student Solidarity Committee
              (*Studencki Komitet Solidarności*)
StB   State Security (*Státní Bezpečnost*)
SzDSz   Alliance of Free Democrats
              (*Szabad Demokraták Szövetsége*)

SZETA	Foundation for Supporting the Poor (*Szegényeket Támogató Alap*)
SZOT	National Council of Trade Unions (*Szakszervezetek Országos Tanácsa*)
SZSP	Socialist Union of Polish Students (*Socjalistyczne Zrzeszenie Studentków Polskich*)
TIT	Society for the Dissemination of Scientific Knowledge (*Tudományos Ismeretterjesztő Társaság*)
TKK	Provisional Coordinating Commission (*Tymczasowa Komisja Krajowa*)
TKN	Society of Scientific Courses (*Towarzystno Kursów Naukowych*)
VONS	Committee for the Defense of the Unjustly Persecuted (*Výbor na Obranu Nespravedlivě Stichaných*)
VPN	Public against Violence (*Verejnost Proti Násilu*)
WTO	Warsaw Treaty Organization
ZMS	Union of Socialist Youth (*Związek Młodziezy Socjalistycznej*)
ZOMO	Motorized Units of Citizens' Militia (*Zmotoryzowane Oddziały Milicji Obywatelskiej*)
ZSL	United Peasants Party (*Zjednoczone Stronnictwo Ludowe*)

PREFACE

In November of 1995 Jeffrey Isaac published an article for *Political Theory* which condemned political theorists *en masse* in the United States for failing to take seriously the revolutions of 1989 in Central Europe, through which "the face of world politics for five decades was transformed" (1995: 636). 1989 was a political milestone equal in scope and importance to both the French and American Revolutions, yet unlike these two previous watersheds which had sparked much debate among political thinkers, and indeed to some extent been provoked by them,[1] the reaction of the professional mainstream had been minimal. Isaac was critical of the pervasive silence and lack of attention paid to both the events themselves, and the activists/theorists and ideas behind them. The statistics are tellingly damning: in the years between 1989 and 1993 in his review of the "major outlets of political theory" (that is, the academic journals *Political Theory*, *Polity*, *American Political Science Review*, *Philosophy and Public Affairs*, and *Ethics*) he found that only two out of 384 articles dealt with 1989, one of which was a review essay (1995: 637).[2] This represents a "shocking indictment" of political theory, and sharply contrasts with the canon. After all, thinkers from Plato and Machiavelli to Hegel, de Tocqueville and Marx were profoundly *engagé* with the events and political realities of their day.

Isaac suggests four possible reasons for "the strange silence of political theory" but in each case finds the explanation unsatisfactory. First, he posits that it is the recency of the events themselves, but then adds that current political theory "itself is so intellectually faddish [that it can] hardly plead patience and caution when it comes to interpreting current events" (1995: 638). Moreover, as Isaac argues, it is hard to maintain such a position in consideration of the great "canonic" theorists, such as Locke, Paine, Kant, Hegel, or Marx, who made it their business to comment on and theorize about the great events, movements, and conditions of their day—from the French Revolution and religious tolerance to the inhumane social conditions of primitive capitalist development. In fact, one could argue that engagement is what made them great political theorists in the first place, and qualified them for subsequent beatification and inclusion in the canon.[3] After all, political theory developed into a professionalized academic discipline long after the real lives and activities of those thinkers. The process of appropriating and institutionalizing their legacies for scholarly consumption has served to retrospectively transform them. An unfortunate result has been the false bifurcation of political theory into questions of "first" and "second" order, that is, theory about politics and metatheory about how we reflect about politics. My examination of the dissidents of East-Central Europe as political theorists is also an exercise in the reintegration of political science and normative political theory. I argue that political theory and theorists properly contextualized and understood are intimately involved in both the enterprise of understanding/explanation as well as prescription/critique.

Second, Isaac postulates the explanation lies in the fact that contemporary theorists are unfamiliar with the cultures and languages of Central Europe, given the strong Western European bias of political theory. On the surface this is more plausible, but Isaac points out that "language barriers have never really constrained political theorists from offering interpretations of texts or the events to which they are related" (1995: 639). Isaac's example is that of Machiavelli:

> Question most self-respecting political theorists ... and they will offer you some interpretation of Machiavelli. Can you imagine many political theorists saying that they could not comment on or write about Machiavelli because they could not read Italian or grasp sixteenth-century Florentine idioms in the original? The writings of the principal Soviet bloc democratic oppositionists Havel, Michnik, Lipski, Konrád, Szelényi, Sakharov, and others—have been amply translated into English. They have long been available to the English-speaking world, and there is no linguistic excuse for having avoided them.

This is especially true for the contemporary political theorist who rushes to publish on Habermas, Derrida or Foucault with research and insight based on translations of their works, rather than interpretations based on the German or French originals (languages far more accessible to the Anglo-American academic context than either Slavic or Finno-Ugric languages!). The "cultural distinctiveness" argument is further invalidated by the fact that any cursory reading of the their works yields an interpretation of their collective *oeuvre* that places it squarely in the broader European context. As Isaac points out (and my interviews corroborate) "... the fact is that the Central Europeans have believed themselves to be, and have been, part of a cosmopolitan tradition of humanistic values with roots in the European Renaissance and Enlightenment" (1995: 639).

The third point raised by Isaac is that the Central European "literature of revolt" although both "historically [and] politically significant" is regarded by those who ignore it as neither "especially innovative [n]or genuinely theoretical" (1995: 639). This criticism is based on a profoundly conservative assumption of what constitutes political theory, all the more ironic in light of post-modernism and its influential critique of the epistemological constructions of such creatures as "authentic theory," not to mention the actual existence of the canon itself. This argument suggests that the work of the Central Europeans is *mere* political commentary, and that the issues dealt with are somehow "casual, uninteresting, [and] *unphilosophical*" (emphasis in original; 1995: 640). Even a cursory glance at the topics covered, however, suggests otherwise. Isaac points out that their work contains arguments about "the ethical and strategic prospects of different forms of resistance, the nature of democratic citizenship, and the importance of civil society" (1995: 640). I would add that the Central Europeans addressed questions of morality in political action (Havel's "living in truth") and the importance of self-limitation and non-violence in the radical transformation of politics (the formulations of Michnik and Kis change the way we conceive of revolution both historically and strategically).

The addition of these topics helps defeat Isaac's fourth possible explanation—that the democratic oppositionists have received too much credit, but are "simply unoriginal, revisiting the themes and concerns of nineteenth-century democratic liberalism with which we are all familiar"; it is not that they are "insufficiently deep, but rather ... simply anachronistic and old hat" (1995: 640). Even if true, this charge would a) require a strong engagement with the theorists themselves, and b) is based on the assumption that re-articulation or being derivative constitutes a reason for intellectual dismissal.

A major purpose of this work is to take up Isaac's challenge, and to analyze seriously the *oeuvre* of the Central European dissidents *qua* political theory. Central and Eastern Europe have been the political laboratory of the twentieth century *par excellence*, the testing ground of both fascism and the many varieties of authoritarian communism. If there is an intrinsic connection between political events and the ideas inspiring or underwritten by them, it stands to reason that this must be a birthplace and breeding ground for indigenous political theory. In fact, much of the Marxian-inspired political theory from the first half of the century (Luxemburg, Lukács, and even Gramsci) as well as the succeeding "critical" and "post-Marxist" variants in recent decades (Adorno, Horkheimer, Arendt, Habermas) can be said to be distinctively Central European in both derivation and content. There are a number of strong commonalities despite the obvious differences—the stress on political and economic equality; the need for humankind to be freed from alienation and instrumental reason and be able to participate meaningfully in politics and society writ large; an analysis of the mental, structural, and historical constraints mitigating such engagement; and finally what one might call the blessing and the curse of post-Enlightenment European thought—the central tenet that human beings as political agents and masters of their own subjectivity can act both individually and in concert to change their circumstances. Not incidentally, these commonalities also extend to the theorists and the activists of dissident movements and the democratic opposition of Central Europe prior to 1989.

The challenge posed by Isaac is not a small one, for I am not merely extending the boundaries of a discipline that has often self-consciously described itself as progressive, radical or indeed revolutionary in scope or implications. Rather, I am conducting a bold experiment to further our understanding of the relationship of political ideas to political change, and to examine how in the late-twentieth century ordinary and extraordinary human beings make this happen.

In order to situate this work into broader metatheoretical discussions in political theory, it is necessary to make explicit my assumptions regarding the nature of political theorizing as an activity and state the hypotheses afforded by this *a priori* declaration. My views on what constitutes political theory, and how it is related to politics—or stated another way, the old issue of the *vita contemplativa* and the *vita activa* debated by Plato and Aristotle—have been formed in reaction to the school of "Cambridge contextualists," most notably Quentin Skinner and James Tully. However, as will be seen below, I have been deeply influenced by contemporary feminist theory in its efforts to broaden the political, and in effect to de-canonize the sacred and elevate the profane. And although I agree with Skinner that ideological context and intentionality of the author are especially paramount in examining the work of self-professed intellectuals, one can no more detach the author from her or his surroundings than detach intention from meaning. Thus the work of Neal Wood and C. B. Macpherson is a powerful corrective to a narrow view of contextualism rather than its materially based deconstruction.

Rather than beginning with the right set of procedures in understanding a particular text, however, the prior question of what is considered political theory requires elaboration. Skinner correctly argues that political life sets the main problems for the political theorist, causing a certain range of questions to become the leading subjects of debate.[4] Thus James Tully states: "Political theory, then, is as Aristotle and Marx would say, a part of politics, and the questions it treats are the effects of political action" (1988: 11). As theorists we end up focussing a great deal on the "big questions," such as justice, liberty, and equality, and most can agree on their relevance, having grown out of political life at certain historical conjunctures. Before going under the surgeon's knife of the political theorist and abstracted beyond reasonable comprehension, the genesis of theory was and is the need to examine and analyze the burning questions of the day critically and comprehensively. For this reason alone I believe it is sufficient to categorize the *oeuvre* of Central European dissident thought *qua* political theory. Writers such as Michnik, Havel, and Kis were pragmatically engaged in politics at the same time as they deliberately not only theorized about it but self-consciously operated within the larger tradition of European political thought.

Following both Foucault and feminist theory, political theory has been expanded notionally but not practically or systematically by the idea that power relations underlie all politics and our attempts to construct and categorize knowledge about politics (and *vice versa*), and that the subject matter of politics is just as easily the household as the public sphere, or the family versus the formal institutions of ruling. The pursuit of political life has conventionally focussed on the *polis*, the explicitly political community from which the responsibilities and rights of citizenship arise. Thus Paul Ricoeur states:

The point of view of philosophy is, on the contrary, that the individual becomes human only within this totality which is the "universality of citizens". The threshold of humanity is the threshold of citizenship, and the citizen is a citizen only through the state. Hence the movement of political philosophy starts with happiness, which all men pursue, moves to the proper end of the state, then to its nature as a self-sufficient totality, and from there to the citizen (1984: 252).

Contrary to Ricoeur, I maintain that political relationships involving mutual responsibilities and structures of obligation and consent can just as easily emerge from the private sphere (especially where it forms a substitute for the public sphere, as arguably occurred in Central and Eastern Europe) or from civil society itself. We need to recognize that programs of thought and action which are not institutionally centered may also constitute political theory. It is political *life* which is at issue, rather than the *polis* or some modern variation thereof.

However, the linguistic and post-modern turn in all forms of philosophy has also meant that our Foucauldian gaze is increasingly directed toward the text, rather than the context, even as we have simultaneously robbed texts of authority and authors of meaning. Thus my metatheoretical critique of both Skinner and Derrida is that simply too much time is spent on interpretation rather than on the power or force of the ideas themselves, and how they were or can be operationalized in a particular ideological *and* social context.

This leads me to my first assumption, which I call the "ideas matter" thesis. Basically, I argue that ideas matter profoundly in delimiting opportunities, helping to formulate political-cultural responses, and, and in predisposing key actors to some decisions and courses of action over others. There is a necessary connection between political theory and political change, and to me there is no better twentieth-century example than the revolutions of 1989. Like Stark (1992), I contend path dependence is indeed important in assessing the processes of transformation, but would add that it has an *ideological* dimension as well. The relevant connection is not simply a logical one, such as that proposed by Alasdair McIntyre, for whom actions have meaning and theories are implicitly and logically necessary to understand those meanings. It is more *causal* in nature, although not in the sense of predictive social science. I suggest we separate institutional history or history-as-events and the history of ideas at our peril; in order to understand complex political phenomena we must understand the dynamic relationship between them. I am not denying the staggering importance of structural determinants rooted in culture, history, or political economy or to suggest that ideas are either independently *Geist*-like and Hegelian, or merely superstructural. There is a compelling complexity of relationships and factors concerning all forms of change, political or otherwise.

Taking ideas seriously means understanding where ideas came from and what they grew out of, as well as a thoroughgoing examination of what happened *after* those ideas were in circulation. Traditional Straussian historiographers of political thought privilege the interpreter; Cambridge contextualists privilege the interpreted. Two metahistorical flaws occur in both approaches. As John Keane suggests, there is the inescapable need to assert the "one true methodology" in both approaches, which is covertly positivist and also ignores the inescapable subjectivity of the interpretation process itself. (Furthermore, these authoritative tendencies tend to result in a curious reproduction of the same political canon regardless of whose gaze is involved.) Second, the focus is usually temporally unidirectional: on the *before* rather than the *after*. Strauss focussed on such arcane issues as how the level of political persecution would lead the author to disguise meaning only to have the sacred truths unveiled later by the clever philosopher. Similarly, Skinner or J. G. A. Pocock discussed the ideological context of the "mirror of princes" literature at the time Machiavelli wrote the *Prince* and how he literally turned the genre on its head. However, I believe strongly that in order to understand the force of ideas in politics, we have to redirect our interpretative gaze to what happened *afterward*. It is hard to even conceive of the twentieth-century unfolding the way that it did, for example, with the explosion of the Russian Revolution at the beginning of our era, if not for the writings and dynamism of Karl Marx.

In making a causal claim for ideas, I cannot in this study focus solely on antecedents, in the same way Hannah Arendt does in *The Origins of Totalitarianism* or Jürgen Habermas in *The Structural Transformation of the Public Sphere*. To give the argument some force and meaning, I must also look at consequences. For this reason, in my conclusion I focus not just on dissident ideas but on the particular impact of these ideas on post-1989 East-Central Europe.

To accept that ideas are powerful motivators of political actors and offer humankind visions of something new or better, is to also implicitly suggest my second assumption—that actors are significant agents of political change. Following O'Donnell and Schmitter (1989), I suggest that human agency plays a more privileged role in moments of magnified and rapid historical change. This is both a theoretical and practical argument against both the scientistic rationalism of orthodox Marxist philosophy (although *not* necessarily political practice inspired by Marx) and forms of post-modernism that for all intents and purposes deny the possibility for human agency. Reclaiming subjectivity and political activism go hand in hand, for without ideas political action has no meaning. With the downfall of authoritarian communism in Central and Eastern Europe came the destruction of a particular ideological vision, no matter how bankrupt and removed from the original source that vision had become. Now we are supposedly in a "global marketplace" where ideas, like goods, move freely. But the magic of markets is in their ever-changing relativities of value; nothing is intrinsically better or worse. Ideas, like consumer goods, are the subject of fad, and are continuously re-tooled, made obsolete, or sold through sophisticated marketing strategies. They are deprived of meaning, which may be just as well in the Nietzschean-inspired universe populated by post-modern academics. Part of the millennial malaise faced by political agents (although curiously not by political theorists) is the search for vision, meaning, and coherence in a world stripped of radical departures and alternatives. Daniel Bell spoke of the end of ideology too prematurely, and Francis Fukuyama applauded the end of history; in my view what we need is more of both. Well-grounded knowledge of the past and some form of political orientation toward the future are necessary if political action is to be anything more than catering to the whims of market economics, whose very purpose is to deny the legitimacy or primacy of politics in the first place. The alternative is that spontaneous protest against injustice remains just that, as hopelessly irrelevant, not disseminated by official or unofficial media, and devoid of any broader purpose. What this is called is less important than that it be called something, if ideas are to serve as rallying cries, and if politics is to maintain its independence into the next century. Ideas only have force in politics if human agents carry those ideas forward.

In terms of research methodology, I rely on the traditional sources of political theory: texts about political ideas. In this case, the texts themselves were not written intentionally as a contribution to the theoretical canon, but as a result of political engagement (not unlike most of the now-canonized tomes of political theory). Many of these texts are not traditional non-fictional histories or programmatic narratives and many of the ideas that constitute the *oeuvre* are contained in unofficial media or in a non-traditional format. By the catch-all term "dissident political theory" I refer not only to such impressive works as Havel's landmark essay "The Power of the Powerless" but also to the novels, plays, poetry, *feuilletons*, unofficial or "flying university" seminars, samizdat newspaper articles, and even various forms of performance art and cultural expression that made the opposition so distinctive, creative and frankly, difficult to penetrate and stop effectively. Thus I am broadening political theory not just in terms of *who* is accepted, but also *what*.

In this respect, I concur with Douglas Williams when he argues that as theorists we should not only "engage with our times" but also consider conducting "political theory by other means." As Williams describes, the traditional labor of professional political theory encompasses "... the reconstruction of the thought of our predecessors; clarification of the languages and concepts we alternately take for granted and debate as citizens and scholars; and the evaluation of the performance and justification of public policies, political institutions and their leaders in light of some pre-established theoretical point of departure" (1991: 91). Williams suggests the arcane methodology of political theorists and the density of their typically rarefied objects of study have combined to produce and sustain a variety of gaps and interstices between the academic world and the real world. By expanding our universe of theoretical discourse beyond "formal treatises and other didactic, systematic sorts of inquiries" to other more experimental and expressive reflections of political thought and life, we give more serious consideration to other narratives and formats which permeate our cultures and daily lives. Williams' view of political theory is expansive, and its objects of study should include films, paintings, novels, sculptures and monuments, poetry, popular music, rock videos, television, and "... a host of other cultural practices [which] are powerful channels of discourse daily traversing those individual and collective narratives we habitually describe as our lives" (1991: 93). In my view, no genre is *intrinsically* theoretical or atheoretical, but each case must be examined seriously and in context. Political theory can and should be much more than what academic political theorists do.

In order to grasp and sustain an argument about the full range of ideas under discussion in dissident circles, I have spent as much time reading novels, watching films and documenting oral histories as reading essays and published works. I have been privileged to supplement this research with personal interviews of many former activists and opposition intellectuals in Poland, Hungary, and Czechoslovakia. These interviews have been helpful in documenting the relationships, both personal and intellectual, among the dissidents of the three countries under discussion and their mutual admiration for or points of departure from each other.

The three countries studied here—Poland, Czechoslovakia, and Hungary—were chosen with considerable deliberation. First, they share a similar historical trajectory in this century. They are all partially or wholly successor states to the Austro-Hungarian Empire. Their inter-war experiences were both formative in setting the context of political debate and the regimes of this period served later as important historical referents. Not by accident was the 1918–1938 Czechoslovak state referred to as the "First Republic," and the post-1989 state as the "Second Republic." Hungary's loss of two-thirds of its territory thanks to the Treaty of Trianon[5] sharply shaped the contours of its interwar agenda: without full knowledge of the Treaty's implications it is hard if not impossible to understand its alliance with Nazi Germany, the very revolutionary demands of 1956, or the persistence of fringe nationalist movements and the important "minorities question" in contemporary post-communist Hungary. The reemergence of Poland after over a century of partition assumed mythic proportions as the successful result of romantic and messianic nationalism; the legend was furthered by the difficult circumstances of state formation and consolidation given the war with the USSR which did not end until 1921. Second, all three countries had indigenous fascist experiences and/or were subject to German fascism. Third, not only were they subject, along with the rest of the nations east of the Yalta divide, to the imposition of Soviet-style authoritarian communism, but all had internationally significant and important movements against Soviet hegemony. Moreover such watershed events such as the Hungarian Revolution of 1956, the Polish October of the same year, the Prague Spring, and the dramatic rise of Solidarity in 1980–1981 reflected an internal regional dynamic of influence and subsequent revision. The "unacceptable" demands that were an outgrowth of the Hungarian revolution of 1956, such as withdrawal from the Warsaw Pact, international neutrality, and the declaration of multiparty competition were countered by the Prague Spring, the apotheosis of reform communism. When the careful Czechoslovak strategy of economic reform, relaxation of censorship, and new openness was met by Soviet "fraternal assistance" in the form of tanks and an occupying force from neighboring countries, internal reforms to the party-state or top-down approaches to changing the system were more or less abandoned by the progressive intellectual elites. Not only did the later normalization pave the way for the alliance and the approach represented by Charter 77, but the twin deaths of the Prague Spring and reform communism profoundly influenced the democratic opposition in Hungary and the worker–intellectual alliance nurtured by KOR, which later came into full bloom with Solidarity.

Opposition movements and activities increasingly from the 1970s onward were mutually influential. Despite the restrictions on travel and on the free circulation of ideas, particularly for those critical of the regime, there were considerable and important connections made, in the form of illicit border meetings, personal visits, public letters of support and condemnation, the funneling of samizdat via internal and external contacts. These bonds are borne out through the use of similar concepts and strategies—diverse in origin yet strong in mutual recognition. Intellectual activists in the region indeed constructed together a coherent *oeuvre* of political theory via a shared sociology of knowledge.

For historical reasons, 1968 is an appropriate and obvious date to begin, as it signaled the end of hopes for a "reformed," or "enlightened" communism in the Eastern Bloc with the crushing of the Prague Spring, an event which reverberated far beyond the borders of Czechoslovakia. The late 1960s in Poland was a time of considerable unrest and protest, especially among students and in universities—a period which resulted in considerable backlash. Most notable was the imprisonment of Jacek Kuroń and Karol Modzelewski for their controversial *Open Letter to the Party*, the expulsion of former Marxist philosopher Leszek Kołakowski from the party after his critical lectures on the events of 1956, the banning of nationalist author Adam Mickiewicz's *Forefathers' Eve* from being performed at the National Theatre in Warsaw, and the resulting anti-Semitic backlash. Meanwhile in Hungary, communist leader János Kádár introduced the "New Economic Mechanism" in 1968–1969, which was intended to partially liberalize the economy, and signaled a loosening of ideological control and a reduction in the level and type of state surveillance and repression with his famous policy "he who is not against us is with us."

These events indicate a series of beginnings; my analysis will commence with this period and continue through the 1970s and the 1980s—for example, from the Workers' Riots in 1971 and 1976 in Poland to the formation of both KOR and Solidarity; the "normalization" in Czechoslovakia and the dissident response in the activities of both Charter 77 and VONS, and later Civic Forum and Public Against Violence; the original (and at first lonely) activism of dissidents such as Miklós Haraszti and author György Konrád, as well as the work of the "Budapest School" of intellectuals, through to the eventual formation of groups such as the Alliance of Free Democrats and the Federation of Young Democrats.

This study focuses intentionally on dissident *intellectuals*. I have deliberately not included worker activists or nationalist anti-communists, not because they were not important, but because it was largely intellectuals who self-reflexively wrote and theorized about their political practice.[6] Many were active in or helped create non party-state organizations.[7] This distinction is especially important in the Polish context, where there existed a large working class opposition, from which many organizers and activists also wrote critically and analytically about their experiences.[8] There are also practical reasons for this approach. First, their writings, both officially published as well as samizdat, are widely available in English, French, or German translation. Second, those more actively and prominently involved exercised considerable intellectual influence over their peers. Finally, marginalized academics, writers, and oppositionally-minded intellectuals were concerned with constructing an alternative to the Yalta division of Europe. Breaking the East–West axis by positing the real and imagined existence of a "Central Europe" was a form of revisionist history, a political goal, and a strategy of increasing the layers of interconnectedness. As a result, a commonality of themes and approaches can be ascertained from a detailed analysis of their work. The most prominent and influential dissidents who were active in opposition movements and who wrote about their experiences and theorized about politics more broadly include Jacek Kuroń, Adam Michnik, and Leszek Kołakowski[9] of Poland; Václav Havel, Václav Benda, Jan Patočka[10], and the Chartists of Czechoslovakia; and János Kis, György Bence, Miklós Haraszti, and György Konrád of Hungary.

Members of the intellectual opposition in all three countries were united by their nuanced and particularly Central European understanding of a grand-historical tradition of political engagement.[11] They self-consciously operated within the traditional roles of moral and political leadership and societal engagement assigned to Central European intellectuals. It can certainly be argued, as do György Konrád and Ivan Szelényi in *The Intellectuals on the Road to Class Power*, that in Central Europe "the intelligentsia, organized into a government-bureaucratic ruling class, has taken the lead in modernization, replacing a weak bourgeoisie incapable of breaking with feudalism" (1979: 10). The intellectual took the place of the entrepreneur as the engine and spokesperson of dynamic change and development. Historically the Central European intellectual faced a dilemma: either become an agent of the state or become completely independent and critical of its authoritarianism and the prevailing *étatiste* form of development—in other words, be a bureaucrat or a revolutionary (1979: 85–86). Thus early dissenters were also the protectors of the ideals of Western Europe, whether as socialists following Lassalle or Luxemburg or after World War I as adherents to the Wilsonian principles of national self-determination and parliamentary democracy (Rupnik, 1988: 13–16). Those who chose the road of collaboration with the state assumed leadership roles often as romantic nationalists or as committed socialists intent on rebuilding their war-torn societies in the postwar period. Characteristic of this pattern has been the commitment to a "social teleology oriented toward growth" (Konrád and Szelényi, 1979: 86), the pursuit of ends without regard to the means employed, which reached its apogee in both the industrial achievements and social degradation of authoritarian communism. This privileged role of the intellectual continued in the post-totalitarian 1970s and 1980s, and thus it is not surprising that such intellectuals became the champions of a distinctive vision of Central Europe. Almost all of the dissidents in Czechoslovakia and Hungary could be described as intellectuals, and although dissent became in Poland an ultimately more widespread phenomenon, many of the leaders and a large core of the activists were also intellectuals.

When Julien Benda published *La Trahison des Clercs* in 1928, he gave substance and meaning to what he perceived as a disturbing trend in modern life: the tendency of intellectuals to play the game of political passions. He compared the *engagé* intellectuals of his day to the earlier masters of critical thought and innovation who, like Kant and Rousseau, when concerned with high principles—such as justice or equality—took a critical and dispassionate stance, abstracting themselves from immediate results and purposefully distancing themselves from the masses. By contrast, the new breed of intellectual he describes

> ... is determined to have the soul of a citizen and to make vigorous use of it; he is proud of that soul; his literature is filled with contempt for the man who shuts himself up with art or science and takes no interest in the passions of the State ...
>
> The time has long past by since Plato demanded that this philosopher should be bound in chains in order to compel him to take an interest in the State. To have as his function the pursuit of eternal things and yet to believe that he becomes greater by concerning himself with the State—that is the view of the modern 'clerk' (Benda, 1928: 32–33).

In Benda's view, the political commitment of the *"clercs"* amounts to a dangerous and inevitably slippery slope toward blind partisanship, xenophobia, and fanaticism, where liberty of thought is swallowed up by closed-mindedness, and the particularism of a cause is substituted for the universal good of humanity.

It is easy to understand how Benda's prescient predictions of ill-gotten political gains championed by intellectuals sure of their positions and surer still of their chosen paths, would ring true for anti-communists living through the consolidation of Soviet-style authoritarian communism in the postwar satellite regimes of East-Central Europe. When Czeslaw Miłosz first published *The Captive Mind* in Cold War America, he helped spawn an intellectual counter-current to which this book remains of biblical importance. Seeringly critical of his Polish compatriots who willingly embraced or who unsuspectingly succumbed to the power of the 'New Faith', Miłosz champions instead an independent intellectual who both refuses all complicity with tyranny and all pressures to conform.

The post-1968 dissidents of East-Central Europe took both Benda and Miłosz to heart. In a sense, they were trying to "reverse" the earlier betrayal, by making a commitment to political and social change that was deeply rooted in independence of thought and action, respect for the rights of the individual, the need to restore human subjectivity, and re-introduce morality into politics. My narrative is thus the latest chapter in the century-old dilemma that has plagued the European "republic of letters" at least since *L'Affaire Dreyfus*. The supreme irony is that, although these dissidents were conscious of their debt to Benda, in many respects they fulfilled their destinies as the same kind of intellectual Benda sought to decry, albeit in the service of a different set of commitments than their predecessors. There is a fickle continuity to the role of intellectuals in this part of Europe, a discussion which I will take up again in my final conclusions.

A Note on Nomenclature

There is the problem of how to describe the regimes of Poland, Czechoslovakia, and Hungary in the 1945–1989 period. In the literature, the generic labels most often encountered are "communism, " "authoritarian communism, " "socialism, " "state socialism, " and "really-existing socialism."[12] Both "socialism" and "communism" *tout court* are problematic as they are more properly ideological constructs rather than geographical locations. To use either term is either to come dangerously close to absorbing the McCarthyist rhetoric of the 1950s, where all socialist or communist beliefs were reduced to and conflated with the sphere of Soviet domination (and by this logic all communists or socialists were inevitably Soviet agents), or to adopting the linguistic codes the regimes used to describe themselves. Invariably, the countries following the Soviet model portrayed their historical progress as moving towards socialism, reaching the stage of advanced socialism, or finally nearing the desired ideal of full-fledged communism. Thus Marx's theory of history was simplistically reduced to a stage-based recipe, where the ingredients of the one stage (socialism) contained the necessary but not sufficient conditions for moving to the next stage (communism). At the same time, in the West both terms came in the postwar period to have historically specific and politically constituted meanings. In Europe, communism was often associated with the phenomenon of "Eurocommunism," and socialism, along with its linguistic relatives social democracy and democratic socialism, were linked to a political project independent of the USSR to resuscitate the socialist ideal either as compatible with a nationally-driven market economy or not (depending on the formulation). "State socialism" came into vogue in the 1970s and 1980s as a *détente* alternative in describing not only the Warsaw Pact countries, but also all countries ruled monopolistically and ideologically by a communist party, and where the economies were centrally planned and controlled by the party-state. Moreover, the term "state socialism" was used to describe the system more in its economic dimensions, with authors such as Alec Nove, Michael Burawoy, and Domenico Mario Nuti applying it primarily or solely to the economic structure and organization of the Soviet model. The term was a victim of its own success—its supposed neutrality fails to distinguish normatively between these systems and other forms of socialism (either real or ideal) which in order to meet their stated requirements must rely significantly on the state. At the same time, the term masks the inability of these systems to meet their own stated *socialist* objectives. Those who hesitatingly use the "socialist" descriptor (with or without the "state") must acknowledge these difficulties, as does János Kornai in his 1992 study *The Socialist System: The Political Economy of Communism*:

> All over the world there are political currents that use the term "socialism" in the normative sense, attaching specific ethical principles to it. Although they interpret the value system of socialism in a number of different ways, most have a constituent in common: they see the combatting of poverty and helping the needy, weak, and disadvantaged as one of the main objectives of socialism. By this definition, a socialist state has a duty to redistribute material welfare more fairly. Now measured by this yardstick, the classical socialist system [read: the Soviet model] just partly fulfills its mission. Some of its institutions help fulfill it, while others hinder; its policy in this respect is inconsistent and self-contradictory. For those who consider this criterion to be the hallmark of a socialist social system, the Scandinavian countries have made far more progress toward socialism than the socialist countries (1992: 327).

This leads to my adopting the term "authoritarian communism" as perhaps the best of a bad lot. First, this term normatively describes the system at hand as "authoritarian" linking it in some respects with other authoritarian regimes and as theoretically and practically distinct from democratic regimes. Second, the term communism manages somewhat imperfectly to unite internal descriptions (by both its dissenters and its official representatives and defenders) with the external description of common parlance.

Communism itself has been widely distinguished as having two chief varieties: Stalinist or totalitarian and post-Stalinist or post-totalitarian. Totalitarianism itself is, of course, a contestable and debatable concept when applied to the region. In Anglo-American social science, this term is usually associated with a) the definition of Carl Friedrich and Zbigniew Brzezinski or b) the writings of Hannah Arendt.[13] The Friedrich/Brzezinski definition is inextricably linked with American Cold War politics, and the desire to paint authoritarian communism as completely monolithic and intrinsically evil. Skilling and Griffiths, in their controversial landmark work *Interest Groups in Soviet Politics* effectively deconstructed this image. In this study, the term "totalitarianism" must be understood initially in its Arendtian sense, as Arendt's work had immense influence on the dissidents active in Central Europe. Havel and Michnik use Arendt as their own point of departure.

Many social scientists have argued that once terror is removed from either the Friedrich/Brzezinski definition or the Arendtian portrayal, totalitarianism no longer properly exists. According to this logic, terror is the only instrument truly effective in the totalization of society. Without the active implementation of a campaign of terror, society, through its inherent complexity and size, is able to differentiate itself through the formation of a multiplicity of competing interests.[14] Different from Western conceptions of pluralism, any formation of active and passive resistance renders the terminology of totalitarianism meaningless. In the spirit of intellectual détente, academics moved toward the adoption of more neutral descriptions, often categorizing the regimes of Central and Eastern Europe as one form or another of authoritarianism.

In describing the governing apparatus or state structures of authoritarian communism, most recent historical literature adopts the term "party-state," and I will be doing the same here. Again, this comes from a need to distinguish the state of authoritarian communism from the state of either democratic or other forms of authoritarian regimes. One of the unique features of authoritarian communism is its fusion of the party as initially a vanguardist and later as a mass mobilizational force with the state itself, such that political positions in the state can only be understood as part of broader relationships of power that include positions in the party as well. Both in the Soviet Union and its satellites in the Eastern Bloc, the highest political position of "president" was often occupied by the same person who was the "First Secretary" or leader of the Communist Party. Like fascism but unlike bureaucratic authoritarianism, the party was at one and the same time in control of and over the state, the only upward mobilizational force in political life, and the most important educational and political instrument in the dissemination of correct history and ideology. This was neatly summarized and understood by all as "the leading role of the party."

So central was the party-state to the functioning of authoritarian communism that once it was threatened, as in Poland by the very existence of Solidarity, the party-state itself was in jeopardy. This self-fulfilling prophecy of the hard-liners—that "giving in" on the leading role of the party or allowing for *any* form of political pluralism that could be dubbed oppositional or even mildly independent of partisan control was the thin edge of the wedge that could bring the system down—was the justification for many of the more lamentable strategies of the Warsaw Pact, as well as some of the more clever tactics of the evolving opposition. Both the Hungarian uprising of 1956 and the Prague Spring were crushed because, among other errors, they allowed independent thought and organizations (more explicitly in the former, more as a result of things "getting out of hand" in the latter). In contradistinction, Gomułka's accession to power in 1956 in Poland was not marked by such independent currents (for criticism and such "opposition" was largely within the party at this time). One of the brilliant insights of Adam Michnik was to realize the importance of an independent civil society in representing a *de facto* challenge to the leading role of the party.

ACKNOWLEDGMENTS

This book would not have been possible without the help, advice, and support of family, colleagues, and dear friends. For making this work emotionally and financially possible, I must first thank my husband Jules, who shares my love of East-Central Europe, from which both our families came over a century ago. I thank my parents Mearl and Faith Falk whose love, understanding, and generosity of time is beyond description. My daughter Alannah has patiently put up with a distracted mother for too many years while I researched and refined this manuscript.

Many mentors, colleagues, and friends at York University read earlier chapters and drafts: Ross Rudolph, Bernie Frolic, Ioan Davies, Leo Panitch, Stephen Newman, Allan Hutchinson, Christian Lenhardt, and Henrik Flakierski. Many others supported me with helpful advice and friendship—especially Stephen and Judy Hellman, Chris Roberts, Mark Baron, Pamela Leach, Gerald Kernerman, Denise Rosenthal, Ruth Groff, Andrew Biro, Greg Chin, David Pottie, John Peters, Andrzej Zaslove, Joanne Wright, Anne Stretch, Marlene Quesenberry, and Lorraine Hardie.

Special thanks go to the past and present members of the Skilling Seminar, most particularly Markéta Doležel Evans, Nadya Nedelsky, Linda Mastalir, Mirella Eberts, Martin Horak, Marta Dyczok, Andrea Harrington, Jim Norman, Marta Karenova, Glenys Babcock, Petr Kafka, Essyn Emurla, Anna Vaničková, and Marci Shore. Gordon Skilling's influence on my work is immeasurable, and thanks also to the support I have received from Peter and David Skilling, and Jane Francis.

Straddling the divide between work, parenthood, and the academy has only been possible by friends who have provided encouragement, advice, and countless acts of kindness: thanks especially to Christine Burton, Nancy Lewis, Lillian Bloch, Linda Gee, Kim Jantzi, Emil Sher, Kathryn Miller, Diane Bull, Wendy Cuthbertson, Nan Weiner, Leslie

Macleod, Linda Kahn, Jane Adams, Barbara Vari, Warren Magnusson, Keith Krause, Jennifer Milliken, Stephen Gelb, Shireen Hassim, Randy Germain, Mike Williams, Paul and Ossi Burger, Jennifer Brown, George Cordahi, Linda Mahaney, Daisy Perry, and Valentina Morgenshtern. Thanks for the support and assistance I have received in the last two years from the Centre for Russian and East European Studies at the University of Toronto, particularly from Peter Solomon, Don Schwartz, Bob Johnson, Edith Klein, and Janet Hyer. Colleagues Niamh Hennessy, Jean Baillargeon, and Tom Olien at Humber College have been especially helpful and supportive. Thanks to Tony Judt for his kind permission in using "The Dilemmas of Dissidence" as the title of this work: his earlier article employing the same clever alliteration was inspiring; his work is impressive and influential on my own. Thanks also to David Ost, Andrew Arato, John Keane, and Margaret Moore for their interest in my work.

Special appreciation goes to Maja Ćatić for her invaluable research assistance, Jeannine Casselman and James Thompson for last-minute editing and index help, Ariel Landau for his technical support and good humour, Jennifer Hammer for her early publication advice, Richárd Rados at Central European University Press for arranging all the details, and Jacek Kochanowicz, Jiří Musil, and András Bozóki for making extensive and useful comments on an earlier draft of my manuscript.

Formative for my understanding of the region was my attendance at the 1995 "Democracy and Diversity" program sponsored by the New School for Social Research in New York. I am grateful to Elzbieta Matynia who made this opportunity possible, and to Jeffrey Goldfarb and Ann Snitow. Many friendships grew from this experience and in particular Jana Juráňová, Gábor Magyar, Michal Vasečka, and Libora Oates-Indruchová stayed interested in my project or helped set up interviews.

Thanks to the Bůžek family in Prague and the Fleps family in Budapest—they welcomed me into their homes and their hearts, sharing difficult and personal memories of life before and after 1989.

The final thank-you must be reserved for the many opposition activists and intellectuals who agreed to be interviewed. I have long admired their collective combination of theory and practice, as well as their courageous commitment. They have generously shared memories, ideas, and their impatience with the past and the future. They were and are extraordinary individuals living and acting on one of the most important stages of the 20th century.

CHAPTER 1

INTRODUCTION

Writing more than ten years hence, one cannot overstate the fact that 1989 represents a historical watershed of immense proportions. History either ended or began again. The defining twentieth-century struggle—between liberal democracies with their apparently superior market economies and authoritarian communist regimes with their ossifying and crumbling command economies—came to a sudden and unexpected demise. The former emperors of the Soviet Bloc were left shivering and cold in their newly-revealed nakedness; the vast political and security apparatus of the party-state crumbled like a house of cards. As if the speed of this revolutionary and transformative process was not enough, the world marveled at its relative non-violence, the impressive level of social mobilization, and the propulsion of a rumpled-looking and naively idealistic group of opposition intellectuals into the media spotlight and critical leadership positions.

Social scientists had to be embarrassed over their collective failure to see what was coming and were quick to fill the shocked silence with a long list of reasons as to why communism fell so spectacularly. The explanations were legion and to some degree self-congratulatory: the United States with its superior system "won" the Cold War, long-suffering Central and East Europeans effectively voted with their feet and opted for Western consumerism, and in any event the old state-run economies were so riddled with inefficiencies and structural contradictions they could not survive the shift to post-industrial technology. Civil society was "re-born." Much credit deservedly landed in the lap of Soviet leader Mikhail Gorbachev, whose leadership and profound restraint under dizzying circumstances was indeed remarkable. The old order was swept away with astonishing speed because Moscow was not prepared to sanction the massive use of force that alone could have "saved" the communist regimes. Moreover, the party-state everywhere was too internally divided to strike the decisive blow against change.

Like other revolutions in centuries past, the events of 1989 had their intellectual forbears and opposition activists, strategists and tacticians. That their collective contribution was and remains as profound as the Federalists were to the American Revolution or the *philosophes* to the French Revolution was not immediately obvious. Intellectuals and dissident writers of the region not only contributed mightily to the unfolding of history, but also collectively bequeathed an *oeuvre* that constitutes one of the most original, insightful, and *useful* contributions to political theory today. Especially in the countries of Central and Eastern Europe, and most particularly in the cases of Poland, Czechoslovakia, and Hungary, the demise of communism was significantly aided and abetted by indigenous grassroots social movements. Unlike the Soviet Union, the impetus for change did not come from above, even where parallel developments internal to the party-state mirrored the efforts of the democratic opposition, as in Hungary.

The specific task of this study is to examine the theory and activism of indigenous intellectuals and dissident writers in Poland, Czechoslovakia, and Hungary from the late 1960s through to 1989. Some of the "philosophers" who effectively became "kings"—like current Czech president Václav Havel and *Gazeta Wyborcza* editor Adam Michnik—are well-known to Western political circles as committed public intellectuals. Much has been written by and about each of the former dissidents *individually*. However, my purpose here to examine their herculean *collective* effort to build a set of ideas and tactics so "outside the box" that they would effectively lead the struggle against authoritarian communism. Through literary and personal connections, the smuggling of *samizdat* across borders, and the dynamic played by a host of external events and players, the dissidents developed their political theory and strategies for change—*together*.

This study will focus on intellectual activists who were most prominent in both non-party-state opposition movements *and* who theorized and substantively reflected upon their experiences. Dramatically evoking the roles they played as dissidents, writers in prison, and actors in the events of 1989, the life and work of Jacek Kuroń and Adam Michnik in Poland, Václav Havel and the Chartists in Czechoslovakia, and finally János Kis, Miklós Haraszti, and György Konrád in Hungary are examined in depth. Taken as a whole, this dissident *oeuvre* contributes mightily to understanding of democratic transformation and consolidation; the tactics, strategies, and indeed moral necessity of non-violence in the social and political arena; responsibility in politics as essential in constructing "thick" citizenship; and civil society as the fulcrum of democratic life. Finally, the dissident *oeuvre* contributes to debates regarding the necessary reinvigoration of Western democracies in the face of globalization, external threats, and citizen anomie. We all require a renewed sense of citizen involvement and community; the revitalization of politics after a decade of market triumphalism is long overdue.

In the Anglo-American West, probably the most any average person knows about history of political opposition in East-Central Europe in the forty years of authoritarian communism that span roughly from the late 1940s to 1989 can be summarized into the names of a country, a city, and an organization—Hungary, 1956; Prague, 1968; and Solidarity, 1980. The implicit assumption is that no opposition existed between these flare-ups, that the leaders involved (such as Dubček) were hopelessly naive, and if one has any understanding of the division of Europe symbolically represented by Yalta, that the West dared not intervene to help these poor doomed souls given the delicate balance of international alliances and the awesome power of the Soviet Union. Indeed, the fact that the aforementioned events attracted massive international attention to a large degree served Western foreign policy interests nicely. The problem that this familiar caricature presents is twofold: 1) it is grossly inaccurate; and 2) it highlights the need of anyone writing *outside* the region, academic or otherwise, *not* to presume a level of general historical knowledge, or even of a cultivated interest.

Although the focal points of Prague in 1968 or the triumphant success of Solidarity in the 1980–1981 period were both critical and equal in scope and complexity, they nonetheless represent much more than a severe blip on the Richter Scale of political opposition. Rather, they denote peaks in a mountain of activity glacial in development and proportion. Obviously, events do not just happen, for *both* reasons of deep structure and individual agency. The voluminous accounts of revolutions that we have from such scholars as Barrington Moore and Theda Skocpol have taught us that broadly comparative analysis combined with the richness and specificity of detail can yield such conclusions as "how could it not *but* happen?" or simply remind us that there is a lot more to history than immediately meets the eye, warning us against simple determinism or easy explanations that enable us to easily slot practice into already existing theories. This is definitely the case when looking at East-Central Europe. The history of the political opposition in each of the countries studied here—Poland, Czechoslovakia, and Hungary—is so full of complexity, detail, and fundamentally *irreducible* to a series of television images of Warsaw Pact tanks in the streets of Prague or Hungarian freedom fighters struggling to keep control of Budapest.

With respect to the lack of assumed knowledge, the two Europes of the twentieth century are brought into sharp contrast. When one refers to "May 1968" in Paris, a series of historical images are brought to mind—students rioting in the streets, massive strikes as they are joined from workers from nearby factories, the overall sense of a social movement *in action*. Unfortunately, for most Westerners, when one refers to "March 1968" in Warsaw, no images immediately appear— one literally draws a blank. North America and the Western half of the European continent have a *shared history* for a multitude of reasons, not the least of which include the postwar division of Europe; the political, economic, and military predominance of the United States throughout the Cold War; the shared hegemony of capitalism and even its tamer aspects as represented in the various postwar settlements and agglomeration of welfare state policies; the ideological intertwining of capitalism and democracy as the ideological twin sisters of freedom and progress; and a network of economic and military alliances and agreements. As these extend eastward, as has already occurred with NATO and will soon happen with the European Union, the continent will knit itself together—not easily, not overnight—but Europe's reality will begin to match its geography.

History—particular in the post-Stalinist Cold War period—remains critical to this study. East-Central Europe was and remains a laboratory for all the political and economic experiments and disasters of the twentieth century. If Eric Hobsbawm is right in characterizing this short century as the "Age of Extremes" then this region is the "Region of Extremes." The collapse of empires at the end of World War I led to the bold Wilsonian experiment of attempting to draw state boundaries around nations or, when that proved impossible (as it was destined to be given the linguistic, religious diversity and mixed historical experience of the region), to attempt to make some innovative combinations— the result being the now-defunct nations of Yugoslavia and Czechoslovakia. The model to be followed—Western democracy and economic liberalism—broke down dramatically in the 1920s and 1930s. The Great Depression ravaged this underdeveloped half of Europe. Hungary, Poland and Slovakia all had their indigenous flirtations with fascism. Even the success story of the region—Czechoslovakia (which in the interwar years was the 10th strongest economy *in the world*)—collapsed from a combination of internal factors and external threats. The Munich agreement in 1938 signaled the cowardly acceptance by the Western powers of the failure of the model they had so boldly and confidently championed at Versailles.

In 1945 the region chose, or as Hobsbawm states "was made to choose," the Soviet model, which he accurately describes "a model for modernizing backward agrarian economies by planned industrial revolution" (Hobsbawm, 1993: 62). Unfortunately, given the intolerance of Moscow for the homegrown Left, it also meant the Stalinist liquidation of indigenous communism and anyone else accused of nationalist or deviationist tendencies. This *de facto* removal of political opposition, even in its most friendly quarters, succeeded only insofar as it cemented together in the minds of its victims the Stalinists with the earlier Tsarist oppressors, as enemies of nationalist aspirations. This was especially the case in Poland. The planned economies of authoritarian communism succeeded and failed most spectacularly in the region, no matter how one looks at it. Moving the largely backward and agrarian economies of Poland and Hungary into Fordist factory production was a major "achievement"; in the minds of the consumer-citizens whose standard of living, education, and employment increased considerably while at the same time their ability to consume could not compete with their Western European neighbors, it was also a colossal "failure." Dubček's "socialism with a human face" was crushed by Warsaw Pact tanks, but more important to the internal opposition, it crushed the possibility for a revisionist model, a more democratically-based and decentralized socialism, one that owed more to Western European Marxism than the Soviet model. At the same time, the "New Economic Mechanism" in Hungary—dubbed "goulash communism" by the West—in the 1970s proved that there may have been life in the old model after all, with some tinkering. Since 1989 the experimentation in political economy continues. Although some of the former oppositionists still maintain the relevance of some sort of "Third Road" between capitalism and authoritarian communism, today the new recipe is neo-liberalism repackaged either in "shock therapy" or "gradualist" terms but in either case a necessary prerequisite for a "return to Europe." With new democratic freedoms have come old and new-old problems—anti-Semitism, xenophobic nationalism, and the general splintering of the body politic.

Thus it is not surprising that in East-Central Europe one encounters a high degree of historical self-consciousness. This has especially been the case with the activists of the political opposition. They have fought against the ideologically-based abuse of their own histories while at the same time they have legitimized their own actions as an effort to reclaim some truth of the past as well as to change the present. Memory and truth are valorized as part of the struggle of the anti-totalitarian project. This was expressed most vividly by Milan Kundera in his famous line that "... the struggle of man against power is the struggle of memory against forgetting" (Kundera, 1987: 3).

This path gave way to grand historically-oriented gestures that on the surface did little to change the present. One example of this phenomenon: the self-immolation of Jan Palach in Prague in January 1969, where a young man dramatically lights himself on fire with kerosene in St. Wenceslas Square in the center of the city to protest the passivity of the Czechs after the crushing of the Prague Spring. It is followed by the brutal mediocrity and repression of the Czech "normalization." The memorialization (and to some degree mythologization) that these events symbolize indicates the power of this truth-recovery. Twenty years later, the so-called Velvet Revolution began with students marching to mark the 50th anniversary of Jan Opletal, a Czech student murdered by the Nazis. A similar experience happened in Budapest: the reburial of Imre Nagy in Heroes' Square, 31 years after his death and one year after a demonstration to mark the anniversary of his execution was suppressed by police violence. At the funeral, mourners join hands and intone the words of the Sándor Petőfi, the poet of the revolution of 1848: "No more shall we be slaves!" Life past and present is neither that simple nor that conveniently dramatic. Yet that is precisely the point: it is only with a knowledge of the valleys of history that we can come to understand its peaks.

My argument in this work primarily concerns political theory, but like many historicists and contextualists in my field, I will be arguing that this theory cannot be separated from the well springs of practice from which it flowed. Most of the activist intellectuals to whose writings I will repeatedly refer would agree, and have done so in a number of personal interviews. Not only has their political theory grown out of their personal experiences, it has been informed by a deep knowledge of and respect for history. In order to understand the meaning of their ideas, explanations, and strategies I have had to learn a great deal of the history of the region. For this reason, I maintain that no accurate and vital analysis of their work even *qua* political theory is possible unless it is historically grounded. This does not mean I have attempted to write the abridged version of postwar history for each of the countries under examination. I have, however, attempted to provide a prelude so that the discussion of theory in the following chapters makes sense to the reader, with or without a prior knowledge of the region. These brief historical sketches also include a discussion of intellectual debates and how they did (or did not) contribute to the climate of oppositional politics. This is important to my metatheoretical argument on two levels. As a political comparativist, I want to demonstrate the theoretical and pragmatic linkages between oppositional ideas and movements in Poland, Czechoslovakia and Hungary. As a political theorist, I want to argue that "ideas matter" to political change, and thus I must be able to illustrate the consequences of ideas, either through references to actual events or by refuting a negative hypothesis by positing historic alternativity. Part of the "proof" lies in my effectively arguing that certain texts appeared as watershed events in themselves, such as the publication of Kuroń and Modzewlewski's *Open Letter*, Kołakowski's powerful essay "On Hope and Hopelessness," as well as Havel's signature piece "The Power of the Powerless". In these cases, the timing and general import of events are discussed in the first section, whereas thorough exegetical analysis takes place in the second section. The study concludes with a long chapter focussing on the contribution of the dissidents to democratic theory and practice.

Too often the revolutions of 1989–1991 narrowly focus on the ramifications for our world today rather than what can be learned in the *longue durée*. The collapse of authoritarian communism in Eastern Europe hastened the demise of the Soviet Union. The geography of Eurasia changed more in a two-year period than in the previous 40 years—with 15 new states created from the former USSR alone. The Cold War was over, and with it the certainties generated by the nuclear arms race and the bizarre logic of mutual assured destruction. The collapse of the bipolar international environment ushered in an era of unquestioned American hegemony in the cultural, political, and economic spheres. Thomas L. Friedman suggests this sea change is so profound he characterizes the 1990s as the new era of globalization. The revolutions also caused a profound crisis of identity for the Left. Although social democratic movements and parties have flirted with "Third Way" politics (with mixed success), radical socialists are increasingly confined to academic rather than electoral quarters. Marxism did not die and was arguably liberated from its ideological and earthly *Doppelgänger*, but Marxism–Leninism as an eschatological and teleological philosophy, as a rigid and determinative set of practices, certainly perished.

In the immediate aftermath of the revolutions in Poland, Czechoslovakia, and Hungary, the dissidents whose theory and practice profoundly affected the type and scope of political change in the region did not seem to offer much in the way of instruction for the present. President Havel could not even keep his country together—although the "velvet" divorce was amicable by regional comparison. Philosopher kings seemed ill suited to "normal" politics, and the era of exceptional moral leadership had passed. There is a false logic, however, to this argument, one I shall return to in depth in the concluding chapter. Havel, Michnik, Kis and their compatriots did not set out to stage-manage revolutions or create liberal democratic societies. If judged on these criteria, they apparently have little "new" to offer. Notwithstanding this critique, their messages were deeper and more universal: the moment Havel's greengrocer reflects on his own phenomenological universe and becomes susceptible to truth, he discovers both responsibility and power. By locating power in the powerless and in such a personal decision, Havel radically democratizes the nature and possibility of such responsibility. Opposition intellectuals found an alternative to authoritarian communism not in traditional armed rebellion nor in typical reformism but in their parallel *polei*, islands of freedom. Moreover, this kind of freedom is more dialogical and solidaristic that the individualism of classical liberalism can reasonably support. Human beings cohabit a common world and in caring for their souls they must care for each other. Accepting political responsibility, acting in concert with others to generate freedom in the Arendtian sense, cannot be the result of a Rawlsian social compact chosen via self-interest from behind a veil of ignorance. Herein lies the deeper and philosophical contribution of the dissident *oeuvre*—not as a recipe for political change but as a moral imperative for political responsibility, regardless of the particular regime or economic order.

An important lesson of 1989 was the unpredictability of history. Humanity can never force-fit its experiences into the determinism of the natural sciences. 1989 was both a reassurance and a reminder that anything and everything can happen. History is neither inevitable nor inexorable. The dissidents lived and acted on one of the most important stages of the twentieth century, and their deft combination of theory and practice demonstrate that human agency is alive and well, and that ideas matter profoundly to our choices and our destiny. Courageous and committed individuals such as Václav Havel or Adam Michnik inform us that human creativity and resourcefulness can topple the most intransigent of regimes, that power indeed belongs to the powerless.

SECTION 1

CHAPTER 2

POLAND: THE HARBINGER OF CRISIS AND COLLAPSE

Intellectual Opposition in Poland: 1956–1965

The frequency of protest and instability in authoritarian communist Poland can be explained according to three competing explanations. First, Polish experiences are seen unique in the region: peculiar factors such as an institutionally strong and independent Catholic Church; the survival of private ownership of land and de-collectivization of agriculture; a history replete with both anti-Russian, anti-Soviet and working class uprisings (in 1831, 1863, 1944, 1956, 1970, 1976, and 1980–1981); the relative power and prowess of intellectuals and the intelligentsia; and the weakness of party-state institutions and elites (Schöpflin, 1983; Ekiert and Kubic, 2001). Second, Poland shares with countries throughout the region all the same structural weaknesses inherent in the logic of the Soviet model. Finally, the *dynamics* of political struggle were shaped by open confrontations between the party-state and social forces that in each case resulted in either a temporary solution or partial accommodation (Ekiert and Kubik, 2001: 24). These narratives are not mutually contradictory but indeed complementary. Clearly Polish exceptionalism is important in understanding both its vicissitudes under and departure from authoritarian communism. Like the Czechoslovak and Hungarian experience, this specificity was always mitigated by the shifting divergence allowed by Moscow, itself sensitive after 1953 to differences in time and space. The postwar history of the Polish opposition seems to illustrate an illusory *ex post facto* quality of inevitability. However, for both the party-state and various resistance leaders and movements, the learning process was neither automatic nor imminent. Clearly, however, Poland served at every juncture of opposition between party-state and society as not only a distinction but also a powerful example. Poland was the only country that sustained repeated waves of mass protest, involving literally millions of people. The exact nature of the coalition of social forces that made Solidarity possible has been endlessly debated and indeed romanticized.[1] Moreover, the Polish experience highlights the actual weakness of party-state institutions in comparison with their perceived strength and power: a realization that assisted intellectuals in theorizing about the scope for and possibilities of dramatic political change well before 1989.

By the mid-1960s in Poland, the hopes that had accompanied the so-called "Polish October" of 1956 had largely dissipated. The 1956 Poznań riots[2] and the leadership crisis which propelled Władysław Gomułka[3] to First Secretary of the *Polska Zjednoczona Partia Robotnicza* (Polish United Workers' Party) or PZPR were hardly promising. The drive for continued agricultural collectivization was abandoned, a fact that would consistently differentiate Poland from its neighbors in the decades to come.[4] Workers' councils formed in response to the uprising continued to exist (although clearly circumscribed by party control).[5] The government failed to heed the advice of Oskar Lange[6] to restructure the economy away from the privileging of heavy industry over the production of consumer goods. Moreover, the cultural and intellectual liberalization in effect from 1955 to 1957 had steadily eroded, even though intellectuals were clearly the winners in the transition to the post-Stalinist environment (Ekiert and Kubik, 2001: 30). Publications such as *Po Prostu* (*Plain Speaking*) were shut down, philosophy professor Leszek Kołakowski was singled out for "excess revisionism," and prominent communist writer Adam Ważyk was publicly censured for his *Poem for Adults*, published in the literary weekly *Nowa Kultura* (*New Culture*). The following lines, along with Ważyk's demands for greater openness and human dignity indicate why this piece was branded as offensive and seditious:

> There are people overworked,
> there are people from Nowa Huta[7]
> who have never been to a theatre,
> there are Polish apples which Polish children cannot reach,
> there are boys forced to lie,
> there are girls forced to lie,
> there are old wives turned away from their homes by their husbands,
> there are the weary dying of tired hearts,
> there are people slandered, spat upon,
> there are people stripped in the streets by common bandits,

for whom the authorities still seek a legal definition,
there are people who wait for documents,
there are people who wait for justice,
here are people who wait very long.[8]

Despite the chill of the late 1950s and the early 1960s, there were
a series of intellectual linkages between the flowering in 1956 and the
activism of the mid-to-late 1960s. Chief among these was the *Klub
Kryzwego Koła* (KKK), or the Club of the Crooked Circle, which operated between 1955 or 1956 and 1962.[9] The club was a forum for discussion and independent thought in Warsaw, dominated by academics
from the city. The KKK was critical from a sociological standpoint,
for as Jan Józef Lipski remarks, "[it] played an important role in the
formation of attitudes and ideologies, and the exchange of ideas among
the large and influential milieu of Warsaw intellectuals" (Lipski, 1985:
10). KKK also provided a generational bridge between the older group
of activists and sympathizers and a younger circle touched by its influence and later prominent in the student movement and *Komitet Obrony
Robotników* (KOR; the Workers' Defense Committee)—including Adam
Michnik. Active members included Ludwik Cohn, Edward Lipiński,
Jan Józef Lipski, Aniela Steinsbergowa, Wojciech Ziembiński, Paweł
Jaisienica, Stanisław Ossowski, and Maria Ossowska (Lipski, 1985:
11)—most of whom were later involved in KOR. The political tone
was leftist in outlook and liberal in openness. It was, as Lipski reports,
"consciously and consistently antitotalitarian" (Lipski, 1985: 11). An
active KKK member, Anna Rewska, was also the first to be tried for
political crimes since the Polish October, in 1958–1959, for reputedly
having sold the Polish monthly *Kultura*.[10]

Various traditions of the Polish scouting movement were also an
important intellectual as well as organizational bridge. Scouting was
a large and popular movement among young boys from the late 19th
century onward and had a long association with Polish nationalism,
however it was coopted in the postwar period.[11] Nonetheless, scouting
was perceived as Polish, independent, and internationally connected
to a larger movement and set of ideas. Activities and outdoor expedi-
tions fostered camaraderie, voluntarism, and mutual trust. Two controversial groups were the *Walterowcy* or "Walterites" and "Black Troop
No. 1" from Warsaw. Jacek Kuroń founded the Walterites, naming the
troop after Karol Świerczewski, the "General Walter" of the Spanish

Civil War (Lipski, 1985:14).[12] Unlike the Baden-Powellism of Western Boy Scout organizations, the Walterites promoted a high degree of social and political involvement, and were radically and uncompromisingly committed to an ideologically pure Marxism. Predictably, this "fanaticist" group was on a collision course with the authorities and was soon dissolved. Membership in the "Walterites" served as a black stain on later dissident "careers," although it is telling that so many had roots in this organization. Kuroń promoted ideological purity and anti-conformism, emphasis on truth, and the importance of a "genuine life"—most hospitably provided by membership and commitment to the scout corps. The second group, "Black Troop No. 1" was a Baden-Powellist troop. Its roots went back to before WW I, when scouting was covertly associated with opposition to partition and Russian domination. It was also associated with the Gray Ranks, a scouting group connected to the Polish resistance and the Home Army during the German occupation during the Second World War. More known was its "alumni" organization, a circle of "old boys" called the "Band of Vagabonds," who met several times a year for discussions of current events, social concerns, and national life. Their implicit social activism was revealed in the later actions of many of its members. Lipski documents this genealogy:

> As many as four members of KOR, and later of KSS KOR, had their roots in the Band of Vagabonds: Antoni Macierewicz, Piotr Naimski, Wojciech Onyszkiewicz, and Andrzej Celiński. Two editors of *Głos* (*The Voice*), Urszula Doroszewska and Ludwik Dorn, also came from the band, as did Marian Barański, who played an important role in TKN, Dariusz Kupiecki, and others. The Band of Vagabonds also put together the original team that organized help for the workers from Ursus in 1976. One might also add that KOR member Mirosław Chojecki, who was for a while the head of the Radom team and later the founder of the Independent Publishing House (NOW-a), had also been a scouting activist, although not a member of the band (Lipski, 1985: 18).

The organizational networks established through scouting proved helpful during the genesis of KOR and later oppositional activities. Even scouts themselves were later mobilized: Piotr Naimski arranged for boy scouts to take care of the children of accused workers in the

Ursus trials in 1976 (Lipski, 1985: 47–48). Boys and girls involved in the Band of Vagabonds assisted also in making contacts with workers' families in Ursus, helping to win their confidence and thus collect information about the nature and extent of the repression in 1976 (Lipski, 1985: 48).

The common prewar history of many intellectuals involved in opposition from the 1950s to the 1970s should not be overlooked. A large number of intellectuals were involved in the *Polska Partia Socjalistyczna* (PPS), or the Polish Socialist Party[13]: Ludwik Cohn, Edward Lipiński, Antoni Pajdak, Józef Rybicki, Aniela Steinsbergowa, Adam Szczypiorski, and Wacław Zawadski were all active in the PPS prior to 1948 and were later important signatories and members of early KOR documents.[14] Many were involved in opposition to both fascism and Soviet domination, reflected in service in the Home Army (Rybicki) or participation in the Warsaw Uprising (Reverend Jan Zieja, Stefan Kaczorowski), the earlier defense of Warsaw in 1920 (Cohn) or wartime resistance (Lipiński, Pajdak).

In the 1960s protest groups which sprung up in response collectively served as an important "training ground" since there was obvious overlap in the personalities involved. In 1965, Jacek Kuroń and Karol Modzelewski (leaders of the Walterites and the Club of the Seekers of Contradictions[15] respectively) were arrested and then imprisoned for the circulation of an essay entitled *Open Letter to the Members of the Basic Party Organizations of PZPR and to Members of the University Cell of the Union of Socialist Youth at Warsaw University.*[16] Written in fiery Leninist rhetoric, the essay demanded that the party uphold the true principles of Marxism–Leninism, and outlined its various deviations therefrom, reinforced by the entire state apparatus, especially the police, political police, and the courts. The supposedly democratic functioning of the party was in practice completely fictional, as decision making was top-down, and structurally organized to exclude the influence or ideas of rank-and-file party members, or society at large. Like Miklós Haraszti's *A Worker in a Workers' State* published later in Hungary, it is a sharp leftist critique of the workers' situation in Soviet-style regimes. Looking at either work today and eliminating the obvious references to authoritarian communism, it is strikingly similar to critiques of Taylorite capitalism. The manuscript, drafted in the summer of 1964 and reviewed by a number of scholars in History, Economics and Philosophy, inevitably aroused the attention of the Interior Ministry. Both students were immediately expelled from the party and its student organization at Warsaw University.

The Catholic Church in Poland

Neither the Polish past nor present can be understood without grasping the complexity of the Church's presence and moral force in Poland, its notions of both the individual and the social order, its mixture of conservative ethics with progressive *and* nationalist politics, and the ongoing battle between Church and State—which both preceded and succeeded forty years of authoritarian communism. The Church is deeply embedded in Polish society, culture, and history, has historically strong church attendance, and over 90% of the population are adherents.

Poland's first Catholic ruler Mieszko was baptized in CE 966, and the existence of Poland as either a real or imagined community is intertwined with the expansion and consolidation of Catholicism. Although the Polish Commonwealth was both multireligious and multicultural, the relationship between Church and nation was cemented during the Third Partition[17] when the struggle for the preservation of the Polish nation, its language and culture was carried out under the auspices of the Church, which systematically opposed both Bismarck's *Kulturkampf* and the forced Russification of the Tsars. From this period developed a peculiar type of religious messianism, to the point where Polish Romantic poet Juliusz Słowacki described his country as "the Jesus Christ of nations."[18] The Church developed a set of survival skills which have been both strengths and weaknesses: rigid conservatism, ethnic exclusivism,[19] and an ability to both resist Poland's temporal rulers or ignore them completely, claiming its source of power and legitimacy was much stronger and could never be overruled by mere secularism. During the Nazi occupation, the clergy and the national resistance movement worked together; thousands of Catholic priests and bishops died or were imprisoned. New postwar Polish boundaries combined with the genocidal policies of Hitler meant that the identification of the Polish nation with Catholicism was increasingly a geographic and cultural reality. The Church's resistance to Nazism and the support of the Vatican to the Polish government-in-exile in London strengthened its legitimacy; in this respect, at least, the Polish Church was considerably different than its French and Italian counterparts. Church legitimacy was strengthened in the postwar period via the refusal to accept any of the doctrinal limitations of orthodox Marxism–Leninism,[20] and the suffering and revocation of Church privileges that occurred as a result. Initial battles gave way to mutual recognition in 1950 when the Episcopate reached an understanding with the party-state: it would acknowledge the authority of the state on all secular matters but would retain its religious autonomy and a number of its privileges, including the Catholic University in Lublin, and the independent functioning of religious orders. Thus Polish opposition to external authority or authoritarianism of any kind—Nazism or communism—becomes associated with the Church. The Church's ability to teach and historicize its role as the savior of the nation from 1950 onward was a distinct advantage, especially since official Polish historiography was revisionist in favor of the regime.

The Church has always been particularly skilful in employing a form of metaphysical symbolism in its self-expression as a counter-weight to the relations of power. An example is the symbolism of Częstochowa, the monastery housing the famous portrait of the "Black Madonna" at Jasna Góra. If Poland is the Christ among nations, doomed to suffer but rise again, the Black Madonna is the marianite icon whose passion, piety, and sublime power make it possible. It was here in the 17th century that the invading armies of Sweden were stopped. August 15 is one of the holiest days in Poland—it is the Feast of the Assumption, and this day is consecrated to the Black Madonna. It is also the anniversary of Piłsudski's defeat of the Bolshevik armies of General Budenny on the outskirts of Warsaw—an event that became known as "The Miracle on the Vistula." Sixty years later, it is also the day that workers all over Poland put down their tools in support of the strikers at the Lenin shipyard in Gdańsk. Signs appeared that read "The Madonna is on strike" (Garton Ash, 1983: 62). Poland's recent history is rife with the fusion of religious celebration with moments of highly charged political significance. Stefan Cardinal Wyszyński was released from prison by Gomułka only days after he became party leader; thus the Polish October became self-identified with freedom for the Primate and greater freedom for Poles. It was the beginning of normalization of church–state relations in the country.

Intellectuals associated with the Catholic Church managed to walk the tightrope between religious expression and political opposition since Stefan Cardinal Wyszyński regained his freedom.[21] Two manifestations of the social activist tradition within the Church were the Catholic group *Znak* (Sign)[22] and the *Klub Inteligencji Katolickiej* (KIK), or Warsaw Club of Catholic Intelligentsia. The *Znak* movement began in 1956 in the spirit of the Polish October, and combined "geopolitical realism" (acceptance of Soviet hegemony) with "a rejection of the Poles' supposed predisposition to revolt" (Michnik, 1985: 139). *Znak* clearly expressed the desire of the mainstream Catholic Episcopate to form an uneasy alliance with the authorities; Michnik states:

> ... the Catholic politicians believed in having concessions and rights "granted" from above rather than in organizing pressure from below. They sought harmony, not conflict; they cared for order, seeking agreement with the party, and sought to avoid imputations of oppositional attitudes (Michnik, 1985: 140).

Znak was largely composed of writers, academics, and journalists. Inspired by French Catholic philosopher-activists such as Emmanuel Mounier and Jacques Maritain, *Znak* was a multi-faceted lay organization, with a publishing house, a monthly journal of the same name and a respected Cracow weekly, *Tygodnik Powszechny* (*Universal Weekly*).[23] *Znak* also had a parliamentary caucus in the *Sejm*, who demonstrated their political allegiance to the emerging opposition by protesting to the prime minister against the harsh treatment of students during the March, 1968 events.[24]

The KIK in Warsaw strengthened the informal alliance between Poland's unofficial opposition and the Catholic Church. Particularly important was the editorial leadership of Tadeusz Mazowiecki in publishing the intellectual monthly *Więź* (*Link*). Mazowiecki's views were critical in laying the groundwork in the early 1970s for the now-famous Church–opposition alliance. Dissidents (including those of Jewish descent) were encouraged to write under pseudonym. Mazowiecki strongly believed that the role of the Church was to stand in defense of the oppressed, against "totalitarian power."[25] Catholic intellectuals like Tadeusz Mazowiecki and Anna Morawska combined Polish nationalism, activism, realism, and religious independence with leftist revisionism. This blending of religiosity and Marxism brought them into conflict with the established Church, but as Adam Michnik observed "[their] ideas also made possible an ideological dialogue with the lay intelligentsia" (Michnik, 1985: 140).

Catholic publications were important, as they had relative freedom of expression. Because of their philosophical nature and moral tone, opinions expressed had enormous resonance. In both his *Letters from Prison* and *The Church and the Left*, Adam Michnik discusses the over-whelming importance of the independent Catholic intelligentsia as laying important groundwork. Polish intellectual life and culture have absorbed much contemporary Christian thought and morality, despite the secularism of many scholars (Michnik, 1985: 140). Moreover, Catholic organizations, publishing houses and journals served as inde-pendent models, creating a base for an independent culture separate from officially sanctioned organizations and "transmission belts." The Church was arguably a proto-oppositional organization simply by virtue of its independent existence. Without intentionally adopting an activist stance, it absorbed societal discontent and was a site for "truth-ful" discussion and criticism, fostering what Michnik described as "ersatz political pluralism" (dependent as it was on the limited toler-ance capacities of the party-state). Finally, Jewish, Left, and secular intellectuals were able to revise their own stereotypes of Catholicism given the examples of analysis and activism from within the Church.

Because the KIK and *Znak* were officially recognized, overt cross-membership between these organizations and later oppositional groups was originally rare, but informally support was strong. Henryk Wujec was a member of both KIK and later KOR, but concerns regarding possible reprisals against these groups made his membership the excep-tion rather than the rule. The publishers and scholars associated with *Znak* (for example, Władysław Bartoszewski, Bohdan Cywiński, Tade-usz Mazowiecki, and Adam Stanowski) were sympathetic politically, but none were among the original members of KOR. However, this group, especially Mazowiecki, emerged as a powerful ally between the Church and Solidarity right from the early negotiations in Gdańsk. Ironically, it was Anka Kowalska, a former activist within the pro-regime Catholic movement PAX who was a member of KOR.

The Students' Protest: March, 1968

In 1966, the Union of Socialist Youth at Warsaw University (ZMS) and in particular students from the history faculty invited Professors Leszek Kołakowski and Krzysztof Pomian to speak in honor of the 10th anniversary of the Polish October.[26] Kołakowski was frank in his assessment of any positive legacies—the opportunities represented by Gomułka's accession to power were lost. He denounced the lack of progress since 1956 in terms of economic planning and political administration, attacked the legal system (since one had "reason to believe certain rightful laws existed in Poland after 1956"), the lack of democratic choice concerning leaders, the unresponsiveness of government, bureaucratic inefficiency and special privileges, the nonexistence of academic freedom, and rights to assembly or free speech (Raina, 1978: 96–97). Kołakowski was subsequently expelled from the party and the university; however, dealing with someone of Kołakowski's stature and reputation was not as easy as dealing with Kuroń and Modzelewski. The university party members took a pro-Kołakowski stand, and 22 prominent Polish writers expressed their disapproval to this expulsion in a letter to the Central Committee. Actions were taken against many of the participants, including Adam Michnik. Many in the Warsaw academic community reciprocated by handing in their party cards, resulting in further suspensions and reprimands (Lipski, 1985: 16). Along with Kołakowski, economist Włodzimerz Brus and sociologist Zygmunt Bauman were expelled. The faculties of economics, philosophy, sociology and psychology were dissolved, and therefore over a thousand students lost their right to continue their studies (Raina, 1978: 146). The affair also attracted international publicity. Czech philosopher Karel Kosík wrote a letter published in *Literarni Listy*, stating:

> A few days ago, my Polish colleagues, the philosophers Bronisław Baczko and Leszek Kołakowski were dismissed, along with some other scholars, from the University of Warsaw because of their opinions. Intellectual Europe knows Baczko and Kołakowski as Marxist humanists and values their work. It would be in keeping with the principles of human solidarity if the Philosophical Faculty of Charles University were to invite these persecuted Polish thinkers to come to Prague, permitting them freely to continue their work and to propagate progressive socialist opinions (Raina, 1978: 146).

Significantly, Kołakowski's speech was the beginning of the end of his commitment to partisanship. His personal journey—from revisionist Marxist intellectual to opposition activist and finally to complete rejection of Marxism as an intellectual project—was indicative of a larger trend across the region.

Another source of state–society antagonism was the national censors' decision to ban the remainder of scheduled performances of the production of Adam Mickiewicz's *Dziady* (*Forefather's Eve*)[27] at the National Theatre in late 1967. Students used the incident to galvanize protest against the state; demonstrations held at both the theatre and at Warsaw University were brutally broken up by police and reserve forces. Both Adam Michnik and Henryk Szlajfer were expelled from the university. Petitions were circulated on the censoring of such a literary masterpiece,[28] and the issue was debated extensively at a meeting of the Union of Polish Writers, who demanded that the production continue. Protests soon followed in other academic centers (Cracow, Lublin, and Gdańsk), complete with street confrontations with militarized police (ZOMO), rallies, and occupation strikes.

The state responded with a campaign of slander, misinformation, and violence that had not been seen in Poland since the end of the war. Hundreds of students were expelled, arrested, or drafted into military service (Ekiert and Kubik, 2001: 33). Leaders of the student movement and the academic community were deliberately portrayed in the media as Zionists, revisionists, American imperialists, and hooligans. The anti-intellectual campaign metamorphosed into a virulent anti-Semitic crusade. Many people lost their jobs and their party membership because of their "Jewish" roots; over 20,000 Jews eventually left the country (Ekiert and Kubik, 2001: 33). Students and leaders (Michnik, Blumsztajn, Szlajfer) were branded as ungrateful troublemakers who lived at the expense of workers—despite the fact that they were from *secular* and *Polish* families. Such anti-Semitic propaganda—designed to sow dissension between workers and intellectuals—went as far as Gomułka himself,[29] who attempted to stymie popular support for Israel during the Arab–Israeli War of 1967 and demonstrate Bloc solidarity with Soviet-supported Arab countries. As Raina states:

> ... the general mood among the Poles was strongly in favour of Israel, because everyone felt that the outcome of the Middle East conflict had been a great defeat for the Soviet Union. *The New York Times* correspon-

dent Henry Kamm, was right when he reported from Warsaw on 13 June 1967 that the sentiments of the population were "running strongly in favour of Israel," and that the Israeli Embassy in Warsaw had received telegrams and letters "overflowing with emotion and sentiments." Cardinal Wyszyński prayed for Israel in a public mass in Warsaw, and the Catholic deputy, Konstanty Łubieński, in a speech to the *Sejm*, disapproved of the Polish Government's policy on Israel (Raina, 1978: 109).

A Ministry of Interior leaflet, written in verse, gives one a flavor of the "debate":

Onward brothers! sabre in hand,
Seize the Jew by his payee [pais]
—And if you well understand—
Hurl him over the sea (cited in Raina, 1978: 116).

The campaign was successful, especially given the ability of the authorities to play on long-standing antipathies of average workers and citizens—both Jews and activists were effectively silenced and "othered." However, in the long run, this served to galvanize oppositional consciousness—as Holzer points out, an entire generation inherited from the March events a sense of hatred and bitterness toward the regime (cited in Ekiert and Kubik, 2001: 34). Former activist Konstanty Gebert tells of how being "beat up as a kid in the playground" for his supposed "Jewishness" following the March, 1968 events fostered his identity as a Jew, and cemented his feelings of anger toward and opposition to the regime.[30]

1968 in Poland was not only about the March movement and its aftermath. Protests and leafleting also followed the invasion of Warsaw Pact troops into Czechoslovakia in August—a pivotal event for Hungary and Poland as well. Compared to the size of earlier events, these responses were marginal given the sense of defeat and organizational disarray. However, the juxtaposition of the two was critical in terms of analysis and the creation of new strategies. In his seminal essay "A New Evolutionism" in 1976, Adam Michnik writes:

Also in 1968, the year revisionism died, the demonstrating students chanted "All Poland is waiting for its Dubček." For a while, the leader of Czech and Slovak communists became the symbol of hope. To this very day, the myth of Dubček and the Prague Spring has played an important role in Poland, and the meaning of this myth is far from simple. It serves to justify both radiant optimism and the darkest pessimism; it provides a defence for attitudes of conformism as well as for gestures of heroism ... .

For me, the lesson of Czechoslovakia is that change is possible and that it has its limits. Czechoslovakia is an example of the fragility of totalitarian stability, and also of the desperation and ruthlessness of an empire under threat. The lesson of Czechoslovakia is that evolution has its limits and that it is possible (Michnik, 1985: 139).

Michnik was hardly the only Pole who came to this conclusion at the end of the 1960s. Prominent intellectuals who were once the jewels in the crown of revisionist Marxism, such as Leszek Kołakowski, Edward Lipiński, and Włodzimierz Brus, moved away from their faith in internal reform. They recognized that the party-state was unreformable given the very nature of its internal contradictions. There was nothing left to revise and nobody was expecting improvement to suddenly spring from a more progressive party faction—this had already failed in Czechoslovakia.

The seeds of political opposition in Poland in the 1970s and 1980s were sown on the *Left*—collectively this is no simplistic anti-communist stance. There were elements of Catholic fundamentalism and Polish nationalism, to be sure, but the general critique grew from disappointed revisionism and the prewar traditions of Polish socialism. Revisionism itself was based on a more radical and democratic reading of Marx and Lenin. This is an important and often conveniently forgotten point in the intellectual history of the Polish opposition, not always due to conscious obfuscation or subsequent ideological conversion. Later many journalists, academics, and foreign policy advisors in the West were keen to present the Polish opposition (especially Solidarity) in a light that suited their own interests—and in a proper "anti-communist" context.

The linkages between 1956 and the 1970s were largely intellectual efforts—discussion clubs, journals, university protests, and the like. Between 1956 and 1970 there was no effective or widespread worker-based resistance to the authoritarian communist regime in Poland; opposition was the privilege of an intellectual and mostly Warsaw-centered elite. Not that the Polish working classes were in full agreement with the Polish state: there are enough indications of tacit and even overt support for the students to quell this claim.[31] Nonetheless, there were no independent mass-based organizations equivalent to the intellectual clubs, nor was there any sense of independent or critical leadership on a national scale. There are a number of reasons for the quiescence of workers during the Gomułka era, not the least of which was the relative expansion and growth of the Polish economy, the continuation of private middle-income farming in what was still a largely agrarian state, and the prevalence of a strong Catholic-based conservatism. Negative manifestations of these factors, such as religious messianism, xenophobic nationalism and anti-Semitism, also help to explain why the state-directed anti-Semitic campaign following the March, 1968 events was passively and in many quarters actively supported by the urban working classes and the peasantry. However unfortunate, it was also the case that the intellectuals so harassed and beaten in the late 1960s were largely silent regarding the December, 1970 massacre in Gdańsk.

The lack of empathy between students and workers in 1968 and 1970 was also a generation gap. The March 1968 events in Warsaw were of the same genus as the student movements in Paris, Berkeley, and Chicago. Adam Michnik, Seweryn Blumsztajn and Jan Lityński *self-consciously* identified with radical student demands worldwide[32] and this extended to their anti-authoritarian style, tastes in fashion, art, belief in sexual freedom, and their identification as "New" (rather than "Old") Left.[33] An excellent illustration is contained in Andrzej Wajda's film *Man of Iron*. The protagonist Maciek Tomczyk is the son of Mateusz Birkut,[34] a Stakhanovite bricklayer and workers' hero who later fell into obscurity as a result of Stalinist purges. Tomczyk rages at his father for not joining him in his radical denunciation of Stalinism (in essence, his father's experience) during the 1968 student demonstrations. In a flashback we hear the narrator (and sympathetic student colleague of Tomczyk) describe the source of tension:

> They didn't get on too well ... in 1968 we were angry with the workers for failing to come round ... Maciek had begged his father to bring the yard out, but couldn't budge him. His father said it was a provocation (Wajda, 1981a).

We then hear Birkut's explanation for not joining the students:

They want a palace revolution. And like sheep you let them use you … .
This thing is a police set-up. It's not the workers' business … . They'll
move when the right time comes … . Lies can't last long. Just stay out of
power politics … .
  When the right time comes, we'll march together (Wajda, 1981a).

He hesitates to join his father at the shipyard in 1970, yet in the
background we hear the workers appealing to the students to join the
workers:

Students! This concerns all of us. Your comrades are still in prison for their
part in the events of 1968. Join us and you can free them! We can now join
common cause. If we join forces 1968 will not be repeated! Our destiny
lies in our own hands. No more oppression, violence, and lies! No more
injustice! Let us gather today … to fight for our human rights! Students!
Will you come with us? (Wajda, 1981a).

Tomczyk is then overcome with grief at his father's death during the
massacre. He effectively channels these strong emotions into political
activism in the 1970s, culminating in the formation of Solidarity ten
years later. It is a story of generational misunderstanding, and the
"passing the torch" to those who finally grasp its full meaning and
their destiny to overcome the mistakes of the past.

The Workers' Protest: Gdańsk, 1970

Virtually every account of Solidarity correctly places the genesis of
the 1980 events in the December protests in Gdańsk in 1970. The
story and its aftermath are now legendary. In a classic move of phe-
nomenally bad timing, the people's state decided to implement a series
of sweeping price increases (including beef, pork, flour, jam, and coffee) on December 13, immediately prior to Christmas in a predominantly Catholic country.[35] The first protests occurred the next day,
outside the Lenin Shipyard in Gdańsk, with the marching crowd moving towards the downtown area. After clashes in the early afternoon
between the militia and the protestors, the crowd attacked local party
headquarters. First Secretary Gomułka responded with force, resulting in street battles between workers and the militia, now backed up

by the security police. After workers left the shipyard to join the fray, shots were fired from the gates, and the fight escalated with Molotov cocktails fired at the obvious symbols of authority: the party building, the municipal council building, and the railway station. The crowd surged to 10,000. The human costs, however, were more devastating and immediately tangible: between December 14 and December 20, 45 people were killed, 1,165 injured and 3,161 arrested.[36] The next show of force involved army tanks and the crowd, subdued by earlier events but still angry, demanded negotiations to redress their grievances.

In Warsaw, the strain of events was beginning to take its toll. Further strikes occurred in Gdynia, and 13 were gunned down in Szczecin.[37] Given the arcane and unwritten code of communist leadership succession, and a lengthy Politburo session, Gomułka was essentially finished. After suffering a minor stroke he agreed to resign, and immediately thereafter, Edward Gierek was announced as the new leader. Less than a month later, however, the strikes resumed, and comprehensive lists of demands were being drawn by hastily-organized strike committees in Gdańsk and Szczecin. In a bold move calculated to win worker support, Gierek traveled personally to the Baltic Coast and acknowledged that the workers had been "provoked beyond endurance." Gierek, a former coal miner who had moved through the ranks to become party boss in Katowice (a mining center in Silesia), made reference to his own roots as a worker, and appealed for their help. At both the Warski Shipyard in Szczecin and at the Lenin Shipyard in Gdańsk, Gierek's personally delivered plea for popular support was well-regarded, even though he made few concrete promises or concessions. Workers reputedly responded with their now-famous conciliatory response: "We shall help!"[38] It was not until after strikes in the predominantly female textile mills in Łódź, that meat prices were rolled back to their pre-December 13 levels.[39] This act was significant in terms of both concrete action and symbolism, for it established the possibility of a popular veto over the policies of the party-state. Gierek's concessions recognized that ultimately worker expectations ought to be met. The regime had to deal face-to-face with both its workers and its consumers, and needed to avert a similar crises in the future.

Gierek essentially "solved" the crisis by postponing it. The government instituted a price freeze for two years, and later extended it for another two years. Real wages increased by 22%, along with family allowances and retirement benefits (Staniszkis, 1984: 257). The cost of the regime's surrender to popular demands was not only high,[40] but also reaffirmed the popular belief that it was done by arbitrary administrative fiat, with no connection to actual economic conditions. This perception reinforced the "us" versus "them" ethos that would come to characterize later conflicts.

Gierek responded by adopting a risky economic strategy of rapid and far-reaching modernization. Whereas the crisis of 1956 was preceded by political liberalization, the crisis of 1970 was succeeded by an ill-thought out and poorly implemented attempt at economic liberalization. Gierek's early achievements as a leader as well as later failures are rooted in the economic policy. The strategy was to initially expand and modernize the Polish economy by credit financing the purchase of Western technology—an approach facilitated both by détente and *Ostpolitik*. From the perspective of Western creditors, financing East European governments meant a convenient merging of economic and political objectives. However, the same conditions that led to the debt crisis in the developing world were also at play: banks flush with petrodollars were easy with their money and increased inflation rates combined with low interest rates made borrowing highly attractive.

The goal was to pay down the newly-accumulated debt with hard currency obtained through increased exports—made possible through the modernization and the improvement of Poland's planning and management systems, with increased efficiency and productivity. New high-quality products would hit the market just as Poland planned to step up the traditional exports responsible for generating hard currency—food products, coal, and steel. The domestic food supply would increase by reforming agriculture and easing supply and distribution restrictions. Modernization would also free up the labor supply, which would then be redirected to re-tooled and new industries.

The plan was a colossal failure. A short-term boom in coal in the early 1970s initially fuelled export earnings, but then collapsed. Wages rose by over 60% between 1970 and 1975, but consumer spending was directed at food, not surprising given the fact that consumer durables were still either in short supply or beyond the reach of the average family. In a few short years, Poland moved from being a net exporter to a net importer of food. Poland's agricultural system did not help—although production was largely private, both supply and distribution was state-controlled, and points of intersection were inefficient and chaotic (by the 1980s the situation was so absurd that Polish farmers began to feed their livestock bread rather than fodder, as it was less expensive given its artificially-lower price). In the industrial sector, where finished goods were produced for export, the markets did not materialize given inferior quality. Put simply, no one in Western Europe wanted to buy a Polish television. Polish industry could not compete globally—it could not simply retool itself fast enough or be flexible enough for the tough and discerning expectations of Western consumers.

In the second half of the 1970s, the regime owned up to some of the economic failures, but placed the blame on the OPEC oil embargo, the quadrupling of energy prices, the stagflation of Western economies which put a downward pressure on the demand for imports. External factors did much to make a bad situation worse. The Soviet Union provided relatively cheap petroleum to the region, but even COMECON rates rose quickly in the early 1970s. Exports initially intended for Western markets were diverted to the USSR for oil credits. Although the energy supply was maintained, this solution did not provide much-needed hard currency to support the mounting debt. Massive corruption and mismanagement of funds were rampant. Lipski succinctly describes the worsening situation:

> The problem of disproportionate prices remained and grew deeper during the later years of pseudo-prosperity achieved in the first half of Gierek's reign. The economic revival had been achieved at the price of a steadily increasing foreign debt. Anyone with ears to listen, or who had a passing acquaintance with economists or engineers, knew that corruption was reaching frightening proportions; that nonsensical licenses were being bought; that low-quality goods, bordering on trash, were being imported at ridiculous prices; that billions were being wasted; that changes in investment were introduced chaotically into various sectors of the economy without regard for the actual needs of the economy, but rather according to the distribution of power among communist palatinates struggling for authority and influence; and that enormous investments, largest among them the Katowice Steel Mill, were economic monstrosities, were badly located, and required miracles of accounting. It was becoming increasingly evident to everyone except those who did not want to know that the censorship and the lack of democracy were serving above all to protect stupidity and theft (Lipski, 1985: 32).

By 1976, the Gierek government ended up exactly where Gomułka had left off—trying to correct the deeply structural problems of the Polish economy with the Band-Aid of removing price supports on key foodstuffs. Disciplining the consumer—the still relatively poorly-paid Polish worker—was seen as a way to begin simultaneously reforming the system and dealing with the debt. It did not help that Gierek himself was grossly inadequate to the task—according to one commentator, "his economic illiteracy was matched only by its contempt for expert economic advice" (Terry, in Curry and Fajfer, 1996: 114). The Polish *apparat* employed no economic rationality in terms of investment and development decisions, but went on an opportunistic and narrowly self-serving buying binge. Structural reforms were watered down; the only new development was the introduction of limited enterprise autonomy for large enterprises.[41]

From the standpoint of the opposition, there were a number of lessons to be learned from December, 1970. First, the workers—in sheer numbers as well as their necessity to the functioning of the economy—had clout. Although lacking any cohesive organizational structure and certainly having no national leadership[42] or strategy, they were a force to be reckoned with. The spontaneity and severity of protest as well as the personal courage and tenaciousness of the participants had brought the regime to its knees, and effectively ended Gomułka's career. The 1970 events also represented a type of ideological challenge: the workers standing up to the obvious contradictions between theory and practice in a *workers' state*. Second, no purely Leninist or vanguardist approach would be successful in terms of building real socialism or achieving lasting structural change. Intellectual dissent was too marginal and deficient in bargaining power. Theirs was the sphere of a political and moral opposition, nonetheless powerful in terms of exposing the regime's weaknesses, as it in turn censored, arrested, and imprisoned its own analysts and academics. Third, leadership, an independent organizational base, a set of objectives, and a long-term strategy were needed if protests were to be anything but reactionary. Fourth, a coalition needed to be built—there were no personal or organizational linkages between the workers' protests of 1970 and the long lineage of oppositional efforts between 1956 and 1970. Moreover, there was no sense of common cause—goals were not seen as the same or even complementary. Peter Raina explains this divergence:

The intellectuals pressed for more freedom of expression, the workers insisted on just distribution of national wealth, higher wages, adequate supply of consumer goods. It looked as if the interests were divergent, hence the continued manifestation of indifference toward each other's cause. In fact, realisation of the desires of one particular group could not be brought about without achievement of those of the other. It was not without sense, then, that in March 1968 the students demonstrated under the slogan, "No Bread without Freedom." While the workers doubtless showed sympathy for this maxim, an open display of sentiments was, nevertheless, lacking. The disapproval of intellectual dissent exhibited in the general cry, "Students Back to Studies, Writers Back to Writing," by the workers' brigades, at the instigation of the party hierarchy, was both alarming and unpleasant. It was unpleasant because the Party oligarchy had, to a large degree, succeeded in creating an ideological chasm between the two dissenting sections of Polish society. It was unpleasant because the intellectuals came to be regarded as a class by itself: egoistic in character, allegedly contemptuous of the working class, idealistic in nature. By propagating this false impression, the oligarchy hoped forever to put an end to any future partnership. In March 1968, the Party almost succeeded in its sinister attempt. The dissidents were driven into isolation; as a result, they assumed a neutral attitude when the workers revolted in 1970. But the intellectuals did not go so far as to shout: workers back to the docks (Raina, 1978: 229–230).

Given the pace of events and the lack of organic sympathy, there was no way of effectively and quickly mobilizing the Warsaw-based intellectual elite.[43] What is most significant about the Polish opposition is that it collectively and reflexively *learned* these lessons, so that by 1976 the response was more unified, and linkages were made with mutual understanding and compassion between the intellectuals and the workers. The response to the June events proved that the opposition began to realize that what united them was much more important than what divided them: defiance of the arbitrary and unchecked power of the party-state.

Gierek would prove to be no more tolerant of criticism and less given to political repression than his predecessors. The regime continued their confrontation with intellectuals in the early 1970s (Raina, 1978: 205–228). The sentences handed down in the *Ruch* trials in late 1971 were unduly harsh—from between one and six years for each of the defendants. *Ruch (Movement)* was a small organization centered in Łódź that managed to produce six issues of a bulletin critical of the system. *Ruch* activists were accused of outrageous plans, including the supposed attempt to blow up the Lenin Museum in Poronin. The cases of Jacek Smykał[44] and Stanisław Kruszyński[45] both demonstrated the continued vigilance of the authorities in exercising political censorship.

The Polish government's effort to amend the 1952 Constitution galvanized opposition to the regime on the part of academics and workers already awakened by the events of 1968 and 1970. At the Sixth Party Congress, the PZPR leadership decided that this process would strengthen current social forces and democratic socialism, and such sacred principles as the leading role of the party and the class character of the Polish state as a proletarian dictatorship be enshrined. The party-state needed to increase its constitutional legitimacy, as the wording of the 1952 document placed sovereignty more directly and vaguely in the hands of the working people. The debate surrounding the constitution continued for several years. Official protests began with Edward Lipiński forwarding the now famous "Memorandum of the 59"[46] and a subsequent letter signed by 300 students and academics to the *Sejm*. This occurred simultaneously with the Helsinki process internationally—prompting demands for the inclusion of basic freedoms such as conscience, religion, and expression. These suggestions were ignored. Rather, in a round of amendments proposed by the party in 1976, the PZPR was entrenched as the "leading political force in society in the building of socialism"; the rights of citizens were declared to be "inseparably linked" to the "conscientious fulfilling of duties to the fatherland" and the section on the friendship with the Soviet Union and cooperation with other socialist states strengthened. Making rights contingent on duties was another way of totalizing the life of the citizenry and erasing the basic meaning of the Helsinki agreements. Poles were affronted by the Soviet friendship clause and the "leading role of the party," effectively drove a constitutional wedge between partisan political activity and independent society. Even Cardinal Wyszyński declared that a "citizen never loses his rights, even if he does not fulfill his duties toward the state" (Raina, 1978: 215). Protests and letters followed, the wording was softened, and with effective blackmail of the *Sejm*[47] membership, the new Constitution was passed in February, 1976.

The Events of June, 1976: Radom, Ursus, and Beyond

Stan Persky called the price hikes of 1976 a serious act of "political amnesia" on the part of the Polish authorities, for in effect, Edward Gierek attempted the same course of action as his predecessor five years earlier (Persky, 1981: 44–45). This round of proposed food price increases was staggering—lending credence to Marx's maxim in the *Eighteenth Brumaire* that history repeats itself only as farce. The impact would have been phenomenal to the average family: sausage, a main-stay of the Polish diet, was to be increased by 90%; other meat cuts and dairy products by 50–70%; sugar by 100% (Persky, 1981: 45; Bernhard, 1993: 49). Wages were adjusted to assist lower-paid workers and pensioners, but at most this amounted to a 23% raise. The speed in which the package was introduced to the *Sejm* and Polish society and the sham of supposed consultation was striking. Polish Prime Minister Jaroszewicz presented the package to parliament on June 24, 1976, and "pledged to hold consultations with representatives of factories and social groups on June 25, before seeking the *Sejm*'s ratification on the 26th" (Bernhard, 1993: 49).[48] The resulting wave of strikes, in hindsight, could have been predicted.

The strikes lasted only for one day—June 25th, the day after the proposals were announced. The reason for the short duration—the prime minister went on national television to indicate the withdrawal of the reform package. The most dramatic events occurred at Radom, a city southeast of Warsaw, and at the Ursus Tractor Factory in the Warsaw suburbs, for it was at these locations that violence occurred. However, Michael Bernhard provides a corrective to the interpretation of events as the "Radom–Ursus" strikes, as he stresses that 1) the strikes took place in more than 130 factories, estimated later by KOR to include approximately 75% of Poland's largest factories, and 2) that the vast majority of the strikes were peaceful and nonviolent in character (Bernhard, 1993: 47). At Ursus, nearly the entire factory supported the impromptu strike, and the workers briefly occupied the major east–west and southwest–northeast rail lines leaving Warsaw, which dramatically increased the level of disruption.[49] In Radom, the strikes were more extensive—workers from a large number of factories participated, gained control of most of the city, ransacked local party headquarters, and towards the end of the day were involved in street battles with security forces.[50] Workers in the *Trójmiasto* were known for their militant actions in 1970–1971, thus army and police patrols were ominously patrolling the streets in advance. There were a number of sit-in strikes and clashes with authorities, but fortunately no repeat of the 1970 massacre.[51] Other strikes occurred in Płock (at the large Mazowiecki Refinery and Petrochemical Works), as well as in Grudziądz, Łódź, Szczecin, Gryfino, Nowy Targ, Poznań, Katowice, Wrocław, and a number of smaller centers (Lipski, 1985: 33–42; Bernhard, 1993: 50–64).

In contrast to peaceful demonstrations, massive police repression followed. A dozen workers lost their lives as a result of the protests themselves, but many more faced reprisals. Thousands were arrested, interrogated, and even tortured.[52] Up to 20,000 workers were dismissed as the result of their alleged participation.[53] Over 1,000 individuals faced misdemeanor or criminal charges. A media campaign was launched which included public rallies (mostly attended by bureaucrats and PZPR members), speeches, and telegrams of praise and support. Despite these efforts, both the symbolic and real uses of violence were so brutal as to alienate not only the victims but created a cadre of sympathizers (Bernhard, 1993: 75)—this in a nation that wore the scars of its repeated victimization proudly and with defiance.

Komitet Obrony Robotników (KOR): The Workers' Defense Committee

KOR was not only the grandest "outreach effort" attempted in postwar Polish history, but it also signaled the beginning of a genuine coalition of workers and intellectuals in opposition to an authoritarian communist regime. Institutionalizing the support for the workers/victims of the June events in a concrete form has been attributed jointly to Jacek Kuroń and Antoni Macierewicz (Lipski, 1985: 43). The original idea was to provide legal and/or financial assistance to workers dismissed or arrested as a result of the riots. KOR boldly and publicly declared its existence, purpose, and membership in September, 1976.

The governing ethos of KOR was based on principles now considered sacred tenets in the mythologized history of the Polish opposition. First, in the words of Lipski, "there was the idea of an action that would appeal above all to ethical values, to general moral standards rather than political attitudes" (Lipski, 1985: 44). Second, there was agreement that the actions of the committee be overt, and that its membership be made public, to the point of publishing members' names, addresses, and telephone numbers. This was sound reasoning rather than simply rash bravery. Although potentially paving the way for reprisals,[54] a policy of openness guaranteed that KOR's documents were considered trustworthy and not the products of possible *agents provacateur*. This helped overcome the "barrier of fear" that existed in Polish society—the elimination of which was one of the committee's basic goals (Lipski, 1985: 45). Finally, KOR decided that it should be not only overt but legal. This was a tricky proposition given the uses and abuses of Polish law, but reference was made to international agreements signed by Poland, such as the Helsinki Accords. Because KOR cleverly never applied to be officially registered, it could not be easily de-registered. It could also claim the legitimacy based on a valid prewar law which allowed for the existence of relief committees. KOR organized itself loosely and without an obvious structure to be criticized or repealed; it had members, but no bylaws, officers, or membership fees (Lipski, 1985: 45).

Principles aside, the major work of KOR was the provision of assistance to workers and their families, especially during trials, including legal advice (and payment for the retention of independent attorneys); medical aid; assistance in finding new jobs (for those whose principal punishment was the loss of income in a country that did not recognize unemployment); child care; financial help; and moral support. KOR called this "social work" for it was both concrete and contextualized in a broader sociological perspective—allowing conclusions to be drawn about the condition of people's lives and pointing to improvements. Defining the work as "social" rather than "political" in nature was a strategic and defensive move, less challenging to the authorities and their political monopoly. KOR—like Charter 77 formed the following year in Czechoslovakia—acted "as if" (to borrow Havel's terminology) it existed in a "normal" open and pluralistic society. This meant acting openly, and attempting to erase any vestiges of secrecy or paranoia from within its ranks. Lipski documents this rationale:

> Also important for the atmosphere in the committee was its attitude toward the possibility that KOR might be infiltrated by the Security Service. Accordingly, it was more difficult to gain access to some kinds of work than others. The rule of overtness could not be extended to the addresses of

print shops and storage places, or to the files of those receiving help. Thus a certain degree of selection was necessary for those granted access to this kind of work. But basically KOR had a different recruitment policy. Anyone could present himself as ready to work. If one came with references from some trustworthy people, so much the better, but references were not required. KOR's doctrine was to trust everyone within the bounds of common sense. Apart from those instances of house searches and arrests in which the hand of an agent could be clearly discerned, any consideration of possible links between a KOR associate and the Security Service was inadmissible. These problems and approaches were formulated with particular clarity by Jacek Kuroń, who gained full approval for his position. There was agreement that in a movement such as KOR, an atmosphere in which everyone suspected everyone else would ultimately be more dangerous than the possibility of overlooking a few agents (Lipski, 1985: 64).

Sociologically, the membership of KOR spanned two important generations. Bernhard describes these as "those who had come to political maturity in the interwar period and those who did so under the communist regime" (Bernhard, 1993: 85). The older generation consisted of those involved in interwar resistance, often having socialist roots in the PPS. They had stature, respect, and provided the historical link to earlier eras of Polish political opposition. Younger members grew up in the sixties, and like their Western counterparts, they were educated, independently critical, and attracted by movement politics. This younger generation also yielded the theoreticians of Poland's new opposition, such as Adam Michnik. Jacek Kuroń was the bridge between these two generations; he was much younger than the old socialist war-horses, and he served as a mentor to the younger activists.

KOR provided documentation and dissemination of information, and thus its publications, principally *Kommunikat* (*Communiqué*) and the *Biuletyn Informacjny* (*Information Bulletin*)[55] were significant sources of accurate reporting. *Kommunikat* was the official organ of KOR—its immediate purpose was to deal with the aftermath of the June events and the publication of the committee's efforts; *Biuletyn* was an independent journal edited by KOR members and associated editorially with its aims. The second issue of the *Biuletyn* published the following statement of support by the Polish Episcopate, greatly boosting the spirits of activists and the moral authority of KOR:

> The Plenary Conference of the Episcopate asks that the highest state authorities cease all repressive acts against workers who participated in protests against the excessive increases in food prices that were announced by the government in June. The rights of the workers who took part in these protests should be restored, along with their social and professional status; the wrongs done to them should be rectified appropriately; and those who have already been sentenced should be amnestied (*Biuletyn Informacjny*, No. 2).

A series of open letters and declarations launched KOR, and the organization attempted to publicize the campaign of repression against the workers.[56] The target audience was the Polish public, the authorities, international media, Polish expatriates, and sympathetic but influential external actors. With respect to the latter, Jacek Kuroń drafted a letter to Italian Communist Party leader Enrico Berlinguer in the hopes that as the leading exponent of the Eurocommunist vision he might hold some sway in obtaining an amnesty. Another appeal was written by prominent novelist and KOR member Jerzy Andrzejewski entitled "To the Persecuted Participants of the Workers' Protest." Given the notoriety and popularity of the author, it was well designed to attract support from participants in the June events:

> There are people in Poland who are immune to deception and hypocrisy and have preserved their ability to discern truth from falsehood and who see in you, the persecuted workers, not only spokesmen for an immediate and specific cause, but, above all, fighters for true socialist democracy and for social liberty, without which all freedom perishes and deceitful cliches reign over public life, the nation is in danger, the life of individuals is stifled (Raina, 1978: 289).

KOR created the groundwork for Poland's rich tradition of underground publishing, and successfully generated the necessary funds to keep its sophisticated range of activities in operation as an entirely self-financed, non-profit organization. Money was first generated within dissident circles in Warsaw to assist the workers and their families. Later, fundraising was conducted nationwide, and parish priests funneled contributions through to KOR members. KOR was also able to raise funds by effectively mobilizing Polish *émigré* communities. Leszek Kołakowski, now in exile and living in the United Kingdom, led one of the external fundraising committees, and the émigré journal *Kultura* in Paris played a strong role. By the spring of 1977, a Fund for Self-Defense was set up to manage and account for monies distributed. (Bernhard, 1993: 80).

KOR defended both itself and the workers successfully. A renewed campaign of repression in May, 1977 led to the arrest of many KOR activists but was ultimately a failure. Facing an innovative combination of hunger strikes (in particular the collective fast held in St. Martin's Church in Warsaw); appeals to prominent international figures such as Willy Brandt and Kurt Waldheim (designed to heighten international pressure); the mobilization of official institutions to intervene on behalf of specific detainees (for example, the Union of Polish Writers for Lipski), open letters, petitions, and protests and demonstrations abroad, the authorities eventually crumbled, and the party-state granted an amnesty for arrested KOR activists and workers still serving their sentences (Bernhard, 1993 : 117–121).

In late 1977 KOR transformed itself into the *Komitet Samoobrony Społecznej* (Social Self-Defense Committee; known by the acronym KSS-KOR), broadening its work from relief efforts to the struggle against political repression, state violence, and the fight for institutionalized human and civil rights (Bernhard, 1993: 123). KSS-KOR published a four-part "Declaration of the Democratic Movement" which, aside from reiterating the expansion of basic freedoms, called upon Polish citizens to take up a number of initiatives fostering democratization. These included: educational reforms; independent workers' representatives (free trade unions); cooperatives for peasants and artisans; economic reforms; support of the underground press; and social support and self-help in the face of further repression (Bernhard, 1993: 124). The agenda became more explicitly political and challenging, and the social milieu of KSS-KOR continued to grow right up until the point its members decided to formally dissolve itself prior to the Solidarity Congress in 1981.

KOR's success lay not only in the concrete material assistance but in its pioneering of "different tools and techniques that permitted the committee to practice oppositional politics effectively" (Bernhard, 1993: 129). The collective experience of KOR was critical to the formation of Solidarity, and was an important role model in both Czechoslovakia and Hungary.[57] By developing and supporting an actual underground press (not just samizdat circulation of carbon-copied typescripts), KOR was able to disseminate its views widely, and foster further press development. Having a visible and prominent open membership with a larger but less visible base of activists and supporters made it difficult for the party-state to a) imprison or stop the prominent players without both antagonizing society and inviting international alarm and b) effectively locate the minor players who provided a grass-roots base and shouldered the burden of much of the relief and support work. Complicated social networks required the development of significant organizational and oratorical skills, and the array of measures employed increased the possibilities for collective action. Friendships, mutual trust, and a collective sense of purpose were built in the process. Through its dogged determination to survive, KOR carved out a public space independent from the party-state—its existence was a living denial of the Constitution of 1976. Social relations in Poland would simply never be the same, for it was at this point the claims of authoritarian communism began to be defeated.

The Alternative Civil Society?

KOR's success was infectious, and nurtured the growth of dozens of independent initiatives, journals, newspapers, and discussion groups. These organs of the nascent opposition expanded the unofficial public sphere. At this point, analysts begin to describe Polish events as the *reconstitution of civil society.*

Of the numerous groups that began almost as offshoots of KOR, most controversial was *Ruch Obrony Praw Człowieka i Obywatela* (ROPCiO)—the Movement for the Defense of Human and Civil Rights. Before the creation KSS-KOR, there were general discussions about a human rights initiative; however, its formation was preempted by the hasty foundation of ROPCiO. Aside from the hard feelings generated by the obvious rivalry, ROPCiO's existence prevented a more "united" front from evolving naturally out of KOR. This was probably inevitable, and in any event ROPCiO's internecine strife led to its own demise. In retrospect, various groups (including *Ruch Młodej Polski*, RMP, or Young Poland Movement) resulting from these controversies helpfully nourished a broader political spectrum and ideological experimentation.

Protests following the death of KOR student activist Stanisław Pyjas resulted in the creation of a new student movement, known as the *Studencki Komitet Solidarności* (SKS), or the Student Solidarity Committee. Furthermore, "Peasant Self-Defense Committees" were organized regionally in response to local grievances and dissatisfaction over new peasant retirement legislation (Bernhard, 1993: 146). Both movements waxed and waned in the late 1970s, but were critical training grounds for future activists and leaders of Solidarity.

Meanwhile, the union of two independent publishing houses in Warsaw and Lublin led to the creation of *Niezależna Oficyna Wydawnicza* or NOW-a, the Independent Publishing House indicating the rapid growth of the underground press.[58] In its heyday, NOW-a employed printers, typesetters, bookbinders, and distributors, as well as an activist-oriented editorial board. Hundreds of people were involved in its operation—their goal was nothing less than to break the party-state's monopoly on printed information. In addition, literally dozens of new periodicals appeared, such as *Robotnik* (*The Worker*), an important underground bimonthly for workers; *Spotkania* (*Encounters*), which catered to independent lay Catholic youth; *Zapis* (*The Register*), an arts and literature review; *Puls* (*Pulse*), another underground literary review; *Opinia* (*Opinion*), *Gospodarz* (*Farmer*), *Bratniak* (also the name of a prewar student fraternity), and *Droga* (*The Way*)—the various official organs of ROPCiO; *Postęp* (*Progress*), a forum for working people to discuss such issues as independent trade unions and workers' self-management; *Krytyka* (*Critique*), a scholarly political quarterly; *Alternatywy* (*Alternatives*), a conservative intellectual journal; and *Res Publica*, a more classically-liberal journal. This list is not meant to be exhaustive, but merely to provide an indication of the volume and variety of publications available; this adds considerable meaning to Lipski's estimate that by 1979 over 100,000 volumes of periodicals, brochures, and books were being produced *each month* (Lipski, 1985: 161–164). After 1978, each issue of *Robotnik* alone reached between 30,000 and 100,000 people (Bernhard, 1993: 161).

KOR engendered this spectacular growth in organizations and publications; a fact not only supported by the literature (Lipski, 1985; Bernhard, 1993), but also obvious from the considerable overlap in membership. For example, Jan Lityński, an active member in KOR, was also a co-editor of *Robotnik*. When *Robotnik* published its "Charter of Human Rights," it was signed by over 100 activists, the majority of which were KOR and ROPCiO members. KOR member Mirosław Chojecki (previously involved in underground publishing in Warsaw) was instrumental in the start-up and operation of NOW-a, which in turn borrowed money from KOR for capital expansion, and employed mostly KOR activists and sympathizers. Adam Michnik sat on the editorial board of NOW-a. KOR members were involved in the formation of ROPCiO and SKS. During the 1977 repression, spokespersons for both ROPCiO and SKS publicly supported KOR detainees. Trying to keep track of which activist belonged to which dozen organizations and was affiliated with how many publications and initiatives is a dizzying experience.

Towarzystwo Kursów Naukowych (TKN): The Flying University

The TKN, or the Society of Scientific Courses, was founded solely by intellectuals and had clearly academic goals. It was also a role model for similar ventures in Czechoslovakia and Hungary. Founded in 1978 by 62 Polish scholars (many of whom were KOR activists) in Warsaw, it was quickly dubbed "The Flying University." Creating independent, advanced education was not a new idea: a similar organization existed in the late 19th century during Russian partition.[59] Locations could be scheduled or rescheduled quickly to avoid authorities—guerilla tactics to enrich the mind. The original Flying University and its 1970s sequel offered the opportunity for like-minded intellectuals and younger students to learn in an open and critical atmosphere conducive to engagement and debate. Both hearken back to the 19th century tradition of what Jerzy Jedlicki has called "national intellectual service," a conception of the role of the intellectual as obliged to keep alive, teach, and defend national ideals, symbols, culture, and history.[60]

The goals of the new Flying University were manifold: first, to find a way to work around the handcuffs of censorship and political restrictions affecting existing universities and thus provide alternative perspectives; second, to provide academic assistance and supervision to those wanting to pursue studies or research not officially acceptable; and finally, to reach out to those for whom university attendance was not possible. No specific criteria for acceptance were required: everyone was welcome, courses were free of charge, and no previous academic qualifications were necessary. The ability of the scholars to get the operation up and running quickly was impressive: between October 1977 and May 1978, over 120 individual lectures were held in Warsaw, Cracow, Wrocław, and Łódź (Bernhard, 1993: 147). Longer courses were held in Warsaw. Courses were partially advertised—through leaflets and through word-of-mouth. The attitude of the lecturers was that if you knew about them, you could attend. In time, this also led to the participation of police agents and student informers, and the occasional break-up of sessions through either physical force or the shouting-down of lectures by agitators.[61] No independent certification process was established and thus one could not earn diplomas or degrees, however, the courses proved popular and were regularly attended by at least several hundred participants.

The continued success of TKN also had a side-benefit: the strengthening of the alliance between the workers and the intellectuals. Esteemed academics willing to take the necessary risks and give their time freely cultivated a sense of trustworthiness to the intelligentsia on the part of the workers and activists—they were seen as "giving back" something to society as a whole (Jedlicki, July 21, 1995). Ultimately, Solidarity drew most of its intellectual advisers to the Inter-factory Strike Committee in Gdańsk from either the TKN membership or from their stable of lecturers (Bernhard, 1993: 148). The obvious overlap in membership between KOR/KSS-KOR and the TKN further enhanced its credibility.

The Pope's Visit, 1979

In 1978 a cardinal little known outside his native Poland shed his identity as Karol Wojtyła and became Pope John Paul II. The following year he made a trip home that arguably had a catalytic effect on the downfall of authoritarian communism. At minimum, the Pope's visit was a "dress rehearsal" for the seemingly spontaneous creation of an independent national workers' movement—Solidarity.

Long before becoming the pope, Wojtyła had made it his business to go to bat with the regime, allying himself with Poland's working class. As Terry states:

> Throughout his years as priest, bishop, and archbishop, the Pope's natural constituency had been the urban blue-collar workforce, a constituency that the party claimed as its own. It was Cardinal Wojtyła who, after years of confrontation with the regime, extracted permission for the construction of the first church in the sprawling, bleak residential districts surrounding the Nowa Huta steelworks outside Cracow ... (Terry, in Curry and Fajfer, 1996: 161).

Given Wojtyła was now the Pontiff, the Church's official attitude toward the regime shifted in favor of a more aggressive stance. Because John Paul II was both determined and charismatic, as pontiff he carved out a role allowing for considerable intervention in temporal affairs.

As the Pope made his tour across Poland in June, 1979, it was clear to observers and participants alike that the visit was something between a pilgrimage and a victory train. It was the largest peacefully assembled gathering in the nation's history. John Paul II addressed literally hundreds of thousands of Polish citizens during a number of carefully planned events, carefully staged for maximum symbolic impact. He spoke in Warsaw's Victory Square; in Gniezno, the birthplace of Polish Catholicism; before the shrine at Częstochowa; inside Auschwitz; and a vast outdoor congregation on the *Błonia* outside Cracow.

For the duration of the visit, the daily-lived realities of the party-state retreated into the background. Renewed faith mixed with national pride. The rebirth of civil society was complete: the Pope's visit demonstrated that a vibrant, unified, and self-conscious public sphere existed as an alternative to the party-state. As Garton Ash states:

> That intense unity of thought and feeling which previously had been confined to small circles of friends—the intimate solidarity of private life in Eastern Europe—was now multiplied by millions. For nine days the state virtually ceased to exist, except as a censor doctoring the television coverage. Everyone saw that Poland is not a communist country—just a communist state (Garton Ash, 1983: 32).

The visit was both a spiritual shot in the arm for the opposition and a logistical triumph. From the papal tour came the realization that self-organization, as defined by Kuroń, was indeed possible. As one Catholic intellectual put it:

It wasn't so much his election as Pope as his visit here that June—in 1979—that really inspired the country. Here we were, facing a tremendously complicated series of logistical tasks—setting the itinerary for his trip, making arrangements for several huge rallies, providing for crowd control, and so forth—and the government was pointedly declining to help us. Generally speaking, the authorities were trying to ignore the Pope's visit as much as possible—television coverage, for instance, was limited. The police pulled back, made themselves scarce, partly out of tact, I suppose. And so, completely independent of anything that John Paul II had to say, we discovered an extraordinary and quite unexpected competence *within ourselves*: we could do all kinds of things by ourselves, we didn't need the authorities. We developed communications networks, planning procedures—all kinds of skills that would become tremendously useful a year later (quoted in Weschler, 1982: 23).

Solidarity *(Solidarność)*

The history of Solidarity—as a trade union, social movement, and powerful force for political and social change in Poland—has become legendary. What began as a wave of strikes in the summer of 1980 grew to become a mass movement of over 10 million members, thus constituting the largest sustained challenge to authoritarian communism since its beginnings in the Russian Revolution in 1917.[62] The history or development of Solidarity cannot be reasonably recounted here,[63] however the contribution made to the political theory and practices of the movement by key intellectuals must be chronicled. Nonetheless, key events are important references in both the literature and this study, thus the incredible victory represented by Solidarity's existence will be briefly examined.

In the early days of the strikes in the Lenin Shipyard in Gdańsk, workers demanded a wage increase (first asking for 1,000-złoty pay raise; this was later escalated to 2,000 złotys); the reinstatement of Free Trade Union activists Lech Wałęsa and Anna Walentynowicz; the construction of a monument to the fallen workers of the 1970 massacre; increased family allowances; publication of their demands; security from possible reprisals; and last but certainly not least the creation of independent trade unions. A tentative agreement was reached on August 16; shipyard authorities agreed to a 1,500-złoty increase, the reinstatement of both Walentynowicz and Wałęsa; and the memorial. The authorities nearly succeeded in buying off the Gdańsk workers and nipping their political demands in the bud when delegates from other striking enterprises began to arrive, accusing them of betrayal. Amidst the confusion, shipyard nurse and activist Alina Pieńkowska courageously spoke to the workers, urging them not to leave but to continue their strike in solidarity with the shipyards and factories in the *Trójmiasto* as well (Persky, 1981: 58–82; Garton Ash, 1983: 42–46; and Ost, 1990: 80–82). As a result, Wałęsa declared the continuation of the strike, issuing his famous line "I'll be the last one to leave the shipyard!"

On August 16 the *Międzyzakładowy Komitet Strajkowy* (MKS), or Interfactory Strike Committee, was born. In formulating a new collective set of demands the recognition of independent self-governing trade unions was at the top of the list.[64] Members of both KOR and ROPCiO were involved almost immediately (for example, Bogdan Borusewicz), as strike leaders such as Andrzej Gwiazda and Alina Pieńkowska kept Jacek Kuroń abreast of events via telephone (until the phone lines were cut, and both Kuroń and Michnik were arrested). At this point, Warsaw intellectuals kept foreign media and press agencies informed about the "real facts" of the strike as events unfolded, challenging the media monopoly held by the official news agency.[65] However, on August 20, 62 prominent Warsaw intellectuals (some of whom were also members of the Party) spoke out publicly in support of a free trade union, and on August 22 medieval historian Bronisław Geremek and Catholic intellectual and editor Tadeusz Mazowiecki delivered a letter of support to the Gdańsk workers. On August 24 a "committee of experts" was formed to assist the MKS in its upcoming round of bargaining with the authorities. It consisted of Geremek and Mazowiecki, as well as Bogdan Cywiński (Catholic journalist from *Znak*), Tadeusz Kowalik and Waldemar Kuczyński (both economists and active in TKN), Jadwiga Staniszkis (sociologist, later author of books about Solidarity and the fall of authoritarian communism), and Andrzej Wielowiejski (of the KKK). These advisors did not take part in actual face-to-face bargaining, but worked with the negotiators (elected directly to the MKS from workers of the various striking enterprises) in reviewing proposals, developing wording,[66] preparing files, and meeting behind-the-scenes with their government counterparts. Intellectuals were also important in the production of the strike newspaper, *Solidarność*[67]—fourteen issues were distributed in only eleven days; the print run of the first issue was 40,000 copies (Touraine *et al.*, 1983: 39).

The historic Gdańsk Accord was finally signed after several rounds of tense bargaining on August 30, when all 21 demands were incorporated into the agreement. Significantly, the MKS held firm and were not railroaded into accepting only wage increases and economic concessions; they held out for *all* their political demands, including the recognition of free trade unions (and the concomitant ability to legally organize workers) and the unconditional release of all political prisoners.[68] Despite the fact that the Accord included a reference to the "leading role of the party" for tactical reasons, the very recognition of the right of existence of independent, self-governing trade unions constituted a challenge to the monopoly of the party-state.[69] It was also an outright rejection of the existing union structure,[70] which had long since been discarded by workers as a potential means of obtaining improvements in wages or working conditions. The fact that the party-state "gave in" at this particular location was significant. As David Ost points out, the factory or workplace and the trade union, like the party cell and its apparatuses, were the essential building blocks of authoritarian communism (Ost, 1990: 98). To emasculate existing trade unions was to deny the party its ability to socialize workers into official structures (Ost, 1990: 98). To provide greater freedom for intellectual dissent was one thing, but to allow some degree of independence for workers was both a symbolic victory for the opposition and an ideological disaster for the regime. Thus initially many intellectuals—such as Kowalik and Strzelicki who were in Gdańsk, and Michnik and Kuroń who were not—either opposed or were sceptical about the demand for independent trade unions, as it was simply too massive a contradiction for the system to sustain for any period of time (Ost, 1990: 77, 98). In the end, they were right on the sustainability issue, but wrong on strategy. The formation of Solidarity was a brilliant strategic move in hindsight because it laid bare the contradictions for all to see, once and for all. It was one thing to confront the regime on its ability to live up to its promises and provide for the well-being of its workers (especially given the consumerist model of Gierek), but another entirely to break down its ideological hegemony, not only among its subjects but its believers as well.[71]

Organizing occupation or sit-in strikes rather than leaving the factory in mass demonstrations was critical to maintaining their position of non-violence and in not providing the authorities a) an easy target and b) the excuse of *prowokacja* (provocation). As in 1970 and 1976, the authorities were in the problematic position of having to deal with workers challenging a state that supposedly privileged their existence. However, the general spontaneity and disarray surrounding the demonstrations in both Gdańsk in 1970 and Radom in 1976 were used by the authorities and paradoxically *by the workers themselves* to dissuade others from protesting in a similar manner. If one wanted to either a) grow to a ripe old age or b) be able to successfully provide for one's family, it simply did not pay to demonstrate, in this type of cost–benefit reasoning. This rationale was successfully undercut by the worsening economic crisis, gains made by the opposition prior to 1980 (including the attenuation of risk given the existence of KOR), and greater societal solidarity (built through the worker–intellectual–Church alliance; the growing self-organization of society; and the powerful sense of community fostered by the Pope's visit).

Although there is considerable debate of the chicken and egg variety[72] regarding who came first and which group was more important initially in terms of formulating demands—the workers or the intellectuals—it is evident from the above analysis that in the ten year period prior to the 1980 strike a strong partnership was being forged. The key event was obviously the formation of KOR, which succeeded in breaking the cycle of separate worker and intellectual protests since 1956, each social group unable to effectively attract the support of the other. With Solidarity, as Eva Hoffman points out ironically, Poles were actually able to realize the Marxist *summum bonum*—a true union of intellectuals and workers mobilized toward the same ends (1993: 45).

Intellectuals played various roles in Solidarity: during the Gdańsk negotiations, throughout Solidarity's most active and legal phase (up until the declaration of martial law by the government of General Jaruzelski on December 13, 1981), and while the movement operated underground (until 1988). Their continued activism set them up not only to be key players in the Roundtable Talks (RT) of 1989, but also as both elected and appointed officials in the first non-communist government. My point is to counterbalance the cynical claim that intellectuals were engaging in farsighted career development with their activism. Rather, the continued relationship of political theory to the overall strategies and tactics of the democratic opposition remained both synchronous and significant. Much of the political theorization of Adam Michnik, for example, grew from direct political experience. Ironically, this process was substantially assisted both in Poland and Czechoslovakia by repeated periods of detention and imprisonment where reflection and writing were one of the few outlets possible. Hence one of the key collections of political essays is Michnik's *Letters from Prison*. To say the least, there was considerable intellectual ferment and counter-education going on in Poland's prisons after 1981.

Intellectuals within Solidarity

In the period of Solidarity's legal existence, from August of 1980 to the imposition of martial law in December 1981, the intellectual side of the newly reconfigured oppositional alliance played a number of critical roles.[73] In the early stage of Solidarity's consolidation, both as a trade union and a broader social movement, the existing *infrastructure* of the opposition—its networks, publishing facilities, administrative and fund-raising capabilities—were vital in getting Solidarity operational in a hurry. For example, Seweryn Blumsztajn, a veteran of 1968 and KOR, was fundamental in developing the nationwide union press agency *Agencja Solidarność*, and became chief editor of its bulletin. In some cases, the offices of the KIK were used to house regional offices of Solidarity for an interim period. Although practice leapt way ahead of theory in the 1980–1981 period, intellectuals were also critical in crystallizing some of the debates leading up to the Solidarity Congress, and in some cases pointing out (sometimes not very helpfully) the contradictions posed by Solidarity's existence and the options available to it.

One of the early debates following the heady days of the Polish August was whether or not the union should be centralized or decentralized in its organizational structure. The semantics of the debate as well as the participants themselves suggest that the pros and cons of both positions were formulated within the parameters of the previous oppositional discourse.[74] Decentralists constructed their positions with reference to greater participatory democracy and grass-roots connectedness—Solidarity, like other efforts in the late 1970s, had to be about the revitalization of the public sphere. This view was consistent with the anti-political and anti-authoritarian stance of the opposition. Centralists argued that the power and unity of *society* against the state could only be achieved with "unified strike action and conciliation with unified assent" (Ost, 1990: 107). In the end, an ambiguous federal structure emerged—so that Solidarity could make good on its promise of a general strike if necessary, but did not rule *over* the workers as had the official union structure.

Alongside the formal creation and legalization of Solidarity (and later Rural Solidarity and Student Solidarity), there was a general resurgence of independent intellectual life. Professional groups and activities spontaneously re-organized, and many academics, journalists, and self-styled experts of all kinds wore the banner of reform, putting forward new demands, sometimes seeking connection with or validation from Solidarity. Under the leadership of philosophy professor Stanisław Szaniawski, a Coordinating Committee of Polish Intellectuals was set up with the self-appointed task of negotiating with the government and Solidarity on various legal issues of particular concern to the academic community, such as censorship and university governance (Curry, in Curry and Fajfer, 1996: 173).

The size and scope of Solidarity meant that there inevitably arose a series of contradictions *vis-à-vis* its initial foundation as a trade union and its reality as a social movement. Proposed solutions differed among key Solidarity activists and advisors. For Karol Modzelewski, Solidarity had no choice but to take a more political and institutional role, given the inefficacy of the government and the worsening economic crisis. Jacek Kuroń's proposal was potentially more substantial and time-consuming: self management through workers' councils in enterprises mirrored by local self-governments in communities. These bodies in turn would be provided representation in a second house of parliament. Bronisław Geremek favored a tripartite arrangement nationally between the government, Solidarity and the Church; this was also the position of Lech Wałęsa.

Differing views as well as fault lines between the interests of the workers and the intellectuals, became more strongly evident during the first national congress of Solidarity in September, 1981. The divisions of the congress reflected a number of processes simultaneously: the presence of generational splits; the crystallization of different views that elections naturally bring forth; the decentralized and radically democratic ethos of the organization, and its resistance to leadership and hierarchy, whether self-appointed or elected; and finally utopian hope mixed with phenomenal ignorance regarding the dismal reality of Poland's economic situation. Because Solidarity was *not* an institution like any other in Poland, its open and antipolitical nature made it appear fragmented and indecisive. Very few concrete proposals were ratified by the second session of the Congress, and this led the National Coordinating Commission to deal with economic reform at the top while restive and impatient members spiraled off into their own alternative worker-based ideas and associations. Polish society was not used to the painfully slow and inconclusive aspects of democratic organizing, and thus many worried that Solidarity was strong or capable enough to tackle the nation's problems. Moreover, in the face of food rationing, strikes, industrial paralysis, and agricultural failure, Poles learned firsthand that economic performance was deteriorating.

Martial Law and its Aftermath

We now know that the party-state had considered the imposition of martial law in the spring of 1981, soon after General Wojciech Jaruzelski was installed as prime minister.[75] Although great pains were made to keep the plans secret, the defection of Colonel Kukliński to the West, meant that the CIA was also apprised of Polish strategy.[76] Soviet pressure for a solution took many forms: in the form of constant telephone calls to Kania from an aging and partially senile Brezhnev, more directly and firmly in the form of an involuntary "summit" in Brest with KGB head Yuri Andropov and Defense Minister Marshal Dmitri Ustinov, military maneuvers along the border and over Polish airspace, and frequent visits from Warsaw Pact chief Marshal Viktor Kulikov to personally push the case with Jaruzelski.[77] Clearly, the Soviets did not trust the PZPR to deal effectively with the problem; in July the KGB even estimated that 20% of the Polish Central Committee was openly pro-Solidarity and that over half the members secretly sympathized with the cause (Rosenberg, 1996: 188).

The Soviets were effectively hamstrung. They knew that a Soviet or Warsaw Treaty Organization (WTO) invasion as had occurred in Czechoslovakia twelve years earlier would be met with the fiercest resistance possible on the part of Polish society, just as they had begun to realize the human and military costs of their entanglement in Afghanistan. The Polish leadership also had reason to worry. Jaruzelski maintains to this day that martial law was the only solution in the end that would appease the Soviets, provide the necessary discipline to get the country stabilized, and eliminate the possibility of an outright invasion. Given détente and European stability, both the Polish and Soviet leaderships knew martial law would be perceived by the Americans as the lesser evil. Jaruzelski also had reason to be concerned about the loyalty of the Polish army and police units whose strength and cooperation were necessary to make the operation a success. Poland was dangerously close to defaulting on its Western debt of over $20 million USD, with endless rescheduling and new credits (Rosenberg, 1996: 229; Sanford, 1986: 8). Other Eastern Bloc countries had already cut financial aid to Poland because of the success of Solidarity.

As a military operation, martial law was an outright success. At midnight on December 12, army tanks and personnel carriers moved out into the streets. Posters tacked up on light posts on street corners announced that a Military Council of National Salvation was now ruling Poland. Overnight virtually the entire Solidarity leadership was rounded up and detained,[78] borders were closed, telephone lines cut, radio and television stations occupied, schools and theatres shut down, all public meetings and gatherings banned, mail censored, and a curfew imposed. By military standards, there were also relatively few casualties. Solidarity fought back with a few noteworthy yet decidedly rearguard actions: occupation strikes in Gdańsk and Katowice were violently and effectively crushed.

Politically, martial law succeeded in stabilizing the country in the short term but in hindsight postponed the inevitable. The party-state could and did exert its power, but could reestablish no form of legitimate authority. No form of post-1968 normalization as had occurred in Czechoslovakia was remotely possible. By attacking Solidarity and blaming it for the country's economic ills, the party-state leadership had only alienated one symptom of a much larger disease. Civil disobedience and a national tradition of passive non-compliance were harder to deal with. Over a million Poles turned in their party cards (Sanford, 1986: 189). The party lost any support it might have still had on the part of reform-minded intellectuals. The West imposed economic sanctions, very little help came from WTO countries, and the Polish economy limped on.

Despite the fact that Soviet pressure on the authorities was assumed by all levels of Polish society, the Solidarity leadership did little to prepare in advance. They took no precautionary measures to avoid detention of key personnel or to set up emergency communications linkages. Moreover, they never directly challenged the barrage of Soviet propaganda that was being constantly fed to the army and police. Despite the ominous atmosphere of threat, they were essentially caught off-guard.

Solidarity Underground

Solidarity did re-emerge as an underground organization after the declaration of martial law, but its existence on this level was sadly paradoxical. The Polish opposition from KOR onward had prided itself on its public face, its openness, its cultivation of civil society that existed *alongside* the party-state and not beneath or hidden from it. Largely under the leadership of Zbigniew Bujak in Warsaw and Bogdan Lis in Gdańsk (who had both escaped arrest), Solidarity was converted into a loose coalition of unevenly organized disparate groups. For reasons of political expediency and the obvious pressures of martial law, they more or less pursued their own oppositional activities by whatever means possible (Ost, 1990: 152). They did manage to form the *Tymczasowa Komisja Krajowa* (TKK), or Provisional Coordinating Commission of Solidarity, in April, 1982.

Although 1982 was a year to simply survive rather than reinstitute vigorous theoretical polemics about where to go from here, an interesting debate did emerge from the underground. An exchange of open letters took place between Jacek Kuroń (then imprisoned) and Wiktor Kulerski and Zbigniew Bujak. Kuroń believed that Solidarity should prepare to overthrow the government and tightly centralize the opposition to this end. Bujak was more in tune with the public mood of mistrust, defeat, and exhaustion. He countered that only an "imprecise and diverse" movement could avoid being crushed by the police state, and that Solidarity had to adopt a "long march" approach (quoted in Ost, 1990: 152). Bujak's approach won out, if only because it was the only practicable means of keeping Solidarity alive.

The TKK put most of its resources into the underground presses and in general information and outreach. In 1982 it managed to install underground radio and television transmitters and penetrate state-controlled airwaves, if only briefly. However, Solidarity's calls for nationwide strikes in 1982 went largely unheeded, just as the organization was formally stripped of its legal status (Ost, 1990: 153). Nonetheless, Lech Wałęsa, the country's most famous political prisoner, was released in late 1982, just after the death of Soviet leader Leonid Brezhnev. Martial law itself was suspended in 1984.[79] Meanwhile, the party-state could not effectively roll back time to the days before August, 1980. Even with the clampdown, cultural policy was relatively open compared to other countries in the Soviet orbit. *Tygodnik Powszechny* resumed publication in 1982 and was quite critical of the regime.[80]

The Church maintained its independence and while sympathetic to Solidarity's aims, officially attempted to mediate in a corporatist manner between opposition and party-state. In fact, the regime and the Episcopate were necessarily conciliatory toward each other, the party-state in terms of recognizing the Church as an institution with which it could bargain (and it sorely needed some partner representative of Polish society), and the Church by taking advantage of the situation by pressing for its own needs. The state attempted to coopt popular national and religious ideology as a result of its own internal legitimation crisis.[81] While the Church enjoyed a construction boom and new primate Józef Glemp appealed to workers not to strike, the situation at the parish level was more uneven. Many priests provided refuge and support to Solidarity underground, and some even preached anti-government sermons.[82]

In 1983, two years after martial law had been declared and Solidarity pushed underground, the Pope's return visit was staged so dramatically and his sermons so well-crafted as to be worthy of a performance of Shakespeare. The climax of the Pope's visit was again his pilgrimage to Częstochowa and the Black Madonna, defender of the Polish nation in times of crisis. Although the papal tour was highly controlled and visually presented as a *state visit*, the Pope was symbolically victorious (Curry, in Curry and Fajfer, 1996: 205). Timothy Garton Ash has captured the spirit of the occasion and the magic contact he established with the crowd during these dark days of the Polish opposition:

And then, as suddenly, the crowd is silent, reverent, half a million people listening with such attention that you could hear a rosary drop. It is a great and simple homily, not a political speech. He preaches a love that is 'greater than all the experiences and disappointments that life can prepare for us.' He shows them that he knows and shares their disappointments, without needing to mention martial law directly. He tells them what they can do:

to begin with the reformation of themselves, which must precede any social or political reform; to listen to their consciences; to 'call good and evil by name.' Then and only then does he mention, for the first time, the word *solidarity*, letting it drop very quietly in the silent crowd, not Solidarity the outlawed movement, but 'fundamental solidarity between human beings' (Garton Ash, 1983: 43).

In the end, the word that best characterized the decade was "stale-mate." Neither side could effectively check-mate the other, and only the Church managed to strengthen its position. With no cards left in the legitimacy game, the regime finally declared an unconditional amnesty in July, 1986 and for the first time since martial law all the former Solidarity leaders and opposition intellectuals could meet and discuss future strategy. However, there was no real consensus as to what that strategy should be. Was Solidarity better off trying to reorganize itself as a more "business–oriented" trade union, or should political reform be first and foremost on the agenda? At this time, a right-wing, anti-trade union critique of Solidarity was being hatched, one that decried the old intellectual–worker alliance and collectivist ethos of the movement (and of the opposition since the founding of KOR) as anti-individualist and anti-liberal.[83] For the first time, Solidarity found itself being described as *too socialist* in nature. Konstanty Gebert, writing under the pseudonym David Warszawski, actively defended the leftist ideals around which the opposition was founded. Warszawski's defence seemed to unravel when it came to the economy, as marketization was increasingly linked to democratic citizenship.[84] By 1987 extensive privatization of the economy was Solidarity policy (Ost, 1990: 168).

By now being an opposition intellectual meant that you were effectively cut off from Polish society. The debates were becoming more arcane and technocratic; gone were the rallying cries of the past. Given the political repression of the 1980s, the costs of being involved were very high in terms of the personal sacrifice, with the likelihood of internment, arrest, dismissal, fines, and confiscation of property. As Castle states:

> Opposition activity became the exclusive sphere of that minority who, for whatever reason, found the nebulous payoffs of intellectual stimulation and/or moral satisfaction worth the significant personal costs. A larger

circle might read the occasional underground newspaper or book, or join a brief march after a patriotic mass, but this had little practical effect (Castle, in Curry and Fajfer, 1996: 219).

The intellectual leadership was also divorced from the shop floor reality of Solidarity as a reemerging trade union in the late 1980s. In 1988, when the biggest price increases since 1982 were implemented, strikes erupted again, beginning with the municipal transportation workers in Bydgoszcz, later spreading to shipyard workers in Gdańsk and Szczecin, the Nowa Huta Lenin steel mill near Cracow, and Silesian miners. The strikes took place under the banner of Solidarity, but it was not the same organization as existed in 1980–1981. Participants were younger, more militant, and had not experienced the defeat of martial law.

Re-Legalization, the Roundtable Talks (RT), and Free Elections

By the late 1980s, optimists outside Poland began to discuss the possibility of political liberalization in Poland, along the lines of the Spanish experience.[85] Ironically, the period of martial law ushered in the most frank and open discussions of economic reform, and the debate took on a tone of harsh realism, and it was clear that economic restructuring would entail loss as well as gain. Among official economists, the words "marketization" and "democratization" began to be used in tandem as a potential solution for the endemic crisis. Efforts by the regime to introduce Kádárism to Poland between 1982 and 1987 were a failure.

Following the introduction of *glasnost* and *perestroika* in the USSR and faced with the waves of crippling strikes in the spring and summer of 1988 from a rejuvenated Solidarity, the party-state was ready to bargain. The PZPR had undoubtedly shifted from its earlier ideological commitment to Marxism–Leninism. Given the depth of the economic crisis and the increasingly technocratic orientation of its leaders, nothing was being ruled out—neither a free market for capital coupled with extensive privatization nor the participation of anti-communists and opposition members in the government itself. It was within this context that on January 18, 1989, General Jaruzelski informed a plenary session of the PZPR that the leadership was now ready to re-legalize Solidarity. Less than three weeks after this announcement, leaders of the party and Solidarity sat down with each other to work out the country's problems and design a blueprint for a more stable future. According to former Interior Minister Czesław Kiszczak, the regime had re-evaluated core beliefs: they overcame contempt for their adversaries; the opposition was recognized as a legitimate partner of whom caution and responsibility could not be demanded without participation in the process; and finally the time had come to end the one-party monopoly (cited in Osiatynski, in Elster, ed., 1996: 24).[86] Nevertheless, by first recognizing and then negotiating with the opposition, the party-state not only relinquished its hold on power, but effectively agreed to a process they could not entirely control. The regime clearly wanted to let the opposition into the system as a junior partner and thus hold it accountable, but they obviously had no concept of the fragility of their own social support.

The Roundtable negotiations were pathbreaking—even if obscured by more spectacular events later in 1989.[87] Most meetings took place in small groups—there were 11 subtables and working groups, where official negotiators were joined by technical experts. This was a purposeful strategy: Solidarity wanted to expand the scope of discussion. Key differences were pushed upward—and resolved—at higher level meetings where top representatives met at the villa of Magdalenka. Throughout the process, each side had to deal with their own hardliners and at appropriate moments issued threats to enhance their bargaining strategies. On the whole, it was understood that neither side would revisit past conflicts, even though the same people on both sides of the table were survivors of 1980–1981. The spirit of compromise and consensus won the day. Negotiating logic demanded that PZPR leaders move beyond the comfort level of the *nomenklatura*, whom they eventually left behind. On April 5, an agreement was signed, re-legalizing Solidarity, Rural Solidarity, and the Independent Student Union. The opposition also gained limited access to power: 35% of seats of the *Sejm* were up for competitive election to any independent candidates who got three thousand voter signatures on a petition. The Senate would be restored with limited parliamentary powers, and all its 100 seats were open to election. A presidency was created with strong executive power. The date for these partially free elections was set for June 4, 1989, and completely free elections were promised four years hence. Events then moved quickly and unpredictably for all the parties involved.

During the campaign, Solidarity reconfigured itself as an electoral machine, the Solidarity Citizens' Committee. Censorship was eased, and an election newspaper—*Gazeta Wyborcza*—was organized, with Adam Michnik as editor (and today it remains the most critical influential daily in the region). Candidates were nominated and Solidarity mobilized all its resources behind its chosen representatives. The candidates from the party-government coalition avoided all ideological and partisan references. In addition, some independents (either putative independents indirectly allied with the regime or non-Solidarity independents) entered the race for the contestable seats. This was of great concern to the Solidarity candidates, who were worried about the fragmentation of the non-communist vote.

In the end, the results of the June 4 elections were resoundingly clear. As Garton Ash stated at the time, "Three things happened at once: the communists lost an election; Solidarity won; the communists acknowledged Solidarity won" (1990c: 29). Far from being syllogistic, he was trying to point out the symbolic importance and interdependence of these three related events. Tadeusz Mazowiecki became the first non-communist prime minister in what was soon to be the former Eastern Bloc. In terms of international events, the Solidarity victory occurred in parallel to another alternative response to communist crisis: the Tiananmen Square massacre in Beijing. This sobering comparison was lost on none of the participants.

CHAPTER 3

CZECHOSLOVAKIA: FROM INTERRUPTED TO VELVET REVOLUTION

Czechoslovak Stalinism and the Role of Intellectuals

The *Komunistická Strana Československa*, or Communist Party of Czechoslovakia (CPCz), assumed power by engineering a coup in 1948, ousting their former coalition partners from power.[1] However, the Czech communists had the strongest indigenous support in the region, a point that cannot be overemphasized. The CPCz had been legally operating in the country since 1921 (although was banned in 1938 and illegal during World War II). Reasons for support are also rooted in the Munich Agreement in 1938—when the Sudeten lands were ceded to Hitler's Germany and Czechoslovakia was effectively abandoned by the Western powers.[2] Germany, not the Soviet Union, was the major enemy. When President Beneš returned to Prague via Moscow with his government-in-exile, the message was a strong one: cooperation and friendship with the USSR. Whereas Polish national independence was perceived at odds with either Russian or Soviet domination, in Czechoslovakia the USSR was seen as the liberator and guarantor of national independence. Even Masaryk was reinterpreted through a socialist lens, accentuating pan-Slavism, and the moral superiority and wartime sacrifice of the USSR. Even before the takeover, communists held many decisive positions in the government.

Moreover, the communists successfully attracted the intellectual elite of the country. As Milan Kundera states:

In 1939, German troops marched into Bohemia, and the Czech state ceased to exist. In 1945, Russian troops marched in Bohemia, and the country was once again declared an independent republic. The people showed great enthusiasm for Russia—which had driven the Germans from the country—and because they considered the Czech Communist Party its faithful representative, they shifted their sympathies to it. And it so happened that in February 1948 the Communists took power not in bloodshed and violence, but to the cheers of about half the population. And please note: the half that cheered was the more dynamic, the more intelligent, the better half (Kundera, 1987: 8).

Many were convinced to support or join the party, for in Milan Šimečka's words, "... almost everyone in that admirable generation of inter-war artists and creators had been in the party ... all the writers we admired, all the poets we loved—cultured people with national standing—were either party members or at least fellow travellers" (1984: 45). The communist generation not only had enormous moral authority but were endowed with *faith* that a new and better community would be built. Utopian idealism was matched with a sense of optimism and social solidarity.

However popular communist ideals and its working class leader, Klement Gottwald, were in the period from 1948 through to his death in 1953, the Czechoslovak party successfully demonstrated its increasing slavishness to the Moscow line. As in Poland and elsewhere, national communists were eliminated. Indeed, Czechoslovak Stalinism reached its apogee with the purges and political trials of the 1950s, especially in the case against Rudolf Slánský and his co-defendants.[3] Those in the party leadership who received the harshest treatment (execution) were overwhelmingly Jewish—a pattern that was unfortunately repeated throughout the region. Both communists and non-communists alike were arrested and imprisoned; the earlier legitimacy of Gottwald and his party was sacrificed in favor of widespread fear and brutal coercion.

The Khrushchev era in Moscow did not lead to either a leadership crisis or open revolt in Czechoslovakia, despite the fact that de-Stalinization in the USSR coincided with new leadership in Prague (unlike Poland and Hungary).[4] The Czechoslovak "New Course" was hardly new at all. Although "cult of personality" was condemned, Gottwald was not personally censured; agricultural and industrial shortcomings were admitted, but no major policy revision took place; the structure of government remained much the same (Skilling, 1976: 31). Signs of protest and dissent were evident—the Pilsen riots, meetings and demonstrations in early 1955 in Prague and Bratislava, and prominent poet Jaroslav Seifert was heavily censured for calling on writers to be the "conscience of the people." Nonetheless, there was relative passivity in comparison to Poland and Hungary, which can be partially accounted for by relative economic progress and the overall lack of a tradition of revolutionary protest or hostility to the USSR. One more factor is critical—at this time there were no large-scale movements of protest or reassessment by intellectuals, first because they were hindered by severe restrictions on expression, but second, they were still, taken as a whole, fairly supportive of the regime.[5]

The active support of prominent intellectuals for not only the events of 1948 but also the purges that followed has been documented both by key players in their personal reflections and diaries[6] and in a number of subsequent analyses. Peter Hruby, in his collection of case studies *Fools and Heroes: The Changing Role of Communist Intellectuals in Czechoslovakia* (1980) paints a picture of the misguided communist supporter slowly awakening to the reality of the regime, moving from anti-democratic hypocrisy to self-correction, democratic support, and anti-communism. The problem with this simplistic political trajectory is that it assumes, and in fact the argument is dependent upon, ideological movement along a left–right axis. People like writer and poet Pavel Kohout and economist Ota Šik did not miraculously transform themselves into anti-communists in either the making of the Prague Spring *or* as result of the Moscow Protocols. Rather, they were exploring a logic intrinsic to democratic socialism, which they had adopted in the 1940s *and continued to support*. If more radically democratic and participatory forms of politics are on the Left even within a socialist dialogue (contrasting, for example, the politics of Rosa Luxemburg with that of V. I. Lenin), then communist intellectuals did not move to the right but rather further *to the Left*. This point is more than simply theoretical nitpicking, as it is central to my thesis that throughout the region much of the opposition to authoritarian communism grew from and remained committed to the Left. The CPCz was able to mount an effective revisionist challenge to the Stalinist model because intellectual opposition remained largely inside the party, at least prior to 1968.

Nonetheless, many intellectuals in the 1950s supported the Stalinist model wholeheartedly as supportive of Czechoslovakia as a national entity, the answer to rapid industrialization and restructuring of the war-torn economy, and responsible for eradication of anti-Semitism and the remaining intellectual and cultural vestiges of the old Hapsburg empire.

The Economic Crisis of the 1960s

By the early 1960s, however, signs of a mounting crisis were evident. Because the old Stalinist guard in the party had remained secure throughout the 1950s, any reform, admission of past errors or responsibility, or rehabilitation of political criminals, was negligible.[7] By 1964, Novotný had carefully rid himself of his more hardline comrades while maintaining his position. This maneuvring had the effect of opening up the party considerably. The question of Slovak discontent in the federation resurfaced, and previous attempts to sweep the problem under the carpet as "bourgeois nationalism" were no longer believed.[8] Under the auspices of Czech and Slovak nationalism, a more relaxed attitude was adopted toward the critical intelligentsia—which was later to prove crucial in the 1967–1968 period. Of more immediate importance, however, was the economic crisis of the early 1960s.

In the 1961–1963 period, the steady economic growth had not only come to a complete halt, but had actually began to reverse itself (Skilling, 1976: 57–58). Between 1962 and 1963 the national income fell and consumer goods were in short supply. Exogenous factors such as the loss of trade with China (as a result of the Sino-Soviet split) and a series of poor harvests also played a role (Williams, 1997: 21). Officially, the party blamed the crisis on earlier decentralization initiatives, which it promptly abandoned in favor of recentralization. The real story was more complicated, and connected to the structure of the Czechoslovak economy.

The war did not bring infrastructural devastation to Czechoslovakia as it did to Poland, Hungary, and Germany. After the communist takeover, this meant both the appropriation and reorientation of industry by the party-state rather than its rebuilding. Although Czechoslovakia was the tenth most highly industrialized country in the interwar period, from 1949–1953 it underwent a second phase of industrialization following the Soviet approach taken in the 1930s (Selucký, 1970: 28). Czechoslovakia was to play the role of the supplier of capital goods to COMECON, which required a major increase in engineering capacities to churn out the necessary machines, weapons, and plant equipment. In the early 1950s, Czechoslovakia was the showpiece of socialist expansion in Europe. Logically, it also meant that the Stalinist model of heavy industrialization and extensive or "easy" economic expansion was exhausted much earlier in terms of economic growth. Industrial expansion was based on outmoded structures; there was no or little necessary long-term planning or economic development aimed at new technologies—nuclear physics, chemistry, electronics, and cybernetics (Selucký, 1971: 28). Such investments would have been necessary to further automatize production processes, generate the mass production of both industrial and consumer goods, and provide a platform for continued growth. Heavy industry and resource extraction (notably mining) yielded much lower returns on productive capacity and efficiency.[9] Moreover, agriculture, distribution, and services did not keep pace with initial growth; the high priority given to heavy industry meant that these sectors were perennially disadvantaged in terms of supply of labor and materials, as well as expansion. Overall, "extensive" economic growth would have to be replaced with "intensive" expansion. However, unlike in Poland where Gomułka had never taken economic reform and the proposals of Oskar Lange and others seriously, a series of drastic changes was proposed within party structures, in particular by the head of the Institute of Economics, Ota Šik.[10]

Proposals for Economic Reform

The party leadership did not easily accept the idea of economic reform. However, mounting economic crisis combined with Novotný's dissociation from the Stalinist "old guard" of Gottwald days created the necessary set of conditions for the acceptance of change. Critical was the appointment of Šik to a team of experts charged with examining economic management and planning in 1963 (Skilling, 1976: 58). Šik was also appointed a full member of the Central Committee in 1962 and through a series of incremental decisions taken from 1964 to 1966 the party-state committed itself to a comprehensive program of economic reform, involving a shift to an intensive-growth, regulated market system.[11] Enterprises would increasingly control their own production through democratically-elected boards, independently formulating their own responses to local and foreign competition, maximizing and reinvesting their surpluses. Šik wanted to dismantle centralized directives in favor of greater independence for enterprises, and managers would set production levels, assess costs, be responsible for technical development and be more responsive to their "customers"

(Golan, 1971: 56). Wages and prices would be adjusted by a partially free market (influenced, but not totally determined by, supply and demand) and regulated by the party-state, but would be allowed to vary according to economic rather than political criteria (skills, productivity, and so on). Planning as a general economic principle was to be revamped—a process whereby investment decisions were to be based on rational estimates of profitability. National economic plans would still exist to provide long-term objectives and facilitate growth in a particular direction. Economic success would be measured against plan targets on the basis of measurable (objective) quantitative *and* qualitative indices. Implicit in these reforms was a critique of the Soviet model as no longer appropriate to the Czechoslovak economy. These proposals were not simply the dreams of economists. Even in the highest ranks of the party, there was a realization that in the Czechoslovak case, the Soviet model had exhausted its potential: even a "conservative" like Jiří Hendrych suggested that there was no longer a socialist model to follow (Golan, 1971: 56). Czechoslovak reformers indeed saw themselves as creating *the new* socialist model, and carefully distinguished themselves from other "variations" such as the NEP or the de-collectivization of agriculture in Poland after 1956, which were not an extension of socialism but a deviation from it (Golan, 1971: 56).

Accepting the proposals was a far cry from actual implementation. Aside from the existing constellation of interests inimical to change, it became increasingly obvious that the reforms required radical institutional and structural change; piecemeal fashion was not likely to succeed (Skilling, 1976: 60). Half-measures taken were compounded by a fear of inflation and price instability. Economists, technical *apparatchiki*, and middle managers (hoping to gain more freedom of action) supported the reforms; resistance came from both the higher echelons of the party (for example Oldřich Černík, planning head, and Drahomír Kolder, chief of the Economic Commission, favored moderation) and at lower levels from party and trade union bureaucrats who naturally feared a reduction in their own levels of personal control (Skilling, 1976: 61). Skilling recounts: "Paradoxically, some sections of the working class were apprehensive, perceiving dangers of dismissals or transfers, greater wage inequalities and the necessity of harder work" (1976: 61). In hindsight, this reaction does not seem paradoxical, given what we know from the fateful experiments of Gorbachev in the latter days of the Soviet Union, not to mention the electoral support for post-communist successor parties.

Meanwhile, as economists such as Šik criticized the "conservatives" for foot-dragging in accelerated reform, others such as Zdeněk Mlynář became convinced of the need for accompanying political reform. As in Poland, the political impetus for reform communism came from the tenets of Marxism, and from a thoroughgoing examination of the discrepancies between theory and practice. Mlynář summarizes this nicely:

> After 1956 [in reference to the Hungarian events], intellectual Communists, who had originally been oriented toward Stalinism, achieved a new state in their thinking, which paved the way for what is called reform communism. Through their study of Marxist literature, they discovered that in Marx, as well as in Lenin, there are many ideas which basically contradict the way Marxism is presented by the official party interpreters. Impressed in particular with Marx's humanism and his unequivocal stand in the cause of freedom and the emancipation of man—the class struggle being only a necessary instrument to attain these higher ends—critically-thinking Communists came to set Marx (and, in some cases, Lenin as well) against official ideology, which they felt had abandoned Marx's scientific methodology and his commitment to truth. This was the basic point of departure at this stage in the development of reform communism (Mlynář, 1980: 45).

As strange as this might seem in today's post-communist context, this viewpoint was both revelatory and revolutionary.

The Writers' Union and the Cultural Renaissance of the 1960s

The *Svaz československých spisovatelů* (SČSS) or Union of Czechoslovak Writers was in structure and organizational intent similar to the other centralized, Soviet-style mechanisms for ideological control. However, the SČSS, which had always been a haven for freer expression, or at least not formulaic participation, began to transform itself from both a literary and political perspective. In the most Stalinist of regimes, the union had by the 1960s partially escaped the most serious restrictions of socialist realism, and had begun to carve out for itself greater freedom, helping to generate a tremendous expansion of cultural life, the likes of which had not been seen since the late 19th century. Both *Kultúrny život* in Slovakia and especially *Literární noviny* in the Czech lands, became known for increasingly frank exchange, political criticism and ultimately as vehicles for reform and rapidly expanded their readerships in the process.[12] The role of the Writers' Union was not unproblematic, and especially in the early sixties as it expanded its political repertoire and tested the boundaries of what was permissible, there were many clashes with the regime, criticisms of the literary and cultural press, and many changes of editorial board members.[13] Censorship continued in an erratic and arbitrary manner, but did not stop the freer expression of views, nor prevent its spread to both radio and television. The atmosphere was one of halting progress. In 1966, a new law proclaimed both the freedom of the press and the obligation of editors "to observe and vindicate the interests of the socialist state and society" (quoted in Skilling, 1976: 68). The process reached its climax at the 4th Congress of the SČSS in June 1967—an event now seen by historians as a turning point in the Prague Spring.

The topics of the discussion during the 4th congress are indicative of this shift. The congress was not simply a forum for rehabilitating the victims of Stalinism, or challenging the tenets of socialist realism as restrictive, narrow and responsible for generating much in the way of bad literature (although this was done as well). Political issues were also hot topics—as in Warsaw during the March 1968 events, the role of Eastern Bloc nations in support of the Arab coalition during the 1967 war with Israel was addressed by Pavel Kohout, Arnoš Lustig, and others. The centerpiece was the contribution by Ludvík Vaculík (subsequently published in English and entitled *The Relations between Citizen and Power*). He offered a thoroughgoing critique of the corrupting nature of power, its internal and inescapable logic of homogeneity and domination, and how its operation serves inevitably to alienate citizens, sponsoring participation based on public suspicion and self-censorship. This is especially so when one of the major tenets of procedural democracy is not met—when governments cannot peacefully be replaced. As Vaculík states:

> Power is a specific human situation. It concerns both the rulers and the ruled and threatens the health of both. Experience of power through the

millennia induced mankind to lay down certain operational rules. This is the system of formal democracy with its feedback controls, switches and regulators. But the interests of certain people interfere with the clearly designed mechanism of government: those who have brute force based on ownership of capital, on bearing arms, on advantageous relationships, on production monopoly, etc. Thus the rules do not prevent the evil and easy distortion of this framework—it can, at second-hand, even lead to the vulgar statement that the rules of formal democracy cause the evil. Those rules by themselves are, however, neither capitalist nor socialist; they do not lay down what should be done.

This is a human invention which on the whole makes it more difficult to govern. It sides with the ruled, but when the government falls it also protects its members from being shot. The preservation of such a formal democratic system does not bring a very firm government—it only brings the conviction that the next government might be better. The government falls, but the citizen is renewed. On the other hand, when the government remains permanently in power the citizen falls (1967: 6–7).

The writers' actions—not just their speeches made at the congress, but their collective development of a more personal and self-reflexive literature[14]—served as both a catalyst and lightening rod for developments in the arts and cultural scene. This was evident from the growth in independent theatrical production (including many of the plays of Václav Havel in his unique Czech adaptation of the genre of the "theatre of the absurd"[15]), new musical currents (the Czech "big beat" and the incorporation of and experimentation with jazz traditions), and perhaps most well known, the Czech "new wave" in cinema.[16] Moreover, to the extent that there were political under- and overtones to these developments, the vast majority were supportive of socialist reform, and with few exceptions (Havel being the most notable) were not anti-communist in nature. In fact, one reason why an officially sanctioned organization such as the Writers' Union could play such a role is that Czech intellectuals largely funneled their energies toward working with and then reforming the regime. Pavel Kohout and Milan Kundera, to use two famous examples, were both committed socialists and party activists. To be sure they moved away from the confining strictures of socialist realism and acknowledged the political shortcomings of the Gottwald era, but many still believed in the "beautiful idea" of socialism.

The politics of the writers, mirroring their own discursive development, were definitely more self-critical and reflexive. As Marci Shore (1998) has succinctly pointed out, they even explicitly reversed their own sense of self-definition from being "engineers of human souls" to existentially rooted bystanders who could not promote politics through culture but through the negation of the very connection between the two. Shore also argues that the transformation of language was not only the most essential aspect of their political transformation, but that this linguistic process was transcendent. However, *prior* to the invasion and the signing of the Moscow Protocols, the evolution of the Writers' Union was still within a socialist discourse. Reform consciousness in the 1960s did not solely have its origins in an essentially apolitical existentialist discourse as Shore contends, but rather was an exercise in testing the limits and, where possible, pushing the boundaries. Politics was at the center of the activities of the Writers' Union; in fact, the transformation of language Shore points to can be seen as inextricably linked to this process.

The Student/Youth Movements and Strahov

As in Poland and Hungary, what is notable about the students' movements in the 1960s in Czechoslovakia is their striking similarity to their Western counterparts. The younger generation felt weighed down by the conservatism of the older generation and their overt disapproval of new forms of cultural expression, whether it be reflected in music, fashion, literary or cinematic style, and even sexual promiscuity. Ironically, most of the students were committed yet independently minded socialists, and had no difficulty in pointing out the discrepancies between the theory of Marxism–Leninism and the actual practise of existing socialism.[17] This generation did not participate actively and with enthusiasm in the organs of the party as did the prior generation of students and committed communists after the war. They were unaffected by the immediacy of the wartime experience and the resistance to fascism. Rather, they were disillusioned and bored with rote political participation and opposed to compulsory courses in Marxism–Leninism. They were searching for a public voice, greater economic opportunity, better quality education, and freedom to travel.

Public meetings and demonstrations became more frequent in the mid-1960s, and often resulted in student arrests.[18] The response of the Party indicates exactly how out-of-touch it was with the students. Students were upbraided by a 1961 Central Committee resolution for their "wrong opinions," "anti-socialist deeds," and "indifference, apoliticalness, and irresponsibility" (Skilling, 1976: 74). Rather than deal with their objections, the Party made a half-hearted attempt to coopt the students, directly supervising the activities of the *Československý svaz mládeže* (ČSM), or Czechoslovak Student Union. New initiatives included "reeducation through work" campaigns, and the promotion of voluntary work brigades and special construction projects. In fostering right thinking, the Czechoslovak regime attempted a sort of voluntary cultural revolution, sending the students to the workers so that their young and vulnerable minds would be correctly moulded. These strategies backfired.

By June, 1967 the party realized modification was necessary but even at the 5th ČSM Congress opposition radicals were not allowed to speak. The net result was that "the union was to remain unified and party dominated and was to support the party's policy rather than to defend youth interests. Its radical critics had failed in their efforts to federalize the Union and to make it a genuine spokesman of youth" (Skilling: 1976: 79). As was often the case during this time, events outside the party began to overtake the situation.

A crisis erupted in 1967 as a result of events at the Strahov student dormitories in Prague. The dormitories were badly constructed and breakdowns in power (both heating and lighting) were common from 1965 onward. In October following ten breakdowns in a row, the students poured into the streets to protest their frustration and anger. Chanting "We want light!" they were met *en route* to the city center by the public security police. The police response was severe, resulting in injuries to 13 students and 3 police officers. Mass protests and meetings followed, and finally a student commission was set up, to be headed by Professor Jiří Hájek.[19] The commission findings only partly satisfied the students,[20] as they were now in a heightened state of mobilization and political awareness.

The Prague Spring

The Prague Spring of 1968 happened more than a decade after the Hungarian Revolution and the Polish October of 1956, and scholars are still asking why it took an additional ten years for reform communism to come fully to fruition. Clearly nationalism was not as powerful in Czechoslovakia as in Poland, nor was there a history and perception of Russia as an imperial invader. The economic situation was initially better in the postwar period. The interwar tradition of democracy, the legacy of Masarykian humanism, and the greater popular support for socialism were influential factors that helped shape the contours of Czechoslovak reformism. After the defeat of the Prague Spring, Radoslav Selucký, distinguished the Czechoslovak experience from that of Poland and Hungary:

> In 1956 Poles and Hungarians had a very clear idea of what they did *not* want. What they lacked, however, was a positive socialist programme acceptable to the general public and expressive of what the public both wanted and what they could realistically hope to get. True, the Polish communists also talked of a new model of socialism and longed for their own Polish model to acquire a more humane appearance. But the level of Marxist thinking at that time was not high enough to allow any realistic solution to be drafted ...
>
> ... It is then significant that these progressive Czechoslovak communists should then have concerned themselves more with analysing the past than with categorically demanding a change in leadership. For they realized that the 'deformations' attributed to the Stalin personality cult lay, not in personalities, but in the system (emphasis in original; Selucký, 1970: 8).

By the winter of 1967–1968, the writers' revolt, Strahov, and the determined efforts of journalists, the technical and scientific intelligentsia, and party members of liberal orientation sped up de-Stalinization and applied pressure for further reform—which took a significant toll on the party leadership. In November of 1967 Novotný had an extended stay in Moscow; and in Prague a strong reform pro-reform bloc was beginning to take shape.[21]   By January 5 the positions of First Secretary and President were split, with Alexander Dubček taking the former and Novotný holding the latter. Novotný then resigned from the presidency.[22] His replacement, General Ludvík Svoboda, was a highly respected soldier who had served as commander of Czechoslovak forces in the USSR during WW II. By the end of April, six of the ten members of the former Presidium were replaced.[23] The winds of the Prague Spring hardly began with the stormy winter weather inside the party, but these personnel changes greatly facilitated the policy shift taking place.

Leadership overhaul and the changing dynamic of party membership was possible in early 1968 partially due to demographics. As Mlynář has pointed out, the pre-1948 leaders of the party (along with their formative experiences) were now of retirement age (1980: 80–81).[24] This lessened the possibility of internal conflict as generational turnover was inevitable. Bureaucrats were better educated, with more to gain than to lose both in class terms and individually by the reform process. Relative social equality and time had erased the necessity of a dictatorial political approach to secure or defend the interests of any given segment or class stratum.

Given the typical snail pace of change within authoritarian communist systems, Dubček and his growing reform team moved very quickly, consolidating their hold on power with new appointments and initiating the construction of a broad reform program, to be called the Action Program. Dubček had been pushing behind the scenes and with his party allies for some kind of program since October of 1967. Its final version was approved in April, and public debate was expected given freedom of the press.

The Action Program and Soviet Response

The Action Program was actually prepared and its 60 pages of text written by a team of five working groups under a commission headed by Kolder. Key participants were Zdeněk Mlynář (who wrote the section on developing socialist democracy), Ota Šik (the architect of economic reform), and Pavel Auersperg (who directed the groups organizationally and wrote on foreign policy).[25] During his speech delivered to the Central Committee in April, 1968, Dubček made it clear that economic success was linked to democracy:

... we are increasingly convinced that the development of democracy is the only way of strengthening a conscious discipline. We also have full confidence in our working people to be able to understand that a newly started tendency of development can be effectively supported by deeds, by purposeful work in factories, in the fields and workshops as well as in scientific thinking and the arts (quoted in Ello, ed., 1968: 9).

Dubček spoke eloquently of economic reform, a new system of management which would raise the standard of living, a renewal of constitutional rights, and the need for an equal federation between Czechs and Slovaks. Of this last point Dubček was particularly proud, given his background as a Slovak participant in the National Uprising of 1944 and his concern over the second-class status of Slovakia. However, the speech was written in the language of collective and continuing struggle in perfecting the ideals of Marxism–Leninism. Dubček situated his vision within the revolutionary tradition:

We consider socialist democracy to be a system in which the working man has his own standing and value, his security, his right, and his future. It is based upon human participation, coherence, and cooperation. We wish to meet people's longing for a society in which they can feel to be human amongst humans. This active, human integrating part of socialism, a society without antagonism, that is what we want to realize systematically and gradually, serving the people. It is a very gratifying task to serve humanity, one which has been waged by Marxist revolutionaries for more than a hundred years. We are carrying out their work and want to link up imaginatively with everything that is progressive and positive in the history of our nations (quoted in Ello, ed., 1968: 10).

Mindful of his external Soviet audience, Dubček was careful to link Czechoslovak success with "proletarian internationalism" and the need for "intensifying cooperation" with both the Soviet Union and her socialist neighbors. He reminded his audience that the "activities of world imperialism" forced "strengthening and maintenance of our armed forces" (quoted in Ello, ed., 1968: 49). Dubček and the authors of the program were careful not to raise any red flags. As Dubček later admitted, the content of the entire package was heretical, but they tried hard not to make it look that way (Dubček, 1993: 148). Even in his later address to Bloc leaders in Dresden and subsequent meetings with Brezhnev, he was careful to use the language of revision, rather than reform.

The Action Program spelled out many facets of reform and implementation. The main points of the document included: 1) national unity and true federal status for Slovakia; 2) a commitment to the leading role of the party as a "guarantee of socialist progress"; 3) the balancing of rights and responsibilities together with the implementation of the freedoms of assembly and association, religion, speech, movement, personal rights, and property of citizens; 4) the rule of law, and a free and independent judiciary; 5) electoral reform based on free elections, the division of powers to provide checks on the role of the party *vis-à-vis* the state, as well as greater freedom for non-communist parties; 6) economic reform based on the protection and relative independence of private enterprises, the revival of the "positive functions of the market,"[26] increased trade, and a new currency policy; and finally 7) a new constitution—to be completed by the end of 1969. The proposals were sweeping in scope and depth, but were carefully articulated as to draw a balance between the old model and unfettered democracy.

In Dubček's memoirs, he describes the content of the program:

The program[me] declared an end to dictatorial, sectarian, and bureaucratic ways. It said that such practices had created artificial tensions in society, antagonizing different social groups, nations, and nationalities. Our new policy had to be built on democratic cooperation and confidence among social groups. Narrow professional or other interests could no longer take priority. Freedom of assembly and association, guaranteed in the constitution but not respected in the past, had to be put into practice. In this sphere, there were to be no extralegal limitations.

The program[me] proclaimed a return to freedom of the press and proposed the adoption of a press law that would clearly exclude prerepublican censorship. Opinions expressed in mass communications were to be free and not be confused with official government pronouncements.

Freedom of movement was to be guaranteed, including not only citizens' right to travel abroad but their rights to stay abroad at length, or even permanently, without being labelled emigrants. Special legal norms were to be established for the redress of all past injustices, judicial as well as political.

> Looking toward a new relationship between the Czechs and the Slovaks, there was to be a federalization of the Republic, full renewal of Slovak national institutions, and compensatory safeguards for the minority Slovaks in staffing federal bodies (Dubček, 1993: 149).

Dubček remained proud of the program to the end. He was adamant in both his memoirs and interviews that he never intended a dismantling of socialism as was later charged.[27] In his view, the Action Program was a collective achievement: an attempt at socialist renewal that was never allowed to run its intended course. He also saw it as the first initiative in an open policy process that would revitalize both socialism and democratic life in Czechoslovakia. Perhaps the best evidence of his determination to hold onto this view is that in the early 1990s before his fatal car accident, Dubček was elected leader of the Social Democratic Party in Slovakia.

The program did serve as a mirror for an increasingly expectant public, and for many it was either too radical or too conservative (Skilling, 1976: 218–224). It was without a doubt a compromise document, but its published existence and the ensuing swirling debate were critical. Like a constitution, it was filled with high-minded principles and much flourish, but lacking in substance and detail. However, like a constitution it could serve as a higher reference point and a standard for debate. Unhappily, the Action Program remained vague on how its proposals would be implemented, and even at subsequent party plenums not much meat was added to the original bones.

It is important to note also what the program did not include: the return to political pluralism or free and fair multiparty elections. Participants in the teams drafting the program were aware of the difficulties and the contradictions inherent in the proposals, such as the question of reconciling transitional freedoms with a single ruling party, and the international repercussions of internal reform for the Soviet Bloc. Political change manipulated from above was seen as a necessary precondition to holding any form of competitive elections; the system would have to be changed by fiat from within. As contradictory as this may sound today, Dubček believed that the only way to revitalize socialism was through the release of a powerful *internal* engine for change.[28]

Finally, the Action Program did not make the "mistake" of constructing an independent foreign policy. The Czechoslovak reformers believed they had "learned" the lesson of Hungary in 1956, when

Imre Nagy called for Hungarian neutrality and withdrawal from the Warsaw Pact in the dying days of the revolution. Not only would such a move be considered anathema to the Soviets, it was clearly not a priority for the reformers either. Domestic problems were the focus of the day—how the economy could be reset on a surer and more productive footing, and how the political system might be overhauled to achieve greater stability, freedom, and legitimacy. Although it is difficult to know the extent to which *ex-post facto* explanations come into play, clearly the Czechoslovaks knew they were up against big odds in trying to sell their program to both the Soviets and the other Bloc leaders. Clearly they underestimated the difficulty of the task at hand, and perhaps the impossibility of their entire project. The Action Program had been prepared without the advice or consent of their Soviet patrons, and they expressed their concern and mistrust from the outset.

The stories about the relationship between Brezhnev and Dubček are legendary. Brezhnev apparently repeated many times that "Our Sasha has come to power in Czechoslovakia. Everything will be all right." He also is frequently reported to have said "*Eto vashe delo*—it's your business" when in Czechoslovakia in December, 1967, thus paving the way for Novotný's successors.[29] However, certainly by the time Dubček was summoned to a meeting of Bloc leaders in Dresden on the pretext of discussing economic reform, the mood of the First Secretary of the CPSU (if ever charitable) had altered drastically.[30]

At the March 23 Dresden meeting, Dubček and advisors discovered that the only item on the agenda were the reform proposals circulating in Czechoslovakia.[31] Gomułka and Ulbricht were harshest in their criticism,[32] with Brezhnev playing the role of the worried father, concerned about the activities of the prodigal son. Following the April plenum and the adoption of the Action Program, response of the Soviet press was distinctly unfriendly. *Pravda* described the program as a "convenient legal platform" for attacking the Communist Party, socialism, and the USSR (cited in Skilling, 1976: 223). At subsequent meetings in May in Moscow and of the Group of Five in Warsaw in July,[33] the situation in Prague was painted as counter-revolutionary. Bloc leaders were particularly concerned about undermining the leading role of the party. Increasingly liberated press reports were cited in order to provide examples of the internal chaos they feared could threaten the entire socialist edifice.

Independent Currents: The Untimely Rebirth of Civil Society

To the extent that the Soviets and other Bloc leaders had legitimate cause for concern, it focused on the growth of independent currents completely out of the control or reach of the party-state. As spring edged toward summer, the flow of activity sped up, a multiplicity of organizations and associations sprang up, and often raced past the measured pace set by the party (Skilling, 1976: 232–237).

In retrospection, the breadth of these organizations and their societal penetration in such a few months is dizzying. Not only did the SČSS revolutionize itself, a non-communist club of independent writers was formed within the union. Intellectuals within the Academy of Sciences were revitalizing institutions of higher learning, and the Philosophical Faculty of Charles University demanded written guarantees of academic freedom and historical revisionism was the order of the day, with new examinations of hitherto ideologically banned discussions of such events as the role of the Czech legions during the first world war, the Slovak question and the Slovak Uprising, the role of Masaryk and Beneš, and even the disputed death of Jan Masaryk in 1948.[34] Organizations banned in the 1950s, such as the Boy Scouts and Sokol clubs, were revived. Unions of scientific workers and collective farmers were organized. Various youth groups and an independent union of university students sprang up. Ethnic minorities found expression in new organizations for Hungarian and German Czechoslovak citizens. Moravian organizations began to suggest that a tripartite federation be established with a new, special place for Moravia alongside Bohemia and Slovakia. On the religious front, the Roman Catholic and Uniate Catholic churches demanded more freedom for their adherents.

Emerging political forces represented the greatest challenge. Attempts to resurrect the independent existence of the Social Democratic Party were problematic and subject to much negotiation under the auspices of the CPCz (with reformer Smrkovský taking the lead) and with the National Front.[35] Smaller parties in both Slovakia and the Czech lands were reviving their membership and claiming a greater say in the activities of the National Front. In many respects, their independent existence could be controlled through the National Front. More "dangerous," however, were independent political currents represented by two organizations, the *Klub angažovaných nestraníků* (KAN), or Club of Non-party Engagés and K-231, an organization of former political prisoners.[36] K-231 was complemented by a similar Slovak organization, the Organization for the Defense of Human Rights. KAN was deliberately formed as an umbrella organization to voice the political interests and engagement of non-party members, and provide an opportunity for political involvement. Outside the CPCz, KAN was formulated as a kind of anti-party, disavowing any desire to establish a formal structure. In reality, the creation of KAN was both a nascent and broad-based social movement, and an important political example for a later movement of much greater importance and impact: Civic Forum. Not unsurprisingly, Václav Havel was a member.

Perhaps the most striking and memorable indication of the new openness was the publication of Ludvík Vaculík's manifesto *Two Thousand Words to Workers, Farmers, Scientists, Artists, and Everyone*. In it Vaculík decries the declining confidence of the people in the party and the state in the postwar period, and holds those in power chiefly responsible. Although acknowledging the revival process, he stated that it had not really come up with anything new, and called for a dramatically improved Central Committee, along with an extension of the democratization process both politically and economically. Vaculík's manifesto had a dramatic impact. It was published in four Prague newspapers, and signed by over sixty people, some of whom were ordinary farmers and workers (Skilling, 1976: 275). Vaculík obviously wanted to stir the pot with his rhetorical statement, both to alert the public and mobilize the public regarding threats to democratization. Successful in this respect, the manifesto also resulted in several weeks worth of stinging recriminations from party officials and a polarization of party reformers from non-party progressives. The most telling indicator of its force was its later citation by the Soviets as evidence of the dangerous dilution of the party's leading role.

Čierna nad Tisou

In the final days of July, the Soviet Politburo summoned the Czechoslovak Politburo to an unusual and unbalanced set of bilateral negotiations at Čierna nad Tisou, a sleepy railroad town close to the Soviet border. The large Soviet delegation was backed up psychologically and militarily (as were earlier meetings in Dresden and Warsaw) by intentional and large-scale Warsaw Pact logistical maneuvres and exercises. Dubček's bargaining power, not strong to begin with, was weakened by his agreement to dismiss Czechoslovak General Václav Prchlík as head of the Department of Defence and Security for the Central Committee (Valenta, 1991: 74). This concession was a tactical error, and certainly prefigured the Soviet "divide and conquer" approach in separating reformers from each other by continually sowing dissention after intervention actually took place. The Čierna negotiations underscored the romantic naiveté and inexperience of the Dubček team; most present were committed reform intellectuals and experts convinced of the rightness of their program in renewing socialism. Even Zdeněk Mlynář later admitted, "... none of the leading Czechoslovak reformists had any experience in the field of foreign policy let alone practical experience with usual mutual relations among socialist countries ..." (Mlynář, 1980).

Brezhnev accused the Czechoslovak leadership of losing political control, endangering regional stability, and warned of inherent counter-revolutionary tendencies.[37] Dubček responded with a skilful and moderate defense of the Action Program, pledged his allegiance to both the WTO and COMECON, and suggested that the renewal of socialism was an important example to Western communist parties. Dubček also tried to convince the Soviets that the popular upsurge in support, represented most recently by a nationwide signature campaign, indicated that he had firm political control and that the people were completely behind him.[38]

The intimidation evident at Čierna was clear not only to Dubček but much of the population. Two days later in Bratislava, a Czechoslovak delegation met with the Group of Five. It appeared briefly that the Bratislava declaration resulted in a brokered compromise where the condemnation of the Warsaw Letter was not accepted and political means seemed to triumph over the threat of a military solution.[39] Each communist party was left to "creatively solve the problems of further socialist development." However, on August 13 Brezhnev ominously called Dubček to complain about the implementation of the Bratislava agreement. On August 17, just three days before WTO tanks rolled over the borders, Kádár summoned Dubček to a private meeting in Bratislava. Dubček claimed he received no direct warnings about the imminent invasion, but it is also just as likely that he was not exactly searching for clues (Dubček, 1993: 169–171). He was never clear from either Čierna or Bratislava how far he was supposed to retreat in order to satisfy the Soviets as allusion and ambiguity were the trademarks of the system. Due to this lack of semantic commonality and the obloquy of ideology, no one could really *clearly* understand anyone else. Moreover, today historians generally concur that the decision to impose a military solution was not made until days before the invasion.[40]

Crisis: Soviet Mobilization and the Moscow Protocols

On August 20, 1968 as the Presidium was in session, about 250,000 soldiers (approximately 30 divisions) from the WTO nations comprising the Group of Five, crossed the Czechoslovak borders in the north, south, and east.[41] Other than for the conservative anti-reformers who were supposed to simultaneously engineer a political coup,[42] the invasion was a complete surprise. From a military point of view, the operation was successful. Within 36 hours the Warsaw Pact armies had complete control of Czechoslovak territory.

From a political standpoint, even from the Soviet viewpoint, it was a short-term disaster, a medium-term success, and in the long run the costs associated with such engagement caused the critical reexamination of the relationship of the USSR to the Bloc. This last process was so underestimated by Western sovietologists that it helps to explain their dumbfoundedness and surprise at the unwillingness of the declining USSR to entertain such a course in 1989. In the short term, the invasion was problematic because the expected alternative government failed to materialize, and there was much initial confusion inside the country. Thus it was not easy for the Soviets to construct a case of counter-revolution against Dubček and his supporters, as they had been able to do with the swift accession of the Kádár regime in Hungary in 1956. After all, the Czechoslovak Presidium declared that the invasion "contradicts not only all principles of relations between socialist countries but also the basic norms of international law" (quoted in Dubček, 1993: 181). The invasion clearly had extremely low support from the general public, and the international media was filled with images of peaceful Czechoslovak protestors attempting to reason with ordinary Soviet soldiers unprepared for what they were encountering. Internationally, the invasion was met with the predictable level of condemnation, but the most devastating and far-reaching critique came from within the communist camp, as had the reform process itself. The ruling communist parties in Albania, Romania, China, and Yugoslavia opposed the invasion. Most importantly, a majority within the powerful French and Italian communist parties were opposed to the invasion, and defended the right of any communist party to define its own path to socialism. Symbolic but key resistance came from within the invading states. In Poland and Hungary, fledgling oppositionists perceived the invasion as the death knell for reform communism. Their protests against the invasion were to signal the beginning of a very different political alternative that would develop in the next twenty years.

The Czechoslovak government offered no military resistance—which in any case would have been costly and futile—but did offer some level of political resistance. The leaders themselves were essentially arrested and taken into "protective custody"—Dubček later described this as "kidnapping." The net result was that all high-ranking leaders were carted off to Moscow and coerced into signing an agreement that legitimized recent events, the Moscow Protocols. Although the "negotiations" were uneven to say the least, many of the Czechoslovak participants sincerely believed that they needed to cooperate in order to salvage the Prague Spring.[43] The Soviet leaders were determined to have concessions in writing, especially in light of the failed coup and the extraordinary party congress then taking place in Prague.[44] In the end, only František Kriegel refused to sign. All those involved, however, were permitted to return to Prague (once a gag order had been placed on revealing the contents of the protocol) and at least initially, to their former posts.

Normalization

"Normalization" refers to the process after the Soviet-sponsored invasion whereby authoritarian communism was reestablished along its originally rigid and Stalinist line. Power was consolidated in the hands of an old communist guard dogmatically loyal in all respects to the dictates of Moscow, and the party was effectively purged of all traces of attempted reform. This was not an immediate result: it occurred gradually over the next few years. At the beginning, normal life appeared to return after the upheavals of tanks in the streets, secret meetings, and work stoppages. Achieving normalizaton represented the "medium-term success" of the invasion.

Certainly the "Big Four"[45] did not immediately lose their positions. Dubček returned as a weakened leader, but he was still in office. It was a time of considerable contradiction: Moscow could not win the hearts and minds of the country even though it occupied and controlled the country. However, the Prague regime could not effectively win support for its compromise with Moscow either (Skilling, 1976: 813; Tuma, interview, 2002). Although it was not immediately clear to outsiders or insiders that the reform process was dead, Ota Šik and Jiří Hájek were removed from their posts, as was Jiří Pelikán, an activist in the 14th Vysočany Congress. By November Zdeněk Mlynář resigned. Legislation was passed by the National Assembly legitimizing the "temporary" presence of the occupation forces and implementing measures for the maintenance of public order, including expanded detention power for the police and extra-judicial procedures. Over time these had a significant deterrent effect.

Peaceful resistance to the invasion was sustained, and in late November, 1968, university students held a successful three-day strike in support of the Action Program, and forwarded their own program of "Ten Points."[46] Demonstrations were held on the important anniversaries of October 28 and November 7.[47] Behind closed doors, party intrigue continued against the backdrop of Moscow's dissatisfaction at Prague's many failures. In retrospect, Dubček's attempt to square a political circle by appeasing the Soviet Union and maintaining the semblance of carrying out reforms, seemed doomed to failure. But this was not immediately evident, although two distinct events brought the hopelessness of the situation into sharper focus.

In January, 1969 a young student named Jan Palach attempted public suicide by self-immolation in Wenceslas Square. He demanded the abolition of censorship and (ironically) the banning of *Zprávy (News)*.[48] This solitary act was highly symbolic, stimulated the spirit of national resistance, and provided the country with a martyr whose importance was amplified exponentially over the next two decades.[49] Palach was immediately compared to the Protestant martyr Jan Hus, who had been burned at the stake in 1415 for his heretical beliefs by the Catholic Church at the Council of Constance. The second event, the victory of the Czechoslovak ice hockey team over the Russians in the World Cup in Stockholm, "led to massive popular demonstrations in many

cities and to violent actions, in several places, against Soviet installa-
tions, including Aeroflot offices in the center of Prague" (Skilling,
1976: 819). This latter political crisis served as a partial pretext for the
ultimate removal of Dubček from power. The Soviet Politburo went
into an emergency session and decided that this incident could be
used to effect a major shift in political personnel in Czechoslovakia
(Williams, 1997: 199–200).

A declaration condemning the "mass hooligan attacks" by "rightist
extremists and counter-revolutionaries" was delivered via letter to
Prague via Soviet deputy foreign minister Vladimir Semyenov. Defense
Minister Marshal Grechko arrived at Miloviče, the main Soviet base,
and rumors swirled about of a possible *coup d'état* by high-ranking
Czechoslovak army officers (Williams, 1997: 200). Dubček was finally
forced to yield power; at a Central Committee plenum in April he
resigned as First Secretary and proposed Slovak Gustav Husák as his
successor. Because the press was tightly controlled, Dubček himself
was perceived as the initiator of the change. As much energy had
already been spent, no great opposition materialized.

Dubček's demise is a metaphor for the failure of reform communism. He was neither able to salvage his program nor political power.
Briefly appointed as Ambassador to Turkey, his eventual expulsion
from the Party prompted his recall to Prague. Completely silenced and
demoralized, he worked as a mechanic in a forest products factory
outside Bratislava until 1989. Unlike earlier political victims, he was
neither tried nor imprisoned, yet remained under close surveillance and
was not politically "rehabilitable"—as late as 1988 editors virulently
attacked him as "that political wreck from 1968" (McRae, 1977: 43).
Reform communism was too dangerous to be seriously engaged with,
even as *glasnost* and *perestroika* were the order of the day in Moscow.

In *The Restoration of Order*, Slovak dissident Milan Šimečka dissected the regime rubric of re-establishing *order* over *disorder*. The "master link" in the chain was the restoration of the "leading role of the
party," which, above all other errors committed in Soviet eyes, was
the gravest mistake made by the Czechoslovak reformers. A heavy toll
was exacted on communist party reformers, beginning with a major
"screening" of all party members, the purpose of which "was not the
creation of some new, ideologically right-minded membership (to do
so would be to reduce the party to a tiny sect and to destroy the illusion of mass membership), but simply to turn the membership into

what it used to be: an apolitical conglomerate of the most varied con-cealed denominations, united only by obedience and a readiness to fulfil its role as a trustworthy receiver of instructions and directives" (Šimečka, 1984a: 37). The cynical goal was to replace activism with passivity. Screening was followed by expulsion, a tragic and soul-destroying occurrence for many who had been brought up in the party, and had dedicated their lives and energies to its regeneration. Many were also blacklisted, subject to "occupational persecution"[50] and various forms of "civilized violence," including police harassment, interrogation, surveillance, and house searches. All of this was accom-plished within a framework of rules—a facade of procedural justice. Restored order constructed reality, with the Prague Spring ideologized as a counter-revolution. (1984a: 121).

The party purges that define the Husák period of normalization began in earnest in the 1970s, and lasted for about four years. The results were staggering: approximately 327,000 members of the party were expelled; another 150,000 left voluntarily. Membership of the party was cut by one third, although the purge was less intense in Slo-vakia. About two thirds of Writers' Union members lost their jobs, 900 university teachers were fired, and 21 academic institutions were closed. A telling result of the depth and breadth of the purges is that in 1971, for the first time since 1821, no literary journals (originally the sponsors of the Czech national revival in the 19th century and long the bastions of critical national Czech culture) were published.[51] Intel-lectual life was frozen. In the twenty years following 1968, over half a million people emigrated (in a country of just 15 million). According to law, their leaving was a criminal act, and they were forbidden to return. Louis Aragon reputedly referred to Czechoslovakia as the "Biafra of the soul."

Implicitly the regime offered its citizenry an unwritten and un-spoken contract. Like the Kádárist "compromise" or the labor peace "bought" by Gierek, citizens were promised the bribe of modest improvement, a decent standard of living, and stable employment in exchange for political silence and labor quiescence. This Faustian bargain was difficult to maintain indefinitely. It required that each citizen accept the state lie and magnify its significance through silence and adaptation, a process Havel later called "living a lie." Constructing new political alternatives ultimately depended the ability to shatter the circular logic of normalization.

The Underground Music Scene and the Trial of the PPU

Normalization was a pervasive and ongoing process throughout Czechoslovak society, and the arenas of music and culture were certainly not immune. The underground music scene was of particular *political* importance for at least two reasons: first, it represented the initial stirrings of alternative culture in the post-1968 period; and second, the arrest and trial of the underground rock group the Plastic People of the Universe (PPU, or "The Plastics") was the catalyst for the formation of Charter 77.

The regime was able to commit "culturecide"[52] in the musical arena largely via its chief tool of normalization repression, the requalification exams. Official music-making was controlled by a series of music agencies in every large city or region under the ægis of the party-state. The ability to perform and receive payment was coordinated through the agencies; in order to qualify as a professional *or* an amateur musician one had to pass an exam and undergo an audition process (Vaničková, 1997: 38–48). In the early 1970s, all musicians were required to pass requalification exams, where their politics, song lyrics, and even mode of dress were as critical as their musical ability. In 1973 the Musician's Union laid off 3,000 of its members; rock music in particular was decimated to the point where only a handful of officially-sanctioned bands were permitted.[53] Guidelines were set up, cultural inspectors attended concerts to ensure compliance, and intimidation and censorship were pervasive (1997: 54–55). Radim Hladík, an official musician working during this period (and who was a member of the examination commission in Prague), commented rather cynically: "There were 3 things one could do in this situation. Either try to continue playing without pissing off the regime, emigrate, or resign professional status" (cited in Vaničková, 1997: 54).

Within this context a musical "underground" emerged in the mid-1970s; however it was not simply an agglomeration of highly idiosyncratic individuals who sought to defy authority in the name of rock music. Rather, over time and under the direction and influence of counter-cultural intellectuals, the underground began to conceive of itself as a constitutive element in an alternative culture and eventually nascent civil society. This is clear in the writings of both Václav Havel and Václav Benda,[54] as well as in the thought and action of the underground's premier theorist, Ivan Jirous.

Ivan Jirous used the term "second culture" to describe the non-conformist and unofficial music-making in which he was involved. Not surprisingly, playwright-dissident Václav Havel and Jirous were friends, and the two were mutually influential. Havel took culture as a departure point for his theorizing about politics; Jirous applied politics to his artistic endeavors, effectively stage-managing political meaning out of counter-cultural activity. Most notably Jirous was both the artistic director and manager of the band, Plastic People of the Universe (PPU). Musically, the PPU were not necessarily the "best" the Prague underground had to offer, but under Jirous' direction they became the center of attention, not only to the small and largely Prague-based community of fledgling dissidents, rock aficionados and 1960s generation leftovers marginalized socially and politically by normalization, but unfortunately also to the *Státní Bezpečnost* (StB), or State Security. The PPU combined a psychedelic sound very reminiscent of the Velvet Underground with ritual theatre; Jirous consciously linked the "authenticity" and "honesty" of the PPU with politics, as their music was not officially sanctioned.[55] As the party-state was not involved in corrupting or manipulating the band, Jirous implied the music itself was free from compromise and commodification. Although Jirous' views may or may not have reflected the feelings of the bands' members, he was definitely a profoundly moving force, encouraging many artists besides the PPU, and wrote extensively in samizdat books and underground journals (Vaničková, 1997: 79–82; Wilson, 1996).

In 1976, after a music festival Jirous held to celebrate his wedding, about 20 musicians were arrested and over a hundred people who attended were interrogated (Skilling, 1981: 8). Following a media campaign of denunciation, three organizers of a 1975 PPU concert and lecture by Jirous were arrested, tried, and convicted in a farcical trial in Pilsen. Later, several band members were tried and convicted in Prague. The authorities linked the musicians to gross indecency, drug use, and alcoholism, describing the PPU as a public disturbance, morally offensive, and opposed to the established order. Song lyrics were cited as incontrovertible proof; underground rock music was depicted as heinous and conspiratorial. The result was the cultural equivalent of the 1950s political trials.

The Prague intellectual community responded quite quickly. Havel approached others of like mind[56] and together they appealed first privately to the President, then to the media and finally to German writer Heinrich Böll (Riese, 1979; Skilling 1981). Böll responded positively, impressed that the prominent intellectuals had taken a public stand against the actions of the regime; presciently he recognized a "new orientation" among the dissenters, and his communication opened up an avenue for discourse with other European intellectuals and writers that would continue right up to 1989.

The trial of Jirous and three of the PPU band members went ahead in a typical perfunctory manner. The verdict was politically determined, and the presiding judge stated that the accused had conclusively been proven guilty, as they "had organized and participated in performances from 1971 to 1976 which had 'manifested their disrespect of society and their contempt of fundamental moral laws'" (Skilling, 1981: 12). Havel attended the trial in place of one of the family members, and later wrote an essay ("The Trial") which was widely circulated in Czechoslovakia, and later translated into English in *The Merry Ghetto*[57] which was included in the Plastics' first album, *Egon Bondy's Happy Hearts Club Banned*.[58] Havel perceived a key shift beneath the predictable drama. He described how although everyone expected the trial to result in the conviction of the defendants, the process took on the nature of a relentless game, one in which all the participants were forced to play their roles but in so doing ironically represented the complete opposite. He states:

> The players in this spectacle found themselves in a paradoxical situation. The more candidly they played their role, the more clearly they revealed its unpremeditated significance, and thus they gradually became co-creators of a drama utterly different from the one they thought they were playing in, or wanted to play in (1991: 103).

Thus the public prosecutor, supposedly the guardian of societal interests and representing the forces of law and morality, was *in fact* the "symbol of an inflated, narrow-minded power, persecuting everything that does not fit into its sterile notions of life, everything unusual, risky, self-taught, and unbribable, everything that is too artless and too complex, too accessible and too mysterious, everything in fact that is different from itself" (1991: 103). Likewise, Ivan Jirous and his friends did not condemn those who condemned them. Despite the efforts of the officials to represent the accused as "repulsive, long-haired hooligans," the PPU ultimately and unintentionally personified the need for self-determination and personal freedom. Finally, the judge was not the "objective arbiter" but tragically symbolized the incapacity of the judiciary to maintain its own independence *vis-à-vis* the party-state.

For Havel, this facade of procedural justice nonetheless began to appear as a smokescreen clouding up what was really going on in the trial:

> [It was] an impassioned debate about the meaning of human existence, an urgent questioning of what one should expect from life, whether one should silently accept the world as it is presented to one, or whether one has the strength to exercise free choice in the matter; whether one should be "reasonable" and take one's place in the world, or whether one has the right to resist in the name of one's own human convictions (1991: 105).

Havel effectively juxtaposed the absurd unreality of staged event with the absurd reality of everyday life in Husák's "normalized" Czechoslovakia. He describes a sea-change in attitudes that has been confirmed and reconfirmed to me by interviews with Charter 77 activists and other Western interlocutors (Skilling, 1981; Skilling, 1994; Urbanek, 1995; Klíma, 1995; Wilson, 1996; Hejdánek, 1997; Šiklová, 1997). The trial presented the "challenge by example," an idea Havel later developed as the now-famous idiom "living in truth." The trial became *the* critical "shared experience" in the founding of a "special, improvised community"—a greater amount of trust, communication, and solidarity grew from those who bore witness, not just inside the courtroom, but more obviously among those who had congregated outside who were not permitted to enter. With no small amount of moral courage, Havel summed up the possible options at this point:

> In this situation, all reserve and inner reticence seemed to lose its point; in this atmosphere, all the inevitable "buts" seemed ridiculous, insignificant, and evasive. Everyone seemed to feel that at a time when all the chips are down, there are only two things one can do: gamble everything, or throw in the cards (1991: 108).

Trite as it may sound, the founding impulse for Charter 77 was this collective sense of "gambling everything."

The Helsinki Accords and Charter 77

As Skilling has aptly pointed out, "Charter 77" referred not only to the document issued by a new coalition of dissidents in January, 1977, but it also "designated a movement for human rights" (1981: 19). The promotion and protection of the human rights of Czechoslovak citizens was the official *raison d'être* of the organization. By focusing on legally ratified rights, the Chartists were brilliantly engaging in the same strategy of self-limitation as the Poles in the founding of KOR, and as the Hungarian intellectuals would later employ in their engagement with the Kádár regime.

In 1975 Czechoslovakia along with other countries in the region endorsed the Final Act of the Helsinki Accord. Article VII, subtitled "Respect for human rights and fundamental freedoms, including the freedom of thought, conscience, religion, or belief" states:

> The participating states will respect human rights and fundamental freedoms, including freedom of thought, conscience, religion or belief, for all without distinction as to race, sex, language, or religion.
>
> They will promote and encourage the effective exercise of civil, political, economic, social, cultural and other rights and freedoms all of which derive from the inherent dignity of the human person and are essential for his free and full development.
>
> Within this framework the participating states will recognize and respect the freedom of the individual to profess and practise, alone or in community with others, religion or belief acting in accordance with the dictates of his own conscience (reprinted in Daniels, 1994: 256).[59]

The idea for creating a human rights group to monitor the implementation of the accords followed the emergence of similar groups in Poland and the Soviet Union. Those involved in the PPU trial clearly wanted to build on the momentum of their growing solidarity. Charter 77 also brought together a number of disparate yet important initiatives of the early 1970s with a new sense of vitality and cohesion.[60] After eight years of normalization and the realization that reform communism was dead, the organizers were also able to create a remarkable consensus. This was evident in the wording of its founding document, as well as by the representative nature of the list of signatures, 239 in all. Almost the same consensus and conclusions, especially regarding the death of reform communism, occurred in tandem with the formation of KOR in Poland.[61]

Charter 77's founding document, the declaration of January 1, 1977, comprehensively details the litany of violations of both Helsinki and the UN covenants.[62] Freedom of expression is described as illusory, given that "tens of thousands of our citizens" are prevented from work in their professions because their views differ from those officially sanctioned and "countless young people" are prevented from attending university because of their own views or those of their parents. The document criticizes the "centralized control of all the communications media and publishing and cultural institutions," the lack of freedom of religion, freedom of association, and the curtailment of civil liberties. Existing legal norms were condemned for their lawlessness, arbitrariness, and disrespect of civil rights.

In the declaration, Charter 77 publicly announced its inception as "a free informal, open community of people of different convictions, different faiths and different professions united by the will to strive, individually and collectively, for the respect of civic and human rights in our own country and throughout the world ..." (Skilling, 1981: 211). From the beginning, Charter 77 was a "virtual" organization—no rules, permanent bodies, formal membership, fund-raising capacity, or legal existence. Anyone who embraced its ideas or participated in its work was essentially a member; although the core group remained the signatories, spokespeople, and those who wrote and disseminated its documents. Its ideals were broad and membership open, but it was nonetheless largely an intellectual phenomenon.

However, considerable diversity was represented by people of very different viewpoints and backgrounds. Skilling (1981) dissected the membership of Charter 77 to include a number of imprecise groupings. First, there were the "ex-communists," (E-club) a few elite party-state functionaries who had wholeheartedly supported reform in 1968 and were stripped of power and privilege in the ensuing period of normalization. Most prominent were Zdeněk Mlynář (former Central Committee and CC Vysočany member) and Jiří Hájek (former foreign minister and one of the three first Charter spokespersons). Although some of the "E-clubs" still held firm their views about the possibilities of the 1968 Action Program, others had moved well beyond reform communism, envisaging true political pluralism as the only legitimate starting point for change. A third tendency wanted to remain close to critical Marxism and international (i.e. Euro)communism, and included Jaroslav Šabata and František Kriegel. Related ideologically were the socialists, of both the democratic and revolutionary variety, including historian Rudolf Battěk, student leader Jiří Müller, and Šabata's son-in-law Petr Uhl. Religious groupings roughly representative of the Evangelical Church of Czech Brethren and the Catholic church were also evident, and over time freedom of religious expression gained greater attention from Charter signatories, and in turn helped to attract more signatures. Many Chartists did not identify with one tendency or grouping, but generically supported the aims of the movement, and supported different declarations and positions independently. Thus Ladislav Hejdánek has been described as a "Protestant" philosopher yet supported socialist aims and declarations. Havel was never a communist, was only peripherally involved in the Prague Spring, made his living as a playwright, but at times described himself as a socialist.

Labeling Chartists as representing tendency X or Y is problematic as they were trying to forge a new kind of consensus politics, not built around a traditional left–right axis. The goal was to emphasize points of agreement rather than disagreement.[63] Over and over, Charter 77 defined itself not as an organization but as a movement, an umbrella under which tolerance for different views would be cultivated and various initiatives proposed. The organizational design of the Charter was made to cohere with its anti-ideological bias and its democratic and pluralistic ethos.[64] Attempts were made to be representative, especially in the selection of spokespersons.[65] However, Charter documents, including the founding declaration, were discussed beforehand, collectively written, and later circulated, commented, and re-commented on. One can accurately speak of the collective position of the Charter, and of its aims and priorities as a whole.

The regime quickly perceived that the Charter was a danger to the regime stability. In late January of 1977, a "voluntary" petition was circulated by the authorities condemning Charter 77—it became known as the "Anti-Charter." All state employees were required to sign the document, and those who did not faced severe repercussions.[66] Despite harassment and interrogation, the Chartists were able to continue effectively, even slowly building up the number of signatories from the original 240 to eventually some 2,000.

Charter 77 was predominantly an organization of writers and intellectuals, and thus its *forté* and principal activity was its endless publication of documents—declarations, open letters, and communiqués. Skilling calculated that during its first decade of existence, Charter 77 "issued a total of some 340 documents" (1989: 47). Underlying this impressive feat are the painstaking details that were involved in preparation of each document: the slow process of collective authorship of many of the pieces as well as time taken for consultation with others, and the even slower process of actual publication and distribution. Constant interruptions to this process were inevitable due to police surveillance and the confiscation of complete or partially-written drafts. The authenticity of Charter materials was ensured through the signature of all three spokespersons on each document.

On an international level, Charter 77 maintained strong linkages with the Helsinki Process. Outreach efforts were made to West European peace activists, spawning a considerable internal and cross-border debate on détente, the stationing of missiles in Europe, and the connections between peace and human rights. Appeals were made to various international and especially UN organizations (such as the ILO on the continued discrimination in employment characteristic of normalization but especially felt by Charter members). Most significant were its associations and linkages with other dissident and social movements in the region. Representatives of KOR and Charter 77 first met on their common frontier in 1978 (Skilling, 1989: 58). Charter 77 expressed strong support for Solidarity in 1980, and condemned the imposition of martial law in 1981. This was formalized through the creation of the Polish–Czechoslovak Solidarity group and later the Circle of Friends of Polish–Czechoslovak Solidarity. Cooperation between dissidents had become so effective that by the 30th anniversary of the Hungarian uprising in 1956 a proclamation was signed by over 122 individuals from four countries (Hungary, Poland, Czechoslovakia, and the GDR). They not only condemned the Soviet intervention, but linked the unfulfilled objectives of the Hungarian revolt historically to the Prague Spring, Solidarity, and the 1953 riots in Pilsen and East Berlin (1989: 59). In order to demonstrate cohesion, "the signatories pledged mutual support in the struggle for political democracy, pluralism based on self-government, the reunification of Europe and its democratic integration, and the rights of minorities" (1989: 59).

Výbor na Obranu Nespravedlivě Stíhaných (VONS)

The role of VONS (The Committee for the Defense of the Unjustly Persecuted) as an alternative organization alongside the Charter but with many of the same members is lesser known. It was founded on April 27, 1978. VONS was conceived on the model of the Polish KOR—a self-help organization which would aid victims of state prosecution, attend trials, document evidence, provide legal advice, and assistance to their families. Rather than replicate the broad sweep of the Charter, the purpose of VONS was to focus on individual cases of persecution.

In 1979 a large-scale police action was commenced against VONS signatories. Six of its founding members were sentenced to prison, making it difficult to continue the work of the organization. Nonetheless, there was no interruption in the regular communiqués (*sdělení*) detailing the monthly specifics of injustice—arrests, searches, trials, beatings, and so on (Skilling, 1989: 27).

In the same way that VONS was modeled on KOR, VONS was an important precursor to later legal defense organizations. For example, in October, 1988, the *Iniciativa Sociální Obrany* (ISO) or Initiative for Social Defense, was formed. Whereas VONS was created to support political prisoners, ISO focused on more subtle forms of persecution, ranging from problems with work, school, travel, and housing to social discrimination and psychiatric abuse (Helsinki Watch, 1989: 10).

The "Underground University"

As in Poland, the Czechoslovak opposition created an impressive array of unofficial seminars. In *The Velvet Philosophers*, Barbara Day describes open and well-organized university-type seminars that were being conducted in Prague in the early 1970s—well before the creation of Charter 77 (1999: 21). In fact, these seminars hearken back to an earlier set of seminars conducted by expelled professor Jan Patočka in the 1950s. Originally, these seminars from the mid-1970s were independent of each other, and rivals in terms of competing for "membership."

One of the earliest seminar leaders, Julius Tomin, sought to establish Western contact and support for his seminar in 1978 by sending a letter to four prestigious universities: Heidelberg, the Freie Universität in Berlin, Oxford, and Harvard. The only copy of his letter to reach receptive ears was that sent to Oxford; it surfaced in a sub-faculty meeting of Balliol College in January, 1979. Tomin requested that Western lecturers come to Prague to provide basic instruction in the classics of Western philosophy. Bill Newton-Smith was friendly to the idea, and it was determined that the first three lecturers to travel to Prague would be Kathy Wilkes, Richard Hare, and Charles Taylor. The first initiatives were so successful that eventually an entire infrastructure was built up in the flow of "goods" (books, equipment, and later office supplies and computers) and "services" (visiting lecturers) from London to Prague. The British academics organized their efforts into a charitable foundation, calling themselves the "Jan Hus Educational Foundation," and similar support was provided by the Charter 77 Foundation in Stockholm.

The Czech seminar leaders never attempted to organize themselves more fully, along the lines of the TKN in Poland. It was simply too dangerous in Prague, where even with the sporadic and disconnected nature of the seminars, the leaders and the students were subject to police harassment.[67] Tomin himself passively resisted arrest and was badly treated; students from the Technical University attending another ongoing seminar were also beaten up. Attending and organizing the seminars was risky business, but considering that a major part of their clientele were the children of dissidents who had been denied university entrance anyway, they continued unabated. A stipend program was even introduced for funding independent research. A number of students completed the entire Cambridge Diploma in Theology, sitting exams in Prague and smuggling out their papers which would be sent to Cambridge professors for correction. Home cinemas were set up; four VCRs were sent over along with a portable television, and over time vast quantities of videos were smuggled into the country.

Prague was not the only site of such seminars. The Jan Hus Educational Foundation also financed a very carefully organized set of seminars in Brno from 1984–1989.[68] Not only were they able to avoid police detection, but over time they were able to offer entire 10–12-week courses in a variety of subjects. In Brno there was also an effort to attract a wider base of students, and many organizers and attendees were either in the "grey zone" or had never been previously involved in any activity deemed illicit by the regime. In 1987 in Bratislava a small but important group gathered for eight lectures of high quality under the stewardship of Miroslav Kusý.

Jan Hus Foundations were set up in Canada and the United States, and other organizations in the Netherlands and France supported the network of independent seminars. Julius Tomin emigrated, taking a job at Oxford, and veteran dissident and philosopher Ladislav Hejdánek took over his seminar. Hejdánek's pupils were extremely fortunate, for through the 1980s the likes of Jacques Derrida, Paul Ricoeur, Jürgen Habermas, Richard Rorty, and Ira Katznelson were to make appearances at his Monday night events.[69] Dangers of participation aside, students in the seminar had better access to the leading minds of European and North American thought than their Western counterparts in graduate schools!

Many of the seminars focused on morality and ethics, with a strong undercurrent of public responsibility and engagement, very much in keeping with the general philosophy of the Czechoslovak underground. To some degree, the seminar graduates—many of whom today hold significant positions in public life—are giving back to their societies today.[70]

Samizdat Publishing and Distribution

After the creation of Charter 77, Zdena Tominová described the veritable explosion of a "typewriter culture" (quoted in Skilling, 1989: 26). First, there was the variety of informational bulletins about Charter 77, and their authorized documents, communiqués, and open letters.[71] Second, a parallel industry of alternative presses focusing on literature, history, philosophy, and music emerged. Academic books, novels, essays, feuilletons, and collections of poetry were all published.

Unlike the Poles, who used regular printing presses and could ensure a mass level of circulation, the typewriter was the technology of choice. Typed manuscripts were permissible under law—and thus in keeping with the principles of the openness and legality that guided the Charter and other organizations (Skilling, 1989: 27). A limited number of copies would be made with each typing through the combined use of onion skin and carbon paper. Later, fax machines and computer disks would be used to transmit files and information, especially to supporters abroad who might funnel paperless documents to Radio Free Europe or Voice of America for maximum exposure.

Independent publishing houses existed, and especially in Slovakia published Catholic books and theological periodicals. Magazines and journals represented all aspects of the underground culture, from music to economics, theatre to history (see Skilling, 1989: 28–30). The most famous independent literary press was *Edice Petlice* founded by Ludvík Vaculík, launched in 1972. Václav Havel started *Edice Expedice* which issued over 300 titles.

One of the most important "independent" presses did not exist in Czechoslovakia at all, but in Toronto in the home of exiled Czech authors Josef Skvorecký and Zdena Salivarová. Salivarová began her publishing house *68 Publishers* on her own initiative, eventually publishing over two hundred titles in Czech. She maintained a brisk mail order business, with a mailing list of over 40,000 names. The goal of *68 Publishers*, however, was not only to reach the emigré community of Czechs and Slovaks worldwide. Salivarová also sought to publish contemporary Czech and Slovak literature and materials that could not be printed in Czechoslovakia, and in turn have these books smuggled back into the country so that they might be more widely available.

Journals published abroad were indispensable channels of information, and were distributed widely. The most well-known were Pavel Tigrid's *Svědectví*, published in Paris, and Jiří Pelikán's *Listy*, published in Rome. In London exile Jan Kávan set up Palach Press.[72] Over the almost 20-year history of Czechoslovak samizdat, most of it was collected and carefully preserved by historian Vilém Prečan in his Czechoslovak Documentation Center for Independent Literature, located at the Schwarzenberg Castle in Scheinfeld, Germany.[73] Elaborate and complicated systems were improvised whereby material would be transported across the Czechoslovak borders both into and out of the country.[74]

Repression and Resistance in the Czech Lands and Slovakia in the 1980s

In 1980 the unremarkable Czechoslovak government did something remarkable: it admitted that for the first time, the country had a negative GNP growth, and announced that only 2% of the country's technological output could possibly match the quality of the developed world. Other cracks in the armor were beginning to show, undermining the tacit social contract. By 1990, Czechoslovakia had one of the lowest per capita expenditures on education in Europe, the mortality rate had been growing for some years, and Czechoslovak citizens had a shorter life span than most Europeans.

Within Slovakia dissent proceeded at lower decibel levels and with less attention than in Prague, but paradoxically was more broad-based. Normalization in Slovakia had never been as severe as in the Czech lands, and it was easier for some opposition currents to plant a seed with the general populace. Being removed from Prague was in some respects advantageous. There was less of a distinction to be made between the Prague Spring reformers in Slovakia—who were not as radical as their Bohemian counterparts—and the anti-reformers, who were similarly not as hardline as the pro-Soviet hawks in Prague.[75] Moreover, some of the token reforms associated with renewed federalism were implemented.[76] Even in the depths of normalization, things could be published in Bratislava that could not be published in Prague. The concerns of Slovaks, associated with nationalist grievances, freedom of religion, and minority issues, were more pragmatic. Right up until 1989, there was less of a sense of the Slovak opposition attempting to occupy the "moral high ground" deliberately claimed by writers and philosophers in the Czech lands.[77] Slovakia's sizeable minority of ethnic Hungarians was a crucial demographic fact. Finally, the Church was a unifying force and a source of public support and mobilization.

In the late 1970s, Hungarian minorities were becoming increasingly outspoken in defence of their human rights and national interests. In 1978, the Hungarians formed a Committee for the Legal Defense of the Hungarian minority and by 1983 their harassed leader Miklós Duray signed Charter 77.[78] The Committee was not created to be anti-communist or united ideologically, but they did agree on the need to pressure the regime to support Hungarian education in schools.[79] In retrospect, however, activist László Szigeti contends that it can be categorized as an independent civic initiative, albeit one that operated partly in the "grey zone."[80] In a smart strategic move at coalition-building, Charter 77 protested discrimination against the Hungarians, and presented a proposal on national minorities to the Vienna CSCE conference. The Hungarians in Slovakia were also an important connection between dissidents in Czechoslovakia (especially Slovakia) and Hungary. Through the Hungarians, Slovaks became acquainted with the works of János Kis and György Konrád, and the efforts of the democratic opposition to align itself with the cause of Hungarian minorities outside the country. Hungarian activists maintained contact with and support for the Czechoslovak opposition, and Fidesz members even traveled to Prague in August, 1988, making a brief statement of support. Given the relative liberalism of the Kádár regime, it was easier for the Hungarians to travel to and meet with their opposition counterparts in Budapest than to make conspiratorial contacts with Slovak oppositionists. The Hungarians did, however, keep in touch with Charter activities—both through signatory Duray as well as Bratislava lawyer Ján Čarnogurský and former philosophy professor Miroslav Kusý. As Čarnogurský was also a Catholic activist, he was a contact point with these two groups. These three groups—Catholics, Hungarians, and Charter signatories—formed the nucleus of opposition in Slovakia and their increasing cooperation paved the way for the formulation and structure of Public against Violence.

By the late 1980s, the solidity of the Husák regime seemed to be crumbling—albeit imperceptibly. Nonetheless, the regime continued its hardline to the bitter end—to the extent that it could and did remain unchallenged. In March, 1987, Gorbachev visited Prague, raising hope for some that perhaps his visit might trigger an accelerated level of reform along the same lines of *perestroika* and *glasnost*. Senior Soviet officials made it known to the authorities that perhaps a revision of 1968 was overdue; these suggestions were rapidly rebuffed and the regime criticized the "fashionable" attitudes of the leadership in Moscow. The same year Miloš Jakeš replaced Husák as first secretary, with the latter maintaining the ceremonial role as president. It became clear, however, that the changeover was merely cosmetic. The Academy of Science's Institute for Economic Forecasting recommended radical reform in order to solve social and economic problems[81] and Prime Minister Štrougal supported the report. The regime responded by ousting Štrougal, replacing him with Ladislav Adamec in 1988.

These official rumblings were also mirrored by extraordinary events which can be read as "clues" of growing discontent with the regime, and the stirrings of public mobilization. On December 8, 1985, for example, on the fifth anniversary of the death of John Lennon, an assembly gathered on Na Kampě to commemorate the day. The original group of about 200 eventually swelled to over 1,000. They marched across the Charles Bridge demanding freedom and peace, and later up to the castle, where a petition was signed by over 300. Like peace activists in END,[82] they demanded an end to the stationing of nuclear warheads in either Western or Eastern Europe. They left peacefully at around 9:00 p.m. (Skilling, 1989: 65). This was not a Charter-sponsored event, although they did comment on it later and called for greater youth opportunities and reduced military service.

John Lennon was a symbolic figure to the flowering opposition, especially among young people. On Na Kampě Island there was an impromptu memorial to Lennon ritualistically spray-painted on a concrete retaining wall. Even though the authorities persisted time and again to secure its permanent removal, it reappeared. Later in 1988 an independent association called the *Mirový Klub John Lennon* (MKJL), or John Lennon Peace Club, was formed. Its aims were to work for world peace generally, human rights in Czechoslovakia specifically, and to encourage independent cultural activity.

Significantly, on the twentieth anniversary of the Soviet invasion, an anti-government demonstration was held in Wenceslas Square, organized *not* by the Chartists but by two groups of young activists: the *Nezávislé Mírové Sdružení* (NMS), or Independent Peace Initiative, and the Czech Children. The demonstration was surprisingly not disrupted by the police. This core group of young people had crossed a line—they were now in direct confrontation with the regime. Moreover, they brought with their commitment new issues (such as conscientious objection to military service) and enthusiasm.[83]

The regime continued its campaign of harassment, and publicly denounced all independent initiatives. From 1981 to 1986 the government launched a campaign of harassment against the *Jazzová Sekce* or Jazz Section, finally culminating in the arrest of seven members, including its head, Karel Srp.[84] The underground and alternative music scenes continued to proliferate; some performances were banned, others operated semi-legally.

In August 1988, what began as a small demonstration on the twentieth anniversary of the 1968 invasion grew to a crowd of about 10,000 in Wenceslas Square, the largest independent demonstration since 1969 (Helsinki Watch, 1989: 43). It was sponsored by the NMS. Perhaps taken by surprise or hesitant to take action given the symbolic importance of the date, the police did not immediately intervene. However, a month later at a similar demonstration called together by NMS, the StB responded in force, emerging from the subway entrances around the square, clubbing and arresting participants (McRae, 1997: 5–6).

Nevertheless, thousands of Czechs took part in a demonstration commemorating the 70th anniversary of the founding of the Republic on October 28 (Helsinki Watch, 1989: 44).

Political trials continued right up until and through the fall of 1989. Václav Havel's third prison term began in January, 1989 after being arrested for laying a wreath on Jan Palach's grave in January on the 20th anniversary of his death.[85] Charter spokesperson Tomáš Hradílek was indicted for "damaging state interests abroad" and tried in April. The trial of Slovak lawyer and Chartist Jan Čarnogurský occurred simultaneously with the onset of the Velvet Revolution in November.

By late 1988 and early 1989, the strides toward reform represented by the Polish elections and the Hungarian negotiations were becoming increasingly problematic for the Czechoslovak regime. Now they had more to contend with than their criticism of trends in Moscow. Deteriorating relations with Hungary throughout 1989 are a case in point. On April 4, much to the chagrin of Czech authorities, the Hungarian television show *Panorama* aired a long and detailed interview of Alexander Dubček conducted by its host András Sugár.[86] Not only was the show able to be picked up in Southern Slovakia, but Radio Free Europe re-broadcast it over the entire country. In the battle of words between the reformers in Budapest and the dinosaurs in Prague, the Czechoslovak government denounced the rehabilitation of 1956 and the reburial of Imre Nagy in June. Acting offensively, in September of 1989 the Hungarian parliament made it their business to condemn the 1968 invasion of Czechoslovakia. The opening of the Hungarian–Austrian border to the West turned out to be the critical proximate cause in the fall of the Berlin Wall (which occurred November 9). Moreover, this decision had concrete consequences for the regime in Prague, as thousands of East German refugees streamed toward the Austro-Hungarian border. By October, 11,000 found a home in the West German embassy in Prague before being allowed to emigrate.

By the summer of 1989, cooperation among dissidents and now former dissidents in neighboring countries had become much more open and widespread. It had been a long haul since the "illicit forest picnics" on the Czech–Polish border, but in July Adam Michnik and Zbygniew Bujak came to Prague as official representatives of the Polish *Sejm*. The *Státní Bezpečnost* (StB) were powerless to stop their visit with Czechoslovak dissidents. On August 11, the new Polish government condemned the 1968 invasion, and apologized for their participation in the process. Andrei Sakharov could now be telephoned openly in Moscow.

The dissidents in Prague were careful throughout 1989, and even when vigorously debating whether or not to advise participation in a demonstration to commemorate the Soviet invasion on August 20, they were extremely hesitant and reluctant. With considerable stamina and a strong moral voice, they were simply unwilling to suggest others get involved in a situation that could turn violent, in which people would likely get hurt. After June 4, a Chinese solution remained a viable possibility. When the regime did crack down on its citizens during the demonstrations on November 17, the dissidents had no blood on their hands; it was not their march.[87]

The Underground Church in Slovakia

Unlike in Poland, the Catholic Church in Czechoslovakia had never managed to fully keep its independence. Many bishops and priests accommodated and supported the regime, even to the point of joining *Pacem in Terris* (Peace on Earth), a pro-regime "peace movement" which was never recognized by the Vatican as a legitimate organization. Religious observance was not high, especially in Bohemia and Moravia. Cardinal Tomášek was no Cardinal Wyszyński or Archbishop Wojtyła, and had historically avoided confrontation with the regime in the normalization period. However, a different story was evident in Slovakia.[88]

Slovakia was the most Catholic and religiously observant part of the Federation, and here the Church suffered the most persecution. In the late 1940s and 1950s, religious orders were forcibly disbanded and hundreds of priests and monks were imprisoned.[89] Rebuilding the Church and religious orders took decades to accomplish, often clandestinely. A secret church was born decades before other independent initiatives were contemplated (Doellinger, 2002). Efforts at spiritual reawakening were a dominant aspect of the Prague Spring as it manifested itself in Slovakia, and Bishop Ján Korec was instrumental in writing a Catholic condemnation of the invasion. Although formally Church leaders were not supportive of dissent and can be categorized as pro-regime, many priests were secretly consecrated.[90] The 1970s can be described as a period of quiet and methodical reconstruction, helped by the more relaxed version of normalization existing in Slovakia. The 1980s, on the other hand, was a time of greater social mobilization; the secret church "went public" with pilgrimages, demonstrations, and petitions for religious freedom. As in Poland, the election of Cardinal Wojtyła was pivotal, and the Slovak Catholics purposefully played up his "Slovak connection."[91]

Over time, Tomášek's willingness to take greater risks also increased. With the tutelage and support of newly appointed Pope John Paul II in Rome, the Cardinal adopted a more independent stance (Skilling, 1989: 85). In 1982, he condemned *Pacem in Terris* as a political organization and became a more outspoken critic of the regime.[92] In 1985 the Cardinal invited the Pope to the 1,100th anniversary of the death of Slav missionary Saint Methodius in Velehrad, Moravia.[93] The Pope accepted the invitation (circulated in samizdat) but was denied permission to attend by the Husák regime. The jubilee year of Saint Methodius was a pivotal event. It was celebrated in every Slovak diocese, and a large delegation of young Slovak believers held a peaceful outdoor meeting the day before the celebration, in defiance of local clergy (Mikloško, 1991). 1985 was also the year that saw the elevation of Slovak emigré Bishop Jozef Tomko to Cardinal. In 1988, more than 600,000 people, both Catholics and lay supporters, signed a petition demanding greater religious freedom (two thirds of the signatories were Slovaks).

Demonstrations took place in both Bratislava and Prague. The March candlelight religious rally organized by Mikloško attracted over 2,000 participants, but was brutally repressed (Kirschbaum, 1995: 248). In July 1988, the Catholic activists had succeeded to such a degree that over 280,000 made the religious pilgrimage to Levoča. In September, 1988, 60,000 traveled to Šaštin in Western Slovakia on pilgrimage. Pilgrimages and demonstrations were increasingly dominated by a younger generation, indicating religious renewal and future continuity.

Although Church activities were not of the Polish scale, the role of Church resistance in Slovakia was particularly significant. By December 11, 1989, one final victory had been secured by Catholic activists. The collaborationist and communist-controlled *Pacem in Terris* was disbanded.

The Tide Turns: "Just a Few Sentences"

On June 29, 1989, both official and unofficial artists signed a petition entitled *Několik vět* (*Just a Few Sentences*). With an ironic reference to the Vaculík's earlier *Two Thousand Words* manifesto, it called for democratization and in particular greater religious freedom. The petition also demanded political prisoners be released, freedom of assembly granted, industrial projects subject to an environmental assessment, and that the Prague Spring and subsequent normalization be openly discussed (McRae, 1997: 50).

The wording of the petition was carefully constructed so as to secure broader support than earlier dissident efforts. Designed to penetrate into the grey zone, it was entirely successful—over 4,000 people signed during the first week. By the time Helsinki Watch in New York reported on the petition, 15,000 people had signed. This was particularly important because many of the signatories were not Chartists or the usual group of dissident suspects, but included employed academics, workers, students, and even police officers. The petition indicated a dissatisfaction and untapped potential for social mobilization.

It was also a daring move at the time, happening just after the Tiananmen Massacre earlier in June, along with the regime's statement of sympathy for the Chinese hardliners. In the five months leading up to the dramatic events of November, it would be signed by over 40,000 people. Prior to November these signatories were also harassed, so much so that on October 25 a group of the signatories, together with official journalists and the Czech Philharmonic Orchestra announced that it would henceforth boycott Czechoslovak television for their attacks and biased coverage.

Just a Few Sentences was also important because of what occurred immediately in its wake. A plethora of independent groups sprouted up, some overtly political, others more conventionally pursuing single interests, such as peace or ecology.[94] In particular, *Hnutí za Občanskou Svobodu* (HOS) or the Movement for Civil Liberties was formed, with the express intention of creating the necessary infrastructure for "normal" political life. It was both overtly political and pragmatic, with a manifesto demanding political and economic pluralism, a new constitution, the restructuring of the legal system, and the installation of basic freedoms. Notably many of its contact persons were also Charter signatories, a direct reflection of the desire of many[95] that the Charter should take a more actively *political* role.

The GDR Exodus and the Fall of the Wall

When the Hungarians ripped open the iron curtain with their decision to permit freedom to travel, many knew it was a bold move with serious and far-reaching ramifications, but few predicted it would go as far as it did. Geographically situated between the GDR and Hungary, Czechoslovakia first experienced a flood of refugees, and then attempted to close their own borders with Hungary. The net result was that thousands sought asylum in the West German embassy in Prague, not only creating a dramatic scene of international tension, but an obvious demonstration for Czechoslovak onlookers. Thousands remained stranded while negotiations took place between Bonn and Berlin, eventually abandoning their Trabants after finally being allowed to leave on specially designated East German trains bound for the West. This interim agreement was short-lived, given the fall of the Berlin Wall on November 9 and the subsequent collapse of the GDR government. After the international media had assembled in the thousands in Berlin to witness the dog days of East German communism, many simply headed south to Prague, hoping for a new set of players to begin a similar drama on another stage.

November 17 and the Birth of Civic Forum and Public against Violence

Neither the media nor the Czech population had to wait long for the action to continue. The demonstration of November 17, that would mark the beginning of the Velvet Revolution, began innocently enough with a legitimate request by some Charles University students to hold a procession commemorating International Students Day.[96] Unfortunately, the local municipal committee rejected their request, so the students decided to set up their own independent students council and go ahead with the march (McRae, 1997: 100). It was significant that it was the students who were the organizers, rather than the older generation of dissidents.

From the many press accounts and the reminiscences of both observers and participants, we know that the demonstration was peaceful and controlled. To be sure, student banners included slogans such as "Democracy for All," the ironic "The Soviet Union Our Example, at Last" and "Democracy, Freedom, and Free Elections." Another banner in the forefront read "We Don't Want Violence"; this is also clearly evident in the photographs of the students facing a wall of police in anti-riot gear on Narodní Avenue on their way to Wenceslas Square. Students were then boxed in on both sides, unable to escape. They peacefully anchored themselves on the pavement with their candles flickering, and many were photographed handing flowers to the police (McRae, 1997; Whipple, 1991; Rosenblum, Turnley, and Turnley, 1990; Garton Ash, 1990b; Gwertzman and Kaufman, 1990).

The police were given a signal, moved toward the crowd and began clubbing and beating the students. Many were seriously injured, and a rumor spread like wildfire throughout the city that one student had been killed. It was later proven incorrect, but it no longer mattered. The children of Prague had been viciously beaten. It was the beginning of the end.

It was historically fortunate that the massacre occurred on a Friday, as it gave various currents within the opposition, as well as the brutalized students, a chance to recover and mobilize for the following week. On Saturday, November 18, representatives from the independent students council declared publicly in the Square that a student strike was being called for Monday, November 20, with a two-hour general strike for all workers to commence exactly one week later. On Sunday afternoon and evening, crowds of protesters and onlookers assembled in Wenceslas Square, a harbinger of events to come.

Meanwhile, an impromptu meeting of opposition groups was also taking place, led by Václav Havel (McRae, 1997: 111). A decision was made to organize all groups under a broad umbrella, to be called *Obcanske Forum*, or Civic Forum. Members of the 1968 reform group were there, along with the two coopted parties still officially part of the National Front (the *Socialistická Strana* or Socialist Party, and the *Lidová Strana* or People's Party).[97] The Chartists were there, members of the NMS, the Jazz Section, as well as other members of the professional intelligentsia not previously linked up with the opposition. They huddled together to prepare a declaration, which was published the following day in the November 20 edition of the Socialist Party newspaper *Svobodné Slovo* (*Free Word*). On November 20 in Bratislava, *Verejnost Proti Násilu* (VPN) or Public against Violence was formed.

On November 20, Havel held a press conference announcing the creation of Civic Forum. Students organized strike committees at high schools and universities *across* the country, not only in Prague. That afternoon Wenceslas Square swelled to hold the crowd of over 200,000. Demonstrations had spread to Bratislava, Brno, Ostrava, and Olomouc (Whipple, 1991: 15).

In Czechoslovakia, the only door that needed to be pushed open to make this possible was that of large-scale public mobilization. When students, workers, professionals, and state workers of all stripes representing all regions, generations, and walks of life took to the streets in defiance of the regime, its days were numbered. The international constellation necessary for such change was in place. Gorbachev effectively sent the message to Western politicians and the Bloc satellites that the USSR was no longer willing to prop up its former puppets. The social contract had long since been eroded; the party-state was unable through mismanagement and economic crisis to keep its end of the bargain. Elections had occurred in Poland, Hungary was peacefully transforming itself, and the Berlin Wall was now an architectural monument to the Cold War; soon it would not exist at all.

Although the Monday demonstration was large and there was definitely an electric current of change in the air, it was largely spontaneous and unorganized. However, the dissidents, after years of underground "training" became effective revolutionaries because, as McRae states, "they got their logistics right" (1997: 124). *By the very next day*, Civic Forum was able to secure a stadium-quality public address system, a speakers' platform, and already had in place an organization to channel the power of the crowd into effective demands. You cannot negotiate with a mob, even a peaceful and euphoric one. The dissidents were accused by a journalist (and later by their fellow citizens) of hijacking the revolution (McRae, 1997: 124). Linkages to workers were there, and it was no accident that on November 23, 10,000 workers from the large ČKD engineering works joined the ranks of demonstrators.[98] Czechoslovak television started to report on the events as they unfolded. These events echo a very perceptive comment by Hungarian dissident Miklós Haraszti. He stated that in order for those in opposition to outwit their adversaries, they had to become paradoxically the best Leninists of all. With characteristic irony he likened the years of underground and semi-legal opposition throughout the region to party cells; at the right moment professionally trained cadres were able to assume their rightful leadership positions at the head of the revolution. They were also operating in a long and historically continuous tradition as Central European intellectuals, assuming both ethical responsibility and moral leadership in bringing their societies with them into a brave new world. The "beautiful idea" of socialism was now replaced by democracy, but the commitment and activism were hallmarks of an earlier time than many would not care to be reminded of, either then or later.

Havel na Hrad

In the weeks remaining in November, events proceeded at a dizzying pace, causing British contemporary historian and journalist Timothy Garton Ash to quip to Havel on the 23rd that, "In Poland it took ten years, in Hungary ten months, in East Germany ten weeks: perhaps in Czechoslovakia it will take ten days!" (Garton Ash, 1990b: 78). Civic Forum moved into the *Laterna Magica*, the home of Prague's legendary black-light theatre, where they formulated demands, convened with the media, went back and forth to the Square, ate, and slept. On November 24, Dubček and Havel appeared on the balcony together in front of the crowd, but it was no longer May Day, 1968 and the crowd wanted something much different than socialism with a human face. On November 26, Cardinal Tomášek conducted a festive mass for Catholics to celebrate the canonization of Ágnes of Bohemia, which took place on November 12, just five days prior to the revolution. The entire service was broadcast live. The same day more than half a million Czechoslovak citizens converged onto Letná Plain, and Prime Minister Ademec promised that all demands would be met "within our competence" (Whipple, 1990: 17). The general strike on November 27 went off without a hitch—with military precision and mass participation. Everyday crowds surged into the Square; jangling their keys, making the "V" for victory sign, and repeatedly chanting *"Havel na Hrad"*—"Havel to the Castle." On November 29 Havel and entourage traveled to Bratislava, to cement the coalition between Civic Forum and VPN, and to give a message to both the people and the authorities that Czechs and Slovaks were acting in concert.

With greater confidence Civic Forum was able to take the lead in negotiation, and substantive changes to their list of demands reflects this.[99] On December 10, International Human Rights Day, President Gustáv Husák swore in the new government and then did what people had been waiting a long time for: he resigned. The transitional government included a communist premier, Marián Čalfa and a few apparatchiks, but was composed mostly of the intellectual activists. Within a few short hours, Jiří Dienstbier *literally* went from being a coal stoker to the nation's foreign minister. It took slightly longer—fourteen days—for Ján Čarnogurský to move from being a prisoner of conscience to being vice-premier.

The New Year's Address and the Consolidation of Democracy

In his New Year's address of 1990, President Václav Havel began with the statement: "*Tvá vláda, lide, se k tobě navarátila!*" which translated means "People, your government has returned to you!" The words were powerful not simply in the obvious sense of a return to democracy. Havel symbolically borrowed this memorable line from the first president of the republic, Tomáš Garrigue Masaryk, who used the same line in his inaugural address.[100] Masaryk himself adapted this quotation from 17th century Czech scholar Komenský (Comenius).

In his speech, Havel expounded on familiar themes. He spoke of the obsolescence of the economy, environmental degradation, and deficits in education. He described the "contaminated moral environment" brought on by 40 years of authoritarian communism. Ten years earlier in "Power of the Powerless" he spoke about the lie running through the hearts and minds of all citizens. On this day he spoke about responsibility for the past:

> We had all become used to the totalitarian system and accepted it as an unchangeable fact and thus helped to perpetuate it. In other words, we are all—though naturally to differing extents—responsible for the operation of totalitarian machinery; none of us is just its victim: we are all also its co-creators (Havel, 1991: 391–392).

The "sad legacy" of communism could not be understood as something alien imposed on the Czechoslovak people by "some distant relative." The message of 1989 was one of both personal responsibility and acceptance. Havel insists:

> ... we have to accept this legacy as a sin we committed against ourselves. If we accept it as such, we will understand that it is up to us all, and up to us only, to do something about it. We cannot blame the previous rulers for everything, not because it would be untrue but also because it could blunt the duty that each of us faces today, namely, the obligation to act independently, freely, reasonably, and quickly. Let us not be mistaken: the best government in the world, the best parliament and the best president, cannot achieve much on their own. And it would also be wrong to expect a general remedy from them. Freedom and democracy include participation and therefore responsibility from us all (Havel, 1991: 392).

Havel's speech was a hopeful one. He talked about the ability of people to make their own history, not in a teleological sense, but in the sense of people not being simply a product of their external world, and their active ability to change themselves and the human condition. Finally, he concluded by restoring Masarykian morality to politics:

> Masaryk based his politics on morality. Let us try in a new time and in a new way to restore this concept to politics. Let us teach ourselves and others that politics should be an expression of the desire to contribute to the happiness of the community rather than of a need to cheat or rape the community. Let us teach ourselves and others that politics can be not only the art of the possible, especially if this means the art of speculation, calculation, intrigue, secret deals, and pragmatic manoevering, but that it can even be the art of the impossible, namely, the art of improving ourselves and the world (Havel, 1991: 395).

The theory and philosophy that lay behind and inspired these events is described and analyzed in the next section.

CHAPTER 4

POST-1956 HUNGARY: REPRESSION, REFORM, AND ROUNDTABLE REVOLUTION

The Hungarian Revolution of 1956: Lessons and Legacies

The failure of the Hungarian Revolution of 1956 was mitigated by the many "lessons" it provided, not only for the reconsolidation of reform communism under János Kádár in Hungary, but also for the generation of communist reformers in Poland and in Czechoslovakia who constructed their programs with an eye to avoiding the "errors" of 1956. Whereas Gomułka's accession to power in Warsaw seemed to indicate how far one could go in nationalist deviation from the Soviet model, Imre Nagy's support for and attempted guidance of an essentially armed uprising and popular revolt certainly demonstrated what was completely unacceptable and would not be tolerated by the Soviet Union. Rather than detailing the events leading up to the Hungarian Revolution of 1956 or analyze its promises or shortcomings,[1] I wish to briefly highlight some of the lessons and legacies, especially as they pertain to the later development of a "dissident" community of people and ideas in Hungary. Decades afterward, a number of key features of the revolution stand out.

First, although the uprising was not the first in the Eastern Bloc since the Yalta division of Europe was consolidated,[2] it certainly garnered the most attention both in the Soviet Union and in the West and was certainly the biggest challenge thus far to Soviet hegemony in the region—measured militarily, by numbers involved, or by scope of the revolution's aims and demands.[3]

Second, because of the size and broad-based support of the uprising—it drove a deep ideological wedge into the workers' state. Workers' councils were among "the strongest and most effective centres of resistance" (Litván, 1996: 108). After resistance was effectively suppressed, new communist leader János Kádár still had to come to terms with widespread strikes, the militant demands of workers that dealt with broadly political as well as economic issues, and the fact that worker

self-organization was becoming an increasingly widespread phenomenon in the ensuing chaos.[4] Indeed a nationwide strike was observed
December 11 and 12, over a month after the Soviet Union had brutally
repressed the uprising (and despite the arrest of workers' leaders, most
notably of the *Nagybudapesti Központi Munkástanács* (KMT), or the
Central Workers' Council of Greater Budapest).[5]

Third, the uprising was significantly an internal matter: Péter Kende
called it an "anti-totalitarian revolution" that "challenged the totalitarian system from inside with the aim to recover the elementary rights
and freedoms abrogated by the dictatorship" (in Litván, 1996: 165).
I would add to Kende's remarks that although it might have been anti-
totalitarian generally, it was specifically anti-Soviet and by no means
anti-socialist. Despite Soviet determination to portray 1956 as counter-
revolution and Western (and Hungarian emigré) perceptions that the
uprising more or less consisted of non- and anti-communist average
Hungarian citizens, the fact remains (and Kende later admits) that
former communists, intellectuals, anti-communist socialists, and many
functionaries of the former regime as well as Imre Nagy and his immediate circle were also a prominent part of the events.[6] However, the
hasty coalition propelled forward by the events themselves moved well
beyond earlier demands and expectations, including demands for Hungarian neutrality (and withdrawal from the Warsaw Pact) and a multi-
party system. Because the Hungarian demands could always be justified by Western pro-Soviet intellectuals and by the Soviets themselves
as a bridge too far, Hungary 1956 did not represent the same crisis of
faith as Czechoslovakia 1968.[7]

Finally, Hungary also heralded events to come, in the sense that
Prague paid attention to avoid the mistakes of 1956, and Poland's
worker-intellectual alliance and development of worker self-organization owed much to the previous Hungarian efforts. The lessons of 1956
were critical for the development of dissident thought, especially in
terms of providing a crash course in the geopolitical realities of Central
and Eastern Europe. From the point of view of intellectual history, the
Hungarian "revolt of the mind" was so influential in the region that,
as Tamás Aczél suggested, "... when the Prague Spring arrived in 1968,
the world simply assumed that it was initiated, led, supported, developed, and spurred on by intellectuals, mainly communist ones, whose
disillusionment became the spiritual axis of that event" (1976: 107).
The lack of effective international response and anything other than

moralizing rhetoric offered by the West[8] also set a pattern and fore-shadowed similar reactions after the WTO invasion of Czechoslovakia in 1968 and the imposition of martial law in Poland in 1981. This pattern, initially disappointing but later predictable, influenced subsequent strategies of dissent: if "liberation" from authoritarian communism was ever going to occur, it was not going to happen with overt Western assistance. The violence and death resulting from the Hungarian uprising[9] also influenced later strategizing; non-violence became the hallmark of all subsequent dissent. Finally, the revolution was important for the instauration of democracy in Hungary itself. It became a moral issue for the democratic opposition, a unifying strategy, a project of recovering historical memory, and even a catalyst for political change.

The Hungarian uprising ultimately represented a distinct departure from and rejection of the Soviet model—which had consequences for the immediate communist restoration. János Kádár had been invited to join the reconstituted cabinet organized by Nagy on November 3. Emblematic of his own equivocation—wanting to eliminate Rákosist elements in the party yet still maintain Moscow's favor—Kádár had issued a press release announcing the reorganization of the communist party on November 1, and traveled the next day to Moscow with Ferenc Münnich for a meeting of the CPSU's presidium.[10] He returned to Budapest on November 4, and was quickly installed as the new leader of the party.[11] The Kádár government dealt harshly with the remnants of the "counter-revolutionary" struggle, reorganized police power, and began a process of mass reprisal, arrest, and judicial prosecution that lasted through to a partial amnesty in 1959. At the same time, the government had to be concerned with its perceived illegitimacy, especially in light of massive popular support for the uprising. Attempting to wrap itself in the cloth of Hungarian history, the regime adopted the Kossuth coat of arms of 1848 as the official state emblem and announced a wage increase. Even during his early period of consolidation, Kádár was laying the groundwork for his own anti-Stalinist but pro-Moscow contract, epitomized forever by his oft-quoted slogan "He who is not against us is with us."[12] With these words and with bloodstained hands over the judicial murder of Imre Nagy and his codefendants,[13] he inaugurated a twenty-year period of "consensus-seeking behavior" (Tőkés, 1996: 11).

There is an old saying that Hungary has historically initiated and lost revolutions (1848, 1956) but gained much from the period of defeat, perhaps not immediately but over time.[14] Thus after 1848 and the brutal murder of the revolutionaries on October 6, 1849, the dual monarchy resulted in 1867, ushering in a period of economic development, cultural advancement, urbanization, and political liberalism. After 1956 and following the period of repression, reprisal, and the execution of Nagy came Kádárite "soft" or "goulash" communism.

Kádárite Communism

Kádárite communism remained as quixotic as its leader. Rudolf Tőkés has periodized his long rule and changing public personae as "the reluctant hostage" (1956–1963); the "risk-taking reformer" (1963–1971); the "good king" (1972–1980) and the "enfeebled autarch" (1981–1988). All of these descriptions are true, but are dependent on events external to Kádár's rule as much as they are connected to any shifts in his personality. In the early years after 1956, he had to straddle Soviet control (and the fearful possibility of a Rákosi return) and the urgent requirement to legitimize his rulership and be perceived as his own political master. Obviously, the recognition of the former tended to defeat the latter, underscoring his own dependence on Khrushchev and his embodiment of the spirit of the XXth Congress. At the same time, Kádár had to avoid internally the types of policies that gave rise to the 1956 revolution in the first place. Given the demise of Khrushchev and the persistent memory and resonance of 1956, this could never be a long-term strategy.

Over time less emphasis was placed on overt administrative coercion as a means of obtaining legitimacy (or simply of preventing dissent). More sophisticated and effective methods were employed to generate tacit support: economic incentives, the selective cooptation of writers, journalists, and intellectuals,[15] the routinization of political and economic life according to criteria of technical efficiency rather than ideological correctness, and the institutional separation of party and state. The regime could even afford, in János Kis' words, to "allow people to discover the cracks and side doors in the wall of official regulation, since it did not have to fear that those who circumvented them would attempt to secure their position with demands of rights" (1989: 14). The Hungarian party became a mass catch-all organization not unlike Western parties of the same period save for its operation in a non-competitive arena. Given the adoption of such measures, life in Hungary slowly adapted; society became more liberal and de-politicized. Thus Kádár legitimized his rule not through a new political approach but by the absence of one—by removing politics and the obtrusive nature of the party from people's daily lives, the perception of liberal and open society could be cultivated. The price to be paid, as Hungarian support for the WTO invasion of Czechoslovakia in 1968 attests, was adherence to the Moscow line in foreign affairs.

Kádár was well suited personally and psychologically to this operational strategy of flexible adaptation. Characterized by Tőkés as a "born follower" he was also an astute survivor, able to carve a place for himself in Rákosi's regime (after being persecuted by it), Nagy's short-lived cabinet, and subsequently as the leader of a still-shaky party reeling from the force and impact of the uprising and the violence attendant on its repression. Whether innately ruthless or not, he was inwardly motivated by situational ethics which allowed him to urge Rajk to confess falsely, knowingly send Nagy to his end by handing him over to the Soviets, and later on appear to support Dubček in Czechoslovakia while agreeing to Hungarian participation in the invasion. Unlike many of his generation who had both suffered and been promoted for their beliefs, Kádár was neither an intellectual nor particularly ideological. Pragmatism was the hallmark of his actions, which probably underscored his willingness to consider and then experiment with sweeping economic reforms. These reforms, which came to be known as the "New Economic Mechanism" or NEM, guaranteed his place as a "reformer" in the annals of authoritarian communism, and generated widespread admiration and even tacit support from outside the Bloc.

The Politics of Economic Reform: The NEM

Like other experiments in economic reform in the region, the NEM was motivated by the need to overcome the structural limitations of Soviet-style industrialization. As in Czechoslovakia, internal resources (measured in terms of capital, material, or labor) had been exhausted by the postwar period of extensive industrialization. Declining growth and productivity by the early 1960s were symptomatic of the diminishing returns that could be obtained if the only policy response available was to throw more resources at the problem.[16] As Nuti (1979),

Burawoy (1985), and Kornai (1992) have shown, any attempt to reform a state socialist economy generates many logical inconsistencies, paradoxes, and above all, political risks. In the first place, to modify resource-allocation strategies is to undermine the command nature of the economy. Second, to decentralize and download economic decision making to the firm or enterprise level amounts to drastically increasing local autonomy. Although such a move may result in greater efficiency, rationality, and thus increased productivity, it will also subvert the centralized command structure and introduce a level of chaos into the picture (remembering that such decentralization would occur across entire industries and thus generate contradictory decisions given differing local priorities). Finally, to introduce wage incentives means allowing a level of societal differentiation ideologically incompatible with the system itself. In a sense, the NEM undertook all of these risks and, intentionally or not, "unleashed a wide array of hitherto latent political and social forces, [setting in] motion a process of complex systemic change that the regime could neither foresee nor control" (Tőkés, 1996: 82).

Proposals for Hungarian economic reform began circulating in the early 1960s, but gained momentum after Rezső Nyers was appointed to the Politburo and as Central Committee secretary for economic policy as a result of the 8th party congress in 1962. The first case for comprehensive reform was submitted in 1965, and importantly the emphasis was not only on achieving economic growth but also *the democratization of public life*.[17]

Ironically, the NEM was based on many of the principles of agricultural reform that were at the center of Imre Nagy's New Course. When finally promulgated in 1968, the implementation of the NEM consisted of the following planks: 1) reform in the industrial sector such that enterprises were to become autonomous and profit maximizing; 2) devolution of planning to the local level; and 3) wage and price reform. The NEM was a bold and far-reaching effort to systematically reform the economy, but from the start it contained a number of contradictions, subject to much debate.[18]

The contradictory nature of the program is evident in Kádár's speech to the 9th Congress of the *Magyar Szocialista Munkáspárt* (MSZMP, or Hungarian Socialist Workers' Party) in 1966 outlining the proposed program. Just a few paragraphs apart, he speaks of how "central planning will continue to have a first class role," however,

"... the state will not generally prescribe compulsory plan indexes for the enterprises." Although he warned that "changes in consumer prices must not entail a lowering of the population's living standard," it was recognized that prices would have to change (that is, rise). Furthermore, Kádár stated "wages should reflect the workers' actual performance more exactly" but then immediately explained this as "... a more direct application of the socialist principle of distribution according to work," all in the context of a discussion to raise wages overall (Kádár, quoted in Daniels, ed., 1994: 228–230).

Price reform was supposed to result in better use of assets and resources, forcing managers to bring prices closer to market levels. However, because of state control over most prices (70% of goods and services were directly regulated) and the general absence of hard budget constraints, enterprise effectiveness (or "profitability") was a chimera, given the opportunities to use the complexity of auditing and accounting procedures to the firm's advantage. Smarter production and better marketing did not result. The illogical relationship between the cost and the price of goods was heightened by the continual state privileging of heavy industry and defense (especially given these could be translated into favorable dollar and rouble exports). Allowing for greater differentiation in wages proved problematic in implementation. Unfortunately, differentiated compensation occurred most effectively in middle and higher management levels, which were largely unproductive and perhaps less deserving of such differentiation. On the shop floor level such policies were often translated into rudimentary and exploitative incentive systems above artificially low base rates. The system of using "piece rates" on the shop floor was effectively analyzed and criticized by Miklós Haraszti (1979) in *A Worker in a Workers' State*. Translated into reality, Kádárist income policies provided for the worst in capitalist-type wage differentiation, with none of the intended benefits.

There were considerable difficulties in implementing the NEM. The party "reds" —largely uneducated working class cadres who owed their upward mobility to their ideological commitment—resented the emphasis on education and technical expertise with good reason given increased job insecurity.[19] The cumbersome and rigidly hierarchical nature of decision-making endemic to all forms of authoritarian communism (not to mention heavily entrenched institutional interests) contributed to the delay between promulgation and implementation, generating a fair amount of policy drift. From 1968 through to 1972 Moscow and other Eastern Bloc countries (most notably normalized Czechoslovakia, the GDR, and Bulgaria; Poland had its own problems in 1968 and attempted new solutions under Gierek in the 1970s) put varying degrees of pressure on Hungary to alter or halt the process. Half-hearted counter-reforms and recentralization were implemented from 1972 onward, with a general lack of success one might have predicted with such a policy turnaround. In the end, the "escape hatch" strategy of Kádár in the 1980s was almost exactly the same as that utilized by Gierek in the 1970s: finance increased expectations and overlook deepening structural constraints by borrowing from abroad.[20] In the West, Hungary found a more than willing partner economically; moreover financial credit was politically supported by governments wanting to "reward" Hungary for its bold experimentation through generous trade conditions (Johnson, 1996: 256).

Regardless of the contradictions inherent in the NEM, it remained the most comprehensive and sustained effort to reform a state socialist economy, only to be surpassed by the grand vision (and failure) of Gorbachev's *perestroika* in the late 1980s. The role of the plan diminished and that of the "market" (such as it was) increased, especially in allocating resources for production. The relationship between plan and market, although not necessarily complementary, meant that a hybrid system was allowed to develop, with features of plan and price bargaining within the context of competing institutional interests (Battaile Hall, 1986). On a bureaucratic level, reform measures were accompanied by gradual emancipation of public administration from direct party control. The rule of experts and debate among them were evidence of what Tőkés calls "institutional proto-pluralism" (1996: 115). The successes and shortcomings of the NEM also generated a regime-sanctioned, serious debate on where it might lead in the future, including proposals for a mixed economy (*gemischte Wirtschaft*), "managerial" or "entrepreneurial" socialism," or some form of syndicalist or worker self-managed economy (Battaile Hall, 1986).

Socialist Redistribution and the Second Economy

An important outgrowth of the NEM was the permitted existence of the "second economy," which consisted of everything from private agricultural plots to small family-run businesses and joint ventures with foreign companies. Elemér Hankiss described the second economy as "the sum total of economic activities outside the state sector," a definition with enough elasticity to include both illegal, semi-legal, and legal transactions (quoted in Skilling, 1989: 165).[21] Moreover, the second economy overall was an integral component of the national economy, contributing up to one third of NMP.[22]

In 1979 the Politburo passed a resolution fully legalizing the second economy, which initiated a renewal of the economic reform process and also served to give a green light for grass-roots privatization (Berend, 1996: 268). In 1981 the private leasing of state-owned shops and restaurants began, and "civil-law companies" and small cooperatives were allowed. During the first half of the decade, the number of private crafts people and shopkeepers increased by up to 40%.

By the late 1980s the second economy was so extensive in Hungary that virtually the entire citizenry engaged with it in the routines of daily life. Many people had at least one job in the second economy, paralleling similar work in the official economy or in a completely separate arena but conducted after "official" working hours. Small independent entrepreneurs played an increasingly important role, but to some degree their influence has been exaggerated by Western economists looking hopefully to Hungary for economic convergence that then might spawn political change.

Ideologically, the second economy encouraged independence, private initiative, personal liberty, existential freedom, and entrepreneurial risk-taking—all this on top of the usual motive of economic gain. From the regime's perspective, this latter function was probably most important, for when it had to face up to the structural nature of its economic crises in the late 1980s, only the second economy was able to smooth the edges by providing consistently high-quality and plentiful consumer goods and foodstuffs.[23] As a socially integrating and legitimizing function for the state, the second economy tolerated and encouraged private initiative and paradoxically the resulting social differentiation increased the public perceptions of *getting ahead* (at least for some).

In the long term, the second economy had considerable corrosive effects. To the extent that participation in the second economy was more profitable, workers engaged in both the official and second economies began to switch their allegiances in terms of a personal investment of time, commitment, and creative energy. The growth of the second economy and its attendant benefits was clearly being undermined by the limits of self-exploitation (Kis, 1989: 17). Structural deficiencies were simultaneously highlighted and camouflaged. The second economy also increased individual autonomy at a time when the post-1956 generation had come of age, a generation for which consolidation, concession, and consumerism were not considered "an unexpected gift, but a natural point of departure" (1989: 17). Kis logically argued that it was from these ranks that the embryonic opposition emerged, not content with grumbling about the shortcomings of economic policies, but demanding a "new start in politics" as well (1989: 17).

Not unlike neo-liberal critics of the Western welfare state, preeminent Hungarian economist János Kornai has subsequently criticized Kádárist economics for creating a welfarist ethos on the part of unmotivated workers, unproductive bureaucrats and parasitic intellectuals. None of these groups would pay for the ultimate costs of *gulyás* communism. However, Kádár was pragmatic enough either to leave alone or encourage the farmers and workers in the second economy; their progress and economic betterment was key to the success of the regime. However, the increase in societal inequality was matched by the inability of the party-state to deal with the implications of success in the second economy by implementing the major structural changes necessary to reform the official economy. Taken together, these factors were in large part responsible for the unraveling of the Kádárite compromise.

Intellectuals: On the Road to Class Power?

If in Czechoslovakia the particular strength of the intellectual opposition lay in its writers and philosophers, if in Poland many of the leading intellectual activists were historians, then in Hungary the strong suit of the democratic opposition could be found in the trenchant analyses of economists and sociologists. A stellar example is György Konrád and Iván Szelényi's *The Intellectuals on the Road to Class Power*: an illuminating account of society in Hungary under authoritarian communism.

Konrád and Szelényi wrote the book as a samizdat essay in 1973–1974, "as an attempt to sum up the results of the studies we had carried on in Hungary since 1965" (1979: xiii). Together they developed the dual thesis that first, under state socialist Soviet-style systems, the workers are in fact the most underprivileged class and second, that the new ruling class is a consolidated class of intellectuals who rule in their own interests but under the banner of "the dictatorship of the proletariat." Moreover, this consolidated class resulted from a class alliance between "free intellectuals" (scholars, artists, teachers) and the technical intelligentsia (engineers, physicians) in combination with the party bureaucracy.

Konrád and Szelényi ground their analysis in the historical experience and development of the intelligentsia in Central and Eastern Europe, where the bourgeoisie was numerically small in comparison with the gentry or nobility. Furthermore, traders and merchants were often of German or Jewish extraction (or both), and thus their "otherness" compounded other difficulties, ensuring that they did not generally "acquire the power and privileges that accompanied the rise of that class in the West" (Rupnik, 1989: 11). Intellectuals and the intelligentsia, replaced the entrepreneur in Central Europe as the engine and spokesperson of dynamic change and development. The authors state: "... the intelligentsia, organized into a government-bureaucratic ruling class, has taken the lead in modernization, replacing a weak bourgeoisie incapable of breaking with feudalism" (1979: 10). The rise of Bolshevism provided the power and even the ideological orientation to defeat local and landed aristocracies once and for all:

> Bolshevism, then, offered the intellectuals a program for freeing themselves of the duty of representing particular interests once power had been secured, and it used particular interests simply as a means of acquiring power. With the expropriation of the expropriators—that is, with the transfer of the right to dispose over the surplus product from landlords and capitalists to intellectuals in power, or to worker cadres whose political positions and functions made intellectuals of them—and with the destruction of the immediate producers' organs of management and control, the Bolsheviks traced the outlines of a new rational-redistributive system and, within it, indicated the position of the teleological redistributors, called to represent the interests of all society expertly and professionally (1979: 142).

The Central European intellectual faced a historical dilemma: either become an agent of the state or become completely independent and critical of its authoritarianism and the prevailing *étatiste* form of development—in other words, be a bureaucrat or a revolutionary (1979: 85–86). The danger inherent in the rule by intellectuals is their claim to possess "transcendent" or "teleological" forms of knowledge. Thus their epistemology coheres easily with economic structures remodeled as "a system of rational redistribution" and political structures that are totalistic and ideological in nature. Such masters of the universe believed not only that politics could be refashioned to achieve desirable social goals, but that this required not simply ownership but *control* over the economic forces of production.

Konrád and Szelényi were able to clarify for themselves the opacity of Hungarian society in terms of latent class conflict, and also account for their own positions within it. More so than any other authoritarian communist regime, Kádár's government was extremely successful in coopting intellectuals *after* a critical episode of dissent (not so in Gomułka's Poland where the intellectuals were disenchanted early on, nor in Husák's Czechoslovakia). By providing for their "class interest" in the bureaucratic hierarchy, intellectuals were effectively demobilized as a force for social change. Miklós Haraszti echoed Konrád and Szelényi when describing the process as follows:

> In Budapest they have come to understand that neither the technocrats, nor the scholars, nor even the artists are necessarily the vanguards of the struggle for liberty. They may become such vanguards but only if their aspiration remains unfulfilled. In general, the regime came to realize that these functionally leading social strata, which in a nationalized industrial society have occupied the place of the bourgeoisie, also have real interests. Moreover, it has remained unperturbed by the recognition that these interests can in fact be satisfied in a monolithic state.
>
> This is how the "Hungarian miracle" came into being. Hungarian society is in the process of demonstrating that it can be transformed from a post-Stalinist crisis-society into a lasting civilization; and with careful concessions, the planning, organizing, directing, and cultural intelligentsia can become supporters of the monolithic state. It is not enough for these strata to serve the state. Security demands that they should also constitute the state. Without relinquishing its monolithic identity, the Hungarian state has reoriented itself to become the real protection of the interests of these new strata that are the products of the process of total nationalization.[24]

Most of the best representatives of Hungarian culture, for example, worked within the system rather than outside it. Kádár's cultural czar György Aczél ruled over a vast *apparat* for over twenty-five years and literally "orchestrated, quite brilliantly, the score, the players, and the instruments of the cultural scene" (Tőkés, 1996: 16). After 1956, when extreme opponents to the regime had either been liquidated, silenced, or emigrated, Aczél oversaw the cultural establishment, encouraging and tolerating an elite of writers, playwrights, poets, and filmmakers. In exchange for being well housed and well fed, the cultural elite propagated the official line but at the same time were given considerable artistic space and license to criticize—within vaguely determinable boundaries, of course. Thus the famed "liberalism" of Kádárite communism had a cultural and intellectual dimension as well.

Even in the late 1980s, when dissident voices were gathering sound, fury, and cohesion, the line between the within-system intellectual and the dissident remained indistinct. There was no Polish division between "us" and "them"; no persecuted community of worthy and recognized writers and activists as in Czechoslovakia. Given the modest improvements (or even the openness of debate) generated by the NEM, the smooth functioning of the cultural aristocracy, and the relative freedom of intellectual debate in the academic sphere, one could well believe that the intellectuals had assumed class power.

The few Hungarians who could later lay claim to the clear-cut label "dissident" had both a subtle appreciation of Hungarian "liberalism" and at the same time were extremely critical of it. In fact, they preferred to speak not of Hungarian "liberalism" but of the chaos or anarchy pervading the system. At issue was not only the fact that strategically it was more difficult to get effectively coopted intellectuals "on side," but that given the fuzziness and mutability of the boundaries, it was never easy to get a clear-cut picture of who stood where. Former opposition activist Miklós Haraszti drew a telling distinction between what he called "the outcast opposition" (of which he considered himself a member) and the so-called "loyal opposition," those who were ensconced in the "velvet prison" of state patronage.[25] Another indication of the Hungarian situation is a cynical joke common at the time: "If Solzhenitsyn had lived in Hungary, he would have been appointed president of the Writers' Union, and *The Gulag Archipelago* would never have been written."

The Budapest School

György Lukács is almost a mythical figure with respect to both the history of twentieth-century Hungary and modern Marxist philosophy.[26] In his long and active life as a philosopher, literary critic, and politician, Lukács managed to play key roles in all three "moments" of Hungarian communism. First, after becoming a committed communist in 1918 he was appointed to the short-lived Béla Kun government of 1919 as "People's Commissar" for Education and Culture. Second, as a leader and theoretician of the Hungarian Communist Party in the interwar period and again after the war, his independent stance, popular-front political strategies, and his compellingly humanistic Marxist philosophy earned him international intellectual influence as well as disdain and official harassment from the Comintern and the gatekeepers of Soviet Marxism. Third, he was appointed Minister of Culture in Imre Nagy's government in 1956, and was deported with Nagy to Romania, lucky to be able to return later to a more "quiet" life in Budapest. In the final decades of his life he returned to earlier themes, specifically aesthetic theory and social ontology. At the same time he nurtured and supported a group of dedicated and highly skilled students of philosophy, and in this role became the unofficial founder and leader of the so-called "Budapest School."

Shortly before he died, in a letter to the *Times Literary Supplement* in 1971, Lukács himself drew the attention of the wider intellectual community to the "accomplishments of a small group of Hungarian marxist philosophers, his own disciples which he called the 'Budapest School'" (Szelényi, 1977: 61). In the early 1960s with the relaxation of the repressive measures necessitated by the uprising, these disciples of Lukács were not only able to develop their ideas with limited political interference,[27] but in fact became full members of the academic community, were published, and acquired a following among younger students. Founded by former prime minister András Hegedüs with the goal of reinvigorating socialism, the Budapest School included a number of prominent philosophers and sociologists, such as Ágnes Heller, Ferenc Fehér, György Márkus, Maria Márkus, and Mihály Vajda.[28]

Lukács was both a problematic and fitting mentor for a generation raised on the philosophical tenets of Marxism as well as having lived through its real-life crises. Lukács always considered himself a party member, funneled his criticism through party channels, took the Stalinist dictates of self-criticism and self-repudiation seriously, and never (unlike Kołakowski) wavered in his belief that Marxism was not irrevocably damaged by Leninist practice. Throughout his life in the various roles he played, Lukács continued his search for a viable and radical *socialist* alternative within the Soviet Bloc.[29] Nonetheless, he continued to be a philosophical iconoclast within the boundaries of Marxist philosophy. One of his major achievements was to root Marxist historiography in its Hegelian origins, and in many respects he remained a philosophical idealist. His treatment of class-consciousness and aesthetics demonstrate his determination that Marxist theory be considered in its subjective and cultural dimensions, and with this approach he strongly influenced the Frankfurt School and the development of a "sociology of knowledge."

As students, and then later as close associates and friends, Ágnes Heller and Ferenc Fehér were among the most faithful Lukács disciples. In the same way that Lukács pushed the envelope of orthodox Marxism, Heller and Fehér moved from Lukácsian Marxist humanism to more broadly philosophical approaches to the problems of alienation and human essence.[30] They were not content to merely comment on the obvious discrepancies between really-existing socialism and the socialist idea, but to move beyond this confrontation to a new critical theory. György Márkus was particularly influential to the younger 1960s generation as a teacher and mentor, fulfilling the same role as Lukács did for his own generation. Much of this intellectual endeavor took place under Lukács' protective umbrella given his personal preeminence in the international community of intellectual Marxists.[31] All those involved in the School sought to utilize Marxism as a methodology to critically analyze the antinomies of the system, from the perspectives of political economy, sociology, and philosophy. In so doing they consciously began to reassess many of the classical tenets of Marxism, a process that led Márkus, Bence, and Kis to write *Is a Critical Political Economy Really Possible at all?* Thus Lukács' disciples moved from a renewal of Marxism by using Marxist methodology to advance a Marxist explanation of state socialist phenomena, to what Szelényi (borrowing from Adorno) called "a negation of the negation."

Originally, as Szelényi points out, the Budapest School functioned like "His Majesty's Opposition": "the humanist critique they presented did not frighten the political establishment" (Szelényi, 1977: 63). It could be tolerated because at this early stage (mid to late 1960s) "it did not offer a structural critique of State socialism" (1977:63).[32] They first began to cross the line with their attacks on the economic reforms envisioned by the NEM, especially with their concerns about widening social inequalities and their fears about the prospect of a technocratic takeover (a dress rehearsal for the thesis more fully developed later by Szelényi and Konrád). Presciently, they emphasized that economic reform without accompanying political reform was an exercise in half-measures that was inevitably doomed to failure. However, when Lukács along with his students openly and publicly protested against Hungary's participation in the WTO invasion of Czechoslovakia, a more obvious and less forgiving barrier had been crossed.[33] Regime retaliation followed and five years later, with Kádár's blessing, they were dismissed from their academic positions as well (Tőkés, 1996: 181). Their ideological transgressions had accumulated to a point where they could no longer be even repressively tolerated, and had indeed become the "problem children" of the regime. In January, 1977, prominent members of the School were among the thirty-four intellectuals who made a public expression of solidarity with the signatories of Charter 77.

By the late 1970s, the *Berufsverbot* had begun to take its toll both individually and collectively on the members of the School. After five years of near-constant police harassment combined with the regime-sanctioned prohibition against academic teaching and publishing, the most prominent members of the Budapest School emigrated.[34] György and Maria Márkus relocated to West Berlin; Ágnes Heller and Ferenc Fehér left for Melbourne, Australia.[35] With considerable Hungarian irony, Minister of Culture Imre Pozsgay paid an eloquent tribute to the foursome, stating that the departure of such highly respected intellectuals was an undisputed cultural loss for the country, but also admitted that the prohibition of their work was necessary given its opposition to the political and economic foundations of socialism.[36] By letting them leave legally and without recrimination, the regime could be seen to be living within the spirit of Helsinki and at the same time ridding themselves of dissenting scholars who had long been a thorn in their side. However, the Budapest School members living abroad formed a small but intellectually influential emigré community of support and external opposition. They continued to focus scholarly attention in the West on the underside of Kádárite communism and the specificities of the Hungarian political situation,[37] which required a more subtle appreciation than the obvious persecution of Czechoslovakia and the periodic popular mobilization of Poland.

"Populist" vs. "Democratic" Dissent

To complicate matters in any discussion of opposition in Hungary prior to 1989, there are a number of cross-cutting cleavages permeating Hungarian intellectual history that are unrelated to the divide between those opposing authoritarian communism and those who worked within the system and to varying degrees may have undermined or supported it (or both). The classic and most important example is the division between the "populist" (*népi*) and the "urbanist" or cosmopolitan writers and intellectuals.

The populists saw themselves as the representatives of *völkisch* Hungarian traditions, epitomized by their valorization of rural and village life.[38] The urbanists, on the other hand, positioned their axis on life in Budapest, were disproportionately Jewish and politically more leftist than nationalist.[39] There are many ways to heighten the differences between the populists and the urbanists: the former were more concerned with the fate of Hungarian *Kultur* and in particular the persecution of Hungarian minorities outside its borders, whereas the latter looked to the West and European civilization, with Budapest representing an island and refuge.[40] Populists tended to be more easily coopted (or more easy for the regime to tolerate), given that their selective use of nationalism was highly functional for the regime. The self-styled "democratic opposition" (*demokratikus ellenzék*) were drawn largely from the urbanists and given their vigorous sociological and economic critiques of the system (such as that of Konrád and Szelényi) as well as their emphasis on human rights and opposition to censorship, they were far more likely to be out of favor with the regime, which even in Hungary had serious and negative consequences.

Following the 1956 uprising, the populist writers "made their peace with the regime" (Tőkés, 1996: 176). Many of the prominent writers sympathetic to the events of 1956 (László Németh, Gyula Illyés and others) were effectively silenced into submission. However, they were not clear-cut victims. Indeed they saw the protectionist and nationalist elements of Kádárite communism as immeasurably preferable to a total loss of cultural statehood, which was represented by *both* Western consumerist capitalism and the Soviet Stalinism already endured under Rákosi. The "modus vivendi" of the relationship between the populists and the party can be found in László Németh's 1962 "Letter to a Cultural Politician" (aimed at György Aczél), wherein he outlined his vision of the future—a society made up of socialist intellectuals, to be sure, but from peasant, worker, and lower-middle-class backgrounds with greater access to education, social mobility and whose voice would be found in patriotism as well as ideology (Tőkés, 1996: 178–179). Needless to say, this unwritten agreement was reinforced by many sweeteners flowing from the regime to the writers: literary prizes, generous financial support, freedom to travel abroad. The regime approach was successful—not only did the populist writers *not* support Charter 77 (as many of the members of the fledgling democratic opposition did), many openly condemned the Czechoslovak signatories (Haraszti, 1979). This stance remained more or less unchallenged until the "leadership" of the populist intellectuals passed from Gyula Illyés' death in 1983 to the next generation, unofficially led by poet Sándor Csoóri.[41] Still, the *népi* writers were collectively not part of the broader East-Central European community of dissent, and did not self-reflexively theorize about the actions or ideas in the same manner as János Kis, Miklós Haraszti, or György Konrád.

The largely urbanist democratic opposition began to take shape in the 1970s, and really crystallized in the 1980s. In many respects, the story of the opposition is the story of two friends and former students of Márkus: János Kis and György Bence. Tőkés accurately claims that both these individuals were more responsible than anyone else "for the transformation of the Budapest School from an esoteric philosophical debating society to what became by far the most influential political opposition movement of the late Kádár era" (1996: 181). In particular, Kis' strategic mind and attitude of philosophical compromise was evident early on in his career, with his suggestion that one must go beyond Marx to a regulated market economy if the freedom of both consumers and producers (as in Marx's original vision) was to be truly achieved. Both Kis and Bence were victims of the 1973 academic purge of the Budapest School. Between 1973 and 1977 they wrote a series of critical essays together under the pseudonym Marc Rakovski, which were later published in Hungarian samizdat and in English as a book under the title *Towards an East European Marxism*. Unfortunately, their intellectual collaboration ended with the acrimonious collapse of their friendship, and in most accounts Kis remained the intellectual leader and strategist of the opposition.

Another key figure in the Hungarian democratic opposition whose roots were *not* with the Budapest School is poet and activist Miklós Haraszti. Haraszti began his "career" as a dissident early, and was on a more obvious collision course with the regime than his counterparts. An avowed and self-described Maoist or "ultra-leftist" and sympathizer with spontaneous and popular democratic struggle, Haraszti came into the spotlight as a student when he published a poem defending Cuban revolutionary Che Guevara.[42] Expelled from university, he went to work for a year in the Red Star Tractor Factory, writing a book about the experience. When he published *A Worker in a Workers' State* it caused a national scandal, as Haraszti had the audacity to claim that Hungarian workers were exploited under state socialism, in the same degree and by the same methods as primitive Taylorite capitalism. His work was declared "subversive agitation against the state" and he was arrested in 1973. A farcical trial ensued, with the widows of Count Michael Károlyi and László Rajk[43] taking part as character witnesses for the defendant. Heller, Fehér, Vajda, and Hegedüs were also in the courtroom. The case captured international attention, and as a result, Haraszti remained an oft-quoted figure in the Hungarian opposition and one of the most well-recognized in the West.

Writer György Konrád straddled many demographic and occupational categories and his novels gave a literary voice to the empirical sociology initiated by Hegedüs and the Sociological Research Group. The personal intensity and confessional quality of *The Case Worker* and *The City Builder* provided fictional yet realistic testimony to the Sisyphean struggles of functionaries employed by the party-state. Konrád was young enough to have remembered and been involved in the 1956 revolution, but played such a minor role that he was neither tried nor imprisoned. After a period of forced unemployment in the early 1960s he found work first as a public guardianship officer and later as an urban sociologist. What Hegedüs studied from the top down, Konrád experienced from the bottom up, an experience which provided fodder for both his writing and his politics. As a writer, Konrád was neither an older nor younger generation populist; his literary style was not local or national but cosmopolitan and modern: ironically, it can be described as realistic socialist realism.[44] Through his friendship and collaboration with Szelényi he became connected with the ideas of the Budapest School. He raised his voice in support of Miklós Haraszti during his 1974 trial, initiating a close friendship between the two men.

As in Czechoslovakia, a catalyst for *organized* dissent was Hungary's participation in the Helsinki process. However, Hungarians did not respond to Helsinki by creating a human rights group; rather, they responded to the Czechoslovak crackdown on the Chartists. On January 9, 1977 thirty-four intellectuals sent the following message to Pavel Kohout in Prague:

> We declare our solidarity with the signers of Charter 77 and we condemn the repressive measures used against them. We are convinced that the defence of human and civil rights is a common concern of all Eastern Europe.[45]

Among those who signed were philosophers, writers, literary critics, and economists and many were of the younger generation, those reared under the promises of communism.[46] The variety of signatories indicated the possibility of an oppositional alliance that went beyond leftist intellectuals. Again, in 1979, Hungarian intellectuals signed a protest supporting their Czechoslovak counterparts, however, this time 184 individuals signed a petition stating, "We protest the trial and sentences of the members of the Charter 77 movement and demand release of the prisoners."[47] The occasion was the trial and sentencing of the six Chartists arrested for the activities in VONS, including Havel, Dienstbier, and Benda.

Similarly, Polish social mobilization—represented at first by KOR and then the spectacular success of the formation of the independent trade union Solidarity—was a powerful incentive for the Hungarians. The regime also took notice and was obviously concerned about a possible demonstration effect: when György Bence and four others attempted to catch a flight to Warsaw on August 27, 1980, they had their passports confiscated at the Budapest-Ferihegy airport. In contravention of the "normal" rules of permissible travel between friendly socialist states, Bence and friends were informed their trip was contrary to the interests of both the Hungarian and Polish governments. The Poles also reciprocated with advice, assistance, and solidarity, especially after the relegalization of Polish Solidarity in 1988 and the increased pace of events in both countries in 1988–1989.[48]

In Budapest as in Poland and Czechoslovakia, a small yet not insignificant underground university was set up in 1978.[49] The so-called "Free University" met on Monday evenings, and lecture courses were held on such subjects as the history of the CPSU, on Hungarian literary policy since 1945, Hungarian social history from 1848 to 1945, the revolutions of 1918–1919, the situation of the Hungarian minority in Romania, and on economic crises both East and West. Typical of Hungarian self-deprecating sarcasm, the oppositionists dubbed their version of the Polish/Czech flying university as the "flying kindergarten" (Lomax, 1982: 3).

A social self-help organization modeled on KOR and entitled *Szegényeket Támogató Alap* (SZETA or Foundation for Supporting the Poor), was set up in 1979. By 1981 they were sufficiently well organized and successful in their fundraising efforts to sponsor a summer holiday in the Lake Balaton area for children from poor Polish families. Strategically, it was a brilliant maneuver, as this charitable act of assistance to a fraternal Bloc member was at the same time an action in support of Solidarity, and was carried out in collaboration with the Mazowsze regional organization.

As in Czechoslovakia, but unlike in Poland, the evolution of the largely intellectual and cultural opposition into a movement of political dissidence did *not* attract widespread popular support. There were no systematic efforts on the part of Hungarian intellectuals to "reach out" to independent worker organizations, as no such organizations existed. Hungarian apathy is harder to explain in retrospect than the attitude of the Czechs given the relative "liberalism" of Hungarian society. However, two important points are in order. First, most Hungarian intellectuals and average citizens knew instinctively that any attempt to resuscitate the worker–intelligentsia alliance of 1956 would be met with harsh reprisals.[50] Second, there was the widely held cynical view that whatever Polish compromise might result from the strikes, it was unlikely to be any better than what had already been achieved in Hungary. Moving beyond the narrow base of intellectuals—even if well represented demographically, regionally, and by profession—would be required if the democratic opposition were to have a meaningful impact. New strategies and ideas were also needed. The best method for allowing for the generation and discussion of new ideas as well as their increased circulation had already been attempted in both Poland and Czechoslovakia: samizdat publishing.

Beszélő and Hungarian Samizdat

Samizdat literature had existed in the 1970s in Hungary, but along the lines of the model of the Soviet dissidents. Typewritten texts circulated within narrow and overlapping circles of friends and acquaintances. Two important samizdat volumes were published in 1977–1978: *Marx in the Fourth Decade* and *Profile*. The first volume was a collection of twenty-one responses to a questionnaire sent out by philosopher András Kovács about the relevance of Marx and Marxism to Hungary in the "fourth decade" of communism in the country. Most expressed their growing disillusionment with the utility of Marxism both in terms of philosophy and political practice.[51] The second consisted of 34 essays which had been previously rejected by official journals because, according to the euphemistic language of Hungarian self-censors, they "did not fit our profile" (Skilling, 1989: 32). This volume was fittingly edited by János Kenedi, a writer who had himself been fired from his position as an editor and prohibited from future intellectual employment.[52]

The turning point in samizdat publishing came in 1980 when Gábor Demszky and László Rajk went to Poland on a course of self-instruction to learn about Polish methods of "mass-market" independent publishing (Short, 1985: 31). Aside from the technical innovation (including the introduction of *ramka*, a Polish screen-printing technique), Demszky and Rajk were equally ingenious in creating new methods of distribution. Their crowning achievement was the establishment of a samizdat "boutique" set up at Rajk's apartment every Tuesday evening where oppositional shoppers could come and peruse the latest offerings.

Operating so openly and brazenly under the watchful eye of the Hungarian authorities was a risky undertaking. However, it was easier for Rajk than others because as the son of the executed yet rehabilitated former Interior minister, he had quasi-political immunity. This was not enough to protect either Rajk or Demszky from police harassment; the first crackdown occurred when the police attempted to evict Rajk from his apartment in central Budapest in 1981. In 1983 both were stopped by a supposedly routine traffic check and when Demszky attempted to recover a personal letter from Konrád he was badly beaten.[53] Prior to the 1848 anniversary on March 15, 1988, Demszky and twenty others were detained by police and the inventory of the boutique was confiscated.

János Kis and Miklós Haraszti were chief co-editors of the most influential Hungarian samizdat periodical, entitled *Beszélő* (*The Speaker*).[54] All articles in *Beszélő* and other samizdat periodicals were published "without official authorization," meaning that the legal process of institutional affiliation, content review, and approval/censorship by officials had been completely avoided. Published from 1981 onward, it had a quarterly circulation of about 2,000 copies. However, the readership of *Beszélő* has been estimated anywhere between three to five times that number (*Uncaptive Minds*, May 1988: 2). Its purpose was to address social, political, and economic issues and provide uncensored news coverage. Its articles were also translated and appeared in Western journals, such as *Uncaptive Minds, East European Reporter, Labour Focus on Eastern Europe, Profil, Gegenstimmen, L'Alternative,* and *Diagonale* (Short: 1985: 31). As in Poland and Czechoslovakia, openness was key to their critical stance: the editors' names, addresses, and telephone numbers were displayed in the journal (Tőkés, 1996: 187).

In the opening editorial of the first issue of *Beszélő*, editors Miklós Haraszti, János Kis, Ferenc Kőszeg, Bálint Nagy, and György Petri announced that their task was to combat the myth that "nothing of note ever happens in Hungary." Naturally, they planned to report on the activities of the opposition and to provide their reading public with a more accurate depiction of events. However, they also wanted to report on the more mundane aspects of resistance:

> *Beszélő* will speak about events that are outside the ordinary run of things: when people, either on their own or together with others, step out beyond the accepted rules of intercourse between the authorities and the subjects, when they refuse to obey humiliating commands, insist on their rights, and exercise pressure on those above them ... We would like to get more information on the motives that inspire people to abandon routine ways of behavior. We would like to know what measures the authorities take to force people back into the machine-like order of daily routines. How is the conflict between the two sides resolved? How do the bystanders react to the out of the ordinary course of events? We would like to see that these experiences don't get lost, and that the people who have been, or could be, the protagonists of such events should come to know more about each other.[55]

What made *Beszélő* the most important organ of the democratic opposition was not its independent news coverage nor even its intended effect in providing a mass audience a communication and connection point to the activists. Rather, its critical role lay in the fact that it sought to mobilize both intellectuals and the wider public around a particular program of radical reform. János Kis reasoned that Hungarians would not be converted to the cause through philosophic posturing, but through an elaboration of basic values illustrated by positions taken on the news events of the day and on the possibilities for future reform.[56] This process reached a pinnacle with the 1987 special issue of *Beszélő* outlining a new program, or "Social Contract."[57] The authors document the breakdown in Hungary's historic golden middle road between Rákosist Stalinism and 1956—as personified in the rule of János Kádár. Going one step beyond "grumbling about the consequences of a bad policy," they formulate a coherent alternative, best summarized as radical and systematic economic change coupled with political reforms consonant with marketization and liberal democracy. On the economic side, proposals included:

- Equal rights for various forms of ownership in the economy. Legal assurances for establishing private businesses and for private investment. Uniform tax rules, credit conditions, business and foreign trade opportunities for every type of business organization and every enterprise.
- Restriction of demand through monetary control, rather than through the arbitrary, administrative withdrawal of income.
- Curtailment of official tinkering with wage and profit mechanisms.
- Development of a capital market, and a substantial reduction in the proportion of centrally controlled investments.
- Dismantling of the proliferating monopolies, the breaking up of other enterprises too large to be economically justified and the establishment of many small and medium-sized enterprises.
- A flexible price policy in the interest of balance-of-trade equilibrium instead of policies to increase particular exports and restrict imports.
- Abandoning of the COMECON program of self-sufficiency, and opening up to the world economy. Within COMECON, the expansion of business relations between enterprises, and turning away from the economically disadvantageous cooperation brought about through political agreements.

On the political side, the *Beszélő* authors noted that the last time Hungary had a comprehensive political program was in 1956. Consonant with those demands, they proposed:

• Political pluralism and representative democracy in government.
• Self-management in the workplace and localities.
• National self-determination and neutrality in foreign policy.

Recognizing that especially the first and third points were unlikely, given Hungary's geopolitical. position, a "compromise solution" was proposed, one that would "fall short of what people aspire to" but at the same time "would produce appreciable changes in the relationship between the power structure and society." Thus the following program was suggested:

• Constitutional checks on party rule, a sovereign National Assembly, and an accountable government.
• Freedom of the press guaranteed by law.
• Legal protection for employees, representation of interests, and freedom of association.
• Social security and an equitable social welfare policy.
• Civil rights.

The Social Contract had both supporters and detractors. As a means of uniting the opposition under a particular (and perhaps feasible) program, it was laudable, and certainly consistent with the editorial perspective of the journal. It was criticized for being too compromising in its recognition of the continuing leading role of the MSZMP for not laying out a path whereby such a compromise might be achieved. Furthermore, the populists (as represented by the Democratic Forum) characterized the program as a Leninist effort to foreclose debate on future opportunities and as a means whereby the intellectual opposition would be able to map its particular agenda onto the rest of Hungarian society.

The most important independent samizdat-publishing house was AB, headed by Gábor Demszky. It was modeled on the independent Polish publishing house NOW-a. Polish texts were very influential, and the works of Adam Michnik, Jacek Kuroń, Karol Modzelewski and others were translated into Hungarian and distributed. By 1988, over sixty books were also in print, each with a circulation of between 2,000 and 3,000. Titles included László Németh's *Hungarians in Romania*, István Bibó's *The Jewish Question in Hungary*, Teresa Toranska's *Them*, György Faludy's *Happy Days in Hell*, George Orwell's *1984*, Arthur Koestler's *Darkness at Noon*, and Milan Kundera's *The Unbearable Lightness of Being*. East-Central European authors, such as Gombrowicz, Miłosz, and Hrabal, were translated and published, as well as the unpublished writings of Hungarian populists. Other publishing houses included Katalizator, which focused on reviving the collective memory and experiences of 1956. Aside from *Beszélő*, other important journals included *Hírmondó* (edited by Demszky) and *Demokrata*. *Demokrata* was more militant than *Beszélő* in its demands vis-à-vis the regime, and generally opposed the idea that the internal system reform. In keeping with this line, *Demokrata* called for a free market economy, popular representative democracy and Soviet troop withdrawal from Hungarian soil.

At times journals would initially attempt official publication, but the insidious processes of self- and overt censorship would drive them into the independent, that is, illegal, camp. One case in point was the journal *Égtájak Között (Between the Points of the Compass)*, published by the VOX HUMANA Circle.[58] Between 1984 and 1986, six issues appeared officially; after the pressures of censorship became "unbearable" in the view of its editorial board, they made the decision to "go independent." The experience radicalized the students, and by the late 1980s, they considered themselves to be "an autonomous group within the Hungarian political opposition" (Bartók, 1987: 62). Their editorial position evolved to the point of promoting "... a democratic, nonaligned, neutral and independent Europe ... close to the independent peace movements and with END (European Nuclear Disarmament, the premiere West European anti-nuclear movement)" (Bartók, 1987: 62).

Other periodicals kept on publishing officially, and simply kept pushing the envelope with authorities. One such journal was *Mozgó Világ (The World in Motion)*, self-styled as an avant-garde literary and cultural periodical, which started publication in 1975. It was extremely popular among students and youth, partially because it gave affirmative expression to alternative lifestyles and discussed taboo topics of the nation's history and culture in a purposefully controversial manner. By 1981 publication had already been suspended for three months, and in the mid-1980s editors were routinely removed. By the late 1980s officially sponsored journals simply began to publish what they wanted. A dramatic example was *Századvég* (*End of the Century*), published by the István Bibó College of Law, whose editors flatly stated that they would cease publication if any attempts were made at censorship.

As in Poland and Czechoslovakia, emigré Hungarians and organizations outside the country also played a role in republishing samizdat literature for an external Hungarian audience, as well as keeping them informed of activities in other East-Central European countries. The Hungarian language newspaper *Irodalmi Újság*, published in Paris, often republished articles from *Beszélő* and *Hírmondó*.

The Hungarians were certainly late entrants to the Central European samizdat scene, but throughout the 1980s more than made up for their slow start. Samizdat publishing in Hungary also had the effect of expanding the limits of what was officially acceptable. Once again, the line between official and unofficial, censored and uncensored could not always be discerned with great clarity.

Toward an Alliance: The Bibó *Festschrift* and Monor

Inevitably if the democratic opposition were to translate their work into something wider and more meaningful, they would have to come to terms with the populists, the regime, and the wider public. A tentative step in this direction was the preparation of a commemorative volume celebrating the life and thought of Hungarian historian and political scientist István Bibó. His death in 1979 was a defining moment for the opposition, and the idea of a *Festschrift* in his honor was a critical symbolic and strategic move.

Bibó himself was a Patočka-like figure for the Hungarian opposition, not for his activism but for his profound social and political analysis of the nation's past, and as a classic representative of liberal thinking in the region. Bibó, like Lukács, was involved and implicated in every stage of Hungarian history in the twentieth century. His first career as a law professor at the University of Szeged was interrupted by the war; he became active in the resistance and in 1945 joined the National Peasant Party. At the time the Peasant Party was relatively radical, and is often described (as Bibó is himself) as seeking a "third road" between capitalism and communism (Jeszenszky, in Bibó, 1991: 6). Bibó was certainly not initially unfriendly to Soviet liberation, which he considered a historic possibility to create politics anew in his country.[59] However, both he and his party were victims of Rákosi's famous "salami tactics" which decimated the opposition slice by slice, resulting in Stalinist consolidation. As a critic of Stalin and as a defender of Hungarian national interests, he was demoted from academician to assistant librarian. In 1956 he briefly assumed the position of Minister of State in Nagy's government. His legendary status was assured when he was the only member of the government who did not leave the Parliament building in Budapest upon the invasion of Soviet troops on November 4. Miraculously, he was mistaken for a clerk and was left undisturbed; under the oppressors' noses he managed to prepare and get out a declaration rejecting the label of counter-revolution and called for passive resistance and international support (Litván, 1996: 105). He later prepared a "Draft Proposal" on how the crisis might be resolved, yet despite its widespread circulation and eventual presentation to the Soviet government (via the Indian ambassador in Moscow) his attempt to broker a peaceful compromise failed (Litván, 1996: 115–116).[60] Unlike many others he remained true to his liberal and democratic ideals, and was not coopted into the system after 1956. After serving a jail sentence (for which he was amnestied in 1963) Bibó was again permitted to work as a librarian, a post held until retirement.

As Tőkés states, "Bibó's funeral serendipitously united everybody who was anybody in the intellectual community and prompted many—whether out of friendship, respect, or guilt—to agree to cooperate on a major samizdat project, the *Bibó Memorial Book*" (1996: 185). The result, edited by dissident sociologist János Kenedi, featured seventy-six authors from a variety of backgrounds. Included, for example, were populist writers Gyula Illyés and Sándor Csoóri, agricultural economist and Imre Nagy co-defendant Ferenc Donáth, and non-dissident historian Jenő Szücs.

The text was submitted to the Gondolat publishing company (an official publishing house) with the veiled threat that if rejected, it would be published abroad (the manuscript had already been sent to the West). This prompted the party to take an unusual move and commission a detailed evaluation of its contents and authors. At first the party appeared to waver towards authorizing its publication, on the condition that five of the authors considered "enemies of the regime" be dropped from the project. After the editorial committee chaired by Donáth rejected the regime's counter-offer, the contents of the examination commissioned by the Politburo were fortuitously leaked and smuggled out of Hungary. With unusual candor and precision, the report expressed concern over the use of Bibó as a "model of public conduct" and as a tool whereby the opposition could begin to form a "consensus among various strata of the intelligentsia" (quoted in Tőkés, 1996: 186). This is exactly what they were trying to do: Bibó's native populism, progressive economic stance, and civil courage could be lauded and at the same time serve as an intellectual bridge to the populists, members of the official intelligentsia, and the generation of 1956.

In the early 1980s, the democratic opposition was particularly sensitive to the charge that it did not care about the status of Hungarian minorities, especially in Romanian Transylvania. As a deliberate coalition-building strategy, members of the democratic opposition, especially those involved with *Beszélő* began to take up this cause, as is evidenced by their many articles on the persecution of the Hungarian minorities and outreach to those representing them (for example, Miklós Duray in Slovakia). To gain popular legitimacy and undermine the regime, they also began to play the 1956 card. In Havelian style, this was raised as an issue not only for political or historical reasons, but as a point of morality. However liberal the Kádárite compromise might be made to seem, it rested on the graves of Nagy and others. Moral indignation generated concrete support for regime adherence to human rights, which in turn highlighted the violation of Hungarian rights outside the country.

The democratic opposition's next foray into coalition building came through their participation in a three-day unofficial conference at Monor, a small village outside Budapest on 14–16 June, 1985. Ferenc Donáth, the moving force behind the *Bibó Memorial Book*, was also the convenor of the conference, and he highlighted the deterioration of living standards and the crisis-ridden economy as both a catalyst for action and a galvanizing force for potentially political change. Participants included members of the democratic opposition, populists, reform-minded socialists, artists, and writers. The agenda consisted of four formal presentations intended to represent the diversity of the conference: the speakers were *népi* writers István Csurka and Sándor Csoóri, economist Tamás Bauer, and philosopher János Kis. The discussion was wide-ranging, and touched on national minorities, the economy, and its attendant social problems. Although the conference was loosely designed to initiate a popular front strategy, no common program or set of aims emerged. There was the usual political nitpicking in terms of favored issues and causes, yet the dialogue was fruitful. Unfortunately, the opposition was unable to keep up the momentum after Monor, partially because of populist agitation over *Beszélő*'s Social Contract, but also because the populists continued to follow their own separate path, culminating at Lakitelek and the formation of the Democratic Forum.

Lakitelek

Now it was the regime's turn to seize the initiative, after it had been dropped in their laps by the populist writers. Stung by their perceived exclusion from the policy preparation of the Social Contract, a number of populist writers set out to arrange their own Monor-style conference on national issues. In 1987 about 150 intellectuals convened at the home of populist writer Sándor Lezsák in the small town of Lakitelek after Zoltán Biró in particular approached Imre Pozsgay (who was his close friend) about engaging in a dialogue with reform-minded senior members of the party-state. Pozsgay, in what was probably a move in his own personal political interests as much as those of the party, assented, and was also a principal speaker at the conference. Others included writers István Csurka, Mihály Bihari, and Csaba Gombár. The problem was simple, as Mihály Bihari put it: "Socialism is in crisis ... a historically institutionalized dictatorial political regime pretends to be democratic ... we have arrived at a crossroads" (quoted in Berend, 1996: 271). The conference was a gamble in terms of both sides attempting to gain support for bipolar political reform—a socialist versus populist two-party scheme. Both György Konrád and economist László Lengyel—two individuals who straddled the divide between the democratic opposition and the populists—vigorously objected, reminding the participants that only multi-party competition was truly consonant with democratic principles.

On another level, the Lakitelek conference represented the resuscitation of the Kádárite compromise. As Tőkés observed:

> The Lakitelek conference was a landmark event: the public renegotiation of the terms of the Kádár–Aczél–Populist compromise of 1958–1962. The

old regime had defaulted on its commitments to Németh, Illyés, and their ideological heirs. This, in turn, presented the reform communists, particularly Pozsgay, with the opportunity to revise the terms of the relationship to their political benefit. The recruitment of Populists for participation in a "democratic socialist" partnership with the political incumbents was an example of communist "rearguard" *realpolitik* at its best (1996: 199).

Even though it might have been strategic politically for Pozsgay, the party was clearly operating on borrowed time—time borrowed from the Hungarian people.

An important outcome of Lakitelek was the creation of the *Magyar Demokrata Fórum* (MDF, or Hungarian Democratic Forum). First envisioned as an intellectual and political movement inspired by the populist message, it was formally set up with official acquiescence in September, 1988. Its program described the MDF as democratic, centrist, committed to Hungarian tradition, and in support of a competitive market economy—no reference is made to a "third way" approach.[61] The MDF initially distanced itself from party identification, but later would be transformed and claim a decisive victory in Hungary's first democratic multi-party elections in 1990.

Monor and Lakitelek are historically representative of the germination of Hungarian political interests along partisan lines. The populists' partisan creation was the MDF, the democratic opposition later transformed themselves into the *Szabad Demokraták Szövetsége* (SzDSz), or the Alliance for Free Democrats.

Intra-party and Election Reform

Although this is a study on intellectual and decidedly non-party opposition, significant efforts at intra-party reform were made in Hungary in the late 1980s. Not that reform socialists in the party-state were ever completely systematic or even organized amongst themselves, but unlike in Czechoslovakia and in Poland, serious efforts were made to ensure some generational renewal within party ranks and some form of policy overhaul.

The reform wing of the party, although hardly unified in practice, consisted of those individuals reared in the *apparat*, usually young or inexperienced enough *not* to have been implicated by 1956 but old enough to have risen through party ranks during the good times of the Kádárist compromise. They were educated, had well-honed political and bureaucratic skills, were influenced by Eurocommunism and had lived through the two steps forward, one step back nature of many previous reform efforts. Aside from veteran economic reform architect Rezső Nyers, the leading lights were Imre Pozsgay, Károly Grósz, and János Berecz.

All their efforts and personal ambitions, both individually and collectively, were stymied by the long-awaited retirement of János Kádár, who had never succeeded in grooming a political successor. His forced retirement was more like a "leveraged buyout" with the outgoing CEO negotiating his own severance package (Tőkés, 1996: 280–281). He essentially demanded that in the process of rethinking the past and in revising the party's role, he *not* be held accountable for the Rajk confession in 1949, his role in 1956, or his responsibility for the unsuccessful counter-reform process of the 1970s.

Although Károly Grósz won the big prize as the country's new prime minister and secretary general of the party in May, 1988, it was Imre Pozsgay who would emerge as the party's best hope for survival and regeneration. A skilled and candid orator and a person willing to seize the initiative, Pozsgay transformed himself by late 1988 (with the help of the media which he largely controlled) into the most popular socialist politician in Hungary. In January 1989 he consolidated his position as a potential leader and confirmed risk taker when he went on television and took on two of the regime's biggest shibboleths. He dared to characterize 1956 as a popular uprising (*népfelkelés*)—and not a counterrevolution—and at the same time suggested that in the future the party would have to learn to coexist not just with another party (an MDF-type popular front) but two or more parties.[62] Reevaluation of 1956 was critical, as the legitimacy of the regime had historically been constructed on its portrayal of events as a counter-revolution and thus its own seizure of power.[63] Thus it was Pozsgay and *not* Grósz or Berecz who played the decisive role on behalf of the party leading up to the Roundtable Talks in 1989.

Intra-party political reform was necessarily a top-down phenomenon, but the 1985 election reforms demonstrated how easily the process could be ambushed from below. Although the regime had modestly experimented with political reform at the same time as the NEM was implemented, 1985 represented the first time Hungarian voters were given a choice of two candidates on the ballot. In what amounted to a harsh condemnation of regime policies and "accomplishments" from local party rank-and-file, a real debate took place on issues of resource allocation in accordance with local priorities. The script was written from above but not followed. All active politicians in leading positions were elected, but many lower-ranking but noteworthy functionaries failed to be elected. Predictably, they were often replaced by locally credible nominees who were not part of the central party machine.

Moreover, a few non-party reform-minded intellectuals attempted to get themselves designated as candidates (such as László Rajk and Gáspár Miklós Tamás), taking advantage of the fact that nominations "from the floor" were permitted during the nomination process.[64] Their efforts were doomed to failure, because after the first few attempts, the party was careful to ensure that the nomination meetings were stacked with their own supporters. However, Rajk's and Tamás's unsuccessful attempts had a demonstration effect, and other independent candidates sought nomination, not only known dissidents but also economists and environmentalists. Moreover, all candidates used the platform provided by the nomination to voice their opinions before a captive audience, thus ensuring a debate on issues usually confined to samizdat.[65] They succeeded in generating discussion and forcing real choices to be made (Demszky, 1985: 24).[66]

The "failure" to nominate independent candidates with oppositional views had two other key consequences. First, the process unmasked the supposed liberality of the Kádárite regime and its mythology of free elections, displaying the actual nature of the "fix" for what it really was. Second, and more positively, the process provided a preliminary sense of democratic antagonism in the electoral trenches; many of those who were defeated in 1985 ran again in 1990. János Kis, writing an election analysis in *Beszélő*, said it best in stating, "The electoral reform was a failure in terms of being a reform, but the process provided an opportunity for the expression of aspirations from below for which there was no precedent for decades" (Kis, 1985).[67]

Yet in the end the party did initiate much of what became regime transformation, and certainly by 1988 was keen to take into consideration opposition forces (Sajó, in Elster, 1996: 70). Thus in Hungary the party leadership promised governance by the rule of law, a constitution-drafting commission, and proposed a constitutional court.

The Rebirth of Civil Society

From the mid-to-late 1980s, the opposition grew in both size and scope, for a variety of reasons. The long and tangled process of economic reform resulted in increasing restratification—Hungary was the first country in the Bloc to introduce a personal income tax and a VAT-type tax in order to deal with the mounting foreign debt. The new phenomenon of unemployment, rising inflation (along with increased consumer and housing costs) and the uneven growth in the second economy meant that Hungarians often had to work several jobs to make ends meet. The Kádárist compromise was dead. The significant growth in both samizdat and officially sponsored publications that refused to self-censor and were ever more critical of the regime coincided with the willingness of intellectuals to add their voices in protest. Demographically, younger Hungarians born after 1956 were less fearful of a draconian Soviet intervention, agitated for reform, especially in the environmental and peace movements. Intra-party reform spawned new hope for some, and for others provided motivation to leave behind the blanket of partisan security and make demands for wider and deeper economic reform with an accompanying process of political reforms. The inability of the Polish and Czechoslovak authorities to put an end to the courageous activities of Solidarity and Charter 77 provided Hungarians with a powerful example of the necessity of continued action under adverse circumstances. Finally, the growth in new and independent associations representing various interests and promoting a wide variety of causes signaled a rebirth of civil society and at the same time pointed to the success, albeit limited, of Kis' strategy of radical reformism.

One of the most important independent initiatives centred around the opposition to the Gabčikovo–Nagymaros Project. The project, first a trial balloon floated in the 1950s as a plan to generate hydroelectric power by building a massive dam on the Danube (also the Czechoslovak–Hungarian border), reemerged as a negotiated possibility in the early 1970s. In 1977 the two countries signed an agreement to start work on the barrage system. Austria was brought in as a third partner, guaranteeing a loan for project construction. Environmental opposition to the project was voiced early on the Hungarian side.[68] Activist and biologist János Vargha began to publicize information about the feared environmental impact of the proposal.[69] In 1983, he founded the Danube Circle (*Duna Kör*), whose purpose was to provide information and generate public debate on the project. Opposition to the dam also had the effect of broadening awareness of other ecological concerns and in 1986 Ferenc Langmár (a Nagymaros activist) set up the first independent environmental journal (VÍZJEL) in the region. The environmentalists had broad public appeal; in September, 1988 over 30,000 citizens demonstrated against the project and in 1989 the Danube Circle gathered more than 100,000 signatures demanding a plebiscite on its continuation. The Danube Circle and other opponents to the project were ultimately so successful that in May, 1989 the government announced that construction would be suspended.[70]

As in the GDR, the peace movement was an important political force, especially in mobilizing young people. It grew rapidly in the early 1980s, and sought to maintain a distinct position, separate and independent from both the democratic opposition and the party-state sponsored peace organizations. As in Czechoslovakia, the response of Hungarian activists to the END appeal for continental nuclear disarmament was tepid. Like their other East-Central European counterparts, they did not want to see a decoupling of human rights, democratization, and (real) national independence from the intense and well-meaning desire of Western activists to achieve a pan-European settlement on arms reduction or even elimination. Secondary school students formed ANC—Anti-Nuclear Campaign Hungary—and peace activist Ferenc Kőszegi founded the Peace Group for Dialogue in 1982. In the same year E. P. Thompson visited Budapest to establish friendly relations with the representatives of different Hungarian groups supporting peace initiatives.[71] The Dialogue group's activities included a number of semi-official public meetings and in 1983 they unsuccessfully attempted to set up a peace camp modeled on Greenham Common.[72]

Similar to the peace activists who sought the protection and encouragement of the Lutheran Church in the GDR, anti-militarism and pacifism were reflected by minority voices in the Catholic Church in Hungary. Efforts by those such as Catholic priests László Kovács and András Gromon, both of whom delivered pacifist sermons and supported conscientious objection to the required 18 months military service, were met with official church reprisals.[73] As in Slovakia, the official church supported the regime, but the Catholic faithful found inspiration within their beliefs to oppose it. In the early 1980s, over a hundred "local communities" of Catholics followed the teachings of György Bulányi, a priest preaching in Franciscan style in favor of the early Christian values of poverty, humility, and non-violence (Lomax, 1982: 30). In 1982, Bulányi's supporters formed the Committee for Human Dignity, and voiced their support for peace movements East and West.

Opposition in Hungary was initially more of a cultural than a political phenomenon, and on the cultural front the range and depth of independent initiatives grew. Originally, such independent artists initiatives as *Inconnu* resulted in underground art exhibitions and events. As early as 1973, the Young Writers' Attila József Circle was created under the auspices of the Writers' Union—unfortunately their demands for radical cultural democratization resulted in official suspension in 1981.

One of the most unusual events took place 1985. The European Cultural Forum was held in Budapest that year, the latest in a series of meetings that were part of the Helsinki process. The official forum was attended by delegations from all 35 countries that had signed the Helsinki Accords. However, parallelling the Forum and coinciding with it, the Helsinki Federation for Human Rights along with members of the opposition organized an unofficial symposium, entitled "The Writer and his Integrity." The goal of the symposium along with its timing was to actively demonstrate that culture was not simply the province of governments, but more importantly involved the writers and artists themselves. Art belonged to civil society, and was not just a function of official regulation. Ten writers were invited to attend the symposium, which was well attended by both international journalists and the democratic opposition.[74] Twenty leading members of the Hungarian democratic opposition (most of whom had attended the unofficial gathering) sent a signed statement entitled "Cultural Freedom for Hungary" to the official Forum. Charter 77 also sent a proxy address to the Forum.

Throughout the 1980s youth culture generally and student activism specifically could be characterized as displaying growing discontent simultaneously with an exertion of greater independence. While Student Solidarity was radicalizing student politics in Poland in the 1980–1981 period, there was an (abortive) effort at democratizing KISZ, the Communist Youth Alliance. In the Karl Marx University of Economics, an overtly political discussion club called Polvax was formed, and it attracted hundreds of students to debates on questions of international and domestic politics, human rights, economic reform, and Eurocommunism.

On March 30, 1988 the *Fiatal Demokraták Szövetsége* (Fidesz, or the Federation of Young Democrats), was founded by several dozen students, drawn largely from the activist student body at the István Bibó College of Law.[75] Lead by Viktor Orbán, Gábor Fodor, Tamás Deutsch and others, it grew within one year to more than 3,000 members. The major issues motivating Fidesz members were political reform, the Nagymaros Dam project, and other concerns specifically relevant to young people, such as conscientious objection to military service.

Encouraged by the success of other groups and discouraged by the ailing economy, the Democratic League of Free Trade Unions was set up in 1989 as an umbrella organization for newly independent unions. Leaflet campaigns were initiated to encourage members of the official National Council of Trade Unions to leave the organization. The unofficial May Day celebration in 1989 was attended by over 100,000 workers, intellectuals, and students. This was in sharp contrast to the official celebration presided over by party leader Károly Grósz, attended by less than 10,000.

Some previously existing groups were able to transform their previously illegal activities into legal organizations. For example, SZETA registered itself as a legal foundation in 1989. Previously extinct "nostalgic" political parties, such as the Independent Smallholders' Party and the Social Democrats, were resurrected.[76]

Although traditionally the groups under the umbrella of party-state sponsorship were of the transmission-belt variety, the late 1980s saw the development of a "gray zone" of organizations that were originally *of* the party-state but not necessarily *for* it.[77] In a sense this was somewhat analogous to events in Czechoslovakia, except that the grey zone there was made up largely of *individuals* acting within their own limited capacities and in so doing enlarging their space for action. One such organization in the Hungarian context was the Endre Bajcsy-Zsilinszky Society. It was established in 1986 under the auspices of the Patriotic People's Front[78] as a discussion group promoting the radical and nationalist agenda of Bajcsy-Zsilinszky.[79] Similar to the populists, one of its main goals was to focus public attention on the plight of Hungarian minorities, especially in Romania. Public activities included co-sponsorship of the June, 1988 demonstration against the persecutionist policies of Romanian leader Nicolae Ceauşescu. The Society had strong links to both reformer Pozsgay and Central Committee Secretary (and conservative) György Fejti, and was certainly more of an "official" nature than, for example, the MDF.

Although the growth of civic initiatives largely occurred in Budapest, other university centers (such as Szeged) became drawn into the ever-larger and overlapping circles of oppositional activities. The production and distribution of samizdat moved outward from the center also, with student activists often taking part in the actual printing processes and transportation of materials in and out of the city.[80]

Ellenzéki Kerekasztal (EKA) and the "Pacted Transition"

The successful initiation and conclusion of the Polish National Roundtable was an instrumental and powerful example. It is hard to imagine, especially given our retrospective knowledge of events, that the Hungarian opposition had enough leverage *on their own* to pressure the regime into such proceedings without the Polish example. The Hungarian authorities, like their counterparts in Poland, wanted to share the increasingly burdensome responsibility of managing the twin problems of a disintegrating economy and barely latent social instability with partners enjoying greater legitimacy than themselves. After all, the now-collapsed Kádárist compromise was built on careful cooptation, and external resources and ideas from outsiders with greater legitimacy and socio-cultural capital were needed now more than ever.

The *Ellenzéki Kerekasztal* (EKA) or Opposition Roundtable began its deliberations on 22 March, 1989, on the heels of massive demonstrations on the March 15 anniversary of the 1848 revolution.[81] The Independent Lawyers' Forum (*Független Jogász Fórum* or FJF) took the initiative in proposing the establishment of an Opposition Roundtable—after previous false starts, it was important to establish some degree of oppositional unity in the face of the regime's own agenda for reform. Although freedom of association legislation had been passed earlier in the year, the status of participants, many of whom were already constituted as quasi-parties, was unclear (Sajó, in Elster, 1996: 72).

Initially, the leadership of the party, now under the command of Miklós Németh, was angry at such a move. With typical divide-and-conquer tactics, their obvious preference was to manage talks with opposition groups separately. Nonetheless, the first stage of the process was successful, and as result the EKA began to meet with the MSZMP on April 22, 1989.[82] Included in the EKA were the MDF, SzDSz, Fidesz, *Független Kisgazda Párt* (Independent Smallholders' Party), *Magyar Néppárt* (Hungarian People's Party), the Endre Bajcsy-Zsilin-szky Society, and the Democratic Trade Union of Scientific Workers. At a later stage the League of Free Trade Unions (*Liga*) and the Christian Democratic People's Party (KNDP) were invited. Like the Polish RT, the nature and progress of both EKA and later the Hungarian RT have been examined elsewhere extensively.[83] However, some salient points about the process are in order.

First, all those involved were devoted to a peaceful and democratic transition. Clearly none of the actors involved wanted to see a repeat performance of 1956—not imminent Soviet invasion but the possibil-ity of uncontrolled popular mobilization. The nervousness about the effects of such mobilization is understandable considering that at this point the Berlin Wall was intact, Solidarity had not experienced its decisive electoral victory, and Czech citizens had not yet gathered *en masse* in Wenceslas Square. Not that the groups involved were unwill-ing to trade on public support if necessary, but to the extent they believed mobilization equaled potential disintegration, they definitely preferred to stay in the controlled realm of negotiations.

Second, all opposition organizations in varying degrees focused on the recognized historic task of engineering a *transition to democracy*— not a retrofit of the Kádárist compromise. Thus the agenda of the talks included a new election law, rewriting the constitution, the modifica-tion of the criminal code in keeping with new legal guarantees, and so on. Political liberalization was front and center, and was considered a prior condition to the discussion of other national issues, such as eco-nomic reform. As László Bruszt stated at the time:

> No one held legitimate power in a country sliding downward in the direc-tion of economic chaos. No one represented "society" and no one was authorized to enunciate the "public will." Under these circumstances the *sole* possible solution became obvious. The apparent crisis could be resolved only by establishing legitimate power, one that possessed appropriate authority. The sole possible path by which this could be accomplished was the holding of free elections (emphasis in original; 1990: 376).

Third, despite the politics-over-economics sequencing that eventually occurred, the party-state tried as in Poland to force shared responsibility early on by emphasizing an economic reform agenda. This process ultimately failed. Even the party had to realize that none of the issues discussed could be easily decoupled from the underlying economic structures, that such issues were mere symptoms of a deeper malaise. This is not to say, however, that the Hungarian economic crisis sat quietly in the background during 1989. The party's desire for economic reform underscored larger pressures looming in the background—from 1987 to 1989 the country's hard currency debt *doubled* in dollar value—the threat of Hungarian insolvency was a real and present danger. Western creditors made it clear that the price for continued financing of the debt was radical transformation of the economy. No side of the triangle had the legitimacy, ability, or resources to go it alone on change of such a major scale.

Fourth, although there were clearly power differentials among the three sides, with the opposition groups still operating in a quasi-legal netherworld between unofficial harassment and official recognition, all the parties to the negotiation had strong interests in staying at the table. The Hungarian example reads like a textbook case in the success of mutual gains bargaining. The party was beleaguered by demands for change from within, as voiced through increasingly active Reform Circles.[84] The regime faced considerable international constraints, such as Soviet meddling in the Hungarian leadership crisis, the increasingly hard-line positions of Honecker and Ceauşescu, and the impending July visit of US President George Bush. This was matched by internal uncertainties, such as the potential impact and outcome of the planned reburial of Imre Nagy—was this to be a moment of uncontrolled revenge or national reconciliation?

EKA effectively had an open-ended agenda for talks, and could effectively veto reform proposals advanced by it—this was more real oppositional power than had ever existed previously (Tőkés, 1996: 336–337). They suddenly had a national forum through which to advance their own platforms, a stage from which to establish their leadership skills and bargaining ability. Although EKA had no institutional power base, they did have the public mobilization card—getting Hungarian citizens onto the streets in large numbers (as the March events amply demonstrated)—this was a veiled threat should a hypothetical departure from the talks be deemed necessary. EKA pressed successfully for open plenary sessions; decisions at the RT were made on the basis of mutual interest and consensus, thus procedurally democratic values were promoted at the outset (Sajó, in Elster, 1996: 79).

The "third side" was acknowledged by all the players to be of less importance both in terms of process and outcome—to extend the metaphor, this was no equilateral triangle.[85] Members of the state agencies obviously had a stake in asserting their independence given the possibility of the once-mighty party becoming an immobilized and rapidly sinking Titanic. To this extent, the "third side" was content *not* to support the party, which automatically destined them to a lesser role in the negotiating process. On another level, however, the "third side" ostensibly represented the non-elites not present at the table, unlike both the party and EKA. Issues included the bread-and-butter concerns of their constituents, such as wages, self-management, the maintenance and extension of the social safety net given the uncertainties of reform and its uneven impact on average Hungarians. By and large, these were only symbolically and not substantively discussed; both EKA and the party sidelined the agenda of the third side in favor of the pressing need for a political solution.

As the national RT talks progressed (and especially after the reburial of Imre Nagy), EKA made its demands more detailed and all-encompassing: guaranteed free elections, free media access during elections, reformation of the criminal code to exclude political crimes, a prohibition on the use of violence, and the depoliticization of the armed forces (Sajó, in Elster, 1996: 80). EKA refused to enter into a Faustian bargain regarding the economy, reasoning that it would be folly to assume any responsibility before actually becoming part of the government.

In the burst of comparativist literature on transitions to democracy following 1989, much has been made of both the Polish and Hungarian cases as examples of a "negotiated" or "pacted" variety.[86] János Kis has suggested that, in fact, such a description calls into question the future plausibility of the old dualism of reform versus revolution.[87] Neither is completely adequate to describe what happened in Hungary, where there was a breakdown in legitimacy but not legality. No clear revolutionary break occurred between the *ancien regime* and the new order. This occurred, in Kis' view, because the avenues of both internal reform and reaction were foreclosed. None of the participants had any long-term *interest* in pushing for a political implosion or explosion, especially given the normative rejection of the violence that such a collapse would likely entail. Thus a fourth option emerged: literally negotiating the transition from one system to another. Making a deal with a counter-power was much more favorable to the ruling party than the inherent unpredictability and instability of a revolutionary moment.[88] The primary condition for the success of this scenario in Kis' view was the degree of popular mobilization. With an apathetic citizenry demobilized by fear, the party-state would have had no interest in making a deal with a counter-elite. Rather, it could have managed its own transition on the economic level foregoing any change on the political side—an East-Central European version of the Asian model. If mobilization had been too high, no deal would have resulted, as negotiation is impossible in a highly-charged environment prone to swings in popular support and instability of the negotiating partners. Such a situation too easily dissolves into regime breakdown.

Tőkés makes the salient point that in Hungary, "patterns of interaction between the political incumbents and the dissidents were substantially different from those elsewhere in communist Eastern Europe and in the USSR" (1996: 205). However true this might be (and it does rest on the generally accepted view that in Hungary the line between dissident and intra-party reformer was indeed highly permeable), Tőkés is incorrect in singling out the Hungarian opposition for special commendation for their "self-limitation and accommodation-seeking behavior" (1996: 205). Certainly self-limitation was a Polish invention if there ever was one (Kis and Haraszti themselves admit to the strong theoretical influence of Michnik here), right from the founding of KOR through to the relegalization of Solidarity and the Roundtable Talks in 1989. The opposition, although profoundly separated from the apparatus of the party-state by near-continuous persecution and a wall of narrow-minded intransigence and near-sightedness on the part of the regime, also stayed well within the bounds of legality (and purposefully so). In all three cases studied here ending authoritarian communism entailed a set of peaceful negotiations, and no one could have predicted at the outset of the process that the oppositional movements in all three cases would end up holding the winning set of cards. Accommodation and compromise were not only geopolitical necessities even well into 1989, they were also an essential and integral planks in their political theorization.

The "Four Yeses" Referendum

As any good negotiator knows, the devil lies in the detail of contractual language. Esoteric points of agreement or disagreement often have huge practical implications. In negotiating the details of a new Hungarian political system, the various participants had to think not only of the big picture, but of the implications of taking certain decisions, and the procedural sequencing of such. A case in point was the fracas over the election of the new head of state.

The MSZMP supported a presidential type of system, and the pro-Pozsgay parties tried to convince others that a semipresidential system be accepted—in either case the president would be directly elected. Aside from institutional reasons of control and centralization, the major *political* reason was an assumed Pozsgay victory. Concerned about the concentration of power in one individual, EKA, particularly Fidesz and SzDSz, wanted a parliamentary democracy. They reasoned that structurally limiting the president's role would be achieved through a parliamentary rather than a direct election. They argued further that presidential elections would have to occur *after* parliamentary elections, theoretically to ensure the legitimacy of the new head of state, but practically to avoid electing Pozsgay.

This issue tore EKA apart—first the Christian Democratic People's Party and later the MDF broke ranks and supported the party's position of presidential elections prior to parliamentary elections. In the end, the agreement signed on September 18, which concluded the phase of the National Roundtable negotiations, was not signed by either Fidesz or SzDSz. In retrospect, this was not exactly a setback, as the agreement signed by the remaining parties did "create legal and political conditions for a peaceful transition"and included six draft pieces of legislation which amended the constitution, provided the organizational and financial rules for multi-party democratic competition, and modified the criminal code and criminal procedure.[89] The refusal of SzDSz and Fidesz to sign on the basis of their political principles set an important example: the opposition was not going to be forced into a pact with communists that would limit the possibility of fully free elections. In this respect, the intellectual opposition wanted to *avoid* what had just happened in Poland, where Solidarity had agreed to partially free elections and whereby Jaruzelski would hold the presidency.

Importantly, the stalemate was resolved in the public realm. On November 28, Hungarian citizens voted in a referendum on four issues: the disbanding of the Workers' Guard, the withdrawal of communist party cells from the workplace, an official accounting of the assets of the party, and the postponement of the presidential elections until *after* national parliamentary elections to be held in March, 1990. The party and the MDF boycotted the referendum, in an offensive enough manner as to generate a voter backlash in favor of the opposition. The SzDSz, Fidesz, *Független Kisgazda Párt*, and the Social Democrats banded together in a campaign asking Hungarians to vote *"Igen"* (Yes) on all four questions, but it was the last question that was to prove most crucial in terms of establishing democratic precedent. The first three issues were in a sense "resolved" beforehand, as the lame-duck parliament had already voted in favor of their implementation; nonetheless the legislative position was upheld by a 95% margin. As to the last question, 58% voted in favor of delaying the presidential election. The timing of the referendum proved to be fortuitous: less than a month after the fall of the Berlin Wall and in the middle of the Velvet Revolution in Czechoslovakia. Expressions of the public will *contra* the party-state were rapidly becoming commonplace. Moreover, the results of the plebiscite were respected and indeed presidential elections were held following the parliamentary elections in March, 1990.

June 16, 1989: The Reburial of Imre Nagy

Unlike the popular upsurge represented by Solidarity in 1980–1981 and the thousands of Czechs in Wenceslas Square in 1989, Hungary did not experience a euphoric moment of popular mobilization in support of a set of political demands. The closest thing to it in terms of emotive symbolism, myth making, and mass participation, was the reburial of Imre Nagy on 16 June, 1989. Exactly one year earlier, demonstrations commemorating Nagy's execution had been suppressed with violence uncharacteristic of the Hungarian regime. The stage was set for a solemn and ceremonial reburial of the national hero of 1956—designed by none other than architect and designer László Rajk (Garton Ash, 1990b: 49). In Heroes' Square five coffins were laid for Nagy and his associates; a sixth was also added to represent the "unknown insurgent."

Over 200,000 attended the "funeral," to which Grósz had assented on behalf of the regime when confronted by representatives of the Hungarian community during his visit to the United States the previous year (Tőkés, 1996: 290). It was also well attended by the Western press, and significant luminaries included Adam Michnik, now in an official capacity as a representative of Poland. A list of the known victims was read to all over loudspeakers, wreaths were laid by public officials, speeches read by such notables as Sándor Rácz (who led the KMT in 1956). The only speech that drew public applause was that of Viktor Orbán, one of the leaders of Fidesz (and later prime minister). More than anyone else, Orbán used the occasion to highlight the extreme irony of the revolution's oppressors now bowing before its victims:

> Friends! We young people fail to understand many things that are obvious to the older generations. We are puzzled by those who were so eager to slander the Revolution and Imre Nagy have suddenly become the greatest supporters of the former prime minister's policies. Nor do we understand why the party leaders who saw to it that we were taught from books that falsified the Revolution are now rushing to touch the coffins as if they were good-luck charms. We need not be grateful for their permission to bury our martyrs after thirty-one years; nor do we have to thank them for allowing our political organizations to function. Hungary's leaders are not to be praised because they have refrained from using weapons against those striving for democracy and free elections, because they have not adopted, as well they could, the methods of Li Ping, Pol Pot, Jaruzelski, and Rákosi [from full English text, reprinted in *Uncaptive Minds* (August–September 1989): 26].

Nor did Orbán hesitate to seize the opportunity provided by the mass audience to advance the aims of the democratic opposition, which at that time had just entered the National Roundtable negotiations. Orbán reminded his fellow citizens to keep their eye on the prize:

> Citizens! Thirty-three years after the Hungarian Revolution was crushed and thirty-one years after the execution of the last legitimate prime minister, we may now have a chance to achieve peacefully the goals that the revolutionaries briefly attained through bloody combat. If we trust our souls and our strength, we can put an end to the communist dictatorship,

if we are determined enough, we can force the party to submit to free elections; and if we do not lose sight of the ideals of 1956, then we will be able to elect a government that will immediately begin negotiations on the swift withdrawal of the Russian troops. We can fulfill the will of the revolution if—and only if—we are brave enough (1989: 26).

SECTION 2

INTELLECTUALS IN POLAND: THE TRADITION CONTINUES

Leszek Kołakowski: A Source of Hope amidst Hopelessness

P olish philosopher Leszek Kołakowski left Poland in 1968 after his expulsion from Warsaw University, and therefore hardly warrants being categorized as a "dissident" in terms of the time frame of this study. However, as a revisionist Marxist who goes beyond revisionism, as a mentor to the generation of Michnik, and as the author of arguably the most important theoretical text of the Polish opposition of the 1970s, he must be included.[1] The influence of his life, his work, and the changing nature of his own philosophical positions was enormous. From outside Poland's borders, as an emigré writing for *Kultura*, as a Central European philosopher engaging with the Western New Left, and as a professor at Oxford or in Chicago bringing the history and ideas of the Polish opposition to new audiences, he personified the importance of East–West dialogue.[2]

Although later one of the regime's harshest critics, Kołakowski enthusiastically joined the ranks of younger-generation party intellectuals who supported the party, even as it consolidated its Stalinist hold on the country in the late 1940s. He quickly advanced upward in the ranks of academic philosophers, first at Łódź and later in Warsaw, aided by the fact that many senior academics lost their positions because of their bourgeois origins or thought. During the 1956 Polish October and the subsequent thaw, Kołakowski gained notoriety as chief intellectual "revisionist."[3] He was increasingly critical of the Marxism institutionalized by the party-state, drawing his inspiration from the newly published writings of the "young" Marx, as well as Gramsci and Lukács, and promoted a more humane and democratic socialism. Revisionist thought developed dialectically—synchronous with the progressive faction within the party, and via its reestablished connections with society and independent non-party intellectuals.

Indicative of this period is Kołakowski's influential essay "The Priest and the Jester," in which Kołakowski posits two possibilities for philosophy in general and for the vocation of the philosopher in particular:

> The antagonism between a philosophy that perpetuates the absolute and a philosophy that questions accepted absolutes seems incurable, as incurable as that which exists between conservatism and radicalism in all aspects of human life. This is the antagonism between the priest and the jester, and in almost every epoch the philosophy of the priest and the philosophy of the jester are the two most general forms of intellectual culture. The priest is the guardian of the absolute; he sustains the cult of the final and the obvious as acknowledged by and contained in tradition. The jester is he who moves in good society without belonging to it, and treats it with impertinence; he who doubts all that appears self-evident (Kołakowski, 1968: 33).

Kołakowski's priest is not simply a religious figure; he represents all efforts in philosophy—both within the *vita activa* and the *vita contemplativa*—to find absolute explanations for human phenomena, or promote a single ordering principle. Thus Plato and Marx can be categorized as priests, for the priesthood is not simply a religious undertaking. As Kołakowski says, "Atheists have their saints, and blasphemers build temples" (1968: 36). Jesters, however, are neither detached nor disinterested intellectuals à la Mannheim or Benda; they must hold court with the rulers and remain engaged with society in order to criticize power or express dubiousness and contempt. The jester rebels, pokes fun, yet knows the limits of rebellion while revealing contradictions in the most unshakable of faiths. The jester "derides common sense and reads sense into the absurd" (1968: 34).

Here Kołakowski is more than cleverly analyzing the metaphorical opposition between priest and jester. His fascination with religion as a historical and cultural phenomenon and his concern with religious dissent of all forms indicates a break with Marxist orthodoxy's view of religion as merely "false consciousness." Moreover, he discusses with considerable insight the role of religious questions in philosophy—as complicated formulations that address the possible reconciliation of human essence with existence (even if postulated in eschatological terms as nature versus grace) or as an attempt to provide a monistic and unifying explanation for consciousness and history. Philosophy cannot escape its theological heritage, and without full understanding the philosopher cannot come to terms with the Cartesian revolution, the Enlightenment opposition of faith and reason, or its logical and radical successors—Marxism, psychoanalysis, and phenomenology. Even at this early stage, Kołakowski brings to his writing an in-depth knowledge of the philosophical currents within Christianity and an unusual affinity for its internal dilemmas for a Marxist intellectual of his generation.[4]

Kołakowski's jester might be read as a defense of Kołakowski as a still-committed yet critical party intellectual. More broadly the jester serves as a partial credo for a nascent opposition. Irony shatters ideology, and can be a potent force in destabilizing existing power relations, but does not provide its own replacement. The events of Kołakowski's life again provide the seeds for his own theoretical reflection. Not until he is in exile does he completely discard revisionism—monumentally and rigorously through his three-volume history of Marxism,[5]—and address the problem of how Poles might remain in opposition to the party-state. The intrigue of the court is ultimately replaced as the home for the jester by society at large. The jester abandons his defining occupational criteria, carving out new social and political space within civil society.

In 1966, Kołakowski published *The Presence of Myth*—not well known outside Poland until its re-publication in France as *Obecność Mitu* in 1972.[6] Setting out to explore the role of myth as central for epistemological enquiry, Kołakowski identifies values—including freedom and responsibility—as part of the ubiquitous mythical consciousness of humanity (1989: 29–33). The essays and fragments which constitute this work, further illustrate Kołakowski's intellectual transition. Still concerned with Marx's demand for the restoration of human dignity and universal emancipation beyond political emancipation, Kołakowski nonetheless locates freedom and self-realization as values or ought statements outside of historical reality in the realm of myth. This divergence becomes clearer in his discussion of indifference and the coercion implicit in the technological appropriation of objects and property ownership (1989: 74–77). Although Kołakowski's portrayal of ownership as degrading is consistent with Marx's theory of commodification, his argument that the determination to possess and subordinate objects to exclusive control disinherits the owner from personal existence (and implicitly freedom) signals a new direction. Myth may have the power to remove indifference and transcend the base empiricism of the world, but this is only possible via a popularization of a sense of responsibility. Moreover, Kołakowski contends that such responsibility can never be generated by the collective.[7] Indeed he suggests collective responsibility is more than an oxymoron; it is a fiction because in collective life the individual is practically speaking absolved from individual responsibility. Obviously, this begs the question of how individual responsibility can be activated and maintained—one Kołakowski answers on a practical level once in exile.

In 1971, Kołakowski published an article entitled "Theses on Hope and Hopelessness," both in Polish in *Kultura* and in English in *Survey*. Written before the wide scale publication and distribution of samizdat, it was nonetheless extremely influential inside Poland—one might even suggest that the existence of such an independent and critical essay necessitated samizdat. Unlike his earlier more philosophical reflections, his purpose was to logically demonstrate the death of revisionism while exhorting his fellow Poles to a new kind of action. Eliminating reform-from-above opened the window for options not centered on the party-state.

Kołakowski begins by summarizing the arguments supporting the thesis that authoritarian communism is, in his words, "unreformable." He claims that as the "main function of the system is to uphold the monopolistic and uncontrolled power of the ruling apparatus"—best expressed by the epithet, "the leading role of the party"—nothing can be permitted to undermine this basic principle (1971b: 37). No monopoly can be partial.

In particular, there are structural features endemic to the Soviet model that make any "revisionist" or elite-centered reform process impossible. Kołakowski outlines these "peculiarities" as his seven "theses of hopelessness":

- Partial democratization is contradictory, as it amounts in the end to "partial expropriation of the ruling class"—impermissible and illogical given the leading role of the party. Dissent is either outlawed or pushed to the margins; discontent takes the form of amorphous social pressure, unorganized, and unrealized.
- Technical expertise, especially in the areas of economic, social, and cultural policy, must always take a back seat to partisan servility. Technical

criteria—such as efficiency or competence—cannot operate independently without eroding authority.

- Freedom and free exchange of information are necessary for the efficient operation of the economy, education, and culture, but cannot be an operative principle given possible discontent. As long as "unfavorable information can prove self-denunciatory" the system must operate on misinformation, as information itself is ideological and never neutral (hence Lysenko's genetics).

- Strict subordination and Soviet conformity promote the following: servility, cowardice, the lack of initiative, readiness to obey superiors, readiness to inform on people, indifference to social opinion, and public interest (1971: 40). Effectively, values which are rewarded run counter to an alternative set of "democratic" values, such as the "capacity to take initiative, concern about the public good, and attachment to truth, efficiency, and social interest" (1971b: 40).

- The Soviet model, like other forms of despotism, produces permanent aggression, either via external wars or an internal state of siege. As with Orwell's *Oceania*, the system must "invent its own enemies, creating real ones in the process" (1971b: 41).

- The principle of monopolistic control requires that "all forms of social life not decreed by the ruling apparatus" be destroyed: thus any form of independent civil society or attempt to promote it must be instantly dismantled. Social life is controlled via its nationalization and is operationalized through the various transmission-belt organizations which are effectively agents of the party-state.

- Citizens' rights can neither be widened nor protected, as the smallest crack represented by the smallest reform would set off an avalanche which could threaten the entire order. Concessions in the face of demands—for democracy or rights—never result in satisfaction, but rather in increased pressure from below (the Prague Spring being the ultimate example). Thus, "the philanthropy of the rulers, even should it exist, could not relieve the political and economic slavery of the population" (1971b: 41).

In Thomist fashion and not unlike Hungarian István Bibó, Kołakowski sets up the arguments against reform before he advances its possibilities. The theses of hopelessness amount to an "ideology of defeatism," for four reasons. First, one cannot possibly predict in advance the "degree of flexibility" of the system, and events have proven that it is not completely rigid. Second, to the degree the system is rigid, it rests on the people's belief that it is so. Third, any arguments claiming total unreformability have in common an "all or nothing" logic not confirmed by actual historical development. Finally, authoritarian communism is rife with a tangled web of internal contradictions which cannot be synthetically resolved.

Kołakowski describes some of these contradictions and how they can present themselves as political opportunities:

> The very nature of this system demands complete concentration of power at the center of command. That is why it is true that Stalin's power (and that of his local miniatures) was the most perfect embodiment of the principles of despotic socialism. However the impossibility of re-establishing it stems from the impossibility of reconciling two values, both important for the ruling apparatus: unity and security. The conflicts for power within the system cannot be institutionalized without threatening the ruin of the whole system, for institutionalization would mean the legalization of fractional activity within the party, which would only differ in an insignificant way from the establishment of a multi-party system. Yet groups, cliques and cabals which organize themselves in accordance with various criteria of choice and with different bonds of interest are an inevitable product of social life (1971: 43–44).

The conflict between the systemic need for control and the inescapable reality of societal pluralism presents the possibility for an external form of political organization. Within the party, the conflict continues to be manifest even where external action does not occur, as there is a contradiction between Stalinist rule and forms of collective or oligarchic leadership. A further contradiction exists between the "need for a radical change in ideology and the impossibility of getting rid of Stalinist–Leninist ideology" (1971b: 45). Thus internal reform is impossible: legitimation requires an ideological rigidity, otherwise its purpose is undercut by itself. Kołakowski uses the example of Soviet internationalism to demonstrate this logic:

> Internationalist phraseology is indispensable to the Soviet authorities, since it offers the only legitimation of their rule abroad; it is indispensable to the local rulers who are dependent on the Soviets, as the justification of their dependence and of their own power. It might seem that the Soviet

rulers can completely disregard the non-ruling communist parties, whom they hardly wish to incite to a real struggle for power, and that their splits and deviations are of no political significance. In reality, this is not the case, for an open and complete abandonment of the communist movement in countries which are not under Soviet control could only occur if they were to abandon the principles which justify this control where it exists. The rulers are thus the victims of their own ideology with all its nonsensical baggage. It is a paradox that this ideology, in which practically everybody has ceased to believe—those who propagate it, those who profit from it, and those who must listen to it—is still a matter of the most vital importance for the continuing existence of this political system (1971b: 46–47).

Attempts by the party-state to reverse the trend through appeals to greater productivity and efficiency through the implementation of better technologies are themselves doomed, because there is inevitably a clash between the requirements of efficiency and the primacy of political values. Nonetheless, the leaders are caught in the trap of pursuing technical solutions to systemic problems:

But technological progress (not limited only to military technique) and even the increase in consumption (in spite of certain political advantages which poverty and an inadequate supply of elementary needs give to the rulers) are in the interests of the ruling class for various reasons; the higher the general level of development, the more difficult it is to achieve outstanding results in one area of production, such as military production, treated as an isolated branch; the expectations of the population depend to a considerable degree on their comparison of their situation with that of highly developed countries, a phenomenon impossible to avoid because a complete blockage of information is, for many reasons, already impossible to achieve. Thus in a situation of stagnation or even one in which the level of consumption is increasing slowly, the level of subjective dissatisfaction and discontent can grow. One can indeed never foresee when it will reach the point of explosion in conjunction with other circumstances; in general it is impossible to avoid a situation of international competition even when this imposes an unfavorable situation, and the conditions of this competition are ever more difficult. Thus the rulers, when they stress their desire for technological progress, and the improvement of the material situation of the population are, in general, stating their true intentions. These intentions are, however, in conflict with a second group of intentions, related to the perpetuation of their own monopoly of uncontrolled power in all fields of life (Kołakowski, 1971b: 47).

Because the rulers get trapped in the need for technology as the ultimate solution to the problem of economic progress and the satisfaction of consumer demand (rather than dealing with the issue structurally which they cannot), there will be an endless cycle of not being able to catch up to their own expectations, or the expectations of the citizenry. However, this disjuncture provides an opportunity and a theoretical basis for the success of the mass protests in 1970 in Gdańsk and in 1976 in Radom/Ursus. The impulse to reform must be selective, strategic, and principled:

> ... a reformist orientation [that can be defined] in the sense of a belief in the possibility of effective gradual and partial pressures, exercised in a long-term perspective, a perspective of social and national liberation (Kołakowski, 1971b: 49).

Only this strategic reformism is the answer because passivity results in increasing inflexibility. Not to commit yourself to resistance is to pull the noose more tightly around your neck. Conversely, repression increases if society maintains passivity and accepts weakness and powerlessness. As Kołakowski states dramatically: "The growth of police methods of rule is the result not of increased resistance, but, on the contrary, of its absence" (Kołakowski, 1971b: 52). In the Polish context, when the intelligentsia moves from a position of revisionism to hopelessness based on the supposed unreformability of the system, drastic consequences result, as occurred in 1970:

> The principle of unreformability can thus serve as an absolution granted in advance for every act of cowardice, passivity and cooperation with evil. The fact that a large part of the Polish intelligentsia has been persuaded to believe in the complete inflexibility of the shameful system under which they live is almost certainly responsible for the regrettable passivity which they displayed during the dramatic action of the Polish workers in 1970 (1971b: 51).

This essay is a compelling call-to-arms, and the combination of tough reasoning and the timing of its appearance on the Polish scene indicate why it was so critical to the political-theoretical development of younger activists, such as Adam Michnik. By shifting the focus of reform away from revisionism and toward resistance, and from the party-state to civil society, he signaled a paradigm shift in oppositional thinking. He does not theorize how societal democratization and resistance might occur, but he does reject dramatic overthrow or revolution as both nonsensical and highly improbable.

Kołakowski's writings on Polish affairs as an émigré continued to inspire the younger generation of Polish intellectuals. In contrast to his deliberately comical condemnation of the radical youth movements of the late 1960s in the West and their "revolutionary farce," Kołakowski's stance was respected in East-Central Europe, and he respected the fledgling opposition in turn. This is doubly ironic since the younger generation in East-Central Europe tended to identify strongly with their Western counterparts. Kołakowski's position is partially reflective of the communications gap between East and West, but it is also a selective lens through which he processed generational change and was willing to privilege and be more forgiving of those struggling against authoritarian communism. In Kołakowski's view, aside from the mass movement against the Vietnam War, the sixties generation in the West discredited itself by agitating for less-than-radical ideas (university reform, the power of rock music, an alternative life-style) or highly euphemistic potentialities (make love, not war), all in highly charged revolutionary and rhetorical language.[8] In the East, the situation was the reverse. As the demands for change grew in strength and volume throughout the 1970s and 1980s, they became less state-centered and more radical—in direct proportion to their shedding the traditional socialist lexicon.[9]

Adam Michnik's Alliance Strategy: The Church and the Left

There are a number of recurrent themes running through Church teaching in Poland that define its philosophy and are worth noting, given that their echoes are also found in the Polish opposition. Not unlike the "liberation theology" of Latin America, this Polish "ethics of emancipation"[10] provide an important moral and religious subtext to political opposition. First, ethics have primacy over politics; a moral order must exist before the founding of a social order. Second, any social order must recognize individual human dignity—people are equal moral subjects and can equally receive salvation. Embodied in human dignity is natural freedom, reason, and right to bear witness to truth—none of which can be deprived by any ideology or political system, or reduced merely to a catalogue of human rights and obligations. Third, religious faith is grounded in hope—as the source of spirituality. Hope finds its human referent in the concept of trust—the placing of one's hopes with another, which is a founding principle of social order. Other founding principles are social love (which precedes justice in the hierarchy of virtues) and solidarity. Love of God and one another together with solidarity are able to overcome the societal hatreds and hardened passions that can accompany the struggle for pure justice without love. Love is fundamentally other-regarding rather than self-regarding, and therefore can absorb social conflict rather than be a source of tension.

Thus the Church's specific teachings and sermons, especially as reflected by activist Catholic intellectuals (Tadeusz Mazowiecki) or clergy (Jerzy Popiełuszko and Józef Tischner), must be understood against this ethics of emancipation. An illustration is the Church's views on labor relations. John Paul II, no doubt with Polish events in mind, published a special papal encyclical on labor relations (relying heavily on his earlier work on the philosophy of labor—*Osoba i czyn*). Tischner also wrote about this subject in *Etyka Solidarnośći*. For both Tischner and John Paul II, the dignity of work is related to the dignity of humankind. This dignity is not fundamentally reducible or alienable—the worker maintains her or his subjectivity and agency despite having been considerably exploited by both capital and the production process. Labor remains throughout history as an ally and not an enemy of human expression. However, the dignity of labor must not be accepted as a divine yoke; workers have rights to a just wage, working conditions, and social care. Unions are understood as "an indispensable element of social life" and the "mouthpiece of a struggle for social justice, for the just rights of working people ..." (Zielonka, 1989: 50). Moreover, unions are an expression of solidarity, the *communion* of working people one with another toward a common set of ends. Tischner goes beyond this religious sanction of unions, to the point where the strike takes on a mystical quality—the collective struggle changes the attitude of the worker to the workplace, and endows work with a form of ownership (not unrelated to the labor theory of value).

At the same time as lay Catholics such as Mazowiecki and clergy such as Tischner were preaching the moral and religious bases for political opposition, those on the secular Left were also coming to terms with the Church. The publication of Adam Michnik's *Kościół, Lewica, Dialog* (*The Church and the Left*) was a watershed.[11] Michnik wrote the book in 1975–1976, and it was originally intended to be part of a special issue of the emigré quarterly *Aneks*, published in London. Michnik's aim, along with fellow contributors Jan Józef Lipski, Antoni Macierewicz, and Father Jacek Salij, "was to reexamine the complex relationship between the Catholic Church and the secular intelligentsia ... to shed light on the new way each side was looking at the other" (1993: xi). Michnik has denied that the book "was an attempt to forge a political alliance with the Church"; rather, he claims, his intention was to "propose a new way of thinking about the Church and its place in the world. I wanted to familiarize a wider audience with the ideas of modern Catholic intellectuals" (Michnik, 1993: xiii). This in turn prompted Michnik to explore intellectually and metaphysically the question "What exactly is religion?" (1993: xii). Along with other members of the nascent political opposition in Poland, he was dissatisfied with official Marxist–Leninist explanations of religion as "ideology" or "false consciousness." Like Havel, he came to understand religion as "an absolute, a mystery, as *sacrum*" (1993: xii).

Michnik's own reassessment of the Church as a potentially *progressive* source of democratic values was instrumental in redefining the relationship between Catholic intellectuals and the secular Left. This new relationship was ultimately reflected by the Church's attitude toward Solidarity, especially during martial law. Church sermons by Jánkowski and Popiełuszko defended those, like Michnik, who were tried and imprisoned by the party-state and church cellars became important meeting places.[12] If the Church was not a powerful ally, then it most certainly was a both a shield and a sanctuary for Solidarity and the democratic opposition more generally.

Christian and particularly Catholic interpretations of Holy Scriptures took on a new tone as the dialogue between the Church and the opposition progressed. Religious questions took on profound existential and political meanings. As Michnik states:

We asked about the meaning of life and suffering, and how to relate to enemies. We were grappling with the relative and absolute nature of values, the meaning of tolerance, the law of love. And all of these questions informed concrete decisions that each of us had to make. For choosing to fight the dictatorship was not a decision to be taken lightly. It was a major decision and exacted a high price. Surely we could not at the time seriously believe that so many of us would be able to trade in our prison cells for the swank offices of state dignitaries. Our questions and reflections thus had a very specific undertone. These were questions about how to live under a dictatorship. About how to avoid the temptations of "normality." In the name of what, we asked ourselves, were we ready to make our own lives and the lives of our loved ones so miserable? (1993: xii–xiii)

Michnik concludes that conflict between the Catholic Church and the secular Left is neither necessary nor inevitable. The struggle for meaning coheres with a practical need to promote dialogue, resulting in an appreciation of Catholicism and religion in the public sphere. Unlike anti-clerical liberals of the past, Michnik is unwilling to falsely separate Church and state, or deny the possibility of a role for the Church in politics. However, he feels that the Church's role is primarily a moral one, as a teacher and carrier of ideals and values. The Church is welcome to publicly censure individual leaders or regimes for abuses of power, and to put forward its vision of humanity as one of the potential sets of ideas circulating in the public realm. However, in both *The Church and the Left* and later writings, Michnik remains fervently opposed to the translation of moral imperatives into juridical reality and the "Julianic" aspirations of the Polish Church today.[13]

Michnik's book is a number of things at the same time: it is an original statement of his political theory (which will be discussed below in the context of his other writings, notably *Letters from Prison*); an historically-grounded revisionist account of both the secular Left and the Church from before the war to the present (and their many errors, mutual misunderstandings and lost opportunities); a defense of the Church's position under totalitarianism and an examination of its role as a defender of human rights and as the source of values underlying many of the commitments of the Left; a highly personal reappraisal of his own (mistaken) assumptions about the Church; and above all a plea for *dialogue* between the Church and the Left. Michnik demonstrated sophisticated mediation skills in his political practice; in this book he applies this same ability intellectually to carefully sketch a common ground that can serve as a meeting place for these previously warring factions of the Polish opposition. In so doing, he was arguing against many of his ideological friends in favor of one of their traditional foes.

Michnik begins with a useful linguistic exercise, particularly helpful to the uninitiated reader of the texts of the East-Central European opposition—he defines what he means by the term "Left" or "Secular Left." From the Spanish Civil War until the end of the Second World War, the term "Left" could be easily summarized: "Its essential features were antifascism, support for a planned economy and for agricultural reform, and the demand for a separation of church and state" (1993: 31). Over the next few decades in the countries in the Soviet orbit, this became increasingly problematic. First, an important rupture occurred between the indigenous Polish (i.e. prewar) Left, most notably the PPS, and the new government installed by Moscow—those who took a more independent and critical stance and those who supported the "new reality." This was not just a Polish dilemma—it was faced by leftist intellectuals and parties throughout the region, and from this division the seeds were planted for the first generation of criticism of and opposition to authoritarian communism. Second, another "Left" faced a crisis of self-definition in 1956, as intra-party anti-Stalinists formulated their position *against* the "conservative" and indeed "reactionary" forces inside the party, as well as *against* the traditional right, represented in Poland by the Catholic Church. This group of revisionists began to make contact with the postwar "independent" Left critics coming out of the PPS and were united in their conflict with the PZPR, but neither group thought it appropriate to engage with the party-state's attacks on the Episcopate. After all, the Church was also painted as the enemy, and in the battle between two enemies, it was thought both amusing and strategically clever to simply stand aside.[14] After the student protests of 1968 and the tragedy of December, 1970, the embattled opposition began to take a new view of what being a "Left" critic of the regime was all about.

In the mid-1970s, Michnik observed that the opposition included those who essentially wanted capitalist restoration, and "those who support the idea of democratic socialism" (1993: 33). Not only does Michnik categorize this second tendency as leftist, but firmly plants himself in this camp. He states:

This Left champions the ideas of freedom and tolerance, of individual sovereignty and the emancipation of labor, of a just distribution of income and the right of everyone to an equal start in life. It fights against national-chauvinism, obscurantism, xenophobia, lawlessness, and social injustice. The program of this Left is the program of antitotalitarian socialism (1993: 31).[15]

Thus Michnik's "Left" is more broadly liberal in its commitment to political freedoms and anti-nationalism, but remains wedded to economic egalitarianism. It is neither teleological nor universalist in its claims about history or the future. It is antitotalitarian, meaning not only that it stands against the authoritarian communist party-state, but also that it attempts to design itself as an opposition that is democratic and decidedly non-statist in character.

This Left is not fundamentally opposed to religion *per se*, but to the historically specific actions and teachings of a conservative Church bent on delivering the message that socialism was intrinsically contrary to God's natural law and ultimately representative of spiritual nihilism (1993: 34). This message was made concrete through the Church's past hostility to social reform and intolerance for both non-Catholics and non-believers. The Church's inherent respect for hierarchy was evident in its own organization and its close relationship with the "earthly oligarchy." Marx advocated the abolition of religion because it was "the sigh of the oppressed creature, the heart of a heartless world, as it is the spirit of spiritless conditions ... the opium of the people." Michnik chose to favorably reinterpret and contextualize Marx rather than to reject him entirely. He states that "... Marx's unshakable atheism stems not so much from antipathy toward the very idea of transcendence as from his opposition to the conservative social doctrines of the Church of his time" (1993: 34). Given a different set of doctrines, the Church might play a different role, and that the Left need not be so unequivocally dismissive. Diametrical opposition between the Left and the Church in the Polish context evolved to a point where intellectual strata on both sides came to have a set of similar goals, learned to speak a similar language, and could thus engage in a dialogue.

For Michnik, secularization is "complete separation of church from state, complete separation of state from church, and complete civil rights for all" (1993: 139). Unlike Cardinal Wyszyński, who defines secularization as "the purging of believers and of religious and Catholic elements" (1993: 139), Michnik wants to redefine secularization so that the Left and the Church can come to terms with each other. This effort is made problematic by the pollution of language by the party-state:

> If secularization is taken to mean censorship and the crippling of a nation's culture by the elimination of its religious traditions; if it is understood as the use of state force to eradicate Catholic customs and interpose other ones; then it is hard to disagree with Cardinal Wyszyński. That kind of "secularization" is merely a mask for totalitarian terror. But the primate's remarks may also be understood as an attack upon the principle of the separation of church and state. There is a terrible confusion of concepts in our language today. Thanks to the work of our official propaganda, more and more words confuse matters rather than explain them (1993: 140).

Michnik is indebted to French clerics such as Jean-Marie Domenach and Jacques Leclerq, who justify the neutrality of the state as a prerequisite for political tolerance. Because the temporal sovereignty of the state is not seriously challenged by the Church, there is no temptation to seek state power. Likewise, the Church, when faced with a neutral state has no need to set up an alternative to the state apparatus. Acceptance of this view, according to Michnik, is the basis of human freedom. He cites J. S. Mill favorably, who sought to ground the principle of liberty first and foremost in freedom of conscience and religious conviction. Absolute freedom of opinion, judgment, and the ability to express and publish one's views flow logically from this premise. This kind of secularization is also necessary if Poland is going to be defended from Sovietization in a culturally pluralistic manner, rather than from a position of Catholic fundamentalism.

Michnik continues the excursus with a discussion of what is meant by "dialogue" in the third section of the book, subtitled "Toward a New Dialogue." He rejects the self-serving and inauthentic dialogue of PAX with the authorities, summing it up as "an encounter between totalitarians, drawing inspiration from a peculiarly understood Catholicism and a specific, very Soviet understanding of Marxism" (1993: 176). Rather, Michnik allies himself with the concept of dialogue advocated by Tadeusz Mazowiecki and *Więź*, whom he quotes:

> A dialogue is made up of three components: people, a common platform, and values. A conversation may be nothing more than a transfer of infor-

mation; a discussion may be merely a debate between differing positions; practical cooperation may entail no more than pragmatic activity pure and simple. A dialogue, on the other hand, depends on the communication and transfer of values. A dialogue thus occurs whenever there is a readiness to understand the validity of someone else's position and to enter into a different way of thinking; that is, whenever there is an openness to the values embodied in other points of view ... A dialogue is not a compromise; the tension of contradiction still exists. It is, instead, an attempt to discover a new dimension of the matter at hand, to find a new plane of discourse in which it is possible to meet ... . Dialogue is a method by which an ideologically diverse society can learn to live together. Based on continual interaction, it is a way to overcome mutual human isolation (Mazowiecki, quoted in Michnik, 1993: 183).

This view of "dialogue" not only permeated the Polish opposition, but set the stage for a self-limiting, and non-violent approach to political change. Negotiation and dialogue were the hallmarks of the Gdańsk agreement, the short official life of Solidarity, and the Roundtable Talks in 1989.

Michnik recasts competing narratives of Polish history so that the secular intelligentsia of the "new" Left and the Catholic intellectuals can see the reasons why they should be talking to one another. Michnik the historian is careful in his attention to detail and evidence, in order to demonstrate that the views that the Church and the Left have of each other have been falsely and ideologically constructed. His revisionist account thus becomes a powerful corrective to these two separate and incomplete histories, and is evidence that *The Church and the Left* was as much a part of the process of dialogue as it was documentation of it. In chapter 2, "The Church Under Totalitarianism," Michnik reconstructs the Church's resistance to party-state domination in the late 1940s as a defense of independent forces in society and of human liberty in thought and practice, rather than as anti-communism *tout court*.

Similarly, in chapter 5, "The Church in 1968," Michnik corrects the commonly held view that the Church viewed the March events as yet one more "settling of accounts" within the Party (1993: 97). He cites Church documents that supported the students, and made veiled references to the regime's anti-Semitic counter-attack, in Cardinal Wyszyński's words, "the monstrous ghost of a revived racism ..."

(1993: 99). Nevertheless, he also harshly criticizes the Church for not having made a "clear and unequivocal denunciation of official anti-Semitism" (1993: 101). Michnik admits the Church to some degree did view the clash between leftist intellectuals as yet another intra-party struggle, tinged with anti-Semitism as had often been the case in the past (1993: 102).

In both cases, Michnik paints a more accurate picture of history and demonstrates how partial accounts have led to past misunderstandings. However, he is not afraid of hitting hard when he feels it is necessary to do so—either to further the cause of historical "truth," or simply to force a combination of awareness and contrition on both sides. Michnik wants both sides to understand how the party-state has carefully promoted the existing divisions between the Church and the independent critics of the regime in its own divide-and-rule approach, a strategy that effectively weakens any potential unity and strength of oppositional forces.[16] Finally, he does not arrive at this dialogue as a passive bystander or as a "neutral" academic carefully balancing the historical record in the interest of "objective" truth. Michnik was invariably involved in the events he describes—as a journalist eagerly interviewing Professor Konstanty Grzybowski on his hostile reaction to the 1965 Pastoral Letter, or as a student leader and activist arrested in March, 1968 and viciously slandered by the regime as an unpatriotic Jewish radical.

In the second half of *The Church and the Left*, aptly subtitled "The Politics of the Church," Michnik illustrates the similarities between Catholic teaching in Poland and the approach that is simultaneously developed among Left intellectuals. He quotes Cardinal Wyszyński at length to demonstrate the Episcopate's support for freedom of assembly and association, essential to individual development and participation in public life (1993: 116). For Michnik, the Church sanctioned the resuscitation of civil society advocated by East-Central European dissidents—all the more relevant given that the sermons he quotes from were delivered in 1974—two years before the formation of KOR. To assuage the concerns of leftist dissidents, Michnik quotes Wyszyński's support for meaningful employment and his distress over the "capitalist spirit" stemming from a "deification of material production" (1993: 116). On the subject of truth and human dignity, Michnik compares the Cardinal's exhortations to "*write the truth, defend the truth*" (emphasis in original; 1993: 120) to both Aleksandr Solzhenitsyn ("Do not live in lies!") and Leszek Kołakowski ("Live in dignity!"). If this book had been written a few years later, no doubt Michnik would have also been making a comparison to Havel's dictum "Live in truth." Notably, he cites Antoni Słonimski's comparison[17] between the ideas expressed in the papal encyclical *Populorum progressio* and the secular principles of the *Declaration of the Rights of Man*.[18] As for the secular Left, Michnik documents the "dramatic shift in attitudes" via the essays and life of Leszek Kołakowski, and his examination of Christian/Catholic doctrine and its meaning for European culture and politics.

For Michnik, the language and teachings of Christ are a meta-narrative woven through the history and culture of Christian Europe. Christian tradition cannot be merely rejected as untrue or invalid. Michnik states:

> For by rejecting Christ's teachings of love for one's neighbor, one rejects the canonical foundation of European culture. By rejecting these teachings, we lose the foundation of our belief in the autonomous value of truth and human solidarity. Belief in the divinity of Christ is a matter of Grace, and in this sense is given only to a few. But belief in the hallowed nature of Christ's commandments is the duty of all, because it is the light that protects human freedom and dignity against violence and debasement, against nihilism and the hell of solitude (1993: 123).

Essentially, Michnik provides the secular Left with political reasons why they ought to support the most basic teachings of Christ and the Church, providing tactical *terra firma* for "A new commandment I give unto you, That ye love one another" (John 13:34) and "Love your enemies, bless them that curse you" (Matthew 5:44). The best example of Michnik's approach is a famous and often retold story from his own life:

> In 1981, in the town of Otwock, Michnik was present when a crowd of Solidarity activists engulfed a policeman suspected of having beaten up two drunks. Members of the crowd threatened to lynch the policeman and burn down the police station. Michnik jumped in the middle. "Listen to me!" he shouted. "I am Adam Michnik and I am an anti-socialist element [the Party's usual term for its enemies]." He quieted the crowd. "And," he wrote to Kiszczak[19] later in a letter from prison, "I would do the same for you." (Rosenberg, 1996: 246)

Michnik may have been willing as a thoroughly secularized and assimilated Polish Jew to practise this expansive and non-dogmatic version of Christ's teaching, but was not always speaking for many of his Leftist compatriots. Encountering God or the universality of Christ's message was entirely different than coming to terms with the Church as an institution. Michnik asks the secular Left to support and recognize the "unique, suprapolitical, and otherworldly apostolic mission of the Church" (1993: 200). The Church not only plays an important *public* role in terms of social criticism based on the biblical moral code, but also reasserts an ethic of personal responsibility. Official Marxist historiography wants to "pass off moral decisions as mere consequences of historical laws"; Michnik recognizes moral responsibility underlying the humanist task of making a better world and acknowledges the possibility of a religious basis for such morality. The secular Left, already in a difficult position for having to defend socialist ideals under authoritarian communism must now embrace the Christian tradition.[20]

Michnik's dialogue is premised upon a notion of *faith* as a place where idealistic belief in a different future merges with fervor and activism in helping to bring it about. Temporal human agency is combined with a very otherworldly sense of faith, buttressed by idealism and optimism. This appears profoundly contradictory, for how can one simultaneously sustain such faith and generate any sense of self-empowerment, when the prevailing relations of power are so obviously uneven? After all, right up until 1989, the goals of the opposition in many respects belonged more to the realm of *faith* rather than any form of concrete possibility, as no constellation of social, political and international forces could be reasonably imagined that might bring about significant political change. Michnik as a non-believer cannot come close to a personal understanding of God or spiritual transcendence, but the dialogue was possible for him because of his romantic yet irreligious acceptance of faith. Faith, as he cites Father Roman Rogowski, "not as a safeguard but as a challenge" can inspire people, promote heroism, and move mountains (1993: 195). Michnik called such a path one of "question and call"—a combination of critique and faith. Such faith demands the recognition of moral rights, as well as the acceptance of responsibility and action as vocation, without which there can be no absolution politically or metaphysically.

Regardless of Michnik's exhortations to the Left to participate in a dialogue, the enemy-cum-friend did not always welcome the gesture with an open embrace. Tischner's seering critique in *Marxism and Christianity* (1987) condemns Michnik for his appropriation of the Church's moral high ground, for misunderstanding and compromising its role in Polish society both historically and in the present, and rebukes his call for dialogue. The Church, in Tischner's view, is *the* site of opposition to communism, and he confidently backs this up with the evidence of church and pilgrimage site attendance, and the overall religious devotion of ordinary Poles. However touching the recognition of some leftists of the good works of the Church, their outsider criticism does not mean the Church has any requirement to reciprocate with its own reevaluation of its past. The secular Left is fundamentally irrelevant to the roots of Polish society, and need not conduct commissions of self-flagellation or inquiry.

Ironically, Michnik's advice was almost too enthusiastically championed by both secular Leftists and Catholic intellectuals—the dialogue was eventually a victim of its own success. Thus Michnik defends the Church in *not* getting *too* involved in politics after the declaration of martial law, given his commitment to the separation of Church and State. Insofar as Michnik wanted increased dialogue with the Church and to morally ground the politics of the opposition with Polish culture (which *ipso facto* means dealing with the Catholic Church), he also wanted the Church to be separate but not removed from politics—for it to have neither the position of outlaw nor have special perquisites.[21]

The alliance between the Church (at least unofficially) and the secular Left can nonetheless be demonstrated by reference to the number of secular initiatives supported by individual priests, Catholic intellectuals, and local parishes. Priests Jan Zieja and Zbigniew Kamiński were both members of KOR. Many others were involved in protest fasts, provided space for meetings, collected money for relief activities (Bernhard, 1993: 138). After the arrest of KOR activists in 1977, both Primate Wyszyński and then-Archbishop Karol Wojtyła addressed the issue in sermons criticizing the repression of those defending human rights and privately intervened with authorities on behalf of KOR (Lipski, 1985: 157–158). Tadeusz Mazowiecki, as editor of *Więź*, played an important role collecting financial support from overseas in 1976 and acted as the spokesperson for the St. Martin's fasters in 1977. Bohdan Cywiński, editor of *Znak* and Aleksander Hauke-Ligowski joined the fast. In 1980–1981, despite the initial calls for the workers to return to work by Primate Wyszyński, Priests Henryk Jańkowski and Jerzy Popiełuszko supported Solidarity from the pulpit, and during martial law their parishes offered sanctuary. St. Brygida's Church in Gdańsk was for a long time the unofficial headquarters of Lech Wałęsa. Officially the Episcopate straddled two worlds—the opposition and the authorities—but the on-the-ground reality reflected the success of the dialogue.

"A New Evolutionism"

After the formation of KOR but before the explosion of Solidarity onto the Polish scene, Michnik was involved simultaneously as an activist and a theorist. He supplemented his public work with KOR and the TKN with another kind of political action: writing. Michnik has the unusual ability to reflect on and write about events in which he is a participant—a skill not unique but common to the dissident-theorists of the region. The facility with which particularly Michnik, Havel, and Kis could move from genuinely creative political theory to innovative action was mutually reinforcing, and thus posed a very real dilemma for the authorities. To imprison the dissidents is to provide a hothouse for writing—as Havel's *Letters to Olga* or Michnik's collection *Letters from Prison*—attest. At large, such activists are equally troublesome, as their periods of enforced reflection add new ideas, vigour, and leadership to the movements to which they belong.

In 1976 Michnik wrote what is probably the most important essay of his dissident "career," entitled "A New Evolutionism." It was both prophetic and programmatic, historically grounded, and politically concrete. In brief, Michnik's argument is that there is renewed hope for Polish opposition to authoritarian communism, to be found precisely in the interstices of Poland's geopolitical reality. Furthermore, the space for action and room to maneuvre can be enlarged through a program of action that addresses itself not to a "totalitarian power" but to "an independent public" (1985: 144). This maneuvrability and the strategy it permits Michnik calls *nowy ewolucjonizm*—new evolutionism.

Michnik accepts at face value Soviet military and political presence in Poland and the parameters this geopolitical reality places on possible evolution. Thus he immediately discards the "reform or revolution" dilemma as "unrealistic and dangerous" (1985: 142). Changing the system from within through either a revisionist or a neo-positivist approach is exhausted theoretically and by experience.[22] The revisionists working within the party, who attempted to graft onto the authoritarian party-state the principles of democratic reform and humane socialism—either in Poland or Czechoslovakia—either petered out or failed. Regardless, failure was guaranteed by the restrictions the USSR historically placed on any variance from the Soviet model. Learning the lesson of the Prague Spring, he explicitly recognizes that any form of military intervention in Poland would be disastrous.

Meaningful political change is ultimately connected to Michnik's analysis of the fortuitous concurrence of interests of the Soviet and Polish leaderships with Polish society. Michnik explains:

> For all three parties, a Soviet military intervention in Poland would be a political disaster. For the Polish leadership, such an intervention would signify dethronement or the reduction of its position of leader of a nation of thirty-four million, with limited sovereignty, to that of policemen acting on behalf of the Soviet imperium. The Soviet leaders, however, certainly remember the international repercussions of their interventions in Hungary and Czechoslovakia, as well as the resolve of the Polish workers in December 1970 and June 1976. If we include the traditional anti-Russian sentiments of the Poles, and their propensity to fight out of sheer desperation (as demonstrated, for instance, in the Warsaw Uprising of 1944), then we can conclude that a decision by Soviet leaders to intervene militarily in Poland would be equivalent to opting for war with Poland. It would be a war that Poland would lose on the battlefield but that the Soviet Union would lose politically. A victorious Soviet war with Poland would mean a national massacre for the Poles, but for the Soviets it would be a political catastrophe. This is why I believe the Soviet leaders, as well as the leadership of the PUWP [PZPR], will go far to avoid such a conflict. *This reluctance delineates the area of permissible political maneuver; this alignment of interests defines the sphere of possible compromise* (my emphasis; 1985: 143–144).

Michnik's innovation is not that "evolutionary change should be planned within the parameters of the 'Brezhnev Doctrine'"—as this was also to some degree the case with the neo-positivists and revisionists. Rather, Michnik's originality pertains to the targeted audience of reform—not the state, but society. Michnik states: "Such a program should give directives to the people on how to behave, not to the powers on how to reform themselves. Nothing instructs the authorities better than pressure from below" (1985: 144).

Michnik's scheme did not involve conventional pressure from the angry or erupting masses to the powers that be—this also had been tried, by the students in 1968 and by the workers in 1970 and 1976. Citizens acting independently in society would take responsibility for their own actions, take control over certain areas of public life, and live and act openly and in solidarity with one another. As Jonathan Schell has stated in response to "A New Evolutionism" and in consideration of KOR, the organization which the essay effectively foreshadows:

> In this deep reach of totalitarian government into daily life, which is usually seen as a source of its strength, KOR discovered a point of weakness: precisely because totalitarian governments politicize daily life, daily life becomes a vast terrain on which totalitarianism can be opposed. It was here that KOR implicitly pitted itself against the regime (Schell, "Introduction" in Michnik, 1985: xxvii).

"New evolutionism" is based on Michnik's faith that particular strata in society will rise to the occasion, most notably the workers, the Church, and the intelligentsia. Four years before the birth of Solidarity, Michnik announced:

> "New evolutionism" is based on faith in the power of the working class, which, with a steady and unyielding stand, has on several occasions forced the government to make spectacular concessions [i.e. October, 1956; December, 1970; June, 1976]. It is difficult to foresee developments in the working class, but there is no question that the power elite fears this social group most. Pressure from the working classes is a necessary condition for the evolution of public life toward a democracy (1985: 144).

The Catholic Church has a special role to play in defending truth, standing up for human freedom and dignity, by encouraging independent thought and nonconformity. The intelligentsia's historical duty is to be rigorously insubordinate, to "formulate alternative programs and defend basic principles" (1985: 147). Within this imagined drama, he even generously scripts a role for the "party pragmatist"—the party insider who may not appreciate democratic ideals but nonetheless is affected by public opinion and economic forces, and understands "the effectiveness of compromising with forces favoring plurality instead of brutally suppressing them" (1985: 146).

Michnik concludes this powerful essay by direct reference to the power of truth and implicitly to civil society as both primary defense mechanisms in the war against authoritarian communism and as bulwarks in establishing a democratic polity:

> In searching for truth, or, to quote Leszek Kołakowski, "by living in dignity," opposition intellectuals are striving not so much for a better tomorrow as a better today. Every act of defiance helps us build the framework of democratic socialism, which should not be merely or primarily a legal institutional structure but a real, day-to-day community of free people (1985: 148).

Michnik did not seek to overthrow the government of the People's Republic of Poland, nor to fundamentally destabilize the Soviet model in the region. His aims were simple and his advice direct—ignore the party-state, be active rather than passive, do what you can rather than what you cannot, take responsibility for yourself, your community, and improve your own life and the lives of those around you. The implications of his approach, far from being ephemeral adjustments to the current reality, were deeply substantive and far-reaching.

Non-violence as Theory and Practice

Violence has been historically connected with social revolutions where political upheaval and regime change were matched and indeed generated by intense and relatively sudden social transformation: in France, Russia, Mexico, and China. Violence has even become one of the defining criteria of the revolutionary process.[23] Marx himself suggested violence was unavoidable in the midst of proletarian revolution. Revolutionary movements historically have employed violence to overthrow an existing regime or government; it is part of their stock and trade. Up until 1989 it was axiomatic that the level of transformation was positively correlative with the level of violence involved in the revolutionary process. That this was so universally accepted among scholars helps to explain the reticence in defining the period 1989–1991 in Central and Eastern Europe as revolutionary at all.

In Poland, intellectual activists such as Adam Michnik and Jacek Kuroń turned this conventional wisdom upside down. Faced with the reality of the post-totalitarian Polish regime—its array of the instruments and methods of violence and deception backed up the overwhelming and inconceivable force of the nuclear arsenal of its Soviet godparent—the *choice* was made to renounce violence in its entirety. The proposition was simple: forget the military-political contest and attempt instead to introduce and increase the multilayered activities and organizations associated with normal civic life. Thus the renunciation of violence and the emphasis on civil society are two sides of the same strategy: they require and reinforce one another.

Since the Polish August and the spectacular growth of Solidarity were dubbed the "self-limiting revolution" through to the Roundtable Talks in Poland and Hungary, the fall of the Berlin Wall, and the oxymoronically titled "Velvet Revolution" in Czechoslovakia, scholars have debated whether the events constitute a revolution at all. The presence or absence of violence is discussed as a necessary but not sufficient condition; arguably "restorative" elements defeat the possibility of revolutionary designation, as does the lack or depth of required social transformation. In my view, Jonathan Schell is completely correct in judging Solidarity as not only revolutionary, but in his assessment that intellectuals like Michnik and Kuroń revolutionized the concept of revolution in the process.[24] Schell suggests that a defining feature of this "revolution in revolution" is the unwavering commitment of the opposition—not just in Poland but in Hungary and Czechoslovakia as well—to non-violent political practice.

A commitment to non-violence among Polish intellectuals was *sine qua non* for the alliance strategy between the Church and the Left promoted by Michnik. Over time non-violence became less of an indispensable condition and more of a morally-inspired credo, inspired not only by Catholic doctrine but the lessons of Polish history. The failed uprisings of the nineteenth century taught the stereotypically insurrectionary Poles that when faced with mammoth force, they could only lose.[25] Within the Polish opposition there was a keen sense of this history, and a purposefully ironic attitude. Much violence had been perpetrated on the Polish people as a result of the partitions and the

German occupation. Yet since 1945 the violence continued under the banner of their "freedom." An analysis of "freedom movements" with the Soviet Bloc after 1945 only served to strengthen the moral and political validity of non-violence. The chaotic brevity of the Hungarian revolution invited crowd-sanctioned lynchings against members of the security apparatus; this was met in turn by the harsh reprisals of the invading Soviet forces and the extent of Kádár's repression. Neither the Polish October nor the Prague Spring, peaceful though they may have been in both reformist orientation and in their ultimate defeats, were successful exercises in either democracy or freedom—primarily because their target was the party-state rather than civil society.

Adam Michnik made his most sustained defense of non-violence in his "Letter from the Gdańsk Prison." Written in 1985 during his second period of incarceration since 1981, he deliberately addresses the renunciation of violence, as a result of constant questioning by foreign observers of the Polish situation. His response is both pragmatic and idealistic. On a military-strategic level, it is obvious:

> No one in Poland is able to prove today that violence will help us dislodge Soviet troops from Poland and to remove the communists from power. The USSR has such enormous military power that confrontation is simply unthinkable. In other words, we have no guns. Napoleon, upon hearing a similar reply, gave up asking further questions. However, Napoleon was above all interested in military victories and not building democratic, pluralistic societies. We, by contrast, cannot leave it at that (1985: 36).

To be sure, the military reality forces caution, yet Michnik suggests a different logic:

> Taught by history, we suspect that by using force to storm the existing Bastilles we shall unwittingly build new ones. It is true that social change is almost always accompanied by force. But it is not true that social change is merely a result of the violent collision of various forces. Above all, social changes follow from a confrontation of different moralities and visions of social order. Before the violence of rulers clashes with the violence of their subjects, values and systems of ethics clash inside human minds. Only when the old ideas of the rulers lose this moral duel will the subjects reach for force—sometimes. This is what happened in the French Revolution and the Russian Revolution—two examples cited in every debate as proof that

revolutionary violence is preceded by a moral breakdown in the old regime. But both examples lose their meaning when they are reduced to such compact notions, in which the Encyclopedists are paired with the destruction of the Bastille, and the success of radical ideologies in Russia is paired with the storming of the Winter Palace (1985: 86–87).

Michnik is concerned with separating the collision of "different moralities and visions of social order" from the attendance of violence on the landscape of political change. The alternative vision can win hearts and minds without violence, and can even provisionally succeed.[26] The *discipline* necessary for non-violence displays an "historical awareness of the possible consequences of revolutionary violence." Acknowledging that terror corrupts is essential to a contemporary freedom movement. Non-violence as a moral and political choice is also characteristic of the contingent nature of the Polish self-limiting revolution. For Michnik, revolutionary terror and violence usually accompany Promethean visions of an ideal society, where "the road to God's Kingdom on Earth led through rivers of blood." Non-violence thus becomes an explicit rejection of Leninism and Jacobinism. Violence is never ennobling nor redeeming, even when deployed by the oppressed in the name of freedom, welfare, or a just society.[27]

Solidarity was not an alternative to the authorities or an instrument in a broader struggle for power, a position which made violence redundant. Michnik states:

> Solidarity has never had a vision of an ideal society. It wants to live and let live. Its ideals are closer to the American Revolution than to the French. Its thinking about goals is similar to that of the resistance against Franco in Spain, or against the "black colonels" in Greece; it is unlike the thinking of those who strive to attain doctrinal goals. The ethics of Solidarity, with its consistent rejection of the use of force, has a lot in common with the idea of nonviolence as espoused by Gandhi and Martin Luther King Jr.

Michnik is also turning conventional twentieth century wisdom about non-violence on its head. According to this argument, non-violence, passive resistance, or civil disobedience can only have a significant political impact in states or societies where boundaries to legitimate authority are recognized and independent political opinion can be formed and expressed as a countervailing measure to arbitrary abuses of state power. Thus passive resistance worked in India because it was imperially controlled by Britain and the civil rights movement was able to galvanize support in America precisely because of the political space afforded free public discourse in both countries. This explanation logically denies the possible success of non-violence under a regime which defines its own limits. The true impact of the Polish opposition was the wide swath of autonomy it cut for itself outside the official realm—as measured by the continuation of Solidarity and other organizations underground after 1981, the persistence of the underground press, the TKN seminars, and the spiritual independence and material aid provided by the Church. It was deliberately inward looking and therefore defined its own success. Thus in his essay "The Polish War," written in 1982 at the nadir of the Polish opposition, Michnik could confidently counter party reformer Stefan Bratkowski's claim that "no one can sit on a bayonet"[28] with the reply that "no one can use a bayonet to wipe fifteen months of freedom from human memory" (1985: 35).

Kuroń: A Bridge between Generations

In 1968 the student activists demanded "real socialism" in the place of the bureaucratically stagnant party-state. Many of those leading the protests—such as Michnik, Lityński, and Blumsztajn—looked to Jacek Kuroń as the kind of activist-intellectual they themselves wanted to be. Unlike Kołakowski, Kuroń was not a privileged party intellectual who first turned revisionist and then rejected the party-state entirely. Kuroń was also too young to have been involved in the intellectual thaw of the late 50s. However, first as a scout leader and later as a scholar-researcher at Warsaw University and coauthor with Karol Modzelewski of the famous "Open Letter," he was a mentor *par excellence* for the generation of '68.

The *Open Letter to the Party* was first published in Polish in Paris in 1966 (*List Otwarty Do Partii*), and thanks to its adoption as credo by the International Socialists, was translated into English, French, German, and Italian and widely distributed. It is a classically Trotskyist critique of authoritarian communism—as statist, anti-democratic, hierarchical, bureaucratic, and responsible for generating contradictions in production and social relations. All political decisions were made undemocratically by a narrow elite possessing monolithic and monopolistic control; counter-organization or opinion and the creation of political alternatives were strictly prohibited.

The party-state had translated its control over the economy into a form of ownership, and worse still, had done so to the overall detriment of Poland's working class. Kuroń and Modzelewski analyzed the economic crises and contradictions endemic to the system. They criticized the overall "class goal of the bureaucracy"—which they describe as production for the sake of production. Industrial saturation worked well in the early postwar period, especially when new infrastructure was desperately needed, but led to over-expansion. Extensive industrial growth meant in practice a "general inadaptation of production to needs" (1982: 41), most profoundly indicated by the low level of household consumption. It generated a deficit in raw materials and fuel, which was, in turn, exacerbated by waste, shortages of key tools and equipment, and inefficient production processes. The system seemed incapable of making the switch to a pattern of intensively-oriented growth, where increased productivity would arise from modernization, technical progress, product innovation, cost reduction, and new methods of organization. This analysis is hardly original given the volumes now published on the inefficiencies of the Soviet economic model. However, its timing and appearance on the Polish scene, coupled with the fact that it was written by two graduate students in disarmingly frank language, *operating within a Marxist framework*, made it especially threatening and in hindsight, more compelling.

Obviously the party elites did not welcome such criticism. What was more damning was the evidence collected by Modzelewski and Kuroń with respect to the sociological condition of the working class. The authors carefully documented everything from how often Polish families consumed meat to the type of clothes worn (how many suits, of what cloth and quality). They included statistics on living space, incidence of hot and cold running water, and health conditions.[29] State-provided housing and medical care were important, but placed in the context of the worker's minimal existence, did little to achieve class betterment. "Benefits" existed to ensure the continued social reproduction of labor power:

> As a rule, the worker has the advantage of living very inexpensively in a government-owned building. His lodging is therefore *part* free. But to live and produce he must stay somewhere. At any rate, his apartment rarely

has any luxuries and in most cases not even the elementary comforts. It is part of his subsistence minimum, supplied to him in addition to his wages.

The workers receive medical care free and can buy medicines at a discount, but these are necessary in order to preserve his labor power: they are ingredients of his subsistence minimum. If free medical care were abolished and rents increased, the worker's wages would have to be raised in proportion to the increase in his necessary expenses. These non-returnable benefits and services are a necessary part of the worker's subsistence minimum, a wage supplement as necessary to the worker as the wages themselves, and therefore a constituent of production cost (1982: 21).

Kuroń and Modzelewski dismiss the much-vaunted benefits of state socialism as a necessary production cost, unrelated to any ideological or altruistic claim about the satisfaction of basic human needs.

What got Kuroń and Modzelewski into real trouble with the authorities, however, were their revolutionary aims and conclusions. They argued that proletarian revolution was inevitable—perhaps not in the sense of a "call to arms" but certainly in terms of societal revolt against the rule of the privileged minority. They foresaw the type of chaos that would result from an uprising of discontented and disorganized masses, as happened in December, 1970. Avoiding such a confrontation required greater and more genuine political participation and democratization via the creation of a "workers' multiparty system," the management of enterprises via workers' councils, peasant control of both land and agricultural products, at minimum the independence of existing trade unions, the abolition of "preventive censorship" and the dissolution of the political security apparatus (1982: 72–76). Taken as a whole, their programme constituted, "an anti-bureaucratic revolution" which they recognized would be threatening for the "established world order"—meaning both the Soviet Union and its satellites *as well as* Western capitalist and imperialist states.

The publication of the letter and the subsequent arrest of the authors served as an important example in terms of formulating an open rather than clandestine political opposition. After drafting their proposals, Kuroń and Modzelewski sought comments from university scholars in the History, Economics, and Philosophy Departments. In accordance with party regulations, they submitted their letter to the Warsaw party organization.[30] Instead of an expected debate, they were arrested the following day on 19 March, 1965. Their arrest, secret trial, and imprisonment initiated a series of shock waves among intellectuals and students, initiating the period of student unrest that came to a head in 1968.

Kuroń himself was sidelined during the March events of 1968, serving the first of a number of prison sentences that did not end until 1972. His removal from the immediate political fray created the conditions for detached observation and reflection on 1968 and 1970, resulting in a new direction in his political thinking.[31] Like Kołakowski, Kuroń saw the need to shift focus away from the party-state in terms of reform efforts. For Kołakowski this was vaguely presented, in terms of the "preservation of Polish culture" and the importance of "living in dignity." Kuroń was able to put some flesh on Kołakowski's theory, suggesting that an independent culture and society is not a precursor to a more organized political opposition, but can *itself* constitute—both formally and informally—an opposition and simultaneously aid in the democratizing process (Ost, 1990: 64). The heart of Kuroń's idea of self-organization—*samoorganizacja*—is that through the constant formation and reformation of initiatives, movements, and organizations citizens create and expand public space, and in so doing build democracy and reinforce democratic values. In the same manner as de Tocqueville and indeed Masaryk, Kuroń saw such "public work" as contributing to social tranquillity, generating positive material results, serving as *de facto* schools in teaching the values of associational freedom, contributing to an appreciation and the actual practise of freedom of the press, and providing engaged citizens with a sense of common good and purpose.[32]

Kuroń's theoretical development can be documented in a number of essays he wrote in the 1970s, such as "Politics and Opposition in Poland" (1974), "Reflections on a Program of Action" (1976), "Notes on Self-government" (1977), and "The Situation of the Country and the Program of the Opposition" (1979).[33] He introduces his ideas about opposition in and through an independent (civil) society and in so doing reconceptualizes his earlier ideas about democratization and emphasizes the significance of the independent social initiatives and organizations, paralleling the thought of Adam Michnik.

Whereas in the "Open Letter" democratization involved bursting open the doors of the party-state and making its organs and agencies responsive and truly participatory, a different notion of democratization is involved in "Politics and Opposition in Poland." Here Kuroń discusses democracy as the continually expanding sphere of non-coerced social activity. As Ost suggests, Kuroń's views are rooted both in Marxist humanist notions of praxis and creative human fulfillment, as well as Isaiah Berlin's (and J. S. Mill's) concept of positive freedom (1990: 65). Democratic strategy is directed away from the party-state and aimed at society. Rather than emphasize the relative autonomy of the parliamentary parties in the *Sejm* (other than the PZPR) or the existence of free and fair elections of the deputies themselves, Kuroń steered clear away from the leading role of the party and the political rigidity of the party-state. He chose to concentrate on citizenship rights and democratic freedoms where the ability to organize autonomous associations is at stake—such as free assembly and association over voting rights.

Because of the false and forced "unity" of politics and society under authoritarian communism, politics itself takes on a new and broader meaning. As the party-state must eliminate independent civil society in order to demonstrate the validity of its rule under the banner of the "universal" class—the proletariat—any action to revive independent activity constitutes political opposition. Thus Kuroń declares at the beginning of his article,

> There are people in Poland today who are intentionally counteracting the fundamental principles of the system, a system that has been imposed on society by state power. These people are so numerous, and occupy such a significant place in society, that we can speak of the movement of political opposition as being a permanent element of life in Poland (cited in Ost, 1990: 65–66).

The participants in this opposition were involved in what Kuroń calls "reconstructing social ties"—that were not viewed as conventionally political.

Ironically, while Kołakowski was in exile trading polemics with the British New Left and taking issue with the aspirations of the "new social movements" produced by the 1960s, a very similar undertaking was being theorized by Kuroń and his Polish counterparts. After the initial success of KOR following the Radom–Ursus riots in 1976, Kuroń became increasingly optimistic about social self-organization. Thus in 1976, after Michnik writes "A New Evolutionism" Kuroń echoes his sentiments in "Reflections on a Program of Action" with a proposition that such organization continue with the interweaving of new social movements:

> It is essential ... that society should organize itself into social movements, interacting on each other [and] expressing as fully as possible the aspirations of all. This is the program for creating in the social movements ... a Poland which is the concern of every citizen and social activity: a country of integrated social action and thought (Kuroń, 1977: 69).

Kuroń differentiates other forms of resistance currently in operation in people's Poland. He discusses the prevalence of illegal enterprise and self-serving fraud and bribery—what political scientists often call clientelism and rent seeking—as well as quasi-official manipulations of institutional budgets, plan targets, and annual results, amounting to a form of political game playing and state planning roulette designed to increase the local share of the national pie. He contrasts this private, individualized, and socially disruptive form of resistance with open, organized protest. By this he refers to the synchronized organization of groups into social movements. The key goal is social solidarity, which is multiplied through the very action of building social movements and independent groups. Democratic values of trust, cooperation and solidarity are so important in Kuroń's view that they overshadow the need for particular demands or a program of action (1977: 67).

Kuroń does not consider such an approach to be utopian. He cites four key experiences from the previous thirty years to demonstrate the possibility of substantive gain. First, successful Polish peasant resistance to collectivization and nationalization remained for Kuroń one of the key lasting legacies of the Polish October. Second, in the periodic protest movements of workers in defense of their pay and social benefits—in 1956–1957, 1970–1971, and in 1976—a heavy price was often paid in terms of casualties and police violence, but many of their demands were ultimately met.[34] Third, the activity of the laity and the Episcopate in maintaining and strengthening the independence of the Catholic Church represented a mass social movement unlike the limited and often compromised role of many other churches in the Bloc. Fundamentally and philosophically through its defense of individual freedom, freedom of conscience, and the dignity of the individual, the Church has reinforced important "universal values" consonant with Poland's national historic culture (1977: 62). Finally, the collective efforts of writers, scholars, artists, and intellectuals in their efforts to maintain and further independent social ideas, keep alive the national history, and preserve and support the values of honesty, non-conformity, truth, and courage, was itself a resistance movement. According to Kuroń, each of these movements

> ... restricts the power of the totalitarian state with a considerable measure of success. But none of them would have been successful, or at least so successful, if it had to operate on its own. The interdependence of all four and their continued existence since 1956 are essential features of our social reality (1977: 63).

Every new organization constitutes a tiny but important ice pick chipping away, at times almost imperceptibly, at the monopoly of the party-state. In the "Open Letter," Kuroń and Modzelewski argued that revolutionary change would have to occur before authentic and meaningful democratic political activity could take place. In the 1970s and 1980s such activity itself constituted democratic action and was profoundly transformative in nature (Ost, 1990: 69). In "Reflections of a Program of Action" Kuroń almost discusses his ultimate goal of "Finlandization"—a parliamentary democracy with limited international sovereignty—in passing, partially because he now finds it impossible to separate political ends from their means of achievement.[35]

Like Michnik, Kuroń argues that although the self-organization of Polish society is a necessary condition for the democratizing process, the opposition must be careful to be "self-limiting" in its aims. The goal must be to improve, not overthrow, due to the ever-present threat of external intervention. Self-limitation, however, has other objectives, such as building social cooperation and solidarity. More dangerous than the threat of intervention is a retreat to apathy on the one hand, or spontaneous anarchic protest on the other. These arguments are seemingly contradictory—how can self-organization be deeply transformative and democratic on the one hand, and self-limiting on the other? The answer lies in the related assumptions that transformative politics need not be revolutionary (in the conventional sense) and that democracy cannot be reduced to institutional arrangements. Both Kuroń and Michnik clearly understood that democracy is as much about process as product, means as ends. Thus they grasped both theoretically and in the Polish context that democracy is something that defies easy categorization or definition.[36]

Kuroń's commitment to self-organization as the primary means of democratization led him to be critical of Solidarity itself, especially in the mid-to-late 1980s during its long and protracted "war of position" with the Polish authorities. In "Landscape after the Battle" he analyzes the deadlock activists felt in their underground existence.[37] He argues against two commonly held views—that nothing had changed (the Polish "war" successfully reversed Solidarity's gains) and that nothing must be changed (in terms of the tightly knit underground survival strategy adopted by Solidarity's Provisional Council).

Against the first claim, Kuroń reminds his readership that "a counter-revolution—and what started on December 13, 1981 could be described as such—never returns the social situation to the time before the revolution" (1988: 30). Despite martial law, significant and lasting gains were made. Solidarity was not completely liquidated, but successfully organized itself underground. Institutional pluralism was defended and indeed flourished—so much so that the official press organs presented social and economic reality in a much truer light. The authorities knew that without a radical improvement in living conditions—perhaps through comprehensive social and economic restructuring—political legitimacy could not be restored. Kuroń wants underground activists to recognize the "complex character of the counter-revolution" and the successes achieved by Solidarity. In particular, he wants to quash zero-sum commentaries that suggest if *all* had not changed, then *nothing* had been achieved (1988: 31).

Against the second claim, Kuroń suggests that activists must adapt themselves to the new situation. In light of Gorbachev's reforms, the release of Wałęsa, and the open publication of *Res Publica*—Solidarity cannot keep itself underground. Anticipating criticism, Kuroń recognizes that while many Poles fearfully avoid involvement with Solidarity as an illegal and banned organization, the vast majority sympathizes with the movement and completely mistrusts the regime. He recommends that Solidarity be involved with new structures in the official and unofficial spheres, and keep pace with a rapidly-evolving reality, given the sprouting of organizations initiated by younger activists not involved in either the rank-and-file or the leadership of the underground movement. He states:

It is the official and unofficial spheres which are now of the greatest significance—all kinds of cooperatives, partnerships, self-governments (particularly local ones)—associations, independent but officially recognized
publishers. Here the movement has the opportunity to regain its popular
character. People truly committed to Solidarity, but fearful of illegality and
all kinds of unrest, can join the official activities which have our support.
What is equally important is that in this way, the extent to which society
makes its decisions concerning itself may be radically increased—it can in
reality start building from the foundations a democratic order. I believe
that Solidarity structures should service this kind of activity—initiating
various actions, organizing professional assistance, and providing publishing facilities to help in organizing all types of actions which put pressure
on the authorities. In workplaces, all possible official means, starting with
meetings and ending with the new unions, should be taken advantage of
(1988: 32).

Reminiscent of Luxemburg's critique of Lenin, Kuroń remained fearful of the "vanguardization" of the Polish movement, which should
strive to remain popular, rooted locally in terms of organization and
orientation. The movement was no "party"—it was the anti-party.

For Kuroń, such an approach is necessary for the Polish opposition
to remain dynamic, willing, and able to push open windows of political opportunity. No matter what happens on the international and
domestic political scene "readiness does not mean merely waiting ... it
means action" (1988: 32). Although he could only guess at the ramifications of his strategy, the approach he takes indicates a shift in the
"us versus them" attitude of the Polish opposition, a necessary step
on the way to the Roundtable Talks.

Theorizing Civil Society: The Polish Case

The Polish conceptualization of civil society was intrinsically tied to
the unfolding of dramatic events—from the workers' massacre in 1970
through to the formation of KOR in response to Radom/Ursus in
1976, culminating in "the Polish August" and formation of Solidarity
in 1980. Solidarity was the proof in the pudding; its independent existence indicated not the formation of a trade union *per se*, but in Michnik's words, "the promise of a civil society" (1985: 124). In August

1981, a year after the Gdańsk negotiations and four months before the imposition of martial law, Michnik wrote:

On the last day of August 1980 the deputy premier of the government of the Polish People's Republic, Mieczysław Jagielski, and the chairman of the Interfactory Strike Committee, Lech Wałęsa, signed an agreement on the grounds of the Lenin Shipyard in Gdańsk; it was clear to all that a new chapter had opened in Poland's history. Much was said at the time about this being a social agreement," although it was only a preliminary one, merely a compromise that could temporarily satisfy both the government and the people. For the first time organized authority was signing an accord with an organized society. The agreement marked the creation of labor unions independent of the state which vowed not to attempt to take over political power.

The essence of the spontaneously growing Independent and Self-governing Labor Union Solidarity lay in the restoration of social ties, self-organization aimed at guaranteeing the defense of labor, civil, and national rights. For the first time in the history of communist rule in Poland "civil society" was being restored, and it was reaching a compromise with the state (1985: 124).

The success of Solidarity lay in the *originality* of its approach. In contrasting the "Polish experiment" with the Hungarian revolution and the Prague Spring, Michnik contends that two essential differences must be stressed; "the first regards the direction of the changes; the second, their reach" (1985: 125). Whereas in Hungary the party apparatus disintegrated in the face of a rebellious popular uprising and the Prague Spring occurred because of a sweeping reformist impulse for change from above, the Polish events were much more limited, and centered on activities *beyond* and *outside* the party-state.

Solidarity signaled the death of revisionism—heralded by Kołakowski and proclaimed by Michnik. The eulogy for revisionism made new forms of democratization thinkable; events in Poland made civil society possible. In his retrospective analysis "The Prague Spring Ten Years Later" Michnik states:

This paradigm [East European revisionism] belongs to history, however, and it will never repeat itself. This is why all those who believe in the democratic evolution of the countries of Eastern Europe and who are waiting for another Twentieth Congress of the CPSU or for another January plenum of the Central Committee of the Czechoslovak Communist party are deluding themselves. I have in mind especially the Italian and French Eurocommunists, who are waiting, once again, for the inspiration of a democratization process to come from the upper strata of the party apparatus. They are wrong because these days joining a ruling Communist party is the choice of opportunists. Those who believe in the ideals of liberty, equality, and the freedom of labor can be found only in the ranks of the antitotalitarian opposition. It is from them that the impulse for democratic actions must now arise. Such actions are unique in that they do not aim to win power but to help society organize itself through the gradual emancipation of groups and individuals from the grip of the all-powerful apparatus. The people have to look after their own interests, the independent flow of information, free learning and culture. Society must transform itself from a "sack of potatoes" (we owe this apt metaphor to Marx) into the executor of its own interests and aspirations. Only such a society can effectively oppose totalitarianism and become a real partner in power (1985: 158).

Michnik and Kuroń appreciated that Solidarity meant many things to many people, especially so in the case of competing intellectual analyses. Western intellectuals and activists flocked to "Solidarity Studies" because in the new union or social movement one could find almost any and every political tendency. Thus Alain Touraine looked to Solidarity to confirm his ideas about social movement form and organization, Reaganite policy wonks found the ultimate people's expression of anti-communism, marginalized Western Trotskyists noted the promise of worker radicalism and applauded the potential for shopfloor organization and revolution, and academics within and on the edges of the American "Slavic Studies" establishment mulled over the meaning of it all for the better part of a decade. This was entirely the point, for as Michnik said:

> ... the Solidarity union is everything at the same time: a labor union that defends the rights of the working people in their places of employment; an office that prosecutes lawbreakers in the power apparatus; a defender of political prisoners, law and order, and an independent culture—a true representative of the people in dealings with the authorities (1985: 129).

Michnik pointed out that Solidarity was definitely *not* a political party in the institutional sense; it had neither the ability nor the desire to take power.

Within Poland, different terms were used to identify this civil society-oriented approach.[38] Michnik was most direct in his appropriation of the term "civil society" and the theoretical heritage that lay behind it. Kuroń preferred to speak of independent social movements rather than an independent or civil society, which fit into his paradigm of activist citizenship. Later he spoke more of self-organization or social self-organization, again privileging process and involvement over static description.

Polish economist Tadeusz Kowalik noted that discussion of an independent society—however it was called—had important precedents in Polish history:

> Similar concepts were used in the nineteenth century when they meant a struggle for state independence. For example, Edward Abramowski (1868–1918), a socialist and cooperativist thinker, whose ideas Oskar Lange called 'constructive anarchism', can be regarded as the first theoretician of an 'independent society' in this sense (unpublished response).

Historian Bronisław Geremek noted the history of civil society *as a form of opposition to the state* had resonance for Poland and consciously linked this project to broader European traditions. Notably he cites the influence of both liberal and socialist—Lockean and Gramscian—lineages of civil society. From the Enlightenment, Locke, and the French *Declaration of the Rights of Man and Citizen*, Poles took seriously the conviction that society must rest on the consent of the governed, that civil society exists prior to the imposition of political rule, and that such rule must rest on some form of contract or mutual agreement. This view of civil society views human beings as free and equal citizens capable of formulating public opinion, expressing some form of Rousseauan *volonté générale*, and establishing a community in defense of the public good. Like Kołakowski, Geremek sees Marx's view of civil society as an instrument of class rule and an unfortunate precursor to the Jacobin model of powerfully centralized state, epitomized in the twentieth century by the Soviet model. However, he finds within Gramsci's writings the vision of a "regulated" society where the state is more marginal in terms of the distribution of power, where political life is focused "on a kind of positional warfare over hegemony in civil society rather than power in the state" (Geremek, 1992: 5).[39] He notes that "in both the liberal and socialist visions of civil society, the organizing principle is some notion of human rights—and by no means only those that concern the political sphere" (1992: 5). The postwar definition of human rights bridged the differences between competing explanations of civil society.

How civil society was defined theoretically had important consequences for how Poles viewed what they were doing as oppositional, and with either potentially profound and deeply structural consequences or responsible for piecemeal change. This relationship between theory and practice is elucidated clearly by Geremek:

> The notion of an independent society also had another meaning, referring to the Gdańsk agreements, i.e. a widening of the sphere of independence of social life, in the economy, and in culture and science, while preserving the principle of the monopoly of party rule in the state. One could say that we were assuming (although the assumption was never confirmed in practice anywhere in Eastern Europe) that the government would be willing to limit its monopoly and for example, to free the national economy, education, science and culture from the system of the *nomenklatura*. Is it possible to achieve this as a result of the evolutionary change of the system? One cannot exclude this, even abandoning revisionist illusions, but it is society itself which is undergoing most important transformations.
>
> Seen on the broadest scale the Polish situation shows so far the possibilities of creating a civil society independently of the will and intentions of the authorities. This is more than a phenomenon of dissidence, and is different from the classical notion of opposition, which was based on striving to take over power. *Société civile*, in Polish conditions, presupposes mass opposition against the structures of authoritarian rule; it assumes the presence of individuals and institutions truly acting in the name of this society and the possibility of group actions aimed at the well-being of the country (unpublished response).

Writing after the fall of authoritarian communism, Geremek similarly reflected on civil society as the *idée centrale* behind the Polish opposition generally and Solidarity specifically:

The concept of civil society, understood as a program of resistance to communism, first appeared in Poland during the late 1970s and early 1980s, primarily in conjunction with the Solidarity movement. At long last there had appeared in the communist world an independent mass movement to contradict the ruling system. Organized as a labor union, Solidarity could boast not only ten million urban members—both workers and intellectuals—but also the support of the peasants, who made up in anticommunist intensity what they lacked in organization. Even Poland's three-million member Communist Party could not be said to be fully outside this movement, for one-third of its members also belonged to Solidarity—and by no means simply as fomenters of internal division. When Solidarity spoke, therefore, it could do so in the name of "We, the People" (Geremek, 1992: 4).

Civil society enabled the dissidents to move from the isolated, marginal, or even hopeless resistance to an effective oppositional force. When Polish dissidents speak of *opozycja*, they connote the mobilization of civil society. *Opozycja* is not about an institutionalized or partisan opposition, nor the isolated activities of a small group of naysayers or disenchanted intellectuals disconnected from society.[40] Michnik and Lipski state:

> In Kuroń's thinking the movement for independent institutions can be classified as political opposition. In our opinion these independent institutions form a part of the broad movement of demands for civil rights, a movement aiming to make our society democratic and autonomous (Michnik, 1985: 150).

Michnik and Lipski were responding to Kuroń's advocacy of a "movement of demands" in the 1970s—practical and non-political pressure on the authorities that would prevent a possible social explosion. Like in his essay "Landscape after the Battle" the question arose of collaboration and exploitation of the semi-official "gray zone" as either possible or desirable. Michnik and Lipski properly clarify the subtleties of Kuroń's argument. The "movement of independent institutions" or civil society and the "program of demands within official institutions" run on parallel rather than intersecting courses. Finally, civil society as a unifying theoretical umbrella brought together the various themes of the Polish dissidents, such as political responsibility,

Kołakowski's early exhortation to "live in dignity," the moral and practical importance of non-violence, and the need bring together the historically disparate strands of Polish opposition. Geremek acknowledges the naiveté of Solidarity's conviction that it might gradually isolate the party-state apparatus and inject more societal involvement in politics, but asks us to realize the power of this potential:

> The naivete of this conviction was obvious, but its power could not be ignored. The simple old ethical injunction "Do not lie" had, after all, enormous political significance in widening resistance to the communist system. Moreover, the cost of such nonviolent resistance was low, while its consequences were far-reaching indeed. Even the crudest totalitarian system requires a certain amount of societal acquiescence. Such systems thrive on political passivity, but they also need a certain amount of participation, even in fictional forms such as voting in fake elections designed to foster the appearance of democratic legitimacy. Moral resistance, though seemingly hopeless against systems that are based on political and military force, functions like a grain of sand in the cogwheels of a vast but vulnerable machine. The idea of civil society—even one that avoids overtly political activities in favor of education, the exchange of information and opinion, or the protection of the basic interests of particular groups—has enormous antitotalitarian potential (1992: 4).

CHAPTER 6

OPPOSITION INTELLECTUALS IN CZECHOSLOVAKIA

Václav Havel's Theatre of the Absurd

Václav Havel did not make his reputation as a political essayist or social critic, but as a playwright. During his eight-year tenure at the Theatre on the Balustrade in the 1960s in Prague, he honed his writing abilities as a master of the Czech theatre of the absurd.[1] In Havel's 1986 interview with Karel Hvížd'ala, he muses about the definition and meaning of absurd theatre:

> [Absurd theatre is] the most significant theatrical phenomenon of the twentieth century, because it demonstrates modern humanity in a "state of crisis," as it were. That is, it shows man having lost his fundamental metaphysical certainty, the experience of the absolute, his relationship to eternity, the sensation of meaning—in other words, having lost the ground under his feet (1990: 53).

Characters in absurd theatre generally and in Havel's plays in particular are in keeping with his down-to-earth views. There is an existential human connectedness and sense of hope despite the chaos and crisis evident in our surroundings. Truth is communicated in everyday, almost trivial situations. Characters are neither overtly nor intentionally philosophical, but in their very banality manage to convey deeper meaning. There is a thread of common and unheroic decency to the good, and unselfaware oafishness to the bad. Havel's characters are neither passionate nor didactic; they know "the phenomenon of endless embarrassment" (1990: 54). His plays from this period are strong, witty, and ironic, somewhat reminiscent of Chekhov, Beckett, and Ionesco and at the same time undeniably Czech in the thought and behavior patterns of the protagonists.[2] One can feel Kafka and Hašek's Švejk looming in the background of his dramas; the sharply comic aspect of many performances owed much to Prague's Liberated Theatre of the 1920s.[3]

Because Havel wrote in both absurdist and philosophical traditions, one cannot neatly separate his dramas from his samizdat writing in the 1970s and 1980s, as "early" versus "later," "fiction" versus "non-fiction," or "drama" versus "essay/critique."[4] In reading Havel's plays and other writings in sequence chronologically, one is struck by the continuous nature of his development as a writer, regardless of the nature of the material. Havel the playwright cannot be divorced from Havel the political thinker—they are the same person. On the basis of plot development and content alone, Havel's plays are *political*. However, they are *theoretical* given their obvious engagement with such themes as the relationship between language and politics, identity and responsibility, and the personal implications of "living in truth." In *The Memorandum* he brings to life the depersonalization of power and the insidious consequences of using language for political ends; in all the "Vaněk" plays we see the what follows from the momentous decision to "live in truth."[5] Earlier plays stand apart from the plays written after his initial prison experiences in their more intensely personal approach, implying a more troublesome and private series of moral choices, rather than simply the engagement of individuals with de-humanizing bureaucracies and the absurdities of modern organizations and life situations. This process reaches a climax in *Temptation*, Havel's confrontation with the Faustian dilemma.

The best known of Havel's early plays is *The Memorandum*. First written and performed in 1966 at the Balustrade, it was quickly translated and produced abroad. American theatre impresario Joe Papp first brought it to the stage in the United States in 1967; it received considerable critical acclaim and won the 1967–1968 Obie Award for Best Foreign Play. The logic of the story is internal to the bizarre twists of partisan orthodoxy and the types of behavior inspired by the bureaucracy endemic to authoritarian communism. Its generality, simplicity, and playful humor resonate with any audience living in a modern mid-century setting. The play addresses both bureaucratic alienation and the impossibility of assigning accountability—reminiscent of Kołakowski's conclusion that responsibility cannot be located in the collective.[6]

In *The Memorandum* the managing director of a large organization catches wind that a new language called *Ptydepe* is being introduced throughout the office, ostensibly at his behest.[7] The new language, based on scientific principles of rationality and thus the theoretical opposite of all "natural" languages, will supposedly erase all possibilities for error and miscommunication. Paradoxically, the language is almost impossible to use and to learn, and an entire apparatus must be constructed for its effective implementation: a translation centre, special methodicians called Ptydepists installed in every office department to monitor correct usage, and of course an array of new rules and regulations governing its procedural deployment. The introduction of *Ptydepe* is actually the brainchild of the deputy director Ballas and his silent sidekick Pillar. He keeps the managing director Gross in the dark to ensure that no obstacles stand in the way of implementation, and as an ingenious method of engineering a management coup.

Ballas is an individual defined by communist rationality. Entirely instrumental in outlook and action, he conflates his own personal interests with the overall good of the organization, with all means justifying any desired end. Gross protests to Ballas about his deviousness and his attempts to "set up" Gross and smear his character. He states: "Good God! Don't you make yourself sick?" To which Ballas predictably and amiably replies: "Of course we don't. When the good of Man is at stake, nothing will make us sick" (1980: 32).[8] As a result of Ballas' innuendo and the false correlations he draws between Gross' motives and his behavior, he forces Gross not to resign but to switch positions, taking the deputy directorship. In a statement completely stereotypical of every partisan victim of a bureaucratic purge trying to retrieve something in the name of a larger cause, Gross explains to an underling: "There was nothing else I could do. An open conflict would have meant that I'd be finished. This way—as Deputy Director—I can at least salvage this and that" (1980: 35).

Havel is incredibly perceptive in this interchange between Ballas and Gross. Art imitates life, for Gross' dilemma is equivalent to that of the Writers' Union in their attempts to quash the literary periodical *Tvář*, where Havel was an editor. In attempting to ban the "independent" periodical that they could not control, the logic of the "antidogmatic establishment" was to make a minor compromise and appease the hard-liners by getting rid of *Tvář*.[9] By this logic, to risk open conflict endangered a struggle of greater importance, such as the general liberalization of conditions and greater "democracy" within the party at all levels.[10] This is not a cute literary device but the epitome of what Havel called "self-destructive politics." As an insider, Gross' moral weakness in *The Memorandum* is his inability to step outside of this logic; by accepting it, he promotes its future usage. This is exactly what

Havel refused to do in his own defining experience of initial dissent in refusing to toe the Writers' Union line *vis-à-vis Tvář*. He revealed this early lesson by reflecting that the model of political behavior exhibited was just as critical as the actual content of the magazine itself:

> We introduced a new model of behavior: don't get involved in diffuse general ideological polemics with the center, to whom numerous concrete causes are always being "sacrificed"; fight "only" for those concrete causes, and be prepared to fight for them unswervingly, to the end. In other words, don't get mixed up in backroom wheeling and dealing, but play an open game (1990: 83).

The logical absurdity of Gross' position is made clearer on the verge of his "rehabilitation" by Ballas. Gross confides in Maria, the secretary of the translation center, and she makes a concerted effort to revive his spirits. His response is telling:

MARIA: If your conscience is clear, you've nothing to worry about. Your innocence will be proved, but you have to fight for it! I believe that if one doesn't give way, truth must always come out in the end.

GROSS: *(walks to Maria, sadly smiles at her and strokes her cheek)*: What do you know about the world, dear child! Still, I wish you could always stay like this! You're right, one really ought to stand firm. The trouble is, I've never been very firm, more of an intellectual, always hesitant, always full of doubts, too considerate, a dreamer rather than a man of action—and that's my bad luck.
(Pause.)

GROSS: When I think back, I see that I muddled up many things in my life myself. I often gave in too soon, yielded to threats, and I trusted people too much.
(Pause.)

GROSS: If I ever have any influence on the course of things again, I'll do everything differently. More real deeds and fewer clever words! I've never been sufficiently matter-of-fact, coolheaded, proud, severe, and critical—especially with myself.
(Pause.)

GROSS: It may be partly because I belong to an odd, lost generation. We've given ourselves out in small change, we invested the best years of our lives into things which turned out not to be worth it. We were so busy for so long talking about our great mission that we quite forgot to do anything great. In short, we were a mess! *(Pause.)*

GROSS: But I believe that now I can at least face all this frankly, without hysteria and without self-pity; that I'll manage to recover from all the upheavals; that I'm still able to forget the past and make a quite new and quite different beginning (1980: 68–69).

We are not surprised to learn that Gross, trained for so long in compromise and complacency, fails the first test of his newly declared courage. He assumes the position of Managing Director once more, but is ultimately unable to purge the organization of Ballas. He cannot "learn" the lesson provided by his earlier experiences of alienation, estrangement, and marginalization. He is exonerated but cannot exonerate himself, unable to take a new stand involving responsibility and courage. Indeed Ballas "sincerely" repents and in so doing manages both to shift responsibility back onto Gross while finagling his way back into his former position of Deputy Director. Furthermore, Maria, the only "humane" person in the organization and the most sympathetic character in the play, is fired because of her act of *personal* loyalty to Gross in finally agreeing to translate the memorandum. Again Gross avoids conflict, hoping that, as Managing Director, he "can at least salvage this or that" (1980: 79).

Ultimately, Gross is representative of all that is wrong with reform communism. Gross personifies the attempt of formerly sincere and stringent partisan intellectuals to absolve their past sins through revisionism. Not only is this effort misguided and mistaken; it is inherently illogical because one cannot step halfway outside the system to reform it, or indeed reform it from within. The "lost generation" thus remains in the wilderness, its beautiful ideals shattered by the reality of their attempted implementation combined with the realization that a new beginning is next to impossible. It is not merely an expression of wistful nostalgia for untainted youth when Gross exclaims at the end of the play, "Why can't I be a little boy again? I'd do everything differently from the beginning!" (1980: 80)

In early plays such as *The Memorandum* and *The Garden Party*, Havel is already contrasting the difference between the internal lie of constant moral compromise and the necessity of "living in truth" as a means of breaking out of this vicious circle. It is indeed this notion of "living in truth" that marks Havel as both a moral philosopher and as a playwright, and sets the stage for a dramatically different form of political theorizing and action within the community of dissent in normalized Czechoslovakia.

The Evolution of "Living in Truth": Its Meaning and Consequences

In *The Memorandum* Havel's portrayal of the absurdities of *Ptydepe* provides the reader or spectator with a humorous sense of the dysfunctional relationship between language and meaning. In his essay "On Evasive Thinking"[11] Havel addresses a similar theme, taking it one step further. "Pseudo-ideological thinking," a "ritualization of language," and what he eventually calls "evasive thinking" disrupt the relationship between language and meaning, causing enormous social damage. The social connectedness language provides by signifying reality and generating mutual understanding of that reality is severed through its ideological misuse. In a direct attack on the writers and journalists who succumbed to the newspeak of authoritarian communism, Havel states:

> This way of thinking, in my opinion, is causing immense damage. The essence of it is that certain established dialectical patterns are deformed and fetishized and thus become an immobile system of intellectual and phraseological schema which, when applied to different kinds of reality, seem at first to have achieved, admirably, a heightened ideological view of that reality, whereas in fact they have, without our noticing it, separated thought from its immediate contact with reality and thus crippled its capacity to intervene in that reality effectively (Havel, 1991: 11).

In this attempt to deconstruct the logic of the political correctness embedded in the language of the system's proponents, Havel examines both underlying assumptions and logical conclusions.

First, false contextualization, at first a praiseworthy attempt to put discrete and local events into a wider context, distorts meaning through nonsensical correlation and disproportion. During the Prague Spring, writers lauded themselves and their ability to engage in public criticism as a great achievement of socialism rather than as a normal aspect of an open and democratic society. A writer censures public criticism over falling window ledges (causing death of passers by), calling his compatriots to free themselves from "petty, local, and municipal matters" and instead deal with "mankind and our prospects for the future." Thus public safety and the degradation of local architecture is demeaned as less important *in comparison with* lofty, higher goals. Not only are honestly expressed concerns of real people given short shrift, the ideological project of building socialism is reduced to empty platitudes.

Second, the "dialectical metaphysics" of evasive thinking results in "vacuous verbal balancing acts," exonerating the speaker of any proposition from either taking a position or assuming responsibility. Here Havel describes this as constant equivocation: "on the one hand—but on the other hand" or "in a certain sense yes, but in another sense no," This linguistic weakness absolves one of responsibility, and at the same time destroys capacity for agency. In Havel's words, "When we lose touch with reality, we inevitably lose the capacity to influence reality effectively" (1991: 14).

Later Havel nicely brings together his work as dramaturge at the Balustrade with his editorial experience at *Tvář* . His advice for the Writers' Union is to act like a good dramaturge, that is, "help literature and authors be true to themselves" (1991: 19). This means avoiding circuitous and platitudinous language, being direct in speech and action, and above all being open to and not suspicious of critique. Havel is sensitive to the paranoia of recently rehabilitated writers who view criticism as the harbinger of neo-Stalinism, but points out that such a view leads to a closed circle.

Havel's engagement with the power structure of the Writers' Union emphasized language, yet signals some key themes he will come back to and refine. First is his generalized emphasis on truth, here explained as honest and direct communication, not muddied by ideologically laden and ritualized obfuscation. Second, truth is linked to self-actualization, the ability of one to live one's life or pursue one's profession authentically, to gain recognition or criticism based on one's owns efforts or outputs, regardless of prevailing political winds. Finally, Havel's own stance—as an independent writer, as an editor of an independent literary periodical, and as a Writers' Union outsider unafraid to challenge directly the *modus vivendi* of the entire organization—serves as an example of a life consistently lived. "Walking the talk" becomes a behavioral standard for dissidents across the region, which Havel will describe more philosophically as living "as if."

Two more articles written during and shortly after the Prague Spring provide us with a more obvious sense of Havel's development as a political thinker. In *On the Theme of an Opposition* he portrays the partisan debate surrounding the notion of political opposition as having one's cake and eating it too.[12] Freedom of speech and public opinion, assisted by the media, is no substitute for an opposition if one-party rule is to continue, states Havel:

> The trouble is, democracy is not a matter of faith, but of guarantees. And although public debate is a primary condition of democracy, the essence of democracy—the real source of those guarantees—is something else: a public, legal contest for power. At the same time, public opinion (as represented by the press, for instance) can act as an effective check on government, and thereby improve its quality, only if it also has the power to influence government, and this can only be done if public opinion leads to a process of public choice—through elections, for example. Ultimately, power only really listens to power, and if government is to be improved, we must be able to threaten its existence, not merely its reputation. [...] (1991: 26–27).

As a statement of support for procedural democracy, this is hardly earth shattering. Havel reasons that alternative sources of an opposition, such as existing organizations and interest groups freed from their Leninist shackles or a reactivation of the multi-partisan National Front, are ultimately flawed because they do not satisfy a basic democratic precondition: the element of citizen choice. The arguments are straightforward, apple-pie arguments in favor of multi-party democratic competition, but the context was anything but straightforward. As the Brezhnevite Soviet realists were to point out to Dubček's administration, this was a direct attack on the leading role of the party. The geopolitical context is neither in the foreground nor the background of Havel's piece, and thus history tempts us to judge it as naive in the extreme. Perhaps less obvious but equally naive is the assumption that effective political opposition must ultimately be mounted through parties, and here Havel changes his position in the 1970s given the extremities of the normalization period and the serious limits placed on any level of independent action.

In his "Letter to Alexander Dubček" Havel advises Dubček—after the signing of the Moscow Protocols but before he was politically deposed—to publicly take a stand against the post-intervention government policies of capitulation.[13] He outlines three courses of possible action and likely consequences for Dubček: 1) renounce his earlier policies and bow to the ideology of his oppressors, thus lending his support for the discrediting of the reform process, all in the name of party solidarity, discipline, and the higher interests of socialism; 2) silence (the route Dubček ultimately took); and 3) resisting all pressure, restate his understanding of and support for the reform policies of the Prague Spring, and take a position openly against the Soviet intervention. In favor of the third option, Havel mounts the following arguments: 1) such a stance would amount to "speaking the truth, keeping to it, and rejecting everything that stands the truth on its head" (1991: 42); 2) by doing so a blow would be struck at the party leadership, revealing at once their "unprincipled distortion of reality"; and 3) it would set an example of "immeasurable moral significance." Although Havel realizes he is a moralizing advice-giver, he takes Dubček to task for shaping his own demise. By signing the Protocols, Dubček merely postponed the fatal moment when he must say yes or no to the invasion; having believed in the leading role of the party, he must now show himself to be the leader. Again, we see Havel express his commitment to the truth as not only morally compelling but politically powerful. By speaking the truth, Dubček would have set a forceful example:

> People would realize that it is always possible to preserve one's ideals and one's backbone; that one can stand up to lies; that there are values worth struggling for; that there are still trustworthy leaders; and that no political defeat justifies complete historical skepticism as long as the victims manage to bear their defeat with dignity. Your act would place before us an ethical mirror as powerful as that of Jan Palach's recent deed, though the impact of what you do will be of longer duration. For many citizens, your act would become a yardstick for their own behavior, a compass needle pointing to a more meaningful future. You would not be forgotten, even were you to live in isolation, and your very existence would be a mote in the eye of all careerists attempting to profit from the occupation. You would enhance the prestige of Czechoslovakia's struggle in the eyes of the world, and you would keep alive one of the more positive aspects of the commu-

nist movement. After some years (especially in the event of changes in the leadership of the Communist Party of the Soviet Union) you would undoubtedly be rehabilitated—quietly, no doubt, as tends to be the case in the Communist Party—because history cannot be halted and time must vindicate you in the end (1991: 43–44).

In his final paragraph, Havel returns to this theme:

> There are moments when a politician can achieve real political success only by turning aside from the complex network of revitalized political considerations, analyses, and calculations, and behaving *simply as an honest person*. The sudden assertion of human criteria within a dehumanizing framework of political manipulation can be like a flash of lightning illuminating a dark landscape. And *truth is suddenly truth again*, reason is reason, and honor (my emphasis; 1991: 48–49).

In retrospect, Havel's analysis of Dubček's errors has remained remarkably consistent. In *Disturbing the Peace* (an interview 18 years afterward), he suggests that the government, "… instead of behaving like the proud representatives of the people … behaved like guilty servants" (1990: 106). As to their hopes of recapturing at least some of the gains of the Prague Spring, he states: "The leadership made concession after concession in the hopes of salvaging something, but all it did was saw off the very limb it was sitting on" (1990: 110).

From Playwright to Dissident in Husák's Czechoslovakia

Ironically, Havel became more involved politically *in an activist sense* after the Soviet occupation in 1968. On 21 August, 1968 Havel was in Liberec in Northern Bohemia, staying with friends. He quickly got involved in local resistance activities, writing and broadcasting declarations from the local television station. Unlike the debates regarding *Tvář*, this was real roll-up-your-sleeves political action. The message of popular participation and resistance was very powerfully conveyed to Havel. In *Disturbing the Peace* he reflected on the unpredictable and unscientific nature of popular resistance:

None of us know [*sic*] all the potentialities that slumber in the spirit of the population, or all the ways in which that population can surprise us when there is the right interplay of events, both visible and invisible. Who would have believed—at a time when the Novotný regime was corroding away because the entire nation was behaving like Švejks—that half a year later that same society would display a genuine civic-mindedness, and that a year later this recently apathetic, sceptical, and demoralized society would stand up with such courage and intelligence to a foreign power! And who would have suspected that, after scarcely a year had gone by, this same society would, as swiftly as the wind blows, lapse back into a state of demoralization far deeper than its original one! After all those experiences, one must be very careful about coming to any conclusions about the way we are, or what can be expected of us (1990: 109).

Havel's writings were blacklisted in 1969. He became a public enemy, in his words, "driven out of every position I'd once held ... indicted for subversion (there was no trial or prison sentence)" (1990: 120). He described the early 1970s as "a single, shapeless fog" (1990: 120). Moreover, Havel linked his own experience of retreat and internal exile to that of the general populace:

People withdrew into themselves and stopped taking an interest in public affairs. An era of apathy and widespread demoralization began, an era of gray, everyday totalitarian consumerism. Society was atomized, small islands of resistance were destroyed, and a disappointed and exhausted public pretended not to notice. Independent thinking and creativity retreated to the trenches of deep privacy (1990: 120–121).

The shared experience of normalization also made for strange bedfellows. Havel and other so-called "independent" writers came to terms with and in many cases developed friendships with, the "antidogmatic" writers of the Writers' Union—such as Pavel Kohout, Ludvík Vaculík, and Ivan Klíma. Cross-generational ties also developed between younger writers and the earlier non-communist writers of the 1950s (such as Zdeněk Urbanek). As Havel stated, "... the differences of opinion that had once separated [us] had long since ceased to be important" (1990: 121). Informal meetings at the Havel family farm house Hrádeček grew into miniature writers' congresses; a ghetto of isolated but like-minded fellow travelers grew out of social atomization and stagnation.

For Havel, the intellectual break from this essentially private activity came in 1975 with a decision to write an open letter to Husák. It was an intentional effort of self-transformation from a passive object of history into an active subject. Reclaiming his subjectivity meant taking a substantial risk, but by public intervention he not only regained his own confidence but also did exactly what the regime despised most. He destabilized the political game, the implicit social contract, by breaking the cardinal rule of silence. Outwardly society was compliant, tranquil, and modestly prosperous; Havel, however, called attention to a profound spiritual, moral, and social crisis lurking just beneath the surface, echoing the analysis of Šimečka's *The Restoration of Order*. Havel sent his letter, addressed to "Dear Dr. Husák," by regular mail to the president's office in April, 1975. He also made copies available to foreign press agencies; it was first published in English in *Encounter* in September, 1975. More essay than letter, "Dear Dr. Husák" is also a defining point in Havel's writing because it is really his first serious piece of philosophy, focussing on fear and consumerism.

Havel notes that life and work have proceeded normally in Czechoslovakia, and that "discipline prevails" (1991: 50). People carry on with the daily routines of work, shopping, and living their lives, but this is not a sign of either success or failure of regime policies, of societal agreement or disagreement. In Husák's Czechoslovakia, people are motivated chiefly by fear—not of imprisonment or execution—but of losing a job, not being able to work in one's chosen field, or not obtaining higher education for one's children. Fear also compels people to do whatever is necessary to gain whatever small advantages they can, by joining a particular organization, spouting whatever platitudes are demanded, or voting for proposed candidates in general elections. Havel defines this fear as ethical as much as psychological:

> We are concerned with fear in a deeper sense, an ethical sense if you will, namely, the more or less conscious participation in the collective awareness of a permanent and ubiquitous danger; anxiety about what is being, or might be, threatened; becoming gradually used to this threat as a substantive part of the actual world; the increasing degree to which, in an ever more skilful and matter-of-fact way, we go in for various kinds of external adaptation as the only effective method of self-defense (1991: 53).

Havel notes "it is not the absolute value of a threat which counts, so much as its relative value" (1991: 53) which motivates people. However, because fear and truth are relativized both are rendered completely meaningless. "Existential pressure" is nurtured and maintained by the security police; meanwhile the regime recognizes only the kind of truth required at a given moment. This second feature departs from earlier periods of Stalinist authoritarianism: "unchangeable creeds" of the past are replaced by "creedless despotism" (1991: 64). The authorities nonetheless justify themselves and their actions in the same revolutionary ideology and language of the past, trapped by this rhetoric from recognizing the multiple levels of contradiction in its extended usage.

Havel discusses the relationship between increasing consumerism and the policies of normalization. He suggests it is functional for the regime to applaud a social orientation toward private needs and desires, not only because of the obvious economic benefits generated by personal industry and consumer goods production (even if via the gray or black markets). The authorities "welcome this transfer of energy" because of what it represents:

> ... an escape from the public sphere. Rightly divining that such surplus energy, if directed "outward," must sooner or later turn against them—that is, against the particular forms of power they obstinately cling to—they do not hesitate to represent as human life what is really a desperate substitute for living. In the interest of the smooth management of society, then, society's attention is deliberately diverted from itself, that is, from social concerns. By fixing a person's whole attention on his mere consumer interests, it is hoped to render him incapable of realizing the increasing extent to which he has been spiritually, politically, and morally violated. Reducing him to a simple vessel for the ideals of a primitive consumer society is intended to turn him into pliable material for complex manipulation. The danger that he might conceive a longing to fulfill some of the immense and unpredictable potential he has as a human being is to be nipped in the bud by imprisoning him within the wretched range of parts he can play as a consumer, subject to the limitations of a centrally directed market (1991: 59).

Havel's concerns have wider resonance, given that consumerist interpenetration of capitalist and "social market" economies of Western

Europe.[14] As Marx pointed out, commodity fetishism is internal to the logic of expansion and growth of capitalism. Many *ex-post-facto* explanations of the downfall of communism have highlighted the failed attempt of authoritarian communist regimes to buy their way out of economic stagnation. Havel states:

> Yet these same authorities obsessively justify themselves with their revolutionary ideology, in which the ideal of man's total liberation has a central place! But what, in fact, has happened to the concept of human personality and its many-sided, harmonious, and authentic growth? Of man liberated from the clutches of an alienating social machinery, from a mythical hierarchy of values, formalized freedoms, from the dictatorship of property, the fetish and the might of money? What has happened to the idea that people should live in full enjoyment of social and legal justice, have a creative share in economic decision making, free participation in political life, and free intellectual advancement, all people are actually offered is a chance freely to choose which washing machine or refrigerator they want to buy (1991: 60).

Havel suggests authoritarian communism will never live up to Marxist idealism. He is particularly concerned about the social anomie resulting from such a strategy, and on an individual level, relativism and moral decay. The influence of French existentialism and German/Czech phenomenology are evident in his discussion of what he calls "the crisis of human identity." The tragedy of human status in modern technological civilization "is marked by a declining awareness of the absolute" (1991: 62). Here Havel's use of "the absolute" can be seen as a moral threshold, not unlike Kant's categorical imperative.[15] The evils of modernity, such as technology and bureaucratic rationality, are not the result of authoritarian communism. In fact, they are implicit in any contemporary political regime, and thus pose a constant and related set of problems for authentic human existence.[16] Consumer behavior literally dulls our senses and encourages the weakening of bonds to the point of epistemological erosion. Over time, the elimination of a social conscience—at first politically dangerous to express, then only possible in the private sphere—is "naturalized," and made normal and everyday. This has historical implications, for removing from humankind the opportunity for meaningful public contact deadens social time. The loss of social space results in the creation of a merely private zone of time governed by rhythmic and cyclical events representing only a microcosm of human interaction—birth, marriage, and death—that Havel characterizes as literally pre-historic (1991: 73).

Before concluding his essay, Havel discusses the liquidation of cultural periodicals to highlight culture as a means of societal expression, a barometer of the regime's openness and ability to tolerate criticism. He answers his silent critics that yes, the "wheels of society continue to go round even without all those literary, artistic, theatrical, philosophical, historical, and other magazines" and that probably only a small fraction of the population truly misses their existence (1991: 68). The forced elimination of such journals, however, is not simply a blow to culture or their readers. He states:

> It is simultaneously, and above all, the liquidation of a particular organ through which society becomes aware of itself and hence it is an interference, hard to describe in exact terms, in the complex system of circulation, exchange, and conversion of nutrients that maintain life in that many-layered organism which is society today (1991: 68).

Knowledge, however compartmentalized by discipline-specific boundaries or technical complexity, always moves beyond a small group of experts and can have profound impact—Havel uses the example of the specific knowledge of nuclear physics and the broader political dimensions of the nuclear threat.

Readers are not likely to "demonstrate in the streets" for the lack of a few extra books, but this is not the real point for Havel. The "real significance" is the long-term impact on cultural self-knowledge, and the negative legacy of such an absence. Rhetorically, Havel asks:

> What mounds of mystification, slowly forming in the general cultural consciousness, will need to be chipped away? How far back will one need to go? Who can tell which people will still find the strength to light new fires of truth, when, how, and from what resources, once there has been such thorough wastage not only of the fuel, but of the very feeling that it can be done?

Later, he restates the issue:

The overall question, then, is this: What profound intellectual and moral impotence will the nation suffer tomorrow, following the castration of its culture today?

I fear that the baneful effects of society will outlast by many years the particular political interests that gave rise to them. So much more guilty, in the eyes of history, are those who have sacrificed the country's spiritual future for the sake of their present power interests (1991: 71).[17]

Finally, Havel characterizes the regime as "entropic." Authoritarian communism increases and generalizes entropy by extending and tightening the mechanisms of social control. The party-state is monolithic, and society is in "a strait jacket of one-dimensional manipulation" (1991: 74). This logic is is ultimately fatal, for like Arendt in *The Human Condition* Havel suggests life has an irrepressible urge to oppose entropy (1991: 74–75). It may seem simplistic to suggest that human life will recuperate and thrive despite being "violently ravished" by such a power structure, but it nonetheless remains a profound statement of human agency. Power such as that wielded by the authoritarian communist regimes of East-Central Europe was ultimately ambivalent despite its ideological pretext and pretensions. Beneath the "heavy cover of inertia and pseudo-events," Havel reminds us that *inevitably* there will exist "a secret streamlet" of seeming non-events, unofficial happenings, private and uncontrolled thought processes, and so on. From the standpoint of Western social science, this cannot be overlooked as it was precisely because scholarship and regional expertise focused largely on the official realm and the heavy hand of power that such resistance was continually downplayed or ignored outright. This essay, written a year and a half before the founding of Charter 77, imagines a range of possibilities for thought and action that normalization had attempted to erase.

Havel neither urged popular revolution nor elite-driven reform. He rather modestly asked Husák to take responsibility and to seriously consider the matters which he brought forward in his essay, and "act accordingly." Havel reported later that he was fully prepared to be arrested for his actions, to the point where he began carrying around with him an "emergency packet" (cigarettes, toothbrush, toothpaste, soap, T-shirt, paper, and so on) wherever he went. The essay received considerable attention—in the foreign press, by the authorities (he even received a reply from the President's office returning his essay), and most importantly by his friends and colleagues. As a catalyst and a call to action, the essay began circulating in samizdat just as Havel and others were organizing on behalf of Jirous and the PPU.

Theorizing Resistance: "The Power of the Powerless"

Without exaggeration, Havel's essay "The Power of the Powerless" was the single most-important theorization of the dissident movements in East-Central Europe prior to 1989. In my interviews, it was repeatedly cited as absolutely seminal and influential; the only piece that ranks close is Michnik's "A New Evolutionism." It circulated widely in samizdat among Czechs, Slovaks, Hungarians, and Poles, and was published abroad in various editions, most notably in John Keane's edited collection titled *The Power of the Powerless: Citizens against the State in East-Central Europe*, as well as in Jan Vladislav's edited collection *Living in Truth*. The best indication of its impact is revealed by Paul Wilson at the beginning of the essay's re-publication in *Open Letters*:

> Here is what Zbygniew Bujak, a Solidarity activist, told me: "This essay reached us in the Ursus factory in 1979 at a point when we felt we were at the end of the road. Inspired by KOR ... we had been speaking on the shop floor, talking to people, participating in public meetings, trying to speak the truth at the factory, the country, and politics. There came a moment when people thought we were crazy. Why were we doing this? Why were we taking such risks? Not seeing any immediate and tangible results, we began to doubt the purposefulness of what we were doing. Shouldn't we be coming up with other methods, other ways?
>
> Then came the essay by Havel. Reading it gave us the theoretical underpinnings for our activity. It maintained our spirits; we did not give up, and a year later—in August 1980—it became clear that the party apparatus and the factory management were afraid of us. We mattered. And the rank and file saw us as leaders of the movement. When I look at the victories of Solidarity and Charter 77, I see in them an astonishing fulfillment of the prophecies and knowledge contained in Havel's essay (1991: 125–126).

The essay was quickly written as an intended contribution to a joint Polish–Czechoslovak volume of essays—one of the outcomes of the border meeting in 1978. Events conspired against the publication of the original volume, as the Polish contributions were not completed and in any event many of the Czech participants, including Havel, were arrested for their work in VONS. Almost a hundred pages in length, it begins ironically:

> A specter is haunting Eastern Europe: the specter of what in the West is called "dissent." This specter has not appeared out of thin air. It is a natural and inevitable consequence of the present historical phase of the system it is haunting. It was born at a time when this system, for a thousand reasons, can no longer base itself on the unadulterated, brutal, and arbitrary application of power, eliminating all expressions of non-conformity. What is more, the system has become so ossified politically that there is practically no way for such nonconformity to be implemented within its official structures (1991: 127).

Although Havel discusses the identity and motives of so-called dissidents and whether or not they might constitute an opposition in what he calls post-totalitarian Czechoslovakia, he focuses on a character who is not the self-appointed dissident.[18] There are two kinds of powerless people Havel talks about—the dissident "as a category of sub-citizen outside the power establishment" but also the non-dissident, non-trouble-maker who goes about his business as efficiently and privately as possible, only doing what the regime demands in the name of a day's work. This second kind of powerless person is famously personified as Havel's greengrocer.

Havel's greengrocer is singled out not because he is extraordinary in any way, but precisely because he is very ordinary, and typical of normalized Czechoslovakia. The act which precipitates Havel's discussion—the placement of a sign in the fruit-and-vegetable shop he manages that boldly states "Workers of the World, Unite!"—is indicative of the behavior both expected and required of the greengrocer. Havel explains that the greengrocer is "indifferent to the semantic content of the slogan on exhibit," he certainly does not "put the slogan in his window from any personal desire to acquaint the public with the ideal it expresses" (Havel, 1991: 132). The slogan is a sign, "and as such it contains a subliminal but very definite message" (1991: 132). It alerts the regime and everyone else that the greengrocer is doing what is expected of him; in his obedience he is fulfilling his end of the social bargain. He is engaging in the mutually reinforcing process of ritual legitimation—in exchange, he has "the right to be left in peace" (1991: 133).

Havel reminds us that the ideological content of the slogan "helps the greengrocer to conceal from himself the low foundations of his obedience"; after all, he is not required to display a sign which states: "I am afraid and therefore unquestioningly obedient" (1991: 133). The greengrocer can hide behind ideology in protecting his own dignity, however debased. Havel suggests that he be allowed to say "What's wrong with workers of the world uniting?" should he in fact be challenged for his display (an unlikely occurrence, but one for which he has a prepared answer nonetheless). For Havel, ideology is an all-too-convenient escape route from human responsibility. Its necessary level of obfuscation and mystification offer us "the illusion of an identity, of dignity, and of morality while making it easier to part with them." He elaborates:

> As the repository of something suprapersonal and objective, [ideology] enables people to deceive their conscience and conceal their position and their inglorious *modus vivendi*, both from the world and from themselves. It is very pragmatic but, at the same time, an apparently dignified way of legitimizing what is above, below, and on either side. It is directed toward people and toward God. It is a veil behind which human beings can hide their own fallen existence, their trivialization, and their adaptation to the status quo. It is an excuse that everyone can use, from the greengrocer, who conceals his fear of losing his job behind an alleged interest in the unification of the workers of the world, to the highest functionary, whose interest in staying in power can be cloaked in phrases about service to the working class. The primary excusatory function of ideology is, therefore, to provide people, both as victims and pillars of the post-totalitarian system, with the illusion that the system is in harmony with the human order and the order of the universe (1991: 133–134).

Ideology is the "glue" that holds the post-totalitarian order together in false harmony. Ideology is effective because its complexity allows for considerable subtlety and flexibility, but its true nature is exposed through the parable of the greengrocer.[19] Havel lays bare the very foundations of ideology through an everyday example to which all can relate. Havel's strategy is reminiscent of the post-modern critique of Marxist ideology; Havel would likely agree with Derrida's layering of Marx's conjuration, or with Baudrillard: [20]

> The 'critique' (not excluding here the Marxist critique of ideology) feeds off a magical conception of its object. It does not unravel ideology as form, but as content, as given, transcendent value—a sort of manna that attaches itself to several global representations that magically impregnate those floating and mystified subjectivities called 'consciousness'.

To imagine communism literally "haunting" Europe is to invoke a range of dualistic options such as present reality/future possibility, threat/utopia, passivity/revolution. For Marx to move from critique to action, and to metamorphosize political theory into a mobilizational call to arms (the point being not to philosophize about the world but to change it) ideology is required. Under authoritarian communism, ideology is not a call to action, but a convenient excuse for passivity. Havel draws our attention to an elemental difference between post-totalitarianism and its Stalinist, Leninist, and revolutionary predecessors.

The regime and its adherents and silent supporters live a continual lie. Ideology masks reality but the dissonance between lived reality and stated ideology reveals the permanent hypocrisy with dark humor:

> ... government by bureaucracy is called popular government; the working class is enslaved in the name of the working class; the complete degradation of the individual is presented as his ultimate liberation; depriving people of information is called making it available; the use of power to manipulate is called the public control of power, and the arbitrary abuse of power is called observing the legal code; the repression of culture is called its development; the expansion of imperial influence is presented as support for the oppressed; the lack of free expression becomes the highest form of freedom; farcical elections become the highest form of democracy; banning independent thought becomes the most scientific of world views; military occupation becomes fraternal assistance (1991: 136).

Because "the regime is captive to its own lies," it must falsify not only present circumstances but also history and the future. One need not *believe*, but one must *behave*, like the greengrocer, as if one actually did. The price to be paid is living the lie, regardless of one's *actual* acceptance of it. Nevertheless, by living the lie, and accepting their life within it, "individuals confirm the system, fulfill the system, make the system, *are* the system" (emphasis original; 1991: 136).

Havel clarifies that the lie runs through each person, though to varying degrees. Everyone is enslaved by the lie and everyone is involved in perpetuating its existence. No one is exempt from complicity or responsibility. Havel states everyone is both a victim and a supporter (1991: 144). This does not mean that all are *equally* responsible or equally unfree. The greengrocer is involved in propping up the regime in a minor way; the prime minister to a much greater extent—their responsibility mirrors the extent to which they are accomplices. Havel reasons that one's position "in the power hierarchy determines the degree of responsibility and guilt, but it gives no one unlimited responsibility and guilt, nor does it completely absolve anyone" (1991: 144).[21] Human capacity to live the lie demonstrates the level of alienation endemic to such degeneration. However, prolonging such existence is neither a matter of fate, nor only subject to determination from above.

Post-totalitarianism is fundamentally at odds with the organic requirements of life. Havel contrasts the "conformity, uniformity, and discipline" of the former with the "plurality, diversity, independent self-constitution, and self organization" of the latter (1991: 134–135). For Havel "every instance of ... transgression is a genuine denial of the system." Logically, if the system commands absolute *prima facie* obedience, then any individual act against the automatism[22] of required roles is, in a sense, meaningful for its very destabilizing quality. Herein lies the real power of the powerless. All human beings, regardless of their moral or actual enslavement, would like to have some moral integrity. The desire for free expression and authentic existence transcends the position in which we find ourselves. But to do something about it takes moral courage and entails some level of risk. To illustrate how a seemingly powerless person might in fact wield power and step out of a preordained existence of servitude, Havel turns again to his friend the greengrocer.

Havel asks us to imagine what might happen if one day something snaps in the mind of the greengrocer and against all prevailing logic, he stops displaying the slogan in his shop window. Moreover, consonant with this initial step he starts to do other things:

He stops voting in elections he knows are a farce. He begins to say what he really thinks at political meetings. And he even finds the strength in himself to express solidarity with those whom his conscience commands him to support. In this revolt, the greengrocer steps out of living within the lie. He rejects the ritual and breaks the rules of the game. He discovers once more his suppressed identity and dignity. He gives his freedom a concrete significance. His revolt is an attempt to live within the truth (1991: 146).

Of course the greengrocer ends up paying the price for his protest. First relieved of his position, he is then forced to take a lower level job in a warehouse. Quite possibly his pay is reduced, holiday plans cancelled, and the possibility of his children attending university vanishes. He will be harassed by his superiors and ignored by others. Indeed, Havel describes the typical scenario of a dissident living in Husák's Czechoslovakia who dares to speak out. Given the heavy hand of the system coming down on the pathetic little greengrocer, why does he bother? What is possibly achieved by his actions? And wherein does his "power" lie? Not easy questions, yet Havel comes up with a philosophically and practically challenging set of answers. Most significantly, the greengrocer has exposed the lie as a lie. This is no small feat:

By breaking the rules of the game, he has disrupted the game as such. He has exposed it as a mere game. He has shattered the world of appearances, the fundamental pillar of the system. He has upset the power structure by tearing apart what holds it together. He has demonstrated that living a lie is living a lie. He has broken through the exalted facade of the system and exposed the real, base foundations of power. He has said that the emperor is naked. And because the emperor is in fact naked, something extremely dangerous has happened: by his action, the greengrocer has addressed the world. He has enabled everyone to peer behind the curtain. He has shown everyone that it *is* possible to live within the truth. Living within the lie can constitute the system only if it is universal. The principle must embrace and permeate everything (1991: 147).

The world of appearances is shattered, for the greengrocer's actions have highlighted an alternative that is, real, reality. As far as the power structure is concerned, it does not matter how tiny or irrelevant the space occupied by the dissident greengrocer; his presence is ominous and threatening.

At bottom, the power of the powerless lies in truth. For Havel, this "singular, explosive, incalculable" political power exists within everyone, at least to the degree that the human order possesses a capacity for and predisposition toward the truth—Havel posits a radical equality in terms of human potential. This is so even in a society alienated by a post-totalitarian regime, and its very alienation is proof of this capacity. Havel explains:

> Individuals can be alienated from themselves only because there is something in them to alienate. The terrain of this violation is their authentic existence. Living the truth is thus woven directly into the texture of living a lie. It is the repressed alternative, the authentic aim to which living a lie is an inauthentic response. Only against this background does living a lie make any sense: it exists *because* of that background (emphasis in original; 1991: 148).

Living in truth thus becomes the most effective weapon against post-totalitarian power, and at the same time is the very essence of a nascent opposition to that power.

Obviously, truth as power is not a weapon on the same terrain as guns or tanks. The "confrontation" between truth and the power of the regime does not take place on the institutional level by conventionally political or military means, but "on the level of human consciousness and conscience, the existential level" (1991: 149). For this reason, the "effective range" of truth as power "cannot be measured in terms of disciples, voters, or soldiers, because it lies spread out in the fifth column of social consciousness, in the hidden aims of life, in human beings' repressed longing for dignity and fundamental rights, for the realization of their real social and political interests" (1991: 149). Its effectiveness as a weapon does not depend on the strength of its own forces numerically, but on the "soldiers of the enemy as it were—that is to say, on everyone who is living within the lie and who may be struck at any moment (in theory, at least) by the force of truth ..." (1991: 149). Havel describes it as "bacteriological" in nature: like an insidious contagion, it does not require a great many carriers to cause an "infection."

However esoteric the notion of truth as power might appear, it is worth pointing out the highly practical dimensions of Havel's strategy.

By the time Havel wrote "The Power of the Powerless," opposition activists and intellectuals had long since recognized that given the geopolitical realities of the Cold War, the stable and unchanging division of Europe guaranteed by Yalta, and the meagre size of the opposition itself, any direct or conventional confrontation with the regimes of East-Central Europe would have been futile. Truth *as* power—which is considerably deeper than simply speaking truth *to* power—is both insidious and pragmatic, and the results of its deployment can be both visible and meaningful, however unpredictable. The consequences can be small or large—"a real political act or event, a social movement, a sudden explosion of civil unrest, a sharp conflict inside an apparently monolithic power structure, or simply an irrepressible transformation in the social and intellectual climate" (1991:150). In short, as Havel would theorize together with his contemporaries, using the weapon of truth or living in truth constituted the germination of civil society.

The effectiveness of truth can also be measured by the reaction of its adversaries. The Husák regime felt it necessary to mobilize its resources against Charter 77 via a harsh media campaign and even an Anti-Charter not because the organization represented a real challenge but because it was a dangerous hole in a leaky dyke. Havel uses the example of Solzhenitzyn being driven out of the Soviet Union, "not because he represented a unit of real power"; rather their reaction was "a desperate attempt to plug up the dreadful wellspring of truth, a truth which might cause incalculable transformations in social consciousness, which in turn might one day produce political debacles unpredictable in their consequences" (1991: 150).

As in his earlier essay "The Trial," Havel also documents the importance of the prosecution of the PPU for the creation of a new truth-based oppositional ethos, critical in the genesis of Charter 77. Charter activity created a new authentic forum for politics by its mere existence.[23] Politics as ideological ritual exists alongside those who attempt to live within the truth, which Havel describes as those "who do not abandon politics as a vocation" (1991: 158), in the true Weberian sense. Politics in this sense does *not* involve "abstract projects for an ideal political or economic order," not just because of their utopian character or likelihood of failure. Those seasoned in the realities of ideological experiments in the 20th century know, according to Havel, that "the more they fix their sights on an abstract 'someday,' the more likely they can degenerate into new forms of human enslavement" (1991:

161). Rather, what Havel describes is more akin to the Masarykian program for nation building based on "small-scale work" (*drobná-práce*).[24] There is no blueprint for such work, but extending the realm of truth and the space for such activity while promoting independent citizens' initiatives were obvious points to begin. Havel is not naive about the results, and coming into conflict with the regime is a likely outcome. To make his point concrete, Havel turns again to the green-grocer:

> Our greengrocer's attempt to live within the truth may be confined to not doing certain things. He decides not to put flags in his window when his only motive for putting them there in the first place would have been to avoid being reported to the house warden; he does not vote in elections he considers false; he does not hide his opinions from his superiors. In other words, he may go not further than "merely" refusing to comply with certain demands made on him by the system (which of course is not an insignificant step to take). This may, however, grow into something more. The greengrocer may begin to do something concrete, something that goes beyond an immediately personal self-defensive reaction against manipulation, something that will manifest his newfound sense of higher responsibility. He may, for example, organize his fellow greengrocers to act together in defense of their interests. He may write letters to various institutions, drawing their attention to instances of disorder and injustice around him. He may seek out unofficial literature, copy it, and lend it to his friends (1991: 176).

The "independent life of society" is like an iceberg—only one tenth is visible. In this respect, "dissent" as that activity practiced by "dissidents"[25] represents the only the tip of the iceberg. The genesis and evolution of independent initiatives and parallel structures operates in a symbiotic and dialectical relationship with the rest of society. Thus over time the post-totalitarian regime is capable not only of repression but also adaptation. Havel uses the example of the Polish flying university (TKN) to demonstrate his point:

> ... the Polish "flying university" came under increased persecution and the "flying teachers" were detained by the police. At the same time, however, professors in existing official universities tried to enrich their own curricula with several subjects hitherto considered taboo and this was a

result of indirect pressure exerted by the "flying university". The motives for this adaptation may vary from the ideal (the hidden sphere has received the message and conscience and the will to truth are awakened) to the purely utilitarian: the regime's instinct for survival compels it to notice the changing ideas and the changing mental and social climate and to react flexibly to them. Which of these motives happens to predominate in a given moment is not essential in terms of the final effect (1991: 198–199).

Havel was influenced by his dissident contemporary, friend (and later fellow political prisoner) Václav Benda in his discussion of how an independent civil society might develop and what its implications might be. He weaves together Benda's notion of a "parallel *polis*" with Ivan Jirous' notion of a "second culture", coming up with a far ranging set of structures that I will later discuss under the Western theoretical rubric of "civil society". Like Gramscian "counter-hegemonic" pockets, the parallel structures in the Havelian formula constitute an alternative civil society where "a different life can be lived, in harmony with its own aims" (1991: 194). Here Havel addresses two important concerns: that of universality and the long-range potential impact of such an alternative.

With respect to the former, Havel is concerned that any parallel polis, second culture, or independent society not fall into the trap of ghettoization. Jirous' "merry ghetto" had all the trappings of the exclusive, "in" group, a status reinforced by persecution and marginalization. The trend is dangerous, because is is inevitably restrictive and implies "... a narrow, self-contained responsibility" (1991: 194). Independent society must be "potentially accessible to everyone; it must foreshadow a general solution" and thus it follows that its participants must have "responsibility to and for the world" (1991: 194).[26]

Regarding the potential for living within the truth and actual systemic change, Havel decries the possibility of engaging in any form of risk/reward or predictive type of analysis. Nonetheless, he realizes he is vulnerable to the objection that "nothing will ever really change" or "not in my lifetime"—so characteristic of the apathy and despair of normalization. He is careful to contextualize the possibility for impact within the crises latent but evident throughout the Soviet Bloc; he argues that unsettling the power structure and accelerating hidden confrontation could result in "climactic change" (1991: 196–197). It is not that such activities *on their own* can cause major systemic change, but taken in conjunction with the shifts outlined above, or a concatenation of unforeseen events (as occurred in 1989), the inter-penetration of independent society into actual and official society can be decisive. The prescient quality of Havel's comments are all the more striking when one remembers this essay was written seven years before Gorbachev's ascension to power. More importantly, for Havel, inde-pendent society has important and intrinsic value *on its own*. Authentic life possibilities not heretofore known open up because of such activ-ity, and on the terrain of "real everyday struggle" changes for a better life occur "here and now" (1991: 205). A "living sense of solidarity and fraternity" is developed through such communities, and this rep-resents a kind of "rudimentary moral reconstitution" (1991: 212–213). Havel argues that the independent life which flourished around the Chartists and their activities was much more than a survival tactic of community-building or experience-sharing for disillusioned writers and academics. They aimed at the concrete expansion of an indepen-dent dimension of space for public and beneficial work, work that at the same time serves to strengthen common bonds and literally to "transform people and the climate of their lives" (1991: 213). The question is not whether such activity will bring a brighter future, but a recognition that by the very fact that this activity is occurring, the future is already brighter (1991: 214).

"Politics and Conscience" and the Destructive Capacities of Technology

"Politics and Conscience" was written as an acceptance speech upon receipt of an honorary doctorate at the University of Toulouse in 1984—a speech he could not deliver personally as he was not able to travel abroad.[27] Havel chose to address his audience more broadly on the relationship between personal conscience and political choices as exemplified in the destruction of the environment. In discussing the dualism of science as both harbinger of progress and destroyer of the natural world (*Lebenswelt*), Havel was influenced by his brother Ivan, a trained computer scientist but in practice a philosopher and critic of modern science.[28] The environmental context of Havel's own life experience is also significant—the forests of Northern Bohemia remain among the most polluted in Europe (a living and dying testament to the impact of heavy industrialization).

Havel argues that environmental degradation by industrial pollution is another illustration of the alienation endemic to modernity. Havel contrasts the adult experience of an average European, no longer rooted by personal experience or life history to the land, with that of either a medieval peasant or a young child, both of whom are existentially centered on the landscape of their immediate horizons in terms of defining the parameters of their experiences and giving them meaning. Havel also likens the "internal coherence" of the natural world to what he calls the "'pre-speculative' assumption that the world functions because there is something beyond its horizon, something beyond or above it that might escape our understanding and our grasp but, for just that reason, firmly grounds this world, bestows upon it its order and measure, and is the hidden source of all the rules, customs, commandments, prohibitions, and norms that hold within it" (1991: 251). The mystery and order of the world are indicative of its very essence, and presupposes the Absolute. Here, the Absolute is not a moral standard or threshold but a reflection of Being.[29] The hubris of humankind, represented by scientific rationality and environmental decay, results from a narcissistic egoism that one can replace the eternal and pre-existing Absolute with a "new, man-made absolute, devoid of mystery ... impersonal and inhuman" (1991: 251). The irony is that the man-made Absolute is inhuman and inhumane, impersonal and destructive, whereas the mysterious and non-human Absolute is more beneficent.

Havel describes the collectivization of agriculture as utopia-building characteristic of authoritarian communism, which brought with it greater productivity and reduced social conflict, but with an environmental price. Erasing the family farm from existence meant abolishing "that humbly respected boundary of the natural world, with its tradition of scrupulous personal acknowledgment." One can extend Havel's analysis: in the same way that human labor was herded into urban factory-based production as a result of the enclosures in rural England (allowing for the prototypical development of modern industrial capitalism), so too were peasants herded onto collective farms through Soviet-style policies of collective agriculture. In both cases, the gods of progress were served at the expense of the accumulated topsoil, natural habitats for birds and other wildlife, and the loss of indigenous species of plant and animal life. Havel is hardly exceptional here—in many respects his diagnosis of the problem is a simple extension of now-familiar social ecology to a political system whose boundaries are hardly recognized by the biosphere in any event. Following Czech philosopher and sociologist Václav Bělohradský, Havel brings environmental destruction to a personal level, and imbue a sense of personal conscience and historic responsibility.[30]

Futile attempts to conquer nature or to save humankind is not only hubris but a denial of "personal 'pre-objective' experience" and its replacement with an ethos of mastery and control. Responsibility is discarded as a "subjective illusion" and "personal conscience and consciousness [is relegated to] the bathroom, as something so private that it is no one's business" (1991: 255). The prerequisite for the retirement of one's responsibility is the total *privatization* of conscience—to the point where one's consciousness cannot inform public actions or one's political choices. Scientific rationality and "an abstract schema of a putative 'historical necessity'" (1991: 255) serve as ideological superstructure, masking the twin rape of environment and conscience with an anonymous, abstract, impersonal, and even utilitarian logic.

This impersonal power, having disposed of human conscience, reaches its apotheosis, says Havel, in [post] totalitarian systems, but warns that it is classically European in every respect, and thus European "civilization" must take responsibility for it:

> As Bělohradský points out, the depersonalization of power and its conquest of human conscience and human speech have been successfully linked to an extra-European tradition of a "cosmological" conception of empire (identifying the empire as the sole true center of the world, with the world as such, and considering the human as its exclusive property). The truth is the very opposite: it was precisely Europe, and the European West, that provided and frequently forced on the world all that today has become the basis of such power: natural science, rationalism, scientism, the industrial revolution, and also revolution as such, as a fanatical abstraction, through the displacement of the natural world to the bathroom down to the cult of consumption, the atomic bomb, and Marxism. And it is Europe—democratic western Europe—which today stands bewildered in the face of this ambiguous export (1991: 258).

The failure of the West European imagination is that it cannot see post-totalitarianism for what it in fact is: "a convex mirror of all modern civilization" (1991: 259). It is much more ideologically convenient to cast Eastern Europe as the anti-democratic "other," the opposite of its achievements rather than a logical extension of its excesses. Extending his argument outward from "The Power of the Powerless," here Havel argues that dehumanizing, omnipresent power may be the hallmark of post-totalitarian regimes, but it is hardly the only birthplace of such power.

With regard to what can be done, Havel suggests the following answer, which he sheepishly admits is "general, very indefinite, and very unrealistic":

> [The] task is one of resisting vigilantly, thoughtfully, and attentively ... the irrational momentum of anonymous, impersonal, and inhuman power—the power of ideologies, systems, apparat, bureaucracy, artificial languages, and political slogans. We must resist its complex and wholly alienating pressure, whether it takes the form of consumption, advertising, technology, or cliché—all of which are the blood brothers of fanaticism and the wellspring of totalitarian thought. We must draw on standards from our natural world, heedless of ridicule, and reaffirm its denied validity. We must honor with the humility of the wise the limits of that natural world and the mystery which lies beyond them, admitting that there is something in the order of being which evidently exceeds all our competence. We must relate to the absolute horizon of our existence which, if we but will, we shall constantly rediscover and experience. We must make values and imperatives the starting point of all our acts, of all our personally attested, openly contemplated, and ideologically uncensored lived experience. We must trust the voice of our conscience more than that of all abstract speculations and not invent responsibilities other than the one to which the voice calls us. We must not be shamed that we are capable of love, friendship, solidarity, sympathy, and tolerance, but just the opposite: we must set these fundamental dimensions of our humanity free from the "private" exile and accept them as the only genuine starting point of meaningful human community. We must be guided by our own reason and serve the truth under all circumstances as our own essential experience (1991: 267).

The reaction Havel favors is the employment of "antipolitical politics"—and here he is echoing common usage from the community of East-Central European dissidents. Havel defines his "antipolitics" as follows:

... politics not as the technology of power and manipulation, of cybernetic rule over humans or as the art of the utilitarian, but politics as one of the ways of seeking and achieving meaningful lives, of protecting them and serving them. I favor politics *as practical morality, as service to the truth, as essentially human and humanly measured care for our fellow humans* (my emphasis; 1991: 269).

Havel's prescription of politics as practical morality is reminiscent of Aristotle's discussion of politics as the practical science. Aristotelian *eudaemonia* requires contemplation, excellence in reason, and moral virtue in action. The practical wisdom implicit in *phronesis* is necessary for the conduct of proper and farsighted political decision-making; it is the virtue of reasoned action with regard to the human good.[31] Aristotle and Havel would be in full agreement on the right conduct of politics as imbued with morality, and that the wellspring of this morality must be a thick notion of personal responsibility.

Largo Desolato, Temptation, and the Vaněk Plays

Not until after his release from prison in 1983 was Havel able to complete another full-length play, *Largo Desolato.* Although published abroad in Czech by *Poezie Mimo Domov* and *Svědectví* and brought to the stage in Bristol, England and in New York and Toronto, it did not reach Czech audiences until late 1989, following the Velvet Revolution.[32] Although somewhat autobiographical—the protagonist is an author returning from prison—the play probes beyond the trauma of the released prisoner. Havel explores the character of his characters— no one is truly good nor bad—and in this respect provides examples of the intermediate position most people occupy under authoritarian communism. He demonstrates the "line" described so vividly in "The Power of the Powerless" running through each person. The play is also about taking responsibility for one's own actions; one's fate is intrinsically connected to the choices made or avoided in the path toward self-understanding and actualization.

Largo Desolato's protagonist Leopold Nettles is an archetypal "Central European Intellectual"—employed as a professor (although this is not necessarily what marks him as an "Intellectual"), a loquacious and cultured individual given to self-agony and irritating equivocation,

likely the descendant of the now-fading pre-war bourgeois establishment. He is a paranoid hypochondriac, whose self-absorption is illuminated by numerous visits over five acts by other archetypal characters—
two workers from a nearby paper mill both named Sidney; Leopold's
nervous, high-strung, and pill-popping lover, Lucy; the emissary of
his concerned friends, Bertram; two nameless male characters who
anonymously represent the regime and appear simultaneously polite
and vaguely threatening; and Marguerite, an earnest but confused
philosophy student who is an admirer.

Largo Desolato is a transitional play. The setting is neither a nameless organization nor a liquidation office, but an apartment, albeit one
that serves as a bustling public space as well as a personal and private
space. The dilemmas of dissidence are fully explored in Nettles' inter-
actions with the other characters and the pressures put on him. The
two Sidneys—"ordinary" workers from a nearby paper mill—visit twice
and make it clear that they are pinning their hopes on the professor to
act accordingly, in the "role" expected of him as dissident. The Sidneys
are willing to "risk" visiting Nettles, even steal supplies and official
documents, but they perceive themselves as both unable and unwilling to directly confront the authorities. They have *vested* their political
agency in Nettles. The two gentlemen who arrive representing "them"
present Nettles with a compromise option to avoid further confrontation and perhaps arrest—to simply sign a document that he is not
himself, that is, not *the* Professor Nettles who wrote papers considered subversive to the regime. Throughout the play, Nettles faces a
crisis of identity and responsibility. If he agrees to sign the paper, he
renounces his identity and denies responsibility for his actions; it may
be a face-saving device designed to give him a "fresh start" but only
as a non-person. As a dissident, Nettles feels fraudulent in any case.
Increasingly he feels like he is "losing his grip," his perspective, his
ability to act as the "self-aware subject" of his own life (1987: 23). He
cannot cope with the expectations of others around him—his wife,
lover, friends, an admiring student—all have built up a public identity
apart from but on the basis of his actions. All the characters take turns
informing Nettles that they will be sorely disappointed if he cannot
meet their expectations. His lover expects a certain commitment he
cannot give, his wife wants him to steadfastly oppose the authorities
and refuse to sign any denial of authorship/identity; his friends are
concerned he might prove "unreliable" and "crack under the strain"

(1987: 16–20). Nettles is forced to consider that an affirmation of his identity involves not simply a personal decision to live in truth, but living up to the expectations of the many "others" who want to live both in safety in his shadow and vicariously through his actions. There is more real-life subtlety, agony, and equivocation to Nettles' choice than we find in the thought-experiment of the green grocer in "The Power of the Powerless."[33]

Largo Desolato is considered by some to be Havel's best play theatrically, but in terms of challenging the audience, it does not come close to *Temptation*. Havel wrote *Temptation* because he had read both Goethe's *Faust* and Thomas Mann's *Doctor Faustus* in prison, and after several false starts, he completed the play after only ten days of tortuous writing—wrestling with both the devil and the literary legend inspired by it. Havel's Faust is Dr. Henry Foustka, a scientist working in an institute with an indeterminate research program who deals with his own doubts about scientific methodology and its dominant and unquestioned role by exploring occult literature. He ponders creation, existence, biology, and survival, and wonders if there is not some deeper design concealed in the "multitude of ... unbelievable coincidences that ... exceed the bounds of all probability" that brought it all about in the first place. Like Czech philosopher Patočka, he is searching for a metaphysical explanation, and blames science for retarding humankind's ability to find one. In his conversation with the Institute's secretary, Marketa, he states:

Foustka: Has it ever occurred to you that we wouldn't be able to understand even the simplest moral action that doesn't serve some practical purpose? In fact, it would have to seem quite absurd to us if we didn't recognize that hidden somewhere in the deepest depths is the presumption of something higher, some sort of absolute, omniscient, and infinitely fair judge or moral authority through which and within which all our activities are somehow mysteriously appraised and validated and by means of which each one of us is constantly in touch with eternity?

Marketa: Yes, yes, that's exactly how I've felt about it all my life! I just wasn't able to see it, let alone say it so beautifully.

Foustka: So there you are! What's even more tragic is that modern man has repressed everything that might allow him somehow to transcend himself, and he ridicules the very idea that something above him might have a higher meaning of some sort! He has crowned himself as the highest authority, so he can then observe with horror how the world is going to the dogs under that authority! (Havel, 1989: 33)

Havel's Mephistopheles is a Švejkian caricature of the devil—the imposing and frightening demon is reduced to the dwarfish and seedy Fistula—a disabled person with questionable habits of personal hygiene living on a state pension. Fistula is definitely slippery and unsavory, but the devil he invokes turns out to be the devil within Dr. Foustka himself. Foustka's "temptation" is not the struggle of a fallen man against the power of evil, but a more modest form of hubris.

In a series of clever plot twists, the audience is led to believe that Foustka's explorations of the supernatural are "betrayed" by his co-worker and lover Vilma. Foustka "rises" to the occasion with a confession and self-defense worthy of a show-trial script, appealing to both higher purposes and the objectivity of truth. In the end, Foustka is foiled by his own gullibility despite his efforts to be too clever by half. Fistula turns out to be the Institute's informer. As this is revealed, we feel less pity and sympathy for Foustka than for Fistula, who is really only the devil's representative, and trying to do a reasonably good job of it. Foustka has betrayed his own ideal to search for some truth apart from science, and has failed his own first test. He reacts with anger and with blame; his reaction is met with a bemused dismissal on the part of the Institute's Director:

Fistula: Wait a minute, now! Hold it! I never said that there is such a thing as the devil, not even while I was engaged in that provocation.

Foustka: But I'm saying it! And he's actually here among us!

Fistula: Are you referring to me?

Foustka: You're just a subordinate little fiend!

Director: I know your opinions, Foustka, and therefore I understand this metaphor of yours as well. Through me, you want to accuse modern science of being the true source of all evil. Isn't that right?

Foustka: No, it isn't! Through you, I want to accuse the pride of that intolerant, all-powerful, and self-serving power that uses the sciences merely as a handy weapon for shooting down anything that threatens it, that is, anything that doesn't derive its authority from this power or that is related to an authority deriving its powers elsewhere.

Director: That's the legacy you wish to leave this world, Foustka?

Foustka: Yes!

Director: I find it a little banal. In countries without censorship every half-way clever little hack journalist churns out stuff like that these days! But a legacy is a legacy, so in spite of what you think of me, I'll give you an example of how tolerant I am by overlooking my reservations and applauding your last testament! (Havel, 1989: 100–101).

With the character of Ferdinand (Bedřich) Vaněk, Havel introduced a unique, multi-authored experiment in Czech drama. Vaněk is the protagonist in three of Havel's plays spanning a ten-year period from 1975 through to 1986—*Audience* (also translated as *Conversation*), *Unveiling* (also translated as *Vernissage* or *Private View*) and *Protest*. Moreover, the character of Vaněk was picked up by three other playwrights and political contemporaries of Havel—Pavel Kohout, Pavel Landovský, and Jiří Dienstbier. Subsequently, Vaněk and the "Vaněk plays" as they came to be called, were emblematic of the twists and turns of the Czech opposition, especially given the fictional Vaněk's occupation as a dissident writer and playwright.[34]

With Vaněk, the transition theatrically and politically, that began with Nettles and continued with Dr. Foustka, is complete. The plays were not written for the theatre, and the character is an anti-character, a complete outsider. Havel wrote the Vaněk plays for his friends and fellow-travelers in the Charter movement, at a time when he knew nothing he wrote could be performed publicly on a Czech stage. As such, they are intimate conversations more than plays—one-act party charades that presume considerable "in-group" knowledge from the participants. Within and between the plays—not only those written by Havel himself—there are references to each other's foibles; the authors are collectively satirical in terms of how they are perceived publicly and to each other. For example, in *Unveiling* we hear about Pavel Landovský's legendary drunkenness, and in *Protest* Havel's "gray zone" writer and television producer Staněk expresses horror at Pavel Kohout's early Stalinist drivel and only dubiously accepts his credentials as a "dissident." Because real-life events and characters are woven into the dialogue of the plays, and the fictional characters play certain archetypal roles, the plays constitute a serialization not only of dissident life, but of normalized Czechoslovakia in the 1970s and 1980s.

Marketa Goetz-Stankiewicz has written that Vaněk himself is the antipode of Švejk, and stands between the positive and negative characters of Hašek and Kafka respectively in Czech literature (1987: xxii). Whereas Švejk is loquacious, colorfully retelling his adventures and subtly questioning authority through his relentlessly dense inquiries, Vaněk tells us almost nothing about himself. We learn he is a dissident playwright who has been imprisoned for his activism, is probably trailed by the security police, and could only find employment in a brewery because of his political stigma through the other characters in the plays. Vaněk is obviously polite, thoughtful, and intelligent but also bumbling and inarticulate—almost all of his sentences end in ellipses, either because he cannot think of the appropriate thing to say, or because his interlocutors constantly interrupt him. Vaněk's values, for which he has suffered so much, are never expressly delineated, nor does he explicitly critique those around him. Rather, he shows his modesty by doing his utmost to accept the decisions of others, not calling into question their integrity or their moral choices. He is obviously a proponent of human rights and has taken some strong public stands, for which he has earned not only the respect but also the agitation of his fellow citizens. In *Protest,* speaking for those in the "gray zone" sympathetic to the dissidents' cause but wary of personal involvement and its consequences, Staněk states:

> Staněk: Now, listen Ferdinand, isn't this a really terrifying testimony to the situation into which we've been brought? Isn't it? Just think: even I, though I know it's rubbish, even I've got used to the idea that the signing of protests is the business of local specialists, professionals in solidarity, dissidents! While the rest of us—when we want to do something for the sake of ordinary human decency—automatically turn to you, as though you were a sort of service establishment for moral matters. In other words, we're here simply to keep our mouths shut and to be rewarded by relative peace and quiet, whereas you're here to speak up for us and to be rewarded by blows on earth and glory in the heavens! Perverse, isn't it? (1993: 257)

To which Vaněk replies with a typical "Mmm ..." only to allow Staněk to continue with his diatribe. A few pages later in the script, however, his begrudging admiration turns to anger:

> Staněk : ... because, as a matter of fact, these people [like Staněk, in the gray zone] secretly hate the dissidents. They've become their bad conscience, their living reproach! That's how they see the dissidents. And at the same time, they envy them their honor and their inner freedom, values which they themselves were denied by fate (1993: 262).

Ultimately, Vaněk is a paradox. He is a writer whose writing we do not read; he seldom speaks; his voice is defined by negation. He is also symbolic of the fate of the Charter signatories. By speaking out publicly, they were effectively silenced, and yet this silence was heard loudly and provoked action from both fellow-citizens and the party-state ranging from outright oppression to sympathy, guilt, and anger. Vaněk also *personalizes* the dilemma of the Chartists, and we appreciate their humanity, humour, and lack of judgment.

Václav Havel's plays blend the aesthetic and the political—the aesthetic not in the sense of *l'art pour l'art* or in terms of subservience to the political, but as a creative exchange within the public sphere. Absurd theatre in Havel's view has neither the "arrogance" of having the "key to anything" nor is it nihilistic nor hopeful.[35] His plays are reminders, warnings, and shared dilemmas. His drama does not stand apart from life but is part of it. Jan Grossman, his mentor at the Balustrade in the 1960s, wrote the following lines in the preface to an earlier collection of Havel's plays entitled *Protocols* in 1966:

> In fact, great theater does not only reveal itself and its own story. It also reveals the audience's story, and through that, the audience's urgent need to compare their own experience—their own "subject matter"—with the subject matter offered them on stage.
>
> This kind of theatre does not end with a performance, but on the contrary, the end of the performance is where it begins. I believe that Václav Havel has shown evidence in his plays of a genuine dramatic talent that very few in contemporary Czech theater possess (quoted in Kriseová, 1993: 47–48).

Letters to Olga: "Being" and the "Absolute"

Letters to Olga is a volume of personal letters first published in the West in 1983 in a deliberate attempt by his supporters to publicize Havel's philosophy, Charter 77, and the plight of Central European dissidents in their various movements of resistance to the state. It consists of a series of 144 letters Havel wrote while in prison from June, 1979 through to September, 1982, as a form of personally-imposed intellectual therapy.[36] Letters to Olga is also a prime twentieth century illustration of the Straussian thesis regarding persecution and the art of writing philosophy.[37] In the preface to the English edition, Havel states:

> The conditions in which I wrote these letters were harsh. All sorts of restrictions imposed by the prison authorities, some possible, some impossible, had to be abided by before the letters could even be sent. There was a desperate lack of space, time, and tranquillity for writing them. At first, my two fellow inmates [Václav Benda and Jiří Dienstbier] and I were allowed only to write about family matters. Gradually, however, we began to smuggle more and more general comments into our letters, and the prison censors gradually got used to these. I soon realized that the more abstract and incomprehensible these meditative letters were, the greater their chance of being sent, since the censors did not permit any comments to be mailed that they could understand. Slowly, I learned to write in a complex, encoded fashion which was far more convoluted than I wanted and certainly more complicated than the way I normally write (1989: n.p.)

Havel even admits that the audience for his letters are, other than friends and family, the most "sensitive and observant readers" (1989: n.p.).

In his "Introduction," Paul Wilson suggests that Letters to Olga is unlike anything else Havel has written, not like the absurd human dilemmas of his theatrical oeuvre, nor like his "intention to stir up discussion around a specific cultural and political situation" which is characteristic of his non-fiction (1989: 17). Consequently, the Letters do not address specific political themes or concerns; they are intensely personal reflections on being, discovering meaning within one's existence, and how personal responsibility follows from this discovery. Havel is at his most philosophic and obscure, but as the Letters contain much personal and mundane information, they represent an effectively stark juxtaposition between the reality of prison life and the intensity of thought provoked by this confinement. For the purposes of this study, the *Letters* provide philosophical background to Havel's overt and openly reasoned "public" arguments, a series of premises or first positions which underscore both his theatre and politics.

Read alongside or in conjunction with "The Power of the Powerless" and "Politics and Conscience" the *Letters* provide us with more information on Havel's view of personal responsibility. In Letter #62 he reflects that the development of his plays reflect his ideas on the crisis of human identity; he states, "All my plays in fact are variations on this theme, the disintegration of man's oneness with himself and the loss of everything that gives human existence a meaningful order, continuity, and its unique outline" (1989: 145). In a similar manner, self-knowledge or understanding of identity gives rise to a sense of responsibility, a key theme in his essays and especially in "The Power of the Powerless."[38] Thus he states:

> ... the importance of the notion of human responsibility has grown in my meditations. It has begun to appear, with increasing clarity, as that fundamental point from which all identity grows and by which it stands or falls, it is the foundation, the root, the center of gravity, the constructional principle of the axis of identity, something like the "idea" that determines its degree and type (1989: 145).

And later:

> ... as an ability or a determination or a perceived duty of man to vouch for himself completely, absolutely, and in all circumstances (in other words, as the only true creator of freedom), *human responsibility is precisely the agent by which one first defines oneself as a person vis-à-vis the universe, that is, as the miracle of Being that one is.* On the one hand, it is only thus that one defines and so infuses meaning into one's dependency on the world; on the other hand, it is only thus that one definitively separates oneself from the world as a sovereign and independent being; it is only thus that one, as it were, stands on one's own two feet. I would say that responsibility for oneself is a knife we use to carve out our own inimitable features in the panorama of Being; it is the pen with which we write into the history of Being that story of the fresh creation of the world that each new human existence always is (my emphasis; 1989: 147).

Carving out one's identity as part and parcel of Being initiates both the processes of authentic existence and responsibility. Havel's metaphysics involves neither a Nietzschean/heroic will to power nor a classically liberal sense of self as a free-floating individual disconnected from other individuals. Authenticity/identity and the taking of responsibility are public acts that occur dialogically in social space. Havel's characters superbly *act this out* in his dramas precisely because they talk through the dilemma that responsibility presents—whether it is Leopold and Marguerite debating Leopold's ability to recapture his "lost human integrity" or Staněk's apologia to Vaněk over signing the petition to release the musician. In his absurdist plays, the ideas of *Letters to Olga* are concretely manifest.

Havel rejects the usual concrete answers to the question, "to whom and to what is a person responsible?" as telling the entire story. If one is a believer, one understands responsibility in relationship to God. Secular understandings reflect responsibility as a network of human relationships rooted in a particular society and culture, as an instinct to self-preservation, or psychoanalytically as sub-conscious calculation, or in terms of love and sacrifice (1989: 145). All of these explanations contain the danger of potentially relativistic, transitory, and even "ideological" responses; in this way we turn over the problem of definition to experts who preside over us with legal codes and religious or ideological commandments. Thus we obfuscate the only possibility for "discovering" responsibility within ourselves. Havel deals with the problem phenomenologically, with reference to his own existence-in-the-world. Responsibility is finally understood when we can express it not only as relativity (in terms of relationships to self and other) but go beyond this relativity to a recognition of what Havel calls "an omnipresent, absolute horizon" which is a measure and a framework which qualifies and defines us and our actions.

At first glance, Havel seems to substitute God conventionally understood with a more existential or Kierkegaardian sense of an absolute, where an intense search inside one's own existence yields the possibility of an overwhelming and demanding commitment to a fundamental yet intensely personal truth. This commitment cannot be wholly rational; rather it is the subjective source of faith, belief, and hope. Havel provides reasons for faith and hope while reinforcing rather than abrogating personal responsibility. He does not want to yield to the ideology of reason in place of faith. In his "Introduction," Paul

Wilson reminds the reader that Havel shares with phenomenology (especially the Czech variety of Husserl, Patočka, and Bělohradský) a concern that through mechanistic determinism we lose our responsibility. The "I" becomes the "they" of the bureaucratic apparatus, of the class enemy, or the imperialist agent. Implicit is a critique of ideology as an "assigner" of blame, an act of negation, rather than a "taker" of responsibility, an act of choice demonstrating ability and agency.

Reading the *Letters* can be a frustrating experience as his ideas are presented in a fragmentary and contradictory manner. However, Havel does not want to be Hobbes or Spinoza and create a consistent theory of the whole or a comprehensive system of knowledge. The multiformity and elusiveness of his presentation is necessarily reflective of his experience as a prison inmate. Havel shared with many of his fellow dissidents throughout the region an abiding suspicion of philosophy that is overly abstracted from real life and experience. Lest we should try to make *too much* "sense" of his thoughts, and remembering his reflections and actions both deny nihilism, he states in Letter #78:

> ... I have never created, or accepted, any comprehensive "worldview," let alone any complete, unified, integrated, and self-contained philosophical, ideological or other system of beliefs which, with no further adjustments, I could then identify with and which would provide answers to all my questions. This was certainly not out of apathy (it is not difficult to take refuge beneath the protective wing of a ready-made system, and it may even simplify one's life considerably), nor on the contrary, out of any overanxious desire to take my stand, come what may, outside all currents of thought. It was simply because something very deep inside me has always resisted such an approach. I simply don't seem to have the internal capacity for it.
>
> The origin of this "inability" is obviously something in my constitution, in how I am internally structured, as it were. I have already written you about what faith means to me: it is a particular state of mind, that is, a state of persistent and productive openness, of persistent questioning, a need to "experience the world," again and again, in as direct and unmediated a way as possible, and it does not, therefore, flow into me from some concretely defined outside object. For me, perseverance and continuity do not come from fixating on unchanging "convictions" but rather from a ceaseless process of searching, demystification and penetration beneath the surface of phenomena in ways that do not depend on allegiance to

given, ready-made methodology. My entire "experience of the world" has persuaded me of the mysterious multiformity and infinite "elusiveness" of the order of Being, which—by its very nature and by the very nature of the human mind—simply cannot be grasped and described by a consistent system of knowledge (1989: 190).

The ultimate irony is that constant questioning yields the ability to have faith and to believe, if only in something as vague as "Being," the "ultimate horizon," or as he often terms it, "the Absolute." Understanding this is simultaneously contradictory and mysterious.

Faith, and in particular faith in Being, provides human beings with a profound sense of meaning. Like responsibility, Being points "toward something that is both beyond things and within them: their 'absolute horizon'" (1989: 154). This "absolute horizon" is a reminder that such concepts as faith and responsibility cannot be understood according to some rational calculus, or on an imaginary scale of relative utility. The absolute horizon or "Absolute" makes ethics possible—like the contradictory reality and unreality of a physical horizon within our eyesight and our experience, it is the outer rim of our existence, which we can see and not see.

Havel admits that contradictions in thought do not "bother him in the least," and goes so far as to advocate what he calls "'parallelism' or 'pluralism' in knowledge" (1989: 191). In the same way that civil or independent society is a concrete manifestation that there are no absolute answers in political organization, least of all within any configuration of a state, philosophical reconciliation is "foolish, impossible, and utterly pointless." We should not even try to attempt reconciliation of Darwin with Christ, Marx with Heidegger, or Plato with Buddha because, in his words:

Each of them represents a certain level of Being and human experience and each bears witness to the world in his own particular way; each of them, to some extent and in some way, speaks to me, explains many things to me, and even helps me live, and I simply don't see why, for the sake of one, I should be denied an authentic experience of whatever another can show me, even more so because we are not talking here about different opinions on the same thing, but different ways of talking about different things (1989: 191).

Epistemological eclecticism may not produce a Leibnizian vision of the whole, but it is personally useful in grounding one's own often problematic and unfathomable experience as a multi-layered being in a complex world. As Havel states in Letter #83 in answer to the question "why live?" he is less concerned about "the different specific values and ideals in life" (which are inevitably arranged in contradiction to each other) than he is *about human existence as the subject of those values and ideals*" (my emphasis; 1989: 208).

Readers familiar with twentieth-century philosophy will note the influence of Heidegger in Havel's choice of terminology, but are probably less familiar with Czech phenomenology, especially the work of Jan Patočka.[39] Like Heidegger, Havel analyzes grand issues like responsibility and truth by looking at the "everydayness" of life. Looking at things simply by how they present themselves to us, not mediated by the lens of science, ideology, or power, can be both liberating and demystifying. He grounds his philosophical reflections in "The Power of the Powerless" by asking us to consider for a moment the tricky dilemma of the greengrocer; in *Letters to Olga* he struggles with his own potential for indifference and resignation in the face of a long prison sentence. He balances his mundane worries and complaints through reflection and writing; when his moods get the better of him, he reflects on these as an expression of his humanity as well. Havel incorporates a Heideggerian view of personal responsibility as a prerequisite for leading an authentic and meaningful existence, and for humanity as a whole to recover from its fallen position and realize its full potential in terms of being. Unlike Heidegger, Havel inserts a strong moral dimension into the idea of personal responsibility. Whereas Heidegger, following Nietzsche, is more bleak in seeing ethics as a negative metaphysical manifestation of modern nihilism, Havel has no problem positing the existence of absolute values. These values—which include the ability to live in dignity or truth, the free expression of interests and beliefs, a prohibition against bodily harm (involving both physical and mental humiliation), responsibility for and to one's self and by extension for and to the community and the world, human solidarity and trust—also form the basis of the Havelian conception of human rights writ large. Finally, both Heidegger and Havel locate alienation and loss of authenticity in modern technology, rationalism, scientific materialism, and Cartesian objectivism.

The Decisive Influence of Jan Patočka

Havel dedicated "The Power of the Powerless" to the memory of Jan Patočka, his friend, fellow Chartist, and philosophical patron. In both life and death, Patočka was to serve as inspiration not only for Havel but for the Chartists generally. Through Patočka, the Chartists also kept alive an important intellectual lineage, for the respected Central European phenomenologist was both a student of Edmund Husserl, who in turn was befriended by Tomáš Masaryk. A student of Henri Bergson and Martin Heidegger, Patočka's work both synthesizes and answers to his mentors.

Patočka's philosophy can be considered a dialectical synthesis of Masaryk's objectivism and Husserl's turn to subjectivity. He sought a philosophical re-working of order in history and of human life and existence neither in terms of Husserlian transcendental subjectivity nor Cartesian rationalism. For Patočka the basic structures of meaning and of life—whether conceived of as the premeditative natural world or as metatheoretical philosophical conjecture and explanation—as *asubjective. Asubjectivity* for Patočka implied that movements of history (facts and belief structures) and human beings themselves were auto-nomous. Patočka held that self-movement—dynamically realizing that potential and change are possible—is the essence of human existence (Tucker, 2000: 24). *Objective* history did not exist for Patočka in either the Marxist or Hegelian sense; human beings were active subjects yet radically contextualized in history and nature. Patočka's concept of self-movement together with asubjectivity provide a compelling argument for human agency. Moreover, this stance had profound consequences for the interpretation of history, philosophy as a vocation, the task of education, and of the possibilities for human action.

Regardless of his attachment to phenomenology and existentialism Patočka, like Masaryk, remained committed to the ethos of the Enlightenment, or at minimum the notion that the development of European culture and ideas created basic standards for behavior and opened up possibilities for human potential.[40] Modernity and rationality were key standard-bearers in Central Europe, where simultaneously the stars of Nietzsche, Jaspers, and Heidegger were ascendant while the small country dedicated to democracy and humanism crumbled under the weight of Munich. Yet his commitment to the idea of reason is more like Habermas', as a means of understanding human connectedness, of providing a philosophical vocabulary. He rejected the narrow reduction of reason to sterile and limited positivist philosophy, in which he felt people fell prey more easily to the irrationalist appeal of ideology, whether national socialism or Stalinist dogma. What Patočka calls the "positivist hypostatization of natural-scientific methodology"—the cult of reason—is symptomatic of a spiritual crisis in European thought and culture. Technical reason might be appropriate for natural or mathematical science, but for Patočka philosophy requires a kind a reason based on holistic metaphysical inquiry.

It is impossible to detail Patočka's many contributions to modern philosophy, for even today he is not well-known or investigated in the Anglo-American tradition, although this is changing given recent efforts to translate and make available his work in the major European languages of philosophy—English, French, and German.[41] However, my task is more limited—to provide some shape and contour to his influence on Czechoslovak dissidents, most particularly the Chartists.

First, Patočka served as a human philosophical connection to the nation's past—from Komenský[42] to Masarykian humanism and Husserlian phenomenology. As a lecturer and writer, Patočka was hardly a neutral transmitter of information. He abhorred the atavistic "cult of Masaryk" that focused on his success as a statesman and nation-builder rather than as a philosopher of humanism and tolerance who acutely appreciated the contradictions of modern existence, the search for a meaningful ordering of the universe, and a moral sense of good and evil in the collapse of religious faith and the rise of modern science. Patočka made his students aware of the conflict of Masaryk's own life experience, as critical of parochial Czech nationalism, yet ultimately destined to serve as the nation's founder and greatest champion. Although he respected the scope of Husserl's phenomenological undertaking, he remained critical of his idea of "transcendental subjectivity," which he felt simply did not do justice either to the autonomy of humankind or to concrete reality.[43] Second, Patočka's ideas of philosophy as a vocation provide valuable insights as to the particularly philosophical orientation of Czechoslovak dissidents—particularly Havel—as well to Patočka's own reasons for signing Charter 77 himself. Patočka has an all-encompassing view of philosophy as providing a metatheoretical framework of intelligibility within which theories and ideas are generated. Like his teacher Husserl and like Plato and Aristotle whom he compellingly taught and admired, Patočka viewed philosophy as a first-order occupation, whose task is comprehension of the whole.[44] It is of a different order than the natural sciences, and thus philosophical theories cannot be verified or falsified in an overall matrix (Kohák, 1989: 19). Philosophical inquiry is also about meaning and morality, about providing human beings with a vision or set of concepts with which to discuss and decide about good and evil. Philosophy may be fundamentally anti-utilitarian but it is not without passion or purpose; the faith of the philosopher is that he or she might with courage and determination speak some truth. Not unconnected to this view is Patočka's rejection of the philosopher who in attempting to be relevant and *engagé* sinks to the level of doctrinaire ideologue, as an intellectual advertisement with all the deception that description purposefully invites. Such philosophical "titans" inevitably play God, doing injustice to ideals and to human faith and frailty in the process.[45] This does not mean, however, that philosophers have no higher calling or purpose. Patočka's philosopher, like Socrates, must pose questions, leave the cave for the blinding light of the ideal, and find in barren soil some way to nurture this ideal. This vocation thrusts a heavy burden onto the philosopher's shoulders, a Promethean task of responsibility. This responsibility is reinforced by ethical absolutism and the requirement to live in authenticity.

Third, Patočka's Platonism and his notion of responsibility are echoed in the works of Havel and the Chartists. Havel's sense of political responsibility is related to Patočka's call of the ideal. Full humanity and autonomy cannot be achieved without assuming responsibility. Husserl's *Lebenswelt* might provide affirmation of one's self in the flesh and a certain subjective gratification and appreciation of the self inserted into an immediate and real context, but for Patočka human responsibility involves the affirmation of choice and action in rising to the task that can only be done by humans, providing an explanatory framework that will ground a moral order (Kohák, 1989: 22).

From Patočka, the Chartists also absorbed the Socratic interpretation of the Delphic oracle—to know thyself is to be aware that this knowledge-seeking is an epistemological task involving the knowledge of the whole. Patočka, like Socrates, was respectful of ignorance, and the careful yet ironic interlocution of his eponymous method. Patočka adopted Plato's "care for the soul" and suggested that it required an ontological investigation into truth as well as the personal demonstration of living in truth (Tucker, 2000a: 34). To "care for the soul" requires seeking the good, the creation of a community in which truth and justice are possible.[46] McRae accurately pinpoints the connection between Patočka's Platonism and his Chartist influence and practice:

> Patočka was influenced by Husserl and Heidegger, but in a more profound way, I think, by Socrates. Patočka's notion of the "care for the soul" and his admonition to act in an authentic manner was a recipe for dissent under the communist regime. The regime enforced artificial obedience from the outward man, but was incapable of penetrating to the essential privacy of inner life, as it found expression in family and among friends (1997: 17).

The Chartists formed a community of knowledge seekers who, through the care of their own souls, and guided by Havel's dictum "live in truth," took seriously politics *as* responsibility. Patočka combined Platonic *arete*—the excellence in being human—with Heideggerian authenticity in a manner not only reflective but exhortative (Tucker, 2000a: 32). Thus dissent was neither private nor restricted to an isolated group of inner selves, but was extended to the public space of the *agora*—in the Czech context the many living room seminars, unofficial cultural performances, written and oral debates that comprised the Chartist community.

Finally, Patočka's modified Heideggerian view of history was important for how the Chartists saw their own activism and their self-conscious awareness of freedom (Kohák, 1989: 28).[47] The definitive task or "movement" of humanity "is the act of freedom in which freedom rises above the anonymity of that overwhelming context and makes a context *for itself*" (Kohák, 1989: 28). We are rooted in our own history, but are not trapped by it. By studying history we are both doing it and transcending it. For Patočka, as for Marx, human beings make their own history. For Patočka, however, human beings can also transform themselves from passively accepting "fate" into freely and actively "choosing" destiny. In the process, the context is also transformed. The ability to act constitutes history. The implicit self-affirmation and agency is an act of freedom and empowerment. Charter signatory Martin Palouš wrote that Patočka's idea of freedom was similar to that of the Ancient Greeks—freedom was not conceived of as liberty or volition, but as *initiative* (Palouš, 1989: 39).

Patočka discusses the "creative energy of history," not as transcendental but set in a particular context of space and time. He accounts for the universality and the particularity of history as theory and discipline.[48] To use the example of freedom, as Palouš states, it cannot "depend on abilities or character of the isolated individual, rather, it [is] based on the existence and freedom of others" (Palouš, 1989: 39). The pursuit and exercise of freedom demands public space and a conversation among citizens. The community where the conversation takes place provides the specific space-time context; the value discussed has universal resonance.

The question is often raised as to why Patočka signed Charter 77 given its obvious and predictable consequences, or conversely, why he waited so long to "resist" the regime. In reading his work, it becomes easier to deflect the question, as it is premised on the notion of a sudden "turn" to politics, or a previous rejection of it. Signing the Charter was an extension of what Patočka had always been doing, whether as a student of Husserl, a clerk in the Comenius archive, or as a lecturer of an underground seminar. Like Socrates, his task was to actively "do" philosophy, not face some forced and false choice between "politics" and "philosophy." The point was not to engage in politics for its own sake, but to logically follow the Socratic dictates of attending to issues of truth and reason in the search for the Good.[49] In a case of life-imitating philosophy, Patočka, also like Socrates, eventually came to a collision with the authorities and lost his life in the process. Withdrawing from "political" life (conventionally understood under authoritarian communism) and devoting himself to philosophical inquiry did not prevent Patočka from taking a political position, one perceived as fundamentally destabilizing to the political order.

Patočka saw in the human-rights orientation of Charter 77 "a moral foundation," and this was likely a minimum condition for his support. In chastising his own society, lacking such a moral foundation, he states:

> No society, no matter how well-equipped it may be technologically, can function without a moral foundation, without convictions that do not depend on convenience, circumstances, or expected advantage. Yet the point of morality is to assure not the functioning of a society but the humanity of humans. Humans do not invent morality arbitrarily, to suit their needs, wishes, inclinations and aspirations. Quite the contrary, it is morality that defines what being human means (Patočka, in Kohák, 1989: 341).

On the intersection of human rights with morality, he states:

> The idea of human rights is nothing other than the conviction that even
> states, even society as a whole, are subject to the sovereignty of moral sen-
> timent: that they recognize something unconditional that is higher than
> me, something that is binding even on them, sacred, inviolable, and that
> in their power to establish and maintain a rule of law they seek to express
> this recognition (Patočka, in Kohák, 1989: 341).

Patočka ties this morality to the philosophical and personal obligation to resist injustice as both an obligation to oneself and out of
respect for "what is higher in humans, a sense of duty, of the common
good ..." (1989: 343). The above-quoted comments were written late
in the philosopher's life, not as an academic treatise, but as a Charter
text, circulated in samizdat, and published abroad as one of the "voices"
of Charter 77.

Václav Benda's "Parallel *Polis*"

Václav Benda was a contemporary, friend, fellow-Chartist and co-
prisoner of Havel from 1979 to 1983. Both a mathematician and a
philosopher, Benda was a student activist in 1968, serving as Chair of
the students' council. He was well known for his strong Catholicism,
Manichean views, and unyielding and defiant commitment to his faith
and his notions of truth and politics. In the post-communist era and
in keeping with his consistently-held views, he was the parliamentarian
who most fervently supported Czechoslovakia's controversial *lustrace*
law, and was briefly Director of the Office for Documentation and
Investigation of Communist Crimes—ironically situated in the old
headquarters of the StB on Bartolomějska Street in Prague. However,
in 1978, shortly before his arrest for his involvement with VONS, and
just prior to Havel penning "The Power of the Powerless," Benda
wrote a brief samizdat essay entitled "The Parallel *Polis*" which had
immense impact on the Chartists and abroad.

Following the teachings of Jan Patočka and with reference to the
ancient Greek model of the *polis*, the centre of the political and democratic community, Benda sought to reinvigorate this ideal by proposing its creation as the centerpiece of alternative politics. Since its pub-

lication, the notion of a "parallel *polis*" has become synonymous with the construction of an independent civil society, and in some ways with its smaller scale and historical resonance, it proved to be both a powerful metaphor and rhetorical rallying point across the region. One of Benda's chief motives in proposing a parallel *polis* was the deep "disillusionment and skepticism" prevalent among Charter signatories after the initial euphoria of its Charter release, combined with the virulent campaign of the regime against the signatories, most symbolically and tragically represented by Patočka's death (Benda, in Skilling and Wilson, eds., 1991: 35–36).[50] Benda's theorization of the parallel *polis* was decisive, especially given his complete and practical theorization of an *expanding* alternate public sphere. He was deliberately pushing the envelope past the semi-exclusive and escapist independent cultural activities of the kind promoted by artist Ivan Jirous.

Regardless of his own personal moral absolutism, Benda saw that expecting the total "moral commitment involved in challenging an evil political power and trying to destroy it" was both suicidal and unrealistic. It was more realistic for a citizen to feel "morally obliged to size up the situation ... and try to bring about partial improvements through compromise and reform" (Benda, in Skilling and Wilson, eds., 1991: 36). Whereas Patočka was firm in his moral foundation, his discussion of the Charter was noticeably abstract and organizationally intangible. As a corrective to Patočka, Benda suggests:

> ... we join forces in creating, slowly but surely, parallel structures that are capable, to a limited degree at least, of supplementing the generally beneficial and necessary functions that are missing in the official structures, and where possible, to use those existing structures, to humanize them (Benda, in Skilling and Wilson, eds., 1991: 36).

His rationale was a compelling re-statement of Michnik's evolutionism:

> This plan will satisfy both the 'reformists' and the 'radicals'. It need not lead to a direct conflict with the regime, yet it harbors no illusions that 'cosmetic' changes can make any difference. Moreover it leaves open the key question of the system's viability. Even if such structures were only partially successful, they would bring pressure to bear on the official structures, which would either collapse (if you accept the view of the radicals)

or regenerate themselves in a useful way (if you accept the reformist position) (Benda, in Skilling and Wilson, eds., 1991: 36).

Benda was careful to propose an alternative that was not zero-sum in character, a strategy of evolutionary reformism which by its very nature cut through radically to the very heart of the system.

Benda's plan was directed and elitist (with its implicit notion of "enlightening the masses" through such activity) and hopelessly naive—both of which he openly admitted. Ironically, it probably took someone of Benda's uncompromising will and faith to push ahead with such an idea, and to do so with a sense of stubborn practicality that it might be achieved after all. To this end, Benda spells out his plan in detail, in effect marketing his proposal to his fellow Chartists.

Benda notes that the already-existing parallel culture is a starting point. In some areas, such as popular music and the plastic arts, these phenomena are so strong and positive that "the parallel culture overshadows the lifeless, official culture" (1991: 37). The second culture, given its dynamism and level of development, would "serve as a model for other areas" (1991: 38), especially related and neglected fields like literary criticism, cultural journalism, theatre and film. He even appeals to the parallel economy (and here he is referring not to an officially-tolerated or semi-sanctioned second economy as in Hungary but in fact the black market) as a factor in most consumer relations, and thus a source of potential. On the intellectual front, Benda promotes a "parallel structure of education and scientific and scholarly life"—indeed this is exactly what developed with the underground university.

With respect to the Charter in such activities, Benda expected it to continue playing a pivotal and central role, but not to limit or control other initiatives. Furthermore, the Charter's work would have to be made more effective and far-reaching through a more dense and efficient information network, ensuring broad circulation of materials internally, especially beyond Prague.

Benda's final suggestions even include the creation of a parallel foreign policy, although he reckoned it would have little chance of success; it was more an expression of the "internationalization of the problem" (1991: 40). He also recommended what he euphemistically called "mutual cooperation between related trends in other East Bloc countries" (1991: 40). At the time this essay was written these cross-border efforts were already materializing: the first Polish–Czechoslovak border meeting took place in the summer of 1978.[51] In the early 1980s Hungarian dissidents were traveling to Poland, and ethnic Hungarians in Slovakia were making contact with the democratic opposition in Budapest.

Aside from this famous and influential essay, Benda applied his very pragmatic and activist orientation to the Catholic Church in Czechoslovakia. Unlike Michnik, who argued for a Left–Church alliance from a secular Jewish perspective, Benda argued for social activism from a deeply religious position as a Catholic philosopher. For Benda, the cultural and political renewal he advocated in "The Parallel *Polis*" also amounted to a reaffirmation of Christian values.[52] Not content to rest on this identification, however, Benda also pressed the Church hierarchy and laity to confront the monopoly of the party-state as an assault not only on religious freedom, but as responsible for isolating and atomizing individuals, making not only Christian community impossible but increasing susceptibility to loneliness and manipulation. He echoes Havel when he speaks of the "Iron Curtain" that separates not only East and West but runs through social classes, the family, and the individual.

According to Benda, a truly Christian attitude requires one not simply to pursue one's own salvation, "imprisoning oneself in a ghetto-like mentality" but also to make "a total commitment to others" (Benda, 1989: 23). Accepting this "mission" as a Christian is not unlike a Charter signatory accepting the responsibility that automatically goes with signing. Benda states: "Uncertainty and risk are part and parcel of the Christian experience" (1989: 25). Similarly, in the same way Benda pushed the Charter to take a more concrete and programmatic stance in making the parallel *polis* come about, he pushes the established Church, in its own program of spiritual renewal, to support independent culture and education, speak out against persecution and coercion, oppose the ineffective and overtly anti-Christian charitable institutions of the regime, and preserve and extend the alliance between the hierarchy and "politically active Christians" like himself. Benda's position does not contravene the Gelasian doctrine of the "two swords"; he paraphrases scripture in his statement, "When Caesar claims everything [as in the case of authoritarian communism]— including what is God's—one may not render him anything whatsoever" (1989: 25). While Benda is careful to oppose "political clericalism" he notes that in the time of opposition the Church must adopt a dual strategy: "as long as we are endangered by external pressure as much as by our own sinfulness, there is a need to confront both equally" (1989: 26). The time is not yet ripe for "political differentiation" between the Church itself and "politically engaged Christians," or between "a purely spiritual renewal and a renewal of civic, national and patriotic virtues"—the two must work hand in hand.[53]

The Collective *Oeuvre* of the Chartists

Charter 77 produced 572 documents over the decade and a half of its existence, mostly in the form of letters, communiqués (*sdělení*), appeals, and short statements or essays. Before "release" by Charter 77, documents underwent a rigorous authorization and review process to ensure authenticity. When documents were signed by one or several persons, they often bore the stamp of collective authorship, given the process of review and commentary. Although the important contributions of Havel, Patočka, and Benda warrant separate treatment, the overall "voice" of Charter 77 is appropriately treated as a collective enterprise.

A number of recurring themes can be discerned through an examination of Charter documents: linkages with and commentary on other dissidents and organizations in Central and Eastern Europe (which implicitly delineate strategy and explicitly outline personal and organizational connections); religious statements underlining not only the importance of religious freedom but also pointing to spirituality as the metaphysical glue between politics and morality; theoretical writings as well as a source of alternative "news" on arts and culture, the social and economic spheres, education, the environment, and statements on international affairs, primarily focusing on the superpower conflict, the peace movement, and the progress of the Helsinki process. Moreover, the Chartists did not only write and think about these issues abstractly; their work collectively *bears witness* to the abuses of an era. They carefully monitored and documented the injustices of authoritarian communism, from the workplace to the prison system, provided evidence of discrimination toward minorities such as the Roma, and compellingly described environmental degradation. However, the predominant theme and underlying ethos of the Charter was its emphasis on human rights. Human rights as theory and practice constitute the primary theoretical contribution of the Chartists to the dissident *oeuvre*.

Charter 77 defined itself as a human rights organization throughout its history, beginning with its initial *Declaration*. In Czechoslovakia (as well as in Poland and Hungary), focusing on human rights served key objectives. Pragmatically and philosophically, human rights are about stripping politics to its naked core. Without respect for the life, belief, and expression of the citizen, authentic politics cannot exist. When we accept the internal logic of democracy, with the extension of the franchise and citizenship rights and responsibilities to adult members of society, we have to premise this involvement with some notion of human rights as natural and inviolable and posit basic equality and mutual respect among human beings. Because human beings are not isolated individuals, such rights must be understood in a community context—thus free expression necessarily entails freedom of association to be practically meaningful. Human rights are thus an essential precondition for public life that is truly inclusive. For this reason, an emphasis on human rights as a basic building block of civilized society could be fundamentally unifying. Charter 77 could and did appeal to a broad range of supporters precisely because ideological differences were nullified in the first-order effort to create a dialogue and level of understanding about the ramifications of accepting the human rights logic. As a result, independent socialists, former revisionists, non-communist writers and intellectuals, religious activists, workers, and professionals came together not simply as signatories but as the originators in a pan-societal *conversation* about what the ground rules of politics *ought* to be.[54]

This discussion on human rights reinforced Western legalism and the constitutional supremacy of law and the legal process. Martin Palouš (1996) argues that the Chartist approach contributed heavily to the post-communist Czechoslovak legal order, literally by comparing Charter documents with the post-1989 Bill of Rights that is now an inseparable part of the Czech constitution and Chartist commentary on human rights abuses around the world. That human rights cannot be contained or protected within national borders underlined a strong element of transnationalization, thus Chartists were concerned and wrote about how international mechanisms must support domestic lines of defense for human rights. International regimes of human rights must be codified in domestic law, and international human rights commitments extend the Havelian notion of personal responsibility to the international arena.[55]

Although the Chartists were careful in neither criminalizing the party-state nor directly challenging its monopoly on power, it remains paradoxically the case that in design and orientation the organization and its authors did just that. Publicizing the Helsinki Accords and the outlining the minimal conditions for the *actual* observance of human rights meant that Charter 77 was a *de facto* subversive organization. Embedded in the notion of human rights is the existence of a legal system founded upon the rule of law that can ensure both protection and implementation—some type of *Rechtsstaat* that is decidedly *not* in keeping with even the most liberal version of the Soviet model.

Beyond human rights, it is difficult to pin down a definitive "Charter position" on anything, and to do so misses the point entirely. The Chartists were an organizational *and a theoretical contrast* to the anonymously ideological bureaucracy of the party-state. Commenting on Charter 77 in *Infoch* as part of an internal discussion on the purposes of the organization, Havel stated:

> ... if Charter documents are not to become depersonalized, shapeless, anonymous, bureaucratic texts, with an official tone as soporific as party speeches and resolutions, then there is nothing wrong with injecting into them a more personal tone, and perhaps even a provocative idea, insight, or formulation, especially when a document has come from a particular pen ... . (1991: 325).

In the same article, he points to the deliberately fuzzy pluralism of the Charter:

> In any case, there is no index of words, expressions, or ideas that are "authentically Chartist," so the territory of what is "authentically Chartist" has no borders. Everything is a matter of a freely determined consensus and agreement, which of course can be influenced by a thousand circumstances both internal and external (1991: 325).

The ultimate irony is that Charter 77 *was* its own "Anti-Charter"; it did not need the regime to provide the organization with its own antithesis.

Theorizing Civil Society: The Czechoslovak Example

In the same way that the existence of Solidarity ultimately represents the originality of the Polish contribution, and provided a living and breathing example of the rebirth of civil society, so too was the case with Charter 77 in Czechoslovakia, albeit on a more limited scale. Czech historian and Charter signatory Vilém Prečan summarizes thus:

> Charter 77's emergence on the Czechoslovak political scene represents the fundamental watershed in the country's development in the period after the defeat of the reform movement of 1968. It was a flash of light which made clear that history never ends, that it remains forever open. This new intellectual orientation, the principle of the indivisibility of freedom and the universal validity of human and civil rights, which Charter 77 professed, was a radical challenge to the totalitarian Communist regime. With the quiet and peaceful arrival of Charter 77 began the era of politics orientated *to the renewal of civil society*, of democracy and the rule of law founded on the unconditional recognition of human and civil rights (my emphasis, 1997: 3).

Similarly, Palouš credits Charter 77 with forcing a political *abertura* through the adoption of a "non-political" stance, one that reinforced public responsibility:

> As the Charter clearly laid out in its opening, it was not and did not try to be a political opposition party. However, its existence created an elementary precondition for a situation in which, in what was then Czechoslovakia, there could begin to emerge from the marasma of the normalised regime a particular phenomenon without which standard political life is unthinkable—civic [sic] society. The "parallel polis" of the Chartists became a key for the renewal of horizontal communication in society, interrupted under the Communist government, a prototype of those "intermediary bodies" which according to de Tocqueville represent a necessary condition for the origin and existence of democracy (1996: 7).

Charter 77 also proved that the actual *size* of a community of dissent mattered less than its existence, visibility, and the societal variegation of its members. For most of the 1980s Western scholars compared dissent in Czechoslovakia as somehow less in quality because its "quantity" could not measure up to the powerhouse of Solidarity. According to Prečan, dissent in Czechoslovakia began and ended with the possibilities inherent in that society under authoritarian communist rule—the normalization process set up the material conditions out of which dissent could both grow but not spread. Charter 77 and the initiatives it spawned did not cause the downfall of the regime, but when the crisis became acute in November, 1989 the "graduates" of its school of dissent and organization acted quickly, enabled the mobilization of social forces, and "stood at the head of the democratic revolution and led it to its conclusion" (Prečan, 1997: 11).

The existence and stubborn longevity of Charter 77 breathed life into the principles espoused by Patočka, Havel, and Benda. Through it a "parallel *polis*" was created, wherein its members and supporters could "live in truth" and act responsibly, in both the moral and political sense. Moreover, this alternative public sphere was neither an *ersatz* creation rendered impotent by the party-state nor a philosophical ideal removed from the lives of average Czechoslovaks. The *modus operandi* of Charter 77 stimulated the growth of the public sphere and encouraged social dialogue. In relation to the institutionalized politics of the post-communist era, Palouš states:

> [Charter 77] created an environment in which people could learn again to live in the public sphere, to examine the state of common affairs and at the same time not to let slip the moment when it was necessary to act; when it was necessary to leave the parallel polis and begin to make—with everything this implied—real, that is "political" politics. The question of communication and the ability to hold a dialogue within our society is essential even today. Even today it is a question of how the non-political and the political politics combine. In my view it is still true that the second cannot exist without the first, that without a moral and civic measure, politics as a mere play of power is bound to degenerate and no parliament or system of politic [sic] parties can save it from its fall (1996: 7).

Finally, although Charter 77 might be seen in retrospect as a "training ground" for future democratic politicians and leaders of civil society, that was not really the point at the time. Because the Charter contained members of differing convictions and strong voices, there was also a tendency, in Havel's words, "to judge the Charter according to the politics of particular Chartists" (1991: 324). In turn, this led to speculative navel-gazing as to whether or not the Charter was leaning to the left or right over time or on a particular issue. As Havel argued in 1986, Charter 77 was not conceived on a left-right axis, nor did it conduct its business two-dimensionally on that axis:

> Charter 77 is neither left-wing nor right-wing, not because it is "somewhere in the middle," but because it has nothing whatever in common with that spectrum, because in essence, it lies outside it. As a civic initiative that is politically undefined and does not seek to implement a political program of its own, it is—if I may say so—"above" it all, or, to put it more modestly, outside it all. It is concerned with the truth, with a truthful description of conditions, and with a free and objective criticism of those conditions. Which means that it is and must be concerned with truth no matter whom that truth favors (1991: 326).

After all, Havel's antipolitics and the supposed "non-political" position of Charter 77 were not about depoliticizing politics *per se*, but rather to expand the political by infusing civil society with authenticity and responsibility.

CHAPTER 7

THE DEMOCRATIC OPPOSITION IN HUNGARY

The Philosophical Legacy of György Lukács

The "first generation" of Hungarian dissidents—for that is really what the Budapest School was—saw themselves not only as Lukács' colleagues or students but described themselves as his *disciples*. Their self-chosen terminology is illuminating, because they both collectively and individually sought to utilize, extend, and reinterpret Lukács' work not only in terms of his own life and struggle but more meaningfully in terms of their own.

It is impossible here to summarize the depth of this scholarly and personal interaction, but some generalizations can be made.[1] From Lukács' early focus on aesthetics (for example, the Heidelberg manuscripts) through to his later work, culture remained a central theme and was also a definitive question for his students and adversaries. Heller has indicated that Lukács' concern went well beyond the possible reconciliation of high and popular culture, to a schema that saw culture as synonymous with authentic life or the "immanence of meaning in life." For Lukács, life could be not lived without alienation unless culture were to be completely transformed (Heller, 1983: 3–4). Lukács promoted the philosophical and existential possibility that life could be shaped through culture—thus it is no mere accident that Hungarian dissidents in their early attempts to create parallel institutions or initiatives called their efforts a "counter-culture," a "second culture," and even a "non-conformist culture." Indeed the double-entendre of the phrase "counter-culture" was intentional, referring not only to their sixties counterparts in the West, but also to this deeper Lukácsian notion.

The same can also be said for the category of class. Although Lukács famously repudiated *History and Class Consciousness* largely for reasons of political expediency rather than philosophical retraction, his ideas regarding class were much more in keeping with Hegel and the writings of the "young" Marx than with the Bolshevism of Lenin and the

258 THE DILEMMAS OF DISSIDENCE IN EAST-CENTRAL EUROPE

Russian revolutionaries. His radically teleological idea of a self-conscious proletariat (or its elite representatives) struggling inevitably toward historical destiny and authentic subjectivity today seems almost ridiculous in its optimism, not to mention universalist assumptions. However, underlying this is a deep understanding of class as a powerful nexus of social relations and identity, one that can be unmasked through a detailed sociological analysis of interests and behaviors. Thus among Hungarian dissidents one finds much more emphasis on class and the class-based nature of authoritarian communism. As might be expected, we find in the Hungarian canon Konrád and Szelényi's *The Intellectuals on the Road to Class Power* as well as the notion of the sub-intelligentsia forming itself into a non-conformist, dissident-friendly class in Kis and Bence's *Toward an East European Marxism*. However, neither of these books was written by the direct "descendants" of Lukács, that is, those most closely associated with him (such as Heller, Fehér, and Márkus).

As was typical for his generation of radical intellectuals east of the Rhine, Lukács demonstrated a deep mistrust of modern science. Unlike Marx, whose beliefs in scientific progress and the emancipatory possibilities of technology were linked to the general intellectual climate of the 19th century, Lukács was formed by the irrational and immoral outcomes of science in the early 20th century—the horrors of the Great War, the inhumanity of industry, the arrogant hubris embedded in the willful replacement of value with fact, subjectivity with objectivity, history with timeless laws. Moreover, Lukács began writing *as a Marxist* (that is, after his sudden "conversion" to Marxism in late 1918) at a time when Marxism itself was being scientized and transformed into methodology, with "scientific" orthodoxy ultimately represented as dialectical materialism. Thus Lukács set for himself the Herculean task of extracting "the latent critique of science from Marx's own method" whereby he could reconcile his own commitment to Marxism with his own experience, and do so within the ever-limiting strictures of the Comintern. Despite his critique of orthodoxy, he was loyal to historicism and the *historical character* of "facts"—reinforcing his concern that scientific rationality thinly disguises a totalizing tendency definitely *not* compatible with human liberation. There are obvious regional parallels with respect to the critique of scientific rationality, and understanding these helps to explain the similarity in content and approach in the dissident oeuvre. One can draw a line from Lukács through his students to the environmentalist concerns of the Hungarian dissidents, just as one can also draw a line from Husserl's critique of science through to Patočka's phenomenology, Bělohradský's condemnation of abstract reason and impersonal objectivity and Havel's call for a reconciliation between impersonal science and the boundaries of the Absolute, along with the reclaiming of human responsibility for the biosphere.

Even if these lineages to the Lukácsian legacy could be demonstrated this simply, it would be misleading to assume that this was either a direct or easy inheritance. Lukács was highly problematic figure on which to model oneself as an *independent* critic of authoritarian communism when he bowed before the authorities so many times in his life. It was not without good reason that Isaac Deutscher referred to Lukács as the ultimate theorist and apologist of Stalinism.

This task was most difficult for his immediate disciples. Without wanting to whitewash his decisions but to understand them in context of his philosophy, Heller and others sought to consider the body of Lukács' thought as a complete whole, refusing to take the easy road of dividing up his life and thought into "young" versus "old," "pre-1918" versus "communist," or "politics" versus "aesthetics." In their search for continuity and with deep respect for the master, however, they often fell into the trap of overcoming his contradictions through higher and higher levels of philosophical abstraction of their own, a process which obviously demonstrated their own erudition and detailed knowledge of Lukács' every word and thought, but which unfortunately has rendered much of the analysis impenetrable to all but the initiated and seasoned expert.[2]

For those more active in the dissident circles of the 1980s and for the most part removed by one generation from Lukács himself (and by his death in 1971), the task of simply taking him for granted, warts and all, was somewhat easier. Thus Gáspár Miklós Tamás was stating the obvious when he claimed in his answer to Heller et al.:

> The exact list of the divergences between you and Lukács ... a lucid summary of the critical aspects of your views formed in the 1960s, is already *lingua franca* of my generation. Together with the results of Kołakowski, Kosík, and the *Praxis* circle, are part and parcel of that secret syntax that shapes the language of all of us (Tamás, in Heller, ed., 1983: 157).

They were at the same time more tolerant of his contradictions (complete philosophical cohesion not being a practicable or desirable goal anyway) and less forgiving of his political errors, especially given the fact that they were clearly taking a different path. To the second generation, taking a stand outside and apart from the insidious tentacles of the Hungarian party-state was as important as it was for Lukács, always and above all a loyal party member, to stay *within* its boundaries.

István Eörsi, the poet-dissident, prisoner of 1956 and friend of Lukács, was in many respects a bridge-builder, both generationally and intellectually. As to the legacy of Lukács, Eörsi did not hesitate in laying bare the embarrassments caused by many of his positions both personal and political but also lauded his fully-developed persona, devoid of pathos, and willingness to take any position regardless of the heresy it might engender. His positions were maddening yet enlightening, but as Eörsi warns, "great enlightenment can also lead to great blindness" (1987b: 15). At the end of his life, Lukács advocated a "complete break" with Stalinism while admitting that Stalin's successors had retained "all the essential points of his heritage"—and also his own (1987b: 15).[3] He knew that Stalinism could not evolve into its opposite, but never saw himself as oppositional. Ultimately, his stubborn ability to live within his own contradictions while philosophically both justifying and rejecting them made him problematic for the regime and a point of departure for the nascent opposition. As Eörsi stated:

> Lukács is not only unacceptable for the general public, but also for official Hungary. His slogan "Back to Marx" implies that the system had deviated from Marx and that its ideological foundations were crumbling. Since Stalin, theory has had no other function than to legitimize everyday tactical decisions. If this is so, then his insistence on the rebirth of Marxism is undoubtedly very embarrassing. Who is interested in such a rebirth? After all, the population of the country agrees with its leaders on only one ideological point: both are indifferent to Marxism (1987b: 16).

Lukács showed that philosophy generally and critical Marxism specifically could be kept alive under authoritarian communism, but at a great intellectual and personal price. His disciples showed that Lukács' own ideas could be extended without personal compromise but only within the realm of philosophy. However, as Marx said, the point was not to philosophize about the world, but to change it. Accordingly the second generation took the critique and attempted to live it, on the margins of society to be sure, but at the same time attempted to reunite theory and practice in open violation of the party-state.

The Influence of István Bibó

István Bibó was far more directly influential on the emerging democratic opposition than was Lukács. He represented a very different type of influence on the Hungarian dissidents, one that was more the result of a conscious political choice. He was neither a *maître-penseur* nor a Marxist. His goal was not to contribute to or mastermind some type of grand theoretical *Verstehen*, but rather to offer much more positional analyses and suggest tactical remedies to seemingly intractable social and political problems. Hungarian journalist, critic (and former editor of *Beszélő*) Sándor Szilágyi accurately, I think, calls Bibó "Central Europe's Political Therapist," and notes that his style was appropriately laden with the language and metaphors of clinical psychology and psychiatry. Bibó did this not to overburden his analysis by adding fear and other human neuroses to already complicated histories, but as a pragmatic choice, a diagnostic tool:

> ... we encounter so many largely fear-induced decisions and political hysterias when analyzing the historical processes of Europe (especially those of Central and Eastern Europe because the preceding periods and generations bequeathed a huge burden of unsolved national social and political problems to the participants and leaders of public life). Thus it is not fear that shapes history—it is history that shapes fear (Szilágyi, in Nagy, ed., 1991: 528).

To extend the metaphor, Bibó was not a medical researcher, but a pharmacologist. His writings contain both historical explanation and underlying examination of social processes but above all "invariably outline the remedy" (1991: 528). Szilágyi explains:

> Bibó always offered a way out, whether the problem arose from the unresolved issues of post-war peacemaking, the border disputes of Eastern Europe's small nations, nationalism, the conflicts between Arabs and Israelis or Irish and British, the democratic political organization of an

occupied Hungary, the situation after the crushing of the 1956 Revolution, or European anti-Semitism. Was he then a kind of political witch doctor, an all-knowing miracle worker, possessing the keys to all solutions, so the rest of us should simply accept his sage counsel? Far from it: Bibó always emphasizes that the solutions he recommends do not promise easy and quick success; quite the contrary, they require more than a little effort from those affected by the unsolved problems. These efforts demand that the participants acknowledge human motives instead of satanic malevolence on the part of their opponents and show a readiness to compromise instead of insistence on total fulfillment of their own wishes. When he talked of the future, Bibó did not present a rose-colored Utopia—all he illustrated, using clear, rational arguments, was that any solution born out of mutual selfishness and the cornering of an opponent does not bode well for the future. He tried to convince opposing parties that they should consider each other not enemies but partners, and that *together* they should seek out solutions to the crises caused by their mutual obstinacy (1991: 528).

An excellent example of Bibó's style and approach to political problem-solving can be found in his essay "The Jewish Question in Hungary after 1944," written in 1948. Amidst angry accusals and denials of Holocaust responsibility, Bibó characteristically entered the fray with a reasoned and balanced essay, carefully excavating some of the most potentially inflammatory issues of his day. With scrupulous attention to historical detail and its human consequences, he addressed Hungarian "collective" responsibility for the events of 1944, going back to the first anti-Jewish legislative measures enacted by the Horthy[4] government to the persecution, forced ghettoization, and deportation of Hungary's Jews to the death camps.

What is particularly striking in reading Bibó's essay so long after the events he described is his dogged effort to locate himself in the middle of a debate marked by hyperbolic extremes. Thus he is *not* willing to blame Hungarians—either individually or collectively—for their inability to reject the discriminatory legislation against Jews or restrictions against their economic activities, because he tries to have the reader understand the social genesis of such action. However, he is absolutely unequivocal in calling the nation morally bankrupt given the majority of Hungarians operated on a continuum from enthusiastic assistance to ignorance and apathy in allowing the rural deportations and urban ghettoization to take place. He does not mince words when he destroys the myth that Hungarians managed to "save" the Budapest Jews through their enlightened and strategic action.[5] Similarly, he does not avoid tackling the inflammatory question of Jewish culpability, and carefully examines how *both* Jews and non-Jews developed mutually negatively-reinforcing views of the other, and how these experiences were both socially and historically constructed and distorted. He examines all the explanations and components of anti-Semitism historically and contemporaneously, including its reemergence in the immediate aftermath of the war. With Thomist logic he considers all of the possible counterarguments to his own position before defending it.[6]

Although he recognizes the infinite complexity of the problem and the inability of any one approach to "solve" it, his recommendations can hardly be improved upon:

> When it comes to the Hungarian situation, our most urgent task is to formulate and disseminate an attitude of *accepting responsibility for the persecution of Jews*, and to create a public conception that takes the issues of responsibility and culpability seriously, while also clarifying the conditions, extent and limits of calling people to account. When it comes to the relationship between Jews and the community, we must recognize the reality and feasibility of both *assimilation* and a *separate Jewish consciousness*, create suitably clear conditions and a benevolent environment for both, and at the same time remove all generalizations, forced attitudes and demands from the entire issue of community identification (1991: 310).

Like Havel, Bibó is adamant in linking responsibility to the (re)establishment of a moral order. Taking such responsibility was a necessary precursor to the creation of a politics where serious and decisive judgments could be made and be trusted. Being *mature, civilized, and in keeping with European values* demanded such action, and Bibó called leaders and the intelligentsia responsible—*because* they were leaders and intellectuals (1991: 187). Avoiding future tragedies would be impossible without an honest and objective recognition of the sins of the past, necessary for any project of national reconciliation. Finally, a strong respect for the human dignity of Jews and their rights should not only be extended to all national minorities but indeed serve as a hallmark for the citizenship of everyone. This would have to be achieved in the context of reshaping the political, economic, and social order toward classlessness and true equality—objectives toward which Bibó felt the postwar national government was making some headway.

A striking comparison which suitably demonstrates Bibó's intellectual heritage can be found in János Kis' essay "On Ways of Being a Jew." Kis wrote the essay in response to an "Open Letter to the Hungarian Jewry and to Hungarian Society" written by *Salom* (*Shalom*), an independent Hungarian Jewish peace group on the fortieth anniversary of the Holocaust and published in *Hírmondó*. *Salom* called for an open examination of the relationship between Jews and non-Jews, which forty years after the Hungarian Holocaust (and nearly that long since Bibó's essay was written) remained unresolved. More controversially, it called into question the automatic assimilationist bias of both Jews and of non-Jewish Hungarians towards Jews which had been prominent since 1867 and hegemonic since 1945.[7] *Salom* gave voice to a growing community of young Jews who were examining their past, felt an affinity for and solidarity with the state of Israel, and wanted to establish and practice secular and religious traditions.

In his response Kis reveals his own bias as a completely secularized and Magyarized Jew, but one who recognizes that in "an environment [that] still recognizes and distinguishes them as Jews ... to strive for complete assimilation is an idle effort [which] can lead only to a compulsion of overcompensation, inferiority complex, and humiliating exposure" (1989: 236). Kis wants to explore why "Hungarian Jews may choose from various life strategies which are all compatible with the coexistence of Jews and non-Jews, a coexistence which is based on mutual respect" (1989: 235). While not recognizing the avenue of conscious Jewish identification as his own, he argues that it is in keeping with the type of liberal democracy he supports. Kis suggests that multiple and overlapping identities do not undermine but rather are part of the very fabric of democratic choice, "... that every individual may choose not only the guiding philosophical and moral beliefs of his life, but also his affiliation with ethnic-cultural communities. ..." (1989: 235). He acknowledges that the problem is one of possibilities—more options are open than the one advocated by *Salom*, though theirs should not be excluded either.

Like Bibó, Kis advocates an "honest confrontation with the past"; he tackles Holocaust responsibility *and* Jewish involvement in the imposition of Hungarian Stalinism. Both speak in the language of "moral responsibility" and are thus compelled to take what might otherwise be unpopular or at least potentially inflammatory positions. Thus Kis writes:

> Is it possible to speak, in this regard, of the Hungarian Jewry's moral responsibility for the Stalinist dictatorship? Up to a certain degree, yes. For whatever opinion a considerable portion of the Jews held about the regime, they accepted it on the grounds that, at least, the persecution of the Jews would not return. This view drove some Jews to a religious identification with Communism, others to a certain conditional sympathy with the regime even during its darkest years. Only a relative few were able to keep their distance (1989: 241–242).

While Kis admits that the parallel with 1944 is inappropriate as Stalinism was hardly construed as its revenge, he reasons that Jews "if they did take part in this terror ... have to face its lessons as well" (1989: 242). Kis shows no hesitancy in taking on *Salom* itself for deviating from its own principles when it comes to the relationships between Israelis and Palestinians. It is contradictory, states Kis, to support the 1948 UN resolution acknowledging the right of Jews to their own state and not recognize that Israel now occupies territory accorded to a sovereign Palestinian state under the same resolution. It is also tactically foolhardy in terms of promoting their own legitimate rights as a minority. Concerned with both the appearance and actuality of proper political conduct, Kis suggests that it is "never good to treat our principles in a casual manner" and certainly "not worthwhile to appear in advance as somebody who violates in thought the fundamental principle of equality among minorities, nationalities and nations. ..." (1989: 243).

János Kis is only one among many in the democratic opposition who have openly in conversation and writing admitted their great debt and obvious appreciation of Bibó. It might be tempting to conclude that Bibó was "selected" by a tactically minded second-generation oppositional elite as a more fitting intellectual forebear than Lukács, and that this reflected the turn from Marxism to liberalism. Aside from the obvious strategy of uniting the populists with the urbanists with such projects as the *Bibó Memorial Book*, what the democratic opposition appreciated more in Bibó was his style rather than any particular content. Bibó was famously characterized as "the most tolerant Hungarian," described himself as "passionately objective," and his writing shows more of a talent for mediation and arbitration than for classical political theory. He believed strongly in the basic tenets of any negotiating process: recognizing your adversaries' interests as well as your own, searching for areas of agreement rather than disagreement, mutual communication as a method of building trust. It should not be surprising that among his many influences and intellectual mentors he counted Dag Hammarskjöld, whose lectures he attended at the Institute on World Peace at The Hague in the mid-1930s.

Bibó was absolutely the opposite of a zealot, completely free of all political illusions and owing no allegiance to anyone for his well-formed and reasoned opinions. It was this position of inner freedom that enabled him to chastise communist leaders for their accusations of class subversion against coalition partners in the late 1940s while telling the landlords and factory owners that democracy in Hungary would never mean a return to the world of *latifundia* and industrial exploitation. This stance of independence and commitment to the idea that direct and open communication can both raise the level of discourse and open up new possibilities was common to those who so actively nurtured Hungarian samizdat and opposition politics.

Bibó was not a liberal in the classical sense, and his principles of social and economic equality have more in common with democratic socialism than capitalism. Throughout his period of political activism, he identified with the Populist Movement, at a time when the movement was at its most progressive phase, representing leftist writers and intellectuals concerned with land reform, grass-roots democratic transformation, and campaigning for a "third way" between the liberalism and Marxism.[8] Indeed, as Kovács has recently argued, Bibó's philosophy—especially his analysis of the social responsibilities of elites in maintaining social solidarity and political legitimation—is particularly instructive under current conditions of globalization.[9]

Kis and Bence: *Toward an East European Marxism?*

János Kis and György Bence published *Toward an East European Marxism* in the West under the pseudonym Marc Rakovski. The English-language version of the book[10] is a collection of essays first published in French journals between 1973 and 1977; only later was it published in Hungarian samizdat under the title *A szovjet típusú társadalom marxista szemmel* (*Soviet-type Society from a Marxist Perspective*). The title of the book and even its subject matter is retrospectively ironic, as it represents the beginning of both authors' turn away from Marxism as a way of coming to terms with Soviet-type societies in East-Central Europe, both analytically and politically.

In their introduction, Kis and Bence suggest that all previous East European Marxist analyses of Soviet-type societies can be basically reduced to three categories: those that accept the *prima facie* self-definition as socialism, those that claim such societies are transitional, or those that maintain that they are in fact some form of capitalism. They propose to take an entirely new approach, for they claim that if "marxism is possible at all in Eastern Europe, it has to stand on a completely new theoretical foundation" (1978: 15). Thus they state:

> The hypothesis which we are going to take as the point of departure for our investigations is therefore the following. Soviet-type society is neither socialist nor capitalist, nor is it a mixture of the two systems. It is a class society *sui generis*, a different kind of class society existing alongside capitalism (1978: 15).

The approach is not without obvious difficulties, because a certain amount of conceptual stretching—if not outright reconfiguration—is inevitable, making a Marxist analysis as conventionally understood difficult indeed:

> In order to approach the fourth hypothesis we have just set out above, it is necessary to reconsider the whole traditional structure of historical materialism. In the generally accepted framework of historical materialism it is impossible to give a description of a modern, non-transitional society where there is not capitalist private property but where the means of production are not at the collective disposal of the producers; where there is no bourgeoisie or proletariat but the population is still divided into classes; where economic priorities are not normally determined by the market, but neither are they chosen by means of rational discussion among the associated producers, and so on (1978: 15).

For Kis and Bence conventional Marxist historiography works best for capitalism, its original intended object, but is very problematic when it comes to the authoritarian communist regimes of East and Central

Europe. Because of the "unilinear evolutionism" Kis and Bence suggest is inherent in Marx's historical materialism, one cannot suggest that Soviet-type societies can exist in and of themselves *as class societies* existing alongside capitalism. Historical materialism permits "no place for a modern social system which has an evolutionary trajectory other than capitalism and which is not simply an earlier or later stage along the same route" (1978: 17).

In fact, Kis and Bence do not take the reader on a voyage of discovery toward a new East European Marxism. The second chapter, "'Market Socialism' in Retrospect" deals with the antinomies of market socialism, both as an ideology and practise. To the extent that the authors analyze the class-basis of those in whose interests the reform processes were initiated and examine the social forces underpinning such efforts, theirs is definitely an effort of critical political economy, but not *necessarily* a project of Marxist historiography. As they admitted later:

> We were looking for classes whose dynamism would lead to socialism, and we were unable to locate them. The fact that socialist movements did not exist, not even in embryonic form, would not have discouraged us. For Marxism has an old—even if only vaguely tested—recipe for such situations. If we could have supposed that the existing tendencies or movements would, in the near future, undergo such a differentiation that the evolution of socialist movements would follow, we could have turned to the old Marxist recipe. But there seemed to have been no ground for such a hypothesis. We had to content ourselves with stating rather empty formulas such as: the observable decentralisation of the economic system, the changes in the consumer habits of the working class or the evolution of an intellectual counter-culture might create more favourable conditions if, at a point, the cause of socialism would seem timely. But why would it become timely? We had no answer to this question (1978: 294–295).

More interesting is the third chapter, "The Intellectuals." Here Kis and Bence try to explain their own existence sociologically and intellectually: how is it that the Soviet-style system they lived under produced non-conformist intellectuals such as themselves? Intellectual workers, in so far as they are "in regular contact with the process of cultural and scientific creation" are permitted a privileged yet narrow and certainly institutionalized form of debate and discussion, for without it such work could not continue. As Kis and Bence suggest, "a minimum of public communication within the academic community is still an irreducible precondition of advancement in learning" (1978: 45). Over time this forms into a *de facto* public sphere, "serving as a functional substitute for political discussion and organization among those who take part in it" (1978: 44). This explains the possibility of open, unofficial and uncensored discussion, but does not suggest an evolution into an *oppositional* ethos. As Kis and Bence state:

> ... the general institutional set-up of scientific and cultural production invests the intelligentsia with the ability to form a collective consciousness of a relatively high level. But the simple existence of this set-up in itself explains nothing more than that. It does not explain the fact that the reproductive process of science and culture produces nonconformist intellectuals who, rejecting the official channels of communication reserved for the intelligentsia, try to work out ideas which by their very nature require a "counter-public sphere," so to speak. Nor do these general conditions of intellectual production explain the emergence of a sub-culture, providing non-conformism with a breathing space (1978: 48).

The development of such an opposition was made possible paradoxically first by the destalinization process's rescinding of physical and ideological terror, and secondly through the death of internal reformism. Ironically, the inherent need of Stalinism to produce and denounce imagined enemies symbiotically generated the ability to produce the real McCoy. The authors maintained that,

> By establishing a symbolic relation between the smallest details of individual behavior and the broadest objectives of social development, the official ideology made any lack of conformity with the expected behavior appear to involve opposition to the ultimate aims, a political crime which demanded terror as a response (1978: 49).

The end of mass terror necessitated elite division within the tight circle of power emanating from the party-state between those who had been directly involved in its deployment and those (often affected by it) who agitated for demobilization. Destalinization as an elite phenomenon necessarily expanded as each side sought cultural products (literature, revisionist historical accounts) to demonstrate the correctness of its position.

At the same time, the professional autonomy granted to the physical sciences (necessary for technological advancement) combined with the "political research control and the social utilization of scientific results" to produce a unique East European phenomenon: the "expert" who with strong moral conviction "intervenes in social questions with a great deal of naïveté but also with a great deal of courage" (1978: 55). The privilege and space afforded the physical sciences initially led to greater possibilities for either open dissent and/or internal marginalization.[11] In the social sciences, such choices were not available—as Kis and Bence suggested, when you are in "direct contact with ideological production, the correlation is far from ambiguous" (1978: 56). Conformism and compromise thus become the hallmarks of most social scientists, faced with dilemma of having to choose between career advancement against the impossibility of conducting research *at all*. More curious and important for Kis and Bence, however, is the post-Stalinist production of a class stratum they refer to as the "sub-intelligentsia"—archivists, interviewers, researchers, translators, and data-processing operators. Made possible by the "factory-type organization of scientific and cultural research," such "auxiliary personnel" make intellectual production possible, but are neither its chief beneficiaries nor dependent on its rigidly hierarchical relations. Nonetheless, they are able to generate enough income to guarantee a modest level of economic security, are in thinking professions, but are liberated from the types of compromises necessary at higher levels. This is the breeding ground for dissidence *par excellence*.

Sociologically, Kis and Bence have begun to explain the genesis of non-conformism at its very roots. Members of the sub-intelligentsia are "plugged into the communication channels of the intelligentsia," allowing both contact and an alliance with non-conformist intellectuals. At the same time, such intellectuals no longer occupy a lonely and largely private marginalized space—they suddenly have a public, and out of this public emerges the counter public-sphere. The process is summarized as follows:

> The work of an interviewer affords contact with sociological research, the work of a translator keeps him in touch with literature or with some field

of social science, etc. Above all, among sub-intellectuals with degrees there are many who are not content with passively satisfying their curiosity, but try to have some autonomous scientific or cultural activity. Their chances of success in submitting their work to the consideration of the scientific community or in having it published in book form or in an official review are clearly much less than the chances of the established intellectuals. They therefore have a very strong motivation to look for a non-official public sphere and to find readers, critics, and people with whom to discuss among their own ranks. This is still true even if we have to admit that for a minority of them their position as sub-intellectuals is only a temporary one, and (the result of a rigid labor market) they are only delayed on their way to joining the intellectual establishment. The nonconformists thus find quite a receptive audience among the sub-intellectuals; it is relatively easy for them to direct their aspirations towards opposition—aspirations which, having no place in the established science and culture, seek fulfillment on their own, outside the official institutions anyway (1978: 61–62).

By the late 1960s, Kis and Bence remind their readers that the "social conditions" were ripe for nonconformism in most East European countries. Post-Stalinist norms were in place, the limits of freedom in most disciplines were more or less clearly delineated, the auxiliary jobs were plentiful and were filled by the dramatic increase in university graduates. Given these conditions, there was also considerable generational as well as sociological coherence to their cohort. This group by their formative political experiences rejected the paths of their mentors and generational antecedents: reforming the system from above was not possible, conforming to its strictures was an intellectual and moral dead end. It is clear in retrospect that Kis and Bence generalize too widely from the specificities of the Hungarian experience;[12] they do much to explain both the possibility and the internal dynamism for the transformation of a "sub-culture of sub-intellectuals" into an "embryonic counter-culture" (1978: 62). In the same way that the system itself began to "produce" nonconformist intellectuals and a sub-culture of the sub-intelligentsia, so too does a counter-public sphere grow into a more formalized political opposition. The existence and extension of such a sphere is guaranteed over time through such innovations as the phenomenon of samizdat publishing. However, Kis and Bence realize that in both their answer and from their experience they beg several additional questions.

First, does the counter-public sphere have any real connection to the workers, the bedrock of authoritarian communist society? As Kis and Bence bluntly state, the workers "have no interest in the elimination of the underground" nor do they necessarily have any direct interest in its continuation (1978: 65). Is a nonconformist counter-culture simply the "irreducible epiphenomenon" of intellectual work, access to which all workers and other ordinary citizens are effectively denied? Their answer to this charge, written before the Polish August but certainly with knowledge of the alliance-building happening through KOR, is that in the first instance workers must organize themselves. Here Kis and Bence are not falling back on Marxist sloganeering. They genuinely could not see how any meaningful communication or political *abertura* could take place *between social classes* unless this precondition were met. This is neither inevitable nor easy, as intellectuals tend to face an uphill battle in terms of workers' perceptions of them as the privileged yet complaining consumers of *their* surplus product. This does not mean that "the sole function of the oppositional ideologies is to talk to the nonconformist intellectuals themselves, to give them moral justification and hope to hold out" (1978: 66). Such a closed conversation would be futile, they admit, and this confession forces the authors to consider the charge (often levied by the conforming intellectuals who in their own way claim to be expanding critical space) that "the underground does more harm than good to the cause of cultural and social freedom" (1978: 66).

This leads Kis and Bence to the second and most critical question. What is the long-range effectiveness of such a development in terms of generating institutional change? They agree that it is practically impossible to gauge the impact of their efforts, as much depended on both internal (systemic) developments and the nature of the external environment (geopolitics, the Cold War). However, they do extol the practical virtue of what they call "propaganda by action" which one can see is extremely close in description and spirit to Havel's dictum to "live in truth":

Propaganda by action means setting an example, showing by one's own actions that it is not necessary to accept the world installed by the regime, that it is possible to act according to norms other than those of the existing institutional system. In societies where the dominated class has the means to create autonomous organizations, no particular significance is attached to this form of propaganda; generally speaking, it does not constitute a separate task but is an integral part of the normal functioning of the class organizations and the everyday life of their members. Its importance is so much the greater in a society in which no one social class is in a position to organise itself, especially when the institutional system manages not only to impose its supremacy externally on all classes but also the models of behavior and attitudes compatible with its reproduction. We are not saying, of course, that the cohesion of the system is ensured only or principally by a belief in the impossibility of change: it is ensured in the first place by institutional mechanisms and by institutionalized interests. However, this belief plays its part in ensuring the system's coherence. Consequently, the counter-public sphere, as well as nonconformism as a mode of personal behavior, decrease not only the coherence of the system, by their very existence (1978: 67).

This counter-public sphere becomes disproportionately important. Walking the talk, living in truth, or propaganda by action becomes both the moral and political means to achieve and extend authentic public space. Nascent civil society is reinforced and encouraged by samizdat literature, which "breaks the monopoly of the ruling ideology's patterns of thought, and introduces new concepts and alternative ideas into the social consciousness" (1978: 67). In turn, "the greater the diversity of the ideologies formed in the underground, the more differentiated social thinking becomes, and the easier it is to relativize the official ideology's *Weltanschauung*" (1978: 67). The worldview and the limitless horizons of the party-state is diminished by the very existence of ideological pluralism.

The remainder of Kis and Bence's book is dedicated to an analysis of the "two systems" of industrial capitalism and state socialism as well as what they call "the detours of East European Marxism." The authors show the inaccuracies and ahistoricity of various convergence theories, both those created to "neutralize" the technological alienation and exploitation inherent in capitalism according to the efficient and necessary dictates of industrial progress, as well as those that are disillusioned with authoritarian communism not leading to real socialism. Because Kis and Bence wanted to chip away at the illusions Western leftists had about Soviet-style societies, their attack on left convergence theories are illuminated by a particular animus. They demonstrate *inter alia* that the ruling class in Soviet societies can never be property-owning as under capitalism, that there are simply no functional equivalents to share ownership or capital/money markets, that institutional decentralization does *not* result in greater economic independence *in practice*, and that the institutions and procedures of formal democracy and freedom of association generate political (and indeed class) competition and a functioning civil society inconceivable in the East.

By way of conclusion, Kis and Bence produce an interesting idealist and materialist analysis of the ideological developments within Soviet Marxism—idealist because they take the force and consequences of the ideological struggle as having great practical meaning (and demonstrate this to be the case), and materialist because they illustrate the social bases of the various positions taken historically and link them to class interests and societal tension. Beginning with Leninism, the debates of the 1920s, and the eventual (and predictable) Stalinist imposition of dialectical materialism, which succeeded in emptying official Marxism of all meaningful content, they tell the story of how the *apparat* succeeded in both adapting Marxism to its own needs while crushing political and ideological alternatives or variations (1978: 110).

Their account of the rebirth of Marxist debates during the 1950s owes much to their own position as both critics and inheritors of the Marxism of the "thaw". Thus they praise and give credit to those who broke radically with "everything that had been used to justify the terror" and their return to original sources, such as Marx, Lenin, and Lukács (1978: 131). They are most harsh in their condemnation of the "Marxism of the thaw" as both naive and lacking in class content. Such Marxists assumed correctly that the political "deformations" of the Stalinist era were not just closely related to but actually stemmed from certain ideological errors, but they were overly credulous in thinking that an ideological purge and a new set of objectives would do the trick in terms of reforming the system. As Kis and Bence state, "the internal structure of this critique is still determined by the object criticized ... by Stalinist ideology itself" (1978: 134). "The critics of the system of terror were insistent on the social homogeneity of Soviet-type societies" (1978: 132) and thus refused to readmit class analysis. To do otherwise would have meant reopening the cans of worms of the 1920s (for example, the peasant versus the industrial worker dilemma) or worse yet to admit the *apparat* itself was based on class interests different from those of the rest of society, most importantly, the proletariat. Their critique was premised on the practical need to *end* the terror, and the limitless and downward spiraling of "objectively" labeling as class enemies all who disagreed with or in some small way deviated from the official course. Acknowledging any level of class antagonism gave credence to conservatives and Stalinist-restorationists who wanted to suppress all disagreement by force.

This all becomes important for how Kis and Bence account for themselves as "underground marxists" in contradistinction to "official Marxists." With great debt to Marx and Lukács, they take a positive view of human potentiality. Human beings are by nature free and social beings, and within certain limiting conditions can "create their own culture by their own interrelated actions" and have the "opportunity for ... conscious and collective control of the evolution of their social life" (1978: 135). Kis and Bence use class analysis to generate a more subtle and valid critique of the actual workings of Soviet-style societies. Thus they disengaged themselves from both the ruling group and the proletariat, opening up the way for "a search for the autonomous social base of Marxism" (1978: 138). However, this concession illuminated the problem of linkages with the working class, still necessary if such ideology were to be a) socialist in form, and b) politically transformative in nature.

In the last five pages of the book that they begin to develop a conception of what critical East European Marxism might look like, but it was too little, too late. With great prescience the authors state:

> Of course, if East European Marxism is to find its connection with the working class in practice, and if by its own theoretical means it is to help the process of practical learning in which the socialist movement—organized and processing a class consciousness—spreads to an increasingly large part of the working class, it is not enough for marxist intellectuals simply to lose their illusions about the ruling class. There must also be such changes in the organization of society and in the situation of the working class so that the institutions of power are no longer strong enough to fragment the working class. Until these changes can be foreseen, the Marxism which has definitively broken away from official Marxism is threatened with disappearance, or with dissolution among the non-Marxist underground ideologies which are better suited to the social isolation of the nonconformist intelligentsia. But at least it has succeeded in avoiding the trap of trying to live as a parasite on official Marxist ideology (1978: 138).

Both phenomena occurred. Underground or unofficial Marxism was doomed to irrelevance as a political ideology for nonconformist intellectuals disconnected from the working class.[13] And as it happened non-Marxist, or more accurately, not *specifically* Marxist ideas were in fact better-suited to the construction of strategy and tactics of dissent.

By the late 1970s, Kis and Bence recognized themselves as Marxists only in the genealogical sense. They retained Marxism methodologically, but not ideologically. They maintained their sympathy for an optimistic "Marxist anthropology" and the philosophy of values they connected with Marx's early writings. Connected to both propositions above is a notion of political engagement which though not exactly teleological in orientation certainly strives toward social betterment. Kis and Bence did not simply "grow out of" their Marxist approach. Rather, their own personal intellectual trajectories led them to a place where the branches of their thought were neither completely determinative nor uniquely Marxist. Their commitment to the development of independent and oppositional social movements was philosophically related to the Marxist coordination of its political and socialist aims through the specific agency of the proletariat. But for Kis and Bence, their program of radical reformism, and the similar projects of other East-Central Europeans, the "autonomous self-organization of society" was also an end in itself, and completely unrelated to either democratic (or the democratizing of) socialism or a philosophy of praxis. Although they might agree with the Marxist conception of humankind that we are all "free, conscious, and universal being[s] ... only held back by ... historically developed circumstances," this belief could not serve as a source of either hope or activism in the 1970s after the defeat of the old style of reformism. They contend that one can likely find more oppositional inspiration in an existentially-rooted concept of humankind as subject to perverse levels of manipulation but somehow equally perversely maintaining the innate ability "to break off from the *Dasein* of manipulation with some kind of a last, desperate effort" (Bence and Kis, 1980: 285). Thus their conception of alienation owes as much to Adorno and Kafka as to Marx, and any notion of mitigating its presence (rather than through some project of liberation) is more modest in scale, such as Havel's notion of living in truth. Kis and Bence never went as far as a "total refusal" of Marxism—a charge explicit in their writing against "Polish ex-revisionists"—and here Leszek Kołakowski is obviously whom they have in mind.[14] No

Marxist of either present or past persuasion would have to disavow all beliefs or history in order to feel comfortable in the new opposition of East-Central Europe, but at the same time "is quite unlikely to derive any relevant theoretical or political guidance from it [i.e. Marxism]" (1980: 266).

The Social Contract of *Beszélő* and "Radical Reformism"

The program of "radical reformism" was premised on being tactical rather than totalizing. Its possibilities may not have been as great or promising as the grand ideological swath cut by Marxism, but it did not set its sights on great heights in the first place. György Bence and János Kis were quite self-effacing on this point, and even suggested that "Radical reformism doesn't offer a political program in the strict sense of the word; it merely expounds some tactical considerations" (1980: 285). By its very nature, radical reformism was intended to be self-limiting and crisis avoiding. "Tactical questions" such as respect for human rights or the expansion of independent social space were "not derived from the need for a different system taking the place of the present one" (1980: 285). Echoing Michnik, the old dilemma of reform versus revolution had been invalidated by East-Central European experience:

> The assumption here is that social aims, worth fighting for in Eastern Europe, are those that can be realized without resulting in a crisis of power; anything else leads to the fabrication of utopias or straight to catastrophe. The alternative of reform or revolution is not a valid one in Eastern Europe, the sensible choice is between two kinds of reformism. The reformers of the 50s and 60s, the 'old evolutionists', wanted to promote their cause 'from the inside', by enlightening and convincing the political leadership. 'Neo-evolutionism', to use the term suggested by the Polish historian Adam Michnik, tries to draw the lesson from the failure of this tactical conception. Michnik concludes that internal criticism is not capable of influencing the leadership effectively: it is exposed to conjunctural changes of power and, in the long run, it is bound to give up its critical content. Serious and lasting pressure on the government can only by exerted by independent social movements (1980: 285).

The most important programmatic statement of "radical reform-ism" remains the 1987 special issue of *Beszélő* outlining the editors' call for a new "social contract." With the possibility of Kádár's depar-ture from the political scene combined with the ever-widening circle of dissent, Kis and others sensed that this would be a key document for discussion and debate. Their intention was not to produce a state-ment of utopian vision or a call for radical grass-roots action, but they *did* want to move beyond the relatively narrow base of largely Buda-pest intellectuals to a wider audience. The contract was intended to have mass-based appeal; it was written simply, with very concrete sug-gestions as to how one might begin to turn from a stance of general-ized dissatisfaction and pessimism to targeted activism. In it they advo-cate utilizing existing opportunities and exploiting them for making new demands and having their voices heard. Under the sub-heading "Don't Just Grumble: Demand" they state:

> Any forum where those below can have their say is acceptable. The briefing sessions that deputies of the National Assembly or council members hold for their constituents are good for this purpose. Programs sponsored by the Patriotic People's Front or the T.I.T. (Society for the Dissemination of Scientific Knowledge), as well as the clubs, political seminars, and open Party meetings are all steps in the right direction. But best of all are the public forums at work: the production conference, the shop meeting, the trade-union meeting, KISZ (Union of Communist Youth) and Party locals. Invite the country's leaders to the factories and institutions. Bombard the headquarters of the political and voluntary public organizations with reso-lutions put into writing. Respond to the announcements of the Central Committee, the SZOT (National Council of Trade Unions), and the gov-ernment. Demand that the materials of the reform debates be made avail-able. Invite the authors. Adopt stances on their proposals. Elaborate con-cepts regarding the future of your workplace. And organize reform clubs at work (reprinted in *Uncaptive Minds* 1.1 (May 1988): 7)

The demand is nothing less than an exhortation for public involve-ment and debate, to join in the recreation of civil society and to par-ticipate in it.

The *Social Contract* was intended to be within the realm of the pos-sible. The first point is almost so obvious as to be overlooked, but it is critical: as the authors state in the introduction, "The 1956 revolution gave Hungary its last political program" (1988: 8). The authors were paying direct homage to the legacy of 1956 and were conscious of resurrecting many of the 1956 demands in a new context. To keep their demands realistic, they recognized that time, and compromises would be needed. Thus they present the demands recognizing that they might fall short of political ideals, but also as a means of allowing the process to advance further. In many respects, the *Social Contract* reads as the opening position of one party in a delicate and complex set of negotiations. The party in question here—the democratic opposition—is concerned to be forceful in making demands, show the other side where they have *already* compromised (thus demonstrating their inherent reasonableness and willingness to bargain), and even generous in giving the other side credit where credit is due. Thus the authors state:

> Political developments since the consolidation [i.e. post-1956] must also be recognized: the government has accepted mass consumption and tolerated certain elements of a market economy; several associations of Western orientation have been formed in the social sciences; the official ideology has been relaxed; specialized knowledge has gained in prestige; and the political differences between the new generation of Party cadres and the professional elite have narrowed. The external conditions have also improved: Hungary is more open to the West than thirty years ago; the threat of Soviet intervention has declined; and the Soviet Union's leaders are more tolerant (1988: 8).

Consonant with this logic, *Beszélő* demanded basic civil and political rights, the rule of law, press freedom and a healthy dose of constitutionalism, whereby there would be institutional checks on the rule of the party. They did *not* demand multiparty competition, institutionalized pluralism, or even abolition of the leading role of the party. There is a bit of political sleight-of-hand in operation, however, because practically the program demanded a functional division of governmental powers, whereby the MSZMP would retain control of foreign affairs and defense, thus ensuring the commitment to the Warsaw Pact. Internal affairs and the justice system—those institutions necessary for the installation of civil and political rights—would be influenced and effectively limited by opposition demands and a new *modus operandi*, to be constitutionally entrenched at some point. On matters more economic and less institutional, the program was more radical on the face of it, but not when one considers that Hungary was the country of great economic experimentation and of the New Economic Mechanism. They boldly ask for "equal rights for various forms of ownership in the economy," the development of a real capital market, the dismantling of monopolies, and euphemistically "a flexible price policy in the interest of balance-of-trade equilibrium instead of policies to increase particular exports and restrict imports" (price deregulation and adjustment to world levels).

The *Social Contract* was immediately successful in sparking debate. A letter published in the more radical *Demokrata* criticized the authors of the *Beszélő* program for creating a logical yet unsustainable compromise—while Soviet troops remained on Hungarian soil and while the party remained in charge, there can be no possibility of cleverly dividing up ministries in a "yours, mine, and ours" fashion. Curiously, this argument, coming from a radical and uncompromising democrat, echoes the same argument of the partisan hard-liners throughout the region that allowing any thin wedge of reform will crack it open, political control was an all-or-nothing game. This critique misses the more important and arguably more deeply democratic point of the authors— that democracy is not about zero-sum games or winner-take-all solutions, but about imperfect compromises and at times an ideologically inconsistent and impure matching of theory and practice.

Gáspár Miklós Tamás advanced a different critique, and gained some renown at home and abroad for his views on the *Social Contract*, as he was a regular contributor to *Beszélő* and other samizdat journals. Tamás held not only that the system was essentially unreformable (again, not unlike the die-hards, but from the opposite perspective), but that the *attempt* to reform it unsuccessfully would, in a sense, erode the moral high ground of the dissidents. Reformed communism might be better than an unreformed one, but in Tamás' view,

> If people don't have to suffer for their views but nevertheless still have no real influence over what happens, the longer such a situation continues the greater the difference develops between words and deeds. We cannot develop a normal political life for the future on such a basis (1988:12).

Tamás argued that it goes against the very nature of the communist system to engage in any form of power sharing, to give concessions, to be anything less than what it is. Poland remained a case in point—

even the weakest communist party in the region cannot allow civil society to become a counter-power, or not for long. This argument confuses the *tactical* position of the compromise with a statement of ultimate aims, which the *Beszélő* program surely was not. Rather, it was a maneuver or an opening position in a nested game.

The *Beszélő* program was not only timely but also expanded the universe of political discourse, to the point where less than two years later, proto-oppositional forces at the Roundtable Talks could move through and *past* these proposals to ones that were far more sweeping. The conditions for such a discussion had already changed radically, the program's significance in helping to construct and shape those new conditions should not be underestimated. Where the *Social Contract* was ultimately less successful was in its call for involvement and participation—a more grass roots flowering of public debate and civic initiatives, at first through existing bodies and then in the transformation of them. Indeed, the Hungarian transition remained a largely elite phenomenon, and to the extent that an alternative civil society was created, it neither inspired mass participation nor was defined by it.

Kis' Democratic Alternative

After the imposition of martial law in Poland, the friendship and intellectual collaboration of Kis and Bence dissolved. At issue was a principled disagreement as to how the Hungarian opposition ought to proceed in the aftermath of 13 December, 1981.[15] Bence felt that moving forward openly and publicly with dissident activities after the brutal suppression of Solidarity was unfairly dangerous, and he was not in favor of risking existential security. Kis was of the opposite view, and felt that the Polish situation showed both the possibility of meaningful political action, and the importance of continuing forward. In a sense, the creation of *Beszélő* was Kis' answer to Bence.

In early 1989, on the eve of the historic transformations that were about to sweep across the region, a collection of János Kis' most important essays (largely from *Beszélő*) were printed in English under the title *Politics in Hungary: For a Democratic Alternative*. Most of the essays were written in response to contemporary events in Hungary from 1983–1988, but woven in and through them can be found Kis' blend of political theory, insightful historical analysis, strategic and positional analysis, social commentary, and critique. In his introduction to the volume, Timothy Garton Ash notes that one reason Kis has such intellectual authority is as a result of his range and diversity. He is a philosopher by training who writes practically and is historically specific and contingent. He is a student of Lukács (and therefore of Marx) who goes beyond this training to encompass Anglo-American liberalism. Finally, as Garton Ash states,

> One particular strength of his political analysis is that he is almost equally good on all elements in the political process or 'game': on the Party as well as the democratic opposition to which he belongs, on the parliament, and on the vital intelligentsia groups—writers, journalists, economists, lawyers, sociologists, political scientists—which came together precisely in these five years (1983–1988) to form a growing, albeit still heterogeneous pressure group for change ("Introduction," 1989: 5).

Reading the collection historically demonstrates the extent to which Kis was able to elucidate paths and alternatives literally in the midst of sweeping change. Hegel's Owl of Minerva would be envious, as only a cursory examination of Kis' exhortations would reveal: writing in 1987 that Kádár must go (shortly before he, in fact, did); supporting Popular Frontism while demanding that ultimately the party-state would have to negotiate some form of social contract with independent mass movements separate from it; and demystifying and discrediting the "specific Hungarian path" represented by the NEM while outlining the extent to which the economy was functioning on borrowed time and money. Finally, Kis describes the window of opportunity for political action cognizant of the possibility of a Soviet response yet minimizes its probability via a carefully-constructed oppositional strategy, understanding that endemic and emergent crises in the Soviet Union itself would militate against such an outcome.

In the essays "Can 1956 Be Forgotten?" "The Restoration of 1956–1957 in a Thirty Year Perspective," and "The Present Crisis and Its Origins," Kis accurately locates the roots of the contemporary political and economic malaise in Hungary in the 1956 revolution. He also looks to the "lessons of the past" as not only delineating political impossibilities but conditioning political possibilities. In "Can 1956 Be Forgotten?" he locates the legitimation crisis of the party not with the popular upsurge in 1956 or with the invading Soviet tanks[16] but rather with the internal disintegration: "... in effect they notified the world that they had to vanish from the scene" (1989: 26). Even under authoritarian communism legitimacy mattered tremendously, and not because it flowed from military force or the threat thereof. Thoroughly understanding this reality was critical to the success of the democratic opposition in terms of pushing the reform envelope during the Roundtable negotiations.

An equally important lesson from 1956 was that Soviet intervention *again* would be neither inevitable nor automatic.[17] By allowing that *many options and outcomes were both available and likely*, he reinvents political opposition by endowing it with the possibility of agency and influence. Kis is brilliant in deconstructing the typical Hungarian refrain in favor of consolidation and concession over political opposition. He unmasks the restorationist view as both a coy and shameful rewriting of history:

> The practices of power which the restoration leadership adopted while breaking the back of the resistance still retain their validity. These could be forgotten during the time of improvement in the consolidation, because the exercise of power was offering palpable improvements. Nowadays in a period of decline no realistic policy is possible without reckoning with the historic burden of the restoration (1989: 34).

Kis argues that Kádár's success ultimately lay not in his restorationist policies of buying off the intelligentsia with perquisites and promoting the quiescence of workers with consumer commodities as well as social tranquillity and a satisfactory standard of living (1989: 69–70). Rather, what Kádár managed to do was to usurp politics from the everyday lives of the people, and to deprive citizenship of meaningful content. It is this cynical elitism rather than its authoritarian window-dressing that makes the regime fundamentally anti-democratic.

Tactically, in terms of constructing an opposition in the 1980s, this analysis was also a bridge-building exercise reaching out to the freedom fighters of the 1956 generation, while providing reasons for opposition and involvement to succeeding generations. By focusing not only on the political and moral leaders of 1956—Imre Nagy, István Bibó, or Tibor Déry—but also on the activists in the council movement, Kis illustrates the political importance of civil society to democracy:

These people and the entire workers' councils movement provided a rare example of political dignity, wisdom and resourcefulness. They proved that a modern society possesses the political capacity for the practice of an effective democracy. This proof was provided by the Hungarian people, and by the generation before ours, though mostly still with us (1989: 75).

Kis also sends his compatriots the message that only by rejecting paralysis and rebuilding civil society can the citizens of Hungary wrest politics back from the party-state and make society *active* again. This is one of the finest legacies of 1956 for Hungary in the 1980s.

Kis marries this emphasis on civil society and its divorce from the party-state with a spirited defense of human rights and the rule of law. Here he appeals not to the past but illustrates the point by reference to the situation of the Hungarian minorities in Czechoslovakia and Romania. In "Hungarian Societies and Hungarian Minorities Abroad" he has two audiences. Externally, he explains and justifies the particular Hungarian obsession with national minorities outside their borders as not only a matter of historic grievance and impractical irredentism, but also more empirically an issue of proportion.[18] Internally to largely populist yet proto-oppositional elites and movements he promotes his oppositional approach and ethos by appealing to an issue close to many hearts. At the same time, he moves populist thinking from potentially narrow ethnocentrism to an embrace of human rights in general, and to minorities living within Hungary as well as those ethnic Hungarians living outside Hungary.

Kis speaks of the Hungarian cultural community rather than a *narodnik* concept of nationhood. He carefully separates issues—if those of Hungarian ancestry assimilate into the dominant cultures in which they now live, this is a source of sorrow but certainly not outrage (1989: 201). This remains a matter of choice, even if structurally limited or skewed in favor of assimilation. Thus he draws a distinction between the systemic preclusion of maintaining one's Hungarian identity from the "flagrant violation of the minority Hungarians' human rights." Here he refers to the denial of state services, the prohibition of education in Hungarian, the abolition of cultural organizations, and professional discrimination against ethnic Hungarians. Finally, he is concerned that the minority question not be falsely linked to border questions, as he wants to avoid his support for Hungarian minority rights becoming fuel for irredentist claims. Even if Trianon might have been unjust, no set of European countries or superpowers would likely agree to another redrawing of boundaries in the region for fear of unleashing yet another set of nationalist passions. Moreover, any new result would still leave minority masses on either side of the border.

Regarding human rights, Kis first wants to connect Hungarian minority issues to human rights more generally speaking:

> What I want is respect of their [Hungarian minorities'] human rights and their rights as a community, and the institutional protection of both. I speak of human rights, that is, rights which belong to every human being—Hungarian or non-Hungarian—and not about special treatment for Hungarians because of their history or cultural eminence. Of course I am particularly concerned if the victims of human rights violations happen to be Hungarians, that is, people who could be in my place and me in theirs if in 1920 the superpowers' arbitrariness had drawn the borders in some other way. But I am also particularly concerned if Hungarians violate the rights of other ethnic communities; that is why I am more preoccupied with the situation of the gypsies in Hungary than in Poland (1989: 201).

Thus in the "Program of Action in Favor of Hungarian Minorities Abroad" published in *Beszélő* an entire section is devoted to the rights of national minorities *within* Hungary, as well as those abroad—the Roma minority is specifically included. Next, Kis wants to link discrimination *against* ethnic Hungarians and minorities to the dehumanization of the system itself. This means recognizing one's adversary—the common citizens of Romania or Czechoslovakia that may be full of hatred for ethnic Hungarians living on their soil—is also a victim. As Kis states: "We have to realize that the minority's special deprivation of civil rights is inseparable from the overall disregard for human rights of every citizen" (1989: 202).

Kis' solution to the minority question is the recognition and the acceptance of multiple identities, which may be ascriptive or chosen, national or civic, overlapping yet not necessarily contradictory. The state must obviously play a strong role in the protection and even advancement of rights but the most difficult and important task happens on the level of civil society—on breaking down hostility, misunderstanding, and stereotypical falsehood and accusation between Hungarians and Slovaks, and between Hungarians and Romanians. Reaching across borders from one civil society to another is critical; the final paragraph of the "Program of Action" states:

> We must seek a dialogue with neighboring countries' democratic-minded circles. They are the ones who could be our collaborators and allies in the slow, gradual process of reconciliation. They must perceive that we are linked to them by commitment to the common cause of democracy, by real solidarity, and not merely by tactical interests (1989: 220).

In "On Our Limitations and Possibilities" Kis reiterates the importance of self-limitation advocated earlier by himself and Bence, but in a more popular and tactical format—this essay was the published form of Kis' contribution to the Monor Conference. The influence of Michnik is obvious; he acknowledges the problem of political mobilization for change categorically in the opening sentence: "Since 1956 the Hungarian public has firmly believed that it is useless to think in terms of comprehensive alternatives to our predicament, for the Soviet state will do with this country whatever it pleases anyway" (1989: 115). From that point there was an "air of contingency" to whatever reform process the Hungarians engaged in under Kádár; small concessions might be rescinded at any time and the weight of Moscow bore heavily and unevenly on any form of within-system bargaining. Furthermore, speculation arose from the fact of this tension, as within the working operations of the Soviet model there was no public debate and thus much was inevitably left to "unverifiable heresy" (1987: 115). Although Kis agrees with the near-certainty that the Soviet State would not tolerate the transformation of system *and* simultaneously concludes that the opposition has reached the point to which "the system's invariables are in question,"[19] he nonetheless concludes that there is considerable room for political reform within such limitations.

That such maneuverability is possible at all is revealed by Kis' careful analysis of the Soviet *imperium* since 1956. As Kis shows, in the first decade after 1948, indigenous Hungarian communists were totally at the mercy of their Soviet sponsors, because of Stalinist terror, the deep chill of Cold War isolationism, and the integration of the Hungarian economy into the Soviet orbit. 1956 in Hungary dramatically illustrated the potentialities and the limits of the post-Stalinist thaw in the region, both in terms of the emancipation of the communist intelligentsia as well as the independence of the populace. After 1956, the stability and power of the leadership "depended on their ability to buy public peace with concessions which were acceptable both to their own apparatus and to the Soviet leaders" (1989: 117). Even though there existed an implicit agreement between the superpowers that the Soviet Union "may use force if one of its satellite governments is in trouble," economic pressures throughout the 1980s made it a less likely occurrence. COMECON could no longer yield an acceptable level of growth, either within the Soviet Union or among its satellites. If the Soviets had been able to extend their capacity to provide cheap raw materials and energy and in return absorb East European products limitlessly into their huge domestic market, the system might have been able to continue, but for reasons endemic and internal to state social-ist economies, the center could no longer hold. If intensifying rather than extending economic growth was difficult, moving to a higher technological platform proved well nigh impossible. Kis explains:

> The only way out of this situation is to transform the wasteful economic system and turn to markets which would link the region's countries to a circuit of faster technological progress. Without such a change Eastern Europe is facing the danger of joining the underdeveloped, stagnating regions of the globe exactly at a time when in the West another technologi-cal revolution is taking place which pulls along some parts of the third world. The Soviet Union has nothing to offer that could substitute for this change, and consequently it is unable to halt the disintegration of its empire (1989: 117).

It is telling that Kis refers not to the overthrow of the system but its *recovery* from the current crisis besetting it:

> I refer to a *recovery*, an evolutionary process, and not to the inducement of political collapse. And I refer to an evolution whose components would emerge from within the organic development of *Hungarian* society (empha-sis in original; 1989: 116).

This notion of recovery implied not only an evolutionary process of structurally significant political reform, but was seen as the only neces-sary way out of the downward spiral of the Hungarian economy.

It was natural for Hungarian dissidents like Kis to make linkages between the political necessity for change with economic reform because of the post-1956 trajectory of economic reform in the country. The NEM and the emergence of the second economy provided a model for nascent civil society:

> It is noteworthy that the shift towards demanding legal rights and codi-
> fied guarantees has begun in the same areas where the loosening of rigid
> forms, the circumvention of regulations, and the bargaining and recipro-
> cation of favors have led to the accumulation of tangible results. These
> demands do not aim at the heights of national politics, rather they are
> directed at certain areas of everyday life. It is no accident that at first they
> emerged in the non-official sector of the economy when the various forms
> of small enterprises became legalized. It is no accident either that apart
> from the economy the primary target of these demands is the right to asso-
> ciation and the realm of cultural and intellectual activities (1989: 122).

For Kis there was a window of opportunity in the late 1980s, with a need and a popular desire to solidify the legal and economic achievements that had added up over the years of Kádárite concessions. *Perestroika* and *glasnost* increased the likelihood of defending "a new compromise against external pressure" (1989: 122). The "crux of the compromise" was the eventual and evolutionary attainment of a clearly defined separation between the state and civil society.[20]

These conclusions are reinforced by Kis' "What Should We Fear," published in *Beszélő* in 1988, three years after "On Our Limitations and Possibilities." Kis addresses a fearful and anxious Hungarian public by telling them what *not* to fear: the diminution of Soviet power, the disintegration of political authority, and most importantly the potential of a mass movement developing out of oppositional clubs, societies, and associations. Although the struggles of the *demos* are necessary to the birthing of democracy, Kis is paradoxically yet typically cautious about either the suppression of isolated demonstrations or the rapid growth of a mass movement that would sweep away the current regime only to be restored by internal or external violence later (a 1980s repeat of 1956 with a Solidarity-type twist). What Kis desires most (and in Hungary actually gets) is a "gradual and orderly transformation" of the system.

One method Kis advocates in moving both the *demos* and the regime toward this goal is the carefully designed and targeted use of strikes. Following the Polish example, he notes that strikes specifically and collective bargaining generally are the practical realization of self-limitation:

> A strike is a form of collective action which has a great deal of built-in self-disciplinary force. A strike makes its participants understand that they are players in a game which demands nerves and patience and has a limited stake. A strike requires organization, and even in the absence of historical traditions, it readily offers effective organizational solutions. A strike offers as its great fundamental experience an education in social solidarity, the recognition of strength born of unity, and the insight that results can be achieved only through negotiations. Strikers learn quickly that they have to face the conflict, and that they need self-moderation and an ability to make concessions in exchange for gains (1989: 184–185).

Ironically, Kis effectively takes the opposite view from Lenin in his landmark essay *What Is to Be Done?* Lenin stressed that left to their own narrow inclinations, workers would never rise above a "trade union consciousness" and reach an understanding where revolutionary aims become paramount. Kis, on the other hand, believes that collective bargaining and the strike experience offer the learning ground for workers (the fundamental ideological and economic units in the state socialist economic enterprise) to move precisely beyond their narrow interests to a broader understanding of what must be done. Kis deftly restates the case for social over business unionism in the context of 1980s Hungary where Solidarity represents the former and the transmission belt unions of authoritarian communism are a bastardized version of the latter. Kis envisages that the movement/union/strike leadership would "have to learn to accept conflicts in a self-limiting manner, but also the party-state would have to learn to accept the curtailment of its power in order to avoid catastrophe" (1989: 185).

Of course, in Hungary popular mobilization did not occur Solidarity-style. History in the form of remembering Nagy and 1956 served as a more powerful motivator by signaling to the regime the memory and restiveness of the population. However, the bargaining metaphor holds, especially in consideration of the fact that the real power shift occurred during the Roundtable Talks in 1989.

Miklós Haraszti:
The Nature of Repression for Workers and Artists

If Kis and Bence became well known for their tightly argued analyses of authoritarian communism, Haraszti can be contrasted as the voice of passion and irony. His two major published works, *A Worker in a Workers' State* and *The Velvet Prison: Artists under State Socialism* tackle different subjects in a highly complementary fashion. The first, originally produced in 1972 in manuscript form, was entitled *Darabbér* (*Piece Rates*). The second was first published in the West in French as *L'Artiste d'État* in 1983, and later in Hungarian samizdat in 1986 as *A cenzúra esztétikája*. Both attracted considerable attention at home and abroad, and cemented the author's reputation—especially outside Hungary—as a leading dissident.

A Worker in a Worker's State was based on Haraszti's own experiences as a millwright after being placed under Police Control in 1970.[21] He obtained a job at the Red Star Tractor Factory in a deliberate effort to experience the daily "reality of working class conditions." Whereas Kis and Bence argued later that the existing theories of Soviet-style societies could not effectively come to terms with the fact that they were *neither* capitalist nor socialist in character, Haraszti in his youthful idealism set out to examine the phenomenon firsthand. Haraszti completed the manuscript of the book at the end of 1972, attempted unsuccessfully to get it published officially,[22] and was arrested and tried for his efforts. He was charged with incitement to subversion, that is "he was accused of having written a book likely to stimulate hatred of the State and of having distributed it in several copies" (1977: 161). The court handed down a guilty verdict and sentenced Haraszti to eight months' imprisonment, suspended for three years.

The harsh treatment meted out by the relatively "liberal" Hungarian regime begs the question as to what the author did write to warrant such a fuss. Essentially, Haraszti writes a first-hand account of the dismal working conditions of the factory, centering on its infamous abuse of piece-rates for workers. Piece rates—or payment based on actual production rather than hourly-based compensation—was justified as the "ideal form of socialist wages." It was logically dressed up by the scions of socialist management science as a bountiful incentive system with possibilities for expanding personal wealth, at least for those industrious individuals who dutifully and efficiently applied themselves. In theory, Stakhanovite work ethic would be matched by material reward. In practice, the worker lost by first playing by the rules, and then by trying to work around them.

Haraszti describes how workers following the instructions for each job can only lose. He states:

> ... if I keep exactly to the time allocations and to the technical directions as laid down in the instructions, the maximum remuneration that I can obtain for uninterrupted work, given one hundred per cent performance on my part, remains less than the minimum payment described as a pure formality. The piece-rate worker who is unaware that he works for a wage per minute theoretically cannot assure himself of a full day's pay, except on the express condition that he does not stop work even for an instant. Obviously, this is impossible (1977: 39–40).

Unhappily Haraszti finds that his colleagues have *internalized* the logic of the piece-rate system, blaming themselves rather than the system when they fall short of full wages:

> When you work, you earn. A lot of piece-workers go along with the idea: very few think that it is because of the system of payment, rather than through a fault of their own, that they may make nothing for the minutes spent studying the blueprint, drinking a glass of water, blowing their noses, resting a little, or changing their tools (1977: 39).

Thus financial insecurity chases the worker to perform, rather than the ability to get ahead.

The sad irony is that when the workers do try to turn the system to their advantage, they cheat themselves in the long run. Haraszti vividly describes the practice of "looting," whereby workers "cheat the norm" by producing more in less time than officially estimated. Only by ignoring "the instinct for good work," that is by producing shoddy goods quickly without reference to either safety standards or respecting the limits of both tools and machine can the worker raise wages beyond the minimal level. Management expects and demands this response to meet production targets, prove increased efficiency, and maintain the long-term viability of the enterprise while officially condemning the practice. Predictably, increased production beyond the norm results in boosting the norms, so the workers ultimately trap themselves in a vicious cycle of continually making more for less.

Writing in the early 1970s, Haraszti did not hold out much hope for the spontaneous development of labor solidarity, and the desperate nature of his description seemed to rule out any intensification of class struggle. More interesting is that Haraszti's analysis forms the ideological background to his later demands for political autonomy. By the early 1980s Hungarian dissidents could look backwards to the Hungarian workers' councils of 1956 or across the border to early demands made by Solidarity activists for the self-management of enterprises. Haraszti clearly allied himself with János Kis as coeditor of *Beszélő* in looking to Poland as a positive example, despite the imposition of martial law. Economic reform could not be considered in isolation, as had largely happened with the NEM. Real trade unions require independence from the state. Freedom of association translated into the economic realm as independent trade unions, a necessary prerequisite for reform, for which the healthy functioning of civil society was an important precondition.

In his later work *The Velvet Prison*, Haraszti turned his attention to a completely different target: the role of artists under state socialism. It seems fitting that, after having examined the experiences of the industrial worker, he turned to the cultural worker. In particular, he articulates the post-Stalinist aesthetics of censorship where "censors and artists alike are entangled in a mutual embrace" (1987: 5). Just as the system makes workers complicit in their own degradation, writers and artists of all stripes were "condemned to collaborate with those that govern them" (1987: 5). In telling this story, Haraszti is not simply making explicit the dynamics of a new and subtler form of state censorship, but is making generalizations about the very essence of post-totalitarianism.

Haraszti compels the reader to understand the differences between the more obvious and "traditional" forms of censorship, that is "meddling [in order to] silence opposition to the state," and newer and more surreptitious forms. He states:

> The old censorship is increasingly being superseded by something altogether new, less visible, and more dangerous. The techniques of the new censorship are fundamentally different from those employed by classical

censorship. The heavy-handed methods of the past are pressed into service only when the new ones fail to function properly. That this occurs relatively rarely in Hungary testifies not to the state's liberalization but to the growing success of more subtle means of constraint. Traditional censorship presupposes the inherent opposition of creators and censors; the new censorship strives to eliminate this antagonism. The artist and the censor—the two faces of official culture—diligently and cheerfully cultivate the gardens of art together. This new culture is the result not of raging censorship but of its steady disappearance. Censorship professes itself to be freedom because it acts, like morality, as the common spirit of both rulers and ruled (1987: 7–8).

For Haraszti censorship is a much more all-encompassing process, involving the entire production of culture and reproduction of cultural norms within the system:

If I still speak of censorship, what I refer to is not merely certain bureaucratic procedures but the whole context of culture, not just state intervention but all the circumstances that conspire to destroy the basis of autonomous or authentic artistic activity, not just political *diktat* but the individual's *Weltanschauung* within an all-embracing and unified society, not only "legal" and "illegal" restrictions but also the secret psychological sources that sustain the state's reach even in the last cell of culture. Hence I will refer not only to punishment but also to reward and sustenance, privilege and ambition. I wish to describe the kind of censorship that is not the skin of our culture but its skeleton. I am interested not only in the outer regulations but also—and primarily—the inner gravitation, the downward pull, of the artist's imagination (1978: 8).

The system placed a special role, with accompanying privileges, on artists. The explosion of cultural production in the postwar era in the region has been well documented: more exhibitions of art, high attendance at the theatre, well financed film studios. Behind the scenes were well-paid cultural workers with access to special retreats of (relative) luxury, decorated with state honors. The picture painted by Haraszti is similar to that of Miłosz's Delta in *The Captive Mind*, who converts his nationalism and subverts his talent to the dictates of socialist realism, finding his ultimate patron saint in the state.

Under Stalinism, "certain anachronistic characters" existed, whose advocacy of personal autonomy resulted in their being branded class enemies. Their intellectual progeny is the current crop of rebels, to whom they have bequeathed "a vanquished civilization whose promise of democracy, individualism, and critical thought has left a lingering, though fading trace" (1987: 10). They are naturally an extreme minority, and unlike Kis and Bence, Haraszti is more tragic in his assessment of their social base and potentiality:

> The new culture of totalitarian socialism has not given observers any reason to accord sociological necessity to these atavisms. I fear that the autonomous spirit is not a necessary product of any institution, class or social relation in the new society. And if this is so, then we have glimpsed the (perhaps only symbolic) sentence of death passed upon these outcasts (1987: 11).

Haraszti is both romantic and realistic—romantic because he realizes that to choose autonomy over the new culture means "influencing the real culture of family, school, and workplace about as much as a malfunctioning traffic light affects the life of a city" (1987: 11), and realistic because he recognizes that "art and power are not natural enemies," and that freedom is not, contrary to popular belief, an essential condition for art (1987: 12–13).

Haraszti's description is highly stylized and ironic; he explains mockingly how artists and censors came to be such cozy bedfellows. He describes how the role of artist-as-vanguard—and absolutely antiauthoritarian in ethos and aesthetics—is transformed in the postrevolutionary political situation into a literate and popular defender of those in power. From the radically independent yet ghettoized artist springs forth the artist as promoter and then defender of the revolution. None of this, including Haraszti's description of socialist realism which follows, is strikingly original, but the manner in which the story is told is both cogent and highly entertaining. What is more original and dark in its implications is the culture of censorship that develops out of this cautionary tale, more insidious because it is embedded in the very behavior of the artist. It is as if Haraszti has drunk deep from the wells of both Chomsky and Foucault, and applies the lessons of manufacturing consent and the subtle operations of the axes of power/knowledge to the production of culture in East-Central Europe.

Stalin suggested that writers were the "engineers of human souls," to which Haraszti adds that as good middle-class bureaucrats, they take their role as organized professionals seriously. They become "corporation artists" and from this material base develops a new mythology and aesthetics. In this respect, Haraszti does not refer to the crass dictates of socialist realism, but to its more subtle post-totalitarian mutations. This new aesthetics perpetuates such absurdities as the all-encompassing functionality of art, the permanent liberation of artists, and perhaps most ridiculous, the notion that within every restriction is some level of emancipation. Artists themselves come to pave the way for censorship as constitutive of the very freedom it seeks to emasculate. Under the mantra "Censorship as Freedom," Haraszti takes on the voice of the state artist and constructs the following apology:

We are tied to a society of progress and necessity by bonds that are stronger than fear. I am one of those who is privileged to articulate my thoughts publicly. Other than the party politician, I am the only individual who can freely remark upon life's complexities and freely use the accepted principles of discourse. What is more, I can be subjective; after all, I am a member of an artistic community that is supposed to express permitted subjective preoccupations. Naturally I come up against restraints. But I am too deeply involved for my position to be explained simply in terms of the barbed wire that surrounds me. I am not a silent inmate of the Gulag.

Why do I not test the limits? Because I am not being forced into a corner. Prohibition plays a different role in a centralized society than in a pluralistic one. No use searching here for a general, amorphous permissiveness that prohibition would diminish. Quite the contrary: here prohibition does not diminish but creates freedom. It provides a standardized satisfaction for the instincts that demand alternatives. In the case of the artist, the choice is between spoken or silent consent, between a fulfilled life and mere existence, between the artists' retreat and the labor camp.

I am not being cynical. The choice available to me is not between honest and lying art, not even between good and bad art, but between art and non-art. The privileges that go with my profession play only as much part in my choices as the gun license does in the vocation of the professional soldier. Art is more important to me than upholding the myth of art's autonomy. In this respect I am not a victim but a true child of my generation. I am the natural successor of the scientist who knew, even before the

296 THE DILEMMAS OF DISSIDENCE IN EAST-CENTRAL EUROPE

advent of state socialism, the pleasures of privilege, security, and influence
that come with being part of an organization (1987: 72).

Censorship becomes "quality control," at best a minor irritation in
the life of the artist. Excuses for state intervention include incompe-
tence, irresponsibility, or corruption. Maintaining the dignity and preeminent place accorded the profession is an important objective, and
thus artists begin to censor themselves and each other. At this point,
the role of the state is limited to rare intervention. Artists are "professionalized" and as state employees they become self-regulating.
Censorship becomes "progressive," defined simply by Haraszti as the
"self-restraint of company artists" (1987: 79).

Haraszti paints a detailed picture. Innovation and creativity are
allowed under the guise of organically making society more manage-
able (1987: 109). Artists are parasitically independent in that artistic
methods and ideas (chiefly from the West) are imported and transformed and generalized to serve the public interest (1987: 114). The
unspoken policy of the "delayed green light" is adopted, whereby
all innovations and imports are cautiously examined and sanitized
before proceeding. As Haraszti states, all new ideas must be allowed to
"mature," that is, they must "be favored by the state." Ideas must not
only be "adaptable, but also banal" (1987: 115). Likewise the "principle of clarity" demands any work of art "*must* admit ... an officially
acceptable interpretation, and nothing must exclude *this* interpretation" (emphasis in original; 1987: 117). Charitably, other interpretations are of course possible, yet context is all-important in sending the
right signals to the recipients of state-sponsored art. The reading and
theatre-going public *knows* a particular work of art is acceptable because
in each case the party-state is a silent coauthor and coproducer.

Haraszti's artist is similar to Havel's greengrocer. Conformity is
expected, but not agreement. While the greengrocer must routinely
display his sign "Workers of the World Unite," the state artist is required
to demonstrate his "sincere participation." For the artist, neither
a "vision of the perfect society" nor "evidence of ideological fealty"
is demanded (1987: 79). Within the expected parameters of performance, freedom of action is the norm. The greengrocer and artist are
complicit in their own agreed-upon servitude to the established order;
"living a lie" runs deep. They are neither passive victims of a post-
totalitarian regime nor its active proponents, but are part of its very

fabric and sustain it. Haraszti explains that state socialism is not like a garment we can take on and off, but is "more like our skin: it grows with us." Artistic cooperation and censorship are two sides of the same coin, both voluntary and involuntary, expressing both self-respect and servitude.

There is a surreal kind of free communication that exists "between the lines" in the system Haraszti describes. Correspondingly, on a societal level, "... it is public life itself that is the space between the lines" (1987: 145). This is not to be confused with real freedom of speech, or legitimately independent trends in either art or society, but is illusory as it is dependent on the state's social base, its widening level of toleration as measured by its own sense of security. Such "social space" was much wider in Kádár's Hungary and much narrower in Husák's Czechoslovakia.

Because Haraszti's deliberately hyperbolically adopts the state writer's voice, he denounces his own cohort of dissidents as atavistic and naive romantics, searching for a new utopia when one has already been found. Their pathetic existence on the margins of society serves only as a cautionary tale to the state artist: "They are living memorials to the sad fate of individualism for a new generation that does not know the misery from which our state culture emerged" (1987: 157). If the dense and careless reader cannot see the twinkle in Haraszti's eye as he makes this dull pronouncement, he makes it altogether clear in the afterward to the English edition:

> I hope that I don't have to defend my treatment of dissent in this book. I intended the very existence of this book to be a denial of its own deliberate exaggerations. I hope that its publication is a proof of the despair that darkens its sentences. For this reason, I chose to speak mostly in the third person, in the voice of a state artist, rather than joining the chorus of my own natural compatriots in the ghetto of romantic individualism. Like a ventriloquist, I adopted this voice in order to deliver the verdict that directed culture confers on the independent spirit. But I hope that the sentence is rendered invalid by the very fact that it has been pronounced publicly by me, and by the fact that you, dear reader, hold this pessimistic book in your hands (1987: 162).

Theorizing Civil Society: Konrád's *Antipolitics*

György Konrád was first and foremost a novelist, but his experience as a banned writer and as a sociological researcher propelled him in the direction of the democratic opposition. Although Kis is more thorough in his theoretical reasoning and his philosophical training is far more evident in his scholarship, it is Konrád who was most well known outside Hungary as its leading dissident voice in the late 1980s. Like Havel, his fiction and its censure brought him both acclaim and notoriety abroad, paving the way for the considerable public and Western acknowledgment of his essay *Antipolitics*. Like Havel's "The Power of the Powerless," *Antipolitics* is a sustained and inspired polemic, and touches upon all the major themes of the East-Central European dissident *oeuvre*.

Not by accident Konrád begins *Antipolitics* with a critique of the Yalta division of Europe. Like Rupnik and Heller, Konrád situates the postwar division of Europe and the ensuing superpower rivalry in the series of military-political conferences culminating at Yalta and Potsdam. It is not simply that Yalta was a death sentence for the independence of the region given inevitable Soviet domination, for it symbolized the logic against which the dissidents fought on both an intellectual and a practical level. As Konrád states: "To question the partition of Europe is dangerous and misleading because it fosters the illusion that it is possible to question it" (1987: 3). These lines have resonance in Hungary precisely because in 1956 the Yalta division of Europe was questioned; Nagy was the only communist leader of the Bloc to try (responding to popular pressure, of course) to remove his state from the Warsaw Pact. Through Hungarian linkages with END and the development of its own indigenous peace movement, dissidents like Konrád were more than willing not only to question the presence of Soviet troops on Hungarian soil, but also the maintenance of American forces and arms in Western Europe as well.

The solution advocated by Konrád is both idealistic and pan-European in scope. Throughout his opening chapter, Konrád alludes to the necessity of an East-West *European* dialogue as an important preliminary step for long-term peace and independence on the continent. Either a Soviet-inspired solution, such as the "gradual, controlled transformation of the Soviet empire ... into a community of nations capable of behaving like a partner towards the countries of Western

Europe" or an American-backed "United States of Europe" are adequate to the task at hand.[23] It is a problem of political vision and conception: "Today's Western Europe has no independent political philosophy, and so it offers none of the transcendence that would give meaning to a common enterprise like integration" (Konrád, 1987: 8). Like Charter 77, Konrád links peace to the dismantling of the Iron Curtain, and chastizes Western European governments accordingly:

> Not a single European government has made the cardinal peace proposal: an appeal for the removal of the Iron Curtain. Europe's politicians have no bold, incisive peace strategy and don't seek to launch any useful debate. This intellectual passivity is simply a retreat before Soviet peace propaganda, which uses military force to make Europeans and the whole world acknowledge that what the Soviets acquired in World War II is theirs. From the Pacific Ocean to the Iron Curtain, their empire is a seamless whole; to contest it from within is counterrevolution, while to contest it from without is to meddle in their internal affairs. The Helsinki Declaration only confirmed, three decades afterward, the validity of the agreements reached at Yalta and, later in 1945, at Potsdam.[24]
>
> It is pleasant to commiserate with the unfortunate Eastern European cousins, but let no one think the West is going to make any trouble on their account. They got détente, they got credits, what more do they want? What more? They want a *creative initiative, a concrete, tangible peace proposal, a plan to take down the Iron Curtain.* They want Western Europeans to understand that while Eastern Europe remains under occupation, Western Europeans cannot live in security. Western Europe is moving toward neutrality of its own accord, without even trying to demand that Eastern Europe be neutralized in exchange. It takes little intelligence to cling to the ideology either of blind loyalty to NATO or of unilateral concessions.[25] Western Europe will find a worthy place for itself in the world only when it no longer allows for the US–Soviet dichotomy to determine its place (my emphasis; 1987: 8–9).

Konrád points out that the "international ideological war" is above all a contest between national political elites, and has little connection with the daily lived experience of citizens on either side of the East–West divide. The sharp contrast between the interests of the superpowers and their respective political elites and the masses of citizens throughout Europe affected by them was of greatest concern. His answer to the impasse, an "historic compromise" whereby the Soviets accept the "democratic practice of Western European communism" and both sides must remove all troops and missiles from the continent, is designed above all to mitigate and perhaps reverse the years of accumulated differences between citizens as a result of the Iron Curtain. The answer is to be found somewhere between the solutions of Finland and Austria. In such a trade-off, however, Konrád was concerned that autonomy and sovereignty be neither partial nor contingent, as he felt resulted from the limited (and later quashed) autonomy granted Solidarity in Poland. Thus he states:

> Better not to bestow any at all formally: we will not barter our salvation for a bowl of lentils. What we want is unlimited self-determination, unlimited democracy, unlimited freedom to speak out. Yes, we want at least as much freedom as the small nations of northwestern Europe have. Yes, we want the Russian troops to go home. If the postwar political situation demands that they be here, and now and then impose or ordain a military dictatorship, then we reject the postwar political situation. Let them go home, and we will go back (or rather forward) to the status quo that would have evolved here of its own accord, without such external disturbances as the communist seizures of power and the counterrevolutions of 4 November, 21 August, and 13 December.[26]
>
> We want that internal process with which East-Central Europe is already pregnant; we want bourgeois civil liberties and an embourgeoisement that is not hedged about with prohibitory decrees. We don't want the authorities to have discretionary rights over us. We want constitutional guarantees; we want it clear that semifreedom is not freedom, half-truth not truth, liberalization not liberalism, democratization not democracy. We want no less than what the most advanced democracies now have.
>
> We will not get it by revolution. We will not get it through gradual reforms.[27] We will not get it by a third world war. How will we get it? I see no other way except for Europe to propose to the two superpowers that they mutually withdraw from the Iron Curtain (1987: 53–54).

Konrád is not content to merely toss out his vision of a peaceful, nonaligned, and democratic future without providing some practical suggestions as what roads might be taken in such a journey. For Western Europeans, the answer lies in broader and deeper integration, both politically and economically. Only by strengthening European identity will the historical anachronisms of national particularism and chauvinism be once and for all discarded, and will the continent develop a new sense of purpose, as well as the political and economic might to carry out its intentions. In the East, the answer is more variegated and complex, given a road less traveled and a decidedly more difficult voyage.

Like his other East-Central European counterparts, Konrád defines the two untouchables—Warsaw Pact membership and one-party rule—as independent variables, but suggests to his readers that these "can be brought into more diverse and more flexible relationship with the dependent variables that are only relatively determined by them" (1987: 73). Thus he raises the following:

How, then, can we make the social status quo more of an independent variable with respect to the military status quo? How can we strengthen the horizontal human relationships of civil society against the vertical human relationships of military society? How can a society adapt to those two fixed facts—the Soviet alliances and the one-party system—in such a way that in every other sphere of life it can display the greatest autonomy: the freedom to express its own individuality, while at the same time cultivating its share of the common European consciousness? (1987: 74)

The goal of freedom is absolute and unequivocal. However, Konrád states, "the road that leads to it is relative" and the trick is to equip society with flexibility, autonomy, and versatility so that it is equal to the task. Konrád declares that society with a strategy is stronger than an armed state (1987: 75). The solution is found not in high politics or diplomatic intrigue but in low politics, in society, or in Konrád's lexicon, *antipolitics*.

For Konrád, *antipolitics* is both noun and verb, vision and action, moral force and political strategy. He refers concretely to the process of resurrecting an independent civil society along side and distinct from the party-state, as well as a system of values that positions political activity and change not in institutions but among active and engaged citizens. Antipolitics discards all narrow and elite-based notions of politics and political change. In Central Europe in the late 1980s, Konrád contextualizes his meaning:

Antipolitics strives to put politics in its place and make sure it stays there, never overstepping its proper office of defending and refining the rules of the game of civil society. Antipolitics is the ethos of civil society, and civil society is the antithesis of military society. There are more or less militarized societies—societies under the sway of nation-states whose officials consider total war one of the possible moves in the game. Thus military society is the reality, civil society is a utopia.

Antipolitics means refusing to consider nuclear war a satisfactory answer in any way. Antipolitics regards it as impossible in principle that any historical misfortune could be worse than the death of one to two billion people. It recognizes that we are a homicidal and suicidal species, capable of thinking up innumerable moral explanations to justify our homicidal and suicidal tendencies (1987: 92).

If politics is ultimately about "the rich network of relationships that we call power" then antipolitics is about constructing and realizing a counter-power. Konrád is concerned that Machiavelli is right in suggesting that power wills its own enlargement; the extension and consolidation of control is contained within its own internal logic. Meaningfully limiting power is thus a difficult if not impossible exercise to either conceive or carry out from within the power structure itself. Like Michnik, Konrád believes that appeals to the Jacobin–Leninist tradition of revolution, struggle, and righteous possession of the truth are both fruitless and misleading. In the region, such a teleological approach *is* the road well-traveled, and unfortunately paved with bloodshed and terror, or at minimum, mediocrity and control. With such demagoguery comes acquiescence to "the inescapable demands of some historical agenda," inevitably resulting in the concentration of power in a newly installed political elite (1987: 114).

Konrád's notion of antipolitics can be compared with the social movement activism of the New Left, as well as postmodern decentered political action, reliant upon overlapping and multiple identities and bases of resistance. Above all, however, Konrád's antipolitics is built upon the philosophical assumption that politics need not and *should* not be enveloped by a ruling ideology or a ruling elite. He criticizes the West for being "captive of its own ideology" in buying into the arms race and superpower struggle and shrewdly suggests that if triumph over the East is paramount, a better weapon is economic policy (1987: 87). Similarly, Soviet-type communism comes under fire for privileging the state and its collective interests and agencies over the rights of human beings generally and minorities specifically. Sadly intellectuals have too often been willing volunteers in authoring the ideological explanations necessary for the sustenance of such regimes.

Antipolitics works as both means and end as it is based on everyday action in everyday life. It is intrinsically oriented toward peace and cooperation rather than violence and war because it is on the micro-level, the level of family, community, village, or neighborhood, that human beings are most often able to help and love one another, make sacrifices if necessary, and resist crime. To be sure, violent acts occur here also, but they are the exception, the interruptions in the flow of daily existence. As Konrád aptly notes: "History takes no note when a woman feeds her family" (1987: 103). Mass violence becomes more likely when these local bonds or communities are torn apart, through some combination of historical and external forces, often including a series of ideologically-twisted exhortations to engage in the process of constructing and demonizing an "other".

Antipolitics presumes and expects a pervasive level of democratization, well beyond the periodic exchange of political elites via free and fair elections. Konrád's ideal of "greater democratism" is consonant with Kuroń's self-organization. As he states, "When there is parliamentary democracy but no self-administration, the political class alone occupies the stage" (1987: 137). Such self-management must include an opening up and democratizing of bureaucratic processes, both within the central state and within local workplaces and communities. Konrád states:

> Workplace and local community self-government, based on personal contact, exercised daily, and always subject to correction, have a greater attraction in our part of the world than multiparty representative democracy because, if they have the choice, the people are not content with voting once every four years just to choose their deputy or the head of the national government. That somehow seems very little when people hope that, by taking a part in the affairs of the community, they can gain a voice in their own destiny (1987: 137).

Following this logic, self-organization according to Konrád (and Kuroń) "means that representative democracy spreads from the political sphere to the economic and cultural spheres as well" (1987: 139).

Democracy is both the prevailing principle of legitimacy and the prevailing principle of societal organization. Citizens are involved and engaged at all levels and in all spheres of social activity.

Moreover, there is historical resonance for this type of approach—the Hungarian Workers' Councils of 1956 were the most spontaneous, vivid, and resistant forms of democratic organization to spring forth from the revolution.[28] Konrád is eloquent:

> The message is clear in the resolutions drawn up by the workers' councils during the Hungarian revolution of 1956: multiparty parliamentary democracy is essential; self-governance in a very concrete community is essential. Democracy is essential at every level. It occurred to no one to expatiate on how this would be a good thing at some levels but a bad thing at other levels. It was the dramaturgical function of 1956 to state the essential, without beating around the bush. Democracy is needed in factory management, in the government, and in relations with other governments. We need it in self-defense, so that others will not be able to humiliate, ruin, occupy and terrorize us (1987: 138).

The resonance lives in the minds of all Central Europeans because of 1956, 1968, and 1981. That these exercises in greater democratization and accountability were arrested does not prove that such approaches are impossible. To the contrary, it enhances "the attractive forces of the ideal" (1987: 140).

Predictably and in keeping with his emphasis on antipolitics, Konrád is extremely sympathetic to the existence and the goals of Solidarity in Poland. For Konrád, Solidarity's "unexpected vigor and popularity confirms the hypothesis that in the state-socialist societies democracy in the broadest sense is now on the historical agenda" (1987: 142). Like KOR and in agreement with his Polish contemporaries, Konrád sees Solidarity as inheriting the role of "social self-defense." Given its improvisational appearance, there was no "ready-made theory and methodology waiting for it." Konrád's affection for the Polish movement is undiminished despite the imposition of martial law and the virtual destruction of the aboveground organization. Although the movement was defeated by Polish tanks (backed by the threat of Soviet ones), the Polish democratic movement to some degree defeated its own self-limited aims by proving that "it is impossible to want freedom a little" (1987: 142). Konrád pinpoints in this failure its ultimate success—that there can be no stable authority in the region unless ultimately terror is resorted to at some level, or some process of democratization is meaningfully initiated. For Konrád, as for Kis and Haraszti, "sensible accommodation" is not a viable option, and thus the Polish experience also serves to invalidate once and for all the historic Hungarian compromise of intellectual acquiescence in exchange for steady embourgeoisement.

Konrád does detail the types of actions or enterprises that might be classified as antipolitical, or furthering the goals of antipolitics. He saves his practical arguments and criticisms for the community of dissenters of which he is a member. He cautions against playing into the hands of the international (read: Western controlled) media, with a footnote to the lack of assistance provided by the West for the freedom fighters of 1956. The West looks only for sensationalism in its ideological war against communism; the foreign press can at best be accorded a limited role, "as auxiliaries in our enterprise." Thus samizdat and the independent word is best targeted at Hungarians themselves—not a bad strategy given the fact that Hungarians were hardly given to social resistance after 1956. Impromptu experimentation is the daily stuff of antipolitics, and is cumulatively important:

> Our real mood is one of neither victory nor defeat, but of experimentation. When I look around I see that everyone is starting something, planning, trying his skills, telling of some small success. It may be an experimental school, an interesting research project, a new orchestra, a publishing opportunity, a screenplay accepted, a little restaurant to open, an association of mathematicians, an attractive private shop, a private gallery, a trip to the West, cultural undertakings, independent publications, semiunderground journals (1987: 166–7).

Both the existence and growth of the second economy, and alongside it, a second culture, enliven and deepen civil society. With such initiatives there is "a slow expansion of the limits" to the point where even in the official realm "an honest documentary appears on TV, a good serious play at one of the theaters, an interesting study in a periodical" (1987: 167). Although the regime's acceptance of a limited form of pluralism is a sign of the system's strength in that it can afford to tolerate some dissent, greater independence in the public realm leads to greater independence in private thought, in the imagining of alternatives. Citizens are more likely to view themselves and each other as participants and subjects, and separate themselves from the party-state—in this respect economic autonomy goes hand-in-hand with what Konrád calls "intellectual self-management":

> Greater independence with respect to redistributive centralism; a brisk circulation in freely associating and self-governing intellectual groups in the marketplace of ideas; alternative enterprises dedicated not to maximum profit but to intellectual activity for its own sake, to make a living without any urge to get rich; in short, an amalgam of the second economy and the second culture—that is the road that beckons to the ablest young intellectuals of Eastern Europe. It is perhaps the only way they can emancipate themselves, step by step, from the rhetoric and intellectual discipline of the state (1987: 176).

For Konrád, antipolitics is the essence of democracy. Democracy conceived and defined by Konrád is strongly participatory in nature, placing strong and active obligations on its citizens. Antipolitics is not only the primacy of local over central, individual over collective, but democracy over its alternatives, and politics over economics. Thus Konrád states:

> In a liberal democracy, socialist reforms can be adopted by parliamentary majority, according to the constitutional rules of the game. Democracy is more important and more basic than the reform of income and property relations. Democracy can include socialism, but one-party state socialism cannot include democracy. If it gives ground, citizens newly awakened to their dignity will destroy the rigidly centralized political structure.
>
> A socialism that benefits the majority—whether by the just redistribution of income or by the just redistribution of power—is possible only in a society where the majority decides and the minority is free to voice its opinion without restriction. If the so-called achievements of socialism cannot be debated there is no democracy. It is a cardinal principle that the values of democracy precede those of socialism (while in no way denying them) (1987: 189).

If antipolitics is key to Konrád's substantive views about democracy, he also makes it clear that the locus of antipolitical action is civil society, not the state. Antipolitics is not about elites and institutions, but rather their opposite:

> Antipolitics is the political activity of those who don't want to be politicians and who refuse to share in power. Antipolitics is the emergence of independent forums that can be appealed to against political power; it is a counterpower that cannot take power and does not wish to. Power it has already, here and now, by reason of its moral and cultural weight (1987: 230–231).

Regarding the relationship between the state and civil society, Konrád states:

> Antipolitics and government work in two different dimensions, two separate spheres. Antipolitics neither supports nor opposes governments; it is something different. Its people are fine right where they are; they form a network that keeps watch on political power, exerting pressure on the basis of their cultural and moral stature alone, not through any electoral legitimacy. That is their right and their obligation, but above all it is their self-defense. A rich historical tradition helps them exercise their right (1987: 231).

Thus Konrád imbues antipolitics with a strong and engaged conception of citizenship, one where involvement in and through the relational and independent networks of civil society provide daily confirmation of the democratic ethos at work. This is not a politics about the circulation or exchange of political elites, or the institutional business of the state. It is about "the rejection of the power monopoly of the political class" because antipolitics posits not only a redistribution of power but also a check on the institutional control of policy and its implementation (1987: 231). Moreover, antipolitics is possible almost anywhere and under any conditions. Even under authoritarian communism, citizens are free to construct their private lives as they wish, to infuse their leisure time, their relationships, and their private conversations with thoughts, ideas, experiences, and criticisms. Civil society can and does survive in harsh times, by retreating into the private spaces of families and circles of friendships. Thus social solidarity is preserved in an official sea of anomie:

> Withdrawal into our huddled private circles enabled us to survive even
> the grimmest years of the dictatorship [during the Stalin era]. We didn't
> really live in a state of constant tension because every evening we could
> be with one another. We talked a great deal; congregating in our lairs, we
> experienced a kind of campfire warmth (1987: 203).

Finally, Konrád in effect "transnationalizes" civil society by suggesting that the worldwide integration of the intelligentsia combined
with the globalization of cultural production and consumption make
this process inevitable. Konrád sees only positive outcomes. The "global
conversation of genius" that began in the hard sciences has now permeated all aspects of intellectual life, which has the twin benefits
of de-nationalizing truth and de-instrumentalizing the bearers of it.
Turning Marx on his head, Konrád wryly suggests: "It appears that the
intelligentsia—not the working class—is the special bearer of internationalism" (1987: 212). The international infrastructure of communication—including personal contacts made through research, conferences, book fairs, film festivals, the international business of publication and distribution of the printed word—has made this possible.
The process has been enhanced by a vast array of technical aids, from
fax machines and photocopiers to the entire telecommunications
industry. Konrád sees freedom and de-ideologization in this process
of marketization and commodification. After all, the intellectual need
no longer be held captive as a spokesperson for a particular ideology,
or some revolutionary of either the Left or the Right. The task of the
intellectual—to create, visualize, inspire, and illuminate—will only be
complete "when there is not longer any institution—state, church,
industrial enterprise, university—that can use him as an instrument"
(1987: 223). As naive as it might sound, Konrád's experience with the
"dissidents' international market of ideas" yields only happy consequences in the service of truth and freedom everywhere.

Konrád's eloquent discussion of a resurrected civil society developing into maturity and opening up "a dialogue with itself" is in parallel
with Havel's "The Power of the Powerless." In his discussion of the
tools and methods of antipolitics, his sympathy for Polish evolutionism is obvious. If anything, Konrád and his Hungarian counterparts
in the democratic opposition are more expansive in their notion of
civil society and its engagement with the state. Politics is a continuum
with civil society at one end and the state at the other, but the processes

of political change require involving the reform-minded intelligentsia of the party-state as partners in this gradualism. Thus antipolitics encompasses not only private, critical conversations between citizens in their non-working hours, but more traditionally social movements, single-issue political organizations with mass memberships (who may or may not conceive of themselves as political) as part of an overall strategy for democratization. In Hungary there was not the "Us versus Them" of the Polish opposition, nor the marked and persistent persecution which permanently ghettoized the Czechoslovak dissidents. This had consequences for their theorizing, most notably their successful theoretical exploitation of the "gray zone" which was neither party-state nor society, but interwoven through both.

SECTION 3

CHAPTER 8

THE DISSIDENT CONTRIBUTION TO POLITICAL THEORY

Defining the Problem: Civil Society and the Shifting Boundaries of Public and Private

In the preceding chapters, I have argued that largely in response to the failure of "reform communism" and the various revisionist approaches taken in Poland, Czechoslovakia, and Hungary, a community of dissident intellectuals began to theorize about and organize against the political and economic stagnation of the 1970s and 1980s in each of their respective regimes. Separately, collectively and with great complementarity they developed an *oeuvre* of political-theoretical approaches, tactical insights, and recommendations regarding not only the possibility but also the probability of political change. Taken as a whole, the most distinctive features of their thought and activism were: 1) the self-conscious creation of a site of resistance which came to be variably known as an "independent society," "civil society," a "parallel *polis*," "second society," or "antipolitics"; and 2) the twin strategies of new evolutionism and non-violence, characterized most succinctly in Kuroń's phrase "self-limitation" or perhaps Kis' "radical reformism."

The majority of key intellectual activists in Poland, Czechoslovakia, and Hungary all wrote and theorized about civil society in the 1970s and the 1980s, and their reflections grew out of personal experiences in attempting to generate a viable space for political change. The dynamics that made political opposition possible were very different in each country: there were significant variations in the ability to hold and make public views contrary to the official ideology, including both censorship and forms of persecution, different religious institutions, different historical traditions more or less receptive to communist (and specifically Russian) ideas, and the very different paths taken after the failure or exhaustion of internal reform processes (normalization in Czechoslovakia versus the New Economic Mechanism in Hungary). However, the overall context was profoundly similar: all were living in authoritarian communist regimes in the Soviet Bloc with planned economies and social orders regimented by Leninist "transmission-belt" organizations, and all three countries had experimented with reform communism, which deeply affected subsequent developments. Operating within their roles as cosmopolitan, urban, Central European intellectuals, they developed a set of ideas about civil society which were connected to a larger project of radical yet piecemeal political reform.

Regardless of what it was called, the following assumptions hold true for the dissidents' description of civil society and can be summarized thus:

1) Invoking the language of civil society was a purposive and deliberate attempt to make a critical linkage with the tradition of Western political thought, and this is evidenced by their references to Locke, Hegel, de Tocqueville, Arendt, and even Plato, both in their writings and in conversation.

2) The use of this terminology and the intellectual tradition it laid claim to was part of a larger argument about the boundaries of Europe, the geographical positioning of Central Europe, and in the post-1989 period, as part of its consequential "return to Europe."

3) The constitutive idea of civil society was the creation and maintenance of an independent space between state and society, through and in which various networks and associations could operate freely and without disruption, such as trade unions, churches, social movements, cooperatives, and free presses and their products, schools of thought and (eventually) political parties. By focussing on society rather than the state and the significance of the *independence* and *openness* of institutions, their approach favored the inclusion of a rich variety of activities, including everyday forms of resistance, passive non-compliance, and participation in (so-called) "non-political" self-help organizations, and cultural activities.

4) Civil society as an interpretative label was also intrinsically connected to and compatible with the strategy of "new evolutionism."

5) Civil society as envisioned by the dissidents is dependent on the cultivation of a culture of mutual tolerance, social solidarity and trust, non-violence, and the right to peaceably assemble and organize. Rebuilding civil society meant rebuilding civic virtue, in both the classical and republican senses of the term.

6) Civil society as operationalized in Central Europe, with its emphasis on *openness* and *consensus,* was democratic in form and function. Moreover, reconstructing civil society was integral to the series of transformations that reached a critical nexus in 1989, and is a necessary but not sufficient condition for consolidating democracies in the region.

It is useful to think of civil society as a particular social formation that both structures and differentiates state-society relations. It names as crucially important and worth examining the intermediate spheres of social existence between the state and the family (and in some versions of the argument, the economy as well). In the Hegelian sense, civil society both mediates public/private domains and is mediated by them. This is a multidirectional phenomenon, described best by Charles Taylor as a "web of autonomous associations, independent of the state, which bound citizens together in matters of common concern, and *by their existence or action could have an effect on public policy*" (my emphasis, 1990: 96). Civil society is also fluid, flexible in terms of time, space, and subject matter, and often it is defined negatively by what it is not. Finally, it is both paradoxical and quixotic: the dissidents were tapping into an intellectual heritage several centuries long, but at the same time appealing to its populist edge. It is as an element of political practice rather than at the level of high theory (where specific resonance is usually lacking) that it has been most successful.

In the Central European context rebuilding civil society was not an idea cleverly construed in an historical vacuum, rather it was twinned with a carefully constructed political strategy which Adam Michnik called "new evolutionism" and János Kis called "radical reformism." First and foremost, this approach meant openly recognizing and working within the boundaries of geopolitical realities as they existed prior to Gorbachev's ascendancy in the Soviet Union. As Michnik stated at the time:

The dilemma of nineteenth-century leftist movements—"reform or revolution"—is not the dilemma of the Polish opposition. To believe in overthrowing the dictatorship of the party by revolution and to consciously organize actions in pursuit of this goal is both unrealistic and dangerous. As the political structure of the USSR remains unchanged, it is unrealistic to count on subverting the party in Poland. It is dangerous to plan conspiratorial activities. Given the absence of an authentic political culture or any standards of democratic collective life, the existence of an underground would only worsen these illnesses and change little. Revolutionary theories and conspiratorial practices can only serve the police, making mass hysteria and police provocation more likely (Michnik, 1985: 142).

Accepting the limits of political reform was also a tacit recognition that the key structural supports and ideological tenets could not be questioned, such as the "leading role of the party" and the role of regional hegemony in prescribing the rules of the game. Second, and no less important, was the core belief that the possibility of internally-generated revisionism or reform communism was terminated by the events of 1968 (both in Warsaw and in Prague). All subsequent efforts to alter (not overthrow) the political system would have to be outside the party-state. Moreover, such movement was to be slow, gradual, and non-violent. By building or re-building civil society, political consciousness would be developed, nonconformity and human dignity championed, and human rights to freedom and truth reasserted. The target of such an approach was not the party-state (this was the grave error of the revisionists in all three countries) but the people themselves. As Michnik states: "Such a program should give directives to the people on how to behave, not to the powers on how to reform themselves. Nothing instructs the authorities better than pressure from below" (1985: 144).

Toward a Reconstituted Public Sphere: Central European and Western Intersections in Theorizing Civil Society

The concept of civil society is one of the key contestable concepts in the Western "canon" of political thought.[1] It is historically critical in understanding both the development of capitalism and liberal democratic practices, and is distinctively within the liberal tradition. Its very existence as something between public and private presupposes a separation of spheres not only functional for but intrinsic to liberalism. This is true of both the Lockean and Hegelian variants of civil society, which correspond to the Anglo-American "rights-oriented" and the continental European "organicist" forms of liberalism. Civil society presupposes liberal political rights and practices—tolerance, the rule of law, autonomy, mutual respect, and basic freedoms. Because independence is a requirement for civil society, there is an implicit sharing and distribution of power, information, and influence in society—a series of the checks and balances most famously described by de Tocqueville in *Democracy in America*. The dichotomy of public and private problematizes the relationship between the individual and the social, and produces necessary tension between public ethics and private interests.[2] Civil society is conceptually appropriated and extended in the dissident *oeuvre*, and signals a key contribution to democratic theory.

Aristotle first used the phrase *koinonia politike* or political union or association to refer to the public sphere. Later translated as *societas civilas* or civil society, the concept generally referred to an independent political entity. Classical political theory did not distinguish between "state" and "society" in the same way as modern political theory: once you exited the private domestic household and entered the Greek *polis*, you were automatically in the public realm, a unique community or social whole which merged political life and the daily public existence of its citizens. Although the *polis* was hardly inclusive and effectively marginalized women and slaves, its strength lay in its overall unity and coherence, a direct mapping of the political onto the public realm, one that modern life cannot permit.

Edward Shils notes that the term *societas civilas* "had a fluctuating presence in medieval political philosophy where it was distinguished from ecclesiastical institutions" (1991b: 5). Adam Seligman has shown how in the historical trajectory between ancient and modern political theory, the tradition of natural law became a crucial component constructing the idea of civil society (1992: 17–20). Particularly important was the fusion of Christianity and natural law—the achievement of Thomas Aquinas and the medieval scholastics. The integration of reason and natural law with Christian morality and divine grace permitted a new legal and political order. The state was seen as furthering and supporting the ends of Christianity, but law was separate and positive in development and implementation. Many other ideological, political, and religious developments came into play before Hugo Grotius could theorize in a modern sense about natural law—debates regarding sovereignty, the legitimacy of resistance to divine rule, and the ramifications of the splintering of the post-Reformation Christianity and the installation of the Westphalian state system. Thus John Locke, with whom we often crystallize the set of ideas that came to be known as liberalism, neither "created" civil society nor exclusively gave it its modern liberal definition.

What makes Locke's view of civil or political society so consistent with liberalism is his theory of property, which prefigures its essential characteristics.[3] In the *Second Treatise* Locke's discussion of property precedes his chapter on civil society. Property exists in the state of nature, but it is not protected. Individual property ownership for Locke is rational, and legitimate.[4] It is based on the necessary appropriation of the goods of nature required for his sustenance and his obligation to God for self-preservation. Property is made *private*, however, by mixing one's labor with it—separating it from both the common fruits of nature and delimiting it from the property of others. Property would be a limited phenomenon in the Lockean account if not for the introduction of money, which allows for significant private accumulation, differentiation according to a universal standard of value, and introduces possibilities for trade. Even *before* the discussion of the appropriate political arrangements, a measure of social organization is presupposed—a framework that includes a natural justification for private property, and by necessity inequality among men.

For Pufendorf, Locke, and Kant, society is natural, but civil society is not. Humankind is naturally sociable; for this reason Locke prefaces his discussion of political or civil society with an analysis of other ties that bind, such as the relations between man and wife (*sic*), and parents and children. However, these are limited and private relations of power and differ considerably from the nature of relations in political society. The state, as an instrument of society, conserves, regulates, indeed *perfects* society. The potential for greater freedom is realized because the state is simultaneously granted powers but at the same time is limited by them. Within the liberal tradition, we see in the development of civil society, as Keane suggests, "a history of attempts to justify might *and* right, political power *and* law, the duties of subjects *and* the rights of citizens" (1988a: 34).

Locke's construction of political society to protect property, premised on the actions of rational and moral men possessing inherent theistically given rights, applied more coherently to the late seventeenth century than to the nascent capitalism of the nineteenth century. Locke's "mutuality of contract and consent" and the potential for the realization of freedom, independence, and equality becomes much more problematic in light of the tumultuous changes wrought by capitalism. How the private accumulation of wealth and property could be reconciled with social stability and the public good was a compelling dilemma for Bernard de Mandeville, Frances Hutchinson, Adam Smith, Adam Ferguson and David Hume. In particular, the writers of the Scottish Enlightenment realized that the new operation of labor and capital meant that individuals acted out their private interests in the public sphere—and therefore had a dangerous level of social autonomy unless grounded in some new form of moral order.

Adam Ferguson, in writing *The History of Civil Society*, has in mind both a realm of urbane civility, punctuated by social and cultural institutions, as well as a flourishing commercial and professional life (Shils, 1991b: 5; Seligman, 1992: 38–40). Ferguson was naturally skeptical about the unintended consequences of economic growth and the division of labor; he was concerned about the effect this would have on a sense of community, neighborhood, and social interconnectedness.

Adam Smith, in *The Theory of Moral Sentiments*, has an answer to this problem. He roots morality in human behavior and nature. His famous "sympathy principle" explains how self-interested human beings can nonetheless act morally. God has fortunately also endowed us with the capacity for "reason, principle, conscience" which in turn guides our ability to sympathize with others. Moreover, human sympathy acting in concert with the invisible hand of the deity ensures that acquisitiveness and the selfish accumulation of wealth will also result providentially in the betterment of the social whole. The unintended promotion of the public good is the *moral* message in *The Wealth of Nations*.

G. W. F. Hegel, in formulating his theory of state and civil society, had read Adam Ferguson and was influenced by the Scottish synthesis of sympathy and mutual reciprocity with self-interest. Disturbed by the Kantian separation between public right and private morality, Hegel sought to resolve the dangerous tension between the particularity and subjectivity of market exchange and property relations by positing an ethically based political community with an eye to the common good. Hegel synthesized individual will and abstract right, illustrating that the various "moments" or elements of *Sittlichkeit*—ethical life—involve a progression from particular to universal where freedom is fully and actually realized in the state. Social life and private interest are not incompatible after all, given the correct structuring of institutions and the harmonization of different aspects of life between them.

In the *Philosophy of Right*, Hegel moves from a discussion of familial love and unity to civil society more broadly because need and interdependence drive the individual from the family into the world. The livelihood of one person is bound up and interwoven with the livelihood, happiness, and rights of all. Families are interconnected and only through this connection are their collective needs and rights actualized and secured. Civil society mediates between the family and the state; it is the level where particularity rather than universality is preeminent, but not exclusively so. This particularity is most evident in the economy, what Hegel calls the "system of needs." It is no accident that Hegel used the term *bürgerliche Gesellschaft* to describe civil society, and Marx picks up this usage. Nascent capitalism gives free rein to accumulation and the fulfillment of desire. Hegel recognizes that this can be both extravagant and degenerative, at odds with self-actualized freedom. Although Hegel accepts Smith's invisible hand, he would state that behind self-seeking lie not God, conscience, nor moral sentiment, but reason. The dialectical unfolding of reason means that the necessary particularity of self-seeking will be transformed and overcome. This "spectacle of extravagance and misery as well as physical and ethical corruption" is tempered somewhat naturally in Smithian fashion by the "system of all-round interdependence (Hegel, 1991: 222)."

The physical and intellectual resources of all individuals in the community form a human infrastructure of "universal and permanent resources" which are drawn upon to ensure both individual livelihood and the economic health of society. Hegel reinforces this moderating influence on subjective self-seeking and in turn makes room for universalizing elements in civil society through his introduction of both estates and corporations.[5] The "police"—better understood as regulatory agencies or public authorities—provide a legal net to ensure public safety, the smooth operation of the market, and so on. Taken together, these institutions are the integrative dimensions of Hegelian civil society, helping to alleviate pauperization and alienation. Ultimately, the reconciliation of the particular and the universal takes place in the ethical community of political life, the Hegelian state. Hegel attempts to square the circle—provide for the operation of private interests but *not* at the expense of the public good.

Marx completely denies the feasibility of Hegel's task. Marx's discussion of civil society begins in the real world of actuality—*Wirklichkeit*—and from this position he wants to demystify Hegel's analysis. For Marx, civil society is nothing more nor less than the equivalent of bourgeois society—literally in this case, *bürgerliche Gesellschaft*—and represents all of its interests as illustrated through the workings of capital. As Keane has shown, Marx's description devalues the distinction between state and civil society while simultaneously conflating all group organization and social stratification to the logic and contradictions of the capitalist mode of production (1988a: 32). The potential independence or activity of other organizations of civil society—churches, scientific and literary associations, hospitals and charitable organizations—is denied because their "fate is assumed to be tied unequivocally to the overwhelming power of capitalism" (1988a: 32). Although Marx correctly insists that we view civil society and other social phenomena not as *natural* but historically *specific* and *contingent*, his theory forgets real civil societies and theorizations of civil society predated capitalism. As a result, the dimensions of some of those earlier meanings, such as the need to mediate or control state power or guarantee its legitimacy, are lost. In the Marxist conception the distinction between the state and civil society is both false and undesirable. Once the victory of the proletariat is assured through class struggle and the means of production is placed under it, social harmony and unity will follow.[6]

Contra Marx, in definite opposition to the Soviet model, yet in sympathy with twentieth century socialist theorists such as Gramsci and Lukács, the dissidents in East-Central Europe *intentionally* and *self-consciously* situated their thought within this European tradition of theorizing about civil society. Moreover, their debt to this tradition is synthetic, as they draw from both what I will call, following my analysis above, the "Lockean" or Anglo-American, and "Hegelian" or continental European, lineages of the concept of civil society. Common and central to Locke, Hegel, and the East-Central Europeans are questions about the appropriate relationship between public and private spheres, the nature of the political and intersections of private rights and public goods, and the dual nature of the individual as an innately social being yet possessing private rights. In this sense, the project of the East-Central European dissidents is what Keane would describe as an exercise in "active democratic memory." Having an "active democratic memory" means constructing future-oriented political theory with eyes in the back of one's head as a pluralistic means of stimulating the imagination:

> [An active democratic memory] can be a subversive weapon in the hands of those who support (often in the name of future generations) the present-day extension of democracy. An active democratic memory recognizes that the development of fresh and stimulating perspectives on the present depends upon the criticisms that break up habitual ways of thinking, in part through types of criticism which remember what is in danger of being forgotten. Hence, the democratic remembrance of things past is neither nostalgic nor atavistic. It turns to the past not for the sake of the past—as if the secrets of present miseries were hidden there—but for the purpose of securing more democracy in the present and future. An active democratic memory knows that past traditions of political discourse can furnish us with more than a few surprises and provoke us into enlightening disagreements. They can remind us of some of the "perennial" problems of social and political life. And thereby, they can help us understand who we are, where we stand, what we might hope for (Keane, 1988a: 33).

Keane suggests that having "an active democratic memory" which looks simultaneously backward at tradition and forward with optimism also confounds the traditional Left–Right historiography of political thought. Moreover, dissident reference to the dilemmas and ideas of the classical texts was a methodological and a strategic project: by laying claim to an ideological shared heritage they were activating an ideological "return to Europe" and highlighting in their own histories various democratic and cooperative traditions and levels of resistance to external power. It was not for nothing that Czech dissidents and Polish activists studied Hegel and Kant in secrecy and under threat of arrest in their various "flying universities."

James Turner Johnson (1992) argues that in their quest for an independent society, Michnik and Havel echo the type of civil society posited by John Locke. Absent from East-Central Europe at the time these intellectuals were writing was a real or imagined social contract where individuals seek freely to come together for common purposes to form a state, whereby those purposes are protected and advanced. For Johnson, Locke's notion of the consent of the governed is central, which he compares with Michnik's celebrated description of the Gdánsk agreement between the Polish government and Solidarity. Although Locke assumes men exit the state of nature voluntarily for both their individual and common good to create a government, Michnik begins with the reality of post-totalitarianism (1992: 44). Michnik's innovation is his discussion of "how civil society might be brought into being within that hostile context" (1992: 44).

Zbigniew Rau (1987) goes further than Johnson, and suggests that what makes the Lockean contractarian approach so applicable to the dissident civil societies of East-Central Europe is their evocation of the morality of Locke's "three-dimensional individualism." In Rau's account, Locke's individualism is composed of the ability of human beings to act morally and self-consciously as subjects in social life; the principles and duties of moral conduct adhere to the individual as an agent, ultimately responsible to God; finally the political and collective expression of these individual moral beings is civil society. Thus conceived, Lockean civil society provides an ideal-type in which the voluntary and collective efforts of individuals give a political and public dimension to their individually-realized concepts of justice. For Rau, the moral conviction which gave rise to the voluntary creation of alternative social groups and movements such as Charter 77 and Solidarity is profoundly Lockean in content. Both Charter 77 and Solidarity were constructed around the central value of individual dignity—from this came moral agency, responsibility, participation, solidarity, and action. Furthermore, the extreme conditions accompanying the rebirth of civil society in East-Central Europe highlight the moral and political consensus important to Locke.[7]

From Locke and the liberal tradition, the dissidents strongly emphasized the rights of citizens to resist arbitrary power. To be legitimate, government *must* rest on the consent of the governed. Resisting illegitimate power is strongly indicative of the freedom of the citizenry. In the East-Central European context, the potential for freedom was actualized and extended through the process of resistance to the party-state. Resistance was part of an authentic life—living in truth—and this resistance was located within civil society, both parallel to and *against* the party-state. The process was self-reinforcing: actualizing freedom meant re-building civil society and re-building civil society actualized freedom.

Following Locke, Hegel, and the Enlightenment tradition, these dissident intellectuals were prepared to view the individual as the key social unit. Individual autonomy and authenticity were inviolable, and could not be reduced to class interests. Many of the former dissidents I interviewed spoke of the social variegation of their movements proudly, as this fact stood in opposition to all they had been taught about the ascriptive nature of class identities. This position was reinforced by the Hegelian notion of the independence of human consciousness, whereby the power of the powerless was possible and a liberal defense of human rights was strategic and necessary.

Unlike Locke, Hegel, and Marx, the dissidents did not focus on property forms or protections. Privacy was usually not conceived according to economic definitions or as ownership, and when it was, the terms were inverted. The workers' state essentially *owned* its worker-citizens, controlling the terms and conditions of more than just their paid employment. More important was an *ideological* opposition and a public space independent of the party-state.

Even though the Hegelian dilemma of squaring private rights with public goods was not explicit in dissident theory, there remains a Hegelian echo in demands for universality in the realm of the particular. For every mention of "rights" in Havel or Michnik, there is also a discussion of social solidarity and of community. As in Hegel, politics is seen as a form of ethical life. In Havel's notion of politics as responsibility, we see a transformation of *Sittlichkeit* through the ideological mediation of Heidegger, Husserl, and Patočka. Morality in politics is an extension of a deeply personal ethic of responsibility which drives the individual into the world, into action in the public sphere.

Civil society for the dissidents was neither apolitical nor beyond politics,[8] as was implied by the Hegelian "system of needs," nor is it synonymous with the class interests of the bourgeoisie, as in Marx. Even liberals who acknowledge civil society as necessary to the healthy functioning of democracy tend to place it outside of representative institutions specifically and outside politics generally. According to the dissident *oeuvre*, civil society is fundamentally antipolitical, which does not mean that it is not political *per se*, but that it provides and generates an alternative non-institutional form of politics. In keeping with Konrád, civil society flows from the wellspring of low politics—not military or diplomatic institutions or processes, but an active and engaged citizenry.

Reappraising Civil Society: Feminist Critiques

There are both implicit and explicit dangers to the civil society approach. Underlying the dissident's model of civil society is a strongly-held but often unstated assumption about the *appropriate* boundaries between public life and the private sphere. To be sure, the dissidents were aggrieved at the over-politicized sterility of official public life as governed by the party-state. Their alternative, breathing new life into civil society—the space between political institutions conventionally understood and the private life of the individual—would reinvigorate an activist notion of citizenship, provide opportunities for an authentic public existence, and strategically serve as a powerful wedge forcing open (and later assist in forcing apart) the closed nature of the system. Both in theory and in practice this process inevitably generated a new kind of line-drawing exercise between the public and the private. The dissidents countered the monopolistic party-state with an "antipolitical" vision to create a parallel set of structures or movements that would serve as a new, authentic public sphere, even though this new public sphere was conducted on previously private terrain. When this alternative "went public" after 1989, it left private terrain and left behind what was most definitively private about it—family life, child-rearing, and social reproduction, as well as an enhanced opportunity for women's participation given its physical location in homes and at times suited to women's roles.[9]

A major part of the civil society project was the re-publicization of what had been pushed into the zone of the private, in not just an effort to recover authentic politics, but also to recapture subjectivity on a profound level. Rethinking political agency becomes as important as the shifting definitions of public and private in the early social processes of the transformations. Nonetheless, as in Western liberal societies, the private sphere under authoritarian communism was *also* the site of depoliticized and feminized activities such as unpaid domestic labor, child-rearing, and cultural and religious reproduction. Not that these activities were simply moved into a "more private private" sphere;

for example, cultural reproduction takes on a decidedly public tone when the "real" (unofficial or alternative) history of the nation is being taught. Nonetheless, women active in the "antipolitics" of the opposition across the region were not proportionately represented at higher levels, and this also reflects both their lower levels of involvement numerically and the fact that their contributions were either less visible or not defined in gender terms (Penn, 1994; Šiklová, 1993a; Šiklová, Matynia, 1995; 1996). Historically, the official public sphere—under the auspices of the party-state—organized the "emancipation" of women and ostensibly legislated and maintained equality between the sexes. However, along with educational opportunities, greater participation in the labor force, and increased political representation, appeared the double burden of home and work responsibilities, and little real independence, choice, or upward mobility.[10]

Feminist political theorists such as Seyla Benhabib (1992), Nancy Fraser (1992; 1994), and Iris Marion Young (1990a; 1990b) criticize the radical democracy, redefinition of the political, and communicative ethics inherent in Western civil society approaches for failing to take into account typically female (and private) spheres of activity, but have also applauded efforts to construct alternative and heterogeneous civic publics where there is no *a priori* exclusion of the proper subjects for political discussion and inclusion.[11] Similarly, Carole Pateman (1988a; 1988b) discusses the exclusion of women from the social contract under the guise of patriarchal rights and the construction of fraternity—itself a false universalism which masks the gendering of both real and imagined civil societies. More recently, Martin J. Matuštík (1993) has explored Habermasian critical theory in light of Kierkegaardian existentialism, suggesting Havelian nonpolitical politics and its implicit multiple public spheres opens up dramatic possibilities for post-national identity formation as well as open non-sexist and non-racist political practices.

One unfortunate result of the reconstruction of "normal politics" in the region has been the privileging of party politics over the parallel discursive arenas represented by the fledgling civil societies prior to 1989, as well as a radical reconfiguration of the meanings of public and private, both of which had significant and gendered consequences (Juráňová, 1997; Watson, 1993a,b, and 1997; Goven, in Funk and Mueller, eds., 1993). Although much lip service is paid to civil society as necessary to successful democratic consolidation, the actual empowerment of social movements and radical pluralism is tenuous. Depressing realities in the midst of transformation do not necessarily invalidate the argument that strong and diverse civil societies or multiple public sphere(s) work best for women *and* men in providing radically responsive and democratic opportunities for social engagement on various levels and a variety of terrains, where there are no real or imagined boundaries in terms of how participation is realized, or what can be discussed. In short, fraternity cannot become social solidarity simply by imagining it as such; it has to be socially and historically constructed from scratch, in the same way that the original civil societies were.[12] In the same way that the dissidents breathed new life into civil society, going beyond the traditional revisionism of post-Stalinism, women's organizations in the region today can go beyond the gendered limitations of civil society, redefining what is meant by "the power of the powerless." The very rejection of the fixed boundaries of politics involved in the civil society approach guarantee its theoretical and practical utility.

Political Economy as Critique:
The Dissidents Meet the Market

The marketization and privatization inherent in the practices of late twentieth-century capitalism threaten to undermine civil society in a potently efficient manner, in much the same way that the Soviet model sought to stamp out independent society as inhibiting its imperatives. Because full employment was taken for granted and the socialization of property remained unquestioned, the dissidents were relatively free to resuscitate the concept of civil society and conveniently side step the issue of the implications of a privately-controlled capitalist market economy. The party-state had effectively liquidated the market and private property yet had also eliminated employment insecurity. Given the guidepost of self-limitation and the reality of the leading role of the party, the dissidents saw no need to re-introduce these elements. The East-Central European emphasis on non-property related forms of human subjugation was in stark contrast with and sometimes in reaction to what they viewed as the obsession of Western European socialists with questions of property, ownership, and class conflict.[13] What the dissidents failed to realize in their conception of civil society is that any attempt to reintroduce "independent" initiatives also involved public/private distinctions, which in a sense brings us back to the Hegelian dilemma.

There is more than an elective affinity between the civil society approach adopted by opposition intellectuals and the subsequent marketization and privatization of Central European economies. Despite their sociological genesis on the Left and past support for egalitarianism, socialist ownership, or at least self-management,[14] post-1989 the morally influential voices of the opposition supported marketization as a *process* and the market as representing a series of desired *outcomes*.[15]

From the mid-1970s onward when dissidents in Czechoslovakia and Hungary began to discuss civil society or initiatives independent of the state as not only widening the space for alternative and open political activity, the "parallel economy" (Benda, in Skilling and Wilson, eds., 1991) or "second society" modeled on Hungary's second economy (Hankiss, 1988) was sometimes offered as either a prominent example or as a constitutive part of the enterprise. Indeed, second or parallel economies were a model given their independence from the state. They provided an example of how parallel structures were capable of supplementing and even supplanting official structures and demonstrated responsiveness to consumer needs. The magic of the market was evident in the fact that, unlike the poor quality goods available through state stores, black or gray markets provided a broader array of high-quality imported goods, albeit at much higher prices. Furthermore, the market was not seen as destructive of the other aspects of an independent society but was conceived as mutually supportive. However, by placing the market alongside the other non-state institutions of civil society, it is neutralized and made benign. In an advanced capitalist economy, the market clearly has more power and penetration than does, for example, the Church or the media. This concern is consistent with the Left critique of the "cult of civil society" among Western academics who see the approach of Keane (1988a, b) and Cohen and Arato (1992) as masking the real exploitation of property relations under capitalism (see especially Wood, 1990).

The predisposition across the region to the market *as a process or mechanism* flowed from formative experiences with reform communism. What united thinkers such as Oskar Lange, Włodzimierz Brus, Ota Šik, and (the earlier writings of) János Kornai was a commitment to a marketization, or some simulation of it, with an economy based on socialist forms of ownership. Under these types of schemes, micro-economic decisions are made independently at the firm level based on shadow commodity prices, operating under the general aegis of rules and procedures prescribed by the center (Altvater, 1993). Because attempts at reforming communism from within could not succeed given Soviet intolerance and the authoritarian nature of the system, this failure was a signal to many that creating a humane socialism out of the communist corpse was impossible.[16]

Construing the market as a process was consistent with the *political* liberalism of the dissidents. According to neo-liberal economic theory, individual actors associate with each other in exchange relationships on the basis of rough equality of opportunity, based on rational calculations of their self-interest. Transactions are assumed to be fair and transparent. Rules of the game are established to ensure that this is the case, and the state serves as neutral third party should any disputes arise. Moreover, the state is also bound by checks on its own behavior. There is a simplicity and efficiency to the overall process, which consists of millions of these freely conducted transactions. Ignoring the possibility of any distortions or externalities that disrupt the perfectly competitive scenario, profits accrue to the most efficient and productive enterprises. Commodity and service prices are set in accordance with the "natural" ebb and flow of supply and demand, and are kept reasonable or appropriate via the forces of competition. Finally, the public good is served through the expansion of industry, the accumulation of capital, the opportunities provided to all. Moreover, if you combine Mandeville's dictum that "private vices equal public benefits" with Smith's famous sympathy principle, you provide a moral as well as an economic basis for capitalism.[17]

The dissidents wanted to be able to "live in truth," so that human relationships would be honest and transparent and politics would be based on authenticity and morality. They wanted rules of fair play to be established, where international human rights agreements would be honored. The rule of law would be established, and individual citizens would be protected from arbitrary arrest and detention. They wanted to associate publicly or privately with whomever they wanted, express themselves freely without censorship, live autonomously without interference, and choose their occupations and lifestyles accordingly. It is not particularly original to suggest the obvious parallels between market economies and political liberalism; however, it bears remembering given the dissidents' debt to the civil society tradition. Havel makes this explicit:

> Though my heart may be left of center, I have always known that the only economic system that works is a market economy, in which everything belongs to someone—which means that someone is responsible for everything. It is a system in which complete independence and plurality of economic entities exist within a legal framework, and its workings are guided chiefly by the laws of the marketplace. This is the only natural economy, the only kind that makes sense, the only one that can lead to prosperity, because it is the only one that reflects the nature of life itself. The essence of life is infinitely and mysteriously multiform, and therefore it cannot be contained or planned for, in its fullness and variability, by any central intelligence (1992a: 62).

Havel assumes that the necessary precondition of market autonomy might somehow act as a protective bulwark for other freedoms. Thus in the Lockean spirit and in the tradition of the Scottish Enlightenment, private right is not separate from public interest—the two coalesce and are indeed mutually supportive. Hence the market became the economic portion of an indivisible package.

Much experience beyond Western Europe suggests that democracy and the market do not always go hand in hand and historical evidence also suggests their uneasy coexistence is the result of unique historical conjunctures (Moore, 1966; Therborn, 1977, 1984a; Przeworski, 1992). However, the dissidents largely focused on the historical nexus of capitalism and democracy as it evolved *in Europe*. The *European* market of the golden postwar age was the focus of attention. The market was a European invention, having a market was thus a precondition for belonging to Europe. The autocracy and inefficiency of central planning was "Eastern" or "Asian" (read "Russian" or "Soviet"). The historical experience of post-war Western Europe was valorized; the market was unproblematically characterized as "normal," and Central Europeans longed for a return to normal (truly European) life. Thus, Michnik naturalizes the market and mythologizes the socialist response in European culture:

> Within the realm of European political culture the market was something *perfectly natural*, but at the same time its by-products—the mentality of

egoism and a respect for the power of money—were embarrassing. Within the realm of this culture, as an answer to this sort of mentality, was created the socialist *myth*. The socialist myth in European culture can be understood, then, as an expression of shame in the face of an uncritical acceptance to the law of the jungle (my emphasis, 1995: 529).

In the Czech context, Havel justifies his original support for the celebrated neo-liberalism of former Czech Prime Minister Václav Klaus:

> ... we wanted a *normal* market system of economics. The program of breaking up the totalitarian system and renewing democracy would founder if it refused to destroy the basic pillar of that system, the source of its power and the cause of the material devastation it lead to—that is, the centralized economy (my emphasis, 1992a: 63).

Normal meant the pricing of labor based on the accumulation and expenditure of human capital ("merit" and "hard work"). Normal meant the opportunity to unburden oneself of politics because a normal situation was one where economics dominated politics, and not the other way around.[18] The construction of the market as a natural entity echoes Hayek's critique of socialism as a dangerous disruption of a "spontaneous" order of freely associating individuals (Wainwright, 1995). Although market economies express a primacy of economics over politics, as long as there are some transformative mechanisms such as democratic institutions or an even limited public sphere or civil society, they can respond to crises of legitimation in a highly elastic way (Altvater, 1993).

The market was also associated with a particular set of desired *outcomes*. Given the demonstrative example of Western Europe next door, the market was associated with the construction of institutional democratic forms, liberal political values, cultural and social freedoms, an open society, and general economic prosperity. In supporting the market or assuming its existence as natural or unproblematic, opposition intellectuals did not have just any market in mind but in particular the social market economy associated with the postwar European welfare state. Implicit in this model are the social entitlements of citizenship outlined by Marshall (1963) as relative economic welfare and security, and the right to share in a civilized life according to prevailing societal norms. The obvious contradiction between the inequality of condition inherent in the market as an outcome and the equality of opportunity associated with the market as a process remained unexplored.

Because the dissidents perceived their own theory and practice as *beyond* traditional left-right cleavages and the contradictions that might be generated by taking different positions on that axis, they were frankly less bothered by their commitment to marketization and privatization than otherwise might have been the case. This is especially revealed in the post-1989 speeches of Václav Havel, where the subtext is not only acceptance but indeed a promotion of the economic reform program of Czechoslovakia and later the Czech Republic. The excesses of unchecked capital are indeed a concern, but Havel tends to place this alongside other concerns, such as environmental disaster, world demographic problems, or the threat of ethno-nationalism and its eruption into regional conflict.

The problem is not the privileging of one conflict over another (such as nation trumping class). More at issue is the recognition that underlying all of the crises dominating the modern era is technological rationality:

> The modern era has been dominated by the culminating belief, expressed in different forms, that the world—and Being as such—is a wholly knowable system governed by a finite number of universal laws that man can grasp and rationally direct for his own benefit. This era, beginning in the Renaissance and developing from the Enlightenment to socialism, from positivism to scientism, from the Industrial Revolution to the information revolution, was characterized by rapid advances in rational, cognitive thinking. This, in turn, gave rise to the proud belief that man, as the pinnacle of everything that exists, was capable of objectively describing, explaining, and controlling everything that exists, and of possessing the one and only truth about the world. It was an era in which there was a cult of depersonalized objectivity, an era in which objective knowledge was accumulated and technologically exploited, an era of belief in automatic progress brokered by the scientific method. It was an era of systems, institutions, mechanisms, and statistical averages. It was an era of ideologies, doctrines, absolute interpretations of reality, an era when the goal was to find a universal theory of the world, and thus a universal key to unlock its prosperity (1997: 89).[19]

Why is this epistemological lesson relevant? For Havel, the end of communism brought this era in human history to an end, and truly initiated the post-modern age. More than indicating the triumph of capitalism over any form of socialist alternative, the fall of communism signaled the end to the epistemological regime that generated both systems. He continues:

> The fall of communism can be regarded as a sign that modern thought—based on the premise that the world is objectively knowable and that knowledge so obtained can be absolutely generalized—has come to a final crisis. This era has created the first global, or planetary, technical civilization, but it has reached the limit of its potential, the point beyond which the abyss begins. I think the end of communism is a serious warning to all mankind. It is a signal that the era of arrogant, absolutist reason is drawing to a close, and that it is high time to draw conclusions from that fact.
>
> Communism was not defeated by military force, but by life, by the human spirit, by conscience, by the resistance of Being and man to manipulation. It was defeated by a revolt of color, authenticity, history in all its variety, and human individuality against imprisonment within a uniform ideology (1997: 89–90).

Marketization and privatization are effectively de-problematized, not because they do not have consequences, but because they are only reflective of a larger set of issues requiring a different set of answers. In the Havelian prescription, there must be a complete paradigm shift in thought, one that rejects universal solutions, accepts mystery and the unknowable, but at the same time makes a profound commitment to absolute and unqualified responsibility. Responsibility remains the bridge between morality and politics, the prime directive of a post-modern politics:

> … we still don't know how to put morality ahead of politics, science, and economics. We are still incapable of understanding that it is the only genuine core of all our actions—if they are to be moral—is responsibility. Responsibility to something higher than my family, my country, my firm, my success. Responsibility to the order of Being, where all our actions are indelibly recorded and where, and only where, they will be properly judged (1997: 19).

Material and market-driven circumstances can devastate the body of humankind, but not its spirit. This makes the power of the powerless possible, and thus he can also claim, "... the salvation of the human world lies nowhere else than in the human heart, in the human power to reflect, in human modesty, and human responsibility" (1997: 18). Capitalism in any of its guises may yet be another reflection of instrumental rationality, but at the same time by Havel's reasoning it cannot be a prison any more than could authoritarian communism. Moreover, for Havel many of the worst excesses of modern society are common to both communism and capitalism: rampant consumerism; excessive and senseless growth; disregard for the environment; continual confrontations based on distinctions of otherness—due to racial, cultural, and religious differences; the loss of subjectivity and thus the inability to assume responsibility.

Dissident Thought as Reconstructed Liberalism

For those who have grappled with the multiple historical "meanings" of 1989 and the dissident thinking that gave theoretical contours to the momentous events wrought during that year, a consensus has emerged, in Jeffrey Isaac's words, "on behalf of an avowedly liberal interpretation" (1996: 292). The basic argument is that the East-Central European dissidents have bequeathed to us—the "West"—either the same-old or a newly reinvigorated form of political liberalism. There are several flaws to this argument, the first of which stems from confusing the theory with the results. Although I argue that ideas have mattered profoundly in the period leading up to post-communist transformation, ideas are not the only forces shaping the political universe. Second, this interpretation ignores the considerable tensions between liberalism conventionally understood as underwriting the political practices of Western liberal democracies and the ideas of the dissidents. A subset of this argument is a tendency to confuse liberalism with democracy, that is, to hold that a pro-democracy perspective must make one a political liberal. Third, the argument is supported by the self-description of many former dissidents as "liberals," misleading to many because it ignores the different connotations of that term in the region from those in the Anglo-American context. Finally, the liberal view tends to serve the agenda of many of the authors themselves, who claim superiority of liberal democracy over authoritarian communism and thus want to infuse 1989 with not only self-validation but even a restorationist impulse. Whereas in the previous section I have shown the dissidents' debt to the Western traditions of political thought, here I hope to demonstrate where the "originality" of dissident theory lies.

Ralf Dahrendorf, in *Reflections on the Revolution in Europe*, suggests that 1989 is a vindication of the tried and true ideals of liberalism, of a tolerant and "open society":

> At its core, the European revolution of 1989 is the rejection of an unbearable and, as we have seen, untenable reality, and by the same token it is a reaffirmation of old ideas. Democracy ... pluralism ... citizenship ... are not exactly new ideas (1990: 27).

This thesis has been strongly sustained by Dahrendorf's student, Timothy Garton Ash. Concluding his "eye-witness" account of the "refolutions" in Warsaw, Budapest, Berlin, and Prague, he claims the dissident intellectuals-cum-politicians have no deep ideological reservoir from which to draw:

> If I am right in my basic analysis, they can offer no fundamentally new ideas on the big questions of politics, economics, law, or international relations. The ideas whose time has come are old, familiar, well-tested ones. (It is the new ideas whose time has passed.) So is all they have to offer us their unique, theoretically intriguing but practically burdensome problems? Or might they have under their threadbare cloaks some hidden treasure? (1990b: 154).

The "hidden treasures" discussed by Garton Ash are tellingly represented as a trove of desirable human qualities rather than as political goods, and for this reason they are immediately conceived as atavistic and sentimental in the post-1989 period:

> Travelling through this region over the last decade, I have found treasures: examples of great moral courage and intellectual integrity; comradeship, deep friendship, family life; time and space for serious conversation, music, literature, not disturbed by the perpetual noise of our media-driven and obsessively telecommunicative world; Christian witness in its original and purest form; more broadly, qualities of relations between men and women

of very different backgrounds, and once bitterly opposed faiths—an ethos of solidarity (1990b: 154).

Dahrendorf and Garton Ash are but the tip of the "liberal interpretation" iceberg. Stephen Holmes describes the radical change post-1989 as a "liberal revolution" (1992: 27); Bruce Ackerman identifies 1989 as the "return of revolutionary democratic liberalism" (1992: 1). Similarly, in his account of 1989 *When the Walls Came Tumbling down*, Gale Stokes writes, "Theirs was not a revolution of total innovation, but rather the shucking off of a failed experiment in favor of an already existing model, pluralist democracy" (1993: 260). François Furet asserted that "nothing else is visible in the ruins of the communist societies other than the familiar repertoire of liberal democracy" (quoted in Sakwa, 1999: 98). Peter Rutland recently stated that in Eastern Europe in the ten years since 1989, "There has been no resurgence of communism nor an appearance of any ideology or philosophy that comes close to mounting a universal challenge to liberalism" and "Liberal democracy, with its ambivalence over final ends and with its agreement to disagree over practical solutions, would be the only game in town" (1999: 27). Even Habermas' description of 1989 as the catching-up revolution (*die nachholende* or *rückspulende Revolution*) implies a restorationist and consumerist impulse (Matuštík, 1993: 187; Arato, 1993b: 622–623).

It is indeed ironic that in many accounts the implicit or explicit standard of theoretical innovation is Marxism, or some variant of the socialist project. In its teleology, revolutionary and counter-hegemonic approach, and incisive analysis of the Old World combined with the brave promise and delivery of something not only new and better but historically necessary, Marxism is presented as grand theory *par excellence*. One reason liberals appropriate the East-Central Europeans unproblematically *as liberals* because they did not engage in a revolutionary project involving cathartic violence and a determined makeover of society and humankind. According to this logic, any more "limited" form of political theory, one that is evolutionary, or non-violent, or does not aspire to total change, must be liberal. Thus underlying the "end of ideology" or "end of history" approach of Francis Fukuyama is the following logical sequence: Marxism has failed, therefore ideology is no longer relevant, therefore we all universally recognize that liberal democracy is the only legitimate alternative.[20] According to this view,

I would add, all "partial theory" must be liberal theory. Marxism is loaded with extra ideological content at the same time liberalism is effectively de-ideologized. Thus it is difficult for those seeking to appropriate the East-Central Europeans as liberals to conceive of their contribution to political theory as anti-utopian yet idealistic; liberal in some ways but not others; radically democratic; strongly moralistic yet pluralistic in outlook; rejecting collectivism yet embracing collective action; inherently contradictory; and on no place on earth fully realized.

There is also an *ex post facto* quality to the liberal appropriation argument. Without 1989 and the triumphalism of American claims about "winning" the Cold War, I suspect dissident theory would be viewed much differently. If the pace of change had been slower, less dramatic—as surely it looked like it would be at the time of the Polish Roundtable Talks—the "spin" might be quite different. It is telling that in the late 1980s, when theorists such as John Keane and Andrew Arato were seriously engaging with the East-Central European dissidents and their *oeuvre*, the project was described as re-democratizing socialism, or looking past Marx to radically participative and Leftist ideas of civil society that both preceded and succeeded Marx. On the book jacket to *Democracy and Civil Society*, published in 1988, Steven Lukes glowingly describes Keane's approach: "Probing, lucid, and historically informed, these fine and timely essays offer new perspectives in rethinking socialism."

Many commentators have confused or conflated dissident theory with the results of the 1989 revolutions in Europe. Looking at the situation more than ten years hence, East-Central Europe *has* provided us with the "best cases" of liberal-democratic transformation. Poland, Hungary, and the Czech Republic have met all the basic polyarchal tests of democratic consolidation: free and fair elections with multiparty competition; peaceful changeover of governments; the establishment of the rule of law and the independent functioning of the judiciary; peaceful resolution of seemingly intractable conflicts (such as the "Velvet Divorce" of the Czech and Slovak Republics). Written constitutions set the rules of the overall game, are seen as legitimate, and all confer considerable rights protection on citizens. A tolerant and liberal conception of citizenship has been challenged by authoritarian populism, religious fundamentalism, and ethnic nationalism, and more or less been successfully defended.[21] Moreover, all three states joined NATO in 1999, and are poised to join the European Union in accordance with the Nice Treaty. Given what has happened in many other parts of the region, from the harshly authoritarian re-communization of Belarus to the downward spiral of ethnic violence in the former Yugoslavia, this is no small achievement. However, it is both facile and misleading to describe dissident thought as liberal and then credit it with the overall result, which also owes much to geography, political culture, relative ethnic homogeneity, a more favorable economic climate and various exogenous factors.

Nonetheless, the dissidents certainly advocated liberalism in terms of over-arching institutional arrangements. They wanted public choice, parliaments, human rights, and the rule of law, and said so on many occasions. They can be described as politically liberal in the sense of attaching great importance to tolerance and pluralism in the public sphere, and it should be said that on this level they have been enormously influential in shaping public debate.

Another central reason for the liberal tag has been what Vladimir Tismaneanu calls the rediscovery and internalization of the values of the American Revolution (1992: 617). As a whole, the dissidents conceived of themselves as the ideological descendants of the Federalists. The French Revolution represented the Jacobin–Bolshevik cult of reason, ideological utopianism and infallibility, a beautiful set of ideas gone perversely wrong. The American Revolution was more usefully symbolic: a revolt of upstarts, pitched against a mighty world power, anti-state in its ethos and modest in its aspirations. The dissidents were seditious according to the prevailing norms of the party-state, but champions of truth and freedom according to their own discourse. Thus Adam Michnik states[22]:

> ... the American Revolution appears to embody simply an idea of freedom without utopia. Following Thomas Paine, it is based upon the natural right of people to determine their own fate. It consciously relinquishes the utopian vision of a perfect, conflict-free society in favor of one based upon equal opportunity, equality before the law, religious freedom, and the rule of law. From the American Revolution also comes the idea of a plurality of exiles. The Revolution was fought by people who had tasted the bitterness of humiliation and servitude. And it brought about a republic of people who have become conscious creators of their own destinies. We see in America the embodiment of the principle of an open society and an open nation (1992: 621).

Like the American Revolution, the revolutionary nature of which at times has been hotly debated, the 1989 revolutions in Central and Eastern Europe do not constitute full-scale social revolution. The dissidents were not revolutionaries wanting to remake society in accordance with their own indubitably correct ideals. Like the American Revolution, theirs was a *political* and not a *social* revolution. They appreciated the American Revolution the same way Hannah Arendt did, as a realization of the capacity for self-initiated freedom within a fully deliberative public sphere. For Arendt, the American Revolution, unlike the French Revolution, epitomized the values of caution, deliberation, dialogue, and judgement. It was neither reckless nor romantic, less inspirational but more pragmatic.[23]

Still, other aspects of the dissident *oeuvre* generate tension with the liberal descriptor, such as the radically anti-political conception of civil society; the notion of politics imbued with morality, authenticity, and active subjectivity; the ethos of social solidarity, the implications for participation flowing from the Havelian understanding of political responsibility; and the broad re-definition of politics itself. There is something more here than the routine and Schumpeterian exchange of competitive elites or the liberal pre-occupation with privacy and the compartmentalization of political life. What Garton Ash describes as the "hidden treasures" of the democratic oppositions of East-Central Europe are just that, and should not be relegated to the museum shelf or be lost in the atavistic sentimentalizing of contemporary historians and journalists.

There are many ways of analyzing this contribution. One possible view is that the dissident *oeuvre* is liberalism-plus, with the above components adding extra value to the basic model. Jeffrey Isaac makes the argument that, upon closer examination, the ideas of the dissidents are fundamentally democratic, but not "unambiguously *liberal* democratic" (emphasis in original; 1996: 303). He elucidates this claim:

> This is *not* to say they are antiliberal. Liberal ideas of individual liberty and liberal institutions of constitutional government are surely valued as the necessary ingredients of human freedom and dignity. But they are not viewed as sufficient for many of the democratic oppositionists. There is, if you will, a democratic "surplus value" that the liberal interpretation of 1989 quietly expropriates (1996: 303).

However, as Isaac demonstrates, liberals such as Ackerman and Garton Ash are uneasy with the implications of dissident thought for the liberal paradigm, on the one hand, and the politics of the transformation, on the other. Ackerman thinks that Havel's hallmark phrase, "living in truth" has an "authoritarian ring"—he is clearly uncomfortable with the notion of *the* truth, that is pursued with a "grim philosophical passion" (1992: 32–33). Good Anglo-American liberals are not philosophically at ease with what they perceive as the moral absolutism in Havel or Konrád. Garton Ash believes that "living in truth" fails at the level of practical parliamentary politics, the daily grit and grime of liberalism, in his view:

> Now we expect many things of politicians in a well-functioning parliamentary democracy. But "living in truth" is not one of them. In fact, the essence of all democratic politics might rather be described as "working in half-truth". Parliamentary democracy is, at its heart, a system of limited adversarial mendacity, in which each party attempts to present part of the truth as if it were the whole (Garton Ash, 1990c: 52).

Another variation on the liberalism-plus model is the argument that what worked well for authoritarian communism does not necessarily translate well into the *realpolitik* of post-communist or existing liberal democracies. Thus Elizabeth Kiss (1992) argues that the antipolitics of the democratic opposition "translates badly into the post-communist era" because it basically depends on individual citizen action and subjecthood. The transformation, on the contrary, has been largely an institutional exercise, steered and managed by elites.

A theoretical dispute arises on the basis of what is privileged—liberalism or democracy. Thus *contra* Garton Ash and Kiss, Jean Cohen and Andrew Arato have argued that it is *precisely* because of the civil society emphasis that the dissidents have something major to contribute to democratic theory. In their landmark study *Civil Society and Political Theory*, Cohen and Arato explicitly acknowledge their debt to the East-Central Europeans, in particular to Michnik, Konrád, and Kis. Cohen and Arato claim to have taken the civil society concept further than the dissidents by taking it "public," that is, developing it from an oppositional strategy to a theoretical approach designed to reinvigorate the public sphere (and by implication, both democracy and democratic theory).[24]

Their debt to the dissidents is displayed in the way they endow social movements with political agency and retain the importance of self-limitation as an effective end and means of political practice. Moreover, they discuss the genesis of rights and legitimacy in civil society, echoing the types of claims made by Charter 77 and KOR. The Cohen and Arato appropriation of dissident theory strengthens the alternative to the liberalism-plus argument, that the dissidents indeed made a contribution to democratic theory beyond adding a little extra to liberalism. Michnik, Kuroń, Havel, Kis, and Konrád never saw civil society solely as an oppositional strategy, but as an end in itself. Process was as important as outcome, hence its fundamentally participatory and democratic content. Antipolitics was not—as it is sometimes interpreted—*against* politics, but *always* about doing politics differently and not simply engineering a clever end to authoritarian communism. The moral imperatives of solidarity, human rights, and "thick" responsibility exist over and against the (often-gendered) compartmentalization and professionalization of partisan politics, as well as the neo-liberal imperatives of marketization and globalization.[25]

Both the Garton Ash–Ackerman interpretation and the liberalism-plus argument reinforce their positions by claiming that since the dissidents have variously described *themselves* as liberals, then it must be so. Thus Isaac praises Adam Michnik and György Konrád for their commitments to civil liberties, parliamentarism, pluralism, and scepticism. After all, writing in the midst of revolutionary change, Konrád stated:

Why am I a liberal? Because I am skeptical about everything human, about our collective self; because for me there are no institutions, persons, or concepts that are sacrosanct or above criticism. Because in human thinking I recognize no obligations or taboos. I demand freedom even among my circle of friends. I have that now; they listen to me with interest. For me, liberalism is, first of all, a style: worldly, civilized, personal, ironic (1990b: 189).

Context here is very important. Liberalism today is often understood in East-Central Europe as an alternative set of values, in opposition to xenophobia, ethnic nationalism, or anti-Semitism. It most often has these connotations rather than referring to a particular ideology or set of institutional arrangements. When Miklós Haraszti discusses the transformation in Hungary ten years later he says that, "... it is a firmly liberal system ... [which] continued to develop in a liberal direction under consecutive partisan administrations" (1999: 33). The liberalism of the "handshake transition" means entrenched respect for human rights and democratic institutions, but it also reflects democratic cultural *attitudes*. To be liberal is to be open to criticism, tolerant of others, civic-minded, and in the region this means bucking historical trends that in the past have favored authoritarianism—of either the communist or the populist-fascist variety. To be liberal is to be progressive, rebellious, and even idealistic. In this sense, one can be politically liberal and many other things at the same time. Perhaps the fact that the dissidents have been embraced in many circles as liberals says as much about the lack of an alternative discourse in America as it does about Central and East European distaste for the lexicon of socialism and social democracy.

Indeed, some commentators have insisted on calling former dissidents liberals even when they called themselves *socialists* (especially in their earlier writings). Thus in his introduction to Michnik's *The Church and the Left*, David Ost decodes Michnik's "socialism" as "liberal communitarianism" or "republicanism." Ost supports his argument as follows:

> The liberal aspect is most clearly on display in his ardent defence of individual rights, freedom of expression, and full religious and political tolerance. Michnik appeals to John Stuart Mill as his authority, not Karl Marx or anyone from the socialist tradition. No political ideology could even be considered socialist if it did not have a communitarian aspect to it. What is special about Michnik's communitarianism, however, is that it too is of an essentially liberal pedigree. He is decidedly unsympathetic to the communitarianism of Leninism and the old Left, with its focus on organic unity between state and society, its vision of a state embodying the needs and interests of all citizens. Michnik recognizes the totalitarian implications of such communitarianism and rejects fundamentalist Catholicism for having similar organicist aspirations. Michnik's communitarianism is based on a free and active citizenry participating extensively in discussing and legislating the issues that confront them. Community is generated through the process of politics, not its outcome (Ost, "Introduction" in Michnik, 1993: 6).

Although Ost does credit Michnik for his critiques of capitalism and strong support for social justice and welfare guarantees, he claims that nothing Michnik demands theoretically could not be accommodated "through primarily a market economy and Western parliamentary structure" (1993: 6). Later on Ost suggests that Western readers "may be surprised that Michnik's socialism is little more than a defense of liberalism and individualism" (1993: 7). Ost has a fairly thick and elastic conception of liberalism—one designed more for American audiences than specifically attuned to Michnik's thought.

For although Michnik does cite Mill extensively in *The Church and the Left* and is making a strong argument for toleration, he also draws extensively from the traditions of Polish socialism. Abramowski's commitment to cooperative socialism, the struggle for an authentic parliamentary tradition by the PPS, and the radically participative views of Luxemburg are just as important to Michnik in defeating a narrowly Leninist view of political involvement and laying the groundwork for social solidarity and coalition politics. In *The Church and the Left* he even acknowledges the problem of maintaining socialist ideals under authoritarian communism, advising his readers to stay the course while embracing religious tolerance:

> The secular Left is in a particularly difficult situation in Poland. It must defend its socialist ideals in the face of an unpatriotic totalitarian power shouting socialistic slogans. Yet it is precisely for that reason that the defense must be firm, consistent, and uncompromising, free from sectarianism, fanaticism, and obsolete scenarios. Leftist thought must be open to all antitotalitarian and pro-independence ideas, and thus open to Christianity and the riches of the Christian tradition (1993: 210).

Parliamentarism and a market economy do *not* alone deliver on the promise of civil society, as both circumscribe the opportunities for direct citizen involvement in the public sphere.

We should, of course, be careful of the various labels the dissidents wore because as they themselves discovered through the process of political action and theorizing about it, *none of the existing labels seemed to fit*. Thus today you have Michnik describing himself as a "radical democrat" and Havel claiming to be a "post-modern politician." Both hesitate to employ the "S" word because it is ideologically and semantically loaded beyond contemporary utility in the region. However they are equally uneasy with the liberal tag, and neither is entirely appropriate to their thought.

Refocusing the lens to look at *democracy* rather than *liberalism* provides us with a better understanding of dissident thought as a whole and the contribution it makes to political theory. The creation of liberal political institutions in East-Central Europe only partially fulfills the promise of the democratic opposition, and what remains cannot be mandated or secured by parliamentary privilege. Here I am referring to the thick notion of responsibility and active citizenship implied in the civil society approach, and the kinds of actions that can and do flow from it. *Liberal* democratic politics in an institutionalized sense is about claims of procedural (and to a lesser degree, distributive) justice—who gets what, when, and where according to a fair, temporally responsive and accountable set of rules. Locating within civil society the nexus of political responsibility and authenticity has different implications entirely. Freedom and responsibility do not begin with a constitution or the right to vote; they are generated from within via self-empowerment. Moreover, this retrieval of subjectivity is profoundly social—it cannot be an interior existential experience but requires ongoing solidarity and open-ended responsibility for others and the multiple publics in which we locate our identities.

Nonetheless, Havel wrote that the injunction to "live in truth" must occur *within each person*—it cannot be coerced. It is only when the greengrocer refuses to put up someone else's sign and finds his own public voice that he takes on political responsibility and becomes a citizen. Thus the dissidents were always insistent that by creating an alternative to authoritarian communism via their parallel *polei*, they were in fact building islands of freedom. As Michnik stated in *The Church and the Left*:

> In Polish intellectual circles it is common to complain about the restrictions on our rights, about the lack of freedom, about censorship. Far be it from me to minimize the importance of these issues. And yet it is not only the political authorities who are responsible for our moral and intellectual life. We all share responsibility. The authorities can expand or restrict the boundaries of freedom, but *they cannot make people free*. Our freedom begins with each one of us, not with the authorities. If we do not circulate our carbon-copy book manuscripts, if we do not publish in uncensored

emigré publications, if we are silent in the face of persecution, then it is not the authorities who are responsible for this but we ourselves (1993: 212).

This kind of freedom is more dialogical and solidaristic than the individualism of classical liberalism can reasonably support. Human beings live together, inhabit a common world, and must care for it through the relationships they begin with each other. Political responsibility is very direct and concrete, unsullied by the type of ideological thinking decried by Havel in his essay "On Evasive Thinking."[26] Ultimately political responsibility involves an ethical or a moral imperative, not a consequentialist, utilitarian, or contractarian account of justice. Thus dissident thought is imbued with such a strong sense of spirituality—it matters less from which faith this imperative arises, only that it does arise. We can paradoxically conceive of a moral absolute that functions not so much as a single criterion of truth or morality, but as an imperative for action that may differ from person to person. Havel's phrasing of an "absolute horizon" is appropriate in this sense because although physical horizons on a landscape change with our perspective, they are nonetheless *there*.

Furthermore, civic initiatives, social movements, and the self-organization of society are necessary not only for building and safeguarding democracies, but this approach simultaneously mitigates countervailing tendencies pulling us in the opposite direction, such as consumerism, alienation, the retreat to tribalism and ethnic or religious particularism, and the self-interested corruption inherent in any form of political clientelism. The fact that these pressures are neither exclusively "liberal" nor "socialist" in character but are indicative of the malaise of our age, highlight the fact that antipolitical politics attempts to leave Left–Right cleavages behind. Traditional paradigms of political organization are also in question; thus Havel speaks a great deal today of the artificiality of borders in a globalized world where states are often the recipients as much as the generators of injustice or inequality.

The strategies and tactics employed by the dissidents in building civil society with a sense of self-limitation are explicitly *not* revolutionary, but neither are they the conventional representative options of liberal democratic politics. Protests—in either written or public form—are by their very nature outside the "normal" political arena and come from somewhere else, usually civil society. "Ruthless criticism of all that exists" in the philosophically Marxist sense combine with peaceful civil disobedience, and purposefully *yet carefully* challenge the legal and political norms of any social order. Yet at the same time, self-limitation requires that the activist never sacrifice means for ends, or push too hard for a confrontation with the authorities, whoever they are. A continual and openly democratic process of judgement is required to determine where the boundaries lay at any given time. The antipolitician abjures violence not only because of its human costs but also because of its political deficits.

John Keane correctly describes the East-Central European dissident commitment to non-violence as antipodean to the classic revolutionary syndicalist recipe for dramatically toppling the state and state power by means of extreme violence (1996: 80). Georges Sorel's *Réflexions sur la violence* and Michnik's "Letter from the Gdańsk Prison" are polar opposites. The Sorelian conception treats violence as necessary and indeed purifying, in the theoretical spirit of the "just war" against interminable evil. The East-Central Europeans were suspicious of the ideological zeal of any Sorelian or Jacobin justification—hence Michnik's comment about storming Bastilles and unwittingly building new ones. Manichean "us versus them" characterization was inimical to democratic oppositions of the region, even in Michnik's Poland where the divisions between apparatchik and dissident were most strongly felt. Violent revolutionary traditions and proponents of direct action are bent on destroying the other, whereas dissident thought is built on tolerance and acceptance of everyone, *especially* the other (Keane, 1996: 80).

Acceptance of the other reflects the fundamentally democratic and democratizing approach of the dissidents. Self-protection was necessary, and if violence was not the answer then the opposition movements looked instead at building social cooperation, solidarity, and trust. Democratization in this sense did not imply *representation* (by others) but *involvement* (of oneself). Experiencing Being in the Havelian sense, living an authentic life, led not simply to personal but *public* and thus *political* responsibility.

In the same way the dissidents rejected revolutionary violence, they similarly rejected the idea of a single revolutionary or universal class. Even though the on-the-ground reality of the democratic oppositions reflected a strong intellectual bias, these intellectuals hardly saw themselves on the road to class power. The antipolitics of civil society was by nature pluralistic, and in the same way power was dispersed throughout society, so too was antipower. No one social group, party, class, or movement could completely represent the oppositional "will" and certainly not any form of absolute, society-wide *volonté générale*. Partisan politics—both in the revolutionary and the parliamentary sense of the phrase—involved speaking and acting on behalf of others, whereas the civil society approach sought initially to locate resistance to the party-state and political responsibility more broadly *within* the individual. Living in truth remained both a local and a personal decision.

Acting effectively and boldly yet non-violently both reinforce the respect for human dignity and human rights, but also requires a fairly high degree of situational creativity. It means you can both "walk the talk"(respect human rights in theory and practice) *and* can truly outsmart the authorities with an endless array of non-violent tactics. This multivalency was more difficult for the party-state both to understand and combat, for it was contrary to its own nature and required a different approach and kind of thinking. After all, fighting violence with violence requires no great innovation on the part of the aggressor or the victim. As the recent conflicts in the former Yugoslavia have demonstrated, the more violence is met with violence, the less likely one can tell the "difference" between the poles of combat.

Isaac refers to this "vigorous yet self-limiting praxis" as "rebellious politics" and places the dissidents on a twentieth century continuum along with Hannah Arendt and Albert Camus. All were and are "animated by the ideals of human dignity, solidarity, and self-determination" and shared a similar distaste for totalitarianism—in fact all were instrumental in fashioning a language through which it could be discussed (1992: 252). Whereas the critical and humane democracy of Arendt and Camus was quashed by the bipolarization of geography and thought after the Second World War, the East-Central Europeans have, in Isaac's view, effectively revived this tradition and extended it.[27]

Dissident thought in East-Central Europe through its praxis involved a rethinking of the sphere of politics itself. At first this was a practical and geopolitical necessity. Because revisionism was effectively dead in the region and the focus of the opposition became *antipolitical* in nature, resistance to authoritarian communism had to be located outside the party-state. With this shift in political tactics came the theorization that meaningful and authentic political life should begin first and foremost at the level of citizen activity. Moreover, this approach was inclusive, democratic, and carried with it a pedagogical dimension. One simultaneously learned and created democratic values of trust, social solidarity, and cooperation through action—the "small-scale" work envisioned by Masaryk, Patočka, and Havel or the "social self-defense" posited by Kuroń, Michnik, and the KOR intellectuals. Furthermore, on this line of reasoning, Kis' argument against Bence was triumphant in the Hungarian opposition. After martial law was imposed in Poland, Bence did not want to go further with an "open" opposition—with samizdat journals, signature campaigns, and other activities for fear of the existential risks involved. To Kis' credit, he saw that it was precisely through the strategy of openness that the opposition could style itself as a *democratic* opposition, rather than the creation of a clandestine elite.

On a second level, and perhaps most concretely in the Czechoslovak case, the dissidents drew a line between politics and morality that effectively changes our perspective on politics. Several reasons account for this redefinition. The dissidents sought to counter a crude line of Marxist–Leninist orthodoxy that sought to situate morality, and in particular individual dignity and respect for individual rights, as an ephemeral reflection of bourgeois ideology and society. Within the intersubjectivity of communication they saw authenticity and cooperation. Respecting individual rights, even as narrowly expressed as the entrenchment of liberal political freedoms, was fundamental to living in truth and creating democratic alternatives. According to McLean *et al.* (1990: 224), the message of morality he reads into Havel is so strong "… that on a deeper understanding of the matter, the sphere of the political is to be understood as contained within that of the moral, and that certain types or aspects of moral behaviour or attitude are of their very nature also profoundly political". By making morality inclusive of politics in this sense, it becomes imperative to political judgement on a very practical level.

Political Theory Engages with Dissident Theory

Support for my argument that dissident thought should be taken seriously *as political theory* is reinforced every time public intellectuals, social critics, and political theorists build on the arguments of Havel, Michnik, and others and in so doing extend the influence and contemporary relevance of the East-Central European *oeuvre*.[28] They conclude, and I concur, that dissident thought has a message for Western democracies as well as continuing relevance for the post-communist regimes of Central and Eastern Europe in a number of crucial respects.

In the West, post-Fordism has bequeathed to theorists and activists alike a number of dilemmas: the neoliberal response to the fiscal crises of the postwar state; the decline of strong nationally- and mass-based, "catch all" parties; the diminishment of parliaments in the face of expanded executive decision-making; globalization and the increasing irrelevance or at least marginalization of the nation-state; the rise of non-state actors with both good and tyrannical ends; and the demographic decomposition of the traditional class identities; and the increasingly documented exit of young people from the traditional institutions of representation and policy formation. In the two decades before the Fall of the Wall, Western "progressive" intellectuals and activists were looking neither to an alliance with the state or particular parties, nor solely to the transformative possibilities of the academy. At the same time as Havel, Michnik, and Kis were challenging the traditional left–right dichotomy, the theory and politics of the "new social movements" emerged as a means of dealing with these dilemmas and an expression of new and cross-cutting political identities.[29] These movements were not seen in the traditional Marxist sense as amorphous precursors to party formation, but as political alternatives *in themselves*. They expressed difference, challenged the notion of class, as a dominant or all-encompassing explanatory variable or as potentially emancipatory, remained within themselves deliberately heterogeneous and open to contestation in both discourse and tactics. Movement politics provided new opportunities for intellectuals to exercise their political responsibility outside the state-party framework.[30] Thus it was reasonable for many environmental scientists, feminists, and African-Americans within the American university system to link up with non-academic constituencies in social movements and pursue their mutually-compatible objectives in a fruitful alliance with one another.

Thus theorists such as Andrew Arato, Jean Cohen, and John Keane have sought to theorize about civil society with *both* the Western experience of new social movements and the East-Central European *oeuvre* in mind. Moving from his earlier discussion of "civil society" *against* the state in Poland, Arato has added the Habermasian public sphere.[31] Keane has utilized the concept of civil society as a means of thinking past what he sees as the outmoded fixations of democratic socialism on the party as the vehicle for change and the "undemocratic ... unrepeatable and therefore obsolete" ideal of full employment. He argues that his civil society approach is more grounded and realistic than the utopianism of André Gorz and more political than the "feasible socialism" of Alec Nove.[32]

To the extent that the "new social movements" theory and practice have reached a stalemate in the 1990s, the civil society *praxis* of the dissidents provides a possible new direction. For even though conservative commentators begrudgingly admit that, thanks to the ethos and politics of the new social movements and their practitioners, they lost the *Kulturkampf*, much remains unchanged. Thanks to feminism, the gay rights movement, and environmentalism, women have greater social and economic equality as much through several decades of consciousness-raising and activism as through legislative and judicial change; our families and societies have become more gay-positive even when our laws are not; and we have no-smoking bistros, recycling bins, and declare municipalities to be nuclear-free even when corporations still get away with massive and continued pollution of our air and land. But both new social movements and parliaments have run into a wall of citizen complacency and apathy that threatens to become more than a serious legitimacy deficit. Increasingly, parliaments, politicians, "special interests," and lobbyists are all held in equal contempt.

Left liberal or "communitarian" thinkers such as Michael Walzer and Charles Taylor have also appropriated the East-Central European discourse on civil society. Writing in 1989, Taylor invoked civil society as not only articulating "the hopes of those fighting to open spaces of freedom" but presciently predicted that the concept would be just as important with the turnover of power in the East as a revitalization of democratic politics in the West (1990: 95). The experience of the dissidents in Poland, Czechoslovakia, and Hungary, according to Walzer, "... invite us to think about how this social formation is secured and invigorated" in the West (1991: 293). As Walzer suggests, we should take heed:

We have reasons of our own for accepting the invitation. Increasingly, associational life in the "advanced" capitalist and social democratic countries seems at risk. Publicists and preachers warn us of a steady attenuation of everyday cooperation and civic friendship. And this time it's possible that they are not, as they usually are, foolishly alarmist. Our cities are really noisier and nastier than they once were. Familial solidarity, mutual assistance, political likemindedness—all these are less certain and less substantial than they once were. Other people, strangers on the street, seem less trustworthy than the once did. The Hobbesian account of society is more persuasive than it once was (1991: 293).

The promise of the East-Central European conception of civil society is that it fills many gaps in alternative political views of "the good life" without completely replacing or supplanting any of them. Walzer outlines four other definitions seeking to create the most supportive environment for "the good life": 1) New Left theories of participation and active citizenship that combine Rousseauian idealism with early American republicanism; 2) Marxist and syndicalist theories which focus on economic activity and the creative and fulfilling value of labor; 3) the capitalist reification of the marketplace where human beings are consumers rather than producers and maximize their preferences through abundant and continual choice; and 4) attachment to "the nation" by "ties of blood and history" (1991: 294–297). The beauty of the civil society approach is that it is not unidimensional, and allows for the complexity of human society and our diverse attachments. Thus both Marxist and capitalist visions undervalue all accounts which do not prioritize *Homo economicus*, and both the New Left ideas of radical participation and Marxism undervalue all associations *except* the *demos* and the working class (1991: 298). According to Walzer, human beings are *social* before being political or economic beings. Moreover, accepting this view does not deny that we are simultaneously entangled in a network of associations, forms of ownership, kinship ties and organizations, religious faiths and institutions, and so on, which are multilayered, involve political and economic choices and conflicts, and account for the actual complexity of modern life. The civil society project points Walzer in the direction of what he calls "critical associationalism" as a means of reinvigorating citizenship and public life without taking away from the need for social (and socialist) economic cooperation, individual autonomy, or national identity. Taken seriously, such a project could aid in decentralizing the state, socializing the economy, and pluralizing and domesticating nationalism (1991: 303).

For both the "socialist" or "post-Marxist" civil societarians like Keane, Cohen, and Arato as well as communitarians like Walzer or

Taylor, the success of civil society in East-Central Europe speaks for itself. In a world defined by endemic crisis and the collapse or theoretical dismemberment of holistic ideological solutions, we do not have many "best practices" in theory or practice to choose from in late twentieth century. Democracy is often isolated as the ultimate political good, but there are so many flaws in existing democracies, and the path to constructing or revitalizing democracy seems so fraught with pitfalls and contradictions, that it is all too easy to conclude that the postwar liberal democracies of the West are a never-to-be-repeated experiment. For this reason alone, the fragile yet stubborn islands of civil society in East-Central Europe in the 1970s and 1980s provide us with more than a glimmer of hope.

The dissident experience points to a recapturing of political agency under seemingly impossible circumstances, where alliances are built on basic yet radically participative democratic goals and stress overarching commitments rather than a collapse into particularistic identities. Significantly, this agency begins neither with group membership nor a narrow or exclusive definition of identity, but with the individual raised to her or his highest common denominator—as a citizen. The citizen is rooted firmly in a community with social obligations and political responsibilities.

As state sovereignty erodes and the power of global capital increases, creating transnational linkages among citizens and looking at the planet and its web of overlapping communities more holistically is an enormous challenge, but not an impossible one. The anti-globalization protestors in Seattle, Prague, Washington, Québec, and Genoa have much to learn from the history of this troubled century past, in particular from the dilemmas of dissidence in East-Central Europe. Lesson one: avoid the storming of Bastilles and focus on on the small-scale work of education and social-self defense—a process that builds confidence and a broad-based constituency, as the KOR activists were to discover in Poland. Lesson two: build transnational coalitions based on similar concerns tempered with mutual respect for and tolerance of inevitable differences. The Czech–Polish border visits, the connections between Hungarian and Polish samizdat publishing houses, the reaching out to Hungarian minorities in Romania and Slovakia by the Hungarian opposition, and even the savvy and timely exploitation of the Western media and "star-quality" intellectuals—all are instructive precedents, replete with tactical successes and pitfalls. A final lesson: aim for a smart combination of theory and practice, concrete in terms of possiblity and idealistic in terms of overall vision. There is no lack of a base for global citizenship: people the world over are increasingly and profoundly uncomfortable with the arbitrariness and democratic deficit of global institutions such as the World Trade Organization and the International Monetary Fund.

Even if "going global" seems an aphorism more appropriate to initial public offerings than citizen-based politics, much remains to be done in the browed-but-not-beaten nation-state of the 21st century. Today in most established liberal democracies we are faced with the twin problems of lies and illusions in politics and the widely perceived immorality of our practicing politicians. At the same time as citizens are increasingly apathetic and retreat into the private sphere, they are also increasingly sophisticated at decoding the strategies of spin doctors, whether in the hire of partisan organizations or media conglomerates. The gap between truth and reality in politics has never seemed larger, but it is also more obvious. The recognition that the semantic content of political speech is twisted beyond recognition to be meaningful to the average citizen is an important first step. Dissident thought and practice points to a critical second step: that authentic politics beginning within civil society and carrying through into the formal institutions of democracy carries with it a strong imperative to truthfulness and respect for truth. One does not have to suggest that there is an absolute standard of truth or morality which should guide citizens and politics in their communications with each other to make this a meaningful requirement. Indeed, competition among truth-claims or different bases for morality—stemming from differing religious and cultural practices—will simply make the process more inclusive and democratic. Kantian judgment and the communicative ethics of Habermas both enter the picture; what is absolute is the sense of responsibility that must flow from the acceptance of morality in politics.

Finally, the first ten years of post-communism in the region have provided us with enough distance to begin an assessment of the revolutions of 1989. Situating post-communism within the discourse of post-modernity and the eschewal of grand projects in favor of limitation and liminality, Richard Sakwa has recently argued that these antirevolutions were not counter-revolutions, but the contrary of revolutions (Sakwa, 1999: 87–88). In roundly rejecting the Enlightenment tradition of revolutionism and societal makeover and bequeathing to political theory and practice their ideas of self-limitation, evolutionism, and radical reform, Kuroń, Michnik, and Kis contributed mightily to the lexicon of political activism. Aiming for less sometimes can mean achieving more. The paradoxical nature of this achievement is not without irony: both Michnik and Haraszti commented to me that in order to be successful, they had to be organizationally vanguardist even while that the old class distinctions and antinomies no longer held. Furthermore, popular mobilization, late though it was, crystallized with a consciousness and sense of purpose that would have made Marx envious. In the aftermath, when academics debated whether or not there had been revolutions after all, the sometimes too-obvious point about revolutionary transcendence and exhaustion was lost. The Gen-Xers that have inherited the revolutions of East-Central Europe are decidedly not the engineers of human souls of an earlier generation, but in their own way have responded to the logic of Havel. The humanism of Patočka and Havel resonates, wittingly or not, with those forging the new Europe through their own email lists, travel patterns, life choices, work habits, and an ability to converse in and maneuver among languages that casually and inadvertently mock the old East–West divide.

Marginalization or Public Engagement: The Role of Central European Intellectuals in the Post-Communist Era

There is a classic story constantly re-told throughout Central Europe in the late 1990s. Like many of the folk and fairy tales emanating from the region, the story has an ahistoric or timeless quality—it could have happened yesterday, a hundred years ago, or ten years ago. The tale begins with a rag-tag group of dissidents huddled around kitchen tables in farmhouses, in local pubs, in urban cellars, and mostly around others who resisted authoritarian communism with great moral courage and not inconsequential personal sacrifice. Many were harassed by the security police. Some were beaten up or imprisoned for lengthy periods. Maybe their children could not go to university, or they lost their own university teaching positions.

These individuals were often quietly supported and their well-worn publications furtively read, passed hand over hand. We still do not know the scope or depth of their influence at this time, for it could not be scientifically measured. They were mostly avoided in the streets and by their acquaintances, as they tended, by their example, to expose the passivity and complicity of the vast majority of the population. A few of them acquired an international reputation—or notoriety— and this gave them a certain immunity which was as much a curse as a blessing.

When the winds of historical change blew in their direction, they were often the only independent players on the political stage with integrity and honor. They spoke passionately in defense of the ordinary citizens of their countries who had so long been under the subjugation of the party-state and warm feelings of camaraderie flowed between them and the crowds in the streets. Human dignity won the day; past collaboration was conveniently forgotten. History was in the making, and magically many of these citizen intellectuals were poised to become philosopher kings. Not for the first time in this part of the world, a new dawn in politics and human history was proclaimed with fanfare, this time immediately witnessed via satellite connections by the rest of the world. The old regime which seemed, despite the cracks and fissures, solid enough to last considerably longer, crumbled like a house of cards.

Conspiracy theories often join the story at this point, going so far as to suggest that the dissidents were in the pay of the previous regime, or at least cleverly manipulated by it, so that the terms and conditions of a transition to liberal democracy and market economy would be written as favorably as possible for the former *nomenklatura*. Regardless of such suspicions, the dissidents suddenly found themselves propelled into positions of power and authority, either by election or the sheer force of popular will.

The political careers of these philosopher kings were both anticlimactic and short-lived. Their ideas—noble and idealistic—were well suited to opposition and even the paradigm shift of regime transformation, but not the *realpolitik* of the normal science of politics. Some were too uncompromising to be good politicians; others were too uncomfortable in the corridors of power. To make matters worse, they began to squabble amongst themselves, and their ensuing political divisions were messy and unseemly. Some stepped down from office; others were defeated in national elections. Once on the margins of society, to the margins of society again they returned.

There were new risks and rewards in the political and economic arrangements which governed society, with new choices but great social

costs. People were disappointed at the slow pace of the *actual* transformation, as opposed to its revolutionary promise. The aftermath of
the euphoria was a series of giant national hangovers. When everyone
woke up, and accommodated her or himself to the new reality, politics
became boring again.

Like many stories, this one is built upon real events and contains
some "truth."[33] It even has several morals—that dissidents do not by
nature make good politicians, or that ideas ultimately cannot triumph
over the impersonal bureaucratic inertia of modern political life. We
may nod sagely at this point, but unfortunately in this story the evidence does not convincingly support many of these claims. What actually *did* happen?

Certainly many former dissidents were propelled into new or newly-
created positions in institutional politics. In Czechoslovakia a playwright became a president, in Poland a Catholic intellectual became
a prime minister. It is also the case that in the "transitional" governments—which contained members of the "old" and "new" regimes—
many former dissidents became members of parliament and cabinet
ministers. It is also true that after this first initiation into high politics,
many left willingly or unwillingly—Miklós Haraszti, Gáspár Miklós
Tamás, Miroslav Kusý, Martin Palouš, Adam Michnik, and Konstanty
Gebert, to name only a few.

However, the myth of the dissidents re-marginalizing themselves
through their political ineptitude or annoying moral superiority is just
that, a myth. Not unsurprisingly, many of the former intellectual activists
found themselves at home in the political arena and have made impressive contributions to building and consolidating democratic institutions and a democratic political culture, by their ideas, commitment,
and office-holding. Jacek Kuroń ran unsuccessfully for president in
1995, but remains an active member of parliament and leader of the
Freedom Union party. Bronisław Geremek was Polish foreign minister. Jan Lityński and Zbigniew Bujak are members of the *Sejm*. Václav
Benda, before his untimely death, was a member of the Christian
Democrats in the Czech Republic and Director of the Office for
Documentation and Investigation of Communist Crimes. Petr Pithart
is vice-chair of the Czech Senate, and Rudolf Battěk is a senator. Peter
Uhl is Government Representative for Human Rights and Minorities.
Saša Vondra is the Czech ambassador to the United States. Jan Čar-
nugurský is head of the Christian Democrats in Slovakia and after the

defeat of Mečiar went from being chair of the opposition to Minister of Justice. Gábor Demszky is mayor of Budapest. And, albeit with little "political" power but considerable moral suasion, Václav Havel will remain in his post as president of the Czech Republic until 2003.

Moreover, those who left high politics hardly retreated into a sedentary private life. Adam Michnik left the *Sejm* to become editor-in-chief of *Gazeta Wyborcza*, the most influential *and* widely-circulated newspaper in the region. Konstanty Gebert left the *Sejm* for a stellar journalistic career, as foreign correspondent for *Gazeta* and has recently founded a periodical which reflects the growth and dynamism of the rebirth of Warsaw's Jewish community, entitled *Midrasz*. Jan Urban was editor of *Transitions*, an important contemporary journal whose reportage covered the entire former East Bloc, and remains an influential journalist. Jiřina Šiklová founded the Prague Gender Studies Center and is currently a professor of sociology at Charles University. Dana Nemcová heads the Olga Havlová Foundation. Martin Palouš was head of the Czech Helsinki Assembly, but returned to the civil service two years ago as deputy foreign minister. Miroslav Kusý is head of the philosophy department of Comenius University in Bratislava. János Kis is no longer a chair of the SZDSZ, but was chair of the Department of Political Science at the new Central European University between 1993 and 2000. György Bence founded the "Invisible College" in Hungary and is a professor of philosophy at ELTE. Miklós Haraszti is currently on the supervisory board of Hungarian Radio and Television and teaches politics and media democratization at universities in both Hungary and the United States. György Konrád was the president of PEN International, and was appointed head of the Institute for Advanced Study in Berlin a few years ago. Again, these are only a handful of examples.

In fact, taking the civil society approach *seriously*, many of the former dissidents have taken up leadership positions within those very independent associations they sought to create in the first place. They know full well that democracy is *not* simply about free elections and parliaments. Many have chosen to build democracy not by sitting as office-holders but by making civil society their job. Thus there has been much *continuity* in the theory and practice of the former dissidents, Western and journalistic accounts notwithstanding.

Although it is incorrect to suggest that intellectuals have withdrawn from political or public life, they do face new kinds of marginality.

The marketization and globalization of mass culture have dealt many a harsh new reality. When samizdat competed in a small and closed market with the agit-prop of the party-state, there was no contest. Carbon-copied manuscripts in Czechoslovakia or journals from the underground presses of Poland or Hungary assumed a disproportionate influence and importance in comparison with their overall number. Today when the speeches of Havel or the editorials of Michnik must compete with *Playboy* magazine, Harlequin romances, American sit-coms on television, and CNN, the airwaves and bookshelves—open and uncensored though they may be—tend to crowd out the moral heroes of another age.

It is an intellectual truism that it is much easier to be against something than for something. Critique is much easier than theory; opposition more dynamic than the implied quiescence of support. This is even more the case with former dissidents as they deliberately avoided promises of redemption and sweeping teleological theories in the first place. The former dissidents *still* do not support ideologies, and their voices are heard strongly against new forms of authoritarianism, anti-Semitism and other forms of ethnic and religious prejudice, and exclusivist nationalism. But this leads average citizens to grumble, "What exactly are they *for*?" Even the clever and aphoristic György Konrád is reported to have said at the 1991 conference of International PEN, "What is left when there is no more devil?" Taking the moral high ground of imprecision, toleration, and distrust of power does not translate well for populations brought up on the slogans of authoritarian communism, only now to be hit with the slogans of advertising.

There is a morose and plaintive tone to the post-1989 international conferencing and intellectual navel-gazing of many former dissidents.[34] One does not quite buy the self-proclaimed happiness of Adam Zagajewski, who made the following remarks at a 1992 conference entitled "Intellectuals and Social Change in Central and Eastern Europe:"[35]

> Now it's all over. Now it's all about money and nationalism. Writers, who once represented mythical entities, now represent just themselves. I welcome this development enthusiastically; it suits me well. What's mythical and visionary hasn't ceased to exist; it has returned to where it belongs: to poetry, instead of nourishing political illusions. Just one thing has become more problematic: literary conferences.

> Who are we writers, those of us who have not entered the administra-
> tion of new, transitional democracies? Now we represent just ourselves,
> our past and future, our mistakes, and *bons mots*. And—as far as political
> struggle against bad, oppressive systems is concerned—we have turned
> into historians who can dwell on their remembrances for decades. I don't
> want to be misunderstood. I am not sneering at the historical function of
> literature, quite the contrary. But we are no longer oracles. We are writers,
> lonely and slightly comical figures, fighting with a white sheet of paper,
> exactly like our colleagues from Australia and Italy, San Marino and
> Andorra (1992: 670).

At least the transformations ushered in by 1989 and a relatively successful first decade of post-communism has assured that in the countries studied here, there is no such thing as a second-generation dissident. Other than being the guardians of memory and truth regarding
authoritarian communism, or as individual writers and poets competing for market share, or philosophers, sociologists, historians, and
economists competing with each other for academic posts, what *now*
is the social role of these dissidents? Former Romanian dissident and
intellectual Andrei Plesu suggests that both the dissidents and the former communists faced the same dilemma of ideological unemployment, and reacted similarly:[36]

> So dissidents after 1989 did something that did also (*sic*) the communist
> party: they renamed themselves. They renamed themselves as intellectuals.
> And this was a very typical renaming of both sides of the old regime. The
> communists became socialists and the dissidents became intellectuals. It
> was safer for both sides (1996: 10).[37]

The participation of these intellectual-activists in the parliaments
and the extra-parliamentary organizations of civil society has nonetheless generated a vigorous debate in the region regarding the appropriate role for intellectuals in politics. Given the deep ambivalence many
feel toward the transformation, perhaps the new role of intellectuals in
the region is to be the critical consciences of their respective societies.
Those involved in the debate differ, however, on the type of critique
or responsibility assumed by intellectuals as well as their appropriate
social location. Tucker, following Weber and Jaspers, draws a distinc-

tion between the ethics of moral conviction adopted by the dissidents and the ethics of social responsibility adopted by intellectual-politicians such as Havel in the post-communist period. He argues that it was easier to adopt an absolutist, non-utilitarian moral stance irrespective of means-ends considerations prior to 1989 than afterward, when in positions of power intellectuals had to take responsibility for the consequences of their actions (Tucker, 2000: 172). By this reasoning, consequentialists are more pragmatic, but could also be interpreted as more cynical. In my view, this argument is unnecessarily dualistic: Havel the dissident may have been more philosophical than concretely political in comparison with Havel the president, but the core values he promotes both prior and subsequent to the Velvet Revolution are the same—responsibility, authenticity, social solidarity—as is his continued exhortation to "live in truth."

Regardless, intellectuals remain both a fact and a social force in East-Central Europe.[38] However, they are no longer associated with radical universalism of any sort, and most especially the Marxist–Leninist variety. Consensus on this point has tended to push intellectuals in one of two directions, either as having a limited "cause" or as defenders of otherness and diversity. Translating this into politics, having a cause can mean having a different level of responsibility, which in turn may require a particular moral stance. Defending otherness or diversity is understood in the liberal sense of promoting tolerance, the protection of human rights and minority rights, and pluralism in civil society. Divided this way, the second definition is more limited, but the first can also include the second. Gáspár Miklós Tamás speaks compellingly of intellectuals as the voices of freedom against all forms of tyranny, regardless of origin, and especially today against all forms of ethnic and religious particularism. Václav Havel speaks more broadly of the modern technology of power endemic to all societies and regimes in the twentieth century, and the requirement of intellectuals to infuse within an open and participative politics a sense of responsibility and a moral dimension. More recently, Havel calls for a "moral minimum" in the face of globalization.

As to whether or not intellectuals should be involved in politics *as politicians*, there are also primarily two camps, haunted by two specters. The first camp argues that although intellectuals may be politicians and many politicians are well read and more cultured than average citizens, there is a gulf that separates the two and ought to be respected.

The differentiation is based in social roles, and reflected through language. As Timothy Garton Ash argues:

> If a politician gives a partial, one-sided, indeed a self-censored account of a particular issue, he is simply doing his job. And if he manages to "sell" the part as the whole then he is doing his job effectively.
>
> If an intellectual does that, he is not doing his job; he has failed in it. The intellectual is not the guardian or high priest of some metaphysical, ideological or pseudo-scientific Truth with a capital T. Nor is he simply the voice of *Gesinnungsethik* (the ethics of conviction) against the *Verantwortungsethik* (the ethics of responsibility) of the politician, to use Max Weber's famous distinction. But he does have a qualitatively different responsibility for the validity, intellectual coherence, and truth of what he says and writes (1995: 36).

There should be, in Garton Ash's view, a naturally adversarial though not necessarily hostile relationship between intellectuals and politicians. Whereas the intellectual seeks truth and warns against the abuses of untruth, the politician speaks in half-truth (1995: 35). The appropriate role of politicians in defending truth is to create and sustain a political environment in which debate and disagreement can take place. *Public* intellectuals should express the conscience of the nation and the voice of the oppressed (1995: 36). Here we are met with the spectre of Julien Benda, and *la trahison des clercs*. As an intellectual you can be a *spectateur engagé* like George Orwell or Raymond Aron, but you can never be an independent critic and a political animal simultaneously. The slippery slope of intellectual service in favor of tyranny—even if a grand end of justice and equality is not promised—remains an inevitable possibility.[39]

Havel has consistently taken the opposite view, arguing for the second camp. He claims there is a necessary fluidity to the roles of intellectual and politician, and his own experience is proof enough. You can be the theater critic, the playwright, the director, and the actor—if not at the same time, then at least sequentially. In fact, the wearing of different hats has a cumulatively positive impact. In essence, it is the theory of a true dramaturge—the actors on stage bring some of their previous roles into their current rules, and the play and the audience are both the better for it.

For Havel, intellectuals in post-communist countries should look at politics not as a dilemma to be shunned but as an opportunity to be embraced. With typical dramatic flourish, he states:

> What if the strange situation in which many independent intellectuals in the postcommunist countries have found themselves is not a dilemma, but a historic challenge? What if in fact it were to challenge them to introduce a new tone, a new element, a new dimension into politics? If may well be that destiny, by thrusting us so unexpectedly into this position, actually meant to entrust us with a special mission (1997: 98–99).

For Havel, contemporary politics needs "a new impulse ... a badly needed spiritual dimension"—one which just might be injected by the former dissident intellectuals as their "something special to offer to the rest of the world" (1997: 99). Intellectuals might possess this capacity because they are not specialists, nor do they represent special interests. However, they do claim to have a "role," one that is informed by social responsibility:

> ... politics should be principally the domain of people with a heightened sense of responsibility and a heightened understanding of the mysterious complexity of Being. If intellectuals claim to be such people, they would virtually be denying the truth of that claim by refusing to take upon themselves the burden of public office on the grounds that it would mean dirtying their hands. Those who say that politics is disreputable in fact help to make it so (1997: 101).

Here Havel throws down the gauntlet. Not only does he think intellectuals *ought* to be involved in politics, but he suggests that principled avoidance does little but make matters worse. His position is consistent with his notion of responsibility, of active citizenship, and the diverse practice of politics. Indeed he takes on Garton Ash directly, whom he suggests as been too influenced by "the banal idea that everyone should stick to his own trade" (1997: 102).

For Havel being an intellectual in politics is not a Weberian calling, but a special task to which East-Central European intellectual activists are uniquely qualified. He takes this view because he sees strong affinities between what the dissidents embodied in their movements and their ideas, and what is needed in politics today. A strong message of dissident theory is the requirement for an injection of morality in the clash of political forces, as an ally of democratic judgement and as an antidote to ideology. Thus he states:

> The dissident movement was not typically ideological. Of course, some of us tended more to the right, others to the left, some were close to one trend in opinion or politics, others to another. Nevertheless, I don't think this was the most important thing. What was essential was something different: the courage to confront evil together and in solidarity, the will to come to an agreement and to cooperate, the ability to place the common and general interest over any personal or group interests, the feeling of common responsibility for the world, and the willingness personally to stand behind one's own deeds. Truth and certain elementary values, such as respect for human rights, civil society, the indivisibility of freedom, the rule of law—these were notions that bound us together and made it worth our while to enter again and again into a lopsided struggle with the powers that be.
>
> By politics with a spiritual dimension, I do not understand a politics that is merely a technological competition for power, limited to what can be practically achieved and seeking primarily to satisfy this or that particular interest. Nor do I mean a politics that is concerned merely with promoting a given ideological and political conception. And I certainly do not mean a politics based on the idea that the end justifies the means. I mean, rather, a politics deriving from a strong and utterly personal sense of responsibility in the world, a politics deriving from the awareness that none of us—as an individual—can save the world as a whole, but that each of us must behave as though it were it his power to do so. I certainly don't need to emphasize that the origin of such a responsibility is metaphysical (1997: 111–112).

Havel's reasoning is made compelling by his consistency. He has not developed the position of the "actively-involved intellectual" post-1989 to justify his assumption and retention of first the Czechoslovak and later the Czech presidency. Rather, his position on the political role of intellectuals flows directly from his dissident writings on responsibility and the concept of "living in truth."

The moment you connect "truth" and "ideas," the question of responsibility is philosophically and pragmatically unavoidable. Truth-claims tend to generate a sense of passion and commitment, which makes the option of disinterest or disavowal not only inconsistent, but on another level unethical or immoral. Havel sets up his own argument so that his conclusions are inevitable. Reverting to "The Power of the Powerless," the greengrocer makes a break with the regime and rejects the ideological obfuscation of ritual slogans such as "Workers of the World Unite" when he begins to *see things as they really are*. The moment the greengrocer reflects on his own phenomenological universe, and becomes susceptible to truth, he discovers both responsibility and power. As long as he remains untouched and uninterested in the semantic content of the slogan and the "pillar of lies" on which it rests, he excuses himself from involvement. But the moment he discovers his identity and dignity by living in truth, he begins to wear the mantle of political responsibility. In this sense, the political responsibility of the intellectual and of the individual citizen are similarly intense. By locating the power of the powerless in such a personal decision, Havel also radically democratizes responsibility. Havel is not suggesting that intellectuals should be in politics as a reflection of their responsibility, but that intellectuals should be in politics because reflecting on this responsibility makes it a moral requirement.

Yet here is where we also find the spectre of Plato. As Garton Ash states, if you ask someone to freely associate the terms "intellectual" and "politics" together in the 1990s, the response almost anywhere in continental Europe or the Anglo-American world would be "Václav Havel" (1995: 36). The connection is even more likely if the question were who comes to mind when you suggest the term "philosopher king." The echoes of Plato we find in Havel are not those of a neo-totalitarian philosopher bent on constructing the ideal city based on the cohering ideals of truth, justice, and the good over and potentially against the citizens of the *polis* who cannot possibly be the judge of such things. Havel's Plato is tamed by the *demos*. The philosopher can be king only because citizens can also be intellectuals—mutual respect and responsibility bind the rulers and the ruled.

BIBLIOGRAPHY

For material originally published in Polish, Czech, Slovak, or Hungarian, I have relied on English translations, especially with respect to the key authors discussed in this study. Secondary and background materials are usually scholarly accounts in English, although some French and German materials have also been used and where appropriate, original language sources are cited. Original interviews were conducted by myself during research trips to the region in 1995 and 1997, and are listed below. I also had the opportunity to consult the Radio Free Europe (now Open Society) Archives housed at the Central European University in Budapest. By permission, H. Gordon Skilling kindly made available to me unpublished responses by Polish and Hungarian dissidents to a questionnaire on independent society conducted in the late 1980s; these are available at the University of Toronto archives, located in the Thomas Fisher Rare Book Library.

Abrams, B. (2002). *The Struggle for the Soul of the Nation: Czech Culture and the Rise of Communism*. Oxford and Lanham, Md.: Rowman and Littlefield, forthcoming.

Ackerman, B. (1991). *We the People*. Cambridge, Mass.: Harvard U. P.

—. (1992). *The Future of Liberal Revolution*. New Haven: Yale U. P.

Aczel, T. (1976). "Between the Awakening and the Explosion: Yogis and Commissars Reconsidered," 1953–1956. *Canadian American Review of Hungarian Studies* 2, 107–114.

—. and Meray, T. (1960). *The Revolt of the Mind: A Case History of Intellectual Resistance behind the Iron Curtain*. London: Thames and Hudson.

Adam, J. (1986). "The Recent Polish Economic Reform and its Results," *Osteuropa Wirtschaft* 31, 287–306.

—. (1989). *Economic Reforms in the Soviet Union and Eastern Europe Since the 1960s*. London: Macmillan.

Adams, T. (1992). "Charter 77 and the Workers' Defense Committee KOR: The Struggle for Human Rights in Czechoslovakia and Poland," *East European Quarterly* 26.2, 219–238.

Ágh, A. (1994). "From Nomenklatura to Clientura: The Emergence of New Political Elites in East Central Europe," *Labour Focus on Eastern Europe* 47, 58–77.

Altemeyer, B. (1996). *The Authoritarian Specter.* Cambridge Mass.: Harvard U. P.

Altvater, E. (1993). *The Future of the Market: An Essay on the Regulation of Money and Nature after the Collapse of 'Actually Existing Socialism'.* Trans. P. Camiller. London: Verso.

A Meeting on the Czechoslovak–Polish Border (1987). *East European Reporter* 3, 24–27.

Ambros, V (1994). "Daniela Fischerová's New Palimpsest between "Living in Truth' and the 'Battle for an Island of Trust'," *Canadian Slavonic Papers* 36, 3–4, 363–376.

Amsden, A. et al. (1994). *The Market Meets Its Match.* Cambridge, Mass.: Harvard U. P.

Anderson, P. (1989). *Lineages of the Absolutist State.* London: Verso.

Antal, L. (1979). "Development with Some Digression: The Hungarian Economic Mechanism in the Seventies," *Acta Oeconomica* 20, 3–4.

Arato, A. (1981). "Civil Society against the State: Poland 1980–81," *Telos* 47, 24–47.

—. (1990). "Revolution, Civil Society, and Democracy," *Praxis International* 10.1–2, 24–38.

—. (1993a). *From Neo-Marxism to Democratic Theory: Essays on the Critical Theory of Soviet-type Societies.* Armonk, N.Y.: M. E. Sharpe.

—. (1993b). "Interpreting 1989," *Social Research* 60.3, 609–646.

Arendt, H. (1963). *On Revolution.* New York: Penguin.

—. (1973). *The Origins of Totalitarianism.* New York: Harcourt Brace Jovanovich.

—. (1974). *The Human Condition.* Chicago: University of Chicago Press.

—. (1977). *Between Past and Future.* New York: Penguin.

Aristotle (1925; 1990). *The Nicomachean Ethics.* Trans. D. Ross. Oxford: Oxford U. P.

— (1995). *Politics.* Trans. E. Barker. Oxford: Oxford U. P.

Aron, R. (1957). *The Opium of the Intellectuals.* Trans. T. Kilmartin. Westport, Conn.: Greenwood Press.

Ashcraft, R. (1986). *Revolutionary Politics and Locke's Two Treatises of Government.* Princeton: Princeton U. P.

Ascherson, N. (1982). *The Polish August: The Self-Limiting Revolution.* Middlesex, U.K.: Penguin Books.

Avineri, S. (1972). *Hegel's Theory of the Modern State.* Cambridge: Cambridge U. P.

Bahro, R. (1981). *The Alternative in Eastern Europe.* Trans. D. Farenbach. London: Verso.

Balassa, B. (1970). "The Economic Reform in Hungary," *Economica* 37.141, 1–22.

Balcerowicz, L. (1994). "Democracy is No Substitute for Capitalism," *Eastern European Economics* 32.2, 39–50.

—. (1995). *Socialism, Capitalism, Transformation.* New York: CEU Press.

Banac, I. ed. (1992). *Eastern Europe in Revolution.* Ithaca, N.Y.: Cornell U. P.

Barańczak, S. (1986–87). "The Polish Intellectual," *Salmagundi* 70–71, 217–228.

—. (1990a). *Breathing Under Water and other East European Essays.* Cambridge, Mass.: Harvard U. P.

—. (1990b). "All the President's Plays," *The New Republic*, July 23, 1990, 27–32.

Barker, C. (1986). *Festival of the Oppressed: Solidarity, Reform, and Revolution in Poland, 1980–81.* London: Bookmarks.

— and Weber, K. (1982). *Solidarność: From Gdańsk to Military Repression.* London: Bookmarks.

Bartlett, D. (1992). "The Political Economy of Privatization: Property Reform and Democracy in Hungary," *East European Politics and Societies* 6, 73–78.

Bartók, G. (1987). "Between the Points of the Compass," *East European Reporter* 3.1, 62–63.

Batt, J. (1988). *Economic Reform and Political Change in Eastern Europe.* New York: St. Martin's Press.

Battaile Hall, J. (1986). "Economic Planning and Economic Reform in Hungary," *Ost-Europa Wirtschaft* 31, 107–116.

Bauer, T. (1976)."The Contradictory Position of Enterprise under the New Hungarian Economic Mechanism," *Coexistence*, April 1976.

—. (1979). "Investment Cycles in Planned Economies," *Acta Oeconomica* 21. 3, 233–50.

—. (1983). "The Hungarian Alternative to Soviet-type Planning," *Journal of Comparative Economics,* September.

Bauman, Z. (1969). "The End of Polish Jewry—a Sociological Review," *Bulletin on Soviet and East European Jewish Affairs,* January 1969. London.

—. (1976). *Socialism: The Active Utopia.* London: George Allen & Unwin.

—. (1987). "Intellectuals in East-Central Europe: Continuity and Change," *East European Politics and Societies* 1.2, 162–186.

—. (1991). "Communism: A Post-Mortem," *Praxis International* 10.3–4, 185–192.

Bell, D. (1973). *Resistance and Revolution.* Boston: Houghton Mifflin Co.

—. (1989). "'American Exceptionalism' Revisited: The Role of Civil Society," *The Public Interest* 95, 38–56.

Bellah, R. et al. (1985). *Habits of the Heart.* Berkeley: University of California Press.

Bence, G. and Kis, J. (1980). "On Being a Marxist: A Hungarian View," *Socialist Register* 1980, 263–297.

Benda, J. (1928). *La Trahison des Clercs (The Great Betrayal).* Trans. R. Aldington. London: George Routledge and Sons.

Benda, V. (1989). "Spiritual Renewal: A Way Out of the Crisis?" *Uncaptive Minds* 2.2, 23–26.

—. et al. (1988). "Parallel *Polis,* or An Independent Society in Central and Eastern Europe: An Inquiry," *Social Research* 55.1–2, 214–222.

Benhabib, S. (1992). *Situating the Self: Gender, Community, and Postmodernism in Contemporary Ethics*. New York: Routledge.

—. (1995). "Response," *Political Theory* 23.4, 674–681.

—. (1996). *The Reluctant Modernism of Hannah Arendt*. New York: Sage.

Berend, I. T. (1990). *The Hungarian Economic Reforms 1953–1988*. Cambridge: Cambridge U. P.

—. (1996). *Central and Eastern Europe, 1944–1993*. New York: Cambridge U. P.

—. et al. (1990). *Hungary and the Transformation to Freedom and Prosperity*. Indianapolis: Hudson Institute, Herman Kahn Centre.

Berger, S. (1979). "Politics and Antipolitics in Western Europe in the 1970s," *Daedalus* 108, 27–50.

Berman, P. (1996). *A Tale of Two Utopias*. New York: W.W. Norton.

Bermeo, N., ed. (1992). *Liberalization and Democratization: Change in the Soviet Union and Eastern Europe*. Baltimore: Johns Hopkins.

Bernhard, M. H. (1993). *The Origins of Democratization in Poland*. New York: Columbia U. P.

Bethell, N. (1972). *Gomułka: His Poland and His Communism*. Harmondsworth, U.K.: Penguin.

Bibó, I. (1991). *Democracy, Revolution, Self-Determination: Selected Writings*. Trans. A. Boros-Kazai. Boulder, Co: Social Science Monographs.

Bideleux, R. and Jeffries, I. (1998). *A History of Eastern Europe: Crisis and Change*. London: Routledge.

Black, N. (1989). *Social Feminism*. Ithaca: Cornell U. P.

Blackburn, R. (1991). *After the Fall: The Failure of Communism and the Future of Socialism*. London: Verso.

Blaive, M. (1999) "1956: anatomie d'une absence," in J. Rupnik and F. Fejtő, eds., *Le printemps tchéchoslovaque 1968*. Brussels: Complexe.

Blit, L., ed. (1968). *The Anti-Jewish Campaign in Present-Day Poland*. London: Institute for Jewish Affairs, with World Jewish Congress.

Bloom, A., ed. (1968). *The Republic of Plato*. Trans. A. Bloom. New York: Basic Books.

—. (1987). *The Closing of the American Mind*. New York: Simon and Schuster.

Boggs, C. (1993). *Intellectuals and the Crisis of Modernity*. Albany: SUNY Press.

Bozóki, A. (1993). "Hungary's Road to Systemic Change: The Opposition Roundtable," *East European Politics and Societies* 7.2, 276–308.

—., ed. (1999). *Intellectuals and Politics in Central Europe*. Budapest: Central European University Press.

—., ed. (1999–2000). *A rendszerváltás forgatókönyve* (Budapest: Magvető–Új Mandátum).

Brabant, J. M. van (1990). *Remaking Eastern Europe: On the Political Economy of Transition*. Boston: Kluwer Academic Publishers.

Bridge, S. (1975). "Why Czechoslovakia? And Why 1968?" *Studies in Comparative Communism* 8.4, 413–444.

Brinton, W. M. and Rinzler, A., eds. (1990). *Without Force or Lies: Voices from the Revolution in Central Europe in 1989–1990*. San Francisco: Mercury House.

Bromke, A. (1985). *Eastern Europe in the Aftermath of Solidarity.* Boulder, Co.: East European Monographs.

Brown, A. (1984). *Political Culture and Communist Studies.* London: Macmillan.

—. and Gray, J. (1977). *Political Culture and Political Change in Communist Studies.* London: Macmillan.

Brown, J. F. (1991). *Surge to Freedom: The End of Communist Rule in Eastern Europe.* London: Duke U. P.

Brumberg, A. (1983). *Poland: Genesis of a Revolution.* New York: Vintage.

Brus, W. (1973). *Socialist Ownership and Political Systems.* Trans. R.A. Clarke. London: Routledge and Kegan Paul.

—. (1975). *The Economics and Politics of Socialism: Collected Essays.* Foreward by Maurice Dobb. London: Routledge and Kegan Paul.

—. (1985). "Socialism—Feasible and Viable," *New Left Review* 153, 43–74.

Bruszt, L. (1990). "The Negotiated Revolution in Hungary," *Social Research* 57, 365–387.

Büchler, A., ed. (1996). *This Side of Reality: Modern Czech Writing.* London: Serpent's Tail.

Bugajski, J. and Pollack, M. (1988). "East European Dissent: Impasses and Opportunities," *Problems of Communism* 37 (March–April), 59–66.

Bunce, V. (1990). "The Struggle for Liberal Democracy in Eastern Europe," *World Policy Journal* 7.3, 393–430.

—. (1995). "Should Transitologists Be Grounded?" *Slavic Review* 54.1, 111–127.

—. (1999). "The Political Economy of Postsocialism," *Slavic Review* 58.4, 756–793.

Burawoy, M. (1985). *The Politics of Production: Factory Regimes under Capitalism and State Socialism.* London: Verso.

—. (1992). "The End of Sovietology and the Renaissance of Modernization Theory," *Contemporary Sociology* 21.6. 744–785.

— and Lukács, J. (1992). *The Radiant Past: Ideology and Reality in Hungary's Road to Capitalism.* Chicago: University of Chicago Press.

Burnheim, J. (1994). *The Social Philosophy of Ágnes Heller.* Atlanta: Rodopi.

Bútorová, Z. et al. (1996). *She and He: Gender Issues in Public Opinion in Slovakia.* Trans. S. Kunová. Bratislava: n.p.

Calhoun, C. ed. (1992). *Habermas and the Public Sphere.* Cambridge: M.I.T. Press.

Canovan, M. (1992). *Hannah Arendt: A Reinterpretation of Her Thought.* Cambridge: Cambridge U. P.

Cerny, A. (1998). "Prague's Reality Check: The Czechs Get Serious," *Transitions* 5.4, 52–55.

Chartier, R. (1988). *Cultural History: Between Practices and Representations.* Trans. L. G. Cochrane. Cambridge: Polity Press.

Chirot, D. (1991a). "What Happened in Eastern Europe in 1989?" *Praxis International* 10.3–4, 278–305.

—, ed. (1991b). *The Crisis of Leninism and the Decline of the Left: The Revolutions of 1989.* Seattle: University of Washington Press.

Cipkowski, P. (1991). *Revolution in Eastern Europe.* Toronto: John Wiley and Sons.

Civic Forum (1989). "What We Want: The Programme Principles Issued by the Czechoslovak Civic Forum," *East European Reporter* 4, 50-51.

Clementis, V. and Clementisová,. L. (1968). *Listy z vasenia.* Prague: Tatran.

Cohen, J. L. and Arato, A. (1992). *Civil Society and Political Theory.* Cambridge, Mass.: M.I.T. Press.

Committee to Defend Czechoslovak Socialists (1977). *Voices of Czechoslovak Socialists.* London: Merlin Press.

Connolly, W. E. (1993). *Political Theory and Modernity.* Ithaca, N.Y.: Cornell U. P.

Cox, R. (1987). *Production, Power, and World Order: Social Forces in the Making of History.* New York: Columbia U. P.

—. (1991). "Real Socialism in Historical Perspective," *Socialist Register* 1991, 169–193.

Crompton, R. J. (1994). *Eastern Europe in the Twentieth Century.* New York: Routledge.

Curry, J. L., ed. (1983). *Dissent in Eastern Europe.* New York: Praeger.

— and Fajfer, L., eds. (1996). *Poland's Permanent Revolution: People vs. Elites, 1956–1990.* Washington: The American University Press.

Cviic, C. (1983). "The Church," in A. Brumberg, ed., *Poland: Genesis of a Revolution.* New York: Vintage.

Dahl, R. A. (1989). *Democracy and its Critics.* New Haven: Yale U. P.

Dahrendorf, R. (1990). *Reflections on the Revolution in Europe.* New York: Random House.

Dallmayr, F. (1993). *The Other Heidegger.* Ithaca, N.Y.: Cornell U. P.

Daniels, R. V. (1994). *A Documentary History of Communism and the World: From Revolution to Collapse.* Hanover, N.H.: UP of New England.

Davies, I. (1989). "The Return of Virtue: Orwell and the Political Dilemmas of Central European Intellectuals," *International Journal of Politics, Culture, and Society* 3.1, 107–129.

—. (1990). *Writers in Prison.* Toronto: Between the Lines.

Davies, N. (1981). *God's Playground: A History of Poland.* Oxford: Clarendon Press.

—. (1991). *Heart of Europe: A Short History of Poland.* New York: Oxford U. P.

—. (1996). *Europe: A History.* Oxford: Oxford U. P.

Dawisha, K. and Valdez, J. (1987). "Socialist Internationalism in Eastern Europe," *Problems of Communism* (March–April), 1–14.

Day, B., ed. (1994). *Czech Plays.* London: Nick Hern Books.

—. (1999). *The Velvet Philosophers.* London: Claridge Press.

Deak, I. "Post-Post Communist Hungary," *The New York Review of Books,* August 11, 1994, 33–38.

Degenharat, H. W. *Political Dissent: An International Guide to Dissident, Extra-Parliamentary, Guerilla, and Illegal Political Movements.* Detroit: Gage Research.

Demszky, G. (1985). "Parliamentarism in Eastern Europe: The Chances of the Independent Candidate," *East European Reporter* 1.3, 23–25

—. (1997). *A Demokratikus ellenzék a külföldi sajtó tükrében: Dokumentumok.* Budapest: M.S.

Denton, G. R. (1971). *A New Economic Mechanism? Economic Reform in Hungary.* London: PEP.

Derrida, J. (1994). *Spectres of Marx: The State of the Debt, the Work of Mourning, and the New International.* Trans. P. Kamuf. New York: Routledge.

—. (1995). *The Gift of Death.* Trans. D. Wills. Chicago: University of Chicago Press.

Deutscher, T. (1978). "Voices of Dissent," *Socialist Register* 1978, 22–43.

Diamond, L. (1994) "Rethinking Civil Society: Toward Democratic Consolidation," *Journal of Democracy* 5.3, 4–29.

—., Linz, J., and Lipset, S. M. (1990). *Politics in Developing Countries: Comparing Experiences with Democracy.* Boulder: Lynne Rienner.

Di Palma, G. (1990). *To Craft Democracies: An Essay on Democratic Transitions.* Berkeley: University of California Press.

—. (1991). "Legitimation from the Top to Civil Society: Politico-Cultural Change in Eastern Europe," *World Politics* 44.1, 49–80.

Dienstbier, J. (1987). "Mikhail Sergeyevich Gorbachev in Prague," *East European Reporter* 3.1, 49–53.

Diskin, H. *The Seeds of Triumph: Church and State in Gomułka's Poland.* Budapest and New York: CEU Press.

Djilas, A. (1991). *The Contested Country.* Cambridge, Mass.: Harvard U. P.

Djilas, M. (1957). *The New Class: An Analysis of the Communist System.* New York: Praeger.

—. (1998). *The Fall of the New Class: A History of Communism's Self-Destruction.* New York: A. A. Knopf

Doellinger, D. (2002). "Prayers, Pilgrimages and Petitions: The Secret Church and the Growth of Civil Society in Slovakia," *Nationalities Papers* 30.2, 215–240.

Downer, W. M. (1996). "Václav Havel on Inequality: Living in Truth and 'The Power of the Powerless' and *Largo Desolato*," paper presented at the Annual Meeting of the APSA, August 29–September 1, 1996, San Francisco (unpublished).

Drakulić, S. (1991). *How We Survived Communism and Even Laughed.* New York: W. W. Norton.

Draper, T. (1993). "A New History of the Velvet Revolution and Goodbye to Czechoslovakia," *The New York Review of Books,* January 14 and January 28.

Dubček, A., with J. Hochman. (1993). *Hope Dies Last: The Autobiography of Alexander Dubček.* London: Harper Collins.

Dubiel, H. (1991). "Beyond Mourning and Melancholia on the Left," *Praxis International* 10.3–4, 241–249.

Dumont, L. (1977). *From Mandeville to Marx: The Genesis and Triumph of Economic Ideology.* Chicago: University of Chicago Press.

Dunn, J. (1969). *The Political Thought of John Locke: An Historical Argument of the "Two Treatises of Government."* Cambridge: Cambridge U. P.

East, R. (1992). *Revolutions in Eastern Europe.* London: Pinter.

Eberts, M. (1998). "The Roman Catholic Church and Democracy in Poland," *Europe–Asia Studies* 50.5, 817–842.

Eckstein, S., ed. (1989). *Power and Popular Protest: Latin American Social Movements.* Los Angeles: University of California Press.

Eidlin, F. (1980). *The Logic of "Normalization."* Boulder, Co: East European Monographs.

Einhorn, B. (1993). *Cinderella Goes to Market: Citizenship, Gender, and Women's Movements in East-Central Europe.* London: Verso.

Ekiert, G. and Kubik (2001). *Rebellious Civil Society: Popular Protest and Democratic Consolidation in Poland, 1989–1993.* Ann Arbor: University of Michigan Press.

Elliston, F.A. and McCormick, P., eds. (1977). *Husserl: Expositions and Appraisals.* Notre Dame: University of Notre Dame Press.

Ello, P., ed. (1968). *Czechoslovakia's Blueprint for Freedom.* Washington, D.C.: Acropolis Books.

Elon, A. (1997). "The Case of Hannah Arendt," *New York Review of Books,* November 6, 25–29.

Elshtain, J. B. (1991). "Sovereignty, Identify, Sacrifice," *Social Research* 58.3, 545–564.

—. (1993a). *Democracy on Trial.* Concord, Ont.: Anansi.

—. (1993b). "Politics Without Cliché," *Social Research* 60.3, 433–443.

Ely, J. (1992). "The Politics of 'Civil Society'," *Telos* 93, 171–189.

Eörsi, I. (1987a). "On the Way to Debrecen with Ginsberg and Company," *Cross Currents* 6, 88–89.

—. (1987b). "The Unpleasant Lukács," *New German Critique* 42, 3–16.

Esterházy, P. (1995). *A Little Hungarian Pornography.* Trans. J. Sollosy. London: Corvina.

Eyerman, R. (1994). *Between Culture and Politics: Intellectuals in Modern Society.* Cambridge: Polity Press.

Falus Szikra, K. (1995). *The Positions and Conditions of Intellectuals in Hungary.* Budapest: Akadémiai Kiadó.

Fawn, R. (1999). "Symbolism in the Diplomacy of Czech President Václav Havel," *East European Quarterly* 33.1, 1–19.

Fehér, F. (1989). "On Making Central Europe," *East European Politics and Societies,* 3.3, 412–447.

—. (1992). "The Left after Communism," in P. Beilharz, G. Robinson, and J. Rundell, eds., *Between Totalitarianism and Postmodernity.* Cambridge, Mass.: M.I.T. Press.

— and Arato, A., eds. (1991). *Crisis and Reform in Eastern Europe.* London: Transaction Publishers.

— and Heller, Á. (1983). *Hungary 1956 Revisited.* New York: McKay.

—, et al. (1983). *Dictatorship over Needs: An Analysis of Soviet Societies.* Oxford: Basil Blackwell.

Feiwel, G. R. "The Standard of Living in Centrally Planned Economies of Eastern Europe," *Osteuropa Wirtschaft* 25, 73–96.

Flakierski, H. (1983). "Solidarity and Egalitarianism," *Canadian Slavonic Papers* 25.3, 380–391.
—. (1993). "Solidarity and the Defeat of Socialism." Unpublished M.S.; used with permission of author.
Foucault, M. (1978; 1990). *The History of Sexuality. Volume I.* Trans. R. Hurley. New York: Vintage.
—. (1980). *Power/Knowledge: Selected Interviews and Writings.* Ed. C. Gordon. New York: Pantheon.
Foxley, A. et al. (1986). *Development, Democracy and the Art of Trespassing: Essays in Honour of Albert O. Hirschman.* Notre Dame, Ind.: Notre Dame U. P.
Fraser, N.. (1992). "Rethinking the Public Sphere: A Contribution to the Critique of Actually Existing Democracy," in Craig Calhoun, ed., *Habermas and the Public Sphere.* Cambridge, Mass.: M.I.T. Press.
—. (1994). *Unruly Practices: Power, Discourse and Gender in Contemporary Social Theory.* Minneapolis: University of Minnesota Press
Frauen Anstiftung e.V. (1994). *Prelude: New Women's Initiatives in Central and Eastern Europe and Turkey.*
Frauen in Ost- und Mitteleuropa. Anstiftung e.V. Dokumentation der Konferenz der Frauen-Anstiftung in Jíloviště bei Prag, October 16–19, 1992.
Frentzel-Zakorska, J. (1990). "Civil Society in Poland and Hungary," *Soviet Studies* 42.4, 759–777.
Friedrich, C. J. and Brzezinski, Z. K. (1965). *Totalitarian Dictatorship and Autocracy.* Second edition—revised by Carl J. Friedman. Cambridge, Mass.: Harvard U. P.
Friedheim, D. V. (1993). "Bringing Society back into Democratic Transition Theory after 1989: Pact Making and Regime Collapse," *East European Politics and Societies* 7.3, 482–512.
Fukuyama, F. (1989). "The End of History?" *The National Interest* 16, 3–18.
—. (1992). *The End of History and the Last Man.* New York: Free Press.
Funk, N. and Mueller, M., eds. (1993). *Gender Politics and Post-Communism: Reflections from Eastern Europe and the Former Soviet Union.* New York: Routledge.
Fuszura, M. (1991). "Legal Regulation of Abortion in Poland," *Signs* 17.1, 117–118.
Gal, S. and Kligman, G. (2000). *The Politics of Gender after Socialism: A Comparative Historical Essay.* Princeton, N.J.: Princeton U. P.
Garnysz, C. (1984). "Polish Stalemate," *Problems of Communism* 5–6 33.3, 51–59.
Garton Ash, T. (1983). *The Polish Revolution: Solidarity 1980–82.* London: J. Cape.
—. (1988). "Reform or Revolution?" *The New York Review of Books*, October 27, 47–56.
—. (1990a) "Revolution in Hungary and Poland." *The New York Review of Books,* August 17, 1990, 9–15.
—. (1990b). *We the People: The Revolution of '89 as Witnessed in Warsaw, Budapest, Berlin, and Prague.* Cambridge: Granta Books.

—. (1990c). "Ten Thoughts on the New Europe," *The New York Review of Books,* June 14, 22.

—. (1991a). *The Uses of Adversity: Essays on the Fate of Central Europe.* London: Granta Books.

—. (1991b). "Poland After Solidarity," *The New York Review of Books,* June 13, 46–48.

—. (1994). *In Europe's Name: Germany and the Divided Continent.* London: Vintage.

—. (1995). "Prague: Intellectuals and Politicians," *The New York Review of Books,* January 21, 34–41.

—. (1996) "Hungary's Revolution: Forty Years On," *The New York Review of Books,* November 14, 18–22.

—. (1999). "The Puzzle of Central Europe," *The New York Review of Books,* 18 March, 18–23.

Gellner, E. (1990). "La Trahison de la Trahison des Clercs," in I. Maclean, A. Montefiore, and P. Winch, eds., *The Political Responsibility of Intellectuals.* Cambridge: Cambridge U. P.

—. (1991). "Civil Society in Historical Context," *International Social Science Review* 43, 495–510.

—. (1994). *Conditions of Liberty: Civil Society and Its Rivals.* London: Penguin.

—. (1995). "The Importance of Being Modular," in John A. Hall, ed., *Civil Society: Theory, History, Comparison.* Cambridge, U.K.: Polity Press.

Gelven, M. (1989). *A Commentary on Heidegger's Being and Time.* Revised edition. Dekalb, Ill.: Northern Illinois U. P.

Geremek, B. (1992). "Civil Society Then and Now," *Journal of Democracy* 3.2, 3–12.

Gerschenkron, A., (1962). *The History of Economic Backwardness.* Cambridge, Mass.: Harvard U. P.

Gill, S. and True, J. (1997). "Europe and the Former East Bloc: Structural Change and Democratic Potentials." Unpublished M.S.; used with permission of authors.

Goetz-Stankiewicz, M. (1979). *The Silenced Theatre: Czech Playwrights Without a Stage.* Toronto: University of Toronto Press.

—, ed. (1987). *The Vaněk Plays: Four Authors, One Character.* Vancouver, UBC Press.

—, ed. (1992). *Good-bye Samizdat.* Evanston, Ill.: Northwestern U. P.

Golan, Galia (1971). *The Czechoslovak Reform Movement; Communism in Crisis, 1962–1968.* Cambridge: U. P.

Goldfarb, J. C. (1982). *On Cultural Freedom: An Exploration of Public Life in Poland and America.* Chicago: University of Chicago Press.

—. (1989). *Beyond Glasnost: The Post-Totalitarian Mind.* Chicago: University of Chicago Press.

—. (1992). *After the Fall: The Pursuit of Democracy in Central Europe.* New York: Basic Books.

Goldstücker, E. (1977). "The Theory and Practice of Communist Internationalism," in K. Coates and F. Singleton, eds., *The Just Society*. Bradford: University of Bradford and the Bertrand Russell Peace Foundation.

Goldthorpe, J. H., ed. (1984). *Order and Conflict in Contemporary Capitalism*. Oxford: Clarendon Press.

Goodwyn, L. (1991). *Breaking the Barrier: The Rise of Solidarity in Poland*. New York: Oxford U. P.

Gorbachev, M.S. (1997). *Peristroika: New Thinking for Our Country and Our World*. New York: Harper and Row.

Goven, J. (1993). "Gender Politics in Hungary: Autonomy and Antifeminism," in Funk and Mueller (eds).

Gowan, P. (1995). "Neo-Liberal Theory and Practice for Eastern Europe," *New Left Review* 213, 3-60.

Granville, J. (2001). "Hungarian and Polish Reactions to the Events of 1956: New Archival Evidence," *Europe–Asia Studies* 53.7, 1051–1076.

Graubard, S. R., ed. (1991). *Eastern Europe ... Central Europe ... Europe*. Boulder, Co.: Westview Press.

Gwertzman B. and Kaufman M. T. (1990). *The Collapse of Communism*. New York: Random House.

Habermas, J. (1991, 1994). *The Structural Transformation of the Public Sphere: An Inquiry into a Category of Bourgeois Society*. Trans. T. Burger. Cambridge: M.I.T. Press.

Hall, J. A., ed. (1995). *Civil Society: Theory, History, Comparison*. Cambridge: Polity Press.

Halliday, F. (1990). "The Ends of the Cold War," *New Left Review* 180, 5–23.

Hankiss, E. (1988). "The 'Second Society': Is There an Alternative Social Model Emerging in Contemporary Hungary?" *Social Research* 55.1–2, 14–42.

—. (1990). *East European Alternatives*. Oxford: Clarendon Press.

Hašek, J. (1973). *The Good Solder Švejk*. London: Penguin.

Haraszti, M. (1977). *A Worker in a Worker's State*. Trans. M. Wright. London: Penguin Books.

—. (1979). "The Hungarian Miracle," *Irodalmi Újság*, July–August, 1–2.

—. (1987). *The Velvet Prison: Artists Under State Socialism*. New York: Basic Books.

—. (1988). "It is not Hopeless if You Demand: An Interview with Miklós Haraszti," *Uncaptive Minds*, April–May, 15–19

—. (1999). "Hungary: Decade of the Handshake Transition," *Transitions* 6.1 (January), 32–34.

Hare, P. G. et al., eds. (1981). *Hungary: A Decade of Economic Reform*. London: George Allen and Unwin.

Havel, V. (1978). "Breaking the Ice Barrier," *Index on Censorship* 7.1, January–February, 25–28.

—. (1980). *The Memorandum*. Trans. V. Blackwell. New York: Grove Press.

—. (1985). *Largo Desolato*. Trans. T. Stoppard. New York: Grove Press.

—. (1986). *Temptation*. Trans. M. Winn. New York: Grove Press.

—. (1987). *Václav Havel: Living in Truth*. London: Faber and Faber.

—. (1989). *Letters to Olga*. Trans. and Introduction by P. Wilson. New York: Henry Holt.

—. (1990a). *Disturbing the Peace: A Conversation with Karel Hvížd'ala*. Trans. P. Wilson. New York: Vintage Books.

— et al. (1990b). *The Power of the Powerless: Citizens against the State in Central-Eastern Europe*. Armonk, New York: M. E. Sharpe.

—. (1990c). *Redevelopment or Slum Clearance*. Trans. J. Saunders. London: Faber and Faber.

—. (1991). *Open Letters: Selected Prose 1965–1990*. Trans. P. Wilson and A. G. Brain. London: Faber and Faber.

—. (1992a). *Summer Meditations*. New York: Alfred A. Knopf.

—. (1992b). "Forget the machines, cut the clichés and get humanity back into politics," *Globe and Mail,* 16 March.

—. (1992c). "A Dream for Czechoslovakia," *The New York Review of Books,* June 25, 8–15.

—. (1992d). "The Honest Politician," *Saturday Night,* June, 62–66.

—. (1993). *The Garden Party and Other Plays*. New York: Grove Press.

—. (1994). *Toward a Civil Society: Selected Speeches and Writings 1990–1994*. Trans. P. Wilson. Prague: Lidové Noviny.

—. (1997). *The Art of the Impossible: Politics as Morality in Practice*. Trans. P. Wilson and others. New York: Alfred A. Knopf.

—. (1998). "The Divine Revolution: Lifting the Iron Curtain of the Spirit," *Utne Reader,* July–August, 56–57.

Havelková, H. (1993a). "Patriarchy in Czech Society," *Hypatia* 8.4, 89–96.

—. (1993b). "A Few Prefeminist Thoughts," in Nanette Funk and Magda Mueller, eds., *Gender Politics and Post-Communism*. New York: Routledge.

—. (1994). "Ignored but Assumed. Family and Gender between the Public and Private Realm," *Czech Sociological Review* 4.1, 63–79.

—. (1996). "Abstract Citizenship? Women and Power in the Czech Republic," *Social Politics: International Studies in Gender, State, and Society* 3.2–3, 243–259.

Hawkes, N., ed. (1990). *Tearing Down the Curtain*. Toronto: Hodder and Stroughton.

Hegel, G. W. F. (1967). *Philosophy of Right*. Trans. T. M. Knox. New York: Oxford U. P.

—. (1991). *Elements of the Philosophy of Right*. Ed. A. W. Wood. Trans. H. B. Nisbet. Cambridge: M.I.T. Press.

Heilbroner, R. L. (1986). *The Essential Adam Smith*. New York: Norton.

Heitlinger, A. (1996). "Framing Feminism in Post-Communist Czech Republic," *Communist and Post-Communist Studies* 29.1, 77–93.

Heller, Á., ed. (1983). *Lukács Revalued*. Oxford: Basil Blackwell.

Heneka, A. et al, eds. (1985). *A Besieged Culture: Czechoslovakia Ten Years after Helsinki*. Stockholm/Vienna: Charta 77 Foundation and International Helsinki Federation for Human Rights.

Hirsch, M. and Fox, E., eds. (1990). *Conflicts in Feminism*. New York: Rout-ledge.

Hirschman, A. O. (1970). *Exit, Voice, and Loyalty*. Cambridge: Harvard U. P.

Hirst, P. and Thompson, G. (1996). *Globalization in Question*. Cambridge: Polity Press.

Hobsbawm, E. (1993). "The New Threat to History," *The New York Review of Books*, December 16, 62–64.

—. (1994). *Age of Extremes: The Short Twentieth Century 1914–1991*. London: Abacus.

Hoffman, E. (1993). *Exit into History: A Journey through the New Eastern Europe*. New York: Penguin Books.

Hoensch, J. K. (1996). *A History of Modern Hungary 1867–1994*. Second Edition. Trans. Kim Traynor. Addison–Wesley Pub. Co.

Holc, J. P. (1992). "Solidarity and the Polish State: Competing Discursive Strategies on the Road to Power," *East European Politics and Societies* 6.2, 121–151.

Holmes, S. (1992). "The Scowl of Minerva," *The New Republic*, March 23, 27–33.

Holzer, J. (1984). *Solidarność 1980–1981*. Paris: Instytut Literacki.

Honig, B. (1995). *Feminist Interpretations of Hannah Arendt*. Pennsylvania: Pennsylvania State U. P.

Hont, I. and Ignatieff, M. (1985). *Wealth and Virtue: The Shaping of Political Economy in the Scottish Enlightenment*. Cambridge: Cambridge U. P.

Horowitz, A. and Horowitz, G. (1988). *"Everywhere They Are in Chains": Political Theory from Rousseau to Marx*. Toronto: Nelson.

Hruby, P. (1980). *Fools and Heroes: The Changing Role of Communist Intellectuals in Czechoslovakia*. Oxford: Pergamon.

Huntington, S. (1991). "Democracy's Third Wave." *Journal of Democracy* 2.1, 12–34.

Iggers, W.A. (1995). *Women of Prague: Ethnic Diversity and Social Change from the Eighteenth Century to the Present*. Oxford: Berghahn Books.

Ignatieff, M. (1993). *Blood and Belonging: Journeys into the New Nationalism*. Toronto: Viking.

—. (1995). "On Civil Society: Why Eastern Europe's Revolutions Could Succeed," *Foreign Affairs* 74.2, 128–136.

—. (1996). "Intellectuals, Between Morals and Politics." Unpublished proceedings of a conference sponsored by the French Institute and Collegium Budapest, 21–23 March; used with permission of organizer (Éva Karádi).

Isaac, J. C. (1992). *Arendt, Camus, and Modern Rebellion*. New Haven: Yale U. P.

—. (1993). "Civil Society and the Spirit of Revolt," *Dissent*, Summer, 356–361.

—. (1994). "Oases in the Desert: Hannah Arendt on Democratic Politics," *American Political Science Review* 88.1, 156–168.

—. (1995). "The Strange Silence of Political Theory," *Political Theory* 23.4, 637–655.

—. (1996). "The Meanings of 1989," *Social Research* 63.2, 291–344.

—. (1998). *Democracy in Dark Times*. Ithaca, N.Y.: Cornell U. P.

Jackson-Lears, T. J. (1985). "The Concept of Cultural Hegemony: Problems and Possibilities," *American Historical Review* 90.3, 567–593.

Jechová, K. (1997). "What was Charter 77?" *The New Presence: The Prague Journal of Central European and World Affairs*, February, 6–7.

Jedlicki, J. (1990). "The Revolution of 1989: The Unbearable Burden of History," *Problems of Communism* 39.4, 39–45.

Jennings, J. and Kemp-Welch, A. (1997). *Intellectuals in Politics: From the Dreyfus Affair to Salman Rushdie.* London: Routledge.

Johnson, J. T. (1992). "Does 'Democracy' Travel? Some Thoughts on Democracy and Its Cultural Context," *Ethics and International Affairs* 6, 41–55.

Johnson, L. (1996). *Central Europe: Enemies, Neighbours, Friends.* New York: Oxford U. P.

Jowitt, K. (1993). *New World Disorder: The Leninist Extinction.* Los Angeles: University of California Press.

Judt, T. (1988). "The Dilemmas of Dissidence: The Politics of Opposition in East-Central Europe," *East European Politics and Societies* 2.2, 185–240.

—. (1990). "The Rediscovery of Eastern Europe," *Daedalus* Winter, 23–54.

—. (1992). *Past Imperfect: French Intellectuals 1944–1956.* Los Angeles: University of California Press.

—. (1996). "Europe: The Grand Illusion," *The New York Review of Books.* 11 July 1996, 6–9.

Jung, N. (1994). "Eastern European Women with Western Eyes," in G. Griffin et al., eds, *Stirring It: Challenges for Feminism.* London: Taylor and Francis.

—. (1995). "About Feminism and Nationalism during the Coffee-break," paper presented at the Vth International Congress of Central and East European Studies, Warsaw, 5–11 August. Unpublished M.S.; used with permission of author.

Jańkowski, H. (1992). *Z teg drogi zejść nie mogę: Wybór Kazán 1983–1991.* Gdańsk, n.p.

Juráňová, J. (1997). "The Boundary between Public and Private in the Space of the Female Body." Unpublished M.S.; used with permission of author.

Kadarkay, A. (1991). *Georg Lukács: Life, Thought, and Politics.* Oxford: Basil Blackwell.

Kafka, F. (1974a). *The Castle.* New York: Vintage.

—. (1974b). *Metamorphosis and other Stories.* Trans. W. and E. Muir. New York: Penguin.

Kagarlitsky, B. (1992). *The Disintegration of a Monolith.* Trans. Renfrey Clarke. London: Verso.

—. (1994). *Square Wheels: How Russian Democracy Got Derailed.* Trans. Leslie A. Auerbach, Amanda Calvert, Renfry Clark, and Masha Gesson. New York: Monthly Review Press.

Kaldor, M. (1990). "After the Cold War," *New Left Review* 180, 25–37.

Kamiński, B. (1991). *The Collapse of State Socialism.* Princeton: Princeton U. P.

Karafilly, I. F. (1998). *Ashes and Miracles: A Polish Journey.* Toronto: Malcolm Lester Books.

Karabel, J. "Polish Intellectuals and the Origins of Solidarity: The Making of an Oppositional Alliance," *Communist and Post-Communist Studies* 26.1, 25–46.

Karpiński, J. (1982). *Count-down: The Polish Upheavals of 1956, 1968, 1970, 1976. 1980 …* Trans. O. Amsterdamska and G. M. Moar. New York: Karz-Cohl.

—. (1987). "Polish Intellectuals in Opposition," *Problems of Communism,* July–August, 44–57.

—. (1995). *Poland since 1944: A Portrait of Years.* Boulder: Westview Press.

—. (1996). "Poles Divided over Church's Renewed Political Role, *Transitions* 2.7.

—. (1997). "In Poland, a Long-standing Tradition of Resistance," *Transitions* 3.3, 14–19.

Kaufman, M. T. (1997). "From Dissidence to Dissonance," *Transitions* 3.3, 5.

Keane, J. (1988a). *Democracy and Civil Society.* London: Verso.

—. ed. (1988b). *Civil Society and the State.* London: Verso.

—. (1996). *Reflections on Violence.* London: Verso.

—. (1999). *Václav Havel: A Political Tragedy in Six Acts.* London: Bloomsbury.

Kemp-Welch, A. (1983). *The Birth of Solidarity.* New York: St. Martin's Press.

Kennedy, M. D. (1991). *Professionals, Power and Solidarity in Poland.* New York: Cambridge U. P.

—. (1994). *Envisioning Eastern Europe.* Ann Arbor: University of Michigan Press.

Kirschbaum, S. (1995). *A History of Slovakia: The Struggle for Survival.* New York: St. Martin's Press.

Kis, J. (1986). "Hungary's Elections: The Wider Implications," *East European Reporter* 1.4, 10–12.

—. (1989). *Politics in Hungary: For a Democratic Alternative.* Introduction by Timothy Garton Ash. Trans. G. J. Follinus. New York: Columbia U. P.

Kiss, E. (1992). "Democracy without Parties? 'Civil Society' in East-Central Europe," *Dissent,* Spring, 226–231.

Klíma, I. (1990). *Love and Garbage.* Trans. E. Osers. London: Penguin.

—. (1991). *Judge on Trial.* Trans. A.G. Brain. London: Chatto and Windus.

—. (1994a). *The Spirit of Prague and Other Essays.* Trans. P. Wilson. London: Granta.

—. (1994b). *Waiting for the Dark, Waiting for the Light.* Trans. P. Wilson. New York: Grove Press.

Koestler, A. (1944; 1970). *Darkness at Noon.* Trans. D. Hardy. New York: Bantam.

Kohák, E. (1989). *Jan Patočka: Philosophy and Selected Writings.* Chicago: University of Chicago Press.

—. (1992). "Ashes, Ashes … Central Europe after Forty Years," *Daedalus,* Spring (1992), 197–215.

Kohout, P. (1969). *From the Diary of a Counterrevolutionary.* Trans. George Theiner. San Francisco: McGraw-Hill Book Company.

—. (1994). *I Am Snowing: Confessions of a Woman of Prague.* Trans. N. Bermel. New York: Harcourt Brace.

Kołakowski, L. (1968). "The Pries and the Jester," in *Marxism and Beyond: on Historical Understanding and Individual Responsibility.* Trans. J. Zielonka Peel. London: Pall Mall Press.

—. (1969). *Toward a Marxist Humanism: Essays on the Left Today.* Trans. J. Z. Peel. New York: Grove Press.

—. (1971a). "Intellectuals, Hope & Heresy: An Interview with Kołakowski," *Encounter* 37.4, 42–47.

—. (1971b). "Theses on Hope and Hopelessness," *Survey* 17.3, 37–52.

—. (1978). *Main Currents of Marxism.* Oxford: Clarendon Press.

—. (1983). "The Intelligentsia," in Abraham Brumberg, ed., *Poland: Genesis of a Revolution.* New York: Random House, 54–67.

—. (1989). *The Presence of Myth.* Trans. A. Czerniawski. Chicago and London: University of Chicago Press.

—. (1990). *Modernity on Endless Trial.* Chicago and London: University of Chicago Press.

— and Hampshire, S., eds. (1974). *The Socialist Idea: A Reappraisal.* London: Weidenfeld and Nicolson.

Kolarska-Bobinska, L. (1991). "The Changing Face of Civil Society in Eastern Europe," *Praxis International* 10.3–4, 324–336.

Konrád, G. (1977). *The City Builder.* Trans. I. Sanders. Introduction by Carlos Fuentes. New York: Penguin.

—. (1983). "Censorship and State-owned Citizens," *Dissent,* Fall, 448–455.

—. (1986). "A Modest Request for Reforms," *Index on Censorship* 15.1, 38–41.

—. (1987). *Antipolitics.* Trans. R.E. Allen. New York: Henry Holt.

—. (1990a). "Ethics and Politics: Nationalism and Intellectuals in Eastern Europe," *Dissent* 37, 474–477.

— (1990b). "Chance Wanderings: Reflections of a Hungarian Writer," *Dissent,* Spring, 189–191.

—. (1995). *The Melancholy of Rebirth: Essays from Post-Communist Central Europe, 1989–1994.* Trans. M.H. Heim. New York: Harcourt Brace & Company.

—. and Szelényi, I. (1979). *The Intellectuals on the Road to Class Power.* New York: Harcourt Brace Jovanovich.

—. et al. (1998). *Central Europe.* Austrian Cultural Institute: London.

Konvička, L. and Kávan, J. (1994). "Youth Movements and the Velvet Revolution," *Communist and Post-Communist Studies* 27.2, 160–176.

Konwicki, T. (1988). *A Minor Apocalypse.* London: Faber and Faber.

Korbonski, A. (1989). "Nationalism and Pluralism and the Process of Political Development in Eastern Europe," *International Political Science Review* 10.3, 251–262.

—. (1993). "The Decline and Rise of Pluralism in East Central Europe, 1949–1989, or How Not to See the Forest for the Trees," *Communist and Post-Communist Studies* 26.4, 432–461.

—. (2000). "Poland: Ten Years After: the Church," *Communist and Post-Communist Studies* 33.1, 123–146.

Kornai, J. (1990). *The Road to a Free Economy. Shifting from a Socialist System: The Example of Hungary.* New York: W.W. Norton.

—. (1992). *The Socialist System: The Political Economy of Communism.* Princeton: Princeton U. P.

Kostrzewa, R., ed., (1990). *Between East and West: Writings from Kultura.* New York: Hill and Wang.

Kott, J., ed. (1990). *Four Decades of Polish Essays.* Evanston: Ill.: Northwestern U. P.

Kovács, G. (1999). "Can Power be Humanized? The Notions of Elite and Legitimation in István Bibó's Political Philosophy," *Studies in East European Political Thought* 51.4, 307–327.

Kowalik, T. (1991). "Marketization and Privatization: The Polish Case," *Socialist Register* 1991, 259–277.

—. (1993). "Can Poland Afford the Swedish Model?" *Dissent*, Winter, 88–97.

—. (1995). "From 'Self-governing Republic' to Capitalism: Polish Workers and Intellectuals," in M. Mendell and K. Nielson, eds. *Europe: Central and East.* Montréal: Black Rose Books.

—. (1996). "On the Transformation of Post-communist Societies: The Inefficiency of Primitive Capital Accumulation," *International Political Science Review* 17.3, 289–296.

—. (1997). "The Polish Revolution," *Dissent*, Spring, 26–30.

—. (n.d.). "The Systemic Presuppositions of the Polish August: Self-governing Socialism or the Restoration of Capitalism?" Unpublished M.S.; used with permission of author.

Kriseová, E. (1991). *Václav Havel: La biographie.* Paris: Editions de l'aube.

—. (1993). *Václav Havel: The Authorized Biography.* Trans. C. B. Crain. New York: St. Martin's Press.

Kucharczyk, J. (1995). "Leszek Kołakowski: An Intellectual between the Two Worlds," unpublished M.S.; used with permission of author.

Kulczycki, A. (1995). "Abortion Policy in Postcommunist Europe," *Population and Development Review* 21.3, 471–505.

Kumar, K. (1993). "Civil Society: an inquiry into the usefulness of an historical term," *British Journal of Sociology* 94.3, 375–395.

Kundera, M. (1984). "The Tragedy of Central Europe," *The New York Review of Books*, April 26, 33–38.

—. (1987). *The Book of Laughter and Forgetting.* Trans. M. A. Heim. London: Faber & Faber.

Kurczewski, J. (1993). *The Resurrection of Rights in Poland.* Oxford: Oxford U. P.

Kuroń, J. (1977). "Reflections on a Program of Action," *Polish Review* 22, 51–69.

—. (1981). "Not to Lure the Wolves out of the Woods: An Interview with Jacek Kuroń," *Telos* 47, 93–97.

—. (1984). *Polityka I odpowiedzialność.* London: Aneks.

—. (1988). "Landscape after the Battle," *East European Reporter* 3.2, 30–32.

—. (1991). *La Foi et La Faute (Wiara i wina)*. Trans. M. Bouvard. Paris: Fayard.

—. (1993). *Maintenant Ou Jamais (Gwiezdny Czas)*. Trans. M. Bouvard. Paris: Fayard.

—. and Modzelewski, K. (1982). *Solidarność: The Missing Link? The Classic Open Letter to the Party*. London: Bookmarks.

Kusin, V. V. (1971). *The Intellectual Origins of the Prague Spring: The Development of Reformist Ideas in Czechoslovakia 1956–1967*. Cambridge: Cambridge U. P.

—. (1978). *From Dubček to Charter 77: A Study of 'Normalization' in Czechoslovakia 1968–1978*. New York: St. Martin's Press.

Laba, R. (1986). "Worker Roots of Solidarity," *Problems of Communism*, July–August, 47–67.

—. (1991). *The Roots of Solidarity: A Political Sociology of Poland's Working Class Democratization*. Princeton, N.J.: Princeton U. P.

Laclau, E. and Mouffe, C. (1985). *Hegemony and Socialist Strategy*. London: Verso.

LaFont, S. (2001). "One Step Forward, Two Steps Back: Women in the Post-Communist States," *Communist and Post-Communist Studies* 34, 203–220.

Laky, T. (1981). "The Hidden Mechanism of Recentralization in Hungary," *Acta Oeconomica* 23, 1–2.

Lane, D. (1996). *The Rise and Fall of State Socialism*. Cambridge: Polity Press.

Lash, S. and Urry, J. (1987). *The End of Organized Capitalism*. Madison: University of Wisconsin Press.

Laslett, P., ed. (1965) John Locke. *Two Treatises of Government*. Scarborough, Ont.: New American Library.

Laux, J .K. (1997). "Double Discourse: National Politics and Global Governance, Fables from Central Europe." Unpublished M.S.; used with permission of author.

Leff, C. S. (1988). *National Conflict in Czechoslovakia: The Making and Remaking of a State, 1918–1987*. Princeton, N.J.: Princeton U. P.

—. (1997). *The Czech and Slovak Republics: Nation vs State*. Boulder, Co.: Westview Press.

Lemert, C., ed. (1991). *Intellectuals and Politics: Social Theory in a Changing World*. Newbury Park, Ca.: Sage.

Lewis, P., ed. (1992). *Democracy and Civil Society in Eastern Europe*. New York: St. Martin's Press.

—. (1994). *Central Europe Since 1945*. London: Longman.

Liehm, A. J., ed. (1970). *The Politics of Culture*. New York: Grove Press.

—. (1974). *Closely Watched Films: The Czechoslovak Experience*. White Plains, N.Y.: International Arts and Sciences Press.

—. (1975). "Franz Kafka in Eastern Europe," *Telos* 23, 58–83.

Liepietz, A. (1987). *Mirages and Miracles: The Crisis of Global Fordism*. Trans. D. Macey. London: Verso.

Lilla, M. (1998). "Still Living with '68," *The New York Times Magazine*, 34–37.

Lipski, J. J. (1985). *KOR: A History of the Workers' Defense Committee in Poland: 1976–1981*. Trans. O. Amsterdamska and G. M. Moore. Los Angeles: University of California Press.

Litván, G. (1996). *The Hungarian Revolution of 1956: Reform, Revolt and Repression 1953–1956*. New York: Longman.

Löbl, E. (1976). *My Mind on Trial*. New York: Harcourt Brace Jovanovich.

Locke, J. (1963). *Two Treatises of Government*. Introduction and Notes by Peter Laslett. Cambridge: Cambridge U. P.

Lomax, B. (1976). *Hungary 1956*. London: Allison and Busby.

—. (1982). "The Rise of the Democratic Opposition," *Labour Focus on Eastern Europe* 5.3–4, 2–7.

—. (1984a). "The Hungarian Peace Movement," *Labour Focus on Eastern Europe* 5.5–6, 35–36.

—. (1984b). "The Dialogue Breaks Down," *Labour Focus on Eastern Europe* 7.1, 23–25.

—. (1990). *Hungarian Workers' Councils in 1956*. Highland Lakes, N. J.: Columbia U. P.

London, A. (1968). *On Trial*. London: Macmillan.

Longworth, P. (1994). *The Making of Eastern Europe*. New York: St. Martin's Press.

Lovenduski, J. (1994). "The Political Status of European Women," Address to Seminar on Womens's Participation in Political and Public Life, Council of Europe, Budapest, Hungary, November 21–22.

Lukacs, J. (1988). *Budapest 1900: A Historical Portrait of a City and its Culture*. New York: Grove Press.

Lukes, S. (1979). *Individualism*. Oxford: Basil Blackwell.

MacLean, I., Montefiore, A., and Wrinch, P., eds. (1990). *The Political Responsibility of Intellectuals*. Cambridge: Cambridge U. P.

Macpherson, C.B. (1962). *The Political Theory of Possessive Individualism*. Oxford: Clarendon Press.

Mahr, A. and Nagle, J. (1995). "Resurrection of the Successor Parties and Democratization in East-Central Europe," *Communist and Post-Communist Studies* 28.4, 393–409.

Mannheim, K. (1959). *Essays on the Sociology of Knowledge*. London: Routledge and Kegan Paul.

March, M., ed. (1990). *Child of Europe: A New Anthology of East European Poetry*. London: Penguin.

Marody, M. (1988). "Antinomies of Collective Subconsciousness," *Social Research* 55.1–2, 97–110.

Marshall, T. H. (1963). "Citizenship and Social Class," in Marshall, T. H. *Sociology at the Crossroads*. London: Heinemann.

Mason, D.S. (1985). *Public Opinion and Political Change in Poland 1980–1982*. Melbourne: Cambridge U. P.

Matuštík, M. J. (1991). "Havel and Habermas on Identity and Revolution," *Praxis International* 10.3–4, 262–277.

—. (1993). *Postnational Identity: Political Theory and Existential Philosophy in Habermas, Kierkegaard, and Havel.* New York: The Guilford Press.

Matynia, E. (1995). "Finding a Voice: Women in Postcommunist Central Europe," in A. Basu, ed., *The Challenge of Local Feminisms: Women's Movements in Global Perspective.* Boulder, Co.: Westview Press.

—., ed. (1996). *Grappling with Democracy: Deliberations on Post-Communist Societies, 1990–1995.* Prague: SLON.

McCauley, M. ed. (1977*). Communist Power in Europe.* London: Macmillan.

McLellan, D., ed. (1978). *Karl Marx: Selected Writings.* Oxford: Oxford U. P.

McRae, R. (1997). *Resistance and Revolution in Václav Havel's Czechoslovakia.* Ottawa: Carleton U. P.

Michnik, A. (1976). "A New Evolutionism," *Survey* 22.3–4, 267–271.

—. (1979). "Poland and the Pope's Visit," *Labour Focus on Eastern Europe* 3.3, 11–14.

—. (1980). "Ticks and Angels," *Survey* 25.1, 179–185.

—. (1981). "What We Want to Do and What We Can Do," *Telos* 47, 65–77.

—. (1985). *Letters from Prison and other Essays.* Trans. M. Latynski. Introduction by D. Ost. Berkeley: University of California Press.

—. (1987). "Towards a New Democratic Compromise: An Interview with Adam Michnik," *East European Reporter* 3.2, 24–29.

—. (1990a). "After the Revolution," *The New Republic,* July 2, 28–29.

—. (1990b). "Dear Alain Besançon," *Uncaptive Minds* 3.4, 11–13.

—. (1991). "Nationalism," *Social Research* 58.4, 757–763.

—. (1993). *The Church and the Left.* Trans. and Introduction by D. Ost. Chicago: University of Chicago Press.

—. (1995). "Market, Religion, and Nationalism: Fundamentalisms in the New European Order," *International Journal of Politics, Culture, and Society* 8.4, 525–543.

—. (1998). *Letters from Freedom: Post-Cold War Realities and Perspectives.* Berkeley and Los Angeles: University of California Press.

— and Habermas, J. (1994). "Ovecoming the Past," *New Left Review* 203, 3–16.

Mikloško, F. (1991). *Nebudete Ich Moct Rosvratit.* Bratislava: ARCHA.

Miller, L. et al., eds. (1993). *Literature and Politics in Central Europe: Studies in Honour of Marketa Goetz-Stankiewicz.* Columbia, S.C.: Camden House.

Miller, S. (1995). "The Case of Abortion in Poland," paper presented at the Vth International Congress of Central and East European Studies, Warsaw, 5–11 August; used with permission of author.

Miłosz, C. (1951, 1953). *The Captive Mind.* Trans. Jane Zielonko. New York: Random House.

—. (1988). *The Collected Poems.* London: Penguin.

Mische, A. (1993). "Post-Communism's 'Lost Treasure': Subjectivity and Gender in a Shifting Public Sphere," *Praxis International* 13.3, 242–267.

Miszlivetz, F. (1990). "Civil Society in Eastern Europe? The Case of Hungary," *World Futures* 29.1–2, 81–94.

Misztal, B. ed. (1985). *Poland After Solidarity: Social Movement versus the State.* Oxford: Transaction Books.

Mlynář, Z. (1980). *Nightfrost in Prague: The End of Humane Socialism.* Trans. P. Wilson. New York: Carz Publishers.

Modzelewski, K. (1992). "Poland: A Temporary Truce?" *East European Reporter* 5, 24–26.

Molnár, M. (1971). *Budapest 1956: A History of the Hungarian Revolution.* Trans. J. Ford. London: Allen and Unwin.

Molyneux, M. (1994). "Women's Rights and the International Context: Some Reflections on the Post-Communist State," *Millennium: Journal of International Studies* 23.2, 287–313.

Moore, B. (1966). *The Social Origins of Dictatorship and Democracy: Lord and Peasant in the Making of the Modern World.* Boston: Beacon Press.

Mueller, C. (1973). *The Politics of Communication.* New York: Oxford U. P.

Mühle, E. (1996/7). "Universitäten und Systemwandel: Der Beitrag akademischer Gemeinschaften zur Wiederherstellung der 'Civil Society' in Ostmitteleuropa seit 1956," *Marburger Universitätsbund e. V.*, Wintersemester, 22–26.

Murrell, P. (1992). "Conservative Political Philosophy and the Strategy of Economic Transition," *East European Politics and Societies* 6.1, 3–16.

Musíl, J. "Czechoslovakia in the Middle of Transition," *Daedalus*, Spring 1992, 175–195.

Nagy, K., ed. (1991). *Democracy, Revolution, and Self-Determination.* New York: Columbia University Press.

Nardin, T. (1991) "Moral Renewal: The Lessons of Eastern Europe," *Ethics and International Affairs* 5, 1–14.

Navrátil, J., ed. (1998). *The Prague Spring 1968.* Budapest: Central European University Press.

Nedelsky, N. (2001). *The Bonds and Boundaries of Nationhood: Political-cultural Roots of Czech and Slovak Definitions of the Nation and Their Implications for Post-Communist Governance.* University of Toronto: unpublished dissertation; used with permission of author.

Nelson, J. M. (1993). "The Politics of Economic Transformation: Is Third World Experience Relevant in Eastern Europe?" *World Politics* 45.3, 433–463.

Nichols, R. (1978). *Treason, Tradition, and the Intellectual: Julien Benda and Political Discourse.* Kansas: The Regents Press.

Nove, A. (1983). *The Economics of Feasible Socialism.* London: George Allen & Unwin.

Nowak, J. (1982). "The Church in Poland," *Problems of Communism* 31, 1–16.

Nowak, S. (1981). "Values and Attitudes of the Polish People," *Scientific American* 245.1, 45–53.

Nuti, D. M. (1979). "The Contradictions of Socialist Economies: A Marxist Interpretation," *Socialist Register* 1979, 229–273.

— and Portes, R. (1993). "Central Europe: The Way Forward," in Portes, R., ed. *Economic Transformation in Central Europe: A Progress Report.* London: European Communities.

Nyiri, J. (1989). *Battlefields and Playgrounds.* New York: Farrar, Straus, and Giroux.

Odden, E. (1984). "Gábor Demszky: Interview with a Non-Existent Publisher," *Index on Censorship* 13.4, 17–19.

O'Donnell, G. and Schmitter, P. (1989). *Transitions from Authoritarian Rule: Tentative Conclusions about Uncertain Democracies.* Baltimore: Johns Hopkins U. P.

Offe, C. (1993). "The Politics of Social Policy in East European Transitions," *Social Research* 60.4, 649–683.

—. (1997). *Varieties of Transition: The East European and East German Experience.* Cambridge, Mass.: M.I.T. Press.

Open Society Institute (1995). *Building Open Societies: Soros Foundation 1995 Report of Activities.* New York: Open Society Institute.

Orbán, V. (1989). "Speech at the Reburial of Imre Nagy," reprinted in English in *Uncaptive Minds* 2.4, 26.

Örkény, I. (1996). *One Minute Stories.* Trans. J. Solossy. London: Corvina.

Orwell, G. (1946; 1980). "Politics and the English Language," *Complete Works of George Orwell.* London: Secker & Warburg/Octopus.

—. (1949; 1980). *1984. Complete Works of George Orwell.* London: Secker & Warburg/Octopus.

Osiatynski, W. (1996). "The Roundtable Talks in Poland," in Jon Elster, ed., *The Roundtable Talks and the Breakdown of Communism.* Chicago and London: University of Chicago Press.

Ost, D. (1990). *Solidarity and the Politics of Anti-Politics.* Philidelphia: Temple U. P.

Otáhal, M. (1992). "Revolution der Intellektuellen? Die tscheschischen Intellektuellen und der Totalitarismus," *Jahrbuch 1991/92.* Berlin: Institute for Advanced Study, 258–272.

—. (1994). *Opozice, Moc, Společnost 1969–1989: Příspěvek k dějinám 'normalizace'.* Praha: Maxdorf, Ústav pro soudobé dějiny. Institute of Contemporary History.

Page, B. B. (1973). *The Czechoslovak Reform Movement, 1963–1968.* Amsterdam: B. R. Grunder B. V.

Palouš, M. (1989). "The Parallel *Polis* after Twelve Years," *Uncaptive Minds* 2.5, 36–40.

—. (1993). "Post-Totalitarian Politics and European Philosophy," *Public Affairs Quarterly* 7.2, 149–163.

—. (1996). "Charter 77 in 1996—a closed chapter or a living heritage?" Unpublished M.S.; used with permission of author.

Panitch, L. (1994). "Globalisation and the State," *Socialist Register* 1994, 60–93.

Paradowska, J. (1991). "The Three Cards Game: An Interview with Adam Michnik," *Telos* 89, 95–101.

Partisan Review 59.4 (1992). Special Issue: Intellectuals and Social Change in Central and Eastern Europe.

Pateman, C. (1988a). *The Sexual Contract.* Stanford: Stanford University Press.
——. (1988b). "The Fraternal Social Contract," in John Keane, ed., *Civil Society and the State: New European Perspectives.* London: Verso.
Patočka, J. (1991a). *Die Bewegung der menschlichen Existenz.* Herausgegeben von K. Nellen, J. Němec und Ilja Srubar. Stuttgart: Klett–Cotta.
——. (1991b). Ausge*wählte Schriften.* Herausgegeben am Institut für Wissenshaften vom Menschen. Wien: Klett-Cotta.
Pech, S.Z. (1982). "Czech Socialism in a Historical and Comparative Perspective," *Canadian Slavonic Papers* 34.2, 138–151.
Pehe, J. (1997). "Reshaping Dissident Ideals for Post-Communist Times," *Transitions* 3.3, 6–8.
Pelczynski, Z. A., ed. (1984). *The State and Civil Society: Studies in Hegel's Political Philosophy.* New York: Cambridge U. P.
Pelikán, J., ed. (1971). *The Secret Vysočany Congress Proceedings and Documents of the Extraordinary Fourteenth Congress of the Communist Party of Czechoslovakia.* Trans. G. Theiner and D. Viney. London: Penguin.
——., ed. (1971a). *The Czechoslovak Political Trials, 1950–1954: The Suppressed Report of the Dubček Government's Commission of Inquiry, 1968.* London: Macdonald.
Penn, S. (1994). "The National Secret," *Journal of Women's History* 5.3, 53–69.
Persky, S. (1981). *At the Lenin Shipyard.* Vancouver, New Star Books.
——. (1996). *Then We Take Berlin: Stories from the other Side of Europe.* Toronto: Alfred A. Knopf.
—— and Flam, H. eds. (1982). *The Solidarity Sourcebook.* Vancouver: New Star Books.
Pickles, J. and Smith, A. (1998). *Theorising Transition: The Political Economy of Post-Communist Transitions.* London: Routledge.
Piekalkiewicz, J. (1972). *Public Opinion Polling in Czechoslovakia, 1968–1989: Results and Analysis of Surveys Conducted during the Dubček Era.* New York: Praeger.
Pithart, P. (1990). "Social and Economic Developments in Czechoslovakia in the 1980s," *Eastern European Reporter* 4, 42–45.
——. (1993). "Intellectuals in Politics: Double Dissent in the Past, Double Disappointment Today," *Social Research* 60.4, 752–761.
——. (1995). "The Division of Czechoslovakia: A Preliminary Balance Sheet for the End of a Respectable Country," *Canadian Slavonic Papers* 37. 3–4, 322–338.
Pocock, J. G. A. (1960; 1989). *Politics, Language, Time: Essays on Political Thought and History.* Chicago: University of Chicago Press.
——. (1975). *The Machiavellian Moment: Florentine Political Thought and the Atlantic Republican Tradition.* Cambridge: Cambridge U. P.
——. (1987a). "The concept of a language and the *métier d'historien*: some considerations on practice," in A. Pagden, ed., *The Language of Political Theory in Early-Modern Europe.* Cambridge: Cambridge U. P.
——. (1987b). "Texts as Events: Reflections on the History of Political Thought," in K. Sharpe and S. N. Zwicker, eds., *Politics of Discourse: The Literature*

and History of 17th Century England. Berkeley: University of California Press.

Pogany, I. (1995). *Human Rights in Eastern Europe.* Aldershot, U.K.: Edward Elgar.

Polanyi, K. (1944). *The Great Transformation: The Political and Economic Origins of Our Time.* Boston: Beacon Press.

Pomian, K. (1982). *Pologne dèfi à l'impossible?: de la révolte de Poznán à "Solidarité."* Paris: Editions ouvrières.

Poster, M., ed. (1988). *Jean Baudrillard Selected Writings.* Stanford, California U. P.

Potter, D. et al. (1997). *Democratization.* Cambridge: Polity Press.

Poznanski, K. Z., ed. (1993). *Stabilization and Privatization in Poland: An Economic Evaluation of the Shock Therapy Program.* Boston: Kluwer Academic Publishers.

—. (1996). *Poland's Protracted Transition: Institutional Change and Economic Growth 1970–1994.* Cambridge: Cambridge U. P.

Prečan, V., ed. (1983). *Human Rights in Czechoslovakia: A Documentation.* Paris: International Committee for the Support of Charter 77 in Czechoslovakia.

—. (1995). *Novoročni filipika 1995: Disent a Charta 77 v pojetí Milana Otáhala.* Praha: Quodlibet, Ústav pro soudobé dějiny.

—. (1997). "Charter 77: Its Past and Its Legacy." Speech Delivered on the 20th Anniversary of Charter 77, 10 January 1997, Prague Castle; used with permission of author.

Przeworski, A. (1991a). *Democracy and the Market: Political and Economic Reforms in Eastern Europe and Latin America.* Cambridge: Cambridge U. P.

—. (1991b). "The 'East' Becomes the 'South'? The 'Autumn of the People' and the Future of Eastern Europe," *PS* 24, 20.

—. (1992). "The Neoliberal Fallacy," *Journal of Democracy* 3.3, 44–59.

Rab, B. (1978), "New Hungarian Samizdat." *Index on Censorship* 7.4.

Raina, P. (1978). *Political Opposition in Poland, 1954–1977.* London: Poets' and Painters' Press.

—. (1985). *Poland 1981: Toward Social Renewal.* London: George Allen & Unwin.

Rakovski, M. (J. Kis and Gy. Bence) (1977). "Marxism and the Analysis of Soviet-type Societies," *Capital and Class* 1: 83–105.

—. (1978). *Towards an East European Marxism.* London: Allison & Busby.

Ramet, S. (1994). *Rocking the State: Rock Music and Politics in Eastern Europe and Russia.* Boulder, Co.: Westview Press.

—. (1995). *Social Currents in Eastern Europe: The Sources and Consequences of the Great Transformation.* Durham, N.C.: Duke U. P.

—. (1996). "Eastern Europe's Painful Transition," *Current History* 95.599, 69–74.

—. (1997). *Whose Democracy? Nationalism, Religion, and the Doctrine of Collective Rights in Post-1989 Eastern Europe.* New York: Rowman & Littlefield.

Rau, Z. (1987). "Some Thoughts on Civil Society in Eastern Europe and the Lockean Contractarian Approach," *Political Studies* 35, 573–592.

Rawls, J. (1971). *A Theory of Justice*. Cambridge: Harvard U. P.

RFE Report (Hungarian Section/KK) (1977). "Thirty Hungarian Intellectuals Express Solidarity with Charter 77," Munich, January 20.

—. (1978): "Prominent Dissident Intellectuals Emigrate from Hungary," Munich, February 10.

—. (1984). "Appeal of Hungarian Samizdat Literature Publisher Rejected," Munich, 24 May (RAD/Reisch).

Ricoeur, P. (1984), "The Political Paradox," in William Connelly, ed. *Legitimacy and the State*. New York: New York U. P.

Richter, M. (1995). *The History of Political and Social Concepts: A Critical Introduction*. Oxford: Oxford U. P.

Riese, H. P., ed. (1979). *Since the Prague Spring: The Continuing Struggle for Human Rights in Czechoslovakia*. New York: Random House.

Rigby, T.H. and Fehér, F., eds. (1982). *Political Legitimation in Communist States*. London: Macmillan Press.

Rödel, U., ed. (1990). *Autonome Gesellschaft und libertäre Demokratie*. Frankfurt am Main: Suhrkamp Verlag.

—. Frankenberg, G. and Dubiel, H. (1989). *Die demokratische Frage*. Frankfurt am Main: Suhrkamp Verlag.

Rosenbaum, W. (1972–1973). "The Background of the Anti-Zionist Campaign of 1967–1968 in Poland," *Essays in History* 17, University of Virginia.

Rosenberg, T. (1996). *The Haunted Land: Facing Europe's Ghosts after Communism*. New York: Vintage.

Rosenblum, M. Turnley, D., and Turnley, P. (1990). *Moments of Revolution*: New York: Stewart, Tabori and Chang.

Rousseau, J. J. (1967). *The Social Contract and the Origins of Inequality*. New York: Simon and Schuster.

—. (1974). *Émile*. Trans. B. Foxley. Toronto: J. P. Dent & Sons.

Rueschemeyer, M., ed. (1998). *Women in the Politics of Postcommunist Eastern Europe*. Armonk, N.Y. and London: M. E. Sharpe. Second Edition.

Rupnik, J. (1989). *"The Other Europe": The Rise and Fall of Communism in East-Central Europe*. New York: Pantheon Books.

—. (1992). "Central Europe or Mitteleuropa?" *Daedalus* Spring, 249–277.

—. (1998). "Risks and Responsibilities: Grandeur, danger, and opportunity," *Transitions* 5.4, 18–20.

Rutland, P. (1999). "The Meaning of 1989," *Transitions* 6.1, 24–28.

Ryback, T. (1990). *Rock Around the Bloc: A History of Rock Music in Eastern Europe and the Soviet Union*. New York: Oxford U. P.

Sachs, J. (1991). "Spontaneous Privatization: A Comment," *Soviet Economy* 7.4, 317–321.

—. (1993). *Poland's Jump to a Market Economy*. Cambridge, Mass.: M.I.T. Press.

—. (1995). "Consolidating Capitalism," *Foreign Policy* 98, 50–64.

—. (1998). "Global Capitalism: Making it work," *The Economist*, September 12–18, 23–25.

— and Woo, W. T. (1994). "Introduction: Experiences in the Transition to a Market Economy," *Journal of Comparative Economics* 18, 271–275.

Safire, W. (1995). "Hello, Central," *The New York Times Magazine*, March 12, 24–25.

Sajó, A. (1996). "The Roundtable Talks in Hungary," in Jon Elster, ed., *The Roundtable Talks and the Breakdown of Communism*. Chicago and London: University of Chicago Press.

Sakwa, R. (1999). *Postcommunism*. Buckingham and Philadelphia: Open U. P.

Sanford, G. (1986). *Military Rule in Poland*, London and Sidney: Croon Helm.

—., ed., trans. (1990). *The Solidarity Congress, 1981: The Great Debate*. New York: St. Martin's Press.

Schmitter, P. C. and Karl, T. L. (1994). "The Conceptual Travels of Transitologists and Consolidologists: How Far to the East Should They Attempt to Go?" *Slavic Review* 53.1, 173–185.

—. (1995). "From an Iron Curtain to a Paper Curtain: Grounding Transitologists or Students of Postcommunism?" *Slavic Review* 54.4, 965–987.

Schöpflin, G. (1983). "Poland and Eastern Europe", in Abraham Brumberg, ed., *Poland: Genesis of a Revolution*. New York: Random House, 123–134.

—. (1985). "Unity and Diversity in Eastern Europe: Poland, Czechoslovakia, Hungary in the Mid-1980s," *East European Reporter* 1.1, 2–8.

—. (1990). "The Political Traditions of Eastern Europe," *Daedalus* Winter, 55–90.

— and Wood, N., eds. (1989). *In Search of Europe*. London: Polity Press.

Schonberg, M. (1992). *Osvobozené*. Praha: Odeon.

Schweitzer, I. (1981). "Some Interrelations Between Enterprise Organization and the Economic Mechanism in Hungary," *Acta Oeconomica* 27, 3–4.

Scott, J. C. (1985). *Weapons of the Weak: Everyday Forms of Peasant Rebellion*. New Haven: Yale U. P.

—. (1990). *Domination and the Arts of Resistance: Hidden Transcripts*. New Haven: Yale University Press.

Selucký, R. (1970). *Czechoslovakia: The Plan that Failed*. Trans. D. Viney. London: Thomas Nelson and Sons.

—. (1975). "The Dubcek Era Revisited," *Problems of Communism* 24 (January–February), 21.

Seligman, A. (1992). *The Idea of Civil Society*. New York: Maxwell Macmillan.

Shils, E. (1991a). "Remembering the Congress of Cultural Freedom," *Encounter* 75.2, 53–65.

—. (1991b). "The Virtue of Civil Society," *Government and Opposition* 26, 3–20.

Shore, M. (1996). "The Sacred and the Myth: Havel's Greengrocer and the Transformation of Ideology in Communist Czechoslovakia," *Contagion: Journal of Violence, Mimesis, and Culture* 3, 163–182.

—. (1998). "Engineering in the Age of Innocence: A Genealogy of Discourse inside the Czechoslovak Writers' Union, 1949–1967," *East European Politics and Societies* 12.3, 397–441.

Short, A. (1985). "Liberal Hungary?" *East European Reporter* 1.2, 34–36.

Šik, O. (1976). *The Third Way*. Trans. M. Sling. London: Wildwood House.

—. (1985). *For Humane Economic Democracy*. New York: Praeger.

Šiklová, J. (1990). "The 'Gray Zone' and the Future of Dissent in Czechoslovakia," *Social Research* 57.2, 347–363.

—. (1993a). "McDonalds, Terminators, and Coca-Cola Ads and Feminism?" in S. Trnka and L. Busheikin, eds., *Bodies of Bread and Butter: Reconfiguring Women's Lives in the Post-Communist Czech Republic*, 7–11.

—. (1993b). "Backlash," *Social Research* 60.4, 737–749.

—. (1996). "What Did We Lose After 1989?" *Social Research* 63.2, 531–541.

Šimečka, M. (1984a). *The Restoration of Order: The Normalization of Czechoslovakia, 1969–1976*. Trans. A. G. Brain. London: Verso.

—. (1984b). "A World with Utopias or Without Them," in P. Alexander and R. Gill, eds., *Utopias*. London: Duckworth.

—. (1993). *The Year of the Frog*. Trans. P. Petro. New York: Simon and Schuster.

—. (2002). *Letters from Prison*. Prague: Twisted Spoon Press.

Skilling, H. G. (1961). "Interest Groups in Soviet Politics," *World Politics* 18.3, 435–445.

—. (1976). *Czechoslovakia's Interrupted Revolution*. Princeton, N.J.: Princeton University Press.

—. (1980a). "Pluralism in Communist Societies: Straw Men and Red Herrings," *Studies in Comparative Communism* 14, 82–88.

—. (1980b). "Charter 77 and the Musical Underground," *Canadian Slavonic Papers* 22.1, 1–14.

—. (1981). *Charter 77 and Human Rights in Czechoslovakia*. London: George Allen & Unwin.

—. (1983). "Interest Groups and Communist Politics Revisited," *World Politics* 27, 1–27.

—. (1985). "Independent Currents in Czechoslovakia," *Problems of Communism* Jan–Feb, 32–49.

—. (1988). "Parallel *Polis*, or An Independent Society in Central and Eastern Europe: An Inquiry," *Social Research* 55.1–2, 211–246.

—. (1989). *Samizdat and an Independent Society in Central and Eastern Europe*. London: Macmillan.

—. (1994). *T. G. Masaryk: Against the Current 1882–1914*. University Park: Pennsylvania State U. P.

—. (1997). "Archive of Freedom," *Acta contemporanea: K pěti desetiletím Viléma Prečana*, 400–419

—. (1997–1998). "Czechs and Slovaks 1998," *International Journal* (Winter), 73–93.

—. and Griffiths, F. (1971). *Interest Groups in Soviet Politics*. Princeton, N. J.: Princeton U. P.

—. and Wilson, P., eds. (1991) *Civic Freedom in Central Europe: Voices from Czechoslovakia*. London: Macmillan, 35–41.

Skinner, Q. (1978). *The Foundations of Modern Political Thought*. Cambridge: Cambridge U. P.

Skocpol, T. (1979). *States and Social Revolutions: A Comparative Analysis of France, Russia, and China*. New York: Cambridge U. P.

Škvorecký, J. (1970). *The Cowards*. Trans. J. Němcová. London: Penguin.

—. (1971). *All the Bright Young Men and Women: Of a Personal History of the Czech Cinema*. Toronto: University of Toronto Press.

—. (1997). *Headed for the Blues: A Memoir with Ten Stories*. Toronto: Alfred A. Knopf.

Smith, A. D. (1995). *Nations and Nationalism in a Global Era*. Cambridge, U.K.: Polity Press.

Smith, D. (1990). *The Conceptual Practices of Power: A Feminist Sociology of Knowledge*. Boston: Northeastern U. P.

Snitow, A. (1990). "A Gender Diary," in M. Hirsch and E. Fox, eds., *Conflicts in Feminism*. New York: Routledge.

Sobell, V. (1988). "Czechoslovakia: The Legacy of Normalization," *East European Politics and Societies* 2.1, 35–69.

Solomon, S.G., ed. (1983). *Pluralism in the Soviet Union: Essays in Honour of H. Gordon Skilling*. London: Macmillan.

Somogyi, L. (1993). *The Political Economy of the Transition Process in Eastern Europe*. Two volumes. Aldershot, U.K.: Edward Elgar.

Sommer, M. (1992). *Living in Freedom The Exhilaration and Anguish of Prague's Second Spring*. San Francisco: Mercury House.

Soros, G. (1997). "The Capitalist Threat," *The Atlantic Monthly* 279.2, 45–48.

Staniszkis, J. (1984). *Poland's Self-Limiting Revolution*. Ed. and trans. J. T. Gross. Princeton: Princeton U. P.

—. (1991). *The Dynamics of the Breakthrough in Eastern Europe*. Trans. C. A. Kisiel. Forward by I. Szelényi. Los Angeles: University of California Press.

Stark, D. (1992). "Path Dependence and Privatization in East Central Europe," *East European Politics and Societies* 6.1, 17–54.

Starski, S. (1982). *Class Struggle in Classless Poland*. Boston: South End Press.

Steinlauf, M. (1997). *Bondage to the Dead: Poland and the Memory of Holocaust*. Syracuse, NY: Syracuse U. P.

Stokes, G. (1991). *From Stalinism to Pluralism: A Documentary History of Eastern Europe Since 1945*. New York: Oxford U. P.

—. (1993). *The Walls Came Tumbling down: The Collapse of Communism in Eastern Europe*. Oxford: Oxford U. P.

Stolzfus, N. (1997). "Dissent under Socialism: Opposition, Reform and the West German Media in the German Democratic Republic in the 1980s," in R. G. Fox and O. Starn, eds., *Between Resistance and Revolution: Cultural Politics and Social Protest*. New Brunswick, N.J.: Rutgers U. P.

Strauss, L. (1952). *Persecution and the Art of Writing*. Glencoe, Ill.: The Free Press.

Streeck, W. and Schmitter, P. C. (1991). "From National Corporatism to Transnational Pluralism: Organized Interests in a Single European Market," *Politics and Society* 19.2, 133–164.

Sugár, A. (1990). *Dubček Speaks.* London: I. B. Tauris.

Svítak, I. (1966). "Kafka as Philosopher," *Survey* 58, 36–40.

—. (1971). *The Czechoslovak Experiment 1968-1989.* New York: Columbia U. P.

Szakolczai, A. (1994). "Thinking beyond the East–West Divide: Foucault, Patočka, and the Care of the Self," *Social Research* 61.2, 297–323.

Szelényi, I. (1977). "Notes on the Budapest School," *Critique* 8, 61–67.

Tamás, G. M. (1988). "There is More to Politics than Human Rights," *Beszélő*, Special Issue, pp. 10–14.

—.(1992). "Socialism, Capitalism, and Modernity," *Journal of Democracy* 3.3, 60–74.

—. (1994). "A Disquisition on Civil Society," *Social Research* 61.2, 205.

Taras, R. (1995). *Consolidating Democracy in Poland.* Boulder, Co.: Westview Press.

Tarcov, N. (1984). *Locke's Education for Liberty.* Chicago: University of Chicago Press.

Tarrow, S. (1991). "Aiming at a Moving Target: Social Science and the Recent Rebellions in Eastern Europe," *PS* 24, 17.

—. (1994). *Power in Movement: Social Movements, Collective Action, and Politics.* Cambridge: Cambridge U. P.

Taylor, C. (1975). *Hegel.* New York: Cambridge U. P.

—. (1989). *The Sources of the Self.* Cambridge, Mass.: Harvard U. P.

—. (1990). "Modes of Civil Society," *Public Culture* 3, 95–118.

—. (1991). *The Malaise of Modernity.* Concord, Ont.: Anansi.

Therborn, G. (1977). "The Rule of Capital and the Rise of Democracy," *New Left Review* 103, 3–41.

—. (1984a). "Classes and States: Welfare State Developments, 1881–1981," *Studies in Political Economy* 14, 7–41.

—. (1984b). "The Prospects of Labour and the Transformation of Advanced Capitalism," *New Left Review* 145, 5–38.

Thompson, E. P. (1980). *The Making of the English Working Class.* London: Penguin.

Thoreau, H. D. (1967). *The Variorum Civil Disobedience.* New York: Twayne.

Tilly, C. (1993). *European Revolutions 1492–1992.* Oxford: Blackwell.

Tischner, J. (1981). *Etyka Solidarnośći.* Wyd. 1. Kráków: Wydawn. Znak.

—. (1987). *Marxism and Christianity.* Washington, D.C.: Georgetown U. P.

Tismaneanu, V. (1989). *In Search of Civil Society: Independent Peace Movements in the Soviet Bloc.* New York: Routledge.

—. (1992). *Reinventing Politics: Eastern Europe from Stalin to Havel.* New York: Maxwell Macmillan.

Tocqueville, A. de (1969). *Democracy in America.* Trans. G. Lawrence. New York: Doubleday.

Tőkés, R. ed. (1979). *Opposition in Eastern Europe.* Baltimore: Johns Hopkins U. P.

—. (1996). *Hungary's Negotiated Revolution: Economic Reform, Social Change, and Political Succession.* Cambridge: Cambridge U. P.

Toma, P. A. and Völgyes, I. (1977). *Politics in Hungary.* San Francisco: W.H. Freeman and Company.

Touraine, A. (1988). *The Return of the Actor.* Minneapolis: University of Minnesota Press.

—. et al. (1983). *Solidarity: The Analysis of a Social Movement: Poland 1980–1981.* Cambridge: Cambridge U. P.

Trensky, P. (1978). *Czech Drama since World War II.* White Plains, N.Y.: M. E. Sharpe.

Trevisani, S. (1978). "Why They are Leaving Hungary," *L'Unita,* February 9.

Trnka, S. and Busheikin, L. eds. (1993). *Bodies of Bread and Butter: Reconfiguring Women's Lives in the Post-Communist Czech Republic.* Prague: Prague Gender Studies Centre.

Trojanowska, T. (1994). "Living in Margins and Mazes or Freedom Worth Considering: Mrożek's *The Emigrants* and Havel's *The Audience*." *Canadian Slavonik Papers* 36. 3–4, 397–411.

True, J. (1995). "Successions/Secessions? Identity, Gender Politics and Post-Communism," *Political Expressions* 1.1, 31–50.

Tucker, A. (1990). "Vaclav Havel's Heideggerianism," *Telos* 85, 63–78.

—. (1998). "Intellectual Responsibility: The Specter of Benda and the Phantom of Bakunin," *Telos* 110: 181–191.

—. (2000b). *The Philosophy and Politics of Czech Dissidence from Patočka to Havel.* Pittsburgh: University of Pittsburgh Press.

Tucker, R. C., ed. (1977). *Stalinism: Essays in Historical Interpretation.* New York: W. W. Norton.

Tully, J. ed., (1988). *Meaning and Context: Quentin Skinner and His Critics.* Oxford: Polity Press.

Tymowski, A.W. (1993). "Poland's Unwanted Social Revolution," *East European Politics and Societies* 7.2, 169–202.

Udovički, J. and Ridgeway, D., eds. (1997). *Burn This House: The Making and Unmaking of Yugoslavia.* Durham, N.C.: Duke U. P.

The Unfinished Revolution (1991). Proceedings of the National Endowment for Democracy's Third International Conference on Democracy. April 15–16, Washington, D.C.

Urban, J. (1997). "Robin Hood and His Merry Band 20 Years Later," *Transitions* 3.3, 9–11.

U.S. Helsinki Watch Committee (1987a). *A Decade of Dedication: Charter 77 1977–1987.* New York: U.S. Helsinki Watch Committee.

— (1987b). *Violations of the Helsinki Accords.* Separate reports for Poland, Czechoslovakia and Hungary. New York: U.S. Helsinki Watch Committee.

Vaculík, L. (1967). *The Relations Between Citizen and Power.* Paper Presented at the Czechoslovak Writers Conference. London: Liberal International British Group.

—. (1987). *A Cup of Coffee with My Interrogator: The Prague Chronicles of Ludvik Vaculík.* Trans. G. Theiner. London: Readers International.

Valenta, J. (1991). *Soviet Intervention in Czechoslovakia, 1968: Anatomy of a Decision.* Baltimore: Johns Hopkins U. P.

Vali, F. A. (1961). *Rift and Revolution in Hungary.* Cambridge: Cambridge U. P.

Vaničková, N. (1997). "Passion Play: Underground Rock Music in Czechoslovakia, 1968–1989." MA Thesis, York University, Toronto. Used with permission of author.

Vargha, J. (1990). "An Interview with Vargha," *East European Reporter* 4.2, 78–79.

Verdery, K. (1996). *What Was Socialism, and What Comes Next?* Princeton, N. J.: Princeton U. P.

Villa, D. R. (1992). "Postmodernism and the Public Sphere," *American Political Science Review* 86.3, 712–721.

Violations of Civil and Political Rights in Czechoslovakia and the Helsinki Accord (1977). Report presented to the Review Second Session of the Conference on Security and Cooperation in Europe, Belgrade, Yugoslavia. Washington: D.C.: Council on Free Czechoslovakia.

Wałęsa, L. (1992). *The Struggle and the Triumph.* New York: Arcade.

Wallace, C. (1995). "Citizenship and Social Policy in East-Central Europe," in M. Mendell and K. Nielson, eds., *Europe: Central and East.* Montréal: Black Rose Books.

Wainwright, H. (1995). "Civic Movements and the Politics of Knowledge," in M. Mendell and K. Nielson, eds., *Europe: Central and East.* Montréal: Black Rose Books.

Walzer, M. (1988). *The Company of Critics: Social Criticism and Political Commitment in the Twentieth Century.* New York: Basic Books.

—. (1991). "The Idea of Civil Society," *Dissent,* Spring, 293–304.

Ward, A. (1985). "Peace, Politics, and Utopia: Václav Havel's 'Anatomy of a Reticence'," *East European Reporter* 1.3, 38–41.

Watson, P. (1993a). "Eastern Europe's Silent Revolution: Gender," *Sociology* 27.3, 471–487.

—. (1993b). "The Rise of Masculinism in Eastern Europe," *New Left Review* 198, 71–82.

—. (1997). "Civil Society and the Politics of Difference in Eastern Europe," in J. W. Scott, C. Kaplan, and D. Keates, eds., *Transitions, Environments, Translations: Feminisms in International Politics.* New York: Routledge.

Webber, M. J. and Rigby, D. L. (1996). *The Golden Age Illusion.* New York: The Guildford Press.

Weigle, M. A. and Butterfield, J. (1992). "Civil Society in Reforming Communist Regimes: The Logic of Emergence," *Comparative Politics* 25.1, 1–23.

Weschler, L. (1982). *Solidarity: Poland in the Season of its Passion.* New York: Simon and Schuster.

—. (1992). "The Velvet Purge: The Trials of Jan Kavan," *The New Yorker,* October 19, 66–95.

Wheaton, B. and Kavan, Z. (1992). *The Velvet Revolution: Czechoslovakia, 1988–1991.* Boulder, Co.: Westview Press.

Whipple, T., ed. (1991). *After the Velvet Revolution: Václav Havel and the New Leaders of Czechoslovakia Speak Out.* New York: Freedom House.

Williams, D. E. (1991). "Political Theory by Other Means: An Introduction," *International Political Science Review* 12.2, 91–99.

Williams, K. (1997). *Prague Spring and its aftermath Czechoslovak Politics, 1968–1970*. Cambridge: Cambridge U. P.

Williamson, J., ed. (1986). "Woman Is an Island: Femininity and Colonization" in Tania Modleski, ed., *Studies in Entertainment: Critical Approaches to Mass Culture*. Bloomington: Indiana UP, 99–118.

—. (1994). *The Political Economy of Policy Reform*. Washington, D.C.: Institute for International Economics.

Wnuk-Lipiński, E., ed. (1995). *After Communism:A Multidisiplinary Approach to Radical Change*. Warsaw: Institute of Political Academy of Sciences.

Wolchik, S. (1991). *Czechoslovakia in Transition*. London: Pinter.

Wolff, L. (1994). *Inventing Eastern Europe:The Map of Civilization on the Mind of the Enlightenment*. Stanford: Stanford University Press.

Wood, E. M. (1990). "The Uses and Abuses of 'Civil Society'," *Socialist Register*, 60–84.

Wood, N. (1978). "The Social History of Political Theory," *Political Theory* 6.3, 345–367.

Woodward, S. L. (1995). *Balkan Tragedy*. Washington, D.C.: Brookings Institution.

Wooton, D., ed. (1993). *Political Writings of John Locke*. New York: Mentor.

World Bank (1996). *From Plan to Market*. New York: Oxford U. P.

Young, I. M. (1990a). *Throwing Like a Girl and other Essays in Feminist Philosophy and Social Theory*. Bloomington: Indiana U. P.

—. (1990b). *Justice and the Politics of Difference*. Princeton: Princeton U. P.

Young-Bruehl, E. (1982). *Hannah Arendt: For Love of the World*. New Haven, Conn.:Yale U. P.

Zamoyski, A. (1995). *The Polish Way: A Thousand-year History of the Poles and their Culture*. New York: Hippocrene Books.

Zielonka, J. (1989). *Political Ideas in Contemporary Poland*. Aldershot, U.K.: Avebury.

Zinner, P. E. (1956). *National Communism and Popular Revolt in Eastern Europe*. New York: Columbia U. P.

—. (1962). *Revolution in Hungary*. New York: Columbia University Press.

Zuzowski, R. (1991). "The Origins of Open Organized Dissent in Today's Poland: KOR and Other Dissident Groups," *East European Quarterly* XXV, 59–90.

—. (1992). *Political Dissent and Opposition in Poland: The Workers' Defense Committee "KOR."* Westport, Conn.: Praeger.

Personal Interviews

Abrahám, Samuel. October 16, 1997. Bratislava.

Ambros, Veronika. July 28, 1998. Toronto.

Arato, Andrew. April 20, 1995. New York.

Benda, Václav. August 30, 1995. Prague.

Białek, Lydia. July 27, 1995. Cracow.

Bauer, Tamás. October 9, 1997. Budapest.

Day, Barbara. March 15, 1998. Toronto.

Eörsi, István. August 22, 1995. Budapest.

Fodor, Gábor. October 14, 1997. Budapest.

Gebert, Konstanty. July 26, 1995. Cracow.

Goldfarb, Jeffrey. November 21, 1995. New York.

Haraszti, Miklós. August 18, 1995. Budapest.

Heller, Ágnes. August 22, 1995. Budapest.

Hejdánek, Ladislav. October 21, 1997. Prague.

Holubová, Miroslava. October 21, 1997. Prague.

Jedlicki, Jerzy. July 21, 1995. Cracow.

Juráňová, Jana. July 25, 1995. Cracow.

Karádi, Éva. October 12, 1997. Budapest.

Kis, János. November 21, 1995. New York.

Klíma, Ivan. August 30, 1995 (by telephone). Prague.

Kowalik, Tadeusz. August 10, 1995. Warsaw.

Król, Marcin. August 10, 1995. Warsaw.

Kusý, Miroslav. October 14, 1997. Bratislava.

McRae, Robert. June 2, 1998. Ottawa.

Michnik, Adam. August 11, 1995. Warsaw.

Mikloško, František. October 17, 1997. Bratislava.

Palouš, Martin. October 20, 1997. Prague.

Pánek, Šimon. August 31, 1995. Prague.

Prečan, Vilém. October 20, 1997. Prague.

Šiklová, Jiřina. October 21, 1997. Prague.

Szigeti, László. October 16, 1997. Bratislava.

Tymowski, Andrzej. November 20, 1995. New York.

Urbánek, Zdeněk. August 31, 1995. Prague.

Vaculík, Ludvík. August 30, 1995. Prague.

Wilkes, Kathy. June 22, 1998. Oxford.

Skilling Seminar, Toronto

Abrahám, Samuel. February 15, 1999.
Ambros, Veronika. March 20, 1999.
Cornwall, Mark. October 28, 2000.
Day, Barbara. March 1, 1998.
Iggers, Wilma. January 10, 1999.
Keane, John. November 18, 1996.
Magosci, Robert. May 7, 2000.
McRae, Robert. January 10, 1997.
Palouš, Martin. January 16, 1999.
Salivarová, Zdena. April 26, 1996.
Schonberg, Michal. March 16, 1997.
Shore, Marci. April 30, 2002.
Skilling, H. G. February 2, 1996; January 10, 1999.
Škvorecký, Josef. June 24, 1996.
Sparling, Don. October 13, 2001.
Tuma, Oldřich. January 19, 2002.
Wilson, Paul. February 25, 1996.

Filmography/Videography

Adams, R., Director (1986). *Citizens.*
Costa-Gavras, A., Director (1970). *The Confession.*
Czechoslovakia after 1989 (1994). Documentary on Public Television (PBS).
Gartner, Hana (1995). Interview with Václav Havel. Canadian Broadcasting Corporation (CBC).
Holland, A., Director (1989). *To Kill a Priest.*
Jaromil, J., Director (1968). *The Joke.*
Kaufman, P., Director (1988). *The Unbearable Lightness of Being.*
Menzel, J., Director (1966). *Closely Watched Trains.*
Němec, J., Director (1968). *Oratorio for Prague.*
Sverák, J., Director (1997). *Kolya.*
Szabó, I., Director (1999). *Sunshine.*
Szabó, I., Director (1993). *Sweet Emma, Dear Böbe.*
Szabó, I., Director (1987). *Colonel Redl.*
Szabó, I., Director (1984). *Mephisto.*
Szabó, I., Director (1970). *Love Film.*
Von Trotta, M., Director (1995). *Das Versprechen.*
Wajda, A., Director (1981a). *Man of Iron.*
Wajda, A., Director (1981b). *Workers '80.*
Wajda, A., Director (1976). *Man of Marble.*

NOTES

Preface

1 For example, the work of Thomas Paine was critical to the thinking behind the American Revolution, and arguably the US constitution is derived from the language and principles of John Locke (Tarcov, 1984). Both Edmund Burke and Alexis de Tocqueville had much to say in the wake of the American and the French Revolutions.

2 Isaac does not "deny that attention has been paid to these events" and cites the work of comparativists in the field of political science, and especially the newly-created *Journal of Democracy*. Moreover, what he calls "public intellectual journals" such as *Dissent, The Nation, Praxis International*, and *Social Research* have published numerous essays relating to 1989. (Isaac might also have added *Constellations, Social Text, Telos, October, Representations, Millennium, Social Anthropology, New Left Review, Socialist Register, International Journal of Politics, Culture, and Society*, and many of the core publications of feminist theory, such as *The Feminist Review, The Journal of Women's History, Women's Studies International Forum*, and *Gender and Society* according to one of his respondents, Kirstie McClure. I would also add *Hypaetia* to the list.) However, his argument is that the "*principal* journals of the field, the main origins of scholarship and intellectual exchange, have been silent" (my emphasis; 1995:637).

3 Although I would argue that engagement is a necessary condition for the production of great political theory, it is obviously not a sufficient condition, as most of the "thinking practitioners" of political life are partisans, hacks, or policy wonks.

4 See the introduction to volume I, Quentin Skinner (1978), p. xi.

5 The Versailles peace treaty signed in the Palais Trianon on June 4, 1920. In the wake of World War I, the victorious powers divided up much of Hungary's former territory among neighboring states which for the most part came into existence for the first time, i.e. Romania, Czechoslovakia, and Yugoslavia. See Hoensch, 1996, especially pp. 98–106.

6 I use the term "self-reflexive" and "self-reflexively" throughout this study. In keeping with contemporary usage in political theory and feminist theory in particular, this term refers to the deliberate and self-conscious reflection

of theorists and activists, especially as they attempt to be sensitive to context and environment throughout the process of critical engagement.

7 Although I would argue that most activities and organizations were broadly and inevitably political in nature, I use this term as not all dissident activities or organizations were considered by their memberships as political. In fact their very existence and belief in "self-limitation" dictated that this be the case. Thus KOR called itself a committee for workers' self-defense, and Charter 77 was described as a human rights organization.

8 Thus I have in mind Michnik and Kuroń, but not Lech Wałęsa. The line I am drawing, of course, is not always so clear, for some, like Zbigniew Bujak, defy easy categorization.

9 I have included Kołakowski because, despite his high-profile expulsion from Poland and his subsequent re-thinking of many of his original ideals, a number of his essays, such as "Hope and Hopelessness," published in the West in 1971 but subsequently available in Poland, was instrumental in helping chart the future course and strategies of a number of the movements.

10 Patočka is included because although he was only briefly a dissident (and suffered a fatal heart attack as a result of an interrogation following his decision to become a Charter 77 spokesperson), his philosophy and unique brand of Czech phenomenology was critically influential on Havel and others.

11 For a complete discussion of intellectuals and their role in political change in the region, see András Bozóki, ed. (1999).

12 This phrase has been attributed to Leonid Brezhnev, the former leader of the USSR who was apparently exasperated with efforts to idealize socialism—it was both more important and more realistic to pay attention to "actually-existing socialism," that is, the socialism of the former Soviet empire. Of course, this catch phrase has been easily converted post-1989 and post-1991 into "previously-existing socialism" to refer to the same in the past tense.

13 See both Carl J. Friedrich and Zbigniew Brzezinski (1956), and Hannah Arendt (1979, originally published 1948). For a thoughtful discussion and review of the concept of totalitarianism, in terms of its essentialist meaning as a tool of American counter-ideology as well as the heuristic, historical, and even metaphysical significance granted to it by Arendt and Camus, see Jeffrey Isaac (1992), especially pp. 37–67.

14 Most influential in formulating and portraying the "interest group" approach is the work of H. Gordon Skilling and Franklyn Griffiths (1971). For Skilling's important contribution to this debate in the literature on comparative communism, see "Interest Groups and Communist Politics," *World Politics* 18.3 (April 1961): 435–45; *Studies in Comparative Communism* 13 (Spring 1979): 6–20 and 21–38 and 14 (Spring 1980):82–88 and

89–90 (Spring 1979) for article by Andrew János entitled "Interest Groups and the Structure of Power" (with comments by William E. Odam, Sarah Meiklejohn Terry, and Zvi Gitelman) and Spring 1980 for article by Skilling entitled "Pluralism in Communist Societies: Straw Men and Red Herrings" with rejoinder by Andrew János); and "Interest Groups and Communist Politics Revisited", *World Politics* 37 (October 1983): 1–27.

Chapter 2: Poland: The Harbinger of Crisis and Collapse

1 I do not mean to hypostasize the categories "worker" and "intellectual," as both were relatively heterogeneous in reality. However, as this study focuses largely on intellectual dissent, it is necessary to draw a distinction— not to be assumed as static or artificial—between those who were valorized by the party-state (its workers) and those who engaged in intellectual labor. For my purpose, a subset of intellectuals can be regarded as political theorists given their written efforts to critically examine and analyze their experiences and possibilities.

2 Domestic and proximate causes of the riots in Poznań were food and housing shortages, a decline in the standard of living since the late 1940s as well as high prices. In June, 1956 because of increased production quotas (and therefore decreased real wages, given a piece-rate payment system), the workers at ZISPO (*Zakłady Imieniem Stalina* or The Stalin Railway Car Factory), Poznań's largest factory, launched a series of strikes and workers' protests. Military force was required to bring the situation under control (although some units of the militia and civil police did side with the demonstrators—over 100 people were killed; 900 wounded, and 750 arrested (Ekiert and Kubik, 2001: 28). The riots were short-lived and the workers did not get an opportunity to present their demands publicly. However, a delegation did travel to Warsaw to demand repayment of taxes, a 20% wage increase, and better working conditions. As in the case of Hungary in 1956, the international atmosphere also played a role. The Korean War armistice had been signed and the Geneva 1954 conference on Indochina at least temporarily settled that conflict. Within the USSR, the declaration of the possibility of peaceful coexistence, the rapprochement with Yugoslavia, Khrushchev's "New Course," and the far-reaching impact of the "secret speech" at the Twentieth Congress of the CPSU were critical milestones on the path to intra-party rebellion and societal conflict in both countries. See Andrzej Korbonski, "October 1956: Crisis of Legitimacy or Palace Revolution," in Jane Leftwich Curry and Luba Fajfer, eds. (1996), and Johanna Granville (2001), "Hungarian and Polish Reactions to the Events of 1956: New Archival Evidence" *Europe–Asia Studies* 53.7, 1051–1076. Korbonski accurately notes that unlike for Hungary and Czechoslovakia, there is no comprehensive landmark study of the Polish events of 1956 akin to Paul Zinner and Ferenc Vali's accounts of the Hun-

garian revolt of 1956 (and the more recently published collection by Litván) or to H. Gordon Skilling's monumental study of the Prague Spring.

3 Gomułka was an indigenous communist who like Imre Nagy had been discredited in the immediate postwar period by Poland's Soviet sponsors, largely because of his demands for a separate and nationalist path for Polish socialism, and his opposition to single-party domination and rapid collectivization. His release from prison in 1954 was fortuitous, as he was untouched by criticisms of the Stalinist leadership, especially the revelations of Józef Światło upon his defection to the West (his confessions were widely broadcast on the BBC and Radio Free Europe).

4 Although Gomułka was strongly opposed to enforced collectivization, the regime was never fully reconciled to the abandonment of socialist agricultural production. The party-state did not grant peasants legal title to their lands until the mid-1970s under Gierek, and modernization of agriculture was always linked in ideology and in public policy to its ultimate socialization. Although the peasants did gain control over land, supplies, equipment, and methods of distribution remained in the hands of the party-state, a fact which encouraged bottlenecks and disequilibrium in the agricultural sector throughout the authoritarian communist period.

5 In 1958 legislation was passed that effectively removed any power held by the workers' councils. See Michael H. Bernhard (1993), pp. 38–39.

6 Lange, one of Poland's leading economists in the 1950s, was aligned with the progressive reform-minded wing of the party and publicly criticized the failures of the economic system to raise the standard of living. Trained at the University of Chicago, he became famous for debates with von Mises and Hayek. He promoted increasing food supplies and consumer goods, providing workers with more control, and encouraging small firms and independent peasants. To what extent such structural reforms would have yielded a more responsive and effective socialist economy is open to debate, one that has been taken up by one of his students and chief biographer, Tadeusz Kowalik.

7 Nowa Huta is one of the new cities built as a result of postwar industrialization. Its location and purpose also had an ideological function as a model for a socialist future. It was constructed immediately next door to the historic seat of royalty and intellectual development—Cracow. The pollution from the steelworks of Nowa Huta and a neighboring aluminum smelter (finally closed down in the 1980s) resulted in considerable environmental damage to Cracow's historic buildings.

8 The entire poem is reproduced in English in Paul E. Zinner (1957), pp. 40–48.

9 Similar clubs of the young intelligentsia operated throughout Poland, and the Warsaw KKK served as a model. These were among the few fora where controversial ideas might be openly discussed. The Warsaw KKK was closed down after an incident in a crowded Warsaw café when a scuffle

broke out between Wadlemar Kasprzak (a suspected *agent provocateur*) and one of the club's members. This, however, was simply the pretext, as club officials were later told by Warsaw City Council that, among other things, they were responsible for right-wing nationalist deviationism, questioning the authority of the party and negatively influencing youth (Raina, 1978: 70–71).

10 *Kultura* was an important Polish emigré journal published in Paris. Peter Raina, in his detailed study *Political Opposition in Poland, 1954–1977*, points out how shocking this was at the time, since *Kultura* was then easily accessible in public libraries, and could be borrowed and read without fear of reprisal (see Raina, 1978: 64–65).

11 My analysis here is much indebted to a conversation with intellectual historian and former TKN activist Jerzy Jedlicki, July 21, 1995.

12 Świerczewski, or "General Walter" was a Polish communist famous for having fought in Spain. Hemingway portrayed him as General Goltz in *For Whom the Bell Tolls*.

13 The PPS was forcibly unified with the Communist Party in 1948—thus the *Polska Zjednoczona Partia Robotnicza* (PZPR: also known by its English acronym PUWP) or the Polish United Workers Party was born. Many PPS members were expelled at this time.

14 The common ancestry of prewar socialism can be inferred from earlier accounts of the political opposition and of KOR but is not dealt with explicitly (for example, Lipski, 1985, and Raina, 1978). Bernhard (1993) mentions PPS membership as having been overlooked by Lipski, but does not discuss the ramifications of this history of activism on the left.

15 This organization, originally founded by Adam Michnik and Jan Gross as high school students, was a sort of short-lived student-successor to the KKK.

16 The *Open Letter* was first published in the original in the West in Paris in 1966. It was later translated into English, French, German, and Italian, often published and disseminated by independent socialist groups.

17 The period between 1795 and 1918 when Poland was divided up by three empires: German, Austrian, and Russian.

18 This peculiar form of religious messianism is so entwined with Polish culture it is not even limited to Catholicism. A number of parallels have also been drawn to the messianic Chassidism of a substantial portion of Polish Jewry during the same period. The only close parallel is the case of religion in Ireland.

19 This chief negative consequence of this exclusivism has been the historical perpetuation of intense anti-Semitism, which unfortunately still remains among some clergy (Father Henryk Jańkowski and even current Primate Józef Glemp)—see Michael C. Steinlauf (1997).

20 Following a Vatican decree in 1949, the Church establishment proceeded to excommunicate members and supporters of communism.

21 Cardinal Wyszyński was arrested in September, 1953 as part of the Stalinist crackdown on the Church.

22 The leading exponent and ideological creator of *Znak* was Stanisław Stomma, who envisioned a dual strategy of working within the system (he and others were members of the *Sejm* from 1957 onward) and providing by their separation from the party a moderate and Catholic-based alternative to it. Michnik describes *Znak* as "neopositivist" in outlook, "... [taking] for granted Poland's loyalty to the USSR while at the same time rejecting Marxist doctrine and socialist ideology"(Michnik, 1985: 135–36).

23 The group around these publications was also instrumental in founding the KIK, the most important of which was located in Warsaw. The editorial board of *Tygodnik Powszechny* included Karol Wojtyła, the future Pope John Paul II.

24 Later, in 1976, *Znak* split as a result of *Sejm* leader Stanisław Stomma's absention during the constitutional amendment process. The pro-regime faction, known as *Neo-Znak*, was deliberately deployed by the party-state in its propaganda efforts. More importantly for the ensuing Church–Left alliance, the progressive elements of *Znak* united with the remaining KIK and developed an increasingly anti-regime, pro-opposition stance. Thereafter politicized lay people and prominent clergy lent their voices and their premises in support of the opposition. Cardinal Wyszyński later spoke out against reprisals against workers dismissed as a result of the protests in June 1976 (see below). In Cracow, Cardinal Karol Wojtyła (later Pope John-Paul II) allowed churches to be used for lectures of the TKN.

25 See Christopher Cviic, ed. (1983), pp. 98–100.

26 In fact, the exact date chosen was October 21, 1966, ten years to the day since the important Eighth Plenum of the party in 1956.

27 Adam Mickiewicz is foremost among Poland's nationalist poets. The play *Forefather's Eve* is thematically about the struggle of the Polish nation to overcome Tsarist oppression during the period of Russian partition. It was staged in 1967 to mark the fiftieth anniversary of the Russian Revolution and, prior to its run in Warsaw, had received favorable reviews in Moscow.

28 Over 3,000 people in Warsaw and 1,000 people in Wrocław signed a petition addressed to authorities decrying the banning of the play (Ekiert and Kubik, 2001: 33).

29 In a number of speeches and remarks Gomułka encouraged Jews to leave for Israel, denounced them for having more than one fatherland, accused them of being a "Fifth Column."

30 Interview with Konstanty Gebert, July 26, 1995.

31 Peter Raina details a number of these in his account: 1) a number of workers addressed the students indicating that they were being "forced" to demonstrate and mobilize against them and in Nowa Huta they actually staged a public demonstration of sympathy for the students; 2) during the sit-in strikes in Warsaw, the public continually delivered packages of food and mineral water to the students lest they be starved out; and 3) during the large student demonstration on March 8th, the strength of the procession grew from about 5,000 to approximately 20,000, and the ever-increasing crowd shouted slogans such as "Workers with Us" and "Warsaw with Us" (see Raina, 1978: 125–43).

32 Adam Michnik once stated in a 1988 interview with French student radical Daniel Cohn-Bendit of May 1968 fame that he remained "loyal to the whole anti-authoritarian project [of 1968] and that in effect Solidarity was a continuation of this same struggle. This self-identification with the 1960s also helps to explain the "disappointment" of many Polish activists and intellectuals toward what they see as the passivity, lack of commitment, and consumerism among "post-communist youth" (Interview with Jan Lityński, August 9, 1995).

33 For a complete discussion, see David Ost, 1990: 2–6.

34 Birkut was the subject of Wajda's earlier masterpiece *Man of Marble*, released in 1976. Wajda's fictional reality is more docudrama than movie— Birkut is killed in the 1970 uprising in Gdańsk.

35 Ironically, the price changes also included decreases in large consumer durables, such as refrigerators and washing machines, but since many Poles could not afford these more expensive items, such decreases were largely irrelevant. For background to the 1970 crisis and a comparison with events in 1956 and 1980, see Luba Fajfer, "December 1970: Prelude to Solidarity," in Curry and Fajfer (1996), especially pp. 70–72 and pp. 95–99.

36 Official data for these and other protests are found in Kubik and Ekiert, 2001: 21–46.

37 Further strikes took place along the Baltic Coast, and in cities inland—in Cracow, Wrocław, Katowice, Łódź, Poznań, and Wałbrzych. The authorities were concerned that if the Baltic situation continued to get out of control, popular discontent would metamorphose quickly into nationwide "counter-revolution." Given the narrow and authoritarian mind set of the Poland's leaders, they could not posit any alternatives between a crackdown and what they perceived as anti-socialism.

38 Although he was greeted with moderate support, neither the workers nor the intelligentsia greeted Gierek's promotion with the same jubilation and hope that accompanied Gomułka's rise to power in 1956. Willingness to help was matched by wariness and mistrust.

406 *Notes to Chapter 2*

39 Persky (1981: 44), Lipski (1985: 31), and Fajfer (1996: 94–95) make references to the Łódź workers. They were among the lowest-paid workers in the entire country, and among the most exploited in terms of overall working conditions. Unlike their male counterparts on the Baltic Coast, they did not opt to form strike committees and arrange lists of demands— their own lives could not afford this amount of time away from work and family (they were also fearful of reprisals that might result from such identifiable organization). As a result, however, their strikes were amorphous and almost impossible to control. The regime could deal with a strike committee or negotiate demands; it could not, however, stop the striking women of Łódź!

40 In fact, Fajfer (1996: 95) makes the salient point that it would have been more politically expedient and economically wise to simply raise the wages of the underpaid textile workers.

41 Giving large organizations control of investment and financial decisions made sense on one level, and was in keeping with the approach employed by Hungary with its New Economic Mechanism. However, the lack of planning and control combined with enterprise irresponsibility simply fuelled the buying binge and the ensuing inflationary wage/price spiral.

42 A number of local leaders did emerge in the Tri-City (*Trójmiasto*) area of Gdańsk, Gdynia, and Sopot who were later to become both instigators and leaders of Solidarity, such as Lech Wałęsa and Anna Walentynowicz. Their legitimacy and authority were considerably enhanced given their début during the 1970–1971 wave of strikes and protests.

43 This is also why the 1970 protests and especially the strikes in 1971 were less known to the outside world than the 1976 Radom/Ursus riots and the rise of Solidarity. Intellectuals such as Kołakowski and Kuroń had links to the international academic community, external media, and so on.

44 A student at the Medical Academy in Szczecin who was expelled for making political comments in a seminar.

45 A student at the Catholic University in Lublin who was imprisoned for insulting Polish authority in private correspondence, as well as possessing prewar "anti-Soviet literature" and copies of *Kultura*.

46 The Memorandum was signed by 59 essayists, poets, novelists, lawyers, priests, and academicians who authorized Lipiński to act on their behalf (Raina, 1978: 212).

47 The constitutional vote was carried out just prior to the *Sejm* elections, thus the party could effectively threaten to strike the name from the ballot of anyone who voted against the new Constitution and offer the carrot of promotion to those who did. This especially raised problems for the *Znak* group; when leader Stanisław Stomma abstained, his name disappeared from the upcoming ballot.

48 Not only did the party leaders not consult with workers (despite Gierek's personal promises to hold "broad social consultations" on food prices only six months earlier), but *Sejm* deputies were informed of the increases only hours before they were expected to grant legislative approval. See Terry, in Curry and Fajfer, eds., 1996: 110.

49 Workers also stopped the Paris–Warsaw express, and distributed to onlookers eggs, bread, and sugar obtained from one of the stopped trains (Bernhard, 1993: 51).

50 For example, workers from the Walter Metal Factory, the Radoskór Leather Factory, the Blaszanka Tin Can Factory, the Telephone Factory, the Tobacco Factories, and the Rolling Stock Repair shop all participated, and were joined by students and women working at home (Bernhard, 1993: 53).

51 A general strike was planned for the following day, but was called off given the withdrawal of the price hikes.

52 As Lipski documents, the chief method was the so-called "Path of Health" whereby the detainee was forced to walk through a line of armed policemen, each of whom would beat the victim with clubs, fists or their boots (Lipski, 1985: 34–36).

53 Bernhard notes that Lipski's estimates match those made independently by the European Trade Union Confederation (Bernhard, 1993: 64).

54 This is the major reason why the majority of the published members of KOR tended to be prominent and in some cases internationally-known intellectuals—it was more difficult for the party-state to retaliate against those whose biographies inspired recognition and respect. Prominence was not a guarantee, and police attacks were not limited to workers only. Ludwik Dorn was severely beaten and abused for being Jewish. Detentions and apartment searches were common, and many prominent members of KOR were arrested in 1977—including Michnik, Kuroń, Macierewicz, Naimski, Blumsztajn, Chojecki, Lipski, and Lityński. In a dramatic event that signalled this new round of repression in May, 1977 (and renewed resistance on the part of KOR) KOR student activist Stanisław Pyjas was murdered in Cracow.

55 *Biuletyn Informacjny* was named after the periodical of the Home Army in Poland during the war. Its editor was Seweryn Blumsztajn; he was assisted by Joanna Szczęsna and Jan Lityński (who later went on to become editor of *Robotnik*, a bimonthly underground journal targeted at workers).

56 The first declaration, "The Declaration of the 14 in Solidarity with the Workers" was sent to the *Sejm*, and significantly did not only address the repression, but called for a broader dialogue and solution to Poland's social problems. It was followed by two more declarations, made by the Warsaw intelligentsia and Warsaw students and graduates, respectively.

Most of the signatories were KOR members and virtually all had a previous history of political opposition.

57 Both VONS, the Committee for the Unjustly Persecuted, in Czechoslovakia, as well as SZETA, the Fund for Support of the Poor, in Hungary, were explicitly modeled on KOR.

58 The acronym NOW-a also spells out the Polish adjective "new."

59 Because of ideological restrictions placed on official education by the Tsarist regime and the requirement to speak Russian and not Polish, well-known scholars began to teach uncensored courses in private homes. Jedlicki has made the point that even this was not an original concept—the idea was borrowed from the private courses set up for girls of wealthy families in East European cities such as Warsaw, as official schools were not open to women prior to Poland re-gaining its independence (Interview with Jerzy Jedlicki, July 21, 1995).

60 Lecture by Jerzy Jedlicki, College for New Europe, Cracow, Poland, 21 July 1995. One might add that the flip-side of this intellectual tradition is the strong desire to promote a correct form of politics, and is a major reason why so many intellectuals were drawn to promote (and later stridently defend) authoritarian communism, as per my introduction. On the collective responsibility of intellectuals for national heritage, see Jerzy Jedlicki, "Heritage and Collective Responsibility" in Ian MacLean, Alan Montefiore, and Peter Winch, eds. (1990).

61 Bullies from the *Socjalistyczne Zrzeszenie Studentków Polskich* (SZSP), or Socialist Union of Polish Students would cause continual disruptions, especially during the larger lectures conducted in 1979—thus causing organizers to shift to a strategy of smaller seminars (Bernhard, 1993: 147). Peter Raina describes one incident in Cracow where over 100 people had assembled in a private home to hear Adam Michnik and police used tear-gas and force to disperse the gathering (Raina, 1978: 546).

62 The power of the workers movement was increasingly obvious in July with an eight-day strike in Lublin—described afterwards as a dress rehearsal for Solidarity (Ascherson, 1982: 131). In the *Trójmiasto* the key group was the KWZZ—Founding Committee of the Baltic Free Trade Unions, a group founded in 1978 in Gdańsk which included a number of workers who played important roles in the shipyard strikes, such as former shipyard electrician (and later Solidarity leader and ultimately Polish president) Lech Wałęsa, Andrzej Gwiazda, Alina Pieńkowska, and Bogdan Borusewicz.

63 See for example, the excellent studies of Neil Ascherson (1981); Stan Persky (1981); Krzysztof Pomian (1982); Lawrence Weschler (1982); Timothy Garton Ash (1983); Alain Touraine et al., (1983); Jadwiga Staniszkis (1984); Jerzy Holzer (1984); Peter Raina (1985); Colin Barker (1986); David Ost (1990); and Michael Kennedy (1991).

64 The full set of 21 demands can be divided into two sets: general political demands and demands more specific to the striking workers in the Tri-City area. In the first set were the following demands: the creation of free trade unions; guarantee for the right to strike and the security of strikers and advisers; freedom of speech and the press, including no repression of independent publications; reinstatement of those dismissed after 1970 and 1976 and renewed status for students dismissed after 1968; the release of all political prisoners; the prohibition of any reprisals; publication in the mass media of both the formation of the MKS and the strikers' demands; full disclosure of information with respect to the socio-economic situation of the country; and the involvement of all social groups and strata in discussions for reform. For further information and analysis see Persky, 1981: 80–91; Garton Ash, 1983: 45–49; Staniszkis, 1984: 43–45; and Laba, 1986: 47–67 and Ost, 1990: 80–90.

65 For example, on August 16, following the official line of the Polish press, Associated Press reported that the strike was over.

66 This was a critical and sensitive task, and in some cases was deftly handled. For example, Mazowiecki and Kowalik were successful in changing the formulaic wording regarding the leading role of the party to "leading role of the Party in the state," whereas in the 1976 Constitution, the party leads over all of society. Similarly, the government agreed that the union would be allowed to defend workers' interests with respect to their *social* needs; the intellectuals knew that much could be included under the umbrella-like rubric of the word social, whereas any reference to political involvement or activity would have been immediately rejected. See Ost, 1990: 84 and Garton Ash, 1983: 62–63.

67 Major roles were played by Konrad Bieliński, who went to the Lenin Shipyard and together with Krzysztof Wyszkowski (the initiator of the Free Trade Unions committee in Gdańsk) produced the first newsletter. See Ost, 1990: 12–13.

68 Andrzej Wajda's film *Workers '80* shows poignant footage of Lech Wałęsa responding to a question from the crowd about political prisoners after the signing of the agreement and shouting in response, "No, no, we don't sell out our friends!" Wajda was detained in 1981—the same day the government submitted *Man of Iron* (which won the Palme d'Or at Cannes) as the official Polish entry for the Academy Awards (Rosenberg, 1996: 224).

69 During the negotiations, the authorities were very hesitant and unwilling to cede to the demand for independent trade unions—rather, they repeatedly offered an overhaul of the existing structure, immediate elections for new leadership, and finally their limitation to the Baltic coast. See Ost, 1990: 79–97.

70 Official trade unions in Soviet-style systems can be understood not only in the traditional sense of "Leninist transmission belts" but also as a form

of interest group or association (Ost, 1990: 98). Unions were responsible for maintaining discipline, providing clarity regarding the boundaries of trades or professions, and coordinating and distributing the provision of social benefits (including paid holiday time, child care, and even vacations). Bargaining was not part of their mandate as it would have presumed the possibility of a particular enterprise *not* acting in the interests of the workers; likewise prior to the Gdańsk Accord there were no provisions in Polish law for a legal strike.

71 The best evidence of the non-belief in the ideology of the party-state is that at its height in 1981, of Solidarity's 10 million members, *fully one-third* were also members of PZPR.

72 There has been considerable debate in the Solidarity literature with respect to the sociological genesis of the political demands—as initiated and championed by the workers or as the brainchild of the intellectual opposition. One view (especially represented by Staniszkis, 1984) contends that workers vacillate between narrow economism (Lenin's "trade union consciousness") and unrealistic utopianism, therefore intellectuals are needed to both politicize and moderate their demands. The other view (especially represented by Laba, 1986) suggests that the workers were capable of formulating sophisticated political demands *by themselves*, as is evidenced by a comparison of the demands made following the 1970 massacre with the 21 demands of August, 1980. Without attempting to simplify the complexity of the debate or its underlying assumptions, however, it is fair to concede in hindsight that both the workers and the intellectuals had a considerable impact on both the Gdańsk Accord and the rapid growth of Solidarity that followed. Moreover, unique to the Polish situation is the degree to which both workers and intellectuals acted in a historically self-conscious manner, with reference to past traditions and events.

73 I am focusing on *intellectuals*, that segment of the intelligentsia who are deliberately theoretical, self-reflexive, and indeed teleological in their deliberations. On the role of the professional classes more broadly in Solidarity, see especially Kennedy (1991). Kennedy points out that engineers and physicians in particular allied themselves *and their own professional interests* with Solidarity in the 1980–1981 period.

74 For complete details of this debate, see Ost, 1990: 102–109.

75 The appointment itself was ominous, as it was the first time in the Warsaw Pact that a military leader was to hold the office of prime minister. Moreover, he retained the post of defense minister.

76 Colonel Kukliński was the former chief of the Strategic Planning Department of the Polish General Staff. Polish leaders knew that his defection guaranteed American knowledge of the plan. See Rosenberg, 1996: 188–198 and Curry, in Curry and Fajfer, eds., 1996: 188–189.

77 Jaruzelski's less-than-liberal counterparts in the GDR and in Czechoslovakia were also pressing for a solution so as to limit the Polish contagion. Erich Honecker even provided Kania with unused plans for a proposed declaration of martial law in 1953 following the Berlin riots.

78 More than ten thousand Solidarity activists were detained and interned without trial. Most of the top leaders were caught in Gdańsk where they had been involved in a national meeting of the organization. Jaruzelski later regretted the detentions as "nasty and stupid"—the biggest mistake of martial law (Rosenberg, 1996: 224).

79 There was a need on Poland's part to be seen to be fulfilling the conditions demanded by the West so that economic sanctions would be lifted. However, this did not stop the regime from formally arresting Jacek Kuroń, Adam Michnik, Jan Lityński, Jan Józef Lipski, and Henryk Wujec for trying to overthrow the state by force.

80 Over time, the party-state effectively gave up monopoly control over media. By the late 1980s, over 1,300 periodicals were regularly published. In 1987 the underground journal *Res Publica* (a prominent liberal theoretical quarterly) was allowed to resume publication. Moreover, *Res Publica's* editor, Marcin Król, was among a group of intellectuals chosen to meet with Mikhail Gorbachev in Warsaw in 1988.

81 On this issue, see Casimir Garnysz (1984).

82 One, Father Jerzy Popiełuszko, paid for his commitment with his life. In October 1984, he was kidnapped and murdered by three policemen. They were clearly acting against official policy and in fact were arrested and prosecuted for their crime. The affair galvanized support for the Church, exposed the excesses of the regime, and laid bare intra-governmental rivalry. See Ost, 1990: 158–159. The story of Popiełuszko's life and martyrdom has been told in Agnieszka Holland's 1989 film *To Kill a Priest*.

83 For a left analysis of the strongly egalitarian and democratically socialist ethos of the original Solidarity program, see Henrik Flakierski (1983).

84 This was a large semantic and theoretical difference from Michnik's early conception of tying active citizenship to a democratic public sphere.

85 See Ost (1990), especially the final chapter "The Viability of an Accord," pp. 187–204. Ost quotes Kołakowski as ridiculing the possibility of a Spanish road for Poland as mere "fantasy"!

86 The party-state contingent included allied, official parties, such as the *Stronnictwo Demokratyczne* (SD), or Democratic Party; the *Zjednoczone Stronnictwo Ludowe* (ZSL), or United Peasants Party; and the *Ogólnopolskie Porozumienie Związków Zawodowych* (OPZZ), the "official" trade union umbrella organization since 1983. Long-time Solidarity activists and intellectuals such as Lech Wałęsa, Adam Michnik, Jacek Kuroń, Tadeusz Mazo-

wiecki, and Bronisław Geremek were at the table, as well as representatives of the Catholic Church.

87 For a detailed discussion of the dynamics of the talks, see Wiktor Osiatynski, in Jon Elster, ed. (1996).

Chapter 3: Czechoslovakia: From Interrupted to Velvet Revolution

1 In the May 1946 elections, the Communists won 38% of the popular vote and a higher number of seats (114 out of 300) than any of the other major contending parties. From 1946 to 1948 the communists participated in a National Front government with Edward Beneš as President. For a more detailed historical description of the period and Czechoslovakia's "national path to socialism," see H. Gordon Skilling, (1976: 22–29); V. V. Kusin, in Martin McCauley, ed. (1977), and more recently Bradley Abrams, forthcoming in 2002.

2 Language is an important indicator of how this event is perceived through Czech eyes. Among Western historians and commentators, reference is commonly made to the "appeasement" of Hitler at Munich by Western allies lead by Neville Chamberlain. Czechs, however, speak of the "betrayal" at Munich or *zrada v Mníchově*, referring to the West's abandonment of collective security guarantees, thus effectively "sacrificing" Czechoslovak sovereignty to National Socialist Germany. Moreover, the Czech use of "betray" is both broader and more intense than in English usage, implying treacherous behavior.

3 Rudolf Slánský was the party's general secretary and a close associate of Gottwald from 1929 onward until his arrest in 1951. He was tried, convicted, and executed in 1952, along with eleven others. Three were sentenced to life imprisonment, and later released. Slánský was not rehabilitated until 1968. For an excellent personal memoir of one of Slánský co-defendants, see Artur London (1968). His book was later made into a film by director Costa-Gavras, entitled *The Confession*. A similar recollection is that of Evžen Löbl (1976). The correspondence of Vlado Clementis and Lida Clementisová (1968) has also been published as *Listy z vasenia* (Prague: Tatran).

4 Originally a duumvirate between Antonín Zápotocký as president and Antonín Novotný as First Secretary, Novotný assumed both positions in 1957 with Zápotocký's death.

5 See Muriel Blaive, "1956: anatomie d'une absence" in Jacques Rupnik and François Fejtő, eds. (1999), on the question of why there was no meaningful dissent in Czechoslovakia in 1956, as had occurred in Poland and Hungary.

6 See for example, Pavel Kohout (1969); Zdeněk Mlynář, (1980); and Radoslav Selucký (1970). All three were prominent communist intellectuals and played a key role in the Prague Spring. The works cited above were published afterward and to a certain extent the authors exonerate and/or explain their previous actions in the 1950s.

7 The findings of the Kolder Commission resulted in the penal rehabilitation of all fourteen Slánský defendants; full rehabilitation and exoneration did not occur until May, 1968.

8 For an examination of the history of both Czech and Slovak nationalism and state formation, see Carol Skalnik Leff (1998). See also Nadya Nedelsky (2001) (unpublished dissertation).

9 Economist Ota Šik came to prominence not only because of his proposals for economic reform (ultimately leading to the expatriate development of his theories of a "Third Way" between capitalism and existing socialism) but also on his assessment of *how* the Czechoslovak economy had deteriorated. He demonstrated that privileging heavy industry leads to a concentration of investment; this level of "consumption" in turn leads to lower plant efficiency, slowed growth of labor productivity, and an increasing proportion of the GNP is absorbed by accumulation rather than consumption. Over time on a macroeconomic level this means that each further increment in productivity demands more and more investment than ever before, that is, productivity is achieved at enormous social and economic cost in an increasingly inefficient manner. See Selucký, 1971: 33–34 and Šik, 1976, 1985.

10 As Galia Golan (1971) points out, much of the debate regarding the necessity for reform was initiated by rehabilitated Slovak economist Evžen Löbl in the pages of Slovak paper *Kultúrny život* (*Cultural Life*). Löbl argued that planning was not intrinsic to the logic of socialism, but became the 'law' of socialism thanks to Stalin. Löbl's view were considered extremely radical, but his charges of dogmatism and demand for creative, independent economists laid the groundwork for others, most notably Šik. Löbl became head of the Slovak National Bank in 1968; afterward he lived in exile in the United States.

11 The ideological shift whereby the market was rehabilitated as a distributive mechanism occurred incrementally with the cautious acceptance of a number of related assumptions: 1) that society was composed of a multiplicity of interests (not simply composed of classes antagonistically at odds with one another); 2) that enterprises and workers require incentives to induce performance; 3) that regardless of the mode of production, consumer demand must be met; and 4) that the commodification of goods and labor would likely continue under centrally-planned socialism. See Williams, 1997: 21.

12 Gordon Skilling describes the literary press at this time as "organs for the intelligentsia as a whole," suggesting that their "outspoken content and somewhat greater freedom from restrictive controls" served to attract a much larger audience than previously—from his investigation in 1967 he reported estimated circulations of 100,000 for *Literární noviny* and 30,000 for *Kultúrny život* (See Skilling, 1976: 64).

13 For example, in 1963 a campaign was launched against "dissident" writers following the outspoken ideas expressed by many during both the congresses of Slovak and Czechoslovak writers in April and May 1963, respectively. For further information on the philosophical transformation of the Writers' Union as well as its members, see Marci Shore (1998). For the details of the backlash that followed, see Skilling, 1976: 64–66.

14 Representative of this literature is Milan Kundera's *The Joke*, Ludvík Vaculík's *The Axe* and Pavel Kohout's *The Hangwoman*. After the invasion of Czechoslovakia the repertoire expanded: Kundera published *The Book of Laughter and Forgetting* in exile in Paris (and subsequently *The Unbearable Lightness of Being*); Vaculík wrote *The Guinea Pigs*.

15 The best example is Havel's *The Memorandum*, written in 1965 and first performed at Prague's Theatre of the Balustrade under the direction of Jan Grossman. Also from this period are *The Garden Party* and *The Increased Difficulty of Concentration*. The Theatre of the Balustrade was in its golden age, with impressive productions of Jarry's *Ubu Roi*. Beckett's *Waiting for Godot*, and Kafka's *The Trial*. For personal reminiscences, see Edá Kriseová (1993), 40–57.

16 The most well known of the young generation of screenplay writer-directors that populated the Czech new wave were Jan Němec, Ivan Passer, Jiří Menzel, Ester Krumbachová, Věra Chytilová, Evald Schorm, Miloš Forman, and Pavel Juráček. Antonín Liehm (1994) has reflected upon this period in *Closely Watched Films: The Czechoslovak Experience*. For a personal account, see Josef Škvorecký (1971).

17 It is important to remember that being permitted to attend institutions of higher learning was considerably dependent on class background and the correct ideological outlook of one's family. Class enemies (that is, of a prewar bourgeois class) or their children were generally not allowed to attend university. Thus this generation was more ideologically predisposed via the selection process to be committed to socialism, making their subsequent disillusion with the restrictions of the regime all the more striking.

18 May Day demonstrations from 1962 onward were a focus of student discontent. In October 1964 demonstrations in Václavské náměstí (Wenceslas Square) were broken up by police. See Skilling, 1976: 72.

19 The same Jiří Hájek who later became Minister of Foreign Affairs under Dubček and one of the founding spokespersons of Charter 77.

20 For example, the police intervention was described as legal, but the measures they took were deemed to be unduly harsh. No disciplinary actions were taken against either the police or the students. The report urged the students to maintain "academic order" and cited efforts to improve their living conditions and the learning environment. See Skilling, 1976: 81–82.

21 Within the Central Committee, Josef Smrkovský, Václav Slavík, František Kriegel, Oldřich Černík all supported reform along with Alexander Dubček. To some degree Jiří Hendrych and Vladimír Koucký held the balance, with Martin Vaculík representing an important defection to the reform caucus. See Dubček, 1993: 118–127; Mlynář, 1980: 70–115; and Skilling, 1976: 161–179.

22 This was partially the result of the so-called Šejna Affair. General Jan Šejna, head of the Czechoslovak Party Main Committee in the Ministry of Defense, was pro-Novotný and a personal friend of Novotný's son. The military prosecutor had compiled considerable evidence that he was profiting from black market sales of army supplies of grass and clover. Given recently re-installed freedom of the press, the story made headlines and the scandal certainly affected public perception of the president.

23 Novotný, Hendrych, Chudík, Laštovička, and Dolanský were replaced; the newly elected Presidium consisted of: František Barbírek, Vasil Bil'ak, Oldřich Černík, Drahomír Kolder, František Kriegel, Jan Piller, Emil Rigo, Josef Smrkovský, Josef Špaček, and Alexander Dubček. Other important appointments of this period include: Miloš Jakeš as chairman of the Party's Central Auditing Commission; Oldřich Černík as prime minister; Josef Smrkovský as head of the National Assembly; Gustáv Husák as deputy prime minister; Ota Šik as deputy prime minister; Miroslav Galuška as new minister of education; Vladimir Kadlec as new minister of culture; and Professor Jiří Hájek (later Charter signatory and spokesperson) as the new minister of foreign affairs. Most of Dubček's close associates remained committed to the reforms and thus suffered for it after August; the exception was Černík who remained prime minister until 1970. Husák, along with Jakeš, Kolder, Alois Indra and Vasil Bil'ak played important roles as "traitors" subsequent to the August invasion. Gustáv Husák later became First Secretary and President, and was chiefly responsible for Soviet-sponsored normalization (see below). Jakeš later became the ill-fated last First Secretary of the Party, and thus presided over its burial during the Velvet Revolution.

24 See also Williams, 1997: 4–6.

25 Auersperg was more of a conservative ideologue than a "reformer" in the same sense as Šik and Mlynář; however, Mlynář states he was involved administratively and in the foreign policy process (remembering, of course, that even the Prague reformers were quite conservative and mindful of the Soviet hegemon in terms of their own external affairs).

26 That is, the use of the market as a regulatory mechanism to ensure a better match between supply and demand. To this degree, command planning would have had to have been significantly modified.

27 See both his memoirs, *Hope Dies Last* (1993: 147–152) and his interview with Hungarian journalist András Sugár, *Dubček Speaks* (1990: 36–42; 84–85; and 98–99).

28 Ideologically, the goal was neither to abandon the Leninist tenet of democratic centralism, nor lessen the leading role of the party. Infusing democratic "content" into this model required the highly disciplined and regulated participation of its members where paradoxically the expression of free opinion was encouraged while factionalism was disallowed. See Williams, 1997: 15–19.

29 In his memoirs, Dubček said that if Brezhnev did make such a comment at their fateful December 9, 1967 meeting, it was not to him directly.

30 Brezhnev personally badgered Dubček repeatedly by letter and telephone about his unhappiness with respect to how the Czechoslovak government was dealing with "rightist forces" and "anti-socialist manifestations." As the summer wore on, Brezhnev demanded that Dubček take "direct charge of the struggle" and later chastised him for not living up to and fully implementing the agreements reached at Čierna nad Tisou and Bratislava. For recently released translations of their correspondence and telephone conversations, see Jaromír Navrátil, ed. (1998).

31 The "Group of Five" leaders were present, i.e. Walter Ulbricht as host from the GDR, Władysław Gomułka from Poland, János Kádár of Hungary, Todor Zhivkov from Bulgaria and of course Brezhnev and company from the USSR. These five nations later made up the Warsaw Pact force that invaded Czechoslovakia in August. Neither leaders Josip Broz Tito from Yugoslavia or Nicolae Ceaușescu from Romania attended the conference.

32 One can understand Gomułka's unease, especially in consideration of student unrest in Warsaw and elsewhere, where one of their slogans was "Poland is Waiting for Her Dubček" (see Raina, 1978: 146 and 162–165). Ulbricht was one of the most conservative and long lived leaders of the Bloc; his slavishness to the Soviet line was legendary; the ultimate vulnerability of his nation to the pull of the West and especially toward a united Germany has perversely proven his paranoia correct.

33 The Czechoslovaks did not attend the meeting in Warsaw on July 14, as Dubček felt bound by a Presidium decision demanding that *all* socialist countries attend, i.e. including Romania and Yugoslavia. The meeting was originally called for July 15, but after Dubček rejected the exhortations of Hungarian First Secretary János Kádár to attend the meeting, it was held one day earlier. The result was a joint letter dispatched to the Czecho-

slovak Central Committee condemning the reforms and expressing alarm at how the situation was getting increasingly out of hand.

34 In 1948 in the midst of the communist takeover, Czechoslovak Foreign Minister (and son of former president Tomáš Garrigue Masaryk) Jan Masaryk "fell" to his death from the Prague Castle. This act of defenestration continues to be debated as either murder or suicide, although Jan's sister Alice maintained until her final days that he committed suicide as a statement of his own dissatisfaction with the government and sense of personal failure.

35 This was an issue of some delicacy as the party, a strong force in politics during the First Republic and after the war, was forcibly "unified" with the CPCz in 1948. CPCz officials were concerned that such a move would be retrograde, and presented a threat to socialist unity. Meanwhile, emerging social democrats argued that the unification was illegitimate, and had not been democratically ratified. As such, the party still existed legally. See Skilling, 1976: 232–235.

36 Membership of K-231 was estimated to be as high as 130,000.

37 Vaculík's *Two Thousand Words* manifesto was cited as proof, along with quotations from the newly liberalized press. Manufactured evidence, such as a letter approving the presence of Soviet troops in Czechoslovakia supposedly signed by Prague auto workers, was also produced. See Valenta, 1991: 77–78.

38 Needless to say, this line of reasoning completely backfired, for identifying oneself with the will of the majority rather than to the bureaucratic elites of the party was tantamount to violating the leading role of the party. Brezhnev was reported to have said, without irony, "How can you claim that you are in control of the situation if the people sign a resolution without your prior knowledge?" (reported by Radoslav Selucký in "The Dubček Era Revisited," *Problems of Communism* 24 (January–February 1975): 41. Nonetheless, Dubček could quote numbers with some certainty in terms of the popular support he enjoyed, as an Institute of Public Opinion had been established during this period. See Jaroslaw A. Piekalkiewicz (1972). In his memoirs, Dubček claims that with respect to the Action Program, 76% were in favor; 7% against. He also stated that at this time public opinion was a "decisive political factor" on which he definitely relied (see Dubček, 1993: 163). See also Skilling's chapter "Non-Communists and Public Opinion" in *Czechoslovakia's Interrupted Revolution* (1976: 526–562).

39 The Bratislava declaration was a contradictory document, citing the right of a socialist state to pursue its own form of socialism while at the same time granting other socialist states the right to intervene if counter-revolution was threatened. Dubček attempted to dispel the confusion and provide his own interpretation of the wording by implying in his public address following the declaration that liberalization would continue and was supported. See Williams, 1997: 103.

40 For an updated discussion of the Soviet decision to intervene and of a critique of earlier explanations, see Williams, 1997: 29–38. Although the crucial shift in Soviet thinking probably occurred mid-August, they were nonetheless preparing for a potential military solution well in advance of the final decision.

41 The vast majority of troops—about 170,000—were Soviet. Polish, East German, Hungarian, and Bulgarian troops were present in token form to convey the message of Bloc solidarity, not because they were necessary militarily.

42 For example, Indra, Kolder, and Bil'ak. They were supposed to constitute the core of a replacement government, which would have helped the Soviets in their efforts to dress up the invasion as of a request for fraternal assistance. However, they were not able to garner the necessary Central Committee support to do so, and the final declaration of the Presidium meeting from the evening of August 20–21 described the invasion for what it was, and claimed that the entry of troops had been made "without the knowledge of the President of the Republic, the chairman of the National Assembly, the chairman of the government, or the First Secretary of the CPCz Central Committee ..." (Skilling, 1976: 716; see also Valenta, 1991: 148–150 and Williams, 1997: 112–143).

43 Motives and explanations for signing as well as their personal reminiscences of the Moscow negotiations are offered by both Dubček (1993) and Mlynář (1980).

44 The military intervention itself was timed to prevent the meeting of the "Extraordinary" Fourteenth Party Congress, originally scheduled to begin September 9. What happened (without the knowledge of the captives in Moscow) is that via a broadcast appeal, over two thirds of the already-elected delegates convened in secret in the industrial district of Vysočany. Their dramatic meeting has been documented by one of the key participants, Jiří Pelikán (1971), *The Secret Vysočany Congress* (London: Penguin). The Congress conceived of itself as legal forum, operating within normal party procedures, and a true reflection of the views of Czechoslovak communists. The records of the Congress give testimony to the fact that the Prague Spring was indeed an exercise in socialist renewal and condemned the invasion as destructive of this process.

45 Here I am referring to First Secretary Dubček, President Svoboda, Prime Minister Oldřich Černík and head of the National Assembly Josef Smrkovský.

46 Students demanded freedom of assembly and association; freedom of research and literary and cultural expression; and personal and legal security. See Skilling, 1976: 816–817.

47 October 28 is the anniversary of the founding of the Czechoslovakia in 1918; November 7 was the anniversary of the Russian Revolution in 1917.

48 *Zprávy* was the major propaganda tool of the occupation forces. It was a Czech-language newspaper distributed by the troops which polemically outlined the WTO position, and ran from August 30, 1968 to May 10, 1969.

49 One can argue that the Velvet Revolution in fact began with activities surrounding the twentieth-anniversary commemoration of Palach's death in January, 1989. The square in front of the philosophical faculty of Charles University was later renamed by the demonstrating students of 1989 "Palach Square." His name and the "honor" of his sacrifice were invoked often by the dissidents and activists in the opposition. See McRae, 1997: 21–25.

50 Šimečka describes this deprivation of meaningful work, a form of economic persecution where targeted individuals were not allowed to make use of the skills or training, but still within the strict boundaries of "humanitarian principles": "none of the victims were forced to starve" (1984: 66).

51 See R. J. Crompton (1994), p. 346.

52 I am indebted to Anna Vaníčková for this phrasing. She documented this process exhaustively in her master's thesis *Passion Play: Underground Rock Music in Czechoslovakia, 1968–1989* (York University, 1997).

53 Rock music was viewed as particularly insidious as it represented the imperialistic influence of the West on culture, not to mention the problems of disaffected youth generally. See Timothy W. Ryback (1990).

54 See especially Václav Havel, "Six Asides About Culture," in Paul Wilson, ed. (1991), and Václav Benda, "The Parallel *Polis*," translated and reprinted in H.G. Skilling and Paul Wilson (1991). For a more theoretical statement, see Petr Uhl, "The Alternative Community as Revolutionary Avant-garde," in John Keane, ed. (1985). For Western comment on the effect of rock music as an independent force undermining the regime, see especially Sabrina Ramet (1994).

55 Not surprisingly, Jirous styled his relationship to the PPU after Andy Warhol's relationship with the Velvet Underground. He was simultaneously an artist, critic, and theoretician. The story of the PPU and their subsequent trial is the subject of Jana Chytlová's recent documentary *The Plastic People of the Universe*.

56 Signatories included poet and former Writers' Union president Jaroslav Seifert, literary historian Václav Černy, philosophers Jan Patočka and Karel Kosík, and writers Havel, Ivan Klíma and Pavel Kohout. All had played a part in the cultural and intellectual renaissance represented by the Prague Spring and were expelled from official life during normalization. Not only were they leading figures, well known in Czech society, but each was both known and published abroad.

57 The term "merry ghetto" was coined by Jirous to describe the Czech cultural underground; it gives some sense of a) the closed or marginal nature

of the alternative cultural community; and b) the fact that its "members" were involved often for less than serious reasons. Pervasive humor, partying, and general entertainment were not only survival strategies, but also a key form of everyday resistance to the regime.

58 From 1977 onward, Paul Wilson played an instrumental role in recording, marketing, and distributing the music of the PPU abroad. He was a vocalist for the band, but as a Canadian national was expelled rather than tried. Given the fact that Wilson became the most prominent translator of Havel and many others, and a tireless organizer for Chartists abroad, this was probably a major error on the part of the authorities! Wilson was not allowed back into the country until late November of 1989, when the Velvet Revolution was in mid-swing (Wilson, 1996; see also McRae, 1997).

59 All the countries of the Eastern Bloc signed at Helsinki, save for Albania. Czechoslovakia also ratified two international United Nations covenants on human rights which had ironically been originally signed in 1968 after the Soviet invasion.

60 For example, the independent existence of samizdat presses (Vaculík's *Edice Petlice* or Padlock Press), the recent founding of Havel's *Edice Expedice* or Expedition Press, the independently mounted performances of Havel's plays (for example, *Audience* and *The Beggar's Opera*), the underground music scene, Ladislav Hejdánek's philosophy seminar, and so on.

61 Although there is no *organizational* comparison in Hungary at this time, Kis and Bence were writing *Toward An East European Marxism* and were in the process of questioning whether or not Marxist critical political economy relevant to the Hungarian situation was possible at all (hence the samizdat title of a similar work, co-written with György Márkus, entitled *Ist eine politische Ökonomie überhaupt möglich?*)

62 This founding document and many of the early documents of the Charter that were translated and disseminated widely abroad can be found in Skilling, 1981: 209–327.

63 The emphasis on agreement and on forging a new political road helps to explain why in the post-1989 period there has been a heated and polemical debate about the meaning and importance of Charter 77 among and between its former supporters and detractors. After the Velvet Revolution, consensus was no longer a perceived necessity, and simmering disagreements over the role of the organization/movement suddenly erupted in an orgy of self-examination and self-criticism. For example, Czech historians Vilém Prečan and Milan Otáhal have conducted a vituperative series of published exchanges on whether Charter 77 was sufficiently political or confrontational. See Milan Otáhal (1992), 258–272, and (1994); and Vilém Prečan (1995). Journalist and former Charter signatory Jan Urban has chastized Czechs for ignoring the contribution of the Chartists yet has also criticized his fellow-dissidents for not having expanded earlier from a narrow human-rights strategy into a more overtly political opposition.

Others have made light of its political intent or impact entirely. Ludvík Vaculík has been widely quoted as describing Charter 77 as "an uprising of characters, not political convictions." Many of these *ex post facto* explanations and critiques are obviously colored by the perceptions of the participants themselves, and in my view miss the key point that the Charter was trying to do politics differently. See Jan Urban (1997). On the reflections of Chartists on the twentieth anniversary of its founding, see (1997), *Charta 77: očima současníků* (Doplněk: Ústav pro soudobé dějiny).

64　Skilling quotes Ladislav Hejdánek who spoke of the Charter as "a platform for people of different beliefs, different professions, different origins and different aims"; he was convinced that had it been differently structured, for example along the lines of a political party, it could not have lasted ten years (Skilling, 1989: 54–55).

65　The first three spokespersons, respected philosopher Jan Patočka, independent playwright Václav Havel, and former communist Jiří Hájek, can be said to be roughly representative of the intellectual community, alternative culture, and reform communism, three important strands of the Charter. Throughout the existence of the Charter, the position of spokesperson rotated each year (sometimes mid-year in the case of arrest or illness), and three people were always assigned to the role, lessening the danger for any one individual and making the organization more accountable and reflective of its collective will. Attempts were later made to include women and Slovaks as spokespersons.

66　Journalist Jan Urban tells the story of being dismissed as a history and civic studies teacher for refusing to sign the Anti-Charter, and of the harassment and interrogation he received following this decision, in "The Politics and Power of Humiliation," in Tim D. Whipple, ed. (1991).

67　This reached a peak in 1979–1980, when Zdená Tominová (spouse of Julius Tomin) was beaten by police, and two Oxford lecturers were unceremoniously expelled, including Anthony Kenny, Master of Balliol College. This last event became a minor diplomatic incident, and was widely publicized in the British press.

68　Key organizers were Jiří Müller and theatre director Petr Oslzlý.

69　Interview with Ladislav Hejdánek, October 21, 1997.

70　Day cited the examples of Jan Ruml, head of the Freedom Union party in the Czech Republic, Marketa Nemčova, who for a time served as Ambassador to Poland, Jiří Schneider, current Czech Ambassador to Israel, and the remarkable Aleš Havlíček who made the transition from manual laborer (when a seminar attendee) to university teacher.

71　Informational material authorized in Charter 77's name was issued by the current collective of spokespersons at the time. Closely associated with the Charter was the bulletin *Informace o Chartě 77* or *Infoch* (*Information*

on Charter 77), issued monthly under the editorship of Petr Uhl and Anna
Šabatová.

72 These external publishers along with František Janouch in Sweden, Prince
Karel Schwarzenberg of Austria, reform communist Zdeněk Mlynář living
in Vienna, and Jiří Gruša and Vilém Prečan active in Germany constituted
an informal network nourishing free thought and discussion, maintaining
the continuity of Czechoslovak traditions, and providing a window through
and from which the dissidents could communicate. For more detail see
H. Gordon Skilling (1997).

73 This was made possible by the support and generosity of Prince Karel
Schwarzenberg, who used his position and hereditary fortune to build the
center and support various human rights activities. In fact, the documentation centre and an apartment for Prečan and his family was constructed
within the Castle at Scheinfeld. Interview with Vilém Prečan, October 20,
1997. This collection has since been relocated to Dobřichovice.

74 Both Kávan and later Prečan smuggled materials into the country, first by
car and later via diplomatic pouch (thanks to contacts at the West German,
Swedish, Canadian and other embassies who often took on these tasks
without their superiors' knowledge and at some risk of being recalled).
Within Czechoslovakia, Jiřina Šiklová was the main and most active contact, often meeting conspiratorially in parks, elevators, or on public transportation to meet fellow activists, diplomats, or even ordinary tourists who
would transport materials. Elaborate code names were worked out and
calls to foreign countries were made from public telephones. Šiklová never
signed Charter 77 as it was too risky given her clandestine work, but over
time she was "found out," her telephones were bugged, and she was followed. From a menial job as a cleaner in a state broadcasting building,
however, she had the ability to work after hours and thus use their telephone lines to play tapes directly to Radio Free Europe in Munich. Working in a hospital also provided her with many contacts; she described it
as "strategic" because she had access to the entire spectrum of society.
Interview with Jiřina Šiklová, October 21, 1997.

75 Interview with Samuel Abrahám, October 16, 1997.

76 The name of the country was officially changed to the Czecho-Slovak
Socialist Republic (ČSSR).

77 As Abrahám describes, even those Slovak dissidents who did take a moral
position, such as Miroslav Kusý, Dominik Tatarka, and Milan Šimečka,
could hardly engage in any level of moral screening with their knowledge
of Slovak society. In later constructing *Verejnost Proti Násilu* (VPN, or
Public against Violence, the Slovak equivalent to Civic Forum), building
a broad coalition to oppose the Husák regime was more critical. However,
the lesser distance between rulers and opposition members meant that the
dividing line between the two was opaque and often meaningless. Former

prime minister Vladimir Mečiar is a good example: he has both a communist past and a record of service in VPN.

78 Duray also publicly thanked VONS for the support he received during his
1982–1983 imprisonment, a testimonial to the ongoing practical work of
the organization.

79 László Szigeti claims that at this time about 40–50% of Hungarian-speak-
ing children were attending schools where the only language of instruction was Slovak. They proposed two alternatives: either have Hungarian-
only schools, or teach Hungarian in Slovak schools.

80 Interview with László Szigeti, October 16, 1997.

81 Both Václav Klaus and Vladimir Dlouhý were employed by the Academy
at this time, and wrote a number of scholarly and technical articles on the
state of economy. Both are good examples of what Šiklová refers to as
"gray zone" intellectuals.

82 European Nuclear Disarmament (END), the largest umbrella anti-nuclear/
peace organization on the continent in the 1980s.

83 For a detailed account of the role of the students and youth movements
more generally in the Velvet Revolution, from 1988 through to 1990, see
Libor Konvička and Jan Kávan (1994).

84 The Jazz Section had for nine years sponsored a jazz festival; in 1981 it
was canceled. Originally officially a part of the Musicians' Union, it had
approximately 4000 members and 100,000 followers. The regime tried
to get the Union to end its activities, but when efforts failed the regime
dissolved it officially in 1984. However, they still managed to carry on
some of their activities, publishing, lending tapes, and having regular open
houses (see Skilling, 1989: 80–83).

85 Havel was released in May after serving five months of his sentence—one
month earlier than expected—probably due to international and even
Soviet pressure.

86 I had the opportunity to speak with Sugár personally in Budapest in
August, 1995. In the hilariously ironic and devilishly critical tradition of
Hungarian television, *Panorama* could only be described as a Central
European version of *60 Minutes* (I am indebted to Rob McRae for this
parallel). Like Mike Wallace, Sugár is a right-of-center populist-nation-
alist who continues to remain a controversial figure in Hungarian society.

87 This fact is important in refuting the popular and oft-quoted conspiracy
theory that somehow November 17 was staged together by dissidents and
hard-liners in order to oust the government from power. The theory was
particularly strong when lists of StB collaborators were published and
contained the names of many former dissidents. For a complete discussion of lustration and retrospective justice in the Czechoslovakia (and

later the Czech Republic and Slovakia) see Rosenberg (1996), especially pp. 3–121.

88 Skilling (1989: 84) cited official statistics showing that most church baptisms, weddings, and funerals occurred in Slovakia. In a sociological study conducted in 1970, almost 71% of the population of Slovakia indicated they were believers (quoted in Kirschbaum, 1995: 246).

89 This has been carefully documented by Catholic activist (and now prominent member of the Christian Democratic Party in Slovakia) František Mikloško (1991). This has been partially translated into English as *You Can't Destroy Them* (1991–1992). Trans. Danielle Rozgon (New York [unpublished M.S.]).

90 This created a thorny issue for the Vatican in the post-1989 period, given that many officially consecrated priests were collaborators (such as those members of *Pacem in Terris*) whereas the unofficially consecrated priests in the secret church argued that they were the true carriers of the message and more worthy of Vatican recognition. On the role of the Secret Church in Slovakia, see David Doellinger, "Prayers, Pilgrimages and Petitions: The Secret Church and the Growth of Civil Society in Slovakia" forthcoming in *Nationalities Papers* 30.2, 215–240.

91 Interview with František Mikloško, October 17, 1997. The Pope had a Slovak grandmother, and for a time rumors were swirling that the he was actually born in a small Slovak village near the Polish border. The drama, which centered around the reputed refusal of the local parish priest in Poland to produce the Pope's birth registration, created much speculation. The rumor, which in any event was useful to the Slovak Catholics, was later proven incorrect.

92 Tomášek had been unsympathetic to Charter activity and in turn Catholic Chartists (such as former priest Václav Malý, and religious lay people Václav Benda and Radim Palouš) were critical of his attitude.

93 Tomášek's collision course with the regime would continue right through to 1989. In June, 1989, for example, he received both Havel and Dubček during his 90th birthday celebration.

94 For example, *Obroda*, or Resistance, a club including former Prague Spring officials wanting to reinvigorate humanist socialism; the *Společenství Přátel*, or Society for the Friendship with the USA; the Czechoslovak Ecology Society; and ecological groups outside Prague such as Brno Forum and *Bratislava Nahlas* or Bratislava Aloud.

95 For example, Rudolf Battěk, Václav Benda, Ján Čarnogurský, Tomáš Hradílek, Ladislav Lis, and Jaroslav Šabata.

96 November 17 had particular resonance, as the British had named International Students Day after Jan Opletal, a Czech student who had demonstrated in 1939 against the Nazi occupation. Opletal was shot to death

and many student leaders were summarily executed by the German fascists. The request was considered legitimate by the authorities as Opletal's act was one of anti-fascist resistance (even if it did occur during the time of the Ribbentrop–Molotov pact).

97 In the fall of 1989 both parties had begun to show signs of independence. For example, on October 14 the "Stream of Birth" was founded in the People's Party and accused the communists of betraying Christian values.

98 It is important to remember that this occurred four days prior to the planned general strike—which in this particular revolutionary time line was quite long. That it happened earlier is at least partially due to the fact that Civic Forum member Petr Miller worked at ČKD.

99 See especially Garton Ash, 1990b, for greater details on this process. Garton Ash was a critical "eye witness" in the *Laterna Magica* yet had considerable depth of understanding, given his long involvement with dissident communities in the region. He documents how Forum members initially "fudged" on of a lot of issues, for example, membership in the WTO and what kind of market economy (or socialist competition) they were asking for. On other issues they were clearer and simply pushed farther as the days went on, in terms of forcing out political leaders, the end of the "leading role" of the party, overhauling government structures, demanding free elections, and liberal political freedoms. The issues on which they were initially less clear obviously came back to haunt the new leaders later, but arguably this was strategically necessary to keep momentum going and coalition members happy. Internally within Forum, there was also disagreement on how it might be structured in the future, which eventually metamorphosed into the debate about political parties versus broader social movements. Since 1989, the former has clearly won out.

100 Havel dramatically injected symbolism in both his speeches and actions, particularly in the early years of his presidency; see Rick Fawn (1999).

Chapter 4: Post-1956 Hungary: Repression, Reform, and Roundtable Revolution

1 The 1956 events have been exhaustively told and retold at several important junctures and from different angles. The most recent "revisionist" account of the Hungarian Revolution, which has had the benefit of access to newly unclassified materials, was the work of a team of historians from the Budapest-based Institute for the 1956 Hungarian Revolution. It has been published in English in 1996 under the title *The Hungarian Revolution of 1956: Reform, Revolt and Repression 1953–1956*, edited by György Litván (New York: Longman). Earlier accounts include Ferenc

A. Vali (1961); Miklós Molnár (1971), Bill Lomax (1976); Paul E. Zinner (1982); and Ferenc Fehér and Ágnes Heller (1983).

2 It was preceded by riots in both East Berlin and Pilsen (Czechoslovakia) in 1953. The Poznán riots occurred earlier in 1956 (June) and the "Polish October" took place immediately prior to the uprising and was to some extent a catalyst. In fact the famous demands of the Budapest students— the "Sixteen Points" formulated at the Technical University—were publicized on October 22, exactly three days after Gomułka was elected first secretary in Warsaw. The revolution proper began the following day (October 23).

3 This was true in spite of the fact that the Suez Crisis was happening simultaneously. Although it is probably true that the muted response of the British and French to the Soviet intervention was to some degree due to their desire for success in the Middle East (Litván, 1996: 94), it is unlikely that any form of Austrian solution would have resulted. Regardless of American posturing, its liberation propaganda aimed at the region and the rhetoric of John Foster Dulles, diverting the issue to the United Nations guaranteed that decisive or unilateral American action was not an option, especially given the limited means of the US to exert any effective pressure on the USSR in its own sphere of influence.

4 The most comprehensive account of the workers' councils by far is Bill Lomax, ed. (1990), which includes detailed information on the workers' proposals and programs, personal and journalistic accounts, and transcripts from the trial of the workers' leaders.

5 The new Kádár regime did not have full control over labor unrest until they issued an order on January 5, 1957 prescribing the death penalty for either refusal to work or "provocation to strike" (Litván, 1996: 113).

6 Imre Nagy himself personifies the level of equivocation surrounding personal decisions and actions during the uprising. Nagy transformed himself and was transformed by the events of 1956 from a lifelong communist partisan and politician into a popular hero. He lived in exile in the Soviet Union during the war, and studied agriculture. In 1944–45 he served as minister of agriculture in the provisional National Government, but fell into disfavor for his go-slow approach to collectivization. Partially due to his close connections with Malenkov and Soviet anxiety over the autocracy of Hungarian Stalinist leader Mátyás Rákosi (and the popular revulsion toward his rule), Nagy was promoted to the position of premier in 1953. Nagy's appointment was short-lived, for after 18 months of political and ideological tug-of-war with Rákosi, Khrushchev's victory provided Rákosi the excuse he needed to oust Nagy from the leadership, charging him and his "New Course" with right-wing opportunism. Throughout 1955 an "unofficial" opposition developed around Nagy, which included Hungarian communists (as opposed to

the Muscovite variety) persecuted by Rákosi, former anti-fascist resistance leaders, writers, and rebellious journalists associated with *Szabad Nép* (*Free People*—the official party newspaper that had dared to criticize the regime). Student unrest and protest in Szeged and Budapest ushered in the mass demonstration of October 23 and the resulting armed conflict; Nagy was personally involved in neither. Initially Nagy took part in Politburo discussions of containing the conflict through radical changes in the program and leadership of the party; not until October 28 did he lend his unconditional support to the uprising. At this point Nagy obviously decided on leading a revolution rather than a restoration; by October 31 he announced Hungary's intention to withdraw from the Warsaw Pact and on November 1 made his now-famous appeal to the United Nations.

7 Kende discusses November 1956 as the "Waterloo of leftist thought" but then admits the Prague Spring "evoked the impression that not all is lost in the Soviet orbit, communism may be redeemable, can receive a 'human face ... '" (in Litván, 1996: 174). In fact, for some of the very reasons Kende expresses–the élan of Czechoslovak reform communism among Western intellectuals, the notion that it was founded on and through socialist market economics combined with greater political liberalism, and the resulting disappointment that the WTO invasion truncated a positive and promising alternative (in Skilling's words an "interrupted revolution")—I would argue strongly that the failure of the Prague Spring was a much greater defeat on an ideological level. This perception has been reinforced through my interviews, and especially by my discussions with János Kis and Miklós Haraszti. To the extent that 1956 did represent a "Waterloo" or more accurately, a watershed, it was more so among Western intellectuals. See for example, Tony Judt (1992).

8 There has been considerable debate, for example, on the role of Radio Free Europe in encouraging Hungarians to believe Western assistance would be forthcoming; a commentary on November 4 declared "a practical manifestation of Western sympathy is expected at any hour" (quoted in Timothy Garton Ash (1996). Of particular contention is whether or not these "false hopes" were generated by Hungarian journalists operating in accordance with US policy guidance at the time and, if so, whether many more lost their lives as freedom fighters as a result.

9 In the early days of the conflict, between 10,000 and 15,000, armed Hungarian "freedom fighters" took part (mostly young people, men and women, mostly from poorer parts of Budapest, especially from worker/apprentice barracks—the most marginalized, oppressed, and poverty-stricken segment of the population in the mid-1950s). It is still difficult to estimate the number of deaths and casualties fighting on either the Hungarian or Soviet side. A minimum of 2,700 Hungarian losses were reported by Litván; recently declassified Soviet documents are also cited which suggest 669 Soviet soldiers died, although this figure may have

been minimized (1996: 102–103). Clearer from Litván is the full extent of reprisals after the installation of the Kádár government. From 1956 to 1959, Litván estimates 35,000 were subject to prosecutorial investigation; between 1957 and 1960 13,000 ended up in internment camps. Approximately 350 people in total were executed (1996: 143–144). The border remained open from the end of October until late November; in less than one month over 180,000 refugees arrived in Austria (more than 200,000 left in total). The emigration after the uprising represented the largest mass exodus and professional "brain drain" ever experienced by the country.

10 The reconstituted communist government formed under the leadership of Kádár between November 2 and November 4 in Szolnok, with Soviet approval.

11 See Robert V. Daniels, ed. (1994), *A Documentary History of Communism and the World,* — 3rd edition (Hannover, N. H.: U. P. of New England), pp. 172–173 and Rudolf L. Tőkés (1996), *Hungary's Negotiated Revolution: Economic Reform, Social Change, and Political Succession* (Cambridge: Cambridge U. P.), pp. 18–19.

12 Kádár was purposefully inverting Rákosi's earlier catch phrase of Stalinist consolidation and paranoia: "He who is not with us is against us." The message was one of live and let live, as long as political quiescence and public acquiescence were the rule.

13 From November 4 to 22, Imre Nagy and close associates obtained refuge in the Yugoslav embassy in Budapest, and refused to either resign or recognize the Kádár government. Although they had been guaranteed safe conduct out of the embassy, they were in fact abducted by the KGB and taken to Romania, where they were both tried and executed.

14 Miklós Molnár (1971) is best known for having described 1956 as "the victory of a defeat." As Ash (1996) pointed out, 1956 was also a turning point in the West's recognition of Hungary and its sympathetic reception. This "positive association" replaced the "negative or non-existent one" Westerners generally had of Hungary, as an oppressor of minority cultures before 1914 (for example, Slovaks, Croats, Romanians) or as the dithering and ineffective ally of Hitler during the Second World War.

15 In fact the regime was so successful in this regard that it goes a long way to explain the smaller size of the intellectual dissident community in Hungary.

16 In fact, because cheap raw materials and economic resources were no longer available by the late 1960s, the USSR and its satellite states had exhausted the possibilities of easy extensive industrialization.

17 I am indebted to Tőkés for highlighting the significance of this "bold coupling"; interestingly he found no compelling explanation for why the latter was included in a program of largely economic reform, but it

clearly had to do with the regime linking political legitimacy to economic performance. See Tőkés, 1996, chapter 2, "Economic Reforms: From Plan to Market."

18 There is a rich literature on the NEM, for example, B. Balassa (1970); G. R. Denton (1971); P. G. Hare and H. Radice, eds. (1981). On the Hungarian debate regarding the failure to implement or correctly enforce the NEM from different points of view, see László Antal (1979); Tamás Bauer (1976) (1979), and (1983); Teresa Laky (1981); and Ivan Schweitzer (1981). A useful summary is Támas Bauer's in Ferenc Fehér and Andrew Arato, eds. (1991).

19 Not in the sense of losing one's job, but being considered ineligible for promotion or new positions given the emphasis on education and expertise.

20 By the end of the 1970s, Hungary already had a 6–7 billion dollar debt and it was increasingly clear that this burden could not be alleviated through successful competition on the world market.

21 Legal activities included the sale of agricultural products by private farmers, cottage goods manufacturing, and licensed transactions by various service workers—crafts persons contractors, repair persons, and professionals, especially in medical and dental fields. Illegal or semi-legal activities were the unlicensed versions of the same activities listed above, and out-and-out illegal activities included the giving and receipt of gratuities, bribery, corruption, black-market and currency speculation or the conduct of entirely underground operations (see Skilling, 1989: 165).

22 Berend (1990, 1996) estimated that by the mid-1980s private businesses accounted for up to 80% of construction work, 60% of the service sector, about one-third of the total agricultural production, and 15% of industrial output.

23 A good example is the provision of privately developed housing units in Budapest which, on the one hand, alleviated the dramatic shortage of urban dwellings but, on the other, generated inflationary pressures on costs such that ordinary citizens were paying an increasingly large share of their net incomes on housing.

24 Trans. from Hungarian, text of a lecture given at international conference in Florence, Italy, "Democracy and Thinking Differently in Eastern Europe." Also appeared as "The Hungarian Miracle," in *Irodalmi Újság* (July–August 1979): 1–2.

25 See "It is Not Hopeless if You Demand: An Interview with Miklós Haraszti," *Uncaptive Minds* (April–May 1988): 15–19.

26 The definitive biography is Arpad Kadarkay (1991), *Georg Lukács: Life Thought, and Politics* (Oxford: Basil Blackwell).

27 This was partially because of Lukács' own influence; he saved Ferenc Fehér from being expelled from university, as he did later with writer and dissident György Konrád (Kadarkay, 1991: 416). Ágnes Heller was expelled from the party in 1959, but was still able to publish. György Márkus was assistant professor of philosophy at Lórand Eötvös University (ELTE) from 1957 to 1959 and later joined the Hungarian Academy of Science's Institute of Philosophy. András Hegedüs founded the Hungarian Academy of Science's Sociological Research Group, of which Mária Márkus, also a noted sociologist and co-author of Hegedüs, was party secretary. Lukács' position in post-1956 Hungary continued to be an ambiguous one: as a towering figure of Marxist philosophy he could not be easily discounted, although he was identified by Moscow as a chief "revisionist" along with Kołakowski in Poland and Lefebvre in France. Despite considerable pressure, he refused to emigrate and over time was more or less tolerated by the authorities. His description of the absurd situation was, "I got stuck in their throat, and they were unable to either swallow or spit me out" (quoted in Kadarkay, 1991: 441). It was not coincidental that the regime crackdown on the intellectuals associated with the School occurred *after* Lukács' death in 1971.

28 Hegedüs was a leading communist politician, served as prime minister in 1955–1956, and was considered a Stalinist hard-liner. However after emigrating to (and then returning from) Moscow in the late 1950s, he organized and was leader of the sociological research group in the Hungarian Academy of Sciences. He first attracted criticism through his editorship of the sociological journal *Valóság*. His own personal process of rethinking the process that led up to 1956 reached a high point with his vocal opposition to the WTO invasion of Czechoslovakia and expulsion from the party in 1973. He later formulated his position for "radical reformism" and "a great historic compromise" together with a proposal for the creation of a new "historical bloc" (in the Gramscian sense) which would transcend existing monolithic social regimes. In a sense, Hegedüs' vision can be considered yet another Hungarian expression of the "third way."

29 A telling reminder of this fact occurred in 1956: as a member of Imre Nagy's government in 1956, he was one of two cabinet members who did *not* support Hungary's withdrawal from the Warsaw Pact.

30 Subsequently, they took on the banner as "post-Marxists."

31 In my interview with Ágnes Heller on 22 August 1995, she noted that from 1957 onward Lukács could and did receive books from the West; being in his circle meant access to contemporary scholarly literature from outside the Soviet Bloc. This fact combined with Lukács' stringent emphasis on being grounded in the philosophical classics—Plato, Aristotle, Kant, and Hegel in particular—meant that his students were well versed not only in Marxist theory but in classical and contemporary debates.

32 This came later, most notably with Fehér, Heller, and Márkus' publication of *Dictatorship over Needs: An Analysis of Soviet Societies* in 1983, after all three had left Hungary.

33 In the summer of 1968 while attending a conference of philosophers at Korcula in Yugoslavia, György Márkus, Mária Márkus, Ágnes Heller, and Ferenc Fehér all signed a declaration condemning the intervention of WTO troops in Czechoslovakia. György and Mária Márkus were both expelled from the party as a result.

34 See Silvio Trevisani, "Why They are Leaving Hungary," *L'Unita*, February 9, 1978.

35 Both Heller and Fehér subsequently joined the Graduate Faculty of the New School for Social Research, where Heller remains currently, as Hannah Arendt, Professor of Philosophy.

36 Quoted in RFE Report (Hungarian Section/KK), "Prominent Dissident Intellectuals Emigrate from Hungary," Munich, February 10, 1978.

37 A good example is the work on and many contributions of Heller and the Budapest School emigrés to the journal *Praxis International*, involvement with NSSR's *Social Research*, and cooperation with the (NSSR) East and Central Europe Program's Democracy Seminars (the Budapest seminars were chaired by former Márkus student György Bence, assisted organizationally by Fehér in New York).

38 Tőkés is emphatic in making the historical comment that the earlier generations of Hungarian populists were "*not* the Russian Narodnik-type urban visionaries bound on a mission to enlighten, or learn from, the poor" (1996: 176). Rather, they tended to be educated provincial intellectuals and writers whose aim was to promote the cultural modernization and development of rural Hungary. In many respects they were radically critical of official policy during the Horthy regime, but to the extent that populist roots were agrarian and anticapitalist, they were also nationalist and inward-seeking, and thus susceptible to both fascist and anti-Semitic sympathies (see Lukacs, 1988: 132–134).

39 On the historical development of these two groups and the antagonism between them, see John Lukacs (1988), especially chapter 4, "Politics and Powers" and chapter 6, "Seeds of Troubles."

40 For a deliberate caricature of the differences, see Timothy Garton Ash, "A Hungarian Lesson" in Garton Ash (1991a), *The Uses of Adversity*, p. 135.

41 Still, the *népi* writers were not considered as part of the regional community of dissent in the same way as the members of the emerging urbanist democratic opposition, and and are not included in this study.

42 The poem, "Che's Errors," first published in *New Writing*, was the subject of a rather polemical rejoinder by regime supporter Rafis Hajdu in *Népszabadság* (*People's Freedom*, the successor to *Szabad Nép*).

43 Károlyi was a prominent Hungarian politician and statesman. In the collapse of the Austro-Hungarian Empire following the First World War, he was briefly declared Prime Minister, and from January 1 to March 20, 1919 he was Provisional President of the Republic. Thus although he had been active as leader of the radicalized Independence Party from 1913 onward (as a potential and popular alternative to the conservative corporatist elite ruling the country), his moment in the political spotlight was sandwiched between the oppressive and short-lived Hungarian Soviet Republic of 1919 and the counter-revolutionary crackdown of the Horthy regime. László Rajk was a prominent "indigenous" communist, appointed to lead the Ministry of the Interior in 1946 and was also briefly deputy secretary general. He was the chief rival of Mátyás Rákosi and in 1949 was arrested and stripped of his positions. Three months later he and several alleged accomplices were tried in what became the first of the famous postwar show trials in the region. He was coerced into falsely confessing that he was a Titoist and Western spy, in regular contact with two Americans ostensibly in the employ of John Foster Dulles—Noel and Hermann Field. Rajk was sentenced to death and executed. His son (of the same name) became a prominent and outspoken member of the democratic opposition in the 1970s and 1980s.

44 Konrád's novel *The City Builder* was rejected by a Hungarian publisher because it was considered "too bleak"! (Konrád, 1995: X).

45 Quoted in RFE Report, "Thirty Hungarian Intellectuals Express Solidarity with Charter 77," Munich, January 20, 1977.

46 Signatories included, for example, Budapest School members such as Mihály Vajda and Ágnes Heller, Miklós Haraszti, established writers such as Miklós Mészöly and Sándor Csoóri, and veterans of 1956 such as poet István Eörsi and historian Ferenc Donáth.

47 "Hungarians Reportedly Protest Prague Trial," October 30, 1979 (Paris: CND/AFP news wire report).

48 For example, on behalf of Solidarity, Janusz Onyszkiewicz sent greetings to free trade unions in Hungary in March, 1989. The organization Polish–Hungarian Solidarity (modelled on the Polish–Czechoslovak counterpart) was formed 18 February 1989, and sent formal greetings on the anniversary of the 1848 uprising, a day of mass action in the country. Polish unofficial and emigré publications published Hungarian samizdat and news of the democratic opposition: typical is the coverage of the Polish Solidarity news magazine *Kontakt*, which provided a revisionist and independent account of the 1956 events, as well as a report on the activities of the opposition and an interview with János Kis ["*Ze Świata Węgry*," *Marzec* 84, 3(23): 44–68].

49 Between 100 and 200 individuals, mostly from the younger generation, met once a month in different private apartments for both lectures and discussions.

50 Tőkés tellingly quotes Kádár's comment at a December, 1980 Politburo meeting: "… should the opposition try to link up with the workers, then all bets are off, for no one can act against the Hungarian People's Republic and remain unpunished" (Tőkés, 1996: 175). There were isolated reports of disturbances, for example, among workers of the Csepel iron and steel works at the same time as the Gdańsk strikes. Fearing a Polish-type reaction, the party-state wisely withdrew a planned price hike. Similarly, fearing a martial-law type reaction, the intellectuals avoided any worker–intellectual alliance.

51 Not surprisingly, one of the most influential entries was that written by György Bence and János Kis entitled *On Being a Marxist*. The authors used the opportunity to explain their philosophical break with the older members of the Budapest School and instead advocated "radical reformism," which owed much to the ideas of Adam Michnik and Jacek Kuroń.

52 See also Balázs Rab (1978).

53 Demszky's trial, like that of Haraszti ten years earlier, generated international attention. He received a suspended sentence for the "assault." In May 1984, 179 individuals signed a "report of public interest" addressed to the Supreme Court expressing concern over the verdict. Significantly, about one quarter of the signatories were students and workers *not* actively associated with the opposition ["Appeal of Hungarian Samizdat Literature Publisher Rejected," RFE Report, Munich, May 24, 1984 (RAD/Reisch)].

54 *Beszélő* has the additional meaning in Hungarian of "prison visiting hours."

55 Entire text of the first issue editorial is translated and appears in (1983) *Index on Censorship* 12.2: 8–9.

56 Personal interview with János Kis, November 22, 1995.

57 For the English translation of the introduction to this issue, see *Uncaptive Minds* 1.1 (April–May 1988): 5–8.

58 A discussion group under the egis of *Kommunista Ifjúsági Szövetség*, or KISZ (the Communist Youth Alliance) organization of ELTE, which focused on Central European Identity. For an insider view, see Gyula Bartók (1987).

59 Many of Bibó's most original and compelling essays were written in response to the events of the early postwar period, and have only recently been translated into English in a volume edited by Károly Nagy (1991), entitled *Democracy, Revolution, and Self-Determination*.

60 Bibó's compromise consisted of substituting for the demand for Warsaw Pact withdrawal a bilateral treaty, an amnesty for Stalin-era transgressions, and a staged removal of Soviet troops. Above all, he wanted both

to protect the achievements of the revolution and to respond to Soviet anxieties over their sphere of influence.

61 The program of the MDF was translated and reprinted in (1990) *East European Reporter* 4.2: 73–75, after their decisive March 1990 electoral victory.

62 At this point Grósz could have initiated proceedings to have Pozsgay expelled from the Central Committee or even resorted to a "scorched earth" policy by declaring martial law. He was dissuaded by the Americans (and likely the Soviets as well) on the second point, and in any event he could not have necessarily counted on internal support for such a move. On the first point, it would have been counter-intuitive at this time to attempt to eliminate the party's most popular leader given the uncertain nature of reform (see Tőkés, 1996: 253–304).

63 This led to the appointment of a four-member expert committee whose task was not only to evaluate the history of Hungarian state socialism, but whose instructions referred explicitly to the "people's uprising" which emerged against the government and the regime (Berend, 1996: 274).

64 The new legislation made it possible for anyone to nominate a candidate who, once nominated, was allowed to speak freely with legal protection.

65 A pleasant surprise for many dissidents was that during the meetings members of the audience raised issues only previously discussed in samizdat, evidence that the illegal publications were reaching a much broader audience than overt supporters of the opposition. See Andrew Short (1985).

66 Demszky's 1985 article, "Parliamentarism in Eastern Europe: the Chances of the Independent Candidate," which appeared in English in *East European Reporter,* is also noteworthy because of its obvious indebtedness to Adam Michnik's analysis in his seminal essay "A New Evolutionism." Virtually every Hungarian activist I interviewed brought my attention to the importance of Michnik's formulation to the Hungarian context.

67 In *Beszélő* 13–14. Translated and reprinted as János Kis (1986).

68 The location of the project, the Danube-bend, is considered to be one of the most beautiful parts of the river landscape. Environmentalists feared such massive intervention would have long-term negative consequences for the soil, water, and vegetation of the area.

69 See interview with Vargha (1990).

70 The story does not end here. The Slovakian government, eager for the economic benefits that the project promised to yield, eventually took their case to the International Court of Justice at the Hague. The court's judgment, released in October, 1997, cannot be easily summarized, but certainly was considered a "victory" for the Slovak side. Negotiations

still continue between the two governments, and Hungary's position in the affair was an issue in the May, 1998 elections (which Fidesz won).

71 Thompson was not allowed to give a planned university lecture, but did deliver it informally to an audience gathered in the flat of György Konrád, and took part in a roundtable discussion with Hungarian participants, including András Hegedüs and Miklós Haraszti. See Bill Lomax (1984a).

72 Four women from Greenham Common arrived in Hungary to lend their organizational support, but once they arrived at the Római camp location, were taken in for questioning and later escorted to the Austrian border and expelled. See Bill Lomax (1984b).

73 Both were suspended by Hungarian Primate László Lékai. He was an outspoken opponent of priests who dared defend the right to object to military service, citing Saint Paul and church doctrine on the use of force in the defense of the nation.

74 They included Susan Sontag, François Bondy, Hans Magnus Enzensberger, Alain Finkelkraut, Timothy Garton Ash, Jiří Gruša, Danilo Kis, György Konrád, Amos Oz, and Per Wästberg. Topics included "Censorship and Self-Censorship," "Writing in Exile," "Ethnic Identity in Literature," "The Rights of Minorities," and "The Future of a European Culture." For an amusing and revealing personal memoir, see Timothy Garton Ash (1991a: 130–141).

75 The Bibó College itself was legendary as a hotbed of student unrest. In the mid-to-late-1980s, the student leaders of the College (the same individuals who founded Fidesz) invited many of the members of the democratic opposition to come and speak to/with them, including Miklós Haraszti, János Kis, and Gábor Demszky. Furthermore, their ideas were made public through the college newspapers' articles. Interview with Gábor Fodor, October 14, 1997.

76 Both parties had participated in the post-1945 coalition government, and had briefly revived themselves in 1956.

77 András Bozóki refers to "independent initiatives" inside the party during its period of "internal disintegration" and the more politicized "social movements" outside the party. The Endre Bajcsy-Zsilinszky Society was an example of the former; the MDF, Fidesz, SzDSz, TDDSZ, and Duna Kör are examples of the latter. See András Bozóki (1993).

78 The *Hazafias Népfront* (HNF, or Patriotic People's Front) was the largest mass membership organization in Hungary, equipped with a national newspaper and a network of local organizations. The role of the HNF was to be a "transmission belt to convey and gain acceptance of the party's policies by the country's non-communist majority"(Tőkés, 1996: 236–237). In the 1980s Imre Pozsgay transformed the organization from this role into a personal power base not bound to the factional and segmented interests of the other transmission belt organizations (built as

they were around particular social constituencies, for example, women, workers, and young people).

79 Endre Bajcsy-Zsilinszky was a prominent politician active in the inter-war period, a populist and nationalist known for favoring closer working relationships with the Social Democrats and the Communists. He was arrested and executed by the Gestapo for his role in the founding of the *Magyar Nemzeti Felkelés Felszabadító Bizottsága*, the Committee of Liberation of the Hungarian National Uprising, in 1944.

80 Interview with Gábor Fodor, October 14, 1997.

81 Over 100,000 Hungarians took to the streets, cheering for the leaders of the democratic opposition. This visual display of support beyond the intellectuals and student activists that had formed its core since the mid-1980s was critical in providing both legitimacy and bargaining power.

82 A "third side" was added in May at the insistence of the MSZMP, and consisted of its traditional agencies and auxiliaries: the *Hazafias Nép-front* (HNF), or Patriotic People's Front; the *Szakszervezetek Országos Tanácsa* (SZOT), or National Council of Trade Unions; the National Council of Hungarian Women, the Ferenc Münnich Society, the *Baloldali Alternatíva* (BAL), or Left Alternative Association; the youth organization of the Communist party (formerly KISZ, now transformed into *Demokratikus Ifjúsági Szövetség* (DEMISZ), or the Democratic Youth Organization); and the Association of Hungarian Resistance Fighters and Antifascists. The inclusion of the "third side" was a regime victory but only a partial one, as the ORT insisted that, like themselves, the third side speak with a unified voice (narrowing the number of options and manoeuvrability of the players). Thus the National Roundtable was not in fact round, but triangular (see Bozóki, 1993: 289).

83 On the details of the talks themselves, see Bruszt, 1990; Bozóki, 1993; Sajó in Elster, ed., 1996; and Tőkés, 1996. Over 150 hours of the talks were videotaped by *Fekete Doboz*, an independent video journal. The footage was edited into a five-hour film, entitled *Ellenzéki Kerekasztal* (Opposition Roundtable). The original 150 hour record is available for public screening in the Széchényi Library in Budapest. Available in Hungarian is an eight-volume account of the Hungarian Roundtable Talks (see Bozóki A., ed. 1999–2000); a short English version has been published in 2002 by Central European University Press.

84 The Reform Circles served not only as an engine for reform within the party, but also undermined the party's legitimacy and centralized apparatus, as many of the reform-circle representatives had great affinity with the opposition, urging talks with and perhaps wanting to join the ORT (Bruszt, 1990: 378; Bozóki, 1993: 287).

85 In the June 10 agreement concluding preparatory talks, the third side stated it would support agreement between the party and the ORT,

and in so doing both acknowledged and limited its bargaining position (Bozóki, 1993: 289).

86 Much of the "transitology" literature of the early 1990s drew on and was inspired by the earlier work of comparativists O'Donnell and Schmitter (1989) in their comprehensive work on comparing the transitions from authoritarian rule in Latin America and Southern Europe, as well as that of Diamond et al. (1990). There ensued a *grand débat*, fought out largely in the pages of *Slavic Review*, between the "transitologists" arguing for the value and utility of broad comparisons and the "area studies" specialists making their case for the uniqueness of the Central and East European transitions. See Philippe C. Schmitter and Terry Lynn Karl (1994); Valerie Bunce (1995); and again Schmitter and Karl (1995). See also Daniel V. Friedheim (1993), and Joan M. Nelson (1993).

87 My summary of Kis' position here is taken from his Democracy Lecture, November 17, 1995, East and Central Europe Program, New School for Social Research.

88 The post-1989 success of the communist successor parties in the region seems to have born out this operating assumption. See Alison Mahr and John Nagle (1995).

89 The text of the agreement is translated as Appendix 7.1 in Tőkés, 1996: 357–360.

Chapter 5: Intellectuals in Poland: The Tradition Continues

1 Kołakowski has been prolific and far-reaching in his philosophy. However, in this section I will be specifically concentrating only on the period in which he questioned his revisionist approach in the context of the emerging Polish opposition. For this reason, I will not be covering landmark essays such as "Responsibility and History," his later comprehensive examination of Marxism, or his most recent turn to Christianity.

2 I am particularly indebted in what follows to David Ost's analysis of Kołakowski's role and thought, as well as to my conversations with Jacek Kucharczyk.

3 As both Marxist revisionist and unofficial intellectual "spokesperson" of this trend, Kołakowski is most well known in the West for his essay "Responsibility and History," which is reprinted in Kołakowski (1969).

4 I make this point in partial refutation of the tendency to view Kołakowski's "conversion" to Christianity as a sudden and clear break with his "Marxist" past. Michnik also discusses the subtle depth of Kołakowski's religious knowledge and arguments in such early essays as "Jesus Christ: Prophet and Reformer." Michnik sees Kołakowski's early engagement with religious thought and Catholic doctrine as a classic missed

opportunity, where dialogue might have ensued much earlier between the Episcopate and the revisionists. See Michnik, 1993: 33–35.

5 See Kołakowski (1978).

6 Issue 224 in the *Biblioteka Kultury*. It was not translated into English until 1989.

7 Like Havel, Kołakowski sees this alienation as a result of the technological imperatives of production and exchange contemporary life—equally problematic in the transnational concentration of capital or the anonymous bureaucracies and planned direction of state socialism (1989: 85–86).

8 Ironically, as Kołakowski's new approach galvanized the Polish opposition, he came increasingly under attack by the Western New Left for *his* despair and hopelessness. See in particular the vitriolic exchange between Kołakowski and veteran socialist and historian in the 1973 and 1974 issues of *Socialist Register*. The debate is much larger than the personal antagonism between Thompson and Kołakowski, and above all signals a fundamental lack of understanding between opposition in the East and West.

9 Jeffrey C. Goldfarb (1982) explains the communications and understanding gap between the oppositions in the "East" and "West" in terms of how dominant values (for example, freedom and quality) are differently produced—defined and administered in the case of authoritarian communism, or created within a shared public realm, albeit flawed by manipulation and coercion, under liberal democracies. Much fallout has occurred from the basic misbelief that oppositions across the political divide between East and West must logically share similar world views. Moreover, Goldfarb maintains that because the conditions for public life are so different in the East from the West, an oppositional ethos and strategy evolves which both transcends and defies traditional Western categories of left versus right, liberal versus conservative, and revolutionary versus reformist. See Goldfarb (1982: 7–13).

10 This phrase and the following analysis owe much to Jan Zielonka's essay "The ethics of emancipation" (in Zielonka, 1989: 35–69).

11 Translated literally, the title is *Church, Left, Dialogue* but it has been rendered by Ost as *The Church and the Left* following the French translation *L'Église et la gauche*, first published in 1979. The English translation did not appear until 1993.

12 See for example, Ksiądz Henryk Jańkowski (1992).

13 Michnik borrows the term "Julianic Church" from Polish historian Bohdan Cywiński, who used it to refer simultaneously to both the history of the Catholic Church under Julian the Apostate in Rome as well as to the current aspirations of the Polish Church. The Emperor Julian

decreed the separation of church and state not by choice but by force. The "Julianic Church" seeks to reestablish its position of power *vis-à-vis* the state; its alliance with a discontented and alienated society is but a temporary and tactical move in a larger game to assure its own power and longevity. See "Introduction" by David Ost in Michnik, 1993: 14–15. For his post-communist views on religion and the Church, see Michnik, 1995.

14 Michnik uses Leszek Kołakowski as the example *par excellence* of a revisionist who categorically refused to take any position toward the Church except that of extreme hostility. He illustrates his point with Kołakowski's reaction to Cardinal Stefan Wyszyński's favorable citation of his essay "Jesus Christ: Prophet and Reformer." In an exploration of historic alternativity, Michnik suggests that this *might* have been the beginning of a *rapprochement* between the independent/revisionist Left and the Catholic Episcopate, but Kołakowski distanced himself from both the Cardinal's interpretation and stubbornly remained silent on party-state persecution of the Church. Later in the book, Kołakowski is again made the example—the atheist revisionist who not only comes to terms with the Church but embraces its teachings.

15 Terminology here is important. Ost translates the Polish term *nacjonalizm* as nationalism-chauvinism to convey the ethnocentric narrowness of the original term. Obscurantism in the Polish context often refers to narrow-minded, traditionally conservative, inaccessible, and obsolete religious reasoning and dogma (in this definition it is commonly used as an epithet hurled against the Church by the prewar Left). It is also used in the sense of being backward, that is opposed to "Enlightenment," "Knowledge," and "Progress."

16 In chapter 4, "The Conflict over the Pastoral Letter," Michnik discusses how the left-wing intelligentsia willingly accepted the regime's propaganda campaign against the Church in the 1965 debate over the Pastoral Letter released by the Polish Episcopate to Germans granting and asking for forgiveness over mutual wrongdoings committed during the war (for example, Nazi atrocities against Poles and the expulsion of Germans from lands east of the postwar Oder–Neisse border). The party-state's clever deployment of xenophobic and nationalistic slogans in its battle with the Church made it easier for the authorities to instrumentally and ideologically suggest an alliance between nationalism and anti-Semitism, or conversely between antitotalitarianism and antipatriotism (1993: 94). Thus the battle with the Church paved the way for the battle with the regime's leftist critics and the student opposition in 1968.

17 Słonimski was a poet, playwright and essayist who was associated with the prewar Left. He was president of the Polish Writers' Association in the late 1950s and a respected moral authority for Polish dissidents generally and for Michnik personally. Michnik worked as a secretary for

Słonimski in the early 1970s and refers to his mentorship extensively in his writing.

18 Michnik initiates a series of repeated comparisons between the values and objectives of the dissidents of East-Central Europe and the goals of the French, and more particularly, the American revolutions.

19 General Czesław Kiszczak was Minister of Internal Affairs at the time martial law was declared and thus was primarily responsible for the round-up and arrest of Solidarity activists and intellectual dissidents such as Michnik. He was also prominently involved in the Roundtable Talks in April, 1989. However, whereas the relationship between Michnik and Jaruzelski has surprisingly developed into a post-communist friendship based on mutual respect, the personal animosity between Michnik and Kiszczak is legendary. See Rosenberg, 1996: 233.

20 In fact, the secular Left did embrace the Church, especially after the election of a Polish pope. They supported the use of religious symbols by the workers in 1980, and sought refuge in the Church during martial law. Arguably the Left moved much closer to the Church than vice versa, a tendency which disturbed both Michnik and his secular critics. See Ost, "Introduction," in Michnik, 1993: 18–22.

21 This is why Michnik has been highly critical of the Church in the post-Communist period, with its demands for mandatory religious instruction, severe restrictions on abortion, and even constitutional recognition. For a comprehensive overview and critique of the Church's role in Poland since 1989, see Mirella Eberts (1998).

22 Michnik uses the term "neo-positivists" in his writing to refer to the Catholic activists in organizations such as *Znak* who were supported by and sought compromise with the communist authorities. Under the leadership of Stanisław Stomma, *Znak* entered the *Sejm* in 1957, signaling the regime's shaky *modus vivendi* with the Church. Unlike the pro-regime PAX, neopositivists did not try to promote a conciliation between Marxism and Christianity—they rejected Marxist–Leninist ideology while recognizing the necessary geopolitical fact of Poland's loyalty to the Soviet Union.

23 See for example, Charles Tilly (1993), and Theda Skocpol (1979).

24 Schell wrote these comments in his introduction to *Letters in Prison* in 1985 but in this author's view are equally valid in assessing the period 1989–1991.

25 Nationalist uprisings that sought to put Poland back on the map during the nineteenth century occurred in 1830–1831 and 1863–1864. Historian Norman Davies calls this period "The Romantic Age of Insurrections" and discusses in detail the great divide in nineteenth century Polish politics as the debate between the "Romantic–Insurrectionary–Idealist" camp and the "Positivist–Conciliatory–Realist" camp. See especially Chapter

IV, "The Legacy of Spiritual Mastery: Poland during the Partitions, 1795–1918" in Davies (1991).

26 In this regard, Michnik regards Solidarity's "loss" after December 13, 1981 as a "victory in defeat." Resistance to martial law was in the form of societal silence (not to be confused with acquiescence), which minimized loss, and allowed for the underground preservation of both Solidarity and the independent organizations it spawned (1985: 88).

27 In a long historical essay entitled "Conversations in the Citadel," Michnik describes and argues against two prominent strains in Polish socialist thought—the universalist, anti-nationalist, and radically democratic utopianism of Rosa Luxemburg and the bureaucratic-revolutionary approach of Edward Abramowski. In different ways, both emphasized the importance of workers's struggle in the eventual attainment of power, and were critical of Lenin and the Russian Revolution—both for the vanguardist approach and the autocratic and bureaucratic result. Although neither renounced violence as a means, Abramowski believed revolutionary methods decisively influenced the shape of political outcomes, and Luxemburg was critical of any attempts to deprive workers of their civil rights, no matter what the goal. See Michnik, 1985: 293–304.

28 Bratkowski purposefully quotes Talleyrand here.

29 The authors relied upon data from the Central Statistical Office and a research project conducted at the Warsaw Motorcycle Factory.

30 At the famous eighth plenum in October, 1956, a resolution was adopted that stipulated members may hold divergent views and submit them to their local party organization, as long as they did not appeal to public opinion outside the party about any decisions taken.

31 To the extent Kuroń developed his thinking in line with Polish reality and possibilities for change, he was also roundly criticized (like Kołakowski) by his former admirers in the West for his "disavowal" of earlier views. According to this Western Trotskyist interpretation, Kuroń's change of heart amounted to a hopelessly reformist perspective, lacking in revolutionary aims and objectives. Such fatal flaws were as responsible for the defeat of Marxist revisionism as (later) for Solidarity itself. See in particular Colin Barker's "Introduction" to the 1982 Bookmarks edition of the *Open Letter*, as well as Colin Barker and Kara Weber (1982).

32 Kuroń's work can be fruitfully compared with Alexis de Tocqueville's *Democracy in America*, especially Volume 2, Book 2, chapters 2–8, where he discusses individualism in democracies, how its revolutionary potential is countered by free institutions and associational autonomy, the important linkages between civil and political associations, and how self-interest is tempered by the common good.

33 "Politics and Opposition in Poland" (*Polityczna opozycja w Polsce*) was first published in *Kultura* in 1974, and later included in Kuroń's 1984

published collection of essays *Polityka i odpowiedzialność* (*Politics and Responsibility*) (London: Aneks); it has not been translated into English. "Reflections on a Program of Action" (*"Myśli o programie działania"*) was first published in Polish in the London journal *Aneks*, Nos. 13–14 (1977); and English translation (cited from below) appears in *Polish Review* 22 (1977). "Notes on Self–Government" (*"Notaki o samorządzie"*) was first published in the Warsaw samizdat journal *Głos* (*Voice*) 1 (1977). "The Situation of the Country and the Program of the Opposition" (*Sytuacja kraju a program opozycji*) was first printed in Warsaw samizdat periodical *Biluletyn Informacjny* (*Information Bulletin*) 29.3 (1979). All three were reprinted in *Politics and Responsibility*.

34 Kuroń makes the important point that the only two periods of relative prosperity for Poland's working class occurred in 1956–1960 and 1971–1975, both following powerful waves of national strikes. He contrasts these strikes, however, from isolated shop-floor protests, revolts by single shifts, or street demonstrations. The strike remains a valuable organizational tool when used strategically and with the force of both discipline and numbers—only when strikes "achieved the caliber of a social movement" were they truly effective in Kuroń's view (1977: 61–62).

35 Kuroń is quick to dispel, however, the party-state rhetoric that parliamentary democracy amounts meaninglessly to "bourgeois democracy" and notes that "the ownership of the means of production is in no way linked with the parliamentary system" (1977: 59). In this context, his commitment to some form of social ownership is implicit when he states: "While I have remained faithful to the essential values I wish to prevail, my views have changed as to the best and most practical methods of achieving our objectives" (1977: 52).

36 A good summary of the competing and overlapping meanings of democracy and the democratization process can be found in David Potter et al., eds. (1997).

37 The article appears in English in *Labour Focus on Eastern Europe* 10.1, *Uncensored Poland News Bulletin* 22, and *East European Reporter* 3.2. It inspired considerable debate within the provisional council, a summary of which is printed in *Tygodnik Mazowsze* 220.16 and which is translated and accompanies the *Labour Focus on Eastern Europe* version. Quotations here are taken from *East European Reporter* 3.2.

38 The analysis below relies not only on published sources, but on a series of questions forwarded to East-Central European dissidents by H. Gordon Skilling in the late 1980s. The Czechoslovak responses were included in Skilling and Wilson, eds. (1991). With the kind permission of H. Gordon Skilling, the unpublished Polish and Hungarian responses have been made directly available to me.

39 Geremek is one of the few dissidents studied here who explicitly refers to the Gramscian re-working of the Marxist idea of civil society, and it

is worth noting that Gramsci himself was heavily indebted in his views to Benedetto Croce, an important Italian interpreter of Hegel.

40 For a discussion of *opozycja* in this sense see Goldfarb, 1982: 11–13.

Chapter 6: Opposition Intellectuals in Czechoslovakia

1 Veronika Ambros denies that Havel is a traditional absurdist playwright by reference to Martin Esslin's distinction between writers who "present their sense of the irrationality of the human conditions in the form of highly lucid and logically constructed reasoning" versus those who write about the "senselessness of human conditions" (à la Beckett). Ambros suggests Havel is heir to the political satire of the *model theatre* given the devices he regularly employs: "distortion of language, reduction of characters to types or even personification of certain ideological vices; and linearity of plot" (Ambros, 365). She emphasizes the influence of Brecht, socialist dramaturgy, and what Jan Grossman called *appellative* drama: "a theatre that wants above all to pose questions to the spectator, often provocative and extreme ones [counting on] the spectator who is inclined to reply to these questions" (quoted in Ambros, p. 364). However, Havel's themes and characters rise above the particularism of time and place, highlighting their rootlessness and meaninglessness. Havel's plays deliberately respond to the reception of Czech audiences to the absurdist plays first performed in Czechoslovakia in the mid-1960s, by Jarry, Beckett and Ionesco, thus I consider Havel (as he regularly does himself) as an absurdist playwright. See Veronika Ambros (1994) and Marketa Goetz-Stankiewicz (1979: 17–28).

2 Most notably *The Garden Party*, *The Memorandum*, and *The Increased Difficulty of Concentration*.

3 Jan Werich and Jiří Voskovec founded the Liberated Theatre (*Osvobozené Divadlo*) in Prague in the 1920s. Their vaudevillian political and social satire was unsurpassed in its day, and tremendously popular; their first show, "Vestpocket Revue" ran for over two years. The Theatre became a progressive social force, with its trenchant comic attacks on national socialism and Czech conservatism. Like Voskovec and Werich, Havel uses many of the same devices: false syllogisms, inverted logical reasoning, and free association (Ambros, 1994: 364). For a complete discussion of the Liberated Theatre, see Michal Schonberg (1992), *Osvobozené* (Praha: Odeon). Werich and Voskovec were forerunners of the later Semafor Theatre of Jiří Suchý and Jiří Slitr; Havel was fortunate to briefly work under Werich as a stagehand during his last season at the ABC Theatre, and notes his debt to him in *Disturbing the Peace* (Havel, 1990a: 39–41).

4 Many current analyses (Matuštík, 1993; Tucker, 2000) of Havel's philosophy focus solely or primarily on his philosophical writings, however

Havel uses his fiction to grasp *from within* "the social mechanisms and the situation of man crushed by these mechanisms ..." (1990: 65). His later plays, especially the Vaněk plays, *Largo Desolato* and *Temptation* examine the internal and highly personal dilemmas of those trying to resist who are caught irrefutably on the outside and must struggle from this position of disconnectedness. Havel sees these latter plays as directly related to his experience of dissent, and the Faustian theme of *Temptation* is powerful evidence of the depth, urgency, and psychological trauma of such an experience. Keane's 1999 philosophical biography *Václav Havel: A Political Tragedy in Six Acts* provides an integrated picture of Havel's philosophy and fiction.

5 My position here follows my "expansive" notion of political theory more generally. In Czechoslovakia under normalization one could also argue that there was no separation of the "aesthetic" and the "political," a logical outcome of the deliberate party-state fusion of culture and politics. Not only was the decision to write independently a political statement *in and of itself*, but authors who wrote "for the drawer" both chose literature as a way of writing about politics and addressed political themes while producing literature. Klíma's *Judge on Trial* captures the essence of normalization as it was internalized and robbed individuals of their authenticity; the publication of Vaculík's *The Czech Dreambook* was a political event that documented the *angst* of a generation. This is a trend in Czech literature, for it would be hard to maintain that Švejk should be taken solely at face value.

6 The sense of spatial alienation of a large bureaucratic establishment is reinforced through Havel's staging directions and the physical arrangement and patterning of the locations of each scene and their repetition. Jan Grossman's first production of *The Memorandum* at the Theatre of the Balustrade included mundane props in order to visually convey bureaucratic ritual and monotony, such as an empty can in which water kept dripping relentlessly, loud outbursts of music, and the movement of the clerk's eating utensils into and out of the filing cabinets symbolizing the symbiotic relationship between physiological need (eating) and bureaucratic routine. With mechanical precision, *The Memorandum* consists of 12 scenes and four locations, with the place of action being repeated four times, always in the same order. One office location is replaced with another; all are within the confines of the establishment. See Marketa Goetz-Stankiewicz (1979: 49–50 and 54–56).

7 In a compelling comparison to Kafka, Marketa Goetz-Stankiewicz likens the absurdist experience of Josef Gross in receiving a memorandum in a new language (and then discovering that the new language has permeated the office and is now officially sanctioned and regulated) to that of Gregor Samsa of *Metamorphosis,* who wakens one morning to discover he has become an insect. See Goetz-Stankiewicz, 1979: 55.

8 Ballas uses the first person plural throughout the play as he literally speaks for himself and his sidekick Pillar. Ballas' individual responsibility is dissolved into the collective "we"; at the same time Pillar's identity is subsumed into that of Ballas given his continual silence and acquiescence.

9 Havel's terminology for the reform-minded but ideologically stringent communists who were in the forefront of the Prague Spring.

10 In *Disturbing the Peace*, Havel maintained that the argument that there is always "a bigger game at stake" is both delusional and endlessly self-propelling. He uses the example of Smrkovský, who in 1968 "argued in exactly the same way to justify having voting [sic] for the liquidation of *Literární Noviny* in 1967; and later Husák, in exactly the same way, would argue for the exclusion of Smrkovský from the political scene" (1990a: 82).

11 Written at about the same time as *The Memorandum* and delivered as a speech in Prague on June 9, 1965 during the Writers' Union Congress (Havel, 1990a: 10–24).

12 First appeared in the April 4, 1968 edition of *Literární listy*, then an influential intellectual weekly in Czechoslovakia. The article attracted attention because it openly demanded the creation of an opposition party, going well beyond the democratizing initiatives of communist reformers who remained wedded to the idea of the leading role of the party.

13 The private letter to Dubček is dated August 9, 1969.

14 In both "Politics and Conscience" and "The Power of the Powerless," Havel suggests that post-totalitarian regimes are species of a larger category—consumer/industrial/technological societies.

15 Here I interpret "the absolute" as moral threshold, yet elsewhere Havel alludes to the absolute in connection with a Heideggerian notion of Being (i.e. *Dasein*), or in reference to a higher consciousness, perhaps consonant with a universal capacity of human beings for moral reasoning and thus responsibility for action. Terry Nardin interprets Havel's "absolute" as "a sense of limit which defines this world and gives it meaning, and which therefore must be respected"—in effect a "natural law" of the world of personal experience and responsibility. See Terry Nardin (1991), "Moral Renewal: The Lessons of Eastern Europe," *Ethics and International Affairs* 5: 10, and my discussion below in *Letters to Olga*.

16 Aviezer Tucker contends that in these statements and in this line of thought (which he comes back to in "Politics and Conscience") Havel is exposing his debt in particular to Heidegger, albeit through the phenomenology of Patočka (who was a fellow student of Heidegger at Freiburg) and especially via the influence of philosophical historian Václav Bělohradský (a student of Patočka who can be described as more Heideggerian than Patočka himself). See Tucker (1990), and more recently, Tucker (2000b).

17 Havel's pessimistic prediction has unfortunately been borne out, at least to some degree. Many of the dissidents I interviewed have lamented the "loss of history" by its citizens, and many journals in the former Czechoslovakia—*The New Presence, Respekt*, and *Kritika & Kontext* have attempted to "fill the gap" with new/old interpretations of history, historiography, and a revisitation of past debates. This is directly related to the "loss of social time" discussed by Havel.

18 Havel's notion of post-totalitarianism varies: at this stage he is referring to post-Stalinism; his post-1989 writings sometimes refer to the period after the fall of authoritarian communism as "post-totalitarian."

19 Havel makes the key observation that the deployment of ideology is a distinctly modern requirement; small and less-stratified dictatorships could exercise power more nakedly. However, with more complex mechanisms of power, with larger and more stratified societies (with greater numbers of individuals, organizational units, and transmission belts), ideology is required to "act as a kind of bridge between the regime and the people, across which the regime approaches the people and the people approach the regime" (1991: 134).

20 See Jacques Derrida (1994). Interestingly, in his proclamation of the death of Marx and Marxism (and his simultaneous announcement that we are nonetheless all heirs to Marx), Derrida infuses his analysis with a Heideggerian phenomenology not unlike Patočka's, and was in fact heavily influenced by Patočka's *oeuvre* in writing his more recent work *The Gift of Death*. To double the irony, if one interprets Derrida's long excursus on ghosts, specters, simulacra and other synthetic images as representative of Marxist double-coding or ideology, one can understand Derrida's defensive stand on behalf of deconstruction as having "never been Marxist" (1994: 75), that is, stringently anti-ideological. To take Derrida at face value one must also accept that the linguistic turn inherent in deconstruction specifically and post-modernism generally with its own many layers of mystification and deliberate double-coding is *sui generis* and not in any way ideological! For a critical comment on the relationship between Derrida, Patočka, and the post-1989 influence of post-modernism on post-communist intellectuals, see Aviezer Tucker (1998).

21 Havel has been remarkably consistent on this point, even during his presidency. He was extremely reluctant to sign the lustration legislation in Czechoslovakia following the Velvet Revolution. See Rosenberg, 1996: 97–101.

22 Havel contrasts individualism not with collectivism, but with automatism. To act as an individual is *not* to act contrary to any collective will or consensus, but to affirm one's authenticity as against non-thinking conformity, or automatism.

23 Havel calls this "pre-political activity" to differentiate it from conventional party-state controlled politics and to signal its importance as a harbinger of greater possibilities.

24 Havel refers to Masaryk's emphasis on education self-improvement (in the sense of *Bildung*), works that would "stimulate national creativity and national self-confidence," humanitarian projects, and a laborist ethos of work done well and with pride (1991: 172).

25 Havel defines dissidents as those citizens of the Soviet Bloc who decide to live in truth and also meeting the following criteria: 1) their open expression of critical opinions means they are well known in the West; 2) despite persecution they enjoy a level of esteem and an indirect level of power; 3) they focus not on narrow contexts or special interests but embrace causes more generally, thus their work and they themselves get branded as "political"; 4) they tend to be writers and intellectuals; and 5) an invisible line is crossed where the dissident is separated from her or his actual profession and thus defined primarily as a dissident (1991: 167–168).

26 In fact, Havel remained critical of Western leftist experiments that smacked of "retreat," whether to an Indian monastery or via the creation of an alternative lifestyle because such a response "lacks that element of universality" necessary for taking responsibility and providing avenues for action. As Havel so tellingly states: "... not everyone can retire to an ashram" (1994: 196).

27 The University of Toulouse was the second university to grant Havel an honorary doctorate; York University in Toronto was the first. In the former case, he was represented by Czech-born British playwright Tom Stoppard (whom Havel had met for the first time in June, 1977; Stoppard later dedicated his 1978 play *Professional Foul* to Havel in admiration). His York degree was accepted by the founder of Sixty-Eight Publishers Zdena Salivarová. Since 1989 he has received scores of additional honors, including the Sonning Prize in Copenhagen, the Onassis Prize for Man and Mankind, the Indira Gandhi Prize, the Jackson H. Ralston Prize (Stanford University), the Philadelphia Liberty Medal and the Catalonia International Prize. He has been repeatedly nominated for, but has not won, the Nobel Peace Prize.

28 Ivan Havel heads the Center for Theoretical Studies in Prague, an independent center for advanced study associated with Charles University. He is a trained mathematician and received his PhD in computer science from Berkeley. In his samizdat writings Havel was very critical of modern science for its assumption of objectivity and impartiality; he has since argued for an interdisciplinary plurality of "modes of cognition," which might include mysticism, metaphor and other non-scientific modes of reasoning.

29 See the discussion of both these concepts in my analysis of *Letters to Olga* below.

30 Before 1989 Bělohradský lived in exile in Italy and taught at the University of Genoa. After his release from prison in 1984, Havel read his book *The Crisis of the Eschatology of the Impersonal*, and later published an anthology of his work and those who analyzed similar themes as *The Natural World as a Political Problem*, through Edice Expedice. He was also a student of Patočka.

31 See Book VI of Aristotle's *Nichomachean Ethics*, "Intellectual Virtue."

32 Tom Stoppard translated the English version of the play, and produced a film version with F. Murray Abraham in the role of Leopold Nettles.

33 For an excellent comparison between the ideas advanced in "The Power and the Powerless" and those acted out in *Largo Desolato* see William Merrill Downer (1996).

34 See especially Marketa Goetz-Stankiewicz (1987).

35 See his discussion of the purposes of absurd theatre in *Disturbing the Peace* (1991: 53–57).

36 This was a result of Havel's first "long" period of incarceration, following the infamous VONS trial of October, 1979 (the others tried and sentenced were Otta Bednářová, Václav Benda, Jiří Dienstbier, Dana Němcová, and Petr Uhl). All except Němcová were imprisoned; she received a conditionally suspended sentence. Surprisingly and perhaps as a result of sheer bureaucratic stupidity, Havel, Benda, and Dienstbier were imprisoned together at Heřmanice, in Ostrava.

37 In *Persecution and the Art of Writing*, political philosopher Leo Strauss advanced the thesis that much of the Western canon of political thought was written by authors so bold and innovative that their ideas themselves were dangerous, and thus they developed the skill of "writing between the lines" to avoid outright censorship. It is premised on the notion that the authors intended their works to address only "trustworthy and intelligent readers" who have the necessary skills to detect the "real" meanings embedded in the text. Although Strauss' thesis has come quite rightly under attack for its generalized ahistoricity and inapplicability to many cases, it is nonetheless partially applicable in the case of Havel's *Letters to Olga*. See Strauss (1952), especially chapter two.

38 Recall that in "The Power of the Powerless" identity is inextricably linked to responsibility. The anomie of the mass is possible in the post-totalitarian regime because identity is surrendered to the "social auto-totality." The "blind automatism" which drives the system is the lie running through each of its constituent parts. By "living in truth" identity is recovered and asserted as part of the process of assuming responsibility for oneself.

39 I am indebted here to Aviezer Tucker (1990), "Václav Havel's Heideg-gerianism," *Telos* 85: 63–78. Although I think Tucker's incisive analysis does much to illuminate the Heideggerian roots of Havel's writing, and he is absolutely correct in suggesting that, taken as a whole, Havel's views and politics cannot be located on a left–right axis, I strongly disagree with his description of Havel's politics as somehow romantic, pre-modern, and atavistically reactionary. I would suggest a counter argument that rooting politics in non-state organizations and looking at the radical empowerment of citizens as the basis for democratic institutions is, if anything, post-modern in orientation. Havel does not look back with a golden eye to a medieval past of structured community interests, or an ordered social whole; rather, he looks forward *past* the organization of interests in political parties to broader and transnational social move-ments.

40 See in particular Patočka's essay "Masaryk's and Husserl's Conception of the Spiritual Crisis of Europe" in Kohák, 1989: 145–156.

41 No complete work of Jan Patočka's writings is available in French, English, or German. Much translation and preparation is currently underway at the Patočka Archive at the *Institut für Wissenschaften vom Menschen* in Vienna, which holds the translation and publication copyrights of all his work in languages other than Czech or Slovak. Complete German and French editions are in preparation and some volumes have been pub-lished (for example, *L'écrivain, son objet* and *Ausgewählte Schriften* and *Die Bewegung der menschlichen Existenz*). In English, aside from short pieces in journals and edited volumes, the only work solely dedicated to Patočka's life and writing is that of Erazim Kohák (1989). Tucker (2000) devotes three chapters to Patočka in *The Philosophy and Politics of Czech Dissidence from Patočka to Havel* (Pittsburgh: University of Pittsburgh Press).

42 Patočka was a major interpreter of Jan Amos Komenský or Comenius, largely thanks to his ban on academic employment and his work as a clerk in the Comenius Archive. Not only was he able to keep "working" as a philosopher through his close study of the life and thought of Come-nius, but he did much to reorient the standard interpretation of Come-nius—from an East-Central European version of Descartes to his alter-native. Patočka's work on Comenius also illustrates practically his histo-riography of ideas (Kohák, 1989: 27).

43 Transcendental subjectivity is Husserl's answer to the post-Enlighten-ment dilemma of subject versus object. Husserl denied the possibility of objectivity completely but realized that simply substituting subjectivity would slide all meaning into a disconnected relativism. Thus he posits the idea of a transcendental subjectivity, which is prior to and more basic than any individual subject and thus provides a shared context for meaning and ideas (Kohák, 1989: 33). See also F. A. Elliston and P.

McCormick, eds. (1977). This volume also contains in English one of Jan Patočka's critiques of Husserl, entitled "The Husserlian Doctrine of Eidetic Intuition and its Recent Critics."

44 Patočka decried the demise of metaphysics—both in terms of its negative connotation as unscientific and its displacement by rationalism, empiricism, and Marxist or Hegelian theories of history. In his essay "Negative Platonism," Patočka discusses how all of these positivist or dynamic and dialectical approaches *presuppose* a metaphysics—some kind of underlying conception of the whole or view of reality and how it operates. See Kohák, 1989: 54–56 and 175–206.

45 Patočka borrows the term "titanism" from an essay by Masaryk of the same name. Patočka likens Masarykian titanism to Dostoyevskian nihilism—one might also add Benda's *clercs*. "In attempting to storm Olympus," writes Patočka, "the Titans ... stress their moral autonomy, in vain they demand the right to live their own life, in conformity with their own free nature; they will never achieve that and will end by destroying their own life and the lives of others; their strivings lead to immeasurable cataclysms which threaten the very life of Europe" (Patočka in Kohák, 1989: 140). Incidentally, the essay was written in 1936!

46 For an interesting comparison of Patočka's and Foucault's notions of the "care of the self" see Arpad Szakolczai (1994). On Patočka's divided care of the self into three grand currents, see Tucker (2000: 34–37).

47 Compare especially with Part One of Division One of Heidegger's *Sein und Zeit* (*Being and Time*), especially where he discusses Being-in-the-World as the basic state of *Dasein* and *Dasein's* encounter and intersections with the worldhood of the world.

48 This explanation of history is also a useful metaphor for my study of the theory of the dissidents. East-Central European dissident "theory" could be meaningful only because it related to a specific space-time context, but it could also be universal to the extent that *through* this engagement this context was transcended.

49 Some Charter signatories, such as Václav Benda and Martin Palouš, saw in Patočka's exhortations important moral, nonpolitical, and personal reasons for signing the Charter, but lamented his lack of an overall political vision. In my view, this critique is based on a narrowly programmatic view of politics, surprising given the overall antipolitical attitude of the Chartists generally.

50 The essay can also be read as taking up more concretely the actual implementation of the ethical position outlined by Patočka before his untimely death.

51 This tradition of border meetings continued up to 1987, when independent civic movement representatives (Charter 77, Solidarity) met on the Polish–Czechoslovak border on the 19th anniversary of the WTO inter-

vention. See "A Meeting on the Polish Czechoslovak Border: Statement of Participants," *East European Reporter* 3.1 (1987): 24–27.

52 The language of "Christian values" is interesting in its use and provides a stunning example of linguistic opposites East and West. For Benda, Michnik, and others writing on the role of the various national Churches in East-Central Europe, "Christian values" euphemistically refers to the belief in individual human dignity, the social tasks of traditional Christian charity—both to heal and to serve, following the teachings of Christ a non-judgmental declaration of love and respect of one's friends and enemies, and on a more philosophical level support for metaphysical claims about the universe and horizons of meaning—*contra* Marxist orthodoxy and the ideology of authoritarian communism. In the West, the term "Christian values" has been usurped by and come to represent the aspirations of the religious right—especially in the United States—and stands for a host of policies from prayer in public schools to the anti-choice movement.

53 Interestingly, Benda did foresee the future possibility and necessity of drawing a "strict line" between a Christian-Democratic political party and the Church itself. This is in fact what happened in Czechoslovakia, and Benda himself was an active member of the Christian-Democratic party in the Czech Republic before his untimely death.

54 It is easy to forget in retrospect what an achievement this loose coalition represented, *simply on its own.* Czechoslovakia was not only under the oppressive yoke of Husák's normalization, it was and had been fundamentally divided along class and political lines since 1948, and the euphoria of the Prague Spring was too short-lived and party-driven to mitigate these divisions. Thus in a twentieth anniversary retrospective article, Miroslava Holubová described the Charter's greatest success as the forging of a new alliance: "For the first time since 1948, people of various backgrounds came together—communists, non-communists, and people of differing religious beliefs. Some people said: 'there are too many Catholics among you.' Others said: 'there are too many communists among you.' But we were happy to be together" (quoted in Jechová, 1997: 7).

55 In this context, the reader should not be surprised to learn that two most recent deputy commissioners of the UNHCR have been former Central European dissidents—Tadeusz Mazowiecki and Jiří Dienstbier. President Havel has been a strong supporter of a new permanent court for crimes against humanity to be established at The Hague.

Chapter 7: The Democratic Opposition in Hungary

1 I am highly indebted in my analysis here to my conversation with Ágnes Heller (August 22, 1995) but also to the insights of Heller and others in her edited collection, *Lukács Revalued* (Oxford: Basil Blackwell) and John Burnheim's edited collection (1994).

2 A telling example is the critique of Lukács' *On the Ontology of Social Being* (the three volume examination was published posthumously in 1976) written by Heller, Fehér, Márkus and Vajda for *Telos* and later republished as part of the *Lukács Revalued* collection. In terms of reverence and detailed textual examination, the authors proceed in an almost Straussian fashion to both clarify and offer a critique of the Lukácsian ontology. Unfortunately, the critical rejoinder authored by Gáspár Miklós Tamás is almost (but not quite) as impenetrable, and leaves the reader completely baffled, especially by the relationship between the six-page excursus on St. Anselm and Lukács, other than the fact that both were obsessed with the intellectual category of being as separate and distinct from religious questions of faith and the existence of God.

3 A few examples of Lukács' political turnarounds: his published 1919 rejection of Bolshevism as "immoral" in surrendering democracy to terror even as he joined the party and as a political commissar ordered the execution of eight men for their refusal to fight; his dogmatic and Stalinist repudiation of *History and Class Consciousness* and his later equation of social democracy with fascism; and his early search for intellectual community in critique which he continued throughout his life despite his self-described "monological way of life" depicted in the self-deprecating slogan "my party, right or wrong." See Istvan Eörsi (1987b).

4 Admiral Miklós Horthy was commanding Admiral of the Austro-Hungarian Navy during the First World War and effective head of state from 1920 through to 1944. His regime was marked early by anti-Semitic tendencies; for example, the mass murders of Béla Kun's "Red Terror" were matched by a "White Terror" where many "leftists" (i.e. Jews) were murdered. In the years of Horthy's consolidation of power, "democracy" was often employed as a code word for Jewish power, which only added to societal confusion and contempt. Horthy rule can be characterized by a number of contradictory actions and policies which in the long run served to heighten anti-Semitism in policy and practice. Supposedly acting in defense of the feudal and conservative interests that supported it, Horthy's government both restricted Jewish participation in politics and the civil service while preserving and in fact allowing them to strengthen their economic activities (many of the most prominent *Ausgleich* industrialists of the country were assimilated Jews; at the end of the first World War their initiative and capital were urgently required to rebuild a nation drastically reduced in size and output by the Treaty of Trianon). Fol-

lowing the *Anschluss* of Austria in March, 1938 and in an ill-conceived attempt to both placate the parties of the right (especially the Arrow Cross, Hungary's version of the National Socialists) and Germany as a formidable ally, the government, the first of many "anti-Jewish laws" was introduced, whereby no more than 20% of public, professional, and business positions could be occupied by Jews. That was later followed by lowering of the threshold to 6% (in 1939) and a "miscegenation law" prohibiting intermarriage in 1941. Despite ongoing persecution and participation in forced labor battalions, however, Jews were not required to wear the yellow Star of David, live in ghettoes or face deportation until March, 1944, at which point the Germans militarily occupied Hungary and swiftly initiated the Hungarian *Endlösung* in the countryside.

5 The Holocaust did not really "happen" in Hungary until late in the war, that is, not until the German takeover and the government of the proto-Fascist Arrow Cross, led by Ferenc Szálasi. Mass deportations began in the summer of 1944. Of the over half a million Hungarian Jews who perished, the vast majority were those from the countryside, and were deported directly to death camps. Approximately 200,000 Hungarian Jews survived, thus making the Budapest community the largest to survive in the entire region. Some have claimed that Horthy "sacrificed" the rural (read: less assimilated) Jews in order to "save" the Budapest Jews; Bibó argues that the only compelling factors that saved the Budapest Jews were a timely delay in the deportation plans due to international pressure, the "confusion of the siege," and finally the liberation by Soviet forces. In the end, Hungarian and German authorities acting cooperatively simply did not have time to finish the job (see Bibó, 1991: 160–162).

6 For example, Bibó discusses the reasons for not accepting responsibility for the persecution and murder of the Jews before advancing his own arguments. Similarly, he gives scholarly consideration to *all* of the possible explanations for anti-Jewish prejudice and anti-Semitism (including the patently anti-Semitic explanations) and *all* of the arguments for and against Jewish assimilation, including those advanced by Jews and non-Jews, both religious and secular.

7 Hungarian Jews were politically emancipated with the *Ausgleich* and the inauguration of the Dual Monarchy in 1867. Both orthodoxy and Zionism resisted assimilation, but both currents as well as the attempted cultivation of an independent secular Jewish culture were effectively eliminated by the combined factors of the Holocaust, emigration, and Sovietization.

8 Bibó was a key author of the 1937 program for the March Front, which called for the elimination of traditional *latifundia*, a peasant cooperative movement, a land reform program whereby estates would be redistributed to the landless poor, opposition to both pan-German and pan-Slavic expansionism (Bibó was clearly against imperialism in all forms),

institutionalized human rights and new radically democratic forms and procedures in keeping with new forms of land ownership and politics.

9 See Gábor Kovács (1999).

10 An earlier version in article form was published as Marc Rakovski (Kis and Bence)(1977).

11 Privileges included the possibilities for private travel or as official representatives of scientific organizations, contacts from abroad, enhanced social status at home etc. Scientific researchers could also effectively self-marginalize by turning their attention to areas not the focus of international competition.

12 For example, it can hardly be suggested that in the Czechoslovak case nonconformists could keep themselves meaningfully employed in auxiliary positions—unless one were to expand the definition to include coal stokers and garbage collectors! Arguably in normalized Czechoslovakia the counter-culture was more completely severed from the officially sanctioned realm. However, given the reprisals from 1970 onward, the ranks of the marginalized swelled to the extent that a counter-public sphere could develop internally without any dynamic interaction with the party-state. Thus many of Kis' and Bence's arguments still hold, if only onward from the point onward where cultural autonomy is concretized into actual opposition.

13 Thus it is no accident that it is in Poland and in the left wing of Solidarity that Marxism persisted ideologically in the 1980s.

14 In their postscript to the English published version of the *Profil* volume, from which this information is taken (which appeared as "On Being a Marxist: A Hungarian View," *Socialist Register*, 1980), the authors respond to E. P. Thompson's famous "Open Letter to Leszek Kołakowski" and Kołakowski's reply, "My Correct Views on Everything" (which appeared in the 1973 and 1974 issues of the *Register*, respectively). Although they agree that by Thompson's terms Kołakowski can in no way consider himself a Marxist, they consider themselves such in terms of Marxism as a heritage or a tradition.

15 My understanding of the subtleties of the conflict between Kis and Bence has been greatly enhanced by my personal and electronic conversations with Professor Éva Karádi of Budapest.

16 Here referring to the first invasion of October 23, 1956 and not the full-scale force which penetrated the country on November 4. Arguably the presence of Soviet army units and their initial rout by poorly-armed and untrained insurgents mainly fighting in the streets of Budapest did much to provoke the rebellion even further. A more measured response on the part of the USSR, claims Kis, might have prevented the complete disintegration of the party, and thus the formation of the national unity government, and thus the movement towards both the multi-party sys-

tem and political neutrality. These last two demands—amounting to the abandonment of the leading role of the party as well as a perceived threat to Soviet national security—virtually guaranteed that the Soviets would respond in force. Kis' lesson is that *things need not have reached this point.* (1989: 26–27).

17 In fact, we now know from both an examination of Soviet archival materials and the investigative work of the Institute for the History of the 1956 revolution that Kis' hypothesis was absolutely correct. There was a real debate in the Soviet leadership; military intervention was seen as a radical option to be exercised only if all other peaceful means of resolving the situation had been exhausted (see especially Litván, 1996: 88–90).

18 As Kis explains, Hungarians living abroad represent a sizeable proportion of ethnic and linguistic Hungarians—between one quarter and one third live outside the country. To drive the point home, he makes a comparison which sadly has more resonance today than when originally written: "Comparable demographic proportions can be found only in the Balkans and a more absurd ratio exists only between the population of Albania and Kosovo" (1989: 200).

19 Kis alludes to the monopolistic control of politics by the party-state (i.e. the "leading role of the party") as well as the primacy of state ownership and direction of the economy.

20 An example of Kis' detailed reasoning and level of understanding is provided in his analysis between "public law" and "civil law" and how the formalization of the latter in conjunction with the reform of the former would substantially advance the idea of public mobility, in his words, "in the sphere of public law towards constitutional state, and in the sphere of civil law towards pluralism" (1989: 125).

21 A form of probation or modified house arrest. Working at a job was permitted, but virtually all public life is forbidden; for example, all forms of entertainment, going to restaurants, and travel. No trial or charge was required, and such control could be extended at the discretion of the authorities.

22 He originally had an agreement with an official publishing house to write about working conditions, but they returned the manuscript as "hostile." *Szociológia* editor Iván Szelényi agreed to publish parts of it in his journal, but by this time the authorities were aware of the situation and Haraszti was arrested. Szelényi appeared as a witness for the defense, and was suspended from the editorship in response (1977: 15).

23 Konrád implicitly critiques Gorbachev's notion of a "common European home" even prior to its introduction into the political lexicon of the West. Existing European unity before 1989—built on the twin pillars of EU economic integration and NATO membership (with minor states opting for or having negotiated neutrality)—was a farce because it was based on American sponsorship and divisive ideological and superpower struggle.

24 The Helsinki Accords were lauded by dissidents as they held the regimes of the Soviet Bloc accountable to international conventions of human rights, but criticized because the *quid pro quo* of the negotiations was Western recognition of postwar boundaries and the national political sovereignty of these governments.

25 Here Konrád refers to the 1980s European peace debate between pro-NATO hard-liners and the "doves" of the various peace movements who advocated unilateral concessions (and especially a moratorium on new missile deployment) in addition to bilateral disarmament.

26 The dates refer to the Soviet invasion of Hungary in 1956, the WTO invasion of Czechoslovakia in 1968, and the imposition of martial law in Poland in 1981, respectively.

27 Konrád is not suggesting that the system itself cannot be reformed, but that it cannot be reformed solely *within*—as the failure of the Prague Spring and the NEM both demonstrate.

28 The emergence and the structure of the workers' councils was the most remarkable aspect of the 1956 revolution, according to Hannah Arendt. In *The Origins of Totalitarianism* she discussed the dissolution of party lines, the imposition of informal but meaningful norms of problem-solving, avoidance of conflict-of-interest and personal abuse of power. For Arendt, the clearest sign of the reemergence of democracy in Hungary in 1956 was not the rapid reestablishment of political parties defunct since the late 1940s, but rather the rise of the council movement.

Chapter 8: The Dissident Contribution to Political Theory

1 For a discussion of the genesis of civil society and its contemporary relevance, see especially Charles Taylor (1990); John Keane (1988a); John Keane, ed. (1988b); and Adam Seligman (1992).

2 In responses to a potential Skinnerian critique of my approach—that I am either a) tracing an ideological line in the history of the concept of civil society that does not exist, or b) that a critique is inappropriate as there is considerable confusion as to linguistic usage (and translation), I would answer to both that the intellectual tradition/use of "civil society" is explicit, and differences in use and shades of meaning are spelled out wherever possible within the limits of brevity. Certainly since the beginning of the eighteenth century, there has been a direct response by one thinker to another in so far as civil society is concerned: Hegel to Locke, Ferguson, and Smith; Marx to Hegel; Gramsci to both Hegel and Marx, and so on.

3 Locke uses these terms interchangeably.

4 It is important to note that Locke's theory of property should not be understood solely in modern economic terms. Locke's theological premises are crucial for his epistemological individualism and his morality. Humankind as part of the Universe is first conceived by Locke as God's property, and from this act of divine creation flow duties and moral principles. See John Dunn (1969) and Steven Lukes (1979).

5 Estates or social groupings are organized around general economic or political functionality, for example, resulting from the specialization of labor, and correspond to the three "moments" of *Sittlichkeit*: the substantial or immediate agricultural class; the reflecting or formal business class; and the universal class of civil servants. Corporations, on the other hand, operate more like a "second family," functioning as both an economic association and a system of welfare, in the broadest sense. The corporation also protects occupational interests and provides and regulates education and training. Hegel makes it clear that if the weakest link in the corporate chain is provided—indeed guaranteed—a measure of subsistence or charity—the chain of society will be stronger as a result (see *Philosophy of Right*, para. 253).

6 For an interesting and controversial discussion on the unity of civil and political society in Marxist thought, see Leszek Kołakowski, "The Myth of Human Self-Identity: Unity of Civil and Political Society in Socialist Thought" and reply by Stuart Hampshire entitled "Unity of Civil and Political Society: Reply to Leszek Kołakowski" in Kołakowski and Hampshire, eds. (1974). Of particular interest to the reader of this study is that Kołakowski predictably takes the view that the forced social unity under authoritarian communism is intrinsic to Marxist thought.

7 Locke's arguments against absolute monarchy in the *Second Treatise*, which Rau takes to be an extreme manifestation of the state of nature, are relevant for understanding the dissident civil societies of East-Central Europe in their parallel but unequal relationship with the party-state. Post-totalitarianism in this context can be read as another state of nature where no laws can be considered just, and thus under this scenario, the alternative political community contained within civil society can makes its own "appeal to heaven." See Zbigniew Rau (1987).

8 Apolitical in the conventional sense, not in the sense of *antipolitics* as conceived by the dissidents.

9 Ann Mische, Hana Havelková and Nanette Funk have all discussed the differences between public and private under authoritarian communism and in the newly democratized and liberalized countries of East-Central Europe. See especially Hana Havelková (1993a, 1993b, 1994, 1996); and Ann Mische (1993); and Nanette Funk (1993), "Feminism East and West," also in Funk and Mueller, eds.: 318–330.

10 For a full discussion of the legacy of state socialism with respect to the 'woman question,' see Barbara Einhorn (1993), chapter 2, pp.17–38. See

also Suzanne LaFont (2001); Susan Gal and Gail Kligman, eds., (2000); and Marilyn Rueschemeyer, ed. (1998).

11 In particular, Benhabib, Fraser, and Young take on the Habermasian public sphere, and Benhabib grounds her critique in Hannah Arendt' s theorization of the public sphere—which she more generally describes as public freedom. See Jürgen Habermas (1994); Craig Calhoun, ed. (1992); and Hannah Arendt (1974). It should also be recognized that Western feminist critiques privilege different goals and emanate from different contexts and experiences. For example, equality remains a central Western dilemma whereas in the region the idea of equality as directed social betterment or *telos* is deeply problematic.

12 In fact, the flexibility of civil society makes it inherently more conducive to women's participation, thus Šiklová (1993a) estimated that early in the transformation process, over 70% of civil society organizations in Prague were headed by women. At the same time, women's participation in traditional political arenas (e.g. parliaments) has fallen across the region since 1989—although this is at least partially due to artificially higher numbers guaranteed by party-state quotas under authoritarian communism (Matynia, 1995; LaFont, 2001).

13 Gáspár Miklós Tamás (1992) has argued that the socialist projects of the two halves of Europe were profoundly different: in the West the overriding emphasis was on social justice and equality whereas in the East ending alienation and oppression was the ultimate goal.

14 Only in Poland did intellectual activists formulate significant proposals for economic reform, both via the Gdańsk Accord and during the Solidarity Congress a year later. Both Kowalik (1995) and Flakierski (1993) have argued that the Solidarity agenda was socialist in character and prescription. Here I leave aside the debate regarding the sociological genesis of Solidarity's demands—as initiated and championed by the workers or as the brainchild of the intellectual opposition. One view (especially represented by Staniszkis, 1984) contends that workers vacillate between narrow economism (Lenin's "trade union consciousness") and unrealistic utopianism, therefore intellectuals need to politicize their demands. The other view (represented by Laba, 1986; 1991) suggests that the workers were capable of formulating sophisticated political demands *by themselves*, as is evidenced by a comparison of the 1971 demands solicited by the party-state following the massacre in Gdańsk–Gdynia with the 21 demands of August, 1980. Without attempting to simplify the complexity of the debate or its underlying assumptions, however, it is fair to concede in hindsight that both the workers and the intellectuals (and these roles were not always static) had a considerable impact on both the Gdańsk Accord and the rapid growth of Solidarity that followed. Moreover, what is perhaps unique to the Polish situation is the degree to which both workers and intellectuals acted in a historically self-conscious manner, with reference to past traditions and events.

15 Havel considered himself a "moral socialist," rejecting "overly fixed categories … empty ideological concepts" in favor of standing on the side of the oppressed, against "… social injustice and the immoral barriers that degraded man and condemned him to the status of one who serves" (1990a: 9–10). Michnik considered himself to be writing in the long-standing Polish tradition of "independence-oriented and democratic socialism" (1985: 330). Because of the history of the Polish workers' movement, the PPS, and the SDKPiL of Rosa Luxemburg, Michnik could speak of belonging to a long-standing socialist tradition, even when he openly acknowledged that the term itself was "discredited and ambiguous" given its association with post-war authoritarian communism. Even Hungarian dissidents such as Kis and Bence who more self-consciously shed socialist vocabulary acknowledged their debt to the Marxist tradition, and Konrád was most apt in stating: "I don't like communism because I see it as a coherent system of pointless prohibitions and abridgments of freedom. (It doesn't follow from this that I have to like capitalism, in reaction to which communism arose, since the fact of communist exploitation doesn't put a prettier face on capitalist exploitation.)" (1987: 236–237).

16 Here I am thinking of not only the failure of the Polish October in 1956 and the Prague Spring in 1968, but also of the limited and contradictory approach embodied in Hungary's New Economic Mechanism, and even the proposals for worker self-management outlined in the Solidarity Congress of 1981.

17 Przeworski (1992) makes the salient point that even as neo-liberal economic theory was being embraced in Central and Eastern Europe, it was being called into question by recent developments in neoclassical economic theory. Claims to the effect that markets efficiently allocate resources or only markets generate growth are undermined, for example, by research confirming the impossibility of a complete set of markets, and the important contributions of state investments in education and public health on economic growth. See 1992: 45–74.

18 There are of course contradictions here, because there was also a repudiation of socialism and economics generally because of the perceived connection between economic planning, centralization, socialized ownership and state control, authoritarianism, the lack of accountability, and so on. Wherever the exigencies of economic necessity were seen as dictating politics, limiting free expression, and prescribing certain approaches for the public good (for example, for writers and cultural workers, the doctrine of socialist realism), economics was seen as a menace.

19 As philosophical as Havel's comments might sound, it should be noted that I am quoting here from his speech to the World Economic Forum in Davos, Switzerland, in 1992!

20 See Francis Fukuyama (1992). One of the reasons Fukuyama in particular received so much airplay with his "end of history" thesis was his
impeccable timing; he first employed this terminology in his article "The
End of History?" published in *The National Interest* in the summer of
1989. Media coverage in the United States during this period, especially
as dominated by correspondents for *The New York Times* and *The Washington Post* was overwhelmingly liberal in interpreting the *annus mirabilus*.
See in particular Bernard Gwertzman and Michael T. Kaufman (1990),
an edited collection of stories written by leading *New York Times* journalists over the course of 1989.

21 In the centuries-old Russian debate between Slavophiles and Western-
izers, or native populists and liberals, the dissidents tend to be lumped
into the "liberal" category. This is definitionally problematic given that
many also exalt religious and national traditions, but at the same time
are supportive of civic communities and post-modern or post-traditional
identities.

22 See *Partisan Review* 59.4 (1992). Special Issue: Intellectuals and Social
Change in Central and Eastern Europe.

23 See Hannah Arendt (1963). For compelling comparisons between the
dissidents' support for the American Revolution and the Arendtian vision,
see both Jean Bethke Elshtain (1993a), and Jeffrey C. Isaac (1992).

24 Cohen and Arato's work is far too complex and multi-dimensional to ade-
quately summarize here, however, it should be noted that in their reconstructed theory of civil society, the concept is part of a three-part framework of social relations. As opposed to the formerly dualistic (Hegelian)
notion of state/civil society, they conceive of state/civil society/economy.
However, these are not clearly delineated or in a necessarily hierarchical relationship to one another. The economy and the state are two sub-
systems, both of which are integrated and mediated by the relations
of money and power. Moreover, the "cultural linguistic" background of
the polity is critical, not in terms of institutions, but on the level of social
resources, as shared normative content. Civil society, according to Cohen
and Arato, involves "all of the institutions and associational forms that
require communicative interaction for their reproduction and that rely
primarily on processes of integration for coordinating action within their
boundaries" (1992: 429). Following Habermas, they discuss communicative action in the operation of civil society, as a "linguistically mediated
intersubjective process" through which norms are questioned and consensus is developed through constant negotiation.

25 Here I agree with Matuštík's interpretation of non-political politics rather
than Tucker, who argues that the dissidents hoped to *depoliticize* politics
and abolish ideology. Arguably antipolitics is about *re-politicizing* politics
by infusing the public sphere with responsibility and authentic subjectivity. See Matuštík, 1993: 196–199 and Tucker, 2000b: 185–187.

26 Jean Bethke Elshtain (1993) has explored the Havelian sense of political responsibilty, and his anti-utopian, anti-cynical idealism in her essay "Politics without Cliché."

27 See especially the chapter "Rebellious Politics Reconsidered" in Isaac (1992), especially pp. 248–259.

28 Over the last decade a debate has blossomed over the meaning of the texts of Patočka and Havel in particular. Havel has been interpreted as a democratic socialist (Keane, 1988b); expressing a post-nationalist and existentialist synthesis (Matuštik, 1993); a post-modernist much in debt to phenomenology and Heidegger (Tucker, 2000); and as transcending traditional left/right distinctions (Elshtein, 1993).

29 An excellent summary which relates the developments in advanced capitalist Europe in the 1970s to the failure of the "transformative vision of the 1960s" and the emergence of new social movements can be found in Suzanne Berger (1979). Classic texts of the 1980s include Ernesto Laclau and Chantal Mouffe (1985) and Alain Touraine (1988).

30 On the connection between political responsibility and the agency of intellectuals in the West from the late 1960s through to the late 1980s, see the survey and analysis provided by Dick Flacks (1991), "Making History and Making Theory: Notes on How Intellectuals Seek Relevance" in Charles C. Lemert, ed. (1991), pp. 3–18.

31 Compare Arato's account of the Polish opposition in "Civil Society Against the State: Poland 1980–81" and "Empire vs. Civil Society: Poland 1981–82" in *Telos* 47 and *Telos* 50, respectively with the complete theorization of Cohen and Arato (1992). Further, Cohen and Arato can be situated in the context of the re-excavation of the concept of civil society (this time purposefully as *Zivilgesellschaft* rather than *bürgerliche Gesellschaft*) within German social theory emanating from the Frankfurt Institute of Social Research and current debates on the "*Rot–Grün*" coalition. See also Ulrich Rödel, Günter Frankenberg, and Helmut Dubiel (1989) and Ulrich Rödel, ed. (1990). John Ely (1992) critically reviews all three in "The Politics of 'Civil Society'" *Telos* 93, 173–191.

32 See in particular Keane's essays "Work and the Civilizing Process" and "Party-centred Socialism?" in Keane (1988a).

33 As recounted above, this a deliberate caricature, but not too far off many contemporary accounts. Within this vein, see Michael T. Kaufman (1997), "From Dissidence to Dissonance" and Jiří Pehe (1997).

34 Aside from my own interviews with former dissidents on this point, my analysis in this section relies heavily on the proceedings of two important conferences on this issue. The first, supported by the National Endowment for Humanities and entitled "Intellectuals and Social Change in Central and Eastern Europe" was held at Rutgers University on April 9, 10, and 11, 1992. The proceedings of that conference were transcribed

and published as a special edition of *Partisan Review*, from which I quote here. The second, sponsored by the French Institute and the Collegium Budapest and entitled "Intellectuals, between Morals and Politics" was held in Budapest on March 21, 22, and 23, 1996, in Budapest. The unpublished and translated proceedings of the conference (which was held in Hungarian, French, and English) were provided to me by Éva Karádi and are used with permission. Some of the contributions were published in Hungarian in the Spring, 1996 issue of *Magyar Lettre Internationale*.

35 See *Partisan Review* 59.4 (1992). Special Issue: Intellectuals and Social Change in Central and Eastern Europe.

36 See *Partisan Review* 59.4 (1992). Special Issue: Intellectuals and Social Change in Central and Eastern Europe.

37 In the East-Central European context specifically, I would maintain that the communists renamed themselves as capitalists—for the most part, socialism is linguistically and politically marginalized.

38 This point might seem banal, but is worth making given that many of the intellectuals involved in the debate have claimed that the idea and tradition of intellectuals—in the sense of having a social stature and in terms of making an expected social contribution—is particularly European. Ágnes Heller, for example, maintains that there is no tradition of intellectuals in America, not simply because of the professionalization of expertise, but also because there is no expectation that they should play a particular role. According to Heller, European intellectuals think transcontextually, reflect on "all the essential things which are going on ... [and] feel some responsibility for these things" (Heller, 1996: 2). Vladimir Tismaneanu, on the other hand, believes there is a American tradition of intellectuals. He concedes ironically, however, that it is primarily a tradition of Central and East-European emigration and exile, one he associates with New York intellectuals, and in particular with the impetus behind the foundation of the New School for Social Research (and publications such as *Dissent*, *Social Research*, the *New York Review of Books*, and so on).

39 There is a naturalistic fallacy inherent in the argument of both Garton Ash and Benda, which is fully explored by Ernest Gellner (1990). In brief, Gellner's position is that the argument that intellectuals should stand apart from practical politics in favour of non-immediate and universal values is wholly pragmatic rather than logical. Gellner suggests that rather than holding up the actions of the *clercs* to the transcendental ethic—in accordance with which they are implicitly measured anyway— Benda paradoxically commits the very sin he preaches against in his sermon. According to Gellner's line of reasoning, it makes *more* sense rather than *less* for those wholly committed to "truth," "impartial objectivity," or "reason" to follow their own conclusions to the extent they necessitate political action.

INDEX

1968 invasion, 79; Hungarian denouncement, 99
AB publishing, 133; *see also* Demszky, Gábor *and* samizdat
Abrams, Bradley, 412, fn1
Ackerman, Bruce, 336, 340, 341
Action Program, 71, 81, 89; defense of, 78; Dubček's description, 72, 73–74; excluded elements, 74–75; objectives, 71
Aczél, György, 121, 126, 138
Aczél, Tamás, 110
Adamec, Ladislav, 97, 106
Adorno, Theodore, xviii, 276
Alliance of Free Democrats, *see* SzDSz
Ambros, Veronika, 443, fn1
ANC (Anti-Nuclear Campaign Hungary), 143
Andrzejewski, Jerzy, 38; *see also* KOR
Antipolitics, 228–229, 256, 298–309, 313, 341, 346; Konrád's definition of, 301–302; *see also* Havel, Václav *and* Konrád, György
anti-Semitism, 6, 358; Holocaust responsibility in Hungary, 262–266; in Hungary, 341, 431, fn37, 453, fn6; use in smear campaigns in Poland, 23–24, 26
Arato, Andrew, 328, 337, 340, 349, 351, 460, fn24

Arendt, Hannah, xviii, xxi, xxxi, 214, 339, 347, 400, fn13, 456, fn28, 458, fn11
Aristotle, xviii, 229, 317
Aron, Raymond, 361
Auersperg, Pavel, 71, 415, fn25

Bajcsy-Zsilinszky, Endre, 439, fn79; "Bands of Vagabonds," 16
Battěk, Rudolf, 90, 356
Bauer, Tamás, 137, 429, fn18
Baudrillard, Jean, 218
Bauman, Zygmunt, 22
Bělohradský, Václav, 227, 239, 259, 448, fn30
Bence, György, xxvii, 123, 126, 128, 286, 290, 294, 348, 357; "radical reformism," 276–277; *Toward an East European Marxism,* 126, 258, 266–277; 327–328; "underground Marxist," 275; *see also* Rakovski, Marc
Benda, Julien; *La Trahison des Clercs,* xxvii–xxvix, 361, 462, fn39
Benda, Václav, xxvii, 128, 356; background, 247; Catholic Church, 250–251; Charter 77, 247–248, 249, 251, 255; Havel, 224, 247, "Parallel *Polis,*" 224, 247–251, 255, 313; Patočka, 247, 248; on underground music, 84
Beneš, Edvard, 59, 76

Benhabib, Seyla, 326, 458, fn11
Berecz, János; economic reform, 140
Berlin, Isaiah, 188
Bernhard, Michael, 34, 39, 403, fn14
Bergson, Henri, 242
Beszélő (The Speaker), 131–133, 134 288, 292; Hungarian minorities, 137; Kis's election analysis, 141; national minorities, 285, 433, fn54, 434, fn67; "Social Contract," 132–133, 137, 138, 278–280; *see also* Bence, György; Haraszti, Miklós; Kis, János; *and* Tamás, Gáspár Miklós
Bibó, István, 134, 161, 283; background, 135–135; *Bibó Memorial Book,* 136, 137, 265; importance for the opposition, 135, 137; influence on Hungarian dissidents, 261–266, 453, fn8; influence on Kis, 264–265; on responsibility, 263; "The Jewish Question in Hungary after 1944," 262–263
Biró, Zoltán, 138
Biuletyn Informacjny (Information Bulletin), 37, 407, fn55; *see also* KOR
Black Madonna, 19, 54; *see also* Catholic Church
"Black Troop No. 1," 15; background, 15–16
Blumsztajn, Seweryn, 23, 26, 49, 184
Böll, Heinrich, 86
Bozóki, András, 400, fn11
Bratislava declaration, 78–79, 417, fn39
Bratkowski, Stefan, 184
Brezhnev, Leonid, 51, 54; "Brezhnev Doctrine," 178; Čierna nad Tisou negotiations, 78; "really-existing socialism," 400, fn12; relationship to

Dubček, 75, 78, 416, fn29, 416, fn30
Brus, Włodzimeriz, 22, 25, 328; on movement away from revisionist Marxism, 25
Bruszt, László, 147
Budapest School intellectuals, xxvi, 122, 126, 128, 257; economic reforms, 124; émigré community, 124; Kádár's dismissal of, 124; *see also* Heller, Ágnes; Hegedüs, András; Márkus, György; Szelényi, Iván
Bujak, Zbigniew, 53, 99, 215, 356
Bulányi, György, Committee for Human Dignity, 144; *see also* Catholic Church, Hungary
Burawoy, Michael, xxx, 114

Čalfa, Marián, 107
Camus, Albert, 347
Čarnogurský, Ján, 97, 356; trial of, 99; vice-premier, 107
Catholic Church, Czechoslovakia, 81; activism, 101; Charter 77, 90, 97; secret church in Slovakia, 424, fn92; status under communism, 100–101; Václav Benda, 250–251
Catholic Church, Hungary; activism, 143–144; attitude towards Solidarity, 167; Catholic Church, Poland; 13, 50; importance in Poland, 18–21; Kuroń, 189–190; Michnik's assessment of, 165–168; Michnik's role as defender of truth, 179; non-violence, 181, 184; opposition, 165, 167; 181, 184; position during martial law, 54; Pope's visit, 43–45, 48; relationship with Left, 168–177, 181; *see also* Black Madonna *and* Michnik, Adam
Černík, Oldřich, 64

Československý svaz mládeže
  see ČSM
Charter 77, xxv, xxvi, xxvii, 2, 36,
  92, 96, 102, 124, 214, 299, 341;
  background, 124; collective
  oeuvre, 251–253; declaration, 89;
  Declaration, 252; civil society,
  254–256, 323; European
  Cultural Forum, 144; Havel,
  236, 255–256; Helsinki Accords,
  88–89, 91; human rights, 252–
  253; Husák, 222; international
  level, 91; KOR, 91; meeting
  with opposition groups, 104;
  membership, 89–91; motivating
  impulse, 87; Palouš, 254–55;
  Patočka, 244, 246; Pavel Kohout,
  128; populist criticism of,
  126; protest by Hungarians,
  128; Prečan, 254; regime
  perception, 90; samizdat
  publishing, 94; Václav Benda,
  247–250
Christian Democratic People's
  Party see KNDP
Čierna nad Tisou, 77–78, 79
Civic Forum, xxvi, 77, 104, 105,
  107; meetings in *Laterna
  Magica,* 106, 425, fn99
Civil Society; in Poland, 40–41,
  192–198; Charter 77, 254–256;
  in Czechoslovakia, 254–256,
  328; dissident contribution,
  313–316; feminist critiques,
  325–327; in Hungary; 283–286,
  307–308, 328; theories of,
  316–325
ČKD, 105
Club of Non-Party Engagés
  see KAN
Club of the Crooked Circle
  see KKK
Cohen, Jean, 328, 340, 349, 351,
  460, fn24
Cohn, Ludwik, 15;
  see also KOR *and* PPS

COMECON, 30, 62, 78, 287;
  Dubček, 78; *Beszélő,* 132
Comenius see Komenský
Committee for the Legal Defense
  of the Hungarian Minority, 96
Committee for the Defense of the
  Unjustly Persecuted see VONS
Communism; definition of, xxx;
  Arendt definition, description
  of, xxi; xxxi; Friedrich/Brzezinski
  definition, xxxi
Communist Party of Czechoslovakia
  see CPCz
Communist Youth Alliance
  (Hungary) see KISZ
CPCz; background, 59, 61, 76;
  history, 59; on KAN, 77; revi-
  sionist challenge, 61
CPSU, 75, 111, 129
ČSM, 69; 5th ČSM Congress, 69
Csoóri, Sándor, 126, 136, 137, 137
Csurka, István, 137, 138
Czechoslovak Documentation
  Center for Independent
  Literature see Prečan, Vilém
Czechoslovak Presidium, 71, 79
Czechoslovak Student Union
  see ČSM

Dahrendorf, Ralf, 335, 336
Danube Circle see *Duna Kör*
Day, Barbara, 92
Democratic Forum, 138
Democratic League of Free Trade
  Unions (*Liga*), 147
democratic opposition, Hungary,
  125, 126; Bibó, 135, 137;
  cultural freedom, 143
Demokrata, 134, 280
Demszky, Gábor, 133, 357; AB
  publishing, 133; trial, 433, fn53
Derrida, Jacques, xvi, xx, 94, 218,
  446, fn20
Déry, Tibor, 283
Deutsch, Tamás, 145
Dienstbier, Jiří, 107, 128, 233

Dissidents' *oeuvre*, 3, 313, 317, 334–348; Havel's definition, 447, fn25; as political theory, 348–354; role in post-communist era, 354–364
Doellinger, David, 100
Domenach, Jean-Marie, 171
Donáth, Ferenc, 136, 137
Dubček, Alexander, 3, 24–24; 113, 416, fn33; Action Program description and opinion, 73–74, 78; attempts to appease Warsaw Pact, 81; becoming First Secretary, 70; Čierna nad Tisou negotiations, 78–79; Civic Forum, 106; during normalization period, 81; Havel, 207–208; *Panorama* interview, 99; in "protective custody," 79–80; on reform 71; relationship to Brezhnev, 75, 415, fn23; removal from power, 82; "socialism with a human face," 5; speech to Central Committee April, 1968, 71–7; *see also* Kádár, János
Duna Kör, 143; *see also* Gabčikovo–Nagymaros Project *and* Vargha, János
Duray, Miklós, 96, 97, 137, 423, fn78

economic crisis; Czechoslovakia, 72–73
Edice Expedice see Havel, Václav
Edice Petlice see Vaculík, Ludvík
Égtájak Között (Between the Points of the Compass), 134
EKA, 56, 66, 151, 153, 181, 281, 289; analysis of, 147–150; background, 146; concerns over head of state, 151–152; conclusion, 191; decision process, 147–148; "third side," 149, 437, fn82
Elemér Hankiss, 117

Elshtain, Jean Bethke, 460, fn23, 461, fn26
Ellenzéki Kerekasztal see EKA
END, 97, 134, 143, 298, 423, fn82
Endre Bajcsy-Zsilinszky Society, 145; EKA, 147
Environmental Movement; Gabčikovo–Nagymaros Project, 143
Eörsi, István; on Lukács, 260
"ethics of emancipation," 165, 438, fn10
Eurocommunism, xxix, 38
European Cultural Forum, 144
European Nuclear Disarmament *see* END

Federation of Young Democrats *see* Fidesz
Fehér, Ferenc, 122, 123, 258; emigration of, 124; Haraszti's trial, 127; *see also* Budapest School intellectuals
Ferguson, Adam, 319
Fiatal Demokraták Szövetsége see Fidesz
Fidesz, xxvi; Hungarian minority, 97; background, 145; EKA, 147; concerns over head of state, 151–152; *see also* youth culture
FJF, 146
"Flying University," *see* TKN
Fodor, Gábor, 145
Foucault, Michel, xv, xvi, xix, 294, 450, fn46
Foundation for Supporting the Poor *see* SZETA
Fraser, Nancy, 326
Free Word, 105
Friedman, Thomas L., 8
Független Kisgazda Párt, 147; EKA, 147; "four yeses" referendum, 152
Fukuyama, Francis, xxii, 336, 460, fn20
Furet, François, 336

Gabčikovo–Nagymaros Project,
142–143; Fidesz agenda, 145
Gandhi, Mohandas K., 183
Garton, Timothy Ash, 44, 54–55,
58, 106, 282, 335–336, 339,
341, 361, 364
Gazeta Wyborcza (Election
Gazette), 2, 58, 357; *see also*
Michnik, Adam
Gdańsk, 19, 43, 47; 1970 protest,
27; 52; analysis of, 29–30;
economic strategy, 28–31;
results of price hikes of 1976,
34; success of Gdańsk agree-
ment, 164
Gdynia, protest in, 28; strikes, 48
Gebert, Konstanty, 356, 357; on
anti-Semitism, 24; writing
under David Warszawski, 55
Geremek, Bronisław, 46, 50, 356;
on civil society, 195–198
Gierek, Edward, 28–32, 47, 83, 116;
price hikes of 1976, 34, 116
Glasnost, 56, 82, 97, 288
Glemp, Józef, 54
Goetz-Stankiewicz, Marketa, 234
Goldfarb, Jeffrey, 438, fn9
Gombár, Csaba, 138
Gomułka, Władysław, xxxii, 14, 19,
22, 23, 31, 109, 120; 1970
Gdańsk protest, 27–28;
background, 402, fn3, 402,
fn4; criticism of Dubček's
proposals, 75; economic
reform, 63
Gondolat (publishing company),
136
Gorbachev, Mikhail, 1, 64, 116,
191, 225, 315; lack of intervention, 105; Prague visit, 97
Gorz, André, 350
Gottwald, Klement, 60, 63, 67
"goulash" communism, 5, 112, 118;
see also NEM
Gramsci, Antonio, xviii, 157, 195,
224, 321

"gray zone," 145–146, 197, 233,
234, 309
Grossman, Jan, 235, 444, fn6
Grósz, Károly, economic reform,
140; celebration of May Day,
145; Imre Nagy reburial, 153;
relationship with Grotius,
Hugo, 317
Group of Five, 75, 78, 79, 417,
fn31
Gwiazda, Andrzej, 46

Habermas, Jürgen, xv, xviii, xxi, 94,
242, 336, 353
Hájek, Jiří, 69, 81, 416, fn23;
Charter 77, 89
Haraszti, Miklós, xxvi, xv, xxvii, 2,
105–106, 126, 150, 305,
341–342, 352, 356, 357;
analysis of Kádár regime, 120;
difference between outcast and
loyal opposition, 121; *Beszélő*,
131–133; discussion of piece
rates, 115, 290–291; dissident
background, 127, 290; *The
Velvet Prison: Artists under State
Socialism*, 290, 292–297; *A
Worker in a Workers' State*, 17,
115, 127, 290–292
Hare, Richard, 93
Hašek, Jaroslav, 199
Havel, Ivan, 225, 447, fn28
Havel, Václav, xvi, xvii, xix, xxii,
xxvii, xxxi, 2, 8, 9, 67, 77, 128,
256, 348, 349, 354, 357, 358,
360, 361–364; antipolitics,
228–229, 256; arrest, 98, 216;
on authoritarian communism,
211–215, 227; background as
a playwright, 199–200; Charter
77, 90, 251, 253, 255–256;
Civic Forum, 105, 106; civil
society, 322, 324, 341; dissident
definition, 447, fn25; *Disturbing
the Peace*, 208–210; economic
reform, 332–333;

Havel, Václav (*cont'd*), *Edice* "On
    Evasive Thinking," 204–206,
    345; *Expedice,* 95; *Havel na Hrad,*
    106; on journal liquidations,
    213; *Largo Desolato* 229–231;
    letter to Dubček, 207–208; letter
    to Husák, 210–215; *Letters to
    Olga,* 177, 282–288, 236–241;
    "living in truth," xvii, 87, 174,
    221, 245, 255, 272, 329, 340,
    341, 347, 360, 363; meeting
    of opposition groups, 104; *The
    Memorandum,* 200–204; New
    Year's address, 1990, 107–108;
    on normalization, 83, 209, 211;
    on Patočka, 242; "Politics and
    Conscience," 225–229, 237;
    "The Power of the Powerless,"
    xxiii, 7, 107, 215–225, 228,
    229, 237, 241, 242, 247, 296,
    298, 308, 364; on responsibility,
    203, 263, 362–363, 364; on
    socialism, 459, fn15; *Temptation,*
    231–235; "On the Theme of an
    Opposition," 206; "The Trial,"
    86, 222; on underground music,
    84–87; on Václav Benda, 224,
    247; the Vaněk plays, 233–235
Hazafias Népfront see HNF
Hegedüs, András, 122, 127; back-
    ground, 430, fn27; Haraszti trial,
    127; *see also* Budapest School
Hegel, G. W. F., xv, 282; Lukács,
    257; civil society, 319–321, 322,
    324; *see also* civil society
Heidegger, Martin, 324, 461, fn28;
    Dasein, 450, fn47; influence in
    Havel's work, 240–241; influ-
    ence on Patočka, 242, 245
Heller, Ágnes, 122, 123, 257, 258,
    259, 298, 462, fn38; emigration
    of, 124; Haraszti trial, 127;
    see also Budapest School
    intellectuals
Helsinki Accords, 36, 88–89, 128,
    144, 456, fn24; Charter 77, 253

Helsinki Watch, 102
Hejdánek, Ladislav, 90, 94
Hírmondó, 134, 264
Hladík, Radim, 84
HNF, 145, 435, fn78
Hnutí za Občanskou Svobodu see HOS
Hobbes, Thomas, 239
Hobsbawm, Eric, 4–5
Hoffman, Eva, 48
Holmes, Stephen, 336
Horkheimer, Max, xviii
Horthy, Miklós, 262, 453, fn5
HOS, 102
Hradílek, Tomáš, 99
Hruby, Peter, 61
Hungarian Democratic Forum
    see MDF
Hungarian minority, 96–97, 145;
    Beszélő, 137; Kis, 284–286
Hungarian People's Party
    see Magyar Néppárt
Hungarian Revolution of 1956,
    xxiv, xxv, xxxii, 70, 74, 91, 109,
    110, 193, 282, 289, 304;
    background 426; classification
    as an uprising (*népfelkelés*), 140;
    importance to development
    of dissident thought, 425, fn1;
    workers' councils, 110, 426,
    fn4
Hungarian Roundtable Talks,
    see EKA
Hungarian Socialist Workers' Party
    see MSZMP
Hus, Jan, 81
Husák, Gustav, 82, 83, 87, 120,
    149, 220, 297; letter from Havel,
    210–215; regime, 97, 101, 222;
    resignation, 106
Husserl, Edmund, 239, 242, 244,
    246, 259, 324

Inconnu, 144
Illyés, Gyula, 125, 126;
    Bibó Memorial Book, 136;
    see also populist writers

Independent Peace Initiative
see NMS
Independent Publishing House
see NOW-a
Independent Smallholders' Party
see *Kisgazda Párt*
Iniciativa Sociální Obrany see ISO
Initiative for Social Defense *see* ISO
Interfactory Strike Committee
see MKS
Intra-party reform, 139, 142, 150;
Hungarian 1985 election, 140;
non-party reform candidates,
141
Isaac, Jeffrey, xv–xvii, 334, 339,
340, 341, 347
ISO, 92

Jaisinica, Paweł, 15;
see also KOR *and* KKK
Jakeš, Miloš, 97, 415, fn23
Jan Hus Educational Foundation,
93–94; *see also* Tomin, Julius
Jańkowski, Henryk, 167; support
of Solidarity, 177
Jaruzelski, General Wojciech, 48;
on martial law, 51–52; re-legalization of Solidarity, 56–57
Jaspers, Karl, 242, 359
Jazz Section, 98, 424, fn84; back-
ground, 424, fn8; meeting with
opposition groups, 104;
see Srp, Karel
Jazzová Sekce see Jazz Section
Jedlicki, Jerzy, 403, fn11, 408, fn59,
408, fn60
Jirous, Ivan, 84–86; influence in
Havel's work, 215, 224; "merry
ghetto," 419, fn57; relationship
to PPU, 419, fn55; Vacláv
Benda, 248; *see also* PPU
John Lennon Peace Club *see* MKJL
John Paul II, Pope, 43–45, 54,
100–101, 176; labor relations,
166; *see also* Catholic Church
Johnson, James Turner, 322–323

Judt, Tony, 428, fn7
Just a Few Sentences, 102–103
see also Vaculík, Ludvík

K-231, 77
Kádár, János, xxvi, 78, 113, 120,
124, 132, 138, 182, 278, 282,
283, 297; analysis by Kis, 283;
background, 113; Kádárist
compromise, 118, 142; Kádárite
communism, 112; Konrád and
Szelényi criticism, 118–120;
NEM implementation, xxvii,
115; post-Hungarian Revolu-
tion, 109, 116; reconstituted
cabinet, 111; relationship with
Dubček, 78, 416, fn33; retire-
ment, 140; second economy,
118; speech to 9th Congress of
MSZMP, 114–115
Kafka, Franz, 199, 276, 414, fn15,
444, fn7
Kamiński, Zbigniew, 176
KAN, 77
Kant, Immanuel, xv, xxviii, 212,
318, 322
Katznelson, Iva, 94
Kávan, Jan, 95, 422, fn74
Keane, John, xxi, 215, 319, 321, 322,
328, 337, 346, 349, 351
Kende, Péter, 110
Kenedi, János, 163; *Bibó Memorial
Book*, 135
Khrushchev, Nikita, 60, 112
KIK, 20, 21, 49
King Jr., Martin Luther, 183
Kis, János, xvii, xviii, xix, xxvii, 2,
8, 96, 123, 127, 150, 177, 294,
305, 340, 341, 348, 349, 353,
357; *Beszélő*, 131–133, 281,
285, 292; "Can 1956 Be
Forgotten?" 282–283; on the
communist regime, 112;
democratic alternative,
281–290; election analysis, 141;
Haraszti, 290;

Kis, János, (*cont'd*), Hungarian minority, 96, 454, fn14; "Hungarian Societies and Hungarian Minorities Abroad," 284–286, 455, fn18; moral responsibility, 264–265; "On Our Limitations and Possibilities," 286–288; "pacted transition," 149–150; "radical reformism," 142, 276–277, 313, 315; second economy, 118; self-limitation, 286, 289; *Toward an East European Marxism*, 126, 258, 266–277; "underground Marxist," 275; "On Ways of Being a Jew," 264–265; "What Should We Fear," 288–289; *see also* Rakovski, Mark

Kiss, Elizabeth, 340

Kiszczak, Czesław, 57; background, 442, fn19

KISZ, 144, 181, 278

KKK, 15, 402, fn9

Klaus, Václav, 331, 423, fn81

Klíma, Ivan, 209, 419, fn56, 445, fn5

Klub angažovaných nestraníků see KAN

Klub Inteligencji Katolickiej see KIK

Klub Kryzwego Koła see KKK

KMT, 110, 153

KNDP, 147, 151

Koestler, Arthur, 134

Kohout, Pavel, 61, 66, 67, 419, fn56; Chartists message, 128; Havel, 209, 233, 414, fn14

Kołakowski, Leszek, xxv, xxvii, 14, 184, 187, 183, 195, 276, 310, 438, fn7; background, 157; on civil society, 457, fn6; on expulsion from the party 22; on Gomułka, 22; "living in dignity," 174, 180, 198; movement away from revisionist Marxism, 25; *The Presence of Myth*, 159; "The Priest and the Jester," 158–159;

responsibility, 159, 200; resistance, 164, "Theses on Hope and Hopelessness," 7, 160–165

Komenský (Comenius), 107, 243, 245, 246, 357, 449, fn42

Komitet Obrony Robitników, *see* KOR

Komitet Samoobrony Społecznej see KSS-KOR

Kommunikat (Communiqué), 37; *see also* KOR

Komunustická Strana Československa *see* CPCz

Konrád, György, xvi, xxvi, xxvii, 2, 124, 125, 126, 138, 258, 340, 341, 357, 358; analysis of Hungary under authoritarian communism, *Antipolitics*, 298–309; 118–120; background, 127–128; civil society, 307–309, 325; definition of antipolitics, 301–302; Demszky, 133; Hungarian minority, 96

KOR, xxv, xxvi, 15, 17, 21, 41–42, 43, 48, 49, 53, 55, 92, 128, 129, 150, 177, 179, 192, 272, 304, 341, 352; alliance between secular Left and the Catholic Church, 176–177; background, 35–37; estimates of 1976 strike, 34; involvement, 46; members' arrest 39, 176; publishing, 33–38; success of, 39–40; underground MKS Charter 77, 89, 91, 128; *see also* Kołakowski, Leszek *and* Michnik, Adam

Koréc, Jan, 100

Kornai, János, 328; regarding Hungarian socialist economy, 114, 118, 328–329; regarding socialism, xxx

Kosík, Karel, 22, 419, fn56

Kőszeg, Ferenc, 131

Kőszegi, Ferenc, 143

Kovács, András, 143, 266; peace activist, 143; *see also* samizdat

Kowalik, Tadeusz, 46, 47, 195, 402, fn6, 409, fn66, 458, fn14
Kowalska, Anka, 21
Kriegel, František, 80; Charter 77, 90, 415, fn23
Kruszyński, Stanisław, 33
KSS-KOR, 39, 40, 43
Kukliński, Colonel Ryszard, 51, 410, fn76
Kulerski, Wiktor, 53
Kulikov, Viktor, 51
Kultura, 15, 157, 160, 403, fn10; KOR funding, 39
Kultúrny život, 66, 414, fn12
Kundera, Milan, 6, 59–60, 67, 134
Kurón, Jacek, xxv, xxvii, 2, 7, 17, 22, 348, 352, 356; civil society, 195, 341; influence in Hungary, 133; KOR activities, 35, 37–38; "Landscape after the Battle," 191–192, 197; MKS involvement, 46; non-violence, 181; *Open Letter to the Party*, xxv, 184–190; "Politics and Opposition in Poland," 187; "Reflections on a Program of Action," 189, 190; self-organization, 187, 190–191, 303, 313; on Solidarity, 50, 194; on *Walterowcy*, 15–17; *see also* KOR
Kusý, Miroslav, 94, 97, 356, 357

Laba, Roman, 458, fn14
Lakitelek, 138–139
Landovský, Pavel, 233, 233
Lange, Oskar, 14, 63, 328; background, 402, fn6
Langmar, Ferenc, 143
Leclerq, Jacques, 171
Lengyel, László, 138
Lenin Shipyard, 27, 44, 194; *see* Gdańsk
Lenin, Vladimir Ilyich, 25, 33, 61, 65, 192, 257, 274; *What Is to Be Done?*, 289
Lennon, John, 97–98

Lezsák, Sándor, 138
Liberated Theater (*Osvobozené Divaldo*), 199, 443, fn3
Lidová Strana see People's Party
Lipiński, Edward, 15, 17; "Memorandum of the 59," 33; on movement away from revisionist Marxism, 25; *see also* KOR *and* PPS
Lipski, Jan Józef, xvi, 15, 30, 39; on "Band of Vagabonds," 16; civil society, 197; KOR, 35–36; *Kościół, Lewica, Dialog,* 167; *see also* KOR
Lis, Bogdan, 53
Listy see Pelikán, Jiří
Literární noviny, 66, 414, fn12
Lityński, Jan, 26, 41, 356; Kurón, 184
"Living in dignity," *see* Kołakowski, Leszek
"Living in truth," *see* Havel, Václav
Locke, John, xv, xvi, 194, 314, 456, fn3, 457, fn4, 457, fn7; civil society, 317–319, 321, 323, 324
Łódź, strikers, 406, fn39
Lukács, György, xviii, 122–124, 131, 135, 157, 265, 274, 282, 321; Kis and Bence, 274, 275; Lukács' disciples, 123, 257; philosophy and background, 257–261, 452, fn3; protest of WTO invasion of Czechoslovakia, 124; relationship with regime, 429, fn26
Lukes, Steven, 337
Lustig, Arnoš, 66
Luxemburg, Rosa, xviii, xxvii, 61, 192, 343, 441, fn27, 459, fn15

Machiavelli, Niccolò, xv, xvi, xxi, 302
Macierewicz, Antoni, 16, 35, 167
MacIntyre, Alisdair, xx
MacLean, Ian, 348
Macpherson, C.B., xix

Magdalenka, 57
Magyar Demokrata Fórum see MDF
Magyar Néppárt, 147
*Magyar Szocialista Munkáspárt
    see* MSZMP
Mandeville, Bernard de, 319, 327
Man of Iron; plot description,
    26–27
March 1968, Poland, 28, 66
Maritain, Jacques, 20
Márkus, György, 122, 123, 258;
    emigration, 124; students, 126;
    see also Budapest School intel-
    lectuals
Márkus, Mária, 122; emigration,
    124; *see also* Budapest School
    intellectuals
martial law; Poland, 51–53, 54;
    amnesty, 64; Church's role, 176
Marx, Karl, xv, xvi, xxi, 25, 34, 65,
    126, 342; on civil society,
    195–196, 320, 321–322, 324;
    commodity fetishism, 212;
    Havel, 218, 240; on history,
    xxix, 245; ideology, 218; Kis,
    282; Kis and Bence, 267–268,
    274–276; Kołakowski, 158, 159,
    216, 245, 308, 337; Lukács,
    257, 258, 260; Michnik on class
    analysis, 194; on religion, 170;
    renewal of, 123; on violence, 180
Masaryk, Jan, 76, 417, fn34
Masaryk, Tomáš Garrigue, 59, 76,
    107, 187, 223, 242, 348;
    Patočka, 242–243
Matuštík, Martin J., 326, 336, 460,
    fn25
Matynia, Elzbieta, 361, 458, fn12
Mazowiecki, Tadeusz, 20, 21, 46,
    166, 167, 171, 176; "ethics of
    emancipation," 165, 409, fn66;
    as prime minister, 58
McRae, Rob, 105, 245
MDF, 139, 140, 146; RT, 147;
    disagreement over head of state,

151–152; referendum boycott,
    151
Mečiar, Vladimir, 357
Michnik, Adam, xvi, xvii, xviii, xix,
    xxi, xxviii, xxxi, xxxii, 2, 8, 9,
    15, 22, 23, 26, 37, 47, 49, 58,
    150, 165, 187, 250, 277, 302,
    340, 346, 348, 349, 354, 356,
    357, 358; on the American
    Revolution, 338; assessment of
    the Church, 167–168; Catholic
    Church, 21; *The Church and
    the Left,* 168–169, 171–177,
    342–343, 344–345; civil society,
    195, 197, 322, 323, 324, 341;
    on the economy, 330–331; defi-
    nition of secularization, 170–171;
    Dialog, 167; dissident writing,
    177; Imre Nagy burial, 153;
    influence in Hungary, 133;
    Kołakowski, 157; *Kościół, Lewica,*
    MKS activities, 46; on "A New
    Evolutionism," 24–25, 177–180,
    215, 248, 315; on non-violence,
    180–184; NOW-a, 42; on
    political movements, 315–316;
    regarding March 1968, 26;
    representative, 99; *Sejm* secular
    Left, 168, 170; on self-limita-
    tion, 190–191, 286; on socialist
    thought, 441, fn27; on Solidarity,
    193–195; on Soviet military
    intervention, 178–179
Mickiewicz, Adam; *Forefathers' Eve,*
    xxv, 23; background, 404, fn27
Midrasz, 357
*Międzyzakładowy Komitet Strajkowy
    see* MKS
Mikloško, František, 101
Mill, John Stuart, 171, 188, 324,
    343
Miłosz, Czesław, xxviii, 134, 293
Mirový Klub John Lennon see MKJL
MKJL, 98; *see also* John Lennon
MKS, 46; Gdańsk Accord, 53

Mlynář, Zdeněk, 422, fn72; Action Program, 71; Charter 77, 89. Čierna nad Tisou, 78; on economic reform, 65; results of normalization, 81

Modzelewski, Karol; influence in Hungary, 133; leader of the Club of the Seekers of Contradictions, 17; *Open Letter to the Party*, xxv, 7, 22, 184–190; on Solidarity, 50

Monor, 137, 138, 139, 286

Moore, Barrington, 3, 330

Morawska, Anna, 20

Moscow Protocols, 61, 68, 80, 207; *see also* Dubček, Alexander *and* the USSR

Mounier, Emmanuel, 20

Movement for Civil Liberties *see* HOS

Movement for the Defense of Human and Civil Rights *see* ROPCiO

Mozgó Világ (The World in Motion), 134

MSZMP, 279; 9th Congress, 114; *Beszélő*, 133; head of state, 151; referendum boycott, 151; "third side," 149

Müller, Jiří, 90

Musician's Union; Czechoslovakia, 84

Nagy, Bálint, 131

Nagy, Imre, 6, 75, 110, 113, 135, 137, 283, 289, 298; background; 426–427, fn6; György Lukács, 122; Hungarian Revolution, 109; importance to RT, 149; New Course, 114; reburial, 99, 152–154; reconstituted cabinet, 111

Na Kampě, 97–98

National Front, 104

NATO, 4, 299, 337

Několik vět see Just a Few Sentences

NEM, xxvi, 5, 112, 121, 124, 140, 280, 282, 288, 292, 313; background, 428–429, fn17; criticisms of, 124; difficulties in implementation, 115; objectives, 113; risks of, 114; second economy, 116–118

Nemcová, Dana, 357

Németh, László, 125, 126, 134

Németh, Miklós, 146

NEP, 64

népi writers, 125–6, 137, 138, 431, fn41; lack of support for Charter 77, 126

New Economic Mechanism, *see* NEM *and* "goulash" communism

New Left, 302

Nezávislé Mirové Sdruženi see NMS

Nice, Treaty of, 338

Nietzsche, Friedrich, 241, 242

Niezależna Oficyna Wydawnicza see NOW-a

NMP, 117

NMS, 98; meeting with opposition groups, 104; Wenceslas Square demonstration, 98, 152

non-violence, 180–184, 314, 316; Michnik, 180–184

normalization, 84, 96, 313; definition, 80; Husák period, 83

Nove, Alec, xxx, 350

November 17, 103; description of, 104–106

Novotný, Antonín, 62, 63, 70, 75, 412, fn4; becoming president, 71; Ota Šik appointment, 63

NOW-a, 41, 42, 133

Nowa Huta, 14, 56, 402, fn7; *see also* Ważyk, Adam

Nowa Kultura (New Culture), 14

Nuti, Domenico Mario, xxx, 141

Nyers, Rezső, 114; economic reform, 140

Občanske Forum see Civic Forum
Open Letter to the Members of the Basic Party Organizations of PZPR and to Members of the University Cell of the Union of Socialist Youth of Warsaw University, 17; *see also* Modzelewski, Karol *and* Kurón, Jacek
Opletal, Jan, 6, 96, 424–425, fn96
Opposition Roundtable *see* EKA
Orbán, Viktor, 145; Imre Nagy reburial, 153–154; *see also* Fidesz
Organization for the Defense of Human Rights, 77
Orwell, George, 134
Oslzý, Petr, 421, fn68
Ost, David, 342–343
Otáhal, Milan, 420, fn63

Pacem in Terris (Peace on Earth), 100–101, 424, fn90
"pacted transition," 146, 149–150
Paine, Thomas, xv, xvi, 338
Pajdak, Antoni, 17; *see also* PPS
Palach, Jan, 6, 81, 99, 419, fn49
Palach Press *see* Kávan, Jan
Palouš, Martin, 245–246, 357; Charter 77, 252, 254, 255
Panorama, 99
"Parallel *Polis,*" 247–251
Pateman, Carole, 326
Patočka, Jan, xxvii, 92, 135, 231, 239 247, 259, 324, 348, 354; *asubjectivity,* 242; "care for the soul," 244–245; Charter 77, 243, 244, 246– 247, 251, 255; on Comenius, 449, fn42; on Havel, 241, 244; on Husserl, 243, 244; influences, 242; on Masaryk, 242–243; on metaphysics, 450, fn44; philosophy, 242–247; on responsibility, 244–245
Patriotic People's Front (Hungary) *see* HNF

PAV *see* VPN
PAX, 21, 171
Peace Group for Dialogue, 142
peace movement; Catholic Church in Hungary, 142; oppositional movements, 144–146
Pelikán, Jiří, 81; *Listy,* 95
People's Party, 104
Perestroika, 56, 66, 82, 97, 116, 288
Petőfi, Sándor, 6
Pithart, Petr, 356
Plastic People of the Universe *see* PPU
Plato, xv, xviii, 158, 240, 243–245, 314, 364; Socrates, 244, 246
Plesu, Andrei, 359
Pocock, J.G.A., xxi
Polish August, 49, 181, 192, 272
Polish–Czechoslovak Solidarity, 91, 249–250, 450, fn51
Polish October, xxiv, 14, 15, 19, 20, 22, 70, 182, 189; Poznań riots, 14, 401, fn2
Polish Roundtable Talks *see* RT, Poland
Polish Socialist Party *see* PPS
Polish United Workers' Party *see* PZPR
Political economy; dissident critique of, 327–334
Polska Partia Socjalistyczna, see PPS
Polska Zjednoczona Partia Robotnicza see PZPR
POLVAX, 144
Pomian, Krzysztof, 22
Popiełuszko, Jerzy, 166, 167, 177, 411, fn82; support of Solidarity, 177
Po Prostu (Plain Speaking), 14
populist writers *see népi* writers
Pozsgay, Imre, 124; economic reform, 138, 140; "gray zone," 146; head of state decision, 151
PPS, 17, 37, 403, fn13, 403, fn14
PPU, 84–87, 88; Havel, 215, 222; *see also* Jirous, Ivan

Prague Spring (1968), xxiv, xxv, xxxii, 3, 6, 25, 61, 70, 71, 80, 83, 90, 91, 100, 102, 110, 178, 182, 193; Jan Palach, 6; 4th Congress of SČSS, 66; Havel's letter to Dubček, 207–208; WTO invasion, 78–80, 418, fn40, fn41, *see also* Dubček, Alexander *and* Moscow Protocols

Pravda (Truth); on Dubček's reform, 75

Prečan, Vilém, 95; Charter 77, 254–255, 420, fn63, 422, fn72, fn73

price hikes (1976), 34; resulting strikes, 35; *see also* Radom *and* Ursus Tractor Factory

Provisional Coordinating Commission of Solidarity *see* TKK

Przeworski, Adam, 459, fn17

Public against Violence *see* VPN

Pyjas, Stanisław, 41

PZPR, 14, 178, 188; ideological shift, 56–57; on martial law, 51; Sixth Party Congress, 33

Radical Reformism, 277–281, 313; *see also* Bence, György *and* Kis, János

Radio Free Europe, 94, 99

Radom, 34, 48, 164, 192; riots, 188; theory for success, 164; *see also* price hikes *and* Ursus Tractor Factory

Raina, Peter, 31–32, 33, 405, fn31, 408, fn61

Rajk, László, 127, 130, 141; Imre Nagy reburial, 152; "samizdat boutique," 130

Rákosi, Mátyás; regarding Bibó, 136, 153

Rakovski, Marc, 126, 266; *see also* György, Bence *and* Kis, János

Rau, Zbigniew, 323, 457, fn7

Reform Circles, 148

responsibility, 8, 146, 148, 255, 330, 341, 360, 398; Bibó, 263–264, 364; Havel, 203, 205, 219, 227, 220, 238, 363–364; Kis, 264–265; Kołakowski's *The Presence of Myth*, 159, 200; moral, 175, 333; personal, 237–238, 251, 253; Patočka, 244–245; political, 245, 233, 344–345, 346, 347, 349

Res Publica, 41, 191, 411, fn80

Rewska, Anna, 15; *see also* KKK

Ricoeur, Paul, xix–xx, 94

RMP, 40

Robotnik (The Worker), 41

ROPCiO, 40, 42; MKS involvement, 46

Rorty, Richard, 94

Rousseau, Jean-Jacques, xxviii, 195, 351

RT, Hungary *see* EKA

RT, Poland, 48, 57, 146, 147, 181, 337

Ruch Movement; trials, 32; background, 33

Ruch Obrony Praw Człowiecka i Obywatela see ROPCiO

Ruch Młodej Polski see RMP

Rupnik, Jacques, 298

Rutland, Peter, 336

Rybicki, Józef, 17; *see also* PPS

Šabata, Jaroslav, 90

Sakharov, Andrei, xvi, 100

Sakwa, Richard, 336, 353

Salivarová, Zdena, 95

Salom (Shalom), 264–265

Samizdat; Czechoslovakia, 94–95

Samizdat; Hungary, 129–135, 142, 352; AB publishing, 133; *Bibó Memorial Book*, 136; circulated books, 134; distribution outward, 146; émigré community, 135

Samizdat; Poland, 352

Schell, Jonathan, 179
SČSS, 65, 76; 4th Congress, 66
second economy; Hungary, 116–118
secular Left, 167–170; Catholic
    Church and Michnik, 165–177;
    definition, 179; non-violence,
    181; Tischner's view, 176;
    see also Michnik, Adam
Seifert, Jaroslav, 60, 419, fn56
Sejm, 20, 33, 34, 57, 188, 356, 357
self-limitation, 88, 190–191,
    232–233, 313, 345; Kis, 286,
    289; Kuroń, 313; *see also* Kis,
    János *and* Michnik, Adam
Seligman, Adam, 317
Selucký, Radoslav, 70
Shore, Marci, 68, 80, 414, fn13
Šik, Ota, 61, 328; Action Program,
    71; appointments, 63; back-
    ground, 413, fn9; economic
    reform, 63, 65; result of normal-
    ization, 81
Šiklová, Jiřina, 357, 458, fn12
Šimečka, Milan, 60, 82, 210, 419,
    fn50, 422, fn77
Skilling, H. Gordon, 64, 88, 89, 91,
    402, fn2, 417, fn38, 418, fn46,
    420, fn62, 421, fn64, 422, fn72,
    424, fn88
Skinner, Quentin, xviii, xix, xx, xxi,
    399, fn4, 456, fn2
Skocpol, Theda, 3, 442, fn23
SKS, 41–42
Skvorecký, Josef, 95, 414, fn16
Slánský, Rudolf, 60, 412, fn3
Słonimski, Antoni, 174, 439–440,
    fn17
Smith, Adam, 319, 320, 329
Smykał, Jacek, 33
Slovak National Uprising, 72
Social Contract, 277–280; *see also*
    Beszélő, Kis, János *and* Tamás,
    Gáspár Miklós
Social Democrats, 145;
    referendum, 152

Socialistická Strana see National
    Front
Society of Scientific Courses *see*
    "Flying University" *and* TKN
Social Self-Defense Committee
    see KSS-KOR
Socrates *see* Plato
Solidarity, xxv, xxvi, 3, 14, 27, 43,
    44, 91, 128, 150, 177, 179, 191,
    192, 300, 304, 323, 408, fn62,
    410, fn73; activism, 191;
    attitude of the Catholic Church,
    21, 54; background, 45–49;
    intellectuals within, 49–51, 409,
    fn66, 411, fn78; Geremek, 196,
    198; Konrád, 304; KOR, 39;
    Michnik, 193–194; as an
    underground organization,
    53–56; RT, 56–58; Solidarity
    Citizens' Committee, 58;
    SZETA support, 124; use of
    non-violence, 181, 183;
    see also Michnik, Adam *and*
    TKK
Solzhenitsyn, Aleksandr, 121, 173,
    222
Sorel, Georges, 346
Soviet Union *see* USSR
Spinoza, Baruch, 239
Srp, Karel, 98
Stalin, Jozef, 70, 162, 286, 295
Staniszkis, Jadwiga, 46, 410, fn72,
    458, fn14
Státní Bezpečnost see StB
State Security *see* StB
StB, 85, 99, 247; crackdown on
    NMS demonstration, 98
Steinsbergowa, Aniela, 15, 17;
    see also KOR *and* PPS
Stokes, Gail, 336
Strahov, 69, 70
Strauss, Leo, xxi, 448, fn37
Štrougal, Lubomir, 97
Studencki Komitet Solidarności
    see SKS student movements;

Czechoslovakia, 69, 82, 93, 98–99; November 17, 103–106, 424, fn96
Student Solidarity Committee *see* SKS
Sugár, András, 99, 416, fn27, 422, fn86
Svaz Československých spisovatelů see SČSS
Svědectví see Tigrid, Pavel
Svoboda, Ludvík, 71
Svobodné Slovo see Free Word
Świerczewski, Karol, 15; *see also* Kurón, Jacek *and Walterowcy*
Szabad Demokraták Szövetsége see SzDSz
Századvég (End of the Century), 135
Szczecin, 56; protest in, 28
Szczypiorski, Adam, 17; *see also* PPS
SzDSz, xxvi, 139, 357; concerns over head of state, 151–152; Opposition Roundtable, 147
Szegényeket Támogató Alap see SZETA
Szelényi, Iván, xvi, xxvii, 125, 128, 258; analysis of Hungary under authoritarian communism, 118–120; Budapest School intellectuals, 127 "negation of negation," 123–124
SZETA, 129, 145
Szigeti, László, 96, 423, fn80
Szilágyi, Sándor, 261–262
Szlajfer, Henryk, 23
Szücs, Jenö, 136

Tamás, Gáspár Miklós, 141, 259, 356, 360, 458, fn13; views on the social contract, 280–281
Taylor, Charles, 93, 350, 352
"third side," 149; *see also* EKA *and* RT
Tiananmen Square, 58

Tigrid, Pavel, 95
Tischner, József, 166–167; assessment of the Church, 176; *see also* Catholic Church, Poland
Tismaneanu, Vladimir, 338, 462, fn38
TKK, 53
TKN, 16, 42–43, 93, 184, 322; Michnik, 177; Havel, 223, 224
Tocqueville, Alexis de, xv, 187, 254, 314, 317, 399, fn1
Tőkés, Rudolf, 112–113, 116, 126, 136, 138–139, 150
Tomášek, Frantisek Cardinal, 100, 101; canonization of Ágnes of Bohemia, 106
Tomko, Jozef Cardinal, 101
Tomin, Julius, 92–94
Tominová, Zdena, 15, 94, 421, fn67
Toranska, Teresa, 134
Touraine, Alain, 194, 408, fn63
Towarzystwo Kursów Naukowych see TKN
Transitions, 357; *see* Urban, Jan
Trianon, treaty of; xxiv, 284, 399, fn5
Tucker, Aviezer, 242, 244, 359, 360, 445, fn16, 449, fn39
Tully, James, xix
Tvář, 201, 202, 205, 208, 208
Tygodnik Powszechny (Universal Weekly), 20, 54
Tymczasowa Komisja Krajowa see TKK

Ulbricht, Walter, 75
Uhl, Petr, 90, 356, 419, fn54, 421, fn71
Union of Czechoslovak Writers, 66, 67, 68, 83; Havel, 205, 209, 209; *see* SČSS
Union of Polish Writers, 23, 39
Union of Socialist Youth *see* ZMS

United States *see* US
Urban, Jan, 357, 420, fn63, 421,
   fn66 Urbanek, Zdeněk, 209
urbanist approach, 125–126
Ustinov, Dimitri Marshal, 51
Ursus Tractor Factory, 34, 215;
   theory for success, 164;
   see also price hikes
US, 1, 7, 148, 153, 200, 298, 299,
   357
USSR, xxix, 7, 30, 33, 59, 71, 72,
   75, 78, 79, 81, 88, 91, 178, 222,
   282, 287, 315; Hungarian
   Revolution, 109, 110; invasions,
   100, 111; Poland, 51, 111, 182

Vaculík, Ludvík, 66–67, 209, 414,
   fn14, 444, fn5; *Edice Petlice*, 95;
   reference to *Just a Few
   Sentences*, 102; *Two Thousand
   Words to Workers, Farmers,
   Scientists, Artists, and Everyone*,
   77, 102
Vajda, Mihály, 122, 127;
   see also Budapest School
Vaničkova, Anna, 84–85, 419, fn52
Vargha, János, 142–143; *see also*
   Danube Circle *and* Gabčikovo–
   Nagymaros Project
Velvet Divorce, 337
Velvet Revolution, 7, 99, 103, 181,
   229, 360, 419, fn49, 420, fn58
Verejnost Proti Násilu see Public
   against Violence
VÍZJEL, 143
Vladislav, Jan, 215
Vondra, Saša, 356
VONS, xxvi; Benda, 247; Charter
   77 support, 128; Havel, 216;
   history, 92
VOX HUMANA, 134
VPN, xxvi, 106; formation of, 97,
   422, fn77; foundation, 105
Vysočany Congress,
   Czechoslovakia, 81, 418, fn44

Wajda, Andrzej, 26, 409, fn68
Walentynowicz, Anna, 45–46, 406,
   fn42
Wałęsa, Lech, 45–46, 50, 54, 191,
   193, 406, fn42, 408, fn62;
   Gdańsk headquarters, 177
Walterites *see Walterowcy*
Walterowcy, 15; *see also* Kurón, Jacek
Walzer, Michael, 350–351
Warsaw Club of Catholic Intelli-
   gence, *see* KIK
Warsaw Pact, xxx, 4, 5, 51, 75, 78,
   79, 110, 279, 298, 301
Warsaw Treaty Organization
   see WTO
Warsaw Uprising, 17
Warski Shipyard, 28
Ważyk, Adam; "Poem for Adults,"
   14–15
Więź (Link), 20, 171, 176
Wilkes, Kathy, 93
Williams, Douglas, xxiii
Wilson, Paul, 215, 236, 238–239,
   420, fn58
Wojtyła, Karol *see* John Paul II,
   Pope
Wood, Ellen, 328
Wood, Neal, xix
Workers' Defense Committee
   see KOR
workers' riots, Poland, xxvi
WTO, 51, 52, 78, 79, 111, 113,
   124
Wujec, Henryk, 21
Wyszyński, Cardinal Stefan, 19, 33,
   100, 172; definition of secular-
   ization, 170; counter to Michnik,
   176, 177; criticism of regime
   repression, 177

Yalta, xxiv, 3, 289, 299
Young, Iris Marion, 326
youth culture; Poland, 68–69;
   Hungary, 144–145;
   see also Fidesz

Young Poland Movement
  see RMP
Young Writers' Attila József Circle,
  144

Zagajewski, Adam, 358–359
Zieja, Jan, 176

Ziembínski, Wojciech, 15;
  see also KOR *and* KKK
ZMS, 22
Znak (Sign), 20, 21, 176, 404, fn22,
  404, fn24; *see also Tygodnik
  Powszechny*
Zprávy (News), 419, fn48

Also available from CEU Press

The Roundtable Talks of 1989
The Genesis of Hungarian Democracy

Editor-in-Chief **András Bozóki**, Central European University and Eötvös Loránd University, Budapest

Associate Editors: Márta Elbert, Melinda Kalmár, Béla Révész, Erzsébet Ripp, Zoltán Ripp

In Hungary the "velvet revolution" of 1989 was prepared, or rather prompted, by a series of negotiations conducted between representatives of the democratic opposition, the ruling Communist party, and a political group called the "third side" comprising organizations close to the Communist regime. As a result of these talks, referred to as the historic "Roundtable Talks," free elections were held in Hungary in 1990, marking the end of the oppressive Communist regime and the beginning of a new epoch in the country's history.

Based on primary sources recently published in Hungarian in eight volumes, this book tells the history of the Roundtable Talks.

The authors believe that in Hungary—as opposed to some other Central European countries—the Roundtable Talks amounted to much more than just a sideshow and in fact they constituted the hub of the revolutionary transformation.

In the first part of the book—a series of analytical essays—scholars of the Hungarian democratic transition discuss the most relevant aspects of the Roundtable Talks, the actors and organizations participating, the tactics and strategies used, institution building, the new electoral system, and constitutional reform. The Hungarian Roundtable Talks are placed into wider historical and international perspectives. In the second part, eight key documents are presented with commentaries. The book has a detailed chronology, biographies of the most important participants, and a glossary.

2002, 520 pages
963 9241 21 0   cloth $65.95 / £39.95

AVAILABLE TO ORDER AT ALL GOOD BOOKSHOPS
OR CHECK OUT OUR WEBSITE WWW.CEUPRESS.COM
FOR FULL ORDERING DETAILS.